Puerto Rican Children in Mainland Schools

A Source Book for Teachers

edited by

Francesco Cordasco

Professor of Education, Montclair State College
Educational Consultant, Migration Division,
Commonwealth of Puerto Rico

and

Eugene Bucchioni

Assistant Professor of Education
Hunter College

The Scarecrow Press, Inc.

Metuchen, N.J.   1968

To

Leonard Covello

for

over one-half century of dedicated service
to youth and the schools.

Preface

The need for this book has been long apparent. In 1960, some 900,000 Puerto Ricans lived in the United States, and the 1960 census reported Puerto Ricans living in all but one (Duluth-Superior) of the 101 Standard Metropolitan Statistical Areas.[1] Historically, the American school has played a major role in the acculturation of the children of communities new to American society and its response to Puerto Rican children has been cast in traditional mold.[2] In an attempt to provide a source book for teachers on the Puerto Rican child, we make no apology for the sociological orientation: too often, the Puerto Rican child has been seen by American educators only in terms of language (non-English speaking), and not in terms of a socio-cultural context which adequately presents him in full dimensional view.[3] It is the socio-cultural context that the collected readings hopefully illustrate, and the school's role as that of one of a number of social institutions which respond to the needs of children.

The collection of readings brings together materials which deal with aspects of Puerto Rican culture (Part I); the Puerto Rican family (Part II); the Puerto Rican experience on the mainland vis a vis conflict and acculturation (Part III), and schools (Part IV). In Part IV we have included materials which afford a historical perspective (J. J. Osuna, Report on Visits to New York City Schools, 1948; Mayor's Committee on Puerto Rican Affairs..., 1951; Leonard Covello, Recommendations Concerning Puerto Rican Pupils..., 1953); and for The Puerto Rican Study, 1953-57 (New York City. Board of Education, 1958),[4] we have chosen to include the unpublished Summary which was issued in mimeograph form (1958) by the Board of Education.

Our first indebtedness in the preparation of this volume is to Dr. Leonard Covello, who served as a basic resource, not only for the form that the book assumed, but for the encouragement that brought it to completion. More than anyone else, Dr. Covello, the originator of the community school concept, demonstrated how effective the schools could be in serving the needs of all children.[5] Valuable counsel was afforded by Joseph Monserrat, Director, Migration Division, Commonwealth of Puerto Rico; by Carmen Dinos, Supervisor of the Education Program of the Migration Division; by Professor Charles Calitri of Hofstra University. and by Dr. Carmen Sanguinetti. Over the years, Professor Mary Finocchiaro has generously shared with us her great fund of knowledge in the field of the non-English speaking child; and our gratitude extends to a whole host of individuals in and out of the schools. In acknowledg-

v

ing with thanks the gracious permissions extended by authors to reprint their works, it is unnecessary to add that we do not necessarily subscribe to all their statements, but we do believe that what is included affords invaluable insight in an area of critical concern.

While the readings are representative, they reflect our choices, and other editors might well have selected certain other articles for inclusion. We hope, however, that the readings presented here will adequately achieve the purposes which this source book is intended to serve.

New York City, 1968   F.C.   E.B.

Notes

1. United States Bureau of the Census, U.S. Census of Population: 1960 Subject Reports. Puerto Ricans in the United States. Final Report, PC (2)-1 D. (Washington, D.C: United States Government Printing Office, 1963).

2. "The cornucopia of Federal legislation of the last few years did not discover poverty as a new or rare phenomenon in American society: what the Congress perceptively recognized was that many of our social institutions (particularly, our schools) were only limitedly successful and that many of our democratic ideals were severely mauled in the grim pathology of social disaffection, cultural assault, and enforced assimilation. It was not that our schools failed but rather that their recorded failures were to be measured in the inadequacy of their response to the child who came to them formed in the context of another heritage, or in the articulation of a strange tongue. If there is a common denominator which must be sought in the millions of American children who presented themselves to a society's schools, it is poverty. And its ingredients (within the parameters of this poverty) were cultural differences, language handicaps, social alienation and disaffection. In this sense, the Negro inmigrant rural poor huddled in the urban ghettoes of the 1960's; the Puerto Rican migrant poor who seek economic opportunity on the mainland; as the Mexican-American poor, largely an urban minority, are not newcomers to the American schools, nor do they present American educators with new problems. The American poor, traditionally, are the ingredients out of which our social institutions have fashioned the sinews of greatness." F. Cordasco, "The Non-English Speaking Child in the American School: Continuing Challenge to Education in a Democratic Society," Hearings Before the General Subcommittee on Education... (House of Representatives) on H.R. 9840 and H.R. 10224, Bills to Amend the Elementary and Secondary Education Act of 1965 In Order to Assist Bilingual Education Programs (United States Govern-

ment Printing Office, Washington, 1967), pp. 270-271. The Bilingual Education Act of 1967 (Amendments, 1967, Elementary and Secondary Education Act) provides support for programs which will give "...financial assistance to local educational agencies to develop and carry out new and imaginative elementary and secondary school programs designed to meet these special educational needs and to preserve and enhance the foreign language backgrounds and culture of such children."

3. For a descriptive tableau of the schools and the urban community, see Maurie Hillson, Francesco Cordasco, Francis P. Purcell, Education in the Urban Community: The Schools and the Crisis of the Cities (New York: American Book Company, 1968).

4. See Appendix II: Bibliography, infra.

5. See Leonard Covello, The Social Background of the Italo-American School Child: A Study of the Southern Italian Mores and Their Effect on the School Situation in Italy and America. Edited and with an introduction by F. Cordasco (Leiden, the Netherlands, E.J. Brill, 1967).

Table of Contents

viii

Introduction

Urban education in many parts of the United States is confronted by a variety of seemingly overwhelming problems. There are serious shortages of teachers, overcrowded classes, an inadequate supply of instructional materials and inadequate space. Alarmingly high rates of academic retardation among urban children and adolescents, especially in reading and mathematics, are of special concern. Greater numbers of high school students in the inner city are leaving school before receiving their diplomas, and those who complete the secondardy school program find that they are not as well prepared for employment as they should be.

Urban education in the last few decades has become sharply characterized by two patterns of development that have affected the traditional program--indeed, the very structure and function--of urban education. The schools are becoming increasingly segregated on the basis of social class. That is, middle class children and adolescents, because of housing patterns in the city, tend to go to certain schools while lower class children and adolescents and other students from poverty areas attend other schools. The general movement of middle class people out of the cities is further contributing to segregation by social class because fewer middle class people are living in the cities and sending their children to urban schools.

The second major pattern of development in urban education that has vital sociological significance is the increased ethnic segregation. White students tend to go to school in predominantly white residential areas. Negro students attend schools that are primarily Negro in enrollment. Discriminatory housing patterns in most American cities have contributed to the increased de facto segregation in urban education.

The heavy influx of Puerto Ricans into some cities such as New York, Philadelphia, Chicago and Newark, presents the schools with the additional important task of assisting the newcomers in adjusting to a new society: a society that generally demands that they function inconspicuously, a society that equates inconspicuousness with adjustment and which tends to suppress, as a mechanism of adjustment, the existing problems within the ethnic group.

The schools in these cities can play an important part in the orientation of Puerto Ricans to North American society as well as providing them with education in the traditional sense. That is, Puerto Rican students can be helped to understand and learn the val-

13

ues, the norms, the culture patterns and the language of urban North America as transmitted by the schools in addition to being taught to read and write English and to master all the other subjects that comprise the elementary and secondary school curricula.

Schools with large Puerto Rican enrollments, however, have become the "difficult" schools in the view of many teachers and urban boards of education. Classes are heavily weighted with transients, with children and adolescents from economically depressed families, with students from broken homes and with "problem" students. In these schools, the reported average I.Q.'s and levels of achievement in reading and mathematics are low. Teachers are reluctant to teach in these schools because they consider that such schools present unrewarding, and even dangerous, teaching situations. As a result, schools with large Puerto Rican enrollments are unable to attract sufficient numbers of qualified teachers and they have extremely high rates of teacher transfer and resignation.

Most Puerto Rican students who come to urban schools are members of lower classes, and they demonstrate characteristic social patterns. In addition, social class patterns are combined with Puerto Rican culture patterns. The result is a social and cultural milieu that is neither understood nor accepted by the middle-class North American teacher. This lack of understanding is evidenced by the failure to modify instruction for Puerto Rican students. The lack of understanding and acceptance of social and cultural patterns that are different is further evidenced through the attitudes of suspicion, hostility, animosity and fear expressed by many teachers.

Many middle class teachers and principals view Puerto Ricans in terms of the prevailing prejudices, clichés and stereotypes. Puerto Ricans are "dirty, lazy, wiry, treacherous, aggressive, 'spics,' potential rapists, and knife wielders." They are viewed as rapidly "taking over" some cities. Many Puerto Ricans are Negro. In the world of many middle class teachers, Puerto Ricans are dark, unintelligible, ominous and threatening. All this is contrary to middle class experience; middle class individuals are not like this. It is much better to teach one's own. If it is not possible to teach one's own, then every attempt must be made to pattern members of the out-group upon models found within one's own group.

The middle class perspective of teachers and principals is reinforced by that of boards of education whose members reflect middle class norms and values. The result is the development of the school as an institution that teaches lower class Puerto Rican students only from its perspective. This middle class orientation of education has so influenced many urban schools that Puerto Rican students lose interest in the programs offered.

Urban education tends to push ahead the mobile middle class individual. Puerto Ricans, however, are not similarly selected and trained for mobility. For most Puerto Rican students, emphasis is placed upon learning the values and norms of middle class people,

14

rather than upon the academic and other related knowledge and skills that are necessary if lower class Puerto Rican students are to compete with middle class North American students.

As a result of the middle class nature of the urban school, a sharp clash of cultural and class values, identifications and loyalties, develops. The meaning of this clash becomes clear when Puerto Ricans are encouraged to shed their identifications and loyalties as Puerto Ricans and assume those of middle class North Americans. In a sense, the school, in requiring Puerto Ricans to suppress and reject their values, loyalties and identifications, is engaging in a direct assault upon the personal and cultural identities of Puerto Rican students.

The education of Puerto Ricans must be understood within the context of this conflict in cultural and social class values. North American middle class teachers like to teach students who are well dressed, well behaved, who study a great deal, and who will follow obediently whatever instructions are given. Teaching is less difficult and students seem to be learning with ease. When lower-class Puerto Rican students are taught, however, the teachers are confronted with many different social and cultural patterns of behavior. Lower class Puerto Rican students are not always oriented to school and they often attend school only because their parents send them to school or because of compulsory education laws. To many Puerto Rican students, much of North American middle class teaching is uninteresting and unrealistic. North American middle class teachers attempt to motivate Puerto Rican students and reward them in an effort to secure their attention and interest. Brightly colored stars or pictures of animals are distributed to reward good work in the elementary school. In the high school there may be talk of future work as doctors or lawyers. But Puerto Rican students are not always motivated by these techniques, partly because of the seeming impossibility of attainment of these goals, and partly because they may not have appropriate parental or other family models that they can emulate. For many Puerto Rican students the urban school becomes a marketplace of unreality and alienation.

Puerto Rican students attempt to escape from the urban classroom through inattention, daydreaming, talking, playing in the classroom, and absenteeism, especially in the high school. Many Puerto Rican students become hostile and resistant to the unrealities in the urban schools and to the assaults made upon their personal and cultural identities by teachers and principals. When resistance and hostility are expressed in the classroom, the urban school teacher reprimands and punishes, often at great length. In addition, certain moral connotations are added to the teacher's response to resistance and hostility, and Puerto Rican students learn, either overtly or subtly, that they are considered bad, immoral, disorderly, evil and unable to succeed in school. When the urban teacher does this, he is exhibiting, in a sociological sense, symbols of higher status, and he is requesting, at the same time, the prestige and deference he believes should be accorded to him by his students.

15

As the culture conflict in the schools becomes more pronounced, a complex arrangement of rhetoric, myth and reality emerges. The rhetoric describes the optimum program of education that is to be provided for Puerto Rican students. The rhetoric further describes the problems that exist in educating Puerto Rican students and the efforts that are being made to resolve those problems. The result, in fact, is widespread academic retardation among Puerto Rican students, failure of the schools to come to grips with the problems and conflicts in the education of Puerto Rican students, and, in general, a breakdown in education for Puerto Ricans. As rhetoric and reality confront one another, a dangerous myth emerges. This myth holds that education for Puerto Rican students is highly successful and that, while there are many problems and difficulties, these problems are the result of inadequate family experience, deprived home conditions and unsatisfactory and hostile attitudes of the students. The myth further states that education for Puerto Rican students is at least as good as, and generally much better than, the education offered to the immigrants who came from Europe decades ago.

What, then, is urban education accomplishing? Insofar as Puerto Rican students are concerned, it is excluding them from the academic channel that is essential if they are to compete with more privileged middle class students. Urban education, as currently constituted, holds Puerto Rican students at a lower class level and prevents upward social mobility that could improve their life chance. A concomitant of this process is increasing social divisiveness and discontent, a result of the inequality in education opportunity offered to Puerto Rican students.

Teachers, principals, school guidance personnel, social workers and other professionals responsible for school programs represent key factors in the education of Puerto Rican students. All too often, however, these professionals lack the sociological sophistication that could improve the teaching of Puerto Ricans. As a result, educational programs often reflect and are built upon stereotypes, misconceptions, prejudicial attitudes and a general lack of knowledge of the realities and significance of social class and cultural differences. Students of the social and behavioral sciences have not given sufficient attention to the specific problems posed by the relationships between the Puerto Rican lower-class culture and the middle class North American urban education programs.

We have reached an impasse built upon ignorance, suspicions and fear. If we begin to learn what we need to know about the realities of the Puerto Rican experience, our ignorance, suspicions and fears can be reduced somewhat, and we may begin to extricate ourselves and the urban schools from their current untenable plight --the failure of North American education to provide effectively for the education of Puerto Ricans.

16

Part I

Aspects of Puerto Rican Culture

No less than any in the world, Puerto Rican culture is saturated with a vast array of attitudes and beliefs about its own way of
life. These attitudes and beliefs are sometimes called metacultural
because, much of the time, they lie beneath the surface of daily experience. They are absorbed into the "bloodstream" of the people
with little awareness that the absorption is occurring readily from
the earliest to the latest years of every normal person.

Theorists have various terms to describe this elusive level
of culture, but the one we shall adopt is configuration, the underlying pattern of order that harmonizes--and sometimes disharmonizes
--the deepest meanings of the culture. The few anthropologists who
have paid careful attention to this phenomenon have had extreme difficulty in delineating any configuration they might investigate precisely because, by definition, it is never fully or accurately expressed in the formal or official language of government, religion,
education, or other institutions.

To put the matter in a different way, metacultural beliefs
are seldom if ever exactly equated with the ideology of a culture--
that is, its symbolic self-portrait is conveyed through such typical
agents as journalists, politicians, priests, and teachers. Yet, despite the difficulty of comparing an ideology with a configuration, no
culture can be understood until the metacultural level is probed and
interpreted. For here, more than anywhere else, the pervasive philosophy of a people living together in a society is to be discovered.
In a genuine sense, it is the key to cultural order.

In this article, we propose to highlight the question by asking
how far the explicit or ideological level on which Puerto Ricans, like
all people, publicly communicate their attitudes, policies and doctrines to one another is or is not compatible with their implicit or
configurational level of experience. We shall not, of course, begin
to exhaust the question. We hope only to become more conscious
both of its significance and of its ubiquity by considering three important areas of belief encompassed by the terms democracy, religion, and morality, and what such consciousness may mean for Puerto Rican education.

17

I. Methodology

Our methodology has required field work in three subcultures
of Puerto Rico: one, a sugar-cane community on the south coast;
two, a coffee community in the mountainous interior; three, a middle-class urban community on the north coast; and, in addition, prolonged interviews with sixteen national leaders selected by a jury of
their peers.[1]

In the three subcultures, attention centered in a total of
twenty respondents, most of whom were democratically chosen by
the groups they represented of teachers, students, parents, and
school administrators. Many of the subcultural or grassroots respondents had lived in their respective subcultures all their lives,
and they were chosen only after careful explanation to their respective groups of the purposes of the study, and of the kind of respondents desired in terms of those purposes. They represented a wide
variety of backgrounds: Catholic and Protestant, rural and urban,
lower and middle class, colored and white. Although such a method of selection was surely unorthodox, it proved to be fruitful when
evaluated by the quality of the material they provided.

National-level respondents included the Governor of Puerto
Rico, leaders of the two opposition parties (one a millionaire indus-
trialist, the other a lawyer), a college president, two university
deans, two novelists, top government officials, and others. The
themes of the interviews were the same for these respondents as
for those in the three subcultures, but the level of communication
varied. The leader panel was addressed in a fairly theoretical way,
though examples were often used. In the grassroots panel an effort
was made to dramatize each problem by couching it in terms familiar to the respondents' experience. Both sets of interviews were,
however, flexible and open-ended. And in both, the issues raised
were invariably placed in the setting of the Puerto Rican culture itself.

To illustrate the approach, a national leader might have been
asked directly: "Is there any considerable discrepancy among Puerto Ricans between their explicitly accepted religious beliefs and their
actual acceptance as revealed by, say, devotion to religious practices?" One of the hypotheses we were interested in testing (within
severe limits, of course) was that the national panel was sufficiently
sophisticated and habituated to abstract thinking to be able to respond significantly to a question of this sort. Looking back at the
sixteen interviews (all of which, incidentally, required more than one
session) our conclusion is that on the whole the degree of meaningful communication was high. This is not too surprising. While of
course there were misunderstandings (the fact that all but one of the
interviews were conducted in English would itself assure that),
nevertheless the questions asked, as well as the many ramifications
and applications encouraged by informal conversation, were close to
their deepest interests. They had apparently thought about most if
not all of these matters in some fashion before, and often theoretically.

On the grassroots panel the approach was less direct and
more concrete. One of the favorite techniques was imaginary role-
playing. The respondent was asked to imagine two or three friends

with familiar names sitting in the room.   One of the friends would
be quoted: "I am sure that..." Then, in vigorous tones and usually
in colloquial Spanish, he would expound his viewpoint on the topic
under discussion, pointing it up with an instance drawn from the respective subculture.   Another friend would next, with equal vigor,
express a sharply different viewpoint.   Sometimes a third or even
fourth imaginary friend would take issue with the others.   The respondent would then be asked whether he agreed with any of the
friends or whether, instead, he believed something quite different.
His answer would often be followed by an effort to discover his
reasons.   Not infrequently he would give very emphatic ones, revealing that he, too, had previously thought about the matter.

Here is a somewhat abbreviated instance related to the same
question asked the national panel in another way:

Senor Rodríguez (the first friend):   I go to church in San
José at Easter and Christmas.   The rest of the time I leave it to my
wife to go.

Senor Sánchez (the second friend):   I think that's wrong.
Everybody should go to church once a week and take confession.

Senor Quinones (the third friend):   I don't believe the things
they tell you in church, so I never go.

Senor Rivera (the fourth friend):   I don't go to church either,
but I believe in God and the after-life.

Interviewer: Now, do you think any one of these four friends
here is right, or do you think all of them are wrong?

Interviewee: Oh, I'm like Senor Rodríguez. I go to the church
in San José about twice a year.   But I think the way Senor Rivera
does, too.

This line of conversation may have continued for some time.   The
technique of imaginary role-playing was not invariably utilized,
however.   Some of the topics did not lend themselves to it as much
as others.   Also, it seemed more effective if not repeated too
frequently.   Nevertheless, it proved successful, if judged by rapport,
indications of interest, and the capacity of respondents to grasp
meanings which might otherwise have been more greatly distorted or
missed entirely.

The Puerto Rican study as a whole is systematically built
upon a theory of culture developed in the author's Cultural Foundations of Education--An Interdisciplinary Exploration (Harper, 1957).
One of the many assumptions is that education can be regarded as a
kind of institutional binoculars through which to focus upon the
several dimensions of culture, such as order, process, and goals
(the three major categories, aided by numerous subcategories, of
the theoretical study).   Equally, it is possible to turn around and
focus upon education through the lens of culture.   To some extent,
both approaches were utilized: the first, through our grassroots
respondents, all of whom were in some way connected with the
schools; the second, through our national leaders who symbolized
more of the attitudes, beliefs, and practices of the total culture.
Or, to epitomize our methodology in still a different way, we wished
to look at Puerto Rico in various perspectives--from the bottom up,
as it were, but also from the top down--using education as a kind of
fulcrum.

The total time devoted specifically to grassroots interviews totalled about two hundred hours--to national-level interviews, about one hundred hours.   In addition, the author has devoted approximately two and one-half years to direct immersion in the culture, including many visits to schools of all types and all levels, among other institutions.

While the study could claim to be primarily anthropological (its findings are therefore essentially qualitative, with all its advantages and disadvantages), we should point out that the methodology as a whole is interdisciplinary.   So, too, are its objectives. The aim is to experiment with a fusion of three disciplines-- philosophy (most familiar to the author), education, and anthropology.   Another assumption of the study, indeed, is that traditional academic divisions are no longer adequate if one is to study the interworkings of human behavior.

The following discussion constitutes only one small part of the total project.   Even this selection, however, should be sufficient to indicate to the critical reader that the study has many limitations.   To mention but three: the data are derived primarily from very small and far from perfectly representative panels of informants; the data are clustered somewhat toward the middle strata of the culture; and they do not succeed in penetrating to the metacultural level by any means as deeply as might have been possible had more time and more skill been available.   It is most important to emphasize, therefore, that this article claims nothing more than our limited evidence permits.   It is one partial profile of culture-and-education in one small, but in revealing ways microcosmic, dot on the global map.

II.   Democracy

Puerto Rico is a democracy-conscious culture.   Its people-- excepting a handful of extreme Nationalists, a portion of those who support the dwindling Independentista Party, and a still smaller number of Spanish expatriates--are publicly proud of their six decades of association with a nation which, since the eighteenth century, has been regarded by the world as one of the greatest of democratic nations.   The Commonwealth Constitution is a model of democratic principles.   The government formally operates according to these principles, and constantly expounds them in its pronouncements.   All religions are free to worship.   Race discrimination is unlawful.   The public schools are modelled upon the North American pattern far more than any other (the doctrine of separation of church and state is one example), and children are taught the rights and duties of citizens living in a democratic country.   Finally, other instruments that shape the citizen's mind, such as newspapers, radio and television stations, enunciate this ideology as loudly as they repudiate all alternatives.   The syndicated columnists in El Mundo, for example, are for the most part the same ones that are read in Continental newspapers, while the magazines most widely circulated are also Continental--most notably, the Spanish and English editions of Time and The Reader's Digest.   Explicitly, Puerto Rican culture is overwhelmingly devoted to the slogans of democracy, and all of our respondents professed this ideology them-

selves.
       Is it equally so on the implicit level?   The answer here, as
it would be in the parent democracy, is far more equivocal.
According to most of our respondents, the bulk of the people have
not yet learned the meaning of such devotion nearly as completely
as they should in at least one major respect--namely, in their
tendency to idolize their present leaders (particularly one, the
Governor), and to leave too much by way of policy and implementation to those they have elected.
       Many voices were heard at the grassroots to the effect that
Puerto Ricans trust their top level leaders too abjectly for the good
of their democracy.   Only a small minority, one a respondent
habituated to the pseudo-feudal life of a coffee hacienda, felt that it
was a proper habit to encourage.   The majority held that other
types of leaders--notably, labor and religious--are also accepted too
abjectly.
       The degree and kind of acceptance varies, however.   Two
respondents pointed to the landslide election as Senator of a well-
known Protestant who had been publicly opposed by the Catholic
Church. This illustrated, they said, that political leaders have a
stronger grip on the people than do religious leaders.   A comparable
point was made by a leader respondent who reported that the Bishop
of Ponce has repeatedly shown his hostility to the party in power,
with little effect.   Labor leaders were also said to have greater
influence than religious leaders, but they, of course, have been
closely affiliated with the dominant political leadership.   Even local
mayors, if a militant Catholic respondent was correct, are usually
"listened to" much more than are local priests.
       National-level respondents, although they usually supported
this general opinion, were more inclined to qualify it.   Whether or
not they were influenced by the fact of their own positions of sometimes high authority, several pointed out that respect by the people
for strong political leadership is not necessarily inconsistent with
democracy.   The real question is whether such leadership represents
the genuine wishes of the people--also, whether they have sufficient
opportunity to criticize and, if they so choose, to repudiate those
they have elected.
       Stated this way, no respondent on any level contended that the
present government leaders are unrepresentative of what the great
majority have thus far considered to be their best interests, and no
one questioned the integrity of the top leadership.   The point was
also made that this leadership has performed a legitimate democratic function in motivating the people, in helping them to understand their own problems, needs, and rights.   In this sense, even
though it has often had to move more slowly than it might have
wished or might have attempted if less democratic, the government
in power has played a tremendous educational role as well as a
strictly political one.
       Nevertheless, even at the national level considerable concern
was manifested by the gap between ideological and underlying
attitudes concerning the leadership issue.   The habit of relying
heavily on leaders, several pointed out, derives from a mixture of
Hispanic, religious, and colonial traditions, a habit symbolized by

the term personalismo, and connoting deep respect for persons in
authority.   Thus, while a larger proportion of adults were said to
go to the polls every four years than in any state of the Union,
they tend to assume that their duty is then over and that it is up to
the chosen leaders to work out a program for their benefit until the
next election.   One subcultural respondent estimated that eighty
percent of the citizens--the least educated majority--think the
leader should decide all crucial questions once they have approved
him.

Some concern arose also over the question of minority dissent
to majority rule--another fundamental democratic principle.   Several
leaders were convinced that Puerto Ricans already respect this
principle, as indicated by their tolerance of unpopular ideas.   One,
for example, mentioned that it is difficult to keep Nationalists in
prison for extended periods, not because of widespread approval of
their views, but because of respect for their right to oppose the
majority.   For the same reason, it would be more difficult to imprison Communists convicted under the Smith Act than in many
North American states.   Likewise, if another leader is correct,
most Puerto Ricans, unlike most mainlanders, are not frightened by
"socialist" or equally unorthodox economic and political proposals;
indeed, they often accept them not only in words but in housing,
agricultural, and other practices.   The reasonableness and tolerance
of ideas even suggested to one leader that the personalismo tradition, with its spirit of arbitrary and sometimes violent authority, is
nowhere nearly as influential as some have tried to argue.

The fact that the American Civil Liberties Union was engaged
by the government to study minority rights in Puerto Rico and to
recommend means of strengthening them--a quite unprecedented step
among democratic countries--would support further the explicit
acceptance of the majority-minority principle.   It would not, however,
prove that no incompatibility with the implicit level prevails.
Censorship by the Department of Education of certain of its publications was cited as one deviation.   Several respondents mentioned
the refusal of majority party mayors, despite the Governor's plea,
to grant minority parties an official voice in municipal affairs.
Repeatedly, too, comments were made at the grassroots to the
effect that dissenters are "afraid" to make themselves conspicuous,
especially if they hold jobs that depend on the good will of party
officers or government bureaucrats.   Finally, according to one
leader, government agencies set up to serve the people are too
often staffed by persons who have feeble understanding of such
methods of democracy as criticism and participation.

But respondents sharply disagreed as to where the greatest
compatibility or incompatibility between democratic ideology and
configuration lies in terms of class and region.   Some were certain
that the lower socio-economic strata manifest the most compatibility
--their argument being that, because ideological beliefs are of minor
concern to people with little education and little guided opportunity
to reflect about so profound a concept, their tendency is to be
democratic simply because it is their "way of life."   One leader
made an intriguing distinction: lower-strata groups especially in
the rural areas are more democratic in their individual relations

(for example, their respect for one another as persons, which is partly the effect of their Christianity) than in their institutional behavior (for example, their careless regard for traffic rules).

A few, however, maintained that the middle urban strata are, on the whole, more consistently democratic than the lower: the former have thought more than the latter about democracy, and so they try harder to equate practice with professed belief, even in the face of insecurities and conflicts that sometimes result from such conscious effort. The fact that in the last election they were more critical than other classes, judging by the size of their vote against the party in power, could be offered in support of this contention. No respondent argued that the greatest compatibility is to be found in the highest social stratum.

Comment is also required with regard to the problem of race relations, viewed in the context of democratic beliefs. Equality among races is not only supported by law but is widely accepted both ideologically and in overt conduct. Respondents did not deny, however, that a limited kind of segregation occurs in restaurants, hotels, swimming-pools and other places where tourists and the well-to-do gather. Any remaining segregation does not result, it was claimed, from official rules established by the management (such rules would be illegal) but rather from the fact that the average colored Puerto Rican cannot afford luxury prices. That he might also feel uncomfortable for fear of being unwelcome in such surroundings may likewise be an intangible factor, as it would be in many northern cities of the Continent. At the same time, a few colored people do appear in the most expensive establishments. More serious in terms of our problem is the fact that they were reported to be excluded by membership qualifications from most if not all upper-class casinos, from certain businessmen's clubs, and from such religious organizations as the Catholic Daughters of America.

Still more serious were the discrepancies between ideology and configuration that appeared in the responses of some resource persons. As anyone knows who has looked into the matter, one of the most revealing tests of such feelings is that of attitudes toward marriage between races. Only one white respondent on the subcultural level would have no serious objection to racial intermarriage for his own children, and three light-skinned fathers insisted they would do all they could to prevent it. Reasons were diverse: one respondent said that it would "lower the race"; another said that "white is for white" and "black for black"; still another feared that his daughter would be boycotted by her friends and that his grandchildren would suffer if they went to the United States. The question was not asked of all leader respondents, but it was possible to infer from related questions that their attitude was typically more liberal. Among all respondents, moreover, only one revealed the kind of extreme inconsistency that is chronic on the Continent: while unusually vocal in professing the egalitarian ideology and insisting that he was not "against" Negroes, he was hostile not only toward miscegenation but toward interracial dancing in high school; he spoke of the "trash," largely colored, that inhabited nearby slums; he thought that Negroes should be excluded from hotel swimming-pools; he wanted them to "keep their distance" in social affairs.

The fact that Puerto Ricans who migrate to the States often experience discrimination would lead one to suppose that insular concern over the problem might increase, particularly since so many travel back and forth. The two army veterans among our respondents both admitted they had experienced discrimination, one at the hands of a private, the second from a Negro officer! Three others at the grassroots said they had heard of prejudiced treatment against Puerto Ricans. Yet no respondent, even among leaders, voluntarily expressed much concern over this problem.

Nor was anti-Semitism, which often develops in North American cities, especially among lower-class people who are seeking a "scapegoat" for their troubles, discernible in the interviews. This is interesting in view of the fact not only that many thousands of Puerto Ricans are employed in the New York garment industry which is manned predominantly by Jewish workers and managers, but that they live in Harlem tenements where anti-Semitism is often rife because of alleged Jewish landlords. The only evidence of anti-Semitism observed in Puerto Rico was the word "kike" splashed on two walls of the metropolis, and symptoms in some university students during class discussions.

Let us draw together our conclusions and inferences from this brief examination of beliefs toward democracy. As would be true of all cultures, even the most democratic, inconsistency prevails between the ideological and metacultural levels. The widest gap was partly attributed to the stubborn persistence of the personalismo tradition, although inadequate appreciation of the principle of minority dissent as the polar principle to majority rule was considered by two leaders as, in long range, even more serious a deficiency. Grassroots respondents were more incensed at their fellow-citizens for relinquishing too much authority and responsibility to leadership than they were at leaders for accepting it. Also, they seemed less concerned with the problem of minority dissent than were most national-level respondents who, interestingly enough, seemed less concerned in turn with the problem of over-concentrated leadership.

In race relations, something of a gap between the explicit principle of equality and implicit attitudes was also discernible. Perhaps because the problem of race relations does not loom large on the Island, little indignation was revealed toward discriminatory treatment even on the Continent. When tested by questions that touched personal sensitivities, however, discriminatory feelings toward colored persons were found to be acute. Whether these could be attributed entirely to the phenomenon that color is explicitly associated in Puerto Rico with lower status rather than with inferior race, or whether (as a minority of leaders insisted) strong ingredients of race prejudice can also be detected in such feelings, was not determined clearly enough to warrant generalization. It would be important to know whether, if racial prejudice does prevail to a markedly greater degree than most respondents were prepared to admit, this would not help to account for perpetuation of the generally lower status of colored people at the same time that the generally lower status of these people helps to perpetuate any remaining prejudice.

Looked at together, both groups of respondents were, nevertheless, convinced that democracy, racially as well as politically,
is far from a mere shibboleth to the people of Puerto Rico, hence
that an impressive compatibility is already revealed between their
explicit allegiance to its principles and their implicit acceptance of
them. Moreover, compatibility has increased rapidly in less than
twenty years, although understanding of some aspects of democracy
is still to be achieved. While strata and regions were considered
unlike in the extent to which they have achieved a democratic configuration that harmonizes with their political ideology, it is a
commentary on the unsettled nature of the problem that respondents
also differed as to which groups have attained the greatest harmony
thus far. They did imply that the upper stratum is the least
compatible both in its political beliefs and in its racial attitudes.
And they would probably hold that the degree of synthesis between
the two levels is already greater, certainly in democratic political
beliefs if not also racial ones, than in any other country south of
the United States.

III. Religion

One of the paradoxes of Puerto Rican culture is the disparity between formal affiliation with the Catholic Church--between
eighty and eighty-five per cent of the population, according to most
estimates--and meager concern for its religious ceremonials and
dogmas. The fact that services of the Catholic Church are
attended regularly by a much larger proportion of women than men--
one leader was sure this was largely due to the tradition that it is
unmasculine to be seen too often in church--and that the most
ardent Catholics, class-wise, are members of the upper stratum,
helps further to sharpen the paradox.

Its significance for our problem is obvious. If the religious
ideology is predominantly Catholic, and yet if only a fraction (ten
to fifteen per cent, according to some informants) are sufficiently
devout to follow the mandates and rituals of Catholicism with any
regularity, can it not then be said that another type of incompatibility appears between the explicit and implicit levels of belief?

Respondents were largely agreed upon a pronounced degree
of incompatibility, but they were equally agreed upon the importance of distinguishing between the theological routines of the
Catholic Church, on the one hand, and the core tenets of Christianity,
on the other hand. If one leader was right, only a tiny handful of
Puerto Ricans could be considered free-thinkers. Virtually all
believe in God; probably as many believe in immortality. Yet,
several others placed the Christian belief in human brotherhood
and sanctity of personality even higher in importance for most
Puerto Ricans. And it is worthy of note that two leaders contended
that the lower strata are more harmonious religiously than the upper
strata, their reason being the same as in the case of democratic
beliefs: though there is the least ideological sophistication on the
lower levels, there is consequently the greatest implicit sincerity.

Another distinction was stressed by both groups of respondents,
including Catholics themselves. The degree of incompatibility be-

tween ideological creed and deeper religious attitudes is strikingly
less among Protestants in Puerto Rico. In other words, the
fifteen to twenty per cent of the population belonging to one or
another of their numerous denominations (the Baptist, to mention but
one, was said to maintain about fifty churches on the island with a
membership of about 150,000) are more successful in relating creed
to behavior than is the Catholic majority. This is demonstrated
not only in a higher ratio of church attendance by both Protestant
men and women, not only in the greater zeal with which they
participate in ceremonials, but especially in their development of
social services such as rural hospitals and agricultural projects.
These were said to dramatize the non-sectarian, non-theological,
and democratic aspects of the Christian faith.

Several explanations were given for the greater gap between
the two kinds of belief among Catholics. One was the reputation
of "clericalism," meaning the affiliation of a politically minded
hierarchy with the colonial rule of earlier centuries, a fact true of
other Hispanic cultures. Such a reputation has lingered long and
helps to explain the continued support of the Church by the top
status level of the population. (Families on this level are often
fervently Spanish in their customs and loyalties.) Also, it at least
partially accounts for a certain half-conscious suspicion if not outright hostility with which many people of lower and even middle
status tend to look upon the Catholic clergy. These attitudes, which
were noted in several subcultural respondents, have been reinforced
by its reputed indifference to the personal and social welfare of the
common people, an indifference related again to the "clerical"
habits of a priesthood imported hitherto largely from Spain itself.
But the situation is now changing, it was reported--indeed, one
Protestant informant went so far as to assert that Catholics are
already surpassing Protestant programs of social welfare.

Traditionally, at any rate, the use of Latin rather than the
Spanish vernacular in Catholic rituals, the remoteness from churches
of many rural settlements, the expense of ceremonials such as
Church marriages, and the great difficulty of living up to the stern
principles of Catholicism (most notably, in sex relations)--all have
been further contributing factors to the disparity.

This last point is underscored by the growing numbers of
Puerto Ricans who practice birth control despite bitter opposition
of the Catholic hierarchy; by the thousands of women, who, though
they may attend church regularly, have also visited one of the many
birth-control clinics established by the Department of Health; and
by the fact that both sterilization and divorce are on the increase.
Only one of the fifteen subcultural respondents who were Catholics
expressed opposition to all forms of birth control as well as
divorce (except for infidelity). This same respondent, a lifelong
rural resident, was also the only one who expressed a wish that
only Catholics would live in his barrio (township). But even this
lone wish was countered by another Catholic respondent in the
same barrio who said he would welcome Protestants as friends
equally with Catholics.

We sum up our evidence concerning the second example
chosen to focus upon cultural configuration by inferring that in-

compatibility between ideological and metacultural beliefs is wider
in the case of religion than in that of democracy. As two respondents put it, Puerto Ricans may be deeply religious in certain
attitudes, but this does not mean that most of them are ecclesias-
tical about these attitudes. If, however, one means by explicit
religious beliefs the kind that would be accepted by earnest Christians everywhere, even though they may seldom be clothed in the
doctrines of ritual or articulated as dogmatic creeds, then in this
sense the degree of compatibility is regarded by our respondents as
extremely high.

IV. Morality

The problem of morality, which was confined in our research
mainly to standards of sex conduct, is closely related to religion
for the obvious reason that the ideological code is influenced by
Christian doctrine, especially the Sixth Commandment. This problem
is complicated by the traditional practices of concubinage and the
double standard. Although both practices were said to be decreasing (most rapidly in the urban middle class) no one contended that
they have become negligible.

Here, then, a conflict even in explicit beliefs inevitably
occurs. The Christian theology completely repudiates both pre-
marital and extramarital sex relations; the secular cultural
ideology tolerates, if it does not openly condone, these relations.
Moreover, while it could not be argued that most women approve, it
did appear evident from several responses that even they tend to
regard the double standard with markedly greater forbearance, albeit
a reluctant one, than would be true in cultures such as the United
States. To cite an example: one woman respondent reported that
upper-class mothers of illegitimate children in her community were
fully accepted socially by others of her class, and that she herself
did so with little reservation.

We must, however, recall that the privilege of the double
standard is limited to the male sex. Because of the so-called
"virginity cult," which is largely unmodified thus far even by the
impact of more flexible Continental standards, respondents would
surely agree that a much higher compatibility prevails between
explicitly approved virginity for unmarried women and implicit
patterns of belief and conduct than it does for unmarried men. Because this compatibility is strongly reinforced by the explicit religious ideology, the degree of consistency between the latter and
the wider cultural ideology is also much higher in the case of moral
standards for women than for those of men.

Among our subcultural respondents, only one was emphatic in
her opinion that women ought to have the same rights as men, and
that if men are entitled to know several women intimately before
marriage, women should have the same privilege. Yet she, too,
concurred in the virtually unanimous opinion of her peers that,
though the double standard is ideologically wrong, either extramarital or premarital relations are "worse" for women than for men.
Whether by "worse" was meant that the man's reputation is less
easily damaged or that it is religiously more sinful for the woman
remained unclear. Possibly one participant came closest to ex-

pressing the implicit belief of the majority when he confessed that
his real reason for looking upon relations out of wedlock as "worse"
for women than for men was that the "norms" of the culture compelled him to think so.

One leader respondent, however, offered the striking argument that within many families a serious disparity may prevail in
another way.   Since neither the average husband nor average wife
admits, much less freely discusses, the husband's extramarital
experiences, the results of trying on both sides to maintain the
appearance of complete monogamy are a good deal of secrecy on the
part of the husband and a good deal of silent suspicion on the part
of the wife.   Often, of course, the husband's relations, especially
in the lower rural classes, become an "open secret," not only because he likes to share his experiences and perhaps boast among
his friends about his virile powers, but because his illegitimate
children and his responsibilities to them quickly become known to
the neighborhood.   By comparison, the operation of a double
standard was said to be oftener concealed effectively, for several
reasons, in upper-class groups.   Concubines are more easily
hidden in the large cities where these groups are concentrated;
more discretion is likely to be exercised in conversation among
friends; and birth control is more frequently and skillfully
practised.   One concomitant effect of such concealment by upper-
class husbands combined with often unconfirmed but unspoken suspicions by upper-class wives could be (although the hypothesis
remains to be tested) a greater degree of intrafamilial tensions
than in the lower classes where covert relations are harder to
maintain and where consciousness of inconsistency may also be less
severe.

Despite these various gaps, several leader respondents were
inclined to the opinion that, in matters of morality, Puerto Ricans
are on the whole more successful in harmonizing their explicit and
implicit attitudes than are Continentals.   Their argument was, of
course, that at least the non-religious aspects of their moral tradition are widely tolerant toward the double standard.   Thus
there tends to be less hypocrisy than in cultures where, though they
too may practice the double standard very widely, no comparably
powerful sanction is available from custom.   The widespread
acceptance of consensual or common-law marriage is another instance: moral stigmatization of either partners or offspring because of earlier failure to perform a religious or civil ceremony is
difficult to discern, certainly in the rural if not also the urban
subcultures.   To punctuate the argument, one respondent drew an
analogy with gambling: here, too, there is less hypocrisy than in
a country such as the United States where, though it is usually
illegal as well as ideologically immoral, its implicit acceptance as
measured by gambling practices was alleged to be even wider on a
"per capita" basis than in Puerto Rico itself.

Whether the argument that moral hypocrisy tends to be less
for these reasons than on the Continent is, however, open to further
inspection.   No respondent raised the question of why, if respect
for female virginity and monogamous relations for the wife is as
universal as the ideology would have us believe, such respect is

violated as often as it apparently is by the polygynous inclinations and activities of the Puerto Rican male. Nevertheless, one leader perhaps came close to encapsulating the moral configuration when he pointed out that the Puerto Rican culture is somewhat "better off" than certain others because it is more modest in its claims. Therefore in the long run it achieves more compatibility between ideology and conduct than if it claimed too much.

V. Education's Role: The Example of Democracy

In the opinion of a respected leader, one of the most important tasks of Puerto Rican education is to narrow the gap between the explicit and implicit culture, a task which cannot, of course, be left only to formal institutions of learning but must be undertaken by all types of institutions concerned with building a unified culture--economic, religious, political, and others.

Can such a complex undertaking "get off the ground" in any deliberate, organized way? To begin again with democracy, the most far-reaching of all recommendations was that the schools and colleges learn how to become democratic by experiencing its principles, by teachers and administrators learning the difference between autocratic and democratic leadership in their own performance, and by students discovering in their classrooms that the right to participate in criticizing and planning is just as important as the duty to accept the plans that are made.

The official ideology of Puerto Rican education would endorse these proposals. At the same time, its own leadership would probably admit that they have not as yet been implemented in everyday practice except to a limited extent. The centralized system with its line-staff administrative structure has not been conducive to wide democratic sharing in the formulation or operation of policies. Curricula, teaching methods, and most rules have been established primarily in the central office for Island-wide adoption. The personnel of local schools have been habituated, in turn, to following prescribed routines with minimum deviation.

Few grassroots respondents were unduly disturbed, however. The majority, on the contrary, seemed to accept this situation as a matter of course. It had not occurred to most parents, for example, that in their parent-teacher associations they might seriously consider matters such as the curriculum of their own schools. When the question was raised, some admitted that cooperative study and recommendations by parents might be beneficial, but others held that all such matters should be left entirely to officials of the school system. Nor was the question of whether teachers and students might also participate in curriculum planning, in formulating rules of discipline, and in offering constructive criticisms, apparently one which had received much previous consideration by subcultural respondents. Thus when they were asked to make their own recommendations for the improvement of education, only a small minority thought to include the strengthening of democratic processes in their own institutions.

This minority did suggest, however, that more decentralization in policies and programs ought now to be attempted. It objected to the frequency with which syllabi, for example, are pre-

pared at the top with little help or guidance from teachers at the
base.   Particularly, it criticized some supervisors for imposing
their own will rather arbitrarily upon principals and teachers who
had deviated from their own directives.

Principals and teachers were also criticized by the same
minority for deficient concern with democratic principles on the
plane of daily practice.   In the estimate of one administrator respondent, considerably less than half of the principals in charge of
local public schools attempt in any significant way to encourage such
practice, a habit that would tend to be reinforced by their own sub-
jection to rules imposed from above.   The more common orientation was thus perhaps expressed by another administrator respondent who, though emphatic in explicitly opposing "traditional methods,"
also opposed student councils with authority to make any rules
except for parties, who felt that students ought not to criticize,
who was content to have curricula made entirely at "headquarters,"
and who would insist on the right to "veto" any suggestions that
parents might make.

The same estimate was roughly applied to the body of teachers, although in their case the fact that they are in charge of
abnormally large classes of children (more than sixty per class
were counted in several of the schools we visited) could help to
account for their frequently rather authoritarian roles.   It would
hardly account entirely, however: considerable insecurity and fear
of "higher ups"; the teacher's strongly traditional "matriarchal"
role; youthful habits of passivity acquired in family relations; the
still chronic practice (despite an official ban) of mild corporal
punishment by elementary teachers; finally, on the university level,
the hierarchical structure of administrative authority and the
European-influenced custom of professorial dignity--these were noted
by various respondents as other contributing though controversial
factors.

Such examples by no means imply, however, that democracy
in Puerto Rican education remains up to now wholly an affair of
words.   While the gap is still a wide one, it is slowly narrowing,
a fact supported by the sensitivity of at least a subcultural minority
to such incompatibilities as we have just listed.   Also, in the
opinion of some leaders, the gap is already closing rapidly in two
fields, both of them concerned primarily with informal and functional rather than formal instruction: first, in the program of
community education on the adult level; second, in the consumer
cooperative movement.   The latter, moreover, is reaching into
some public schools where cooperative savings clubs and supply
stores are being organized and run primarily by students themselves.

Nor should it be forgotten that individual schools and individual teachers vary markedly in their application of the democratic
ideology.   Thus, in one of the three subcultures, participation by
teachers in limited curriculum planning, the operation of a high-
school student council with some authority, as well as group methods
of learning, were becoming accepted, if still unevenly practised,
in schools of the municipality.   Also, the fact that many grassroots
respondents were willing when asked to endorse more participation

and other democratic processes for parents, for teachers, and even
for children, might indicate a potential readiness that has not yet
found opportunity for actual expression.   The fact, too, that
several of these same respondents, including teachers, were unsure
whether to admire or to condemn Franco as a leader might indicate
lack of sophistication in democratic political principles rather than
reasoned opposition to them.

Perhaps most revealing, the explicit concept of equality of
races has moved far in education toward complete achievement as
an implicit cultural pattern.   Colored teachers are as commonly observed in charge of classes of predominantly white children as
white teachers are observed in the converse situation.   A great
preponderance of all public schools contain some mixture of colored
and white students as well as teachers--a phenomenon so taken for
granted that school people showed surprise when it was called to
their attention.

Many respondents would probably consider a more serious
discrepancy between ideology and configuration to be the divisions
that arise between classes due to the rapid growth of private schools
--divisions that have the effect also of tending to separate racial
stocks in so far as white children in larger proportion than dark
children belong to the upper classes that can afford private school
tuitions.   Whether or not another limiting factor is, as one
respondent contended, that qualified personnel who are conspicuously
Negroid are less frequently promoted in administrative positions by
the Department of Education than are Caucasoid personnel, the
racial situation when appraised by democratic standards probably
reveals as little discrepancy as in any comparably sized area under
the American flag.   No respondent on any level expressed the
slightest opposition to racial integration in the public-school system.
Rather it was wholeheartedly accepted.

Much of the evidence presented thus far concerning education
as a configurational expression of democracy in Puerto Rico has
been derived from the three subcultures.   National-level respondents
agreed with many of the same points, but they both limited and
enriched them.   One leader, particularly, insisted that a wider gap
exists between the explicit and implicit levels in formal education
than it does in most other institutions, a weakness he attributed
more to over-verbalization and middle-class biases operating in
professional teacher-training programs than to any other cause.

Two other leaders differed almost diametrically from each
other on the proposal that one way to narrow the gap would be to
remake classrooms into miniature laboratories of democratic living
and learning, with special regard for experience in majority rule-
minority dissent.   The one who opposed was afraid that children
would learn the meaning of democracy in a naive and superficial
manner.   Maturity, he argued, must be attained first--especially
the capacity to reason--an argument he supported by reference to
classic thinkers in political philosophy, of whom Plato might have
been one.   The respondent who as strongly favored the proposal
would avoid superficiality by giving teachers and children daily
opportunity to learn democratic principles through practice.

We shall not here examine the issues for learning and teach-

ing that arise from our second and third examples--religion and
morality--except to assert that incompatibilities between explicit
and implicit beliefs were equally discernible.   They were most conspicuous in religion where the ideological principle of separation
of church and state is neither strictly manifested in daily school
activities nor supported on the implicit level by the beliefs of
many respondents.   As for morality, the fact that sex instruction
is only slightly touched upon by most curricula, hence that sex
morality is not as yet widely regarded as a fit subject for formal
learning, makes it doubtful whether the gaps between ideological
and metacultural beliefs that we have observed in the broader
culture would be less pronounced in education.

One leader did insist that cheating is widespread on the
college level and that this is symptomatic of a deeper moral
challenge than the evils of the practice itself.   It is due, he contended, to the "artificiality" of much Puerto Rican education, to the
stress upon paper-work, verbalization, and grades, and hence to
the separation between those and the real interests of typical
learners.   Cheating will cease to be a problem, he predicted, when
students become excited by the intrinsic importance and worth of
what they are learning--a prediction that would be equally relevant
to education in other cultures.

His point, however, is germane to the problem of sex
morality as well.   If the failure of many students to respect in
conduct a code of honesty which they accept as ideology is much
less of a reflection upon the code itself than upon the lack of
functional relationship between it and the educations they continue
to receive, then perhaps the deceits and other effects of customary
sex morality are traceable to relationships that are equally
dichotomous.   One implication surely is that education should afford
no less opportunity for scrupulous examination of disruptions caused
at least partly by incompatibilities for any other cultural behavior--
the political, say.   Just as cheating will diminish, this leader
believed, when Puerto Rican education is vitalized in terms of such
behavior, so will the tragic effects of inharmonious relations between men and women also diminish.

Looking, finally, at our theme as a whole and recalling that
its purpose has been to sample rather than to exhaust the difficult
issues it has raised, we may nevertheless contend that the overall
configuration of Puerto Rican culture-and-education can now be
perceived in both negative and positive terms.   Negatively, this
configuration according to our evidence is decidedly less democratic,
less religious, and less moral than we should expect were we to
be guided by typical ideological formulations such as those taught
by the schools.   Positively, it appears according to our evidence to
be more implicitly democratic than other Central American or
South American cultures; it is manifestly more religious in basic
Christian attitudes than in ecclesiastic allegiances; and it is more
consistently moral according to its secular traditions than its
religious ones.   In important respects, moreover, there is perhaps
a higher positive relationship between its metacultural democratic
and religious attitudes than there is between these and its moral
attitudes, although the contention could be argued further.   At any

rate, we may be reasonably sure that much the same congruities and incongruities that prevail in the Puerto Rican cultural configuration prevail also in education.

Notes

1. All the respondents on both levels, with the exception of two leaders, were born in Puerto Rico and have lived there, except for brief periods, since birth.

Long before the ice-cream man comes down the block
(twice a day) you can hear his truck playing Brahms's "Lullaby"
over the loudspeaker, and after he is gone, the sweet and gluey
tones (a little like the tasteless local ice cream itself) still linger
maddeningly on the air. Over and over and over, the music box
repeats the treacly phrase--tum-te-tum, tum-te-tum, tum-te-tum
tum tum tum!--and you think, probably that's what Chinese water
torture used to be like, only you didn't think it would come
to the cadence of Brahms's "Lullaby"! But finally he takes
himself down the street of identical pink and blue stucco
houses, and the nothingness of the long day takes over.

Time is longer here than elsewhere; the day begins early,
as it does in all the hot Latin countries; at 7 a.m. people are already walking across the garbage-strewn fields next to our house
that are a short cut to the 65th Infantry Road, the highway to the
airport; they are beginning to lay out streets on these fields;
soon there will be more identical pink and blue stucco houses;
the men are already at work. And already it's hot: the even late
summer heat of Puerto Rico that before noon clamps you around the
back and chest, and that will go on all day and late into the evening
interrupted only by the sudden rains that stop as quickly as they
come, and that end always in the same heavy clamping late-summer
heat.

The day begins early and it begins indistinguishably from the
rest of the day and from all the other days. Across the empty
fields back of street number 1, house number 14 (there are so
many new developments in Puerto Rico that they no longer bother
to give names to such streets), the brown-faced men and women
are already going to work, and as you look at the faces, the
curious stillness is already on them--the stillness that always
seems inertness in the presence of the "continental," the "American",
the stillness that in my students at the University I can no longer
tell from a deeply resistant shyness. "Feed my lambs.". . . There
is a lamb in the official seal of the Commonwealth of Puerto Rico,
and in truth these people are lamblike. We laugh when an outbreak of rapings in Santurce calls out headlines in the <u>Island Times</u>:
'New York-Type Gangs"; but as they say, there was no such
violence here until Puerto Ricans came back to the Island. I
believe them, for their famous docility (which can also be interpreted as the apathy of tropical countries and the Step'n Fetchit sloth
in the presence of Americans barking questions in the language
they do not know and no longer even pretend to know) shows itself
all day long and every day in a variety of silences and withdrawals.

Even on the road--and they are the most erratic drivers in the
world, with a sickening record of accidents--they will commit every
fault but that of excessive speed.   They drive, in fact, as if they
were on muleback; they drive en famille, arms perpetually hanging
out of the car, talking and eating as if they were home;   but they
are not aggressive.   They are used to waiting on life, waiting on
other people; they are used to taking orders; they are "sensitive"
beyond endurance, but not stormy.   The long long hot day long ago
took them over, and the sudden rainstorms--to say nothing of the
Spanish generals, the Spanish bishops, the Spanish slave owners
and feudal owners, and now.... And now the bishops are still never
Puerto Ricans but are American Irish, and the girl behind the
automatic cash register at the supermercado (run by Grand Union,
development by Laurance Rockefeller) may not speak English but
she has learned to say "okay, you bet, next aisle, please," and my
lambs are reading Emerson and Thoreau, you bet! "In transcen-
dentalism is implied that there is knowledge of transcendental
elements.   In these three passages are implied in the following
way: Emerson: During these days the people is getting rid of
the traditional feelings...."
         Are they "docile" because someone has always taken them
over--or are they just docile?   To me they are the waifs and
wards of big power politics, the submerged colonial mass incarnate,
the emerging masses in Africa and South America and the East
Indies--the mass just getting itself up through the crust of poverty,
racism, and the bush, and which, as it gets up, is immediately
handed a television program and a subscription to Confidential.
The Puerto Ricans are always being reformed, educated, studied,
analyzed, worked on, "developed" by others.   Just now they are
being worked on by the most intelligent and social-minded administration in Latin America, and thanks to the massive infusion of
American capital and the rapid industrialization of the island, Puerto
Rico is now the most prosperous and fastest growing economy in
this area.   But as I see from the complaints of Puerto Rican
students who have been to the States, they are very quick to
suspect, to misunderstand, to be hurt--and somehow I hear from
them more of what they have suffered from Americans than of
what they think of Americans.   It must be this passivity that explains the hilarious number of anthropologists and sociologists
forever prowling this island.   I am told that there is still no
really good history of Puerto Rico.   But let a young American
loose with a foundation grant and a manual of behavior patterns,
and he doesn't need to know any history, for he can always look
into breast-feeding patterns in the purely Negro areas, or study
spiritualism.
         It's all such a gold mine, either for the American sociolo-
gist or the American chain store; two and a half million Puerto
Ricans waiting to get into Woolworth's, Franklin's, Kresge's,
Grand Union, and as they wait, they can get their resources
counted and their "patterns" studied.   They won't object: why should
they?   The boy who stands all day long outside the big hotel on
the Avenida Norte trying to get rid of the few coconuts he brought
down this morning will before long move into the hotel and learn

to serve ten different kinds of rum drinks to the alrightniks in the
swimming pool--and he will still have the same far, faraway look
on his face. The alrightniks will never see him, any more than
they see his cousins and brothers in New York; and truth to tell,
he doesn't have the information and undoubtedly lacks the curiosity
with which to see them. The Puerto Ricans live on an island in
every sense of the word: they are here, and their minds don't
roam around much. Talking with university students about American writers, I have been struck by their refusal to visualize New
England landscape or wintry weather. It's not simply that they
haven't seen snow: neither had the young heroine of Carson
McCullers' novel who so longed to see some. It's that they are
here and cannot easily imagine anything too different from their
island, their town. For centuries they were wrapped round in the
torpor of the Spanish Empire, and their island was never of major
significance to the Spaniards themselves. Puerto Rico was largely
the taking-off place for Spain, the "rich port," in which anchored the
galleons bearing the gold back to Spain from Mexico, a last place
to which Spanish royal troops retreated from South America after
losing to Bolivar.

Richard Morse, head of the institute at the University for
regional studies of the Caribbean, has written a paper on "The
Deceptive Transformation of Puerto Rico" in which he points out
that there was less transplantation of Spanish society here than anywhere else in Latin America. This explains why even the most
ignorant foreigner somehow senses the lack of any real cultural
tradition here, of any firm national identity. Not only was there
no strongly organized society here under the Spaniards, says Morse,
but Puerto Rico even lacked the spontaneous spirit of organization
and economic thrift which produces a flourishing class of independent farmers. No wonder that there have been no real group
identities here for the sociologists to seize on, not enough "rituals
of celebration": even Catholicism has never been an all-dominating
cultural force here, for the Spanish priests were always regarded
as agents of Madrid, and evangelical Protestantism has taken hold
here as it has nowhere else in Latin America. Morse believes
that the island itself has usually been subject to violence from without, whether by hurricanes or buccaneers or French, British, or
Dutch invaders. It has always depended for its sustenance and
progress upon more highly organized institutions and societies
abroad, and even in the heyday of the Spanish Empire depended on
a periodic financial subsidy from vice-regal Mexico (the famous
situado), on contraband trade with European ships and with the
plantation islands of the lesser Antilles. Now it depends on the
skills, capital, and industrializing organization of the United States.

Morse's paper, which I discovered thanks to sarcastic
comments on it by a columnist in the Island Times, explains a
good deal of what troubles me about Puerto Ricans--as much here
as in the United States. If there is no strong local tradition on
the part of migrating groups, if there is no articulated and
positive ideal in their own history for which they seek expression
and fulfillment in the new country--as was true of the Irish with
their longing for political emancipation and religious tolerance, of

the German democrats and liberals who loved the republican idea,
the land-hungry Italian peasants and the oppressed East European
Jews--then it follows that some of these "newcomers," as Oscar
Handlin calls them, will not consciously seek any real attachment
with American culture.   Handlin thinks that for Puerto Ricans the
"break of migration" is not "as sharp as it had been for Europeans.
...Such newcomers did not feel the complete and total sense of
foreignness that overwhelmed the European immigrants, and, therefore, did not feel called upon to create the institutions which were
the response to the shock of separation." But in Puerto Rico itself
one discovers on every hand that these cultural institutions have
never existed, and so cannot arbitrarily be created in New York.
As many a schoolteacher in East Harlem has learned, Puerto
Rican kids are often as illiterate in Spanish as they remain in
English; and judging from the frenzied missionary effort of the
Catholic church to reclaim Puerto Ricans in New York for the faith,
they often arrive without any real religious traditions at all.
Handlin thinks that Puerto Ricans have a sense of connectedness
with the United States because they are already American citizens.
But I think that it is because citizenship has simply been granted
en bloc, because they have not had to earn it as a voluntary and
individual act, that they lack connectedness with the United States
and even with its language.   During the Korean war many Puerto
Ricans in the American forces were killed, Dan Wakefield says in
Island in the City, almost as a direct result of not knowing English,
and he suggests that the American army was at fault at not assign-
ing these troops to officers who could give orders in Spanish.   But
it must be a powerful feeling of separation from the United States
that will keep a soldier from learning enough English to keep
himself alive, as so many refugees did.   And lecturing in English
here in Puerto Rico, I can testify that this feeling of separation
exists; I have taught American literature all over Western Europe,
but have never had such trouble communicating with my students
as I do here.   The United States figures here simply as Big
Brother, and my boys and girls don't quite believe in what I am
saying--or in its possible relevance to them.   The more prosperous
ones do, of the class from which José Ferrer came.   In 1949,
when Ferrer was given the medal of the National Academy of Arts
and Letters for the best diction by any actor on the American
stage, I heard him deliver a bitter and powerful attack on in-
tolerance against Puerto Ricans, and truly, his diction was beautiful.
But his complaints against the inhumanity of the city don't help me
much when I go over a page of Thoreau or Melville with my
students.   I have never cared for the humor of H*Y*M*A*N K*A*P-
L*A*N, but he tried, didn't he?   Yes, yes, my students try, too,
and the babble from the speech clinic is all around me as I teach.
But let us say that they try without hope; they don't really believe,
as J. Robert Oppenheimer once said of his German-born father,
that being an American citizen seemed to him the greatest privilege in the world.   And why don't they believe it?   Because individuals among them are treated with disrespect, as are individuals
among Negroes, Italians, Jews, California-born Japanese?   It is
because they see themselves as wards of the state, as colonials,

not as immigrants; it is because they are "associated" with the
United States, not attached to it.   They are in no position to see
what they can make of the United States; they are in positions only
to suffer from it.

Historically, the great achievement of the United States
as a civilization has been its creation not of a tradition but of a
promise; it has been extraordinary in its ability to suggest to all
peoples the fulfillment of their particular hopes.   If anything, it
has promised the fulfillment of too many; this is why immigrants
jokingly curse Columbus, for having prepared the frustration with
the promise.   There is a kind of bitterness about America which
is the other side of the universal and infinite hopes connected with
it.   As F. Scott Fitzgerald said, France was a land and England a
people, but America, "having about it still that quality of the idea,
[is] harder to utter."   Even Mark Twain, who like all his generation in the West was an immigrant from a fabulous natural world
to the era of Mark Hanna and Rockefeller, spoke like an immigrant
when he said crossly that wonderful as it was to discover America,
it would have been more wonderful to lose it.   No country can
disappoint like America, for no other country has aroused so many
hopes.   But such hopes can arise only from an identity of one's
own and a specific tradition sharp enough to arouse the possibility
of its fulfillment in this country.   Otherwise there is no spiritual
marriage at all between America and its newcomers, and the great
epic of immigration simply becomes a picture of the lesser breeds
attached to the white Protestant majority.

Richard Morse says that the essential lack of direction
behind the "spillage" of American capital and techniques into Puerto
Rico has merely perpetuated and deepened the instability of the
Puerto Ricans, and that the industrial boom has significantly lacked
any counterpart in agriculture or education or city planning.   Now
"the hard shell of top-level technocrats covers an underbody of
soft institutions."   Needless to say, Governor Muñoz Marín is
worried about this situation, and now that massive industrialization,
"Operation Bootstrap," is so brilliantly under way, he has called
for "Operation Serenity," for a massive cultural and spiritual effort
to close up the gap behind Puerto Rico's industrial progress.   If
Puerto Rico is "the Formosa of the New Dealers," Muñoz Marín --
and his equally brilliant wife--are certainly not the Chiang Kai-
sheks.   Muñoz Marín's salary is astonishingly modest; he has
refused pay increases, and he is as imaginative and dedicated to
the welfare of his people as an administrator can be.   The United
States would be fortunate indeed if it were led with half as much
imagination and eloquence as Puerto Rico is by the present commonwealth government.   But in Puerto Rico all such operations,
whether toward industrialization or "serenity," seem to percolate
downward; and Luis Muñoz Marín, with his warm heart and his
quick brain, is still in the tradition of a famous father and of the
Puerto Rican intellectual elite, a teacher and reformer from the
governor's palace.   And because he represents so much of what is
best in the American Democratic party, New Deal wing, his friends
worry over what may happen to Puerto Rico in Washington--where
its fate has so often been decided--if the Republicans, some of

whose leaders have repeatedly expressed their contempt for Puerto
Rico and all its works, win again in 1960.

When a people has never had a chance to work out a deep
national identity of its own, when its experience has fundamentally
been that of dependency, when even in its religious practice it
shows an inner mutinousness against the beliefs imposed by the
conqueror--then it must seek in external political solutions at
least the sign of the independence and unity it has lacked in the
past.   Whether under the Spaniards or under the Americans, the
Puerto Ricans have always debated the same problem--whether to
be "associated" with the larger country, or to be independent of it,
or to become directly part of it.   The Puerto Ricans were granted
autonomy within the Spanish Empire just as the Spanish-American
war broke out.   Since this was followed by American domination
of the island, Puerto Ricans think that the everlasting problem of
their political status might have been solved if it had not been for
the war of 1898.   But even if one grants the closer ties to Spain,
it is obvious, from the continued restiveness of the Puerto Ricans
under commonwealth status and a native administration, that Muñoz
Marín's hope--to deflect the agitation for purely formal solutions
into a massive effort to raise living standards--has in the first
respect not succeeded.   The Puerto Ricans are very busy debating
statehood versus commonwealth status, and there is still a core of
intellectuals with strong faith in Puerto Rico's national culture who
are simply for independence, while the hard-bitten extremists who
tried to kill Truman and shot up Congress are still represented by
the Nationalist party.   Muñoz Marín, who was once simply for independence and now of course strongly backs commonwealth status,
tried to detour the statehood movement by coming up with a new
formula: there would be time to consider statehood only when the
per capita wealth of the islanders reached that of the poorest state
in the union (Mississippi); it was calculated that this would happen
in the 1990's.   Without directly opposing statehood, Muñoz Marín
managed to give the pro-commonwealth forces a handle against it,
and the next day the New York Times editorially applauded Muñoz
Marín for his brilliant and thoughtful solution.   But while the Times
drew a sigh of obvious relief at being able to put the problem off
for thirty years, at least a few Puerto Rican intellectuals pointed
out that even considering statehood wholly in economic terms was
distinctly not complimentary to the United States.

The demand for statehood is probably strongest in the
prospering new middle class.   Now that they travel like Americans
between San Juan and New York, or gaily study psychoanalysis in
Iowa City and the theatre arts in Dallas (unlike the poorer and
darker-skinned Puerto Ricans, who arrive on the hideous economy
flight that seems to be the airlines' effort to duplicate the steerage
in mid-air), many businessmen and doctors and lawyers are all for
statehood, and you can see in the rear windows of the newer and
bigger cars stickers asking for admission of Puerto Rico as the
fifty-first state.   But obviously statehood is spiritually inconceivable
to Governor Muñoz Marín--and many Puerto Ricans--and how else
should it be?   They are Latin Americans; their language is Spanish;
and Governor Muñoz Marín, one of the principal advisers to Wash-

ington on Latin American policy, is, as head of the Commonwealth
of Puerto Rico, a far more dignified and significant figure than he
would be as head of just another American state. Understandably,
since by now many Puerto Ricans feel closer to the elites on the
mainland than they do to the peasants in the hills, statehood
promises more secure personal status. So with one thing and
another, the everlasting argument about what Puerto Rico is to be
still boils over. And how it fascinates and enthralls! How many
stickers in the back of how many cars! What endless excitement!
Like the Russians of the 19th century debating Slavophil against
Westerner, the Puerto Rican may yet discover that debates about
which culture to join up with are a symbol of national powerless-
ness. But in Puerto Rico these debates cannot conceal the fact
that there is no positive, rich, and glowing national past either to
save from the Americans or to affiliate with them.
    And to make the situation even drearier, the American
businessmen and technical experts and supermarket designers who
in typical American fashion have "expertise" without culture, who no
longer have any intellectual convictions of their own with which
they can either challenge, or adopt, or reject the culture of others,
are now all "liberals" to a man, sympathetic to Puerto Rico as a
matter of course, and sit around the bars discussing affiliation
versus independence as if this gummy question were one that they
could answer. If ever proof were needed that Americans do not
have enough pride and self-knowledge even to think of themselves
as "imperialist" custodians of the "lesser breeds," it can be found
in Puerto Rico. The manager of a soft-drink company told me
that he thought the United States should "hold on" to the island,
whatever the cost to us, only in order to show the world how
beneficent and richly devoted to the welfare of other peoples we
can be. This would show up Russia in the eyes of the world and
give us a higher score in the cold war. Most of the Americans I
meet here don't even think of themselves as "holding on" to Puerto
Rico. The intellectuals at the University, many of whom came
expecting a breath of Latin culture, a whiff of the mother continent,
by now either feel like Puerto Ricans or just feel sorry for them;
whereas the technical experts, the airlines personnel, and the
journalists find it all too easy not to think beyond their jobs. This
in part I can understand, since the heat, the perpetual need of a
lift, the lack of the more oppressive stateside taxes on liquor and
the bathfuls constantly being flown in from the free ports of the
Virgin Islands--to say nothing of the fact that you can conveniently
buy your liquor in the supermercado and that the rum is cheap and
the local beer excellent--make this place a perpetual New Year's
Eve party. The swimming pool is never far from the bar, and
all you need to cover your nakedness is a credit card.
    Of course there are other Americans who do not drink at
all. There is a whole group of evangelical young American physicians who have given up big incomes in the United States to build
up medical stations like Castaner, in the middle of the island--
which can be reached only by mountain roads so winding that people
in small cars often take dramamine. And there are young writers
and artists at the university in Rio Piedras who are there out of a

deep interest in Hispanic culture, who know their Lorea and their
Machado as well as they know their Hart Crane, and so are not as
homesick as I am when I read my students' papers on The Great
Gatsby. They do not believe in the press-agent talk of Puerto
Rico as a "hybrid" of two cultures; they are there for the Spanish,
like the wonderful Spanish Loyalist scholars you run into at the
University. But between the young American officers here and in
the Virgin Islands, who like the medical scientists here seem
virtually the last Americans with a keen professional edge to their
lives, there is a whole group of Americans who have come here in
flight: from broken marriages, from the lifelong stigma of having
once belonged to the Communist party, from. . . the difficulties and
pains of not being better than they are. An American Somerset
Maugham could do a picturesque novel on the drifters, the ex-
radicals, the drunks, the queers, the invalids seeking the sun,
the missionaries, the Southern crackers who have gravitated here
as a matter of course and interestingly have learned to be civil
to their Negro neighbors. And what I mind most about Puerto
Rico is not that this island absorbs so many Americans, but that
it enervates them, gives them no mark to shoot at, nothing hard,
clear, perfect of its kind to be equal to. The torpidity I mind as
I mind it anywhere, whether in Latin America or in those parts of
the United States where insularism makes itself felt, sooner or
later, in the same peculiarly thin, two-dimensional quality of a
society wholly "modern," without tradition and without ideas. The
Spanish Republicans in Puerto Rico do not have this peculiar
sensitiveness without pride, this readiness to take offense from a
stranger; the Englishwoman at the University speech clinic, who
has spent much of her life teaching Latin Americans, does not
have it. But with Puerto Ricans one always finds oneself discussing
their feelings and their sufferings, never their ideas and their
hopes.
      And so history always repeats itself here as the sterile
tale of the bigger nation and its Puerto Rican victim. Unfortunately,
there is not as much time left for Puerto Ricans as there used to
be, for as everything moves faster and faster even as the subject
nations and peoples come forward, there is barely a chance to
make up for the centuries of intellectual numbness before the
smoothing out process of mass culture takes over. Independence
will not create in Puerto Ricans the past they lack; statehood,
should it ever be granted, will not automatically create the self-
respect they seek; the present commonwealth status of "association"
will continue to symbolize the uneasiness that must persist so
long as the people do not know what to hope for--or the direction
from which their hope is to come.

Anthony Lauria, "Respeto, Relajo and Interpersonal Relations in
    Puerto Rico." Anthropological Quarterly 37:53-67, April 1964.
    Reprinted by permission.[1]

        Every universe of discourse has its clichés.[2] Ordinary
speech is full of trite statements which describe and evaluate the
behavior of individuals. Among these cultural forms are two poorly
explored classes: one refers to the way in which all roles must
be played; the other refers to the way in which kinds of individuals
play all their roles--that is, to a general styling of all their interaction. The first class refers to the characteristics which any encounter between all persons must possess, and which any actor
must demonstrate; the second class refers to the characteristics of
specific personae, or social personality types. Students of Latin
American anthropology have not devoted enough discussion to this
type of analysis[3] with one significant exception: Edwin Seda's
codification of Puerto Rican social personality types (1957: 32-63).
        Our examination of some of these clichés utilizes a concept-
ual scaffolding derived from Erving Goffman's work,[4] who in turn
builds upon earlier insights provided by G. H. Mead (1934). In
ordinary social intercourse, the participants mutually present and
maintain a certain image of self which pertains to each of them.
Men seek to communicate certain information about themselves
and each other; they establish and convey impressions about certain qualities of the self. In this process, men give each other
value: "the person . . . is allotted a kind of sacredness that is
displayed and confirmed by symbolic acts." (Goffman 1956b:473)
The self, and the image of self built up in action is endowed with
the sort of ritual value discussed by Radcliffe-Brown (1939). This
is accomplished through the use of a ceremonial or ritual idiom,
by which individuals express their character and also convey their
appreciation of the other participants in the encounter. If, through
the proper use of this idiom, a man shows himself as committed
to, and capable of, maintaining another person's image of himself,
he demonstrates what Goffman terms proper demeanor. In doing
so, he will use a component of the ceremonial idiom which serves
to express the positive value with which the participants in any
situation endow each other. Goffman describes this component of
activity as "deference" (op. cit. 477). The idiom also provides for
profaning the self; it contains equally elaborate rituals of defamation.
        1. Seda's analysis of a number of clichés of Puerto Rican
speech ordered them into sets delineating social personae.[5] Our
discussion begins with another of these linquistic labels, respeto.
Rather than being associated with a specific social personality type,
respeto is a quality of self which must be presented in all inter-

personal treatment.

In attempting to describe this self, we must have recourse to an additional set of clichés. Besides the set containing those of Puerto Rican social discourse, we add that of many observers of Puerto Rican social discourse. Such commentators have placed considerable emphasis on the folk aspects of dignidad (literally, "dignity"), honor ("pride," "honor"), upon the courtesy of adult males, upon the impression given that each man seems to conceive of himself as always being primus inter pares; the image of the haughty Hispanic individualist, conserving within himself an inviolable residue of pride. Many of these comments appear in discussions which implicitly or explicitly postulate a uniform Puerto Rican "national character."[6] They are hackneyed comments, but we submit that they can be endowed with heuristic value precisely because they are hackneyed. They are clichés because they refer to clichés; i.e., the most general definition of a social situation which Puerto Ricans present to each other is also presented to outsiders. Both sets overlap.

Respeto is a quality ascribed to the properties. It signifies proper attention to the requisites of the ceremonial order of behavior, and to the moral aspects of human activities. This quality is an obligatory self-presentation; no Puerto Rican is considered properly socialized unless he can comport himself with respeto.

The verb form, respetar, indicates that in any encounter, one expresses deference to the person whom he confronts. Failure to convey this is termed una falta de respeto ("lack of respeto").

Un hombre de respeto is a man who projects the kind of self which is capable of maintaining the ceremonial order. He demonstrates proper demeanor; his comportment gives the impression that he can be a proper "interactant," committed to, and capable of, maintaining another man's image of himself. He is said to be un hombre de consideración--one who has consideration for the self-images of others.

But the quality of possessing proper demeanor is also something which must be presented to the individual; he alone cannot legitimize his claim to it. Others' communication of their regard for him in turn endow his self with proper demeanor. It is frequently said "Hay que darse a respetar antes de ser respetado," alternatively, "El que no se da a respetar, no lo respetan"--one must evidence proper demeanor, show oneself worthy of being respected before another will defer to him; he who shows no respect will not receive it. When a man does show it, él considera --he shows "personalized deference,"[7] he is de carácter ("of character"), possessing the requisite self-attributes. He is also de vergüenza, capable of knowing shame, of taking responsibility for his acts. Carácter and vergüenza denote "self-respect"; one shows that one has sufficient regard for one's self, to be allocated a self in society.

Thus, in their daily intercourse, Puerto Rican men give each other value; they treat each other as if they were sacred. Through their mutual enactment of the ritual, they establish and convey impressions concerning certain highly valued self-qualities.

And it is here that the clichés of Puerto Rican social discourse
coincide with the clichés of those who have commented upon this
discourse. Both sets overlap. We have the picture of men who
stand off from each other, players in an elaborate game where no
one may come too close for fear of offending, who treat each
other as potential duelists, ferocious in self defense. And the man
who is indeed de respeto, possessing dignidad, or who is truly
macho, [8] who is serio, taking the moral and ceremonial order
seriously, and cumplidor, who complies with the obligations of
proper inter-personal treatment, is the hombre completo, the
integral or complete man. He possesses, as one Puerto Rican
anthropologist has described this, "an almost fanatical conviction
of his self value" (Seda 1957:40).

In treating with others, one is always careful not to step on
the other's dignidad. Men might kill for many reasons in Puerto
Rico, but their reasons are usually phrased in this idiom; violations of the basic right to respeto, either in personam or in rem,
can lead this far.

Further, one must treat all men with respeto. To be sure,
the concrete deferential acts of respeto communicate many kinds
of regard in which a person may be held--awe, trust, esteem for
technical capacity, recognition of superior rank, and affection.
But the element of respeto which must be communicated in the
most minimal message of this ceremonial idiom concerns the
person's basic right to a self. This element of respeto obtains
between those who are, otherwise, social equals, superiors, and
subordinates. One's very social existence is predicated upon the
bonds of respeto.

However, respeto is a homonym. In describing this term,
it is necessary to differentiate between the sort of generalized
deference which we have been discussing, and various particular-
ized forms of respeto which are the concomitants of particular kinds
of social relations in Puerto Rico. The two categories must not
be confused. The first category of respeto is that which must be
present as a quality of all social relations, regardless of their
content. The second category contains a wide variety of kinds of
regard, all defined as respeto. One deserves special mention:
deference in the ordinary sense of the term, as we use it--giving
place to a person of superior authority or prestige. But no
matter how much the subordinate is expected to respetar his
superior, in this sense, the latter must always express deference
as well, using the first form of respeto. Even if the superior
comports himself with an overbearing hauteur, he is obligated to
express his deference to the subordinate's self through the proper
symbolic acts. [9]

Just as the kinds of regard which are expressed through
respeto vary, so do the symbolic forms which communicate them.
There is a universal ceremonial idiom, in which all adult Puerto
Ricans can communicate; there are other idioms which are more
specific to certain segments of Puerto Rican society. In either
case, respeto is the basic prop of the deference game. But not
all Puerto Ricans are capable of manipulating the forms of all of
the special idioms. Embarrassment, loss of face, shaming, and

other breaks in communication are created by the contact of these differing ceremonial orders. The well-known examples of the peasant who cannot mesh with the bureaucracy of the State; and the nouveau riche who cannot get on with the visiting technical specialist from the capital are illustrations. Yet both these examples of dissonance are evaluated in terms of the universal idiom. The peasant avoids the use of State services because the clerks do not express respeto properly: 'no consideran a uno''; the nouveau riche is ''misunderstood'' and refuses to take the advice of the specialist.

2. As Puerto Ricans have developed an elaborate set of honorific rituals around the conveyance of respeto, so have they developed an equally elaborate idiom of defamation. We may examine one aspect of this idiom in considering the semantics of the verb relajar and the associated noun el relajo. They have a wide variety of behavioral referents, a few of which we will briefly illustrate before examining one set of these referents in detail.

Most usages of relajar refer to joking, and to a kind of joking interaction whose elements parallel the content of the classical joking relationship--privileged insult, banter, and so forth. The topics are numerous; reference can be made to the personal, political, occupational idiosyncracies and sexual habits of a participant in the interchange, or some close relative or friend, or of some absent person. Ribbing, riding, kidding all come under the purview of un relajo. The derogatory nickname with which a person is endowed may sometimes be used. Many Puerto Ricans have two nicknames: one, the apodo or sobrenombre serves as an alternate, or sometimes the only name by which a person is addressed; the other, the mal nombre, is wounding and derogatory, unless the situation in which it is used is otherwise carefully defined. Use of either type of nickname is a relajo. One may also 'put one over'' on another man, making him swallow a tall story, or cogerle de bobo (take him for a sucker, make a fool out of him); an alternate form is to catch him out in some set joking gambit. If a man falls for the gambit, the reply is ''Me cogiste'' ('you caught me off guard,'' 'my face slipped'), and/or a sally in kind. 10

The telling of jokes, obscene or otherwise, the use of obscenity regardless of the interactive context is described as están diciendo relajos. Friendly grappling, punching, slapping also rate this epithet, which also serves to describe a somewhat unruly or disorderly gathering or party, (''se formó el gran relajo en el baile''). Sexual intercourse is also described--e.g., ''Cogieron a Chuito y Pepa en el relajo en el monte'' ('they found Chuito and Pepa making out in the bush'). Impious or inappropriate behavior with reference to religion is another example. In one case, a man described what he deemed to be a faked trance on the part of a young member of a certain revivalistic sect as 'el niño estaba relajando con los ojos abiertos. Estaba relajando con la religión.'' ('the kid was faking it with his eyes wide open; he was fooling around with religion').

There are more neutral uses; an excessively sweetened cup of coffee will evoke the comment 'Este café relaja''; a woman,

commenting on a dress which is in fashion, but owned by too many
women, may say "Esa moda está relajada." The connotation, in
common with most uses of the term, is of excess.

Cogen las cosas a relajo is said of those who do not take
things seriously, of those who fool around, in our parlance. Some
men can take nothing seriously; they attempt to turn everything
into a joke; such a one is described as un relajón. Frequently,
the adjective un exagerado is added, signifying one who always
exaggerates some aspect of behavior, some aspect of his role
playing--one who continually and consistently goes too far.

The full array of meanings assignable to relajar and un
relajo may be paralleled, in colloquial New York speech, by the
full array of uses of "to fool with/to fool around/to fool around
with"; "to mess with/to mess around/to mess around with"...

Space permits the detailing of only one of these behavioral
complexes: the confrontational joking game, where the object of
the relajo is a direct participant in a social encounter. The behavior which constitutes part of a joking game, in which all adult
male Puerto Ricans are seemingly capable of participating, may be
observed to take place between the occupants of practically any
position in the structure of any Puerto Rican social grouping.
Such passages may occur between any type of kinsmen, peers,
colleagues, "buddies," friends, and neighbors, and even between
compadres (co-godparents), subordinates and superordinates, and
men of quite disparate ages. It occurs among and between
representatives of any segment of Puerto Rican society. Only one
significant difference is notable; where the overall social position
of the participants is symmetrical, then any one has the right to
initiate the relajo; where the overall status is assymetrical, only
the superior may generally initiate the game.

The settings and occasions for such interaction are legion.
They occur in bars, in the plaza, at race-tracks and cockpits,
around baseball diamonds, in clubrooms, in private homes, in
the streets, or any place of work. Indeed, any place where men
congregate is an appropriate context. The joking most often takes
place when men are at their leisure, or where the place of work
is in a temporary locus of "leisure" activity. We must emphasize
that joking, riding, kidding, banter, the ironic sally, are among the
salient characteristics of all encounters between men, except in the
courtroom, in churches, and during parts of the work process.

When the content of the message would be considered
offensive or insulting, a consensus must be established between
the participants, allowing someone to begin the relajo, knowing
that the person he confronts will maintain a poised line of action--
that he will take it as a joke. A rich vocabulary of speech and
gesture aids in so defining the situation. Tone, gesture, laughter,
and the time and place of the confrontation convey the impression
that the statement is not meant as an affront. The other will
immediately indicate just how he accepts the sally. In general, he
is obliged to accept it--cogerlo como relajo; he may laugh at his
own expense, and usually returns the treatment in kind. From

there, the game continues.   If he is angered, he is obliged not to
express it.

Sometimes, he cannot reply--the sally may have hit him
too hard, or his repertoire of retorts is exhausted.   He may say
"Ah, deja eso" or "Deja el relajito ese" ("Ah, cut it out, get off
my back!"), making it clear that he is not offended.   He may attempt to stop the interchange by expressing the faintest hint of
anger via intonation and a stiffening of the body.   Or he says
"tumba ese relajo," a usage specifically showing that he means it
this time; "ho relajes mas commigo," "don't mess around with me
anymore."

The mutual "fooling around," described as "se relajaban uno
al otro" (kidding each other) can occur as a sustained interchange,
remaining at the level of a simple game whose vocabulary is part
of the ritual of defamation and humiliation, but no one takes it
seriously.   At other times, the participants may take it very
seriously, yet maintain the facade of the friendly joke.   For analytical purposes, two categories may be distinguished: a simple
"joking game" and the much more serious, and consequently infrequent "joking contest."   In the second case, the mutual relajo
becomes a joking contest, a full-blown contest of defamation, a
ritual of degradation whose players are aggressively engaged in
scoring points against each other, in seeing how far they can go
and still retain the superficial consensus of amiability.   All the
devices, gambits and insults are used, successively becoming more
dangerous.   The winners are those who do not express their anger,
who do not become embarrassed or flustered.   In such a contest,
the self maintained in interaction is attacked on two levels: its
positive qualities are assailed; in addition, one is treated by the
rest of the participants, not as a participant, a full social person,
but as a mere focus of attention. [11]

In the contest, the standardized techniques of withdrawal
from the particular line of interaction cannot be used without losing
face.   One cannot become embarrassed, nor can one demand,
with various degrees of severity or mock-severity, that the op-
ponent stop there, or stomp out in a righteous rage, or become
angry and curse, or even resort to the ultimate sanction of violence.   The game continues until someone breaks, or the participants are somehow satisfied that they cannot break through
the other's reserve, or some witness succeeds in intervening.
Such intervention takes numerous forms; frequent tactics include
outright criticism of the line of interaction being followed by one
of the participants; re-direction of the joking at a different level,
with different objects and referents; a new alliance between those
who are temporarily onlookers; an attempt to shift the focus of
attention to matters outside the frame of the relajo.   Of course,
the game may end in mutual recrimination and fighting.

The obligation to take it as a joke can produce different
lines of interaction: the joking game, and the much less frequent
joking contest.   Either one may terminate in a serious rupture of
relations, or in actual fighting.   As the limits of tolerance are approached, el asunto coge calor (things get hot), the participants
ponen color al asunto--they color it red-hot.   If the limits are

passed, men storm at each other, fight, or retire from the scene.
Others comment on the incident: it has gone beyond joking; the
relajo has been converted into un abuso, una ofensa; una falta de
respeto has been committed. Se han pasado de la raya.[12]

Defamation contests, or profanation games, are described
for several cultures, the best known being several varieties of "the
dozens" and "jiving" among North American Negroes, and La
Passategla of Southern Italy.[13] Both examples seem to be examples
of a defamation contest that, as recurrent types of social situations,
are more formally instituted than the relajo "contest." The rules
of the "dozens" and La Passategla constitute sets which contrast
sharply from milder forms of profanation. But the difference
between the Puerto Rican joking game and joking contest is less
a matter of special rules and symbolic forms and more the way
in which the rules are manipulated. Joking game and joking
contest are analytic constructs, in this case; Puerto Ricans do
not define this as a game.

3. To indulge in relajos of any sort in the presence of
anyone is to engage in a relation of confianza--of trust and familiarity with that person. The significance of confianza is quite
complex, since it does not merely denote an absence of formality
as it would amongst North Americans. Thus, certain kinds of
social relations are characterized by a great degree of both respeto
and confianza. In general, however, confianza refers to an invasion of that social space surrounding the self which is demarcated
by the ritual avoidances enjoined by the maintenance of generalized
respeto. And confianza implies that one's image of self is even
more committed into the hands of others. Conflict, or its threat,
follows upon an abuse of such trust, or when one presumes to
inject an element of confianza in a relationship where there should
be none. And the relajón is frequently called un confianzudo, one
who presumes too much familiarity.

4. The aspects of the ceremonial order discussed above are
symbolically coherent. Respeto refers to a set of deferential
rituals; relajo subsumes, among other things, the symbols of
defamation, counters in transactions of mutual degradation and
profanation. Respeto and relajo are sometimes seen as antithetical;
"si tú no respetas y te pones a relajar con cualquiera, nunca te
respetarán a tí" ("if you do not defer properly to others and fool
around with everyone, no one will respect you") is a statement
frequently made to children--and to ethnographers.

Considering the standard meaning of relajar (to relax, to
stretch, to loosen) the choice of this term to describe rituals of
defamation becomes significant. A man who indulges in such behaviors figuratively does just that to the obligation of respeto
which should rigidly bind the confrontational self-presentations of
Puerto Ricans. The rule of conduct is stretched; avoidances are
relaxed; the precincts of the self are invaded. In acceptable joking,
one presumes upon the respeto due to one's self and that of another;
and one can, relajando, stretch things too far. One can pasarse
del límite and commit a true falta de respeto. In such cases so
much metaphoric strain, in the logic of the ceremonial order, has
been placed upon the rule of conduct that it ceases to obtain. The

consensus which maintains the worth of each participant's social
image is disrupted, and can no longer be restored through embarrassment or further banter. Only withdrawal, violence, rupture
of relations or apology can restore the situation.

Other uses of relajar are consistent with the metaphor of
strain upon the proper order of things or of excess beyond that
which is seemly or satisfactory. [14]

5. We have stated that all adult male Puerto Ricans are
capable of manipulating the symbols of respeto and relajo. In
generalizing about elements which pertain, at least as a minimal
or background element to all interaction among all Puerto Ricans,
we introduce considerations which raise the same thorny problems
presented by the national character studies. In discussing problems
met in the study of Mexico as a complex society, Wolf (1956: 1075)
suggested:

> It seems possible to define "national character" operationally
> as those cultural forms or mechanisms which groups in-
> volved in the same overall web of relations can use in their
> formal and informal dealings with each other. Such a view
> need not imply that all nationals think or behave alike, nor
> that the forms used may not serve different functions in
> different social contexts. Such common forms must exist
> if communication between the different constituent groups
> of a complex society are [sic] to be established and
> maintained.

The ceremonial idiom under discussion is one such device.
In Puerto Rico, we can demonstrate the existence of different cultural codes for various segments of the society. We postulate that
all male adult Puerto Ricans, regardless of character or personality type, or the specific symbolic idiom of their particular
social segment, are capable of communicating in a common ceremonial idiom. Each of the sub-groups of the society has its own
ritual idiom, part of a symbolic order reflecting the peculiar social
structure of the group; a symbolic order which produces differing
cognitive models of the structure of the total society. But, using
the symbolic small change of the universal ritual idiom, all Puerto
Ricans may make statements to each other concerning their
ceremonial and moral worth as social persons. Although, at times,
the different orders may clash, the clash is evaluated in the same
terms by the participants, using the idiom of respeto. They can
tune in on a common network. Representatives of different segments of the society can converge upon one another, regardless of
cognitive and emotional differences presupposed by the idiom of
their particular social segment. Thus the element of respeto and
the associated ceremonial order is one of a number of forms which
allow us to speak of Puerto Rico as constituting a single society, as
well as being a relatively homogeneous socio-cultural system. [15]

We have not attempted here any psychodynamic analysis of
these situations. The image of self predicated upon respeto is an
outcome of the confrontation of men in society; there is no need to
postulate a particular set of psychic mechanisms at this level of
analysis.

It is possible that the segment of the network which turns

upon respeto may cease to be a stable mechanism in the articulation of Puerto Rico as a single society. New ritual forms, and a new symbolic idiom are apparently emerging. Through migration to the mainland, through the new educational system, and especially through the emergence of new religious systems, individual Puerto Ricans are differentially exposed to alternative symbol systems. The nature of the self which will be a product of the new systems of ceremonial discourse is changing; new sets of self-presentations are emerging. And the code built upon respeto, as well as the concept itself, may well become one of several partly antagonistic idioms mediating relations in the same social field.[16]

6. Summary. Respeto and relajo have been discussed as composing a symbolic idiom that serves to integrate Puerto Rican society. The relation of the term relajo to the crucial self-property of respeto has been demonstrated. This included showing why Puerto Ricans use relajo to designate those behaviors to which it refers. The conceptual scheme developed by Erving Goffman has proven useful in ordering data from another culture, although a systematic test of his formulations in cross-cultural perspective was not attempted. Using Goffman's framework, it is possible to operationalize at least some aspects of the notion of national character. The framework conveniently orders data in an attempt to delineate the kinds of messages which constitute the universal components of the circulation of symbols, cartes d'identité and self-presentations through a complex society. Further, the approach used in this paper seems to allow the anthropologist to bring together the microstructural and the macrostructural aspects of the study of complex societies. On the basis of this tentative analysis, a uniquely Puerto Rican symbolic idiom is postulated. In the absence of comparative studies of sufficient rigor, it is not yet possible to specify the degree to which the idiom is unique.

References Cited

Abrahams, R.
    1962--"Playing the Dozens." Journal of American Folklore.75: 209-220.
Albizu Miranda, C. & H. Marty Torres
    1958--Atisbos de la personalidad puertorriqueña. Revista de Ciencias Sociales 2:383-403.
Berreman, Gerald D.
    1962--Behind many masks: ethnography and impression management in a Himalayan village. Monograph No.4, Society for Applied Anthropology.
Brameld, T.
    1959--The remaking of a culture. New York.
Cochran, T.
    1959--The Puerto Rican businessman. Philadelphia.
Dexter, L.
    1949--A dialogue on certain Puerto Rican personality patterns and the social psychology of colonialism. Human Relations 2:49-64.

Dollard, J.
    1939--The Dozens: dialect of insult. American Imago 1:
        3-25.
Goffman, Erving
    1955--On face-work: an analysis of ritual elements in social
        interaction. Psychiatry 18:213-231.
    1956a--Embarrassment and social organization. American
        Journal of Sociology 62:246-271.
    1956b--The nature of deference and demeanor. American
        Anthropologist 58:472-502.
    1959--The presentation of self in everyday life. Garden City.
    1962--Encounters: two studies in the sociology of interaction.
        Indianapolis.
Hotchkiss, J. C.
    1962--Children errand-runners: their roles in the social life
        of a small Mexican community. Paper read at the
        61st annual meeting of the American Anthropological
        Association, Chicago, Illinois, Nov. 1962.
Hymes, D.
    1962--The ethnography of speaking. In T. Gladwin and W.
        C. Sturtevant (eds.) Anthropology and Human Behavior.
        Washington: Anthropological Society of Washington,
        13-53.
Kany, Charles
    1960--American-Spanish euphemism. Berkeley.
Kaplan, B. (ed.)
    1961--Studying personality cross-culturally. Evanston.
Lauria, A.
    1960--The effects of migration on the processes of cultural
        stability and cultural change in contemporary Puerto
        Rico. MS.
Luquín, E.
    1961--Análisis espectral del mexicano: el lambiscón, el
        madrugador, el pica-pedrero, el pistolero. México,
        D. F.
Manners, R. M.
    1956--Tabara: subcultures of a tobacco and mixed crops
        municipality. In Steward 1956:93-170.
Marqués, R.
    1962--El puertorriqueño dócil. Cuadernos Americanos 120:
        140-195.
Mead, G. H.
    1934--Mind, self, and society. Chicago.
Mintz, S. W.
    1956--Cañamelar: the subculture of a rural sugar plantation
        proletariat. In Steward, 1956:3]4-417.
Padilla, E.
    1956--Nocorá: the subculture of workers on a government
        owned sugar plantation. In Steward, 1956:265-313.
    1958--Up from Puerto Rico. New York.
Paz, Octavio
    1950--El laberinto de la soledad. México, D. F.

Pedreira, A. S.
    1934--Insularismo. Madrid.
Petrullo, V.
    1947--Puerto Rican paradox. Philadelphia.
Radcliffe-Brown, A. R.
    1939--Taboo. Reprinted In Structure and function in primitive
        society, 1952:133-152. Glencoe.
Reuter, E. B.
    1946--Culture contacts in Puerto Rico. American Journal of
        Sociology 52:91-101.
Seda Bonilla, Edwin
    1957--Normative patterns of the Puerto Rican family in
        various situational contexts. Unpublished doctoral
        dissertation, Department of Anthropology, Columbia
        University.
Steward, J. H. (et. al.)
    1956--The people of Puerto Rico. Urbana.
Stycos, J. M.
    1955--Family and fertility in Puerto Rico. New York.
Tugwell, R.
    1947--The stricken land. Garden City.
Vailland, R.
    1959--The Law. (P. Wiles, trans.) New York.
Wallace, A. F. C.
    1961--The psychic unity of human groups. In Kaplan 1961:
        129-164.
    1962--Culture and personality. New York.
Wolf, Eric R.
    1956--Aspects of group relations in a complex society:
        Mexico. American Anthropologist 58:1065-1078.
    1962--Cultural dissonance in the Italian Alps. Comparative
        Studies in Society and History 5:1-14.
    1963a--Review of M. Kenny, A Spanish Tapestry. American
        Anthropologist 65:432-434.
    1963b--Kinship, friendship, and patron-client relations in
        complex societies. Read at the Conference on New
        Approaches to the Study of Social Anthropology,
        Cambridge, U. K.
Wolf, Kathleen L.
    1952--Growing up and its price in three Puerto Rican sub-
        cultures. Psychiatry 15:401-433.

Notes
1. A shorter version of this paper was selected by The Central
   States Anthropological Society as the outstanding student
   paper presented at its annual meeting held in May, 1963
   at Detroit, Michigan.
2. This study is based upon field materials gathered in Puerto
   Rico during the summer of 1958 and the period from August
   1960 to August 1962. I am deeply indebted to Esther
   Santiago Lauria, my wife and colleague, for her advice and
   comments during the preparation of this paper, and grateful
   for the comments and suggestions of John C. Hotchkiss,
   Irving L. Horowitz, Julian Pitt-Rivers, James Silverberg,
   Eric R. Wolf, and Alvin W. Wolfe.

3. Anthropologists have generally left this to the belle-lettrists, who sometimes systematize the linguistic labels into types of personnae, and dialectologists and folklorists, who do not. See for example Luquín (1961), Paz (1950). An interesting compendium of the terminology associated with aspects of self in American Spanish is found in Kany (1960).

4. This brief exposition of Goffman (esp. 1955, 1956a, 1956b, 1959, 1962) serves only to introduce our discussion; it does not do justice to the value of his work. His ideas were developed in the study of North American behavior; we are attempting to utilize his ideas in ordering data on another culture, as have Berreman (1962) and Hotchkiss (1962). However, this paper does not attempt a systematic test of all his formulations in cross-cultural perspective.

5. He shows certain sets of these clichés to be descriptions and evaluations of the individual "...not as an actor in a particular social role but generalized to apply to the personal stylization of the individual in all life activities...and person playing roles...may be described not with reference to a particular role but rather to a general description of his actions. Examination of these overall descriptions used in a culture may spell out clusters of attributes of high or low desirability. Such social personality forms provide ready-made styles in which individuals portray themselves and by which they 'size-up' and accordingly respond to others." (1957:32-33) In our terms, these are "self-attributes." Without Seda's codification, the present analysis could never have been written.

6. Almost everything written about Puerto Rico touches on this. The more important statements are to be found in: Brameld (1959) Cochran (1959) Dexter (1949) Petrullo (1947) Tugwell (1947) and a host of cultural nationalist exegises. The imagery of passivity employed by Albizu and Marty (1958) and Marqués (1962) contrasts with the picture painted by the first group. K. Wolf (1952) and Landy (1960) present analysis of personality systems per se.

7. Seda's rendering (1957:42).

8. For present purposes, the usual translation labels "He-man," "real man" may be used to render macho.

9. This point is best documented in studies of the relations between workers and their superiors. Cf. Mintz (1956:368) who mentions that a mayordomo should show workers on a sugar plantation "the respect (respeto, not deference) they believe appropriate." Generally the treatment of the concept of respeto in the literature consists of noting nothing more than the concomitant of respeto peculiar to a specific social relation. (Eg. Padilla 1956:292, 295; 1958:177; Stycos 1955:38n, 75, 79, 122-123; Mintz 1956:386). Manners (1956:144-45) apparently recognized some of the elements stressed in this paper: a 'word generally used to describe the proper behavior and response to others in social situations...there are no absolutes determining what constitutes respectful behavior in all situations...When the forms

are observed, the participants in the vis-á-vis situation are
said to be behaving properly towards one another. When
they are violated it is because either or both behaved with
falta de respeto."

10. The usual translation equivalent of <u>bobo</u> is "fool." The term is
used throughout Puerto Rico to describe a baby's rubber
pacifier. This is perhaps significant, since the term in
e.g. Northern Mexico is the more neutral chupón. This
makes our rendering--"sucker"-- doubly significant.

11. Compare Goffman 1962:58-59.

12. Of course, these matters are extremely subtle; the cues, the
messages, which convey various degrees of <u>relajo</u>, intent,
and reaction cannot be expressed in a paper of this length.
Nor was I equipped to record them adequately. All of the
methodological problems posed by this paper are reviewed
in Hymes, 1962.

13. For "The Dozens," see Dollard, 1939; Abrahams, 1962. For
<u>La Passategla</u>, see Vailland, 1959. Among whites of
various ethnic groups in New York City, "ranking" or "sound-
ing" an individual represents a similar phenomenon.

14. There are a number of labels which are partial or complete
synonyms for <u>relajo</u> and <u>relajar</u>. Some are as yet im-
perfectly understood. The following are listed as examples
only: (subs.) un pasamacho, un chacoteo, una burla, una
burla, una broma; (verb) pasar el macho, burlar, bromear,
molestar, chavar, joder, chacotear.

15. See also Wolf, 1962, 1963a, 1963b, and parallel discussions
by Wallace 1961, and 1962, Chapter 1.

16. An analysis of changes in the idiom of personal confrontation
resulting from conversion to the Pentecostal church is
currently in preparation. We do not mean to imply that,
e.g., migration necessarily changes the idiom which a
person uses; migrant returnees use the old patterns. Certain aspects of this problem are analyzed by Lauria (1960).

L. H. Rogler and A. B. Hollingshead, "Puerto Rican Spiritualist as a Psychiatrist." American Journal of Sociology 67:17-21, July 1961. University of Chicago Press. Reprinted by permission. [1]

[Abstract: Preliminary study of schizophrenia in the lower class in San Juan, Puerto Rico, suggests that spiritualists often serve as psychiatrists and that spiritualism functions as a therapeutic outlet for mental illnesses. A mentally afflicted individual, alienated from his social groups by his deviant and enigmatic behavior may find that a group of spiritualists accepts his behavior. Participation in a spiritualist group serves to structure, define, and render the aberrant behavior institutionally meaningful. Spiritualism serves the afflicted without the stigma of attending a psychiatric clinic.]

In recent years social scientists have made a number of studies of interrelations between the social system and mental illness, some of which discuss the role the psychiatrist plays in society. [2] This paper focuses on the therapeutic role of a quasi-professional group only rarely thought of as being in the medical sphere--the spiritualists. [3]

Currently, we are doing research on mental illness in the lower classes of the San Juan metropolitan area of Puerto Rico. Early in our study we learned that persons afflicted with mental illness frequently come into contact with spiritualist mediums before, during, and after their visits to psychiatrists. Local psychiatrists are aware of these folk therapists. Likewise, spiritualist mediums have some understanding of the functions of psychiatrists. In some cases, a psychiatrist and a medium may share a patient: one psychiatrist, for example, told us that relatives brought a patient to him for a "special" purpose--they wanted him calmed so that he could be taken to a "genuine" therapist, a spiritualist medium! Psychiatric clinics in the San Juan area are known to have been used surreptitiously by local mediums to treat ambulatory patients. Furthermore, outpatients at one psychiatric clinic have been heard to refer to psychotherapy as pases. (Pases are the symbolic gestures performed by mediums for curative purposes; the term is rich in connotation.)

Our experiences have led us to the tentative conclusion that persons in the lower class rely upon spiritualist beliefs and practices as therapeutic outlets for mental illnesses. We hope to furnish here illustrative materials on the interrelations between the culture of the lower class and the identification and treatment of mental illnesses by non-medical practitioners. The materials are

drawn from systematic interviews with mentally ill persons, ranging from mild neurotics to severe psychotics, with their spouses,
and with a series of individuals diagnosed by qualified psychiatrists
as having "ho mental illness." In addition, we have interviewed
spiritualist mediums and participated in many of their sessions in
order to observe their patients acting and being reacted to in these
settings.

        Spiritualism is the belief that the visible world is surrounded
by an invisible world populated by spirits. The latter are "good"
or "bad."[4] Spirits have the power to penetrate the visible world
and to attach themselves to human beings. They may manifest
themselves as a reincarnation of some other person or thing. As
metaphysical beings they are able to coerce and influence human
affairs, often very dramatically. Persons may develop special
faculties (facultades), "mystical antennas," which enable them to
communicate with spirits. In this sense the person with facultades
has gained a measure of control over the spirits. Consequently,
an individual with facultades may influence human affairs by
commanding the obedience or favor of the spirits.

        The beliefs and practices of spiritualism are distributed
throughout the society with, perhaps, a relatively pronounced
tendency to concentrate in the lower classes. However,
spiritualists and their followers in the upper classes are careful
to distinguish their type of spiritualism from that of the lower
classes. Upper-class spiritualists insist on the scientific and experimental character of their beliefs, arguing that lower-class
spiritualism is irrational and superstitious.[5]

        Spiritualism actively provides social meanings to its troubled
participants. In the lower class, it is coterminous with social life,
woven into the intimate trials, strife and personal turmoil that
enmesh the members of a socially and economically deprived stratum,
where its function is to discharge the tensions and anxieties generated in other areas of social life. For example when, as often
happens in spiritualists' sessions, a married woman complains of
the infidelity of her husband, the medium may call upon the spirit
of her rival and assume her role. The medium indicates this
change in her personality by gesticulating, changing the quality of
her voice,and in general acting "como una mujer de la calle" (like
a woman of the street), it being assumed that that is the kind of
woman that would lure married men from their spouses. The
troubled wife then attempts to convince the spirit that she should
leave the husband alone and cease causing untold suffering. The
effect of the dramatic exchange appears to be that the wife believes she has begun to cope with the problem.

        "Crazy" (loco), "bad in the mind" (mal de la mente), and
"weak in the brain" (debil del cerebro) are common expressions
for mental illness in the vernacular of the persons studied. The
words denote unusual and idiosyncratic behavior. One of our
schizophrenic subjects said:

        'A mentally ill person is one who has no control and can kill
someone else. It is a person who is irrational, like an animal,
one who does not use his mind. Such a person can do any horrible
thing. They must be treated like children, otherwise they may fall

upon you like a ray of lightning. Would I marry such a person?
Absolutely not. Why would I want to bring a piece of worthless
furniture into my house? It would be best to put such a person
in a hospital where she could die.

"I am uncomfortable when I speak to [friends] about my illness. They may misinterpret what I say about my illness. They
will laugh at me. They will not trust me. They will avoid me."

This man, and others, realize that the very act of going to a
psychiatric clinic may be the first step in the assumption of this
feared role, for the psychiatric clinic is known as a place where
locos go.

The spiritualist, as believer and participant, takes the
stigma from an afflicted person. The spiritualist may announce to
the sick man, his family, and friends that the patient is endowed
with special psychic faculties, a matter of prestige in this social
class. Spiritualism is a form of folk psychiatry. It serves its
believers without their suffering the stigma associated with psychiatric agencies.

Spiritualism claims competence in the interpretation and
treatment of pathological symptoms. Does the individual report
hallucinations? This clearly indicates to the believer in spiritualism that he is being visited by spirits who manifest themselves
visually and audibly. [6] Does he have delusions? He is told that
evil spirits are deceiving him about himself as well as others.
His thoughts are being distorted by interfering bad spirits. Or,
through the development of his psychic faculties, spirits have informed him of the true enemies in his environment. Is his talk
incoherent, rambling, and cryptic? This indicates that he is
undergoing a test, an experiment engineered by the spirits to see
if he is of the right moral fiber. Does he wander aimlessly
through the neighborhood? He is being pursued by ambulatory
spirits, unmercifully tormenting him. To illustrate: a thirty-
seven-year-old woman, subject, according to the psychiatric diagnosis, to "hysterical hyperkinetic seizures," stated:

"Yes, I went to consult a spiritualist to see what the attacks
meant. The medium told me that there was a young man who was
in love with me. The mother-in-law of this young man bewitched
me through an evil spirit. This evil spirit takes me over in a
violent way.

"Did I believe the medium? Of course I did. She described
many events in my life that were true. When I would see the
mother-in-law of this young man I would get an attack. This proves
that she [the medium] was right."

The basis for the medium's claims of competence is the
assumption that all individual problems are material, or spiritual,
or a combination of both material and spiritual things. The latter
may have little or nothing to do with the outstanding complaint;
rather, it classifies the source of the problem. Consequently, if
the etiology of the illness is traced to the invisible world, it is
a spiritual problem and, as such, within the control of the medium.
Material problems, in contrast, have their causes in the visible
world of "hard" facts. These, consequently, fall within the com-

petence of doctors, druggists, nurses, and other professionals.
        Few behavioral or medical problems have a conspicuous
"material cause," immediately apparent to the subject, to the
medium, or to others; therefore, problems are classified invariably as spiritual by the medium. Thus, the spiritualist medium
effects a rough division of labor, relegating to herself (mediums are
usually women) therapeutic competence to deal with a vast range of
problems, many of which are disorders of personality in the broad,
non-technical sense of the term.
        The contacts between the medium and a patient take place
variously in, to mention two possibilities, a private consultation
or a session involving, usually, from fifteen to twenty participants.
These meetings are organized explicitly to serve the participants;
social interaction, consequently, is channeled toward the solution
of problems they bring.
        The room in which the session is held may be decorated with
portraits of Franklin D. Roosevelt, Mahatma Gandhi, and banners
of "Charity and Humility." A sober-faced, almost life-sized figure
of a cigar-store Indian with arms crossed, looking ominously to the
ceiling, may be a part of the setting. The odor of burning incense
may pervade the room. The head medium opens the session with
a long prayer, frequently from one of Allan Kardec's works, [7]
directs herself to the auxiliary medium(s), and asks them to concentrate. Preparations are designed to develop the "correct"
mood to welcome the spirits. As the session develops, the head
medium may direct her attention to the participants' order of seat-
ing as they face the table where she and the auxiliary medium(s)
are seated. The head medium then proceeds to probe, interpret,
treat, and prescribe for the ills and maladies afflicting the individual. Prescriptions include a variety of herbs, ointments,
medicated hot baths, massages with symbolic meaning, and prayers.
The session generally requires intense participation by the members,
which the medium frequently relieves by joking.
        Participants who have developed psychic faculties show
through their contortions, spasms, screeching, babbling, and deep
breathing that they have been possessed: the behavior varies in
accordance with the kind of spirit that has communicated with the
one possessed.
        The group meeting then is structured around four social
roles: those of the head medium, the auxiliary medium(s), and
participants with and those without faculties, [8] the four being
arrayed according to the participants' alleged degree of influence
over spirits. The roles are differentiated and co-ordinated by the
charisma imputed to the incumbents: we have observed psychiatri-
cally diagnosed schizophrenics effectively play each role. [9] Moreover, their performance was enthusiastically received by the others
at the session.
        Although we lack direct evidence bearing on the therapeutic
effect on mental illness of participation in spiritualist sessions, we
have abundant information describing the manner in which participation served to cope with specific problems. To illustrate: the
wife of a paranoid schizophrenic described to us the disrupting
effect her husband's incessant and pervasive suspicions were having

on her. Were she to get up during the evening to take one of
their children to the outside toilet, her husband would accuse her
of conspiring to see a lover, waiting outside. Were she to leave
the house to feed the chickens, a similar charge would be made.
In short, she had to be within the radius of her husband's vision
or suffer accusations of unfaithfulness. As she says:

"Then I decided to take him to see a spiritualist medium
since his suspicions had created an impossible situation. She [the
medium] and the other people in the session advised him. He has
not been suspicious since then. They explained to him that it was
a test that he was undergoing since he was in the process of developing facultades. They told him that he should devote himself
to charity and to the good and that he should concentrate on the
development of his facultades. My husband is now a medium, and
when he does not feel well he performs pases on himself in front
of the mirror. He feels better afterward."

Another schizophrenic reports that, when he feels restless
and fearful inside, dissatisfied with himself and others, and not
wanting to see anyone, he turns to the spiritualist for help:

"I go to sessions because they make me feel good and rested
inside. They bring me peace. I go to them because the medium
is the maximum authority in knowing how to rid one of those evil
spirits and demons that upset one inside."

Another with a severe psychotic illness reports:

"Before I go to a session I feel very unhappy. When I get
to the group I talk to the medium and the others, and I feel good.
When the others begin to talk about their problems I feel as if
I am not alone. They [the group] make me feel sure of myself."

Such reports so often come from the mentally afflicted individuals in our study that we are led to the conclusion that
attending group sessions serves, at least, to ease and alleviate
personal stresses.

We do not have the research design to test the proposition
that spiritualist sessions alter the personality of the mental patient
in the direction of mental health. However, we believe that
spiritualist sessions have a good many of the therapeutic advantages
of group psychotherapy.[10] In addition to the presumed advantages of
group psychotherapy as practiced in clinical settings, spiritualist
sessions are coterminous with the values, beliefs, aspirations,
and problems of the participants: no discontinuity in social contacts is required or participation. Little social distance separates
the afflicted person from the medium, but, in contrast, visiting
a psychiatrist involves bringing persons together who are separated
by a vast social gulf. The others in the session are often neighbors, and so the spiritualist and her followers form a primary
group where problems are discussed in a convivial setting, classified, interpreted, and rendered understandable within a belief
system that is widely accepted even by those who profess not to
believe in it.[11]

Persistent hallucinations to the believer in spiritualism are
not symptoms of a deranged mind experiencing things unperceived
by others--a definition which serves to isolate the sick. Rather,
they demonstrate the development of psychic faculties that may

eventually put the lucky person in more permanent contact with the invisible world. Thus, participation in a spiritualist group serves to structure, define, and render behavior institutionally meaningful that is otherwise perceived as aberrant.

Notes

1. Expanded and revised version of a paper read before the
    Section on the Sociology of Medicine at the annual meeting
    of the American Sociological Association held in New York
    City, 1960. The research reported here is being done
    by the Social Science Research Center of the University of
    Puerto Rico and is supported in part by a research grant,
    M-1750, from the National Institute of Mental Health,
    United States Public Health Service. We wish to acknowledge
    our debt to the members of the staff responsible for the
    interviews: Eugenia D'Acosta Ruiz, Francisca Santos de
    Limardo, Esperanza Acosta, Ricardo Márquez Rivera, Elsa
    Torres de Dávila, and Juan Muñoz Valentín. We would
    like to thank Dr. Charles Rogler, Mrs. Margot P. de la
    Cruz, and Mrs. Ann Richardson for reading and criticizing
    this article.
2. Ivan Belknap, Human Problems of a State Mental Hospital (New
    York: McGraw-Hill Book Co., 1956), pp. 205-7; G. Morris
    Carstairs, The Twice Born (London: Hogarth Press, 1957);
    Elaine Cumming and John Cumming, Closed Ranks (Cambridge,
    Mass.: Harvard University Press, 1957), pp. 36-44; Joseph
    W. Eaton and Robert J. Weil, Culture and Mental Disorders
    (Glencoe, Ill.: Free Press, 1955); August B. Hollingshead
    and Frederick C. Redlich, Social Class and Mental Illness
    (New York:John Wiley & Sons, 1958), pp. 161-67, 353-55;
    Melvin L. Kohn and John A Clausen, "Parental Authority
    Behavior and Schizophrenia," American Journal of Ortho-
    psychiatry, XXVI (April, 1956), 297-313; Alexander H.
    Leighton, My Name Is Legion (New York: Basic Books, Inc.,
    1959); Alexander H. Leighton, John A. Clausen, and Robert
    N. Wilson, Explorations in Social Psychiatry (New York:
    Basic Books, Inc., 1957); Jerome K. Myers and Bertram
    H. Roberts, Family and Class Dynamics in Mental Illness
    (New York: John Wiley & Sons, 1959); Alfred H. Stanton
    and Morris S. Schwartz, The Mental Hospital (New York:
    Basic Books, Inc., 1954), pp. 143-44; Marion Radke Yarrow,
    Charlotte Green Schwartz, Harriet S. Murphy, and Leila
    Calhoun Deasy, "The Psychological Meaning of Mental
    Illness in the Family," Journal of Social Issues, XI (Septem-
    ber, 1955), 12-24.
3. Joseph Bram, "Spirits, Mediums, and Believers in Contempor-
    ary Puerto Rico," Transactions of the New York Academy of
    Sciences, 1957, pp. 340-47; also Morris Siegel, "A Puerto
    Rican Town" (unpublished manuscript).
4. See Allan Kardec, El libro de los espiritus (Mexico City:
    Editorial Orion, 1951), pp. 147-80.

5. The type of data required to determine the prevalence of spiritualism and its class distribution is unavailable.

6. Allan Kardec discusses the different ways in which the spirits may communicate and the corresponding facultades that spiritualists may have in El libro de los mediums (Mexico City: Editorial Orion, 1951), pp. 183-224.

7. For an official biography of Kardec see Henri Sausse, Biografia de Allan Kardec (Buenos Aires: Editorial Victor Hugo, 1952). This biography contains its own review (pp. 138-39), allegedly provided by Kardec's spirit, which spoke through one of the participants in a session attended by the author of the biography.

8. This fourfold role structure has been derived from observations of problem-oriented sessions in small spiritualist groups; other spiritualist groupings may be different.

9. Lee R. Steiner, who has made the same observations in New York City, says: 'I've encountered psychopathic personalities with Jehovah complexes, at the lowest rung in both integrity and knowledge, who have effected emotional cures. It is my very definite impression that there is not very much correlation between validated knowledge and emotional cures. And I feel that this same condition obtains, at the moment, in professional therapy as well as in the occult" ("Why Do People Consult the Occult?" The Humanist, XIX [January-February, 1959], 27).

10. On the therapeutic advantages of group therapy see Marvin Opler, "Values in Group Psychotherapy." International Journal of Social Psychiatry, IV (Spring, 1959), 196.

11. 'If you ever talk to a Puerto Rican who says he doesn't believe in spirits, you know what that means? It means you haven't talked to him long enough''--statement attributed to a Puerto Rican in Dan Wakefield's Island in the City (Boston: Houghton Mifflin Co., 1959), p. 59. Though an exaggeration, it offers a very valuable hint to the interviewer. Often respondents will deny their belief in spiritualism when first questioned. However, once the interviewer has established a warm relationship with the respondent, the latter may not only admit his belief but may describe incidents that substantiate it dramatically. It is our impression that members of the upper class are more hesitant to admit to such beliefs than are lower-class individuals.

C. J. Bodarsky, "Chaperonage and the Puerto Rican Middle Class."
Journal of Marriage and Family, 26:347-348, August 1964.
Reprinted by permission. 1

[Abstract: Attitudes toward the custom of chaperonage are examined in
a sample of Puerto Rican students and their parents. Predominantly favorable attitudes indicate that the custom, although more
relaxed, still persists and is viewed as functional by its adherents
despite the influence of American culture.]

A frequently expressed belief in Puerto Rico is that the
traditional Spanish customs are disappearing under the onslaught of
the American cultural invasion. Although the precise nature of
chaperonage has been modified to meet the needs of the current
tempo of Puerto Rican life,[2] the custom of chaperonage, as a
psychological commitment to external controls to assure acceptable
behavior, does not appear to be an immediate victim.

Methodology and Sample. A sample of 10 Puerto Rican high
school seniors, half boys and half girls, was selected for participation in a cross-cultural study. All students chosen for the study
had demonstrated superior competence in academic, extracurricular,
and social behavior during high school. The students were interviewed four times during their senior year in order to determine
psychological factors influencing their superior performance.
During their freshman year at college, an interview was conducted
with the student's parents, focusing upon areas such as their goals
for the son or daughter, changes in the student since college, and
how the college was chosen. Several additional interviews with the
students were conducted during freshman and sophomore years. The
author visited the 18 Puerto Rican families in the study (two students had North American parents residing in Puerto Rico) over a
period of almost two years (1960-62). These visits took place in
the families' home and afforded an opportunity for an intensive
introduction to a Puerto Rican cultural stratum which has not been
significantly studied: the middle class.

Results. Only one of the fathers in the study said that he
disapproved of the custom of chaperoning; only two mothers stated
that they did not approve of it. The one mother who disapproved
of the custom had been divorced and was interviewed at her home
in the United States where she and the student were living. The
other couple who disapproved of chaperonage consisted of a Puerto
Rican husband and his American wife who had resided for some
time in the United States. The remaining parents, irrespective of
the sex of their children, were clearly in favor of the custom and
expressed themselves at various levels of enthusiasm and sophistication.

All of the parents who expressed approval of chaperonage actually practiced it. The mothers of the girls expected to accompany their daughters on dates or to arrange for some member of the family or friend to do so. In some instances, the father accompanied the young people. The parents of sons expected that their sons would have chaperoned dates. Frequently, mothers arranged the dates for both girls and boys, especially if an important dance was scheduled.

The male students were almost equally divided in their acceptance and rejection of being chaperoned, and all but one of the girls accepted and approved of being chaperoned. The one disapproving girl was also the one female Puerto Rican student attending a university in the United States, and her mother was the only parent who disapproved of chaperonage.

Four themes were presented by the parents as rationale for continuing the custom of chaperoning their young people. The most frequently expressed were: (a) the fear that people would gossip if it were not done; (b) young people were considered less responsible now; (c) it was necessary to teach good behavior and how to control oneself; and (d) since Latins are more passionate by nature, the girls require protection.

The concern that people would gossip was generally accepted as sufficient reason for protecting the girl's reputation by chaperoning her. This anxiety about gossip was often presented as being so strong that only a native Puerto Rican could appreciate its importance. The most meaningful way to appreciate the intensity and tenacity of these families' feelings about chaperonage is to consider their often passionately expressed comments.

The point was frequently made that the parents trusted their son or daughter but did not feel comfortable about "other young people." These "other young people" were considered to be wild and dangerous, and it was against them that their own sons and daughters had to be protected:

'I think chaperoning is necessary because it seems to me boys behave differently now from when I was a boy. There is more drinking, and they drive cars very wildly, and as you know, I think that Latins are more passionate than North Americans, and if you mix this with alcohol...''

Another couple indicated their trust in their daughter, their concern about gossip, and the mother's general wariness of boys:

"My daughter has been chaperoned by me up to last year, but now I permit her to go out in groups, never alone. Sometimes we permit her to go to a dance in groups, and chaperoning is necessary or one's daughter will be free on the lips of everyone. We are sure she wouldn't do anything wrong, but the harmful gossip...If I lived in New York City, I would want to chaperone her. I know that I couldn't but I would have to know the boy very well, because I trust girls but not boys."

The study did not attempt to study the frequency with which chaperonage was practiced throughout the island and among various classes of Puerto Ricans. Most of the parents did report that the

precise nature of chaperonage was changing in the direction of less
restrictiveness.   Groups of girls may now go to the movies or a
dance together, and a girl may go unchaperoned to the library or
a church activity during daylight hours with a boy friend.   The
rigidity of the process which many parents described as characteristic of their own youth (for example, a daylight trip to the drug-
store by a young girl occasioned parental involvement) no longer
seems representative of the custom, and this former fierce pro-
tectiveness and total control has been ameliorated.

      Conclusions.   The custom of chaperonage may have become,
for this class of Puerto Ricans, a status symbol which represents
their aspirations in society.   Chaperonage does require leisure
time, money, an automobile, and access to clubs, and it assures the
social movement of the young people within an acceptable group.
Its practice could be considered as evidence of the family's socio-
economic level.   Chaperonage frequently requires that the parents
socialize with each other while the young people dance, and
these occasions probably provide reassuring contacts for the parents.

      The ideology of freedom of mate selection with its corres-
ponding courtship practices does not appear to be characteristic
of this sample.   However, it should not be assumed that the
chaperonage system necessarily militates against a self-expressive
process of mate selection.   Most of the dates of the subjects
reflected personal preference and choice.   Within the dating experience, however, experimentation is limited and privacy curtailed.
This tends to limit interpersonal experiences and to surround them
with obstacles which act to discourage the less aggressive youth.

Notes

1. Supported by USPH (NIMH) Grant No. 3M9175 (C1) at the Puerto
    Rico Institute of Psychiatry.   E. D. Raldonado-Sierra,
    C. J. Bodarky, P. B. Field, S. E. Wallace, R. Fernandez-
    Marina, G. V. Coelho, Richard D. Trent, Arlene Cohen,
    and Francisco J. Umpierre constituted the professional
    research team for the project.   Carol DeDov has aided in
    the preparation of this paper.   See E. Silber, G. V. Coelho,
    E. B. Murphey, D. A. Hamburg, L. I. Pearlin, and M.
    Rosenberg, "Competent Adolescents Coping with College De-
    cisions," AMA Archives of General Psychiatry, 5 (1961), pp.
    517-527; and E. Silber, D. A. Hamburg, G. V. Coelho,
    E. B. Murphey, M. Rosenberg, and L. I. Pearlin, "Adap-
    tive Behavior in Competent Adolescents," Ibid., pp. 354-365.
2. Reuben Hill, "Courtship in Puerto Rico: An Institution in
    Transition," Marriage and Family Living, 17 (February
    1955), pp. 26-35.

Poverty and the so-called war against it provide a principal
theme for the domestic program of the present Administration. In
the midst of a population that enjoys unexampled material well-being
--with the average annual family income exceeding $7,000--it is
officially acknowledged that some 18 million families, numbering
more than 50 million individuals, are below the $3,000 "poverty
line." Toward the improvement of the lot of these people some
$1,600 million of Federal funds are directly allocated through the
Office of Economic Opportunity, and many hundreds of millions of
additional dollars flow indirectly through expanded Federal expenditures in the fields of health, education, welfare and urban affairs.

Along with the increase in activity on behalf of the poor indicated by these figures there has come a parallel expansion of publication in the social sciences on the subject of poverty. The new
writings advance the same two opposite evaluations of the poor that
are to be found in literature, in proverbs and in popular sayings
throughout recorded history. Just as the poor have been pronounced blessed, virtuous, upright, serene, independent, honest,
kind and happy, so contemporary students affirm their great and
neglected capacity for self-help, leadership and community organization. Conversely, as the poor have been characterized as shift-
less, mean, sordid, violent, evil and criminal, so other students
point to the irreversibly destructive effects of poverty on individual
character and emphasize the corresponding need to keep guidance
and control of poverty projects in the hands of duly constituted authorities. This clash of viewpoints reflects in part the infighting
for political control of the program between Federal and local officials. The confusion results also from the tendency to focus study
and attention on the personality of the individual victim of poverty
rather than on the slum community and family and from the consequent failure to distinguish between poverty and what I have called
the culture of poverty.

The phrase is a catchy one and is used and misused with
some frequency in the current literature. In my writings it is the
label for a specific conceptual model that describes in positive
terms a subculture of Western society with its own structure and
rationale, a way of life handed on from generation to generation
along family lines. The culture of poverty is not just a matter of
deprivation or disorganization, a term signifying the absence of
something. It is a culture in the traditional anthropological sense
in that it provides human beings with a design for living, with a

65

ready-made set of solutions for human problems, and so serves a
significant adaptive function.   This style of life transcends national
boundaries and regional and rural-urban differences within nations.
Wherever it occurs, its practitioners exhibit remarkable similarity
in the structure of their families, in interpersonal relations, in
spending habits, in their value systems and in their orientation in
time.

Not nearly enough is known about this important complex of
human behavior.   My own concept of it has evolved as my work has
progressed and remains subject to amendment by my own further
work and that of others.   The scarcity of literature on the culture
of poverty is a measure of the gap in communication that exists between the very poor and the middle-class personnel--social scientists, social workers, teachers, physicians, priests and others--
who bear the major responsibility for carrying out the antipoverty
programs.   Much of the behavior accepted in the culture of poverty
goes counter to cherished ideals of the larger society.   In writing
about "multiproblem" families social scientists thus often stress
their instability, their lack of order, direction and organization.
Yet, as I have observed them, their behavior seems clearly patterned and reasonably predictable.   I am more often struck by the
inexorable repetitiousness and the iron entrenchment of their life-
ways.

The concept of the culture of poverty may help to correct
misapprehensions that have ascribed some behavior patterns of ethnic, national or regional groups as distinctive characteristics.   For
example, a high incidence of common-law marriage and of households headed by women has been thought to be distinctive of Negro
family life in this country and has been attributed to the Negro's
historical experience of slavery.   In actuality it turns out that such
households express essential traits of the culture of poverty and are
found among diverse peoples in many parts of the world and among
peoples that have had no history of slavery.   Although it is now
possible to assert such generalizations, there is still much to be
learned about this difficult and affecting subject.   The absence of
intensive anthropological studies of poor families in a wide variety
of national contexts--particularly the lack of such studies in socialist countries--remains a serious handicap to the formulation of de-
pendable cross-cultural constants of the culture of poverty.

My studies of poverty and family life have centered largely
in Mexico.   On occasion some of my Mexican friends have suggested
delicately that I turn to a study of poverty in my own country.   As
a first step in this direction I am currently engaged in a study of
Puerto Rican families.   Over the past three years my staff and I
have been assembling data on 100 representative families in four
slums of Greater San Juan and some 50 families of their relatives
in New York City.

Our methods combine the traditional techniques of sociology,
anthropology and psychology.   This includes a battery of 19 questionnaires, the administration of which requires 12 hours per informant.   They cover the residence and employment history of each
adult; family relations; income and expenditure; complete inventory
of household and personal possessions; friendship patterns, particu-

larly the compadrazgo, or godparent, relationship that serves as a
kind of informal social security for the children of these families
and establishes special obligations among the adults; recreational
patterns; health and medical history; politics; religion; world view
and "cosmopolitanism." Open-end interviews and psychological tests
(such as the thematic apperception test, the Rorschach test and the
sentence-completion test) are administered to a sampling of this
population.

All this work serves to establish the context for close-range
study of a selected few families. Because the family is a small
social system, it lends itself to the holistic approach of anthropology. Whole-family studies bridge the gap between the conceptual extremes of the culture at one pole and of the individual at the other,
making possible observation of both culture and personality as they
are interrelated in real life. In a large metropolis such as San
Juan or New York the family is the natural unit of study.

Ideally our objective is the naturalistic observation of the
life of "our" families, with a minimum of intervention. Such intensive study, however, necessarily involves the establishment of deep
personal ties. My assistants include two Mexicans whose families
I had studied; their "Mexican's-eye-view" of the Puerto Rican slum
has helped to point up the similarities and differences between the
Mexican and Puerto Rican subcultures. We have spent many hours
attending family parties, wakes and baptisms, responding to emer-
gency calls, taking people to the hospital, getting them out of jail,
filling out applications for them, hunting apartments with them, helping them to get jobs or to get on relief. With each member of
these families we conduct tape-recorded interviews, taking down
their life stories and their answers to questions on a wide variety
of topics. For the ordering of our material we undertake to recon-
struct, by close interrogation, the history of a week or more of
consecutive days in the lives of each family, and we observe and
record complete days as they unfold. The first volume to issue
from this study is to be published next month under the title of La
Vida, a Puerto Rican Family in the Culture of Poverty--San Juan
and New York (Random House).

There are many poor people in the world. Indeed, the poverty of the two-thirds of the world's population who live in the underdeveloped countries has been rightly called "the problem of problems." But not all of them by any means live in the culture of
poverty. For this way of life to come into being and flourish it
seems clear that certain preconditions must be met.

The setting is a cash economy, with wage labor and production for profit and with a persistently high rate of unemployment and
underemployment, at low wages, for unskilled labor. The society
fails to provide social, political and economic organization, on either
a voluntary basis or by government imposition, for the low-income
population. There is a bilateral kinship system centered on the nuclear progenitive family, as distinguished from the unilateral extended kinship system of lineage and clan. The dominant class as-
serts a set of values that prizes thrift and the accumulation of
wealth and property, stresses the possibility of upward mobility and
explains low economic status as the result of individual personal in-

adequacy and inferiority.

Where these conditions prevail the way of life that develops among some of the poor is the culture of poverty. That is why I have described it as a subculture of the Western social order. It is both an adaptation and a reaction of the poor to their marginal position in a class-stratified, highly individuated, capitalistic society. It represents an effort to cope with feelings of hopelessness and despair that arise from the realization by the members of the marginal communities in these societies of the improbability of their achieving success in terms of the prevailing values and goals. Many of the traits of the culture of poverty can be viewed as local, spontaneous attempts to meet needs not served in the case of the poor by the institutions and agencies of the larger society because the poor are not eligible for such service, cannot afford it or are ignorant and suspicious.

Once the culture of poverty has come into existence it tends to perpetuate itself. By the time slum children are six or seven they have usually absorbed the basic attitudes and values of their subculture. Thereafter they are psychologically unready to take full advantage of changing conditions or improving opportunities that may develop in their lifetime.

My studies have identified some 70 traits that characterize the culture of poverty. The principal ones may be described in four dimensions of the system: the relationship between the subculture and the larger society; the nature of the slum community; the nature of the family, and the attitudes, values and character structure of the individual.

The disengagement, the nonintegration, of the poor with respect to the major institutions of society is a crucial element in the culture of poverty. It reflects the combined effect of a variety of factors including poverty, to begin with, but also segregation and discrimination, fear, suspicion and apathy and the development of alternative institutions and procedures in the slum community. The people do not belong to labor unions or political parties and make little use of banks, hospitals, department stores or museums. Such involvement as there is in the institutions of the larger society--in the jails, the army and the public welfare system--does little to suppress the traits of the culture of poverty. A relief system that barely keeps people alive perpetuates rather than eliminates poverty and the pervading sense of hopelessness.

People in a culture of poverty produce little wealth and receive little in return. Chronic unemployment and underemployment, low wages, lack of property, lack of savings, absence of food reserves in the home and chronic shortage of cash imprison the family and the individual in a vicious circle. Thus for lack of cash the slum householder makes frequent purchases of small quantities of food at higher prices. The slum economy turns inward; it shows a high incidence of pawning of personal goods, borrowing at usurious rates of interest, informal credit arrangements among neighbors, use of secondhand clothing and furniture.

There is awareness of middle-class values. People talk about them and even claim some of them as their own. On the whole, however, they do not live by them. They will declare that marriage by law, by the church or by both is the ideal form of marriage, but few will marry. For men who have no steady jobs, no property and no prospect of wealth to pass on to their children, who live in the present without expectations of the future, who want to avoid the expense and legal difficulties involved in marriage and divorce, a free union or consensual marriage makes good sense. The women, for their part, will turn down offers of marriage from men who are likely to be immature, punishing and generally unreliable. They feel that a consensual union gives them some of the freedom and flexibility men have. By not giving the fathers of their children legal status as husbands, the women have a stronger claim on the children. They also maintain exclusive rights to their own property.

Along with disengagement from the larger society, there is a hostility to the basic institutions of what are regarded as the dominant classes. There is hatred of the police, mistrust of government and of those in high positions and a cynicism that extends to the church. The culture of poverty thus holds a certain potential for protest and for entrainment in political movements aimed against the existing order.

With its poor housing and overcrowding, the community of the culture of poverty is high in gregariousness, but it has a minimum of organization beyond the nuclear and extended family. Occasionally slum dwellers come together in temporary informal groupings; neighborhood gangs that cut across slum settlements represent a considerable advance beyond the zero point of the continuum I have in mind. It is the low level of organization that gives the culture of poverty its marginal and anomalous quality in our highly organized society. Most primitive peoples have achieved a higher degree of sociocultural organization than contemporary urban slum dwellers. This is not to say that there may not be a sense of community and esprit de corps in a slum neighborhood. In fact, where slums are isolated from their surroundings by enclosing walls or other physical barriers, where rents are low and residence is stable and where the population constitutes a distinct ethnic, racial or language group, the sense of community may approach that of a village. In Mexico City and San Juan such territoriality is engendered by the scarcity of low-cost housing outside of established slum areas. In South Africa it is actively enforced by the apartheid that confines rural migrants to prescribed locations.

The family in the culture of poverty does not cherish childhood as a specially prolonged and protected stage in the life cycle. Initiation into sex comes early. With the instability of consensual marriage the family tends to be mother-centered and tied more closely to the mother's extended family. The female head of the house is given to authoritarian rule. In spite of much verbal emphasis on family solidarity, sibling rivalry for the limited supply of goods and maternal affection is intense. There is little privacy.

The individual who grows up in this culture has a strong feeling of fatalism, helplessness, dependence and inferiority. These traits, so often remarked in the current literature as characteristic of the American Negro, I found equally strong in slum dwellers of Mexico City and San Juan, who are not segregated or discriminated

against as a distinct ethnic or racial group. Other traits include a
high incidence of weak ego structure, orality and confusion of sexual identification, all reflecting maternal deprivation; a strong present-time orientation with relatively little disposition to defer gratification and plan for the future, and a high tolerance for psychological pathology of all kinds. There is widespread belief in male superiority and among the men a strong preoccupation with machismo,
their masculinity.

Provincial and local in outlook, with little sense of history,
these people know only their own neighborhood and their own way of
life. Usually they do not have the knowledge, the vision or the
ideology to see the similarities between their troubles and those of
their counterparts elsewhere in the world. They are not class-con-
scious, although they are sensitive indeed to symbols of status.

The distinction between poverty and the culture of poverty is
basic to the model described here. There are numerous examples
of poor people whose way of life I would not characterize as belonging to this subculture. Many primitive and preliterate peoples that
have been studied by anthropologists suffer dire poverty attributable
to low technology or thin resources or both. Yet even the simplest
of these peoples have a high degree of social organization and a
relatively integrated, satisfying and self-sufficient culture.

In India the destitute lower-caste peoples--such as the Cha-
mars, the leatherworkers, and the Bhangis, the sweepers--remain
integrated in the larger society and have their own panchayat institutions of self-government. Their panchayats and their extended
unilateral kinship systems, or clans, cut across village lines, giving them a strong sense of identity and continuity. In my studies
of these peoples I found no culture of poverty to go with their
poverty.

The Jews of eastern Europe were a poor urban people, often
confined to ghettos. Yet they did not have many traits of the culture of poverty. They had a tradition of literacy that placed great
value on learning; they formed many voluntary associations and ad-
hered with devotion to the central community organization around
the rabbi, and they had a religion that taught them they were the
chosen people.

I would cite also a fourth, somewhat speculative example of
poverty dissociated from the culture of poverty. On the basis of
limited direct observation in one country--Cuba--and from indirect
evidence, I am inclined to believe the culture of poverty does not
exist in socialist countries. In 1947 I undertook a study of a slum
in Havana. Recently I had an opportunity to revisit the same slum
and some of the same families. The physical aspect of the place
had changed little, except for a beautiful new nursery school. The
people were as poor as before, but I was impressed to find much
less of the feelings of despair and apathy, so symptomatic of the
culture of poverty in the urban slums of the U.S. The slum was
now highly organized, with block committees, educational committees, party committees. The people had found a new sense of power and importance in a doctrine that glorified the lower class as the
hope of humanity, and they were armed. I was told by one Cuban
official that the Castro government had practically eliminated delin-

quency by giving arms   to the delinquents!

Evidently the Castro regime--revising Marx and Engels--did not write off the so-called lumpenproletariat as an inherently reactionary and antirevolutionary force but rather found in them a revolutionary potential and utilized it.   Frantz Fanon, in his book The Wretched of the Earth, makes a similar evaluation of their role in the Algerian revolution: "It is within this mass of humanity, this people of the shantytowns, at the core of the lumpenproletariat, that the rebellion will find its urban spearhead.   For the lumpenproletariat, that horde of starving men, uprooted from their tribe and from their clan, constitutes one of the most spontaneous and most radically revolutionary forces of a colonized people."

It is true that I have found little revolutionary spirit or radical ideology among low-income Puerto Ricans.   Most of the families I studied were politically conservative, about half of them favoring the Statehood Republican Party, which provides opposition on the right to the Popular Democratic Party that dominates the politics of the commonwealth.   It seems to me, therefore, that disposition for protest among people living in the culture of poverty will vary considerably according to the national context and historical circumstances.   In contrast to Algeria, the independence movement in Puerto Rico has found little popular support.   In Mexico, where the cause of independence carried long ago, there is no longer any such movement to stir the dwellers in the new and old slums of the capital city.

Yet it would seem that any movement--be it religious, pacifist or revolutionary--that organizes and gives hope to the poor and effectively promotes a sense of solidarity with larger groups must effectively destroy the psychological and social core of the culture of poverty.   In this connection, I suspect that the civil rights movement among American Negroes has of itself done more to improve their self-image and self-respect than such economic gains as it has won although, without doubt, the two kinds of progress are mutually reinforcing.   In the culture of poverty of the American Negro the additional disadvantage of racial discrimination has generated a potential for revolutionary protest and organization that is absent in the slums of San Juan and Mexico City and, for that matter, among the poor whites in the South.

If it is true, as I suspect, that the culture of poverty flourishes and is endemic to the free-enterprise, pre-welfare-state stage of capitalism, then it is also endemic in colonial societies.   The most likely candidates for the culture of poverty would be the people who come from the lower strata of a rapidly changing society and who are already partially alienated from it.   Accordingly the subculture is likely to be found where imperial conquest has smashed the native social and economic structure and held the natives, perhaps for generations, in servile status, or where feudalism is yielding to capitalism in the later evolution of a colonial economy.   Landless rural workers who migrate to the cities, as in Latin America, can be expected to fall into this way of life more readily than migrants from stable peasant villages with a well-organized traditional culture, as in India.   It remains to be seen, however, whether the culture of poverty has not already begun to develop in the slums of

Bombay and Calcutta. Compared with Latin America also, the strong corporate nature of many African tribal societies may tend to inhibit or delay the formation of a full-blown culture of poverty in the new towns and cities of that continent. In South Africa the institutionalization of repression and discrimination under apartheid may also have begun to promote an immunizing sense of identity and group consciousness among the African Negroes.

One must therefore keep the dynamic aspects of human institutions forward in observing and assessing the evidence for the presence, the waxing or the waning of this subculture. Measured on the dimension of relationship to the larger society, some slum dwellers may have a warmer identification with their national tradition even though they suffer deeper poverty than members of a similar community in another country. In Mexico City a high percentage of our respondents, including those with little or no formal schooling, knew of Cuauhtémoc, Hidalgo, Father Morelos, Juárez, Diaz, Zapata, Carranza and Cárdenas. In San Juan the names of Rámon Power, Jose de Diego, Baldorioty de Castro, Rámon Betances, Nemesio Canales, Llorens Torres rang no bell; a few could tell about the late Albizu Campos. For the lower-income Puerto Rican, however, history begins with Muñoz Rivera and ends with his son Muñoz Marin.

The national context can make a big difference in the play of the crucial traits of fatalism and hopelessness. Given the advanced technology, the high level of literacy, the all-pervasive reach of the media of mass communications and the relatively high aspirations of all sectors of the population, even the poorest and most marginal communities of the U.S. must aspire to a larger future than the slum dwellers of Ecuador and Peru, where the actual possibilities are more limited and where an authoritarian social order persists in city and country. Among the 50 million U.S. citizens now more or less officially certified as poor, I would guess that about 20 per cent live in a culture of poverty. The largest numbers in this group are made up of Negroes, Puerto Ricans, Mexicans, American Indians and Southern poor whites. In these figures there is some reassurance for those concerned, because it is much more difficult to undo the culture of poverty than to cure poverty itself.

Middle-class people--this would certainly include most social scientists--tend to concentrate on the negative aspects of the culture of poverty. They attach a minus sign to such traits as present-time orientation and readiness to indulge impulses. I do not intend to idealize or romanticize the culture of poverty--"it is easier to praise poverty than to live in it." Yet the positive aspects of these traits must not be overlooked. Living in the present may develop a capacity for spontaneity, for the enjoyment of the sensual, which is often blunted in the middle-class, future-oriented man. Indeed, I am often struck by the analogies that can be drawn between the mores of the very rich--of the "jet set" and "café society"--and the culture of the very poor. Yet it is, on the whole, a comparatively superficial culture. There is in it much pathos, suffering and emptiness. It does not provide much support or satisfaction; its pervading mistrust magnifies individual helplessness and isolation. Indeed, poverty of culture is one of the crucial traits of the culture of poverty.

The concept of the culture of poverty provides a generalization that may help to unify and explain a number of phenomena hitherto viewed as peculiar to certain racial, national or regional groups. Problems we think of as being distinctively our own or distinctively Negro (or as typifying any other ethnic group) prove to be endemic in countries where there are no segregated ethnic minority groups. If it follows that the elimination of physical poverty may not by itself eliminate the culture of poverty, then an understanding of the subculture may contribute to the design of measures specific to that purpose.

What is the future of the culture of poverty? In considering this question one must distinguish between those countries in which it represents a relatively small segment of the population and those in which it constitutes a large one. In the U.S. the major solution proposed by social workers dealing with the "hard core" poor has been slowly to raise their level of living and incorporate them in the middle class. Wherever possible psychiatric treatment is prescribed.

In underdeveloped countries where great masses of people live in the culture of poverty, such a social-work solution does not seem feasible. The local psychiatrists have all they can do to care for their own growing middle class. In those countries the people with a culture of poverty may seek a more revolutionary solution. By creating basic structural changes in society, by redistributing wealth, by organizing the poor and giving them a sense of belonging, of power and of leadership, revolutions frequently succeed in abolishing some of the basic characteristics of the culture of poverty even when they do not succeed in curing poverty itself.

Part II

The Puerto Rican Family

J. M. Stycos, "Family and Fertility in Puerto Rico." American
Sociological Review 17:572-580, October 1952. National
Council of Family Relations. Reprinted by permission.

The past decade's development program in Puerto Rico has
aided but far from solved the island's population problem. With
the present rate of natural increase at 29 (United States, 8) Puerto
Rico's population will double by 1985 if the birth rate continues at
its present rate. With a population density 15 times that of the
United States, with a population characterized as "rural, landless
and wage-earning," and with less than 1,000,000 acres of tillable
land for its 2,100,000 inhabitants, Puerto Rico's "problem" is
clearly Malthusian.
　　Various studies have aimed at providing information which
could assist in effecting a rapid solution of the population problem.
Insular and mainland anthropologists, economists and demographers
have pursued research projects which have thrown valuable light on
reduction of high fertility. Considerable research can still be
profitably directed, however, at the institution most strategic to
the regulation of fertility--the family. This paper, consequently,
will describe and analyze the salient characteristics of the Puerto
Rican family, in an attempt to establish the kind of hypotheses
fruitful for research in the area of human fertility.

Background Information
　　The considerable advances in industrialization made by the
Popular Government in the past ten years have not yet altered
Puerto Rico's status as an underdeveloped economy. In 1948 about
39 per cent of the labor force was directly engaged in farming. [1]
Despite the fact that real income has increased 80 per cent from
1940-1950, [2] three quarters of the families of Puerto Rico still have
an annual income under 1000 dollars, while 44 per cent earn less
than 500 dollars. [3] While this is considerably higher than average
incomes for families of other Caribbean islands, it ranks well
below the income of our poorest states. The per capita income of
Mississippi, for example, is twice that of Puerto Rico.
　　Unemployment is high, the yearly average usually totaling
around 10 per cent of the labor force. [4] Yet this disguises the true
picture, for sugar harvesting and refining is a seasonal occupation.
Approximately three quarters of the sugar workers are employed
about 175 days a year, and the remainder work only about a hundred

75

days during the peak harvest season.

While the insular economy is still strongly agrarian the
situation is now changing, particularly with respect to urban migration.   At the time of American occupation a half century ago,
Puerto Rico's population was 14.5 per cent urban.   Urbanization
has grown steadily, accelerating in the past decade, and now
stands at 60 per cent.   Literacy rates have also increased greatly.
While only one-fifth of the population over ten years of age could
be classified as literate in 1900, three-fourths of the present day
population can read and write.[5]   Even in many rural areas, the
degree of contact with the large cities is such as to promote a
degree of modernization not characteristic of Puerto Rico's agrarian
economy of two or three decades ago.

We may assume too that family ideals are undergoing rapid
change.[6]   Whereas the _jibaro_ once wanted "all the children that God
sends," his ideal is now three,[7] and he feels that a family has the
right to limit the number of its children.[8]   Despite such changes
Puerto Rico's birth rate has not dropped appreciably.

We are left with a difficult task--that of reconciling Puerto
Rico's high fertility rate with the small-family preference among
its population.   Before attributing this anomaly solely to the relative absence within the lower class of technical means to achieve
lower rates of fertility, it is desirable to examine those institutions
and cultural patterns which may work counter to low fertility
ideals.   Two principal patterns help explain the relationship between
family and fertility in Puerto Rico.

(1)   Differential sex statuses and roles are such as to encourage family limitation on the part of the wife and to discourage
it on the part of the husband.   These roles and statuses are
often sufficiently disparate to limit adequate communication between
husband and wife on matters of family limitation; and to frustrate
the wife's desires where such communication may exist.

(2)   Subsequent to high fertility performance in a given
family, certain individual and institutional mechanisms operate to
alleviate the pressure of numbers on resources.

Differential Sex Statuses and Roles

Rigorous subordination of the women is a normal concomitant
of rural living where a sharp division of labor relegates wage-
earning activities to the male.   Spanish-Catholic patterns fit neatly
this type of economy.   The virginity cult,[9] fostered by religious
ideology[10] and accompanied by severe limitations on the freedom of
the female, helps to insure continuing dominance of the male in the
economic and political spheres.

Even in the middle and upper class families where the subordination patterns are less emphasized[11] but none-the-less effective, male dominance is partly insured by secrecy on the part of
husbands.   There appears to be a great deal of separate sex rec-
reation--a pattern of "going out with the boys," and illicit affairs.
This privilege of privacy concerning the husband's business and
pleasure enshrouds much of his life with mystery and enhances his
role as an authority figure.

For the lower class the differential statuses and roles have

other manifestations, the consequences of which have a more direct
effect upon fertility.   This is not because the double standard is
more strictly enforced in the lower class but because there are
fewer compensating institutions.   For the lower class it is principally the combination of marginal economic subsistence and the
disparate masculine and feminine statuses which succeeds in aggra-
vating the fertility rate.   It is hypothecated that the discrepancy
between male and female statuses and roles is widened subsequent
to marriage, that this forestalls the establishing of adequate communication between the marital pair, and results not only in an unstable marital relationship, but in high rates of fertility.

In the pre-marital period the double standard takes several
important manifestations.   The society and particularly the males
put a high premium on masculinity and virility.   To be a macho
(a virile male) is one of the dominant values which is inculcated
into the male child and which continues to be valued in manhood. [12]
This male ethic is supported by permissiveness in regard to
behavior.   The society allows the male a great deal of freedom
for socio-sexual exploration with prostitutes and mujeres baratas
(cheap women).

For the women precisely opposite proscriptions exist.   The
cult of virginity puts a premium on modesty and sublimation or
repression of sexual drives.   Relative to the lower class male her
behavior is heavily circumscribed.   She is surrounded by cultural
obstacles to socio-sexual experimentation and her experience with
males may be largely confined to her own kin.   The male, tan=
talized by his erratic and expensive contacts with prostitutes, has
a decided sexual appetite at marriage.   But the woman, due to
thorough childhood training, tends to regard sex as a necessary
evil, and enters the marital relation with an attitude toward sex
ranging from ignorance to revulsion. [13]

The already existent gap between the sexes may be further
emphasized upon marriage.   The male sexual interest may only
serve to increase his wife's indifference or distaste.   Also, his
attempts to compartmentalize his sexual attitudes towards prostitutes and toward his wife (una buena mujer) may serve to increase
his own conflict or frustration, and so result in diminished understanding between the sexes.   The gulf is not only present with
regard to sexuality but with regard to procreation as well.   Here
again it may be supposed that the male has more immediate
gratifications to derive from children than does the woman.

For the lower class male there are few available channels
for prestige.   The most important, economic advancement, is unavailable to him.   Due to the scarcity of land, the seasonal nature
of employment, and the surplus of labor, he can scarcely provide
the basic necessities of life for himself and his family. [14]   Consequently, two of his chief sources of prestige are virility and
fatherhood.

Machismo will provide him with respect from his peers,
and being un buen padre respect from his community.   Both show
that despite his poverty he is after all a man.   Thus the institutions which once had meaning for the survival of the species and
for survival of the family unit have been exaggerated beyond their

original meaning and now function as a perhaps compulsively desired substitute for masculine achievement in the economic world.
"Mira como la tengo" (Look at what I have done to her) brags the
lower class male about his pregnant wife, and the more pregnancies
he can point to, the better he has proved his machismo. [15]
      Economically derived prestige is not normally a part of the
female expectations. She is not expected to provide for the family--
the double standard places her firmly in the home as wife and
mother, thereby protecting her against the frustrations attendant
upon contact with the economic world. To be a macho (a positive
demand) a man must continue to prove himself. For the female,
however, the demand is negative: "Don't be a machorra" (a barren
woman) and one child is sufficient to dispel all fears. She thus has
none of the additional motivations for having a large family, and
indeed must suffer the brunt of the hardships entailed in the production and rearing of children.
      For such reasons we would expect that the woman be more
"small-family minded" than the male. Hatt's study has shown this
to be true, although the sex differences do not seem as marked as
would seem likely from the foregoing analysis--6.6 per cent of
the married women interviewed reported that their husbands desired
more children than they, but only 1.8 per cent of the husbands
wanted fewer. [16] On the basis of a number of such indices, Hatt
concluded that "Women seem to have adopted what we might call
the low fertility value system more strongly than their husbands."
      Thus the evidence gives some support to the hypothesis that
the female is more small-family minded than the male. Why then,
does she not utilize contraceptive techniques herself? Contraception is not employed because of the combination of male resistance
to contraceptive techniques and male dominance in the sexual relation. This position of dominance includes the prerogative of initiating sex activity and of determining its frequency and form.
This means not only that there will be a higher frequency of relations than the woman desires, but that usually contraceptives will
not be used.
      The woman, on the other hand, must not only meet the male
sexual needs, but cannot resort to contraception for herself, for
the pre-marital circumscriptions concerning sex information prevent a knowledge of birth control for large numbers of lower class
women. Also, since the male controls the sexual situation, even
if she desires contraception, she is not in a position to demand its
implementation, [17] and in several ways the modesty complex,
stemming from indoctrination with the virginity cult, impedes the
use of birth control.
      Modesty may reduce the likelihood that she discusses the
matter with her husband ('Such things are not talked about'), and
the modesty pattern plus the crowded bedroom of the lower class
home discourage employing the usual methods designed for women.
Also it discourages her from soliciting birth control information
from clinics with male physicians. [18] Thus the gulf between the
sexes is both manifested and aggravated by the inability of the
female to communicate or to realize her family ideals.
      Given culturally reinforced sex and reproduction drives on

the part of the male, given his reluctance to use contraception and
the inability of his spouse to deny his wishes, the net result is a
high degree of marital stress and a high rate of fertility.   The
high fertility pattern itself is both productive of further tension in
the marital relationship, and of drastic personal and institutional
means to alleviate the consequent psychological and economic hardships.[19] The now obvious pressure of family numbers upon scant
resources may induce wives to resort to sterilization and sexual
denial and may impel husbands to desertion or marital infidelity.
Furthermore it may lead to a reliance upon the extended family to
drain off the excess number of children.

Individual Responses

Sterilization is one of the most popular birth control measures
on the island.   Though less than 3 per cent of the lower rental
group mothers in Hatt's study had been sterilized, it is among this
group that sterilization is becoming increasingly popular.[20]   Cofresĭ
found it to be the second most popularly used method of birth control for the lower income group, far outranking other methods.[21]
Sterilization is popular because it obviates the necessity for contraception, is a sure technique which solves the problem of contraceptive defects and male caprice, and is a method upon which both
parties can agree.   The male who has proved his virility by several
past pregnancies[22] can avoid the economic pressure of children
without losing his pleasure or his sense of respect for his wife.

But sterilization may be considered too expensive, too
difficult to arrange, or too dangerous.   One other drastic technique
may finally be used by the mother of a large family--that of complete sexual denial.   The incidence of such a technique is not
known but its frequency in a selected Puerto Rican town probably
indicates that it is not uncommon.   King, in reporting on 37 cases
of women difinitely willing to limit their families, cites examples of
13 cases expressing "rather typical attitudes."[23]   Five of these
statements clearly indicate that sexual denial was employed.   In two
of the cases the women actually suggested that their husbands satisfy
their sex urges by consorting with other women.   In three of the
cases the avoidance led to separation.   We may speculate then,
that the reputedly high rates of male promiscuity and desertion
in the lower class may result not only from the desire to escape
the responsibilities of a large number of children, but additionally
from sexual denial on the part of the wife.

Institutional Mechanisms: The
Extended Family and Familism

Because of easy shifting of funds and personnel from one
nuclear family to another within a broad kinship system, it is
largely the extended family that provides relief from the pressure
of numbers upon resources.   Before describing the shock-absorbing
qualities of the extended family, it seems desirable to demonstrate
to what extent such a structure exists in Puerto Rico.

There is some evidence indicating that as many extended kin
live under the same roof as the income permits.   Thus, while
fertility drops as income increases, size of household shows the
opposite trend.   Roberts and Stefani found that 17.5 per cent of the

households in the less than 500 dollar yearly income group had one
or two members only.   In the 2000 dollar income bracket only 6
per cent had such small households. [24]   The situation may be
similar to the Chinese pattern, in which the large household is expected of all groups but practiced by those with means. [25]

Another evidence of familism is the extent to which children
and relatives contribute to the family income.   In only about half
of the households is the father the sole source of support.   Sons
and daughters contribute to family income in about a quarter of the
households, and relatives in about 5 per cent. [26]   Since in both
rural and urban areas (though more so in the former) the father
tends to be the chief breadwinner in higher economic groups, it is
clear that children and relatives play an important economic role
in the lower class household.   This is not to say, however, that
they are more of an asset than a liability, for the statistics do not
show how many children in a family help or how much they contribute. [27]   On the other hand the figures do give some credence to
the popular belief that children help provide for parents' old age.
Less than 6 per cent of Robert's and Stefani's sample was composed of individuals sixty years of age and older, yet children are
recorded as sole sources of support in about 8 per cent of the
households.   While this does not, of course, prove that these cases
are actually supporting the aged, when considered along with Hatt's
data showing that many parents think of their children as security
for old age, [28] it seems likely that filial devotion is still strong
in Puerto Rico.

Another index of familism is the degree to which the family
relationships operate at the expense of the community.   While no
concrete data are available at this time, we may speculate that in
rural areas the community is subordinate to the family.   The
jíbaro's sense of individualism with regard to property and marriage
precluded much of a sense of community responsibility.   For example workers in the new Title V Communities [29] report that their
greatest difficulty in the successful organization of these rural
villages is a lack of community spirit on the part of the participants.   That kin solidarity operates to the exclusion of easy identification with non-kin is also visible in regard to attitudes toward
the children of non-kin strangers.   Originators of a foster home
care plan for homeless children a few years ago encountered powerful resistance on the part of donors who did not want their young
relatives given to strangers and on the part of prospective care-
takers who did not like taking "strangers" into their homes. [30]
Finally, the cleavage between family and community is given particular emphasis by another characteristic of family living in
Puerto Rico--the seeming lack of concern for privacy.   Given the
physically cramped living quarters of the lower class Puerto Rican
(58 per cent of Puerto Rico's rural families average two or more
per room), [31] the crowded sleeping quarters (76 per cent of the
rural population sleep with three or more to a room, 39 per cent
with 5 or more), [32] and the general intimacy of family members,
it is not surprising that lower class Puerto Ricans in the United
States startle social workers by their desire for interpersonal
contacts and a seeming unconcern with privacy.   This pattern may

lead to an interesting end product--the standardization of the personalities of any given family. The unusually high degree of interpersonal relationships, plus the wide range within the family toward whom these relations may be directed, may result in greater identification with the group than in dependency upon the mother or father, as characteristic of the small, privacy-conscious nuclear family typical of industrial Western society. This greater degree of personality standardization within the family might contribute to tighter family organization or at least to greater dependence on the family--another pattern which would reinforce the familistic pattern at the expense of identification with the larger community.

 We may conclude then that familism exists to a high degree in Puerto Rico. What specifically is its relation to fertility? Disregarding the fact of family economic pools, the relation occurs in the easy and frequent transferring of excess children from one nuclear family to another, within a structure of blood and ritual kin. Such informally adopted children are frequently taken by their god-parents--these latter are frequently ritual rather than blood kin. Since the institutions of ritual kin (compadrazgo) and informal adoption[33] are among the few which articulate the family with non-kin, both are here interpreted as devices for relieving the pressure of fertility, and as structurally significant institutions in the Puerto Rican family system.

Hijos De Crianza and the
Compadrazgo System

 Within the extended family in Puerto Rico, children are shifted around from home to relatives with a great deal of ease. The period for which a child is sent to a relative may vary from months to life. The latter case, in which parental rights and duties with respect to a child are handed over to the relative, is quite prevalent,[34] and the children in such a system are designated as hijos de crianza.

 At the death of the father or mother of a family, it is quite usual in rural areas for the members to be dispersed to kin or ritual kin,[35] but such a family crisis is hardly needed for the adoption of children. For example, a very young child may be sent to live with a relative or friend who is better off economically, or to live with grandparents who may be lonely. The latter will informally adopt the child, feed and clothe it, and in return may expect it to assist in the housework.

 Looking at the institution broadly we can hypothesize three functions. First, the pattern serves both as a manifestation of the extended family and a cohesive force in preserving and intensifying it. When one segment of the family has migrated to the city or to the United States, the hijo de crianza may form a bridge between a widening gap in extended family relations.[36] Second, it may have certain important functions for the donor of the child, serving both as a means of social mobility and as a kind of human investment which might bring dividends in old age. Given the sense of futility of improving his economic status that faces the average rural Puerto Rican, and given the tradition of respect and care for the aged kin, the giving of a child to a relative or friend of better status, preferably in the city or in the States, may be partly

based on the estimation of the child's future value. The hijo de
crianza may provide a wedge into urban society which the parents
may eventually use for migration or at least support. Third, it
can be seen as a means of giving a more equitable distribution of
scarce goods--as a society's crude way of relieving population
pressure in relation to resources. Since hijos de crianza are
usually from homes poorer than those of the foster parents (except
in cases of broken homes where children may be farmed out to
class contemporaries), it can be assumed that this provides some
relief for the lower class population pressure.

One of the most frequent institutional channels used for this
transfer of children is compadrazgo. The god-father relationship,
in the United States now an empty ritual, is a living and vital part
of social relations among Puerto Ricans. It acts as a security
mechanism for children in a land where life expectancy is low (46
years in 1940) and where economic security is always tenuous. If
a family has an excess of children for which it desires a better way
of life,[37] it is not unusual that a child or children be sent to a
compadre whose economic position is slightly better.

Probably even more important for an understanding of the
Puerto Rican family is the compadre relationship established between age contemporaries which binds the participants in a net of
reciprocal aid and friendship. As country women say once they
enter into such a relation, "Los siete sacramentos están entre
nosotros." (The seven sacraments are between us.) Not only is
the relation sacred, but it taboos fighting and quarreling and establishes reciprocal rights and obligations such as aid in time of
sickness, and in economic and other crises. In a society where
social mobility is encouraged and where the pattern of land tenure
makes this virtually impossible for the bulk of the population, the
compadrazgo system theoretically could form a convenient channel
for upward mobility. To what extent compadrazgo is used for
such purposes is not known in any statistical sense, and would be
an important area for research. What concerns us here is the
fact that compadrazgo may be used where the individual feels insecure or dissatisfied with his present status. In such cases, the
way out for the individual with Spanish heritage but without a
history of community action or a high degree of community relations, is to deal with the situation in the only terms he knows--
family terms. In effect he may extend his family to encompass
non-blood-related individuals who will be bound by family mores.
He may thus construct a large artificial family as an additional
bulwark against ever-present misfortune in Puerto Rico.

Fianlly, compadrazgo, as hijos de crianza, may be used as
a tool for cementing family relationships where these are threatened
by mobility;[38] or it may be increasingly employed as a mechanism
to wean the individual from the family and toward a more secular
society.[39]

Summary

The discrepancy in lower class Puerto Rico between low
fertility aspirations and high fertility performance can be partly
explained by the dynamics of family life. It is hypothecated that the

wide gulf between the sexes may become widened or aggravated
upon marriage and result in a breakdown of adequate communication between the pair. The male is almost compulsively concerned
with sex and procreation while the woman, at least relatively, is
indifferent to birth. High fertility may result then, not from
planning on the part of the parents, but as a natural by-product of
an interpersonal situation in which the woman's effective role is
minimal.

       As palliatives both for the pressure of numbers on resources
and for the psychological disequilibrium between the marital pair,
certain individual and institutional mechanisms are operative.
Sexual denial and sterilization are drastic personal means used to
reduce fertility while desertion functions as an escape from it.
The extended family, by means of informal adoption and through
channels such as compadrazgo, serves to cushion the impact of
high fertility on any given family. By a process of supply and
demand, a situation is brought into equilibrium in a manner which
relieves the situation of a particular family, though not that of
the society.

       The value of the foregoing paper will consist in its provision
of an analytical model of the lower class Puerto Rican family which
can be employed in research, particularly in the area of human
fertility. It provides the researcher with the defined task of testing three areas of hypotheses: (1) The differential extent and
quality of certain marital interrelationships and familial institutions
among varying social groups in Puerto Rico; (2) The functional
articulation of such patterns and institutions with other parts of
the society; (3) The relation between such patterns and institutions
and the prevailing rates of fertility.

                                Notes

For stimulation and information the author is indebted to Carmen
Alvarado and Maria Echandi of the school of Social Work, University of Puerto Rico, and to the project's director, Reuben Hill.

1.   Harvey S. Perloff, Puerto Rico's Economic Future, Chicago:
     University of Chicago Press, 1950, p. 54.
2.   Economic Development of Puerto Rico, Puerto Rico Planning
     Board, January 1951, p. 13.
3.   Lydia J. Roberts and Rosa Luisa Stefani, Patterns of Living in
     Puerto Rican Families, Rio Piedras: University of Puerto
     Rico, 1949, p. 8.
4.   Harvey S. Perloff, op cit. p. 145.
5.   1950 Census of Population, Preliminary Reports, Series PC-6,
     No. 12 Washington, D. C. , May, 1951, p. 7.
6.   The implications of changing family ideals and organization in
     Puerto Rico's rapidly industrializing economy is not con-
     sidered in this short paper. Attention is concentrated on
     that large proportion of the population which has been least
     effected by the changes--the rural lower class. Additionally,
     such factors in family life as are considered, are treated

largely as if change were not occurring.

7. Hatt's study of 13,000 Puerto Ricans disclosed that three or
    fewer children is the ideal for about 75 per cent of the
    population. Paul K. Hatt, Background of Human Fertility in
    Puerto Rico: A Sociological Survey, Princeton: Princeton
    University Press, 1952, Table 187, p. 219.

8. Less than 13 per cent of Hatt's sample felt that no couple
    has the right to practice family limitation. Ibid., Table 60,
    p. 79. In another recent study of 2,125 Puerto Rican
    women, it was found that religious scruples were mentioned
    in less than 5 per cent of the cases not employing birth
    control methods. Emilio Cofresí, Realidad Poblaciónal de
    Puerto Rico, San Juan, Imprenta Venezuela, 1951, Table 36,
    p. 95.

9. A phrase used by Seigel to describe "a set of ideas and practices
    which . . . dominates the relationships between the sexes
    in Lajas and determines the role of the males and females
    in pre-marital and post-marital life." Morris Seigel, A
    Puerto Rican Town, 1948, unpublished, p. 148.

10. Observers report that the popularity of the Virgin as a direct
    or inter-cessional object of prayer and ritual is increasing
    in Puerto Rico, probably at the expense of Christ and male
    saints. Whether or not the cult of the Virgin is increasing,
    its manifestations are easily evident all over the island.

11. The inordinate number of "Queen" contests, particularly in the
    middle class, may represent the culture's response to the
    threat of the modern, competitive career woman. The
    queens appear to be chosen more for modesty and grace
    than for glamor, suggesting something of the Queen of
    Heaven, the Virgin Mary. The lavishness and publicity which
    accompany such contests also suggest a channeling both
    of resources and ideals away from the utilitarian and toward
    the pure but useless.

12. Dynamically, the strong emphasis on "being macho" may repre-
    sent an effort on the part of the male to escape the strong
    mother-son bonds which have been formed as a result of
    the deficient role of the father in socialization. Patterns of
    desertion, drinking, separate sex recreation, etc., are a
    few of the lower class patterns which keep the father
    physically removed from the children. On the part of the
    female child these same absence patterns may lead to con-
    siderable fantasy, the consequent misconception of the male
    sex increasing the gap between masculine and feminine
    worlds.

13. "So much is intercourse considered in terms of obligation (un
    deber) that one woman who enjoyed sexual intercourse 'for
    its own sake' was considered sick by the other women of
    the barrio." Eric Wolf, Culture Change and Culture Stability
    in a Puerto Rican Coffee Community, Cambridge: Eagle
    Enterprises (offset), 1951, p. 94.

14. "Sixty–two per cent (of the population) have less than the amount
    needed to buy a minimum adequate diet ($140 per year)."
    Roberts and Stefani, op. cit., p. 13.

15. 'The importance of beginning a family soon is a value rather
    more generally accepted throughout the society than are any
    principles with regard to either the size of the family or
    the acceptability of planning the family." Paul Hatt, op.
    cit. Hatt reports that such a large proportion of his sample
    felt that the first child should come "as soon as possible"
    that correlation with other factors was rendered impossible.
    At this point both machorra and macho complexes coincide
    to insure a rapid first birth:"(Because) working people here
    do not regard a marriage as truly consummated before the
    birth of the first child, consensually married couples will
    seek to have a child...within a year of their union." Sidney
    Mintz, Cañamelar, The Contemporary Culture of a Puerto
    Rican Proletariat, unpublished doctoral dissertation, 1950,
    Chap. VI, p.21.
16. Paul Hatt, op. cit., Table 276, p. 324. It is possible that the
    high percentage (76.5) of women reporting the concurrence of
    their spouses on this item may be exaggerated by the
    desire to present a united front to the interviewer.
17. Cofresí found that half of the failures to employ birth control
    methods were due either to ignorance on the part of the
    women or objections on the part of the husband.   Emilio
    Cofresí, op. cit., Table 36, p. 95.
18. "A number of women expressed horror at the prospect of
    being subjected to a vaginal examination, particularly by a
    male physician....Several women declared that they pre-
    ferred a midwife, even though inadequately trained, to a
    male doctor whose services might be obtained free of charge,
    specifically because of shame at being seen by a man."
    Marguerite King, "Cultural Aspects of Birth Control in
    Puerto Rico." Human Biology, Vol. 20 (February, 1948),
    p. 32.
19. At this point class differentials operate to the disadvantage
    of the lower class. Whereas all classes see the small
    family as an ideal, it is the upper class which comes
    closest to achieving the ideal. Consequently, the greater
    frustration on the part of the lower class is more produc-
    tive of this drastic palliative measure.
20. P. Hatt, op. cit., Table 318, p. 444. About 8 per cent of
    the "upper class" women had been sterilized; this rate is
    doubtlessly affected to some degree by their greater ability
    to pay a private fee and by the fact that lower class women
    usually have their children at home.
21. Cofresí, op. cit., Table 34, p. 90. From three to four
    thousand sterilizations are performed every year in Puerto
    Rico.
22. Although the trend over the past thirty years has been toward
    earlier sterilization 86 per cent of the sterilizations of the
    women married between 1940 and 1947 occurred subsequent
    to at least two births. Hatt, op. cit., Table 320, p. 446.
23. Marguerite King, op. cit., pp. 26-27.
24. Op. cit., Table V., p. 272. It is possible that a greater
    number of wage-earners in the upper income households have

exaggerated the picture. Rosario's data by average monthly
wage, however, show the same trend, the average number
per household ranging from 5.3 to 6.7, as average monthly
wage varies from 13.76 to 22.73 dollars. José C. Rosario,
The Development of the Puerto Rican Jibaro and His Present
Attitude Towards Society, University of Puerto Rico: 1935,
p. 85.

25. Olga Lang, Chinese Family and Society, New Haven: Yale
University Press, 1946.

26. Roberts and Stefani, op. cit., Table 12, p. 275.

27. Unpaid family workers cannot be considered a major source of
income in Puerto Rico. Whereas a total of 37 per cent of
Hatt's household heads were engaged in agriculture, only
3.9 of the total male sample were classified as non-paid
family workers.

28. Roughly 47 per cent of Hatt's respondents mentioned assistance
in old age when asked why they had not picked a smaller
number for ideal size of family, Table 42, p. 59.

29. A program initiated in the early 40's, the Title V Communities or parcelas are composed of a few hundred families,
each with an acre or so of land for subsistence farming.

30. Not only is it particularly humiliating to accept charity from
non-kin but there appears to be an equal aversion or at
least indifference to giving it. Philanthropy, as opposed to
paternalism, is not a part of the culture, for it is held that
the needy should be cared for by their "own people."

31. Roberts, op. cit., p. 52.

32. Ibid., p. 86.

33. The neighborhood is of course another institution which ar-
ticulates the family with non-kin, but little can be said of
this with any certainty. Contradictory norms and behavior
patterns are found with respect to the relation of family and
neighbors. Some claim that there is a clear line between
neighbor and relative and that reciprocal rights and obligations are more extensive with the latter. In other instances neighborhood ties parallel or exceed those of family.
'Quién es tu hermano? Tu vecino más cercano." (Who is
your brother? Your closest neighbor.) Actually, the general
situation may be such that there is a fine line between
neighbor and relative. In country areas the visiting patterns
are so liberal that people have a great deal to do with the
socialization of their neighbors' children, to the extent
that close bonds are formed between the former, the
children, and the children's parents. In a transitional
society such as Puerto Rico, the neighborhood may serve as
a "weaning" institution which makes the transition from
family to society less painful.

34. Six and a half per cent of Puerto Rico's households have one
or more such informally adopted children. Additionally,
13.4 per cent have grandchildren, living in the home.
Roberts and Stefani, op. cit., Table 17, p. 279.

35. 'If a man who has a family and no property dies, his brothers
and sisters will either support the family, keeping it as a

unit in their own homes, or will apportion the different
members among themselves...It is a rather common spec-
tacle in the rural regions of Puerto Rico to see two or three
children from a compadre, brother or sister joining an
already numerous brood in another family." José C. Rosario,
op. cit., p. 81.

36. Children are sent to urban centers for the enhanced levels of
living and educational possibilities there. But city residents
also send children back to the farm. City households have
fewer hijos de crianza and grandchildren living with the
family. See Roberts and Stefani, op. cit., Table 17, p. 279.

37. Levels of aspiration for children are high. About 80 per cent
of the island's parents want their sons at least to complete
high school, and only about three-quarters of one per cent
want their sons to be laborers. Paul Hatt, op. cit., Tables
56 and 58, pp. 75 and 77.

38. "...compadrazgo...may be a valuable social mechanism even
when families are quite unstable, and families or family
heads geographically very mobile," Mintz, op. cit., Chap.
VI, p. 64. Mintz also states, however, without citing
sufficient evidence, that compadre relationships break down
if they cease to be face-to-face.

39. 'Where families are no longer tightly knit, all-encompassing
networks of relationships, compadrazgo may be understood
as a mechanism to facilitate the transition to a more individualized and less familistic type society." Ibid., p. 65.

Clarence Senior, "Research on the Puerto Rican Family in the
United States." Journal of Marriage and Family 19:32-37,
February 1957. The National Council on Family Relations.
Reprinted by permission.

The Importance of Research on
The Puerto Rican Family Here

The Puerto Rican is the newest "stranger in our midst" in
many towns and cities throughout the United States. He comes to
perform essential functions toward the bottom of the base of the
economic pyramid; he is the entrant into what are euphemistically
labeled the "entry trades." He competes for scarce housing; his
children compete for scarce seats in overcrowded schoolrooms. He
is likely to be more highly visible in his new community than are
the far more numerous other migrants from the "underdeveloped"
areas of the United States. Politically, he is a citizen; culturally,
he is an alien. This duality is likely to puzzle, irritate, and
frustrate even those institutionally delegated to help the newcomer.

He is just as likely as most of our forty million working-
class immigrant ancestors to become a convenient scapegoat for
a society in which belief in adequate education, recreation, housing,
et cetera is verbalized, but in which actual distribution of the
national income does not leave sufficient money for enough schools,
playgrounds, housing, and other community facilities for persons
and families in the lower income brackets.

Finally, there comes the attack on human dignity in being
treated as a "problem"--in being labeled a "minority." This fate
the Puerto Rican shares with many other citizens.

Few areas of civic affairs today cry out more urgently for
attention by researchers whose equipment contains the tools of the
cultural sciences than that of internal migration. Each recent
year has seen at least five million persons move their homes
across state lines; many of these cross regional lines. The
Spanish-speaking internal migrants, the Mexican-Americans of the
Southwest and Pacific coast, and the Puerto Ricans in the North-
eastern, Middle Atlantic, and North Central regions, usually
recapitulate the experiences of our immigrant ancestors.

But there is a big difference for the social scientist; he can
read and admire one of the few scientific studies ever made of the
immigrant (Thomas and Znaniecki's, The Polish Peasant in Europe
and America 1918-1920); he can study the critique of that work
produced by the Social Science Research Council,[1] but he can't go
back to the days of mass immigration to apply the more developed
research tools of today to the crucial human problems tackled by
Thomas and Znaniecki. The Puerto Rican supplies a reasonably

close facsimile of the immigrants of the past so far as family life
is concerned. Furthermore, he and his family are often found in
areas inhabited by other recent arrivals, including Southern Negroes,
Southern mountaineers, Mexicans, Texas-Mexicans, Midwestern
farm families, et cetera. Cross-cultural studies of families
arriving at more or less the same time in more or less the same
socioeconomic environment would yield rich results for social
theory as well as for purposes of prediction and control in an
important field of social policy.

Some Demographic Factors

There are probably around 750,000 Puerto Ricans, first and
second generation, in the United States today--an increase of 249
per cent since the 1950 census was taken.[2] Close to 80 per cent
live in New York City, although the proportion of new migrants
settling in the nation's largest city is declining and now stands at
about 60 to 65 per cent of the total migration. Puerto Ricans were
found in thirty-nine of the forty-eight states in the 1910 census, in
forty-five states in 1920, and in all states in the past three censuses.[3]

The more important settlements outside New York City are
Chicago; Philadelphia; Bridgeport; Cleveland; Hartford; Newark;
Camden; Trenton; Gary; Milwaukee; Youngstown and Lorain, Ohio;
Rochester and Buffalo, New York. All important industrial centers
east of the Mississippi and north of the Ohio have Puerto Rican
communities. Miami is the only Southern center of any importance.

Net migration in recent years has risen from an annual
average of 18,794 between 1941 and 1950 to 49,624 between 1951
and 1955. The drop from 69,124 in 1953 to 21,531 in 1954
dramatically illustrates the story that is told statistically by a .82
coefficient of correlation between the migration and United States
business conditions from 1908 to 1952.[4] Continuation of fairly high
levels of employment will mean a continuation of fairly high levels
of Puerto Rican migration, in spite of considerable progress in
economic development on the island itself.[5]

The rate of natural increase in Puerto Rico is one of the
highest in the world. The birthrate is 34.8; the death rate 7.1,
making a rate of natural increase of 27.7. It is far exceeded by
that of the migrant, however, if one may judge the reproductive
behavior of those outside New York City by the record of the New
York Puerto Rican. The crude birth rate in 1950 was 49.1; the
death rate 4.2, making a rate of natural increase of 44.9 per
thousand! This extraordinary rate is partly a function of the age
structure, of course. The median age of 29.2 years per person
born in Puerto Rico and living in the states, shown by the 1950
census, helps make the crude rate understandable, but the standardization afforded by using the fertility ratio shows a genuine high
fertility pattern, unmatched in our culture for several generations.[6]
Comparative ratios of birth per thousand women fifteen to forty-four
years of age, for the three major ethnic groups in New York City
were, in 1950, as follows:

Total white women 82
Total non-white women 100
Puerto Rican born women 135

Source Material For
Research Planning

The only full-scale study of the Puerto Rican family in the
United States is still under way; other studies, and there are few
of them, deal with the family incidentally as they investigate some
other aspect of Puerto Rican life here. A review of sources of
background material may suggest at least the gaps in the field. As
a matter of fact, the gaps seem to have more substance than the
field.

Studies in Puerto Rico itself have achieved a high level of
sophistication and have been extremely helpful to administrators
and policy personnel. No attempt will be made here even to catalog
them. Millard Hansen, director of the Social Science Research
Center of the University of Puerto Rico, described the program in
some detail at the 1951 Milbank Memorial Fund annual conference. [7]

The first important publication of the Research Center
was Paul K. Hatt's impressive Backgrounds of Human Fertility in
Puerto Rico, [8] based on interviews in 5,579 households reached, out
of a probability sample of 6,000 households. "The Family in Puerto
Rico Research Project" was started under the direction of Reuben
Hill in 1951. [9] J. Mayone Stycos, a sociologist from Columbia,
was made assistant director in charge of one phase of the project,
"Family and Fertility." His report appeared last year. [10] David
Landy, a Harvard anthropologist, was in charge of another phase,
labeled "Child Rearing in a Puerto Rican Community." Other material on child rearing in Puerto Rico has appeared as a result of
a series of ethnographic studies under the general direction of
Julian S. Stewart. [11] One of the most succinct and perceptive
statements of a changing institution in the field is "Courtship in
Puerto Rico," by Reuben Hill. [12] These provide essential background
for research among families from Puerto Rico in the United States.

Puerto Ricans in New York City's two "core areas" (East
Harlem and the Morrisania area of the Bronx) were studied by the
Bureau of Applied Social Research of Columbia University during
1947 and 1948 and the report published in 1950. [13] It is based
largely on lengthy interviews conducted in 1,113 households in an
area sample believed representative of the two major clusters of
Puerto Ricans in New York City. The author's preface states the
aims of the report:

> It begins on the island and ends with the aspirations of the
> Puerto Ricans in New York City. We try to tell who the
> migrants are and why they came; how they compare with
> their compatriots who remain at home; what their journey
> to the continent means in their occupational and income as
> well as life stories; what kind of social world they inhabit
> in New York, and how that world compares with the kind
> of world New York has been for previous migrants; what
> seem to be their solidarities and their conflicts with other
> ethnic and racial groups in the city of New York; what is
> meant by "adaptation" for a group at this level of living,
> and how the Puerto Ricans are involved in this process in
> the middle of the twentieth century.

The major emphasis in the study was on the economic
transition, but enough was learned of the effect of this transition
on the structure and functions of the family in the new surroundings
to have been of great value to welfare workers, teachers, and
others involved in action programs in New York City, according to
reports from them.

The report shows, of course, that there is no such entity
as the Puerto Rican family.   Factors influencing the status of the
family in the community and the roles that its members play both
inside and outside the home are numerous.   They vary widely in
their impact.   However, five major factors influencing the
adaptation of the Puerto Rican in New York City were summarized
as follows: "...having a job, being a male, having more education,
being younger in age, and being white."

In spite of the bias inherent in interviewing only in slum
areas, 87 per cent of earlier arrivals (before 1942), and 78 per
cent of more recent arrivals were found to be either "fairly well" or
"well adapted" on an index which was constructed to give an empirical basis for judging adaptation.   Adaptation was defined as
"inconspicious functioning with psychic contentment."

The first extended research which focuses on the family itself has been under way for the past two and a half years in
East Harlem.   This is a pilot study designed to investigate qualitative relationships between ways of life and health, according to the
prospectus.   It proposes to draw a comprehensive picture of the
ways of life of a neighborhood in East Harlem, with particular
emphasis on the Puerto Rican migrants who live there.   The study
has been designed to produce a detailed description and analysis
of family life, formal and informal associations, values, ideologies,
social goals, the nature of social and cultural conflicts, social
and cultural change, and how these factors in the culture and in the
organization of the society relate to conditions of health.

The study is sponsored by the Foresight Foundation, and
carried on under the auspices of the Department of Anthropology,
Columbia University.[14]

Interviews are being conducted with a sample of five hundred
families, and fairly detailed case studies are being made of five
Puerto Rican families.   The publication of the study should greatly
increase the possibility that further studies will be made in other
slum subcultures of our cities in such a manner that comparative
results may be obtained.

Relevant incidental information on the Puerto Rican family in
the new environment is found in several recently completed studies
which would be of value for certain projects.[15]   One of the   findings of studies made outside New York City which confirms one of
the major results of the Columbia 1948 study is the crucial role
played by the "pioneer" members of the family in helping motivate
the "stay-at-homes" to come to the states and to smooth the transition for them.

None of the studies, to the best of the writer's knowledge,
has shown any significant variation in the essentials of the Puerto
Rican migration which would distinguish it sharply from patterns
established by the immigrants of the past.   One who knows Oscar

Handlin's The Uprooted[16] will already have some insight into the
difficulties faced by the Puerto Rican family here today.

Suggestions on Further Research

The structure of the situation into which the Puerto Rican
family moves, and the pressure for "practical" results, quickly,
are likely to lead to undue attention being paid to the pathology of
the migration. Adequately representative samples of Puerto Rican
families, so constructed that various factors can be controlled for
length of residence, are essential.[17] Publication of the results of
research which concentrates on the pathological aspects of the life
of any group makes living more difficult for the "normal" members
of the group.

There would be great advantages in starting research on the
Puerto Rican family as it arrives in a new area, in various parts
of the country, using a common outline. The studies should be
continued over a period of at least ten years. This would obviously
be costly.

Another difficulty which may face the prospective researcher,
not so much in himself as among the membership of boards of trus-
tees, administrative committees, et cetera, is the white middle
class Protestant background, sometimes flavored with more than a
dash of xenophobia. This may be especially true in dealing with
groups in which comparatively high percentages of illegitimacy and
of consensual marriage are found; for example, the Puerto Rican,
the Southern Negro, and the "hillbilly."

Few social questions are more full of meaning for the
future of the world than the application of intelligence to the control
of births as well as to the control of deaths. It has been noted
that a large amount of research on this subject has been conducted
in Puerto Rico. It has also been reported that, at least in New
York City, the high fertility habits characteristic of Puerto Rico
are maintained.

A whole complex of fascinating and important research problems revolves around the question of the "demographic transition"
of the migrant family. How soon does the pattern begin to change?
What are the major factors? What part does the new role of the
woman play? Is the housing factor as important as it is for the
receiving population? Where do husband and wife get information
and advice? Is the heavy emphasis on sterilization found in Puerto
Rico continued when there is easier access to less drastic methods
of contraception? Dozens of similar questions will suggest themselves.

Another fruitful area urgently needing research concerns the
role played by skin color in the adjustment process of the Puerto
Rican family. Puerto Rico, while not completely free from race
prejudice, has little discrimination. The dark-complexioned Puerto
Rican is puzzled and frustrated by color barriers; he was never
taught at home to "act like a Negro." The role of color within
the family which contains a range of skin colors provides a delicate field of research which should be most rewarding. Comparisons of the personal relations among Negroes of varying shades,
raised and "socialized" in this country, with similarly situated

persons among the Puerto Rican group might well add significantly
to our knowledge of the color factor in human relations. Many
Puerto Ricans feel they have a more enlightened attitude in this
field than many persons in the receiving community. [18]

Reference group theory might well be called upon in studying
a key phenomenon of culture conflict in this and many other migrations. "Second generationitis" afflicts the Puerto Rican child,
as it did his earlier immigrant equivalent. When the family is
displaced as the reference group, what group takes its place and
what factors influence the choice?

The problems of bilingual children have given rise to a
fairly extensive literature which has left some questions still open
for discussion. Although there is now a fair consensus on the
deleterious role of invidious comparisons, factors connected with
the internal stresses and strains of the family faced with the problems of culture conflict as expressed by the language used at home,
at school, at work, and in the neighborhood do not seem to have
been adequately covered.

We know, for example, that in general the darker the skin
of a Puerto Rican in New York City, the longer he clings to his
mother tongue. We know that often a difficult family situation is
exacerbated when one or more of the children learn English faster
than the parents. English then may be used to assure higher
"bargaining power" in a family situation in which the parents were
already losing some of their authority because of culture conflict.
These are only two illustrations of the complexity of the relationships between language and the "adjustment" of the family.

The list of fields awaiting cultivation in connection with the
Puerto Rican family in its new environment is long. Such research
must, of course, be considered within the framework of other
research awaiting consideration in allocation of time, energy, and
funds. There are important "practical" and scientific purposes to
be served by research work with the families of the newcomers
from Puerto Rico. The migration increases the importance of the
family to its members while, at the same time, it causes it to be
submitted to a bombardment from the new culture which often
seems to the participant as if it were malevolent. Those families
which do disintegrate deserve the aid which action-research could
give them. Those which do not disintegrate may help point the
path, or paths, to a more satisfactory family life for others.

Notes

1. Herbert Blumer, An Appraisal of Thomas and Znaniecki's
        The Polish Peasant in Europe and America, New York:
        Social Science Research Council, 1949. 210 pp.
2. "Puerto Ricans in the Continental United States," 1950 Census,
        Special Report P-E No. 3D, 1953, 18 pp.
3. Clarence Senior, "Patterns of Puerto Rican Dispersion in the
        Continental United States," Social Problems, 2 (October,
        1954), pp. 93-99.

4.   Ibid. p. 93; Clarence Senior, "Puerto Rican Migration to the
      Mainland," Monthly Labor Review, 78 (December, 1955),
      pp. 1354-58.
5.   See Earl Parker Hanson, Transformation: the Story of Modern
      Puerto Rico, New York: Simon and Schuster, 1955. 416 pp.
6.   A. J. Jaffe, ed., Puerto Rican Population of New York City,
      New York: Bureau of Applied Social Research of Columbia
      University, 1954, p. 11.
7.   Millard Hansen, "The Family in Puerto Rico Research Project,"
      in Approaches to Problems of High Fertility in Agrarian
      Societies. New York: Milbank Memorial Fund, 1952.
      pp. 50-61.
8.   Princeton: Princeton University Press, 1952. 512 pp. A
      previous "domestic science" type study of real importance in
      the field of nutrition, health, housing, etc. also was spon-
      sored by the University of Puerto Rico: Lydia Roberts and
      Rosa Luisa Stefani, Patterns of Living in Puerto Rican
      Families, Rio Piedras: University of Puerto Rico, 1949.
      411 pp.
9.   An interim report appeared in 1955: Reuben Hill, "Family
      Structure and Fertility in Puerto Rico," Social Problems,
      3 (October, 1955), pp. 73-83.
10.   J. Mayone Stycos, Family and Fertility in Puerto Rico: a
      Study of the Lower Income Group, New York: Columbia
      University Press, 1955, 332 pp.
11.   Kathleen L. Wolfe, "Growing Up and Its Price in Three Puerto
      Rican Subcultures," Psychiatry, 15 (November, 1952), pp.
      401-33. Several doctoral dissertations have been presented
      as a result of Stewart's project for the Center and a general
      book is scheduled for publication soon.
12.   Marriage and Family Living, 17 (February, 1955), pp. 26-35.
13.   C. Wright Mills, Clarence Senior, and Rose Kohn Goldsen,
      The Puerto Rican Journey, New York: Harper, 1950, 238 pp.
14.   Dr. Charles Wagley, chairman of the Department, is consultant
      to the project; Beatrice Berle, M.D., is medical director;
      and Dr. Elena Padilla (who participated in the Stewart
      studies in Puerto Rico) heads an anthropological staff of
      eight persons. The anthropological phase of the study has
      been divided into various projects: (1) Changing patterns of
      family structure of Puerto Ricans in the neighborhood: to
      establish the types of acculturation to American society and
      the factors underlying it. (2) The social roles of the family:
      socialization of the child from birth to six, with particular
      emphasis on the contrast between traditional practices and cur-
      rent concepts of child rearing. (3) The roles of the school in the
      neighborhood: focusing on how the school system operates to af-
      fect the ways of life of the people, its role in changing attitudes
      and ideologies, and the ways in which the home life and
      neighborhood relate to the schools. (4) Youth lifeways in
      the neighborhood: the study of formal and informal associa-
      tions of youth with reference to the ways in which youth
      relates to family, neighborhood, and value orientation in the
      society. (5) Social and cultural roles of old age: the defini-

tion of the aged person, the role of the aged in the family, and the expectancies of the behavior of old people.

15. For example, Samuel M. Goodman, Lorraine K. Diamond, and David J. Fox, Who Are the Puerto Rican Pupils in the New York City Public Schools? New York: Board of Education, 1956. 88 pp.; Isham B. Jones, The Puerto Rican in New Jersey, Newark: State Department of Education, 1955. 48 pp. Robert W. O'Brien, A Survey of Puerto Ricans in Lorain, Ohio, Lorain: Neighborhood House Association; 1954. 77 pp.; Arthur Siegel, Harold Orlans, and Loyal Greer, Puerto Ricans in Philadelphia, Philadelphia: Commission on Human Relations, 1954. 135 pp.

16. Boston: Little, Brown, 1951. 310 pp.

17. For a warning from a closely related field see Clark E. Vincent 'The Unwed Mother and Sampling Bias," American Sociological Review, 19 (October, 1954), pp. 562-567.

18. See a folder published by the Migration Division of the Puerto Rico Department of Labor, 88 Columbus Ave., New York 23, New York, "A la Tierra Que fueres..." (When in Rome...") which emphasizes that, although there are many habits and practices the migrant should copy from his new neighbors, color discrimination is not one of them!

Reuben Hill, "Courtship in Puerto Rico: An Institution in
Transition." Marriage and Family Living 17:26-35,
February 1955. The National Council on Family Relations.
Reprinted by permission.

When Ponce de León first colonized the island of Puerto
Rico for Spain in the early fifteen hundreds he brought with him
more than a band of adventurers looking for gold, he brought also
the Iberian ideologies about courtship, marriage and family life.
This ideological heritage prescribed segregation of boys and girls
from childhood until marriage. It also supported a differential
child training which rendered boys knowledgeable and assertive and
girls innocent and submissive with respect to the facts of life and
the relationships of the sexes. Contacts between girls and boys
from puberty on were carefully limited and supervised through a
system of chaperonage. To enter courtship boys had to meet
criteria of acceptability authored essentially by the girls' parents.
In effect, mate selection was really "parental choice " by veto
rather than "free choice" by the young people themselves, since
parents determined so carefully who would be permitted to enter
courtship with their daughters.
　　Once courtship began, couples were rarely permitted to be
alone until the wedding night. Thus was it possible to insure that
girls came to the altar virginal and properly dependent upon their
husbands for tutelage in matters of sex and reproduction.
　　Once married the "good wife" remained in her home unless
accompanied by her husband or someone who could vouch for her
conduct. Husbands were encouraged to maintain strict supervision
of their wives. An old saying demonstrates the restrictions which
were once placed on the "free life space" of Puerto Rican women:
"la mujer honrada, las piernas quebradas, y en su casa (An
honorable woman has no need of legs, for she always remains at
home)."[1]
　　With the transfer of Puerto Rico from Spain to the United
States at the turn of this century, a new source of cultural definitions was opened to its people. Sex segregated education was
among the first of the Spanish patterns to lose support as a program
of free universal education was instituted. Literacy increased from
20 per cent in 1900 to 75 per cent at the present time, making
Puerto Ricans highly accessible to ideas and patterns carried by
the mass media of the mainland.[2] Urbanization has increased
steadily from 15 per cent at the time of the American occupation
to 40 per cent today. The admission of women to schools, to professional positions and to the labor force generally as well as to
positions of power in government has gone far to alter the traditional cultural definitions of the proper relations between the

sexes. Not the least of the influences in recent years have been
the pictures of American patterns of courtship and marriage provided by Hollywood movies, which in Puerto Rico are more
popular, even though in English, than Mexican and Latin American
produced films.

The island is not only a meeting place of hispanic-catholic
and North American cultures but it is also a country in transition
from a traditional agrarian way of living to a dynamic planful
type of existence. It is within this context of rapid social change
that I propose to examine the Puerto Rican courtship system.
Agrarian traditional hispanic values clash with urban American
norms wherever parental control of courtship occurs. As the
cultures clash, I want to ask, which is most compelling, the
ideology of freedom of mate selection of America or its corresponding courtship practices? Which American practices, if any, have
been adopted and with what modifications? What traditional beliefs
and practices have survived? To what extent does the resulting
mélange serve the objectives of mate selection in a democratizing
society? It is to these questions that the balance of the article will
be addressed.

Sources of Information and Background

My observations of the contemporary courtship system in
Puerto Rico are based on two years of intermittent visits to Puerto
Rico, 1951-53, and thirteen months of continuous residence, 1953-54,
during which I have been director of the Social Science Research
Center's four year study of the Puerto Rican family at the University of Puerto Rico. During my stay in Puerto Rico I have been
able to observe the processes of accosting, sorting, and involvement among the high school associates of my teenage daughter and
the students of the University of Puerto Rico whom I have served
as teacher of an experimental "marriage course."

My observations of courtship patterns in the interior of the
island have been limited to occasional evenings spent there during
field trips and to the special reports of practices on the island
provided by my students in the marriage course. My generalizations about dating and chaperonage practices on the campus are
drawn from a survey in the spring of 1954 of 275 students in
classes in all divisions of the university, a sample reasonably
representative of the student body by sex, year in school, and
field of concentration.

My occasional references to courtship in the lower class are
drawn from the researches undertaken with Dr. J. Mayone Stycos
in 1951-53 which concentrated on seventy-five lower-class families
distributed in city slums, hill villages and the open country out in
the island. [3] With the exception of these generalizations the data
collected probably apply primarily to the middle classes of metropolitan San Juan and the communities between twenty and fifty
thousand population in which the majority of the university students
surveyed were reared.

Contemporary Patterns of Courtship

From an examination of the language usage in Puerto Rico it

is apparent that certain stages of involvement between the sexes
are unnamed in Spanish whereas other stages have names in
Spanish but are unknown in English.   The word for the phenomenon
of dating without serious intentions is not found in Puerto Rican
Spanish.   Likewise, the Puerto Rican practice of plante or dressing colorfully and then placing one's self strategically to attract
attention from members of the opposite sex is unidentified by an
English term.

Even such a general term as courtship does not translate
directly into Puerto Rican Spanish.   The dictionary translation,
galanteo, is unused here.   The term noviazgo is as close as the
language comes, and it refers only to the affianced relationship,
not to all the broad range of processes understood by the word
courtship in America.

It will be seen that Puerto Ricans give names to the early
stages of accosting and of attracting attention which Americans
ignore. [4]   Americans for their part have made subtle distinctions
between the various types of dallying, non-serious relationships
which occur before marriage-oriented courtship usually begins.
These dating practices are almost entirely absent from the Puerto
Rican experience so far as being named is concerned, such as the
distinctions we make between group dating, double dating, blind
dating, dutch dating, solo dating, and steady dating.

Objectives of the Contemporary System.   In any cross-
cultural comparison of courtship systems it would be possible to
identify a few common and many uncommon objectives.   Puerto
Rico minimizes certain objectives and maximizes others in its
courtship system.   To illustrate, let us identify the overriding and
subsidiary objectives of courtship in the United States.   The most
generic objective of most courtship systems is to sort eligible
young people into culturally if not psychologically compatible pairs
while bringing about a progressive commitment to marriage.   Four
subsidiary objectives which are not so generic to all societies but
are important to realize freedom of mate selection in democraticiz-
ing America are:

1.   To offer abundant opportunities for eligibles to meet
     under conditions which would promote wide range of
     acquaintances.
2.   To provide places of reasonable privacy and periods
     for being alone during which planning can occur and
     personality and cultural differences can be made
     explicit and resolved.
3.   To provide controls to introduce responsibility into
     the behavior of courting pairs to keep conduct within
     safe limits and to commit them to a marriage-oriented
     relationship.
4.   To provide a method of mediating back into circula-
     tion incompatible combinations by providing facesaving
     means of withdrawing from commitments to marry.

Of these four objectives the Puerto Rican system maximizes
number three at the expense of the other three objectives.   Free
choice of mate implies some range of choice among eligibles.
Actually opportunities are scarce as yet in the Puerto Rican situa-

tion for meeting a number of persons under conditions which might lead toward friendship and close acquaintance. It is clear from my explorations that little merit is seen in girls knowing many young men. On the contrary, too many novios suggests the girl may be fickle. Open field dating with many boys, such as is common in the United States, is virtually unknown here.

Among the 160 women students surveyed at the University of Puerto Rico 31 per cent had had no dates at all while in college and 74 per cent had experienced fewer than nine dates all told. Fifteen per cent of the 115 men surveyed had never dated in college and fifty-three per cent had had fewer than nine dates in college. What about no date affairs, mixed recreation events to which men might come as a group without dates and girls might come similarly? Not more than four such events a year are scheduled for this campus of 8500 students. Most student social affairs are for couples primarily. The U. S. phenomenon of the "mixer" is alien to the Puerto Rican campus.

The systematic postponement of involvement until one has played the field is discouraged in Puerto Rico. In the interior of the island, even more than on the campus, efforts are made to narrow the field of unpaired young people early. There is no special merit for females, at least, in being unattached, "free, white and single" as Americans put it. The ideal is to get into a novio or steady boy friend relationship. [5] Relatively little time is lost in exploring persons as possible companions or friends before becoming identified as novios. University students averaged only one dating contact before becoming novios. Forty-five per cent moved directly to the novio status without any previous dating appearances. Indeed, there is no guarantee of extensive dating or novio experiences before becoming engaged. Among the engaged we surveyed, the average couple had had one novio experience and a total of five dates while in college on which to base their choice of one another.

Additionally the Puerto Rican system is not concerned with providing opportunities for testing the compatibility of temperament by offering unsupervised periods alone during which quarrels and heated discussions might occur. On the contrary, in the interest of safeguarding the virginity and innocence of the unmarried girl, the system conspires to keep the couple from ever being alone before marriage.

Needless to say, with so much parental management little opportunity is provided to break up and withdraw from the relationship; once the parents have been advised of its existence the door begins to close on any change of partners. In effect, this cripples the engagement as a possible testing period before marriage.

In summary, the overall objective of the Puerto Rican system is to bring about a commitment to marry early while supervising the courting pair so that their sex conduct is above reproach. The ultimate objective of the system is to make sure that the girl arrives at marriage virginal and unimpaired by the experiences of the courtship--if the parents fail in this they feel no other man will be likely to show honorable interest in her thereafter. Hence the overconcern in Puerto Rico for objective number three at the expense of the other three objectives listed above.

Parental Supervision and Chaperonage. How is the objective
of providing controls to introduce responsibility into the behavior of
courting pairs to keep their conduct within safe limits implemented?
Parents, especially the girl's parents, undertake the responsibility
of much more supervision of the courtship process than one would
find in the United States. Good parents are actively concerned for
the safety of their daughter, for her reputation and for her conduct. [6]
The father of the girl serves as a powerful conscience to whom
the suitor must answer if his conduct has been unseemly. While
he doesn't actually choose the suitor he may still exercise the
power of elimination since he can deny the right of entrance into
the home.

A colorful extension of the parental control of courtship is
the chaperonage system which persists today in various forms in
Puerto Rico. The parent delegates to a chaperon the task of
supervising and escorting the courting pair to events away from
the family home. The system has been eroded by the demands of
the times but its services continue. There are fewer unmarried
tias (aunts) available today so that formal chaperons are rarely
used except for accompanying the couple to major balls, public
fiestas or grand affairs where formality is the order of the evening. [7]
Informal chaperons, more indulgent and less powerful, such as
older brother or sister, or younger sibling or cousin, or even
an extra girl friend may fulfill the purpose. It is not infrequent
to see threesomes, couples and "extra lady" at beaches, plays,
shows, night clubs, and picnics. Few girls risk being seen in
public alone or in the company of a young man alone without someone who can vouch for their conduct while away from home.

On the university campus chaperonage has been even more
eroded by substituting a system of group dating for the system of
informal chaperons described above. Group dating is a system in
which several couples will go to movies, dances, or other recreational events together. Obviously this does not fulfill all of the
functions of supervision of conduct which chaperonage originally was
designed to serve. [8] Parents and their daughters have come to
accept this type of chaperonage as a sufficient measure of protection. Chaperonage in this transitional stage in Puerto Rico has lost
most of its supervisory functions and has become primarily a
reputation-vouching service. In group dating each couple vouches
for every other couple and reputations are thereby kept intact.

Some indication of the distribution of chaperonage services
for present day university students is provided in the tabulations of
our survey. Men report not only a greater volume of dates (although low by U.S. campus standards) [9] but also have freed themselves substantially more from the supervision of the formal
chaperonage system. Nevertheless few men can really report that
they are as free as U.S. students, only eighteen per cent confining
their dates to unchaperoned situations. The double standard
of sex morality has its counterpart in Puerto Rico in a double
standard of supervision, women being chaperoned much more
closely than men students. Seventy-four per cent of the women
students indicated they had experienced up to this moment no un-

chaperoned dates.

The number of unchaperoned experiences with a novio (steady boy friend) was even more varied among university students. Twenty-five per cent of the men and forty-two per cent of the women students have never attended a party, movie, or recreational event alone without another couple, extra person or official chaperon along. Only thirteen per cent of the women students and thirty per cent of the men students have had this experience of being alone with one's steady fifteen times or more. Yet college students are the most Americanized, in this respect, of the young people in the island.

Readers may feel that the chaperonage system is surely costly and burdensome to the participants. This would be true if recreation were the major objective of heterosexual activity. But chaperonage in its transitional form persists in Puerto Rico because other objectives are more important that recreation. Men want to marry women of unblemished reputations, unspoiled by too much contact with too many men before them.[10] Chaperonage serves this aim well enough since it functions to discourage open field dating, and minimizes the opportunities for sexual contact before marriage.

Stages of Involvement and Commitment

The Puerto Rican boy and girl follow a well blazed path from single irresponsibility to married felicity. Each stage is named and the roles appropriate to the stage are well known. The Spanish terms for the stages and brief descriptions are shown in Table 1.

Accosting Stages. Plante. Much more time and attention are devoted to the initial stages of accosting than in the United States. The stage is institutionalized more clearly in the interior of the island than in the metropolitan area of San Juan, where the evidences of transition are apparent. In the towns of the interior the public square is the center for plante and picheo activities. Girls dress and make up their faces and adorn their appendages colorfully with jewelry, pendants, and costumery that is designed to be eye-catching--then they converge as a group on the town square where they will walk round and round to be seen by as yet unattached boys. It is the "strutting of the male cock wooing the hen" in reverse!

The young men will walk together in the opposite direction, calculated to meet the girls once every turn of the square. Others will sit on the benches of the square eyeing the girls as they pass and leaving no doubt in the girls' minds that they are noticed. Some boys will do no more than smile and try to catch the eye of a girl they favor. Others more daring will launch into the picheo stage of accosting, which consists of throwing compliments and yearning comments called piropos or flores, which the girls may pretend not to hear or may acknowledge ever so slightly by a word to their sisters.

Other versions of plante by girls may be observed on the college campus and in the metropolitan area, where girls are to be seen congregated at the playing fields, at ROTC exercises, or near the library entrance, wherever boys are likely to be found.

Boys engage in plante, too, by planting themselves where

Table 1.   Stages of Accosting, Involvement and Commitment
In Middle Class Puerto Rico

I	II	III	IV	V
Plante and Picheo	Acompañar	Salir Juntos, Pretendiente, & Novio stage	Novio Serio	Novio de Compromiso
Dressing to attract attention and going where boys are	Accosting and possibly escorting girl from dance or fiesta without prior arrangement	Special boy friend girl friend stage Steady dating	Private family understanding Going steady Exchange of class rings Boy gains official entrance to girl's home Informal and unannounced engagement	Formal engagement Public announcement
Flirting, throwing compliments called Piropos at passing girls				

Period of window shopping, uninvolved and uncommitted looking around	Period of increasing involvement and commitment with stress at beginning on winning the consent of the girl and her parents
Little opportunity to talk or visit because of close supervision of girls by parents and chaperons	Little opportunity to talk or visit alone, or to quarrel long enough to discover basis for differences, because of close chaperonage
	Difficult to withdraw from the relationship once it enters the Novio Serio stage

specific girls may see them standing on the street   corner near the
girl's home, or even boldly directly across the street from her
balcony.   The stance he takes is attention getting, and is called
hacer varilla or "making himself stiff like a ramrod." His military
bearing as he walks, his stiff attention when standing are designed
to attract attention.   The tradition of serenata, while serving a
variety of purposes of rendering honor and homage to deserving
persons, was clearly once an institutionalized expression of plante and
of picheo since it combined the attracting of attention with the art
of throwing one's sentiments as flowers before the desired one. [11]
     Picheo.   Inextricably related to plante is the phenomenon of
picheo to which we have already referred.   It involves "pitching"

compliments at walking señoritas, at specific or unknown women
whose dress or bearing hint they merit a comment. Picheo is an
art less direct than the American "line" in that the girl does not
openly acknowledge the piropo. Examples of well known piropos
used by university students are given herewith:

Masher Type
    Qué bombón! Y yo con diabetis! (What a sweet dish and me
with diabetes)
    Qué curvas peligrosas y yo sin frenos! (What dangerous
curves and me without brakes)

Wistful Yearning
    If a girl passes eating a cone.
        Quién fuera esa barquilla (If I could only be that ice
        cream cone)
    If a girl is in black.
        Haría todo lo que hizo el muerto menos morirme!
        (I would do everything for her he did except die for her)
        Qué viudita, aunque el muerto me salga!
        (What a beautiful widow! I say it at the risk of her
        dead husband coming back to punish me)
    If the girl is dressed in red.
        Me casaría con ella aunque los hijos me salgan
        bomberos!
        (I would marry her even though the children would be
        born firemen)
    Que Dios bendiga el rosal que dió esa rosa! (May God bless
the bush which produced that rose)
    Que Dios bendiga todo lo que esta bien hecho! (May God
bless all that is beautifully put together)
    Parece que San Pedro ha dejado las puertas del cielo abiertas
porque los angeles han bajado a la tierra! (St. Peter must have
let the doors of heaven open because the angels have come to
earth)
    Dios te bendiga y te guarde para mi! (May God bless you
and keep you for me)
    In time the piropos may be rewarded by an acknowledge-
ment by the girl that she notices the boy and gives him the
opportunity of seeing her later. Both girl and boy exchange co-
quettish remarks in the period that follows, the girl playing the
teasing-disbelieving role and the boy playing the eloquent, sentimental and convincing part. At this point their picheo does resemble
the exchange of lines in American persiflage. Usually the relationship moves quickly to the novio stage without many intervening
contacts of a picheo nature. The boy may however utilize the
mechanism of "acompañar" or escorting the girl home from a no-
date affair to gain access to the girl and her parents.
    Acompañar. With the exception of the freshman no-date
"mixers," for a boy to escort a girl home from a party or dance
that he hasn't escorted her to in the first place is not quite in
good taste in the United States. It is not a majority pattern in
Puerto Rico either, but may be a product of the discomforts and in-
effectiveness of a courtship system in transition. It serves a
definite purpose when it is used.

Groups of girls will go to a fiesta or an informal ball with an older lady along who supervises their conduct carefully. Boys will appear and ask to dance or to sit with a girl they have not dared to bring to the ball. If encouraged a boy may ask for several dances and end up by escorting the girl and the chaperone home. This is an honorable form of "pickup" or acompañar.

According to my informants the accoster may be quite direct. Immediately upon starting to dance he will put pointed questions to the girl: "¿Tienes novio? (Do you have a fiancé?)" or "¿Cómo va tu noviazgo? (How is your courtship going?)" or "¿Cuándo te casas? (When are you marrying?)" or "¿No tienes ningún plante o picheo?) (Aren't you carrying a torch for someone?)." The discussion almost always centers on whether the girl is already spoken for. The girl may answer directly or avoid the issue but eventually must indicate her status.

In many cases a novio relationship may be established directly from such situations without further dates. Before accosting the girl he has already made inquiries about her from friends. Once started he has no disposition to dally. University students report an average of only one appearance together before becoming novios. Indeed the largest group of respondents moved directly into the novio status without any previous public appearances together. [12] Once he gets the ear of a girl, the Puerto Rican boy is a "fast worker!"

Salir Juntos, Pretendiente, and Novios. The status of salir juntos, or "going out together" is rarely acknowledged as a stage in its own right, as "just dating" is in the United States. The term pretendiente, is reserved for the persistent caller who has not yet been accepted by the girl as novio. These two indefinite statuses have been merged for this discussion with the phenomenon of "novios (going steady)" as the first stage in involvement and commitment. The stage is very short, even for university students who have inaugurated dating on the island. One does not "go out together" with more than one boy at a time, or keep more than one pretendiente in uncertainty long, and very soon people begin talking, defining the couple as novios after a minimum of public appearances together. And the couple soon accept the designation themselves.

The stage of being novios or steady dating is the only one in which it might be possible to break the relationship and withdraw gracefully into circulation again. It is used too infrequently for this purpose, however, to constitute an effective screening device in the sorting of mates into compatible pairs.

There are good explanations for failure of the novio status to eliminate incompatibles from the marriage mill. It is first of all a period during which the boy is seeking a secure attachment. He is at a disadvantage in bargaining; it is the girl who grants the favors. Back of the girl are the all powerful parents who have not yet granted him the right to officially launch his courtship. He still feels too much like a pretendiente, a pursuer engaged in a chase in which he wins only if he continues the relationship. Obviously, the relationship during this period is too onesided for the male to initiate a break, and it has not reached a point where

the girl knows enough about the boy to bring about an open break.
And words of discouragement from her, moreover, merely serve
to heighten his persistence.   For these reasons calculated withdrawals from the relation are not likely to occur in the early
novio stage.

     The insecurity of the pretendiente and new novio relation-
ships is the basic theme of the popular songs of Puerto Rico,
melancholic, yearning, despondent and doleful.   The bolero music
typifies the mood of the boy and is often sung by male tenors who
specialize in lloriqueo or crying tones which rise in plaintive
fashion to plead for the loved one's consideration.[13]   Titles of
some of these songs communicate the sentimental pleading of the
Puerto Rican male who feels not fully appreciated by his loved
one: "Engaño (Deceived)," "Perdida (Lost)," "Piensalo Bien (Think
it Over)."

     The humiliations of the period make for more insecurity in
the male ego than any other stage of courtship.   He is easily
activated to jealousy and presumes to be possessive even before it
is appropriate to do so.   He is not nearly so likely to share his
partner with associates as his American counterpart who is "going
steady."   Actually, novios who go to dances sit apart with their
chaperon or the other couples acting as reputation vouchers, never
trade dances, and the boy may be very surly if asked to share his
partner in a dance.   He resents nothing more than to have friends
or strangers attempt to cut in on him while he is dancing with his
novia.[14]   Later, if they become engaged the possessiveness   of
the young man is exalted into a virtue.

     Novios Serios.   The uncertainty of the steady dating period
is usually broken by acknowledgement of the relationship by the
girl's parents.   Although he may have called for the girl at their
home before, he now asks her father for authorization to call
("pedir la entrada de la casa") and if accepted is assigned certain
nights that he will be welcome.   When the girl's parents officially
invite the boy to dinner everyone knows that he has been accepted
in the status of novio-serio.   The couple may have exchanged
pictures or pins before this, but now they usually also exchange
their class rings.   If, however, the boy is satisfied to remain in
the going steady status and doesn't make the steps to declare his
intentions the girl's mother may bring pressure on her to crystallize
the relationship or break it off quickly.

     From this point on the novio may not withdraw from the
relationship without risking sanctions from the father, the girl's
brothers and relatives.   His conduct becomes their concern now.
In some ways he is now adopted into the girl's family so far as
answerability for his conduct is concerned.   In sheer time lapse,
the novio-serio stage is longest of all, sometimes lasting several
years until the boy is financially in a position to marry.

     Novio de Compromiso.   The compromiso or engagement is
the most formal of the statuses in the Puerto Rican system.   It
may not be announced for several months or years after the couple
have been adopted by both sets of parents and it is understood that
they are going to marry.   Instead of a "private understanding" as
we speak of it in the United States, the novio-serio affianced have

a "family understanding" shared with both sets of parents which they
do not communicate to the general public until the formal announcement of their engagement.

When marriage is an immediate possibility financially the
boy's parents pay a formal call on the girl's parents and ask for
her hand in marriage.   The agreement reached, the girl's
parents make a formal announcement.   In Puerto Rico it is frequent
for the boy's parents to purchase the engagement ring, which is
expected to reflect in its size and setting the financial position of
the family.

Some parents give the engaged couple increasing privacy and
freedom of action.   Movies at least are events to which they may
go without chaperonage.   Parents thus express their confidence in
the integrity of the boy and tell him he is responsible for the
safety and good reputation of their daughter.

Other parents respond to this situation of courtship in
transition by moving in the opposite direction toward more and
more strict supervision of the pair--back to the traditional patterns
of old Spain.   They conspire to keep the engaged pair from any
opportunity to be alone.   Where before the engagement they allowed
the couple to leave under supervision of informal chaperons, they
now undertake to supervise the pair night and day.   They regard
this period as the most dangerous of all from the standpoint of
morality and reputation and act accordingly.   Elopements are not
unheard of in response to these restrictions.

Interesting changes occur in the couple's relationship during
engagement.   Both are inclined to be somewhat possessive and
easily activated to jealousy.   Although they are now cut off from
their friends they have little time alone by themselves without
chaperons present.   The inevitable engagement tensions build up
but can't be released by quarrels or heart to heart talks, because
of the presence of third parties.

Whereas the girl has had the upper hand during the early
stages of the courtship, the situation is now reversed.   She now
must ask permission to change her hairdress, to wear decolletage,
to go shopping or to leave town to visit relatives or friends in the
island.   She may be asked to discontinue certain female friendships;
she has long since discontinued all male friendships.   She may no
longer appear in public places with other girls where she may be
exposed to piropos.   She may no longer tease her fiancé or question
his judgment in public.   The role of the masterful husband is
required of the engaged man, not only by the girl's father and his
male friends, but by his fiancée.   It tells her she has betrothed
a strong forceful man who will exert substantial leadership in their
future family affairs. [15]

The incidence of engagements is probably lower among university students in Puerto Rico than in the United States and the
proportion of married students is demonstrably lower. [16]   Only
twenty-seven per cent of the seniors surveyed had ever been engaged.
There is a tendency for engagements here to be between senior girls
and men now in business or professional practice rather than among
students in residence.   Thus, the frequent practice in the states
of engagement of college seniors with a June marriage after gradua-

tion is not customary here.   Senior men are not as likely as United
States seniors to regard themselves as economically marriageable,
and are therefore less prone to engagement while in college.

Conclusions About the System

The pattern of sorting, involving and committing young
people to marriage in Puerto Rico is still predominantly more
Spanish than American.   The two systems have merged at a number
of points with interesting results.   The American ideology of free
mate choice has been largely accepted but parents still hold veto
power.   Moreover, the acceptance of the ideology has not brought
sufficient change in the parental management of the courtship to
permit much latitude in choice among young people.   The opening
of opportunities to meet and evaluate the suitability of members
of the opposite sex has lagged behind the acceptance of the principle of freedom of mate selection.   There are few places to meet,
few places for talks with privacy provided.   The continued use
of chaperons discourages much mutual exploration.

The American belief in the desirability of permanent
marriage may not be as inflexible as the hispanic-catholic doctrine
but the ideology is common to both cultures.   Nevertheless Puerto
Rico's courtship system provides little opportunity for sorting
couples out into compatible pairs which might be expected to live
permanently in marriage.   After becoming novios there is very
little chance to test their compatibility by meeting marriage-like
situations together.   The Puerto Rican engagement is a "promise
to marry," not a testing period which will determine whether
marriage should follow.   Puerto Ricans become committed to
marriage early in the courtship and have no face-saving chance to
withdraw gracefully.

For the moment the system neither fulfills the requirement
of the Spanish ideology of insulation of the sexes until marriage nor
the American ideals of free mate choice and equalitarian investment
in a relationship destined to foster mutual growth of personalities.

The system is ideologically oriented increasingly toward the
beliefs of North America but its forms and practices remain predominantly those of the hispanic-catholic world.   It is a system in
transition which is trying to straddle two incompatible goals, the
traditional goal of bringing women to marriage chaste and innocent
and the goal of freedom of mate choice based on experience and
knowledge of the opposite sex.   The machinery set up to insure the
first objective obstructs and interferes with the achievement of the
second.   Little evidence is available to justify a prediction that
the dilemma will be resolved in the immediate future.

Notes

I wish to acknowledge help in preparing this article from many
    of the faculty and students of the University of Puerto Rico,
    especially Dr. Carlos Albizu, Dr. Kurt Back, Sra. Celia
    Núñez de Bunker, Dr. Millard Hansen and Dr. J. Mayone
    Stycos.

1. José C. Rosario, <u>The Development of the Puerto Rican Jíbaro</u>
    <u>and His Present Attitude Toward Society</u> (Río Piedras,
    University of Puerto Rico Press, 1935).
2. The most popular magazines in the bookstores and sales
    counters of the island are published in the United States.
3. J. Mayone Stycos, <u>Family and Fertility in the Lower Class of</u>
    <u>Puerto Rico</u> (New York: Columbia University Press, in press).
4. See our description later of the early stages of involvement in
    Puerto Rico, particularly, <u>plante</u>, <u>picheo</u>, throwing of
    <u>piropos</u> or <u>flores</u> and <u>acompañar</u>.
5. My daughter was taken aside by her high school peers and
    advised to select one boy for attention rather than to play
    the field so she wouldn't get the reputation of being fickle.
    She remonstrated that she couldn't tell that much difference
    between the boys, that she liked them all the same. "Judy,
    it isn't natural to like all boys the same--they aren't the
    same," she was told. It didn't take Judy long to discover
    that her friends were right and to adapt by concentrating
    her time with one special boy who is of course sure that
    he chose her. Precisely the opposite counsel is given the
    freshman girl on most stateside campuses, where to settle
    down to one boy too soon may kill a girl's popularity. The
    newcomer is urged to play the field, to build the illusion of
    being in great demand and above all not to "fall" for any
    one boy. Puerto Rican girls who come to the states to
    college are understandably bewildered by the American system
    of dating primarily for recreation or for popularity's sake.
6. The responsibility falls clearly on the parents of girls. My
    informants tell me that Puerto Rican parents of boys serve
    notice to the world with an expression: "Ellos que recojan
    sus pollitas porque mi gallo anda suelto (Gather in your
    chicks, my rooster is on the loose!)."
7. At the formal balls of the upper class Casa de España in
    San Juan a special gallery for chaperons, equipped with
    comfortable chairs, is provided from which the conduct of
    the couples may be observed. At a student cadet dance
    given by the Air ROTC this spring we counted fifty chaperons
    for roughly one hundred couples, many of whom came in
    groups.
8. Couples tell me that mild necking and goodnight kissing are
    quite possible when out on group dates, which would be un-
    likely under the informal chaperonage of the "extra-lady"
    or little brother, and would be unheard of with formal
    chaperons about.
9. See estimate of an average of three dates a week in Ohio by
    Marvin R. Koller, 'Some Changes in Courtship Behavior
    in Three Generations of Ohio Women," <u>American Sociological</u>
    <u>Review</u>, 16:366-70, 1951.
10. Puerto Rican men want no "warmed-over kisses or left-over
    love," as a popular song goes. Mothers of boys discourage
    their sons from becoming serious with girls who have had
    more than two or three <u>novios</u>, regarding them as "<u>fáciles</u>
    (too changeable)," and possibly less likely to be faithful

after marriage.

11. Once an integral part of the attention getting phase of court-
    ship, today there is an ordinance requiring a municipal permit
    at a cost of two dollars to serenade a loved one in any town
    in Puerto Rico. The police usually monitor such serenades
    and check to make sure they have been authorized. Here
    is another evidence of the transition from folk to secular
    practices reaching into the realm of the rituals of accosting.
    No wonder the custom is disappearing in Puerto Rico!

12. On the campus students may have many informal contacts, not
    properly termed dates, walking to the library or to the
    cafeteria, before becoming _novios_. The point is, however,
    that even the informal contacts are oriented toward becoming
    novios rather than toward companionship or friendship with
    several members of the opposite sex as in the states.

13. I am indebted to my colleague J. Mayone Stycos for this inter-
    pretation of Puerto Rican popular music.

14. At a dance recently an interesting exchange of this order took
    place. A boy and his _novia_ were approached by a mutual
    friend for a dance. The boy turned to the girl as if to let
    her make the decision and then because she accepted feuded
    with her for the balance of the evening. In his jealous state
    he didn't have the insight to recognize that he had given her
    no cue that he didn't wish her to accept the dance.

15. Although she will frequently be as well educated as he and
    will expect to continue her employment in business or in a
    profession after marriage she relishes the prospects of
    exalting her man publicly. I have no evidence of com-
    petition by women for the leadership role in engagement or
    marriage among Puerto Rican couples. And Puerto Rican
    women are strong characters in the economic and political
    life of the island! This phenomenon would bear further ex-
    ploration.

16. Only four per cent of the Puerto Rican students are married
    compared with ten per cent of students in colleges of the
    Middle West, see, Ray E. Baber, Marriage and The Family
    (New York: McGraw-Hill, 1953), p. 148.

Francesco Cordasco, "The Puerto Rican Family and the Anthropologist: Oscar Lewis, La Vida, and The Culture of Poverty." Urban Education 3:32-38, 1967. Reprinted by permission.

Few European scholars (and fewer American savants) have managed to scale the ramparts of academe and carry their intellectual wares into the lay market place: those who have, almost inevitably, have earned the envy and suspicion of their professional confrères, and the countless dollars of dilettantish lay readers who have acquired fashion and prized erudition in frenzied pursuit of the erstwhile academicians. Most often, historians and sociologists (Cesare Lombroso, Guglielmo Ferero, Oswald Spengler, H. G. Wells, and W. G. Sumner come easily to mind) have made the trek from Parnassus into the valley of discord. Successively, they have titillated, infuriated, amused and mesmerized their lay audiences: they have cast dazzling pearls before raucous crowds, and they have counted ducats; and few have remembered to return home to their Olympian lairs. The latest of the academic itinerants is the anthropologist Oscar Lewis, who has studied Blackfeet Indians in Canada, farmers in Texas, and the culture of the Indian subcontinent. And all of this he has done well; but with the publication of La Vida,[1] Professor Lewis has disappeared into the lay gethsemane to which, with some timorous flirtation, his Five Families (1959), The Children of Sanchez (1961) and Pedro Martinez (1964) had earlier brought him.

La Vida (an enormously thick, nondescripto Teutonic volume) is the first of a series on Puerto Rican slum families in San Juan and New York which Professor Lewis plans. It is part of the burgeoning literature on the Puerto Rican community, and beyond the accolades it has received from book distribution clubs (which have been ecstatic in their praises), La Vida has been hailed as "...one of the most important books published in the United States this year;" cautioned against, in that "(its) insights...will depend upon the compassion and perception of the reader;" and energetically questioned: "Is he (Professor Lewis) describing Puerto Ricans, ...or is he describing exceptional people, leading exceptional lives, who resemble their fellow Puerto Ricans only in limited ways?"[2]

The Plan of La Vida

Basic to any of these considerations is Professor Lewis' plan for La Vida, and his theory of the "culture of poverty" out of which the plan evolves. If the plan of La Vida is deceptively simple, Professor Lewis' "culture of poverty" is not; yet one is meaningless without the other, and it is not the portraiture of La

Vida (a vast pathological Eloge) which gives validity to the theory, but rather the theory which is the deus ex machina of Professor Lewis' vast social tableau.

The plan for La Vida takes on Zolaesque proportion: some three hundred individuals cross its pages. While preparing the volume, Professor Lewis studied nineteen related households, eleven in San Juan and eight in New York; and data on twelve other households appear in the book. The Ríos family which is presented "consists of five households, a mother and two married daughters in Puerto Rico and a married son and daughter in New York. The mother, Fernanda Fuentes... is now living with her sixth husband in La Esmeralda, a San Juan slum. Her children-- Soledad, twenty-five; Felicita, twenty-three; Simplicio, twenty-one; and Cruz, nineteen--were born to Fernanda while she was living in free union with her first husband, Cristobal Ríos, a light-skinned Puerto Rican." Professor Lewis' family kaleidoscope revolves about Fernanda in San Juan; Soledad in New York; Felicita in San Juan; Simplicio in New York; and Cruz in San Juan. It is a harrowing tale of two cities of life-styles largely recorded on tape which Professor Lewis has edited to present the details of the way of life of the Ríos family with Karamazovian affectlessness. And there is no absence of detail. What emerges is a vast panorama of social and psycho-pathology: cruelty and violence; deceit; the subtleties of human degradation; endemic social deviance; the "game" of prostitution; consensual unions; and abandonment; and omnipresent sex, never missing from the lives of the protagonists, and recorded with such literalness of language and an unrestrained abundance of detail by Professor Lewis that it initially shocks and, then, revolts the reader.[3] The Ríos family are a dramatis personae in search of an author and in a curious Pirandellean twist, Professor Lewis not only furnishes a play, but a theory as well. It is this theory (the "Culture of Poverty") which translates La Vida into Balzacian reality or into grotesque illusion.

Professor Lewis and The Culture of Poverty

Professor Lewis (by his own statement) originated the concept of the "Culture of Poverty"; as a conceptual model, he has attempted its precise definition. The trick lies in distinguishing between "poverty" and the "culture of poverty": for the Ríos family is not representative of the poor, but rather of the subculture of poverty (Professor Lewis uses the shorter form); and this subculture of poverty focuses upon the individual personality rather than upon the group (that is, upon the family and the slum community).[4] Lewis defines the "culture of poverty" as,

"... both an adaptation and a reaction of the poor to their marginal position in a class-stratified, highly individuated, capitalistic society. It represents an effort to cope with feelings of hopelessness and despair which develop from the realization of the improbability of achieving success in terms of the values and goals of the larger society. Indeed, many of the traits of the culture of poverty can be viewed as attempts at local solutions for problems not met by existing institutions and agencies because the people are not

eligible for them, cannot afford them or are ignorant or
suspicious of them." (p. xliv)
However, Professor Lewis is quick to add that the "culture of
poverty" is "...not only an adaptation to a set of objective conditions of the larger society.   Once it comes into existence it tends
to perpetuate itself from generation to generation because of its
effects on the children.   By the time slum children are age six
or seven, they have usually absorbed the basic values and attitudes
of their subculture and are not psychologically geared to take full
advantage of changing conditions or increased opportunities which
may occur in their lifetime." (p. xlv).   Daniel Moynihan refines the
theory and adds still other ingredients: "...these families and the
communities they make up (in the culture of poverty) tend to
transmit from one generation to the next, traits and circumstances
which help perpetuate their condition.   There is nothing absolute
about this: as many individuals, no doubt, leave the culture as
remain in it, and on one level the proposition amounts to little
more than the assertion that the poor rarely inherit large estates."
(Commentary, February 1967, p. 36.   The italics have been added.)
        This adaptive ambience, Professor Lewis finds both crea-
tive and the source of great strengths (with its own structure and
rationale, as a way of life), but with the key traits of fatalism and
a low level of aspiration,"(which) helps to reduce frustration, (and
with) the legitimization of short-range hedonism (which) makes
possible spontaneity and enjoyment." Within these theoretic constructs, Professor Lewis analyzes the "culture of poverty" against
four sets of characteristics: (1) the lack of effective participation
and integration of the poor in the major institutions of the larger
society; (2) poor housing, crowding, gregariousness, and a minimum
of organization beyond the level of the nuclear and extended family;
(3) the absence of childhood as a specially prolonged and protected
stage in the life cycle;   early initiation into sex, free unions or
consensual marriages, high incidence of abandonment of wives and
children, female-centered families, lack of family stability, authoritarianism; (4) marginality, helplessness, dependence and inferiority.
In essence, if one is disposed to accept the thesis, Professor
Lewis' discussion is a major contribution to the "culture of poverty."
        Lewis develops the thesis and basic methodology in a lengthy
introduction (pp. iv-ix) which must be read if the book is to be kept
in its proper setting.   The socio-economic correlates of the theory,
mutatis mutandis, vis à vis the Negro community were developed by
Daniel Moynihan in The Case For National Action (1965).   Although
Lewis, at no point in any substance, relates his "culture of poverty"
to the schools and education, Moynihan does.   In a review of the
controversy spawned by The Negro Family (the Moynihan Report), he
gives the theory a significant and new dimension: "At the moment
Negroes are placing enormous confidence in the idea that quality
education can transform their situation.   But it is not at all clear
that education has this potential.   Last summer, the U.S. Office
of Education issued its report on "Equality of Educational Opportunity" based on the study...ordered by the Civil Rights Act of
1964 of the educational facilities available to Negroes and other
minority groups as compared with the white majority.   The report

(The Coleman Report)...radically confounded expectation. Negroes, it turned out, tested badly at the outset of their schooling, and worse at the end of it. But the quality of the schools they attended--shockingly segregated schools--was not in fact significantly different from that of schools attended by whites and others. More important, the regression analysis carried out for the study produced the astounding proposition that the quality of the schools has only a trifling relation to achievement...the two great determinants of outcome turned out to be family background and social peer group." (Commentary, February 1967, p. 44)

The Vast Slough of "La Vida"

Caught in the vast slough of La Vida, the central question for the Ríos family is their typicality: is Professor Lewis describing exceptional people, leading exceptional lives, who resemble their fellow Puerto Ricans in only limited ways? The very viability of Lewis' theory of "the culture of poverty" depends on the answer to this crucial question. Unfortunately, Professor Lewis is ambiguous in his answer. Although he disclaims the representativeness of the Ríos family ('I should like to emphasize that this study deals with only one segment of the Puerto Rican population and that the data should not be generalized to Puerto Rican society as a whole '), he still claims a much larger significance and typicality: "The Ríos family would probably be classified as a multi-problem family by most social workers, but it is by no means an extreme example nor is it the worst I have encountered in the Puerto Rican slums;" and he extends his observation by noting, "The history of the Ríos family...suggests that the pattern of free unions and multiple spouses was not limited to the poor. It has been a widespread pattern among wealthy rural families." (pp. xxviii-xxix). In much of the data, the tendency is always the cultivation of a special perspective even if this leads Professor Lewis to distortion.

Continuing Doubts

Clearly, continuing doubt frames a crucial question: is La Vida a study of the culture of lower-class Puerto Rican life; or is it a study of the culture of radically disorganized forms of slum life? Does all poverty lead to Professor Lewis' culture of poverty? For the theory must, if it has any validity, be more than the adaptation to the urban ambience which is its nexus: is it (for Professor Lewis) culture itself? All of the indices of Professor Lewis' "culture of poverty" (its marginality, and its helplessness, its sex and its prostitution) are related to poverty, but is the microcosm which Professor Lewis sketches in the macabre vignettes of the Ríos family the very substance of poverty itself?

The controversy which surrounds La Vida will obscure many of the important questions it raises. It will, unhappily, overshadow the tremendous struggle of the Puerto Rican community (both on the mainland and in the island) to confront the realities of the grim social and economic problems;[5] it will minimize the gains achieved in mainland schools;[6] it will register as crude parodies the poetic pathos of the Puerto Rican poor.[7] And it will be widely read, misinterpreted and misused.

References

1. La Vida: A Puerto Rican Family in the Culture of Poverty--
   San Juan and New York. By Oscar Lewis. Random House
   (1966). 669 pp.

2. See the reviews, respectively, of Michael Harrington, New York
   Times Book Review, November 20, 1966, p. 1; Rev.
   Joseph P. Fitzpatrick, America, December 10, 1966, p. 778;
   and Nathan Glazer, Commentary, February, 1967, p. 83.
   See also the negative sentiments in the review by Joseph
   Monserrat, "A Puerto Rican Family," Natural History
   (April 1967).

3. See the description of Soledad's relationship with Benedecto as
   an illustration of the pervasive luridity, pp. 217 ff.

4. cf. Michael Harrington's definition of the "culture of poverty"
   in his The Other America (1961). See also Elizabeth Herzog,
   'Some Assumptions About the Poor." The Social Service
   Review, December 1963, pp. 389-402; and Nathan Glazer,
   loc. cit., supra. Professor Lewis is not without historical
   predecessors who have attempted to fashion a viable theory
   out of the poignant evocations and delineations of human
   misery: Henry Mayhew's London Labour and the London
   Poor (1861-62) is an analagous tableau; and so is the literary and sociological canon of Mid-Victorian England.

5. See particularly, Dorothy D. Bourne and James R. Bourne,
   Thirty Years of Change in Puerto Rico (New York: Frederick
   A. Praeger 1966); and The Puerto Rican Community
   Development Project: Un Proyecto Puertorriqueño De Ayuda
   Mutua Para El Desarrollo De La Comunidad (New York:
   The Puerto Rican Forum 1964).

6. 'Most of our children are brought up in homes where the language and culture is still mostly shaped along the way of
   life parents lived in Puerto Rico. This is good and positive
   and it has to be so because parents themselves cannot
   transmit what they do not know, but here is where the school
   enters as the institution that will help transmit the new
   culture into a child's life, and for that matter into the home
   as a whole. We pledge our support in all aspects where
   community support will be needed." Statement of Carmen
   Dinos (Supervisor of the Education Program of the Migration
   Division of the Commonwealth of Puerto Rico) before the
   Board of Education of New York City, March 11, 1966.
   See also, F. Cordasco, 'Puerto Rican Pupils and American
   Education," School and Society, vol. 95 (February 18, 1967),
   pp. 116-119.

7. 'Ricardo Sanchez came from where the sugar cane is higher than
   a man to the plaza in old San Juan where the buses marked
   Aeropuerto stop. He came with his wife and two daughters
   and three suitcases and a paper bag and the promise from
   a brother in Harlem, New York, that there was work to be
   found in fabrica. The work in the sugar cane was over for
   the season and Ricardo had found nothing else. The government would pay him $7 every two weeks for thirteen weeks

before the season began again, and then with the season
he would get $3.60 a day for eight hours in the sun. He
had done it before, as his fathers had done it but this time
he told himself he wanted something more. 'It is,' he said,
'no good to be poor.'" Dan Wakefield, <u>Island in the City.</u>
<u>The World of Spanish Harlem</u> (New York: Houghton Mifflin,
1959), p. 23.

Joseph Bram, "The Lower Status Puerto Rican Family." Un-
    published paper, Graduate School of Arts and Sciences,
    New York University (March 1963).

(1) In discussing the Puerto Rican family, one must remember at all times that the society of this West Indian island is part
of a wider Spanish-speaking world, which in turn is part of our
Western civilization. Thus, in the final analysis, the family in
Puerto Rico should be expected to have a great deal in common
with the family in Spain, Ireland, Sweden, the United States, et al.
    Our interest in this disucssion, however, is focused on
Puerto Rico, and consequently we shall deal with specific local-
historical pecularities found in Puerto Rican society. In so doing
one should be careful not to overstate the significance of these
peculiarities, as over against the more widely shared characteristics of family life in the total European-American culture area.
    (2) In concentrating on one particular national society out
of several dozen constituting the European-American world one
runs into more differences of degree than those of structure. Thus
all societies of that area are monogamous. Some of them, however,
are more rigorous in opposing adultery, concubinage, divorce and
pre-marital experimentation than others. None of the Western
societies has placed the wife's and mother's authority legally or
socially above that of the father's and husband's. Yet it is known
that male authority is weaker in Denmark than, let us say, in
Greece.
    (3) It is also important to keep in mind that statements re-
garding national or class characteristics are at best probabilistic
in nature. When we say that the cult of gastronomy is typically
French, we actually mean that we are likely to find more individuals
valuing the refinements of cuisine among the French than, for instance, in England. Thus all statements about Puerto Rican modes
of behavior made in this essay must be understood as referring to
their relative frequencies.
    (4) The title of this article points out that our concern
here is with the lower status Puerto Rican family. One knows that
comparative social status can be defined in terms of numerous
criteria, such as income, housing, occupation, education, clothes,
manners, peculiarities of speech, racial origins, church membership, etc. In most cases the identification of social status must
be based on several such criteria, which occur in consistent and
meaningful clusters.
    (5) When dealing with the social status of an immigrant
group one must consider one at a time the standards of status
rating applied to it by the majority society (mainland Americans in
our case) and those of the immigrant group itself. To many

prejudiced mainland Americans all Puerto Ricans in the United
States are low status people with just a few individual exceptions.
A member of the Puerto Rican community, on the other hand, may
be keenly aware of a wide range of status differences among his
fellow islanders.

(6)   The status rating of individual immigrant families by
their own community is never identical with the one they enjoyed
on native grounds.   When moving from the island to New York
City many a Puerto Rican family undergoes a loss of "accumulated
social assets".   In its new position as occupant of a cold-water
flat on Tenth Avenue in Manhattan it finds itself down-graded, with
no neighbors aware of the good social standing it enjoyed in the
native environment.

(7)   The same process, however, may operate in reverse
and be described in terms of a loss of "accumulated social
blemishes."   Thus a family which at home had labored under an
established unfavorable reputation, may, under the protection of
metropolitan anonymity, be able to make a fresh start and move
upwards on the socio-economic ladder.

(8)   Of the many criteria of lower social status listed above,
poverty seems to us the most significant one.   If one excepts the
cases of recent and accidental reverses of fortune, poverty is most
meaningfully related to other such earmarks as housing, clothes,
manners, level of literacy, etc.

(9)   How much poverty is there on the island of Puerto
Rico today?   The economic advances made by the island society
since the establishment of the semi-autonomous Commonwealth of
Puerto Rico in 1952 have been quite spectacular.   At the same time,
the well-deserved publicity given them by the press has obscured
the picture of mass destitution which remains widespread.   Here
are some figures based on the population census of 1960:   (Based
on Boricua, La Revista de Puerto Rico.   Diciembre 1962, p. 31)

18. 2 per cent of the families have an
         annual income of more than $3,000

33. 8 per cent of the families have an
         annual income between $3,000-$1,000

16. 9 per cent of the families have an
         annual income between $1,000-$ 500

31   per cent of the families have an
         annual income of less than $500

The extreme forms of poverty are alleviated by various
Commonwealth programs: free school lunches, free shoes for
impecunious school children, free outpatient clinics, free hospitali-
zation, visiting nursing services, pension and relief plans, low
income housing and the distribution of surplus food made available by
the Federal Government.

Well-planned and generous as these policies have been they
have not done away with mass poverty and all its usual concomitants.

(10)   It is sometimes assumed that the cost of living in

Puerto Rico must be much lower than in the continental United
States. This is only partially true. The climate of the island,
of course, makes it unnecessary to own warm clothes or to
spend money on heating the homes. The alimentary needs of the
body are also somewhat lower in the sub-tropical Caribbean area.
On the other hand, Puerto Rico is dependent on imported foods
including such national staples as rice, beans, wheat flour and
dried codfish (bacalao). The cost of freight is added to the
prices of these staples. Clothes, domestic appliances and cars
also cost more on the island than in the United States.

(11) One could claim, nevertheless, that extreme poverty is
a bit more bearable in a place where temperature is never below
68°. Children have no lack of natural playgrounds; the aged
lounge on benches around the plaza of their community, neighbors
spend long hours socializing outside their small and inadequate
dwellings, and many a homeless man may find a shed or a driveway
where no one would disturb his sleep. Streams and water-holes in
the mountain areas and the beaches along the coast provide accessible facilities for bathing and swimming. Cooking can be done on
open-air improvised stoves (fogon). Furthermore starchy fruits
such as panapen (breadfruit) are plentiful and inexpensive as emer-
gency resources. There is no intent in these remarks to play
down the drama of poverty, disease and loneliness to which many
human beings fall prey in Puerto Rico. Yet for purely comparative purposes attention is being called to the relatively less tragic
fate of the poor in the less inclement climate of the Caribbean area.

(12) The poor of Puerto Rico are of two basic types--urban
and rural. Rural folk are in turn divided into those of the low-
lands of the coast, and the dwellers of the highlands. The urban
poor may be either of recent rural origin or with an older urban
background.

Town people tend to call all rural folk jíbaros. Coastal
rural groups feel insulted by this term and apply it to the farmers
of the mountainous interior. But even these farmers would sometimes use the term in referring to another hamlet or community
while excluding themselves from this category. Thus not many
people openly identify themselves as jíbaros while the term is used
loosely with regard to a wide range of socio-economic types.

(13) The reluctance to regard oneself as a jíbaro conflicts
with the idealization of this type by the literati and intellectuals of
the island. The jíbaro has been portrayed by them as the true
carrier of the Puerto Rican folk tradition. He was the authentic
native "son of the earth" marked off by his own inimitable sense
of humor, practical wisdom, shrewdness in his dealings with city
people, and a strong spirit of independence. All jíbaro proverbs,
sayings, songs, games, superstitions, tales of supernaturalism and
works of craftsmanship (e.g. home-made string instruments,
figures of saints, i.e. santos, carved out of wood, et al) have been
reverentially collected and enshrined in the public mind or in public
collections.

(14) What sober statements can one make about this sizeable
and yet elusive element in the population of Puerto Rico? "True"
jíbaros appear to be descended from the predominantly white early

settlers of the interior of the island.   Geographical isolation
combined with poverty has made them the least literate element in
the insular society, and the least familiar with the urban way of
life.   Not many true jíbaros have had the daring, for instance, to
migrate to New York City.   Those who did had spent first a few
years in one of the coastal shanty-towns or slum suburbs in Puerto
Rico, where they underwent a bit of acculturation to city ways.
      The well-known drama La Carreta (1952) by René Marqués
portrays the social fate of such a family.   In the first act they
are shown leaving their home in the mountains under the pressure
of economic circumstances.   In the second act we witness their
trials and tribulations in the coastal slums of Puerto Rico.   The
third and last act of the play portrays them as "adjusted" to the
urban ways of The Bronx as well as victims of unscrupulous individuals
and of industrial accidents.
      (15)   Many jíbaros are landless and propertyless agricultural
workers who meet their subsistence needs by selling their labor
power.   Some of them own their homes but do not always own the
lot on which the dwelling is located.   Others live rent-free in the
home provided by their employer.   Occupying a house erected on
lands belonging to another person qualifies them as "squatters"
(agregados) and implies various customary obligations with regard
to the owner of the holding.
      Those jíbaros who are agricultural wage-earners without
property or any outside income are often forced to play a subser-
vient role with regard to their potential or virtual employers,
the store-keeper from whom they buy their groceries on credit
between the harvest seasons (zafras), the wealthier neighbors who
may give a temporary job to their wife or son, and to many
others.   They teach their children to behave with proper humility
and to render services to their more powerful neighbors and even
playmates.
      (16) In a somewhat different category are those jíbaros who
own enough land to depend for survival on subsistence farming.
They raise marketable crops of fluctuating value (such as tobacco
or coffee) and supplement cash income with some vegetables, fruit,
chickens and pigs grown and raised by their own efforts.   In
jíbaro families of this type the father finds himself in the role of
task-master and foreman, whose job is to extract as much work as
he can from his small family group.   At the same time, he also
controls the family expenditures and is thus cast in the role of an
occasional "kill-joy."   The same function, however, gives him a
chance to make a show of generosity and affection by buying things
for the home or clothes for his wife and children.
      (17)   Halfway between the wage-earner and the small land
holder is the share-cropper.   In the tobacco growing area he splits
with the owner of the land the costs of production and shares in
the half of the proceeds.   Traditionally share-croppers press the
members of their family into work in the fields or into services to
the landlord and thus again they are found in the role of task-
masters and disciplinarians.
      (18)   As elsewhere in the Spanish-speaking world, the Puerto
Rican jíbaro family is also giverned by male authority.   The jíbaro

man who has limited claims to social and economic prestige is
strongly dependent on his wife's and children's deferential attitudes
(particularly in the presence of outside observers) for his ego-
gratification. Many a jibaro's wife does not begrudge her husband
this privilege since indirectly it enhances her own social standing
as well. She feels that there is no honor attached to being married
to a weak and unmanly husband. In fact, she may even tend to
exaggerate his dictatorial masculinity and portray herself as a
masochistic victim in the hands of a strong virile tyrant.

(19) Where male authoritarianism appears to be a socially
recognized norm, women quite commonly evolve indirect methods
of defense and compensation. The ailing wife and mother (without
being an outright malingerer) often uses her afflictions to secure
sympathy and a more lenient treatment. Threats of suicide and
frequent unsuccessful attempts at suicide (suicides manqués) by
Puerto Rican women have been diagnosed by careful observers as
attention-getting devices. Quite often, however, suicide in Puerto
Rico is committed in an irretrievable manner. The Anglo-American
imagination is particularly struck by those cases where the victim
soaks her clothes in gasoline and sets herself on fire. Several
such cases occur every year along with more numerous but less
spectacular forms of self-destruction.

(20) The jíbaro mother makes up for her inferior social
position by gaining her children's (her sons' in particular) affection and attachment. She may do that by protecting the guilty boy
from his father's anger, by passing small amounts of spending
money to him and in many other ways. The image of his
"suffering mother" has been found deeply embedded in the mind of
many a Puerto Rican adolescent boy or grown man. Most Puerto
Rican men regard themselves as natural protectors of their
mothers when they are victims of desertion, widowhood, poverty or
social abuse.

(21) The jíbaros are known to be proud of their numerous
progeny, which symbolizes the father's procreative vigor and also
represents the poor man's only "wealth." It is indeed a proud day
in an individual jíbaro's life when he walks to a fiesta in the nearest
center surrounded by his small flock of four or five children.

(22) The rural folk of the coastal plains are not drastically
different from the jíbaros of the highlands. Nevertheless, several
points of distinction should be brought out. To begin with, most of
them are employed by either government operated or privately
owned sugar cane plantations. They thus are landless laborers
entirely dependent on their wages for a living. They more than
often live in primitive barracks where each family occupies a one
or two-room dwelling (without indoor cooking or toilet facilities) or
a section in a similarly inadequate multiple dwelling. They are
surrounded on all sides by temporary tenants like themselves and
have no illusions of independence that go along with the ownership
(by a jíbaro) of a small home in the relatively inaccessible mountain
fastness. The comparative crowding which characterizes their life
deprives them of all privacy and affects their sense of dignity.

(23) The family of a sugar cane worker is more a unit of
consumption than of production. The head of the family does not

have to act as a task-master since he rarely has access to any
gardening or poultry raising facilities where members of his family
might be engaged in productive work.   As soon as his sons or
daughters reach the age of marriage or become employable they
tend to strike out for themselves and drift away to wherever work
can be secured.

   (24) Workers in the cane and their families are also in a
much less personal relationship with their employers (private
owners, corporation representatives, supervisers, foremen, et al)
than the rural folk of the highlands.   For practical and traditional
reasons the jíbaros of the interior have to live up to the standards
of conduct acceptable to wealthier neighbors on whose goodwill they
often depend, i. e. the store-keepers who sell to them on credit,
landowners on whose land they build their homes, local politicians
and other power-wielders.   This may account for a somewhat
higher rate of the more respectable church weddings and for more
regular attendance at church services in the mountain area, also
for a somewhat stronger resistance to the inroads of Protestantism.

   Correspondingly, the sugar-cane workers of the coast have
a much higher incidence of the less respectable consensual or
common-law unions and have proven more receptive to the appeals
of Protestant proselytizers.

   (25) The urban poor of the island are much more open to
observation on the part of the middle class and upper class people
of the cities than are the jíbaros. The slums and shanty-towns of
Puerto Rico are adjacent to the more respectable neighborhoods
and no one can escape the sight of human misery which they harbor.
The city poor more often come to the attention of medical men,
hospital personnel, social workers, police authorities, school
teachers, members of the clergy and other professional people.
This being the case it is rather surprising to discover that
sociologists and other researchers in Puerto Rico have given them
less attention than to rural populations.

   (26) This element in the population of the island is of
course much more diversified than anything one would observe in
the countryside. We find among them widows with or without
dependent children, abandoned wives, jilted girls, orphans, invalids subsisting on small pensions, uprooted jíbaros, unemployed
and unemployable individuals of every possible origin, mentally
inadequate persons, women of easy virtue, and many aged people
(single or in couples), et al.   They survive by engaging in a wide
variety of small and often temporary occupations as pedlars,
delivery men, unskilled repairmen, gardeners, part-time domestics,
lottery ticket salesmen, newsboys, etc.   Some of their activities
conflict with municipal regulations, police rules and law in general.
This would be true of illegal number games (bolita), the sale of
privately manufactured rum (canita), prostitution, etc.   Centuries of
existence under indifferent and inefficient administrations combined
with widespread poverty have resulted in much more lenient attitudes toward these "marginal" and outlawed occupations than a
moralist conditioned by life in prosperous democratic communities
would expect.   Here is an area where one has to approach human
behavior with a bit of historical perspective and the faculty of

empathy.

(27) Government relief, municipal aid, private charity and sporadic contributions by relatives keep many of these city poor not only alive but less unhappy than one might imagine them to be. In part this is due, as pointed out earlier, to the climate of the island, but also to the gift of sociability with which the people of Puerto Rico are so richly endowed.

(28) One of its expressions is their extreme fondness for children. In giving their care and affection to children, the Puerto Ricans are less proprietary than other Europeans and Americans. They easily make room in their poor and crowded homes for children of divorced parents, illegitimate offspring, orphans, abandoned children and foster children (hijos de crianza) in general. Many people enter marriage while having children by previous common law or legalized marriages. It is not unusual to have a family with three or four children none of whom are the offspring of the married couple. As a rule such adopted children or children by previous marriages are treated as well as their adoptive parents' joint progeny.

(29) A special type of relationship known as godparenthood (compadrazgo) can also be considered as a partial corrective to poverty and loneliness among lower status Puerto Ricans. A person sponsoring a child at baptism and christening becomes his life-long godfather (padrino) or godmother (madrina). Where two godparents (compadres) preside over the same ritual this co-participation establishes a special social tie between them. Similarly all godparents are bound in a special way to the biological parents of their godchild. Thus most Puerto Ricans have ritually sanctioned friends, allies, protectors and confidants. The practical value of such a relationship may vary from case to case. Nevertheless, the institution of godparenthood obviously extends the individual's trust and reliance beyond the immediate family, and in some cases provides a person with a substitute for a defaulting family group.

(30) The love of children so common in Puerto Rico appears in a somewhat less idyllic light if viewed against the background of demographic statistics. In 1940 the population of the island was 1,869,255. In 1950 it had reached the figure of 2,210,703 and in 1960 it was 2,349,544. The total land area of the island being 3,421 square miles, the population density of Puerto Rico is nearing the ratio of 700 per square mile, one of the highest in the world. Considering the slender natural resources of the island, the situation is rapidly reaching the point of critical intensity.

(31) There are three basic ways of relieving this growing population pressure: birth control through contraception, emigration and industrialization. All three have been encouraged by the government of the Commonwealth, unfortunately with inconclusive results. Contraception has met with strong opposition on the part of the Roman Catholic Church, which has, however, failed to reverse its growing popularity. Industrialization, combined with tourism, has created numerous jobs and indirect sources of income for the island treasury with its heavy programs of social welfare. And, finally, emigration has relieved some of the immediate pres-

sure on the island economy by reducing the number of unemployed and encouraging the flow of subsidies by emigrants to their needy kin.

(32) The advocacy of contraception has also run into non-religious opposition. Some Puerto Rican men have been reported as feeling that the use of contraceptives was humiliating to their wives or to their own male dignity (or both). Other observers have claimed that shyness and awkwardness in communication between married people made the use of contraception difficult. The provisional figures of birth rate for 1961 give 23.4 (per 1,000 population) for the United States, 31.0 for Puerto Rico. Neverthe-less there has been a steady decline in the successive birth rate figures over ten years. The much sharper rate of decline in the rates of mortality, however, has neutralized the limited gains made by the application of birth control.

(33) We have mentioned earlier the frequency of common law (consensual) marriages among lower status Puerto Ricans. Dr. Sidney Mintz in focusing on one specific rural area (which he calls Barrio Jauca) has established the fact that out of 183 marital unions 134 were of the consensual variety. (1) For the island at large the ratio of such common law marriages has been variously estimated between 25 per cent and 35 per cent of the total. The historical roots of this practice go too far to be examined here. The pehnomenon is not restricted to Puerto Rico but has been ob-served throughout the Caribbean area and in parts of South America.

(34) Dr. Mintz shows very clearly that such marriages are as a rule initiated by means of a socially standardized procedure (a "ritualized elopement") which is viewed by the community as equivalent to more traditional legal and religious observances. (2)

(35) Children born to such unions suffer only minor social disadvantages in their home areas, but run into inconveniences and embarrassments when they migrate to the cities or to the main-land of the United States. This is due to the growing importance of pension plans, social security benefits, veteran pensions and insurance policies, all of which have to rely on properly legalized relationships between spouses and between parents and children.

(36) In the meantime people say that "vale mas un buen amancebado que un matrimonio mal llevado" (a good consensual union is worth more than a bad marriage). The prohibition of divorce by the Roman Catholic Church has also been used to justify consensual unions where the two parties are not tied to each other for life. The growth of Protestant congregations in Puerto Rico may be in part due to the toleration of divorces by most of them, even though their strong emphasis on personal morals obviously checks the trend toward easy divorces.

(37) From the Anglo-American point of view one of the striking features of Puerto Rican marriage relationship is the prevalence of jealousy. As could be expected, male infidelities are somewhat more frequent and less rigorously condemned by the community. When the woman's husband shows a decline of personal interest in his wife she is likely to seek "professional" advice from a spiritualist medium or a practitioner of folk-medicine (or folk-magic).

When a man suspects his wife of growing indifference he looks around for a possible rival and is very likely to challenge and even assault the presumed seducer.   Painful and dramatic as they are these tensions and actions are indicative of somewhat higher romantic and erotic expectations on the part of married lower status Puerto Ricans than what we observe in our more placid and sedate society.

(38)   The Puerto Rican family as we find it in New York (or Philadelphia, Chicago, Boston, etc.) should not be expected to be a duplicate of its counterpart on the island.   To begin with, mainland Puerto Ricans are keenly aware of the social prejudice they encounter on the mainland.   Two conflicting reactions to social hostility may take place.   The members of a family group may, so to say, "close their ranks," i.e. experience an intensified sense of solidarity and view their home as a haven of refuge.   The other possible reaction is that of resentment against the group to which they belong, whose characteristics are the alleged cause of its rejection by the outside world.

(39)   Where local prejudice against Puerto Ricans assumes racialist undertones (which seems to be always the case), it may have a divisive effect on family unity and solidarity.   Puerto Rico is a land of racially mixed marriages (particularly in the lower social strata), and children in many homes run the whole gamut of pigmentation from the very dark to the Mediterranean light.   In the North American social environment lighter-complexioned young-sters have a better chance of social and occupational acceptance than their darker siblings.   Brothers and sisters are thus separated by differential opportunities, and envy and resentment enter their life.

The same factors may invade the relationship between two differently colored spouses or in-laws, or grandparents and grand-children.   The dark grandmother who hides in the kitchen while her lighter granddaughter, a high school girl, entertains her class-mate in the living room, could serve as a symbol of the impact of race prejudice on the Puerto Rican family in New York.

(40)   Another source of anxieties among mainland Puerto Ricans is constituted by their gradual loss of influence over their children.   In the natural course of events, Puerto Rican children learn English better and faster than their parents.   With the lan-guage they acquire a whole world of values, attitudes and rules of adolescent etiquette which remain incomprehensible to their elders. Before long, the English-speaking child may serve as an interpreter in his mother's or father's dealings with the outside world and may come to feel that his parents are unsuited to the American way of life, or even "inferior."

(41)   Quite often Puerto Rican women have an easier chance of finding employment than their husbands in our city economy, and thus become principal family providers.   With this economic change goes a re-definition of male authority, and many a family head feels that something has gone wrong in his domestic life. Some accept their new dependence on their more successful wives and turn to a half-way justifiable idleness.   In the meantime, the unemployed man's children lose their traditional respect for him,

and refuse to accept his attempts at reasserting his authority.

(42)   Many other changes take place in Puerto Rican family
life in the new social environment.   At home they lived under what
sociologists call "primary social controls," i. e. in small close-
knit communities, where neighbors, relatives, storekeepers, school
teachers and all others exercised a restraining influence on individual behavior.   The anonymity of New York life makes them feel
uncomfortably free, "on their own," and also fearful of how this
might affect those loved ones (wife, daughters, sons, etc.) whose
behavior they would like to supervise.

(43)   The easy and casual sociability of the island has also
been affected by the new urban world.   The climate of the mainland and big city traffic have made street life of the Caribbean
type next to impossible.   Instead of occupying small family homes
with doors and windows open on the outside world, New York
Puerto Ricans find themselves living in isolated apartments behind
closed doors.

(44)   Numerous other material details undergo far-reaching
changes, e. g. methods of laundering, patterns of cooking, sleeping
arrangements, shopping practices, etc. ad infinitum.   None of these
taken by itself may be viewed as profoundly significant; in combination they change the whole style of living.   Eventually the values
of the island give way to something new and different.

(45)   When an entire ethnic group is undergoing such a
change, it should not be assumed that its individual members will
move along at the same pace or will react to the challenges of
transformation in the same manner.   Family circles may thus be
expected to be torn between nostalgic homesick old-timers, ambitious and pushing opportunists and the more rational synthesizers
between the old and the new.   The island home which was left
behind becomes idealized and/or vilified quite realistically, just as
the urban world of mainland America is extolled or run down in
accordance with the fluctuating circumstances and changing moods.
The influx of new migrants from the island keeps alive the overall
ambivalent attitudes of the Puerto Rican community.   Numerous individuals get tempted by the short distance and the low airplane
fares and go home, only to turn around and come back to New York.

(46)   Trying to describe and understand the lower status
Puerto Rican family of our day is on the whole not easy.   The
island society is undergoing numerous changes, briefly identifiable by
such terms as urbanization, industrialization, secularization, welfare economy, diffusion of literacy, growing life span, increasing
population, etc.   When individual Puerto Rican families fly over
to the mainland and attempt an adjustment to the new socio-economic
world of the United States, they find themselves subjected to
numerous additional pressures.   Neither back home nor here in the
States can their existence be described as stable and secure.   Thus
in order to understand any specific Puerto Rican family group one
has to "locate" it on the total map of social change which this
national society is undergoing at this time.

Selected Bibliography

Bram, Joseph   Spirits, Mediums and Believers in Contempo-
                        rary Puerto Rico, Transactions of the New
                        York Academy of Sciences, Ser. II, Vol. 20,
                        No. 4, pp. 340-347, February 1958
Hansen, E.   Transformation: The Story of Puerto Rico,
                        1955
Hatt, R. K.   Backgrounds of Human Fertility in Puerto
                        Rico, 1952
Landy, David   Tropical Childhood, Cultural Transmission and
                        Learning in a Rural Puerto Rican Village, 1959
Mills, C. W., C. Senior and R. Goldsen.
                        The Puerto Rican Journey, 1950
Mintz, Sidney W.   Worker in the Cane. A Puerto Rican Life
                        Story, 1960
Roberts, L. J. and R. L. Stefani
                        Patterns of Living in Puerto Rican Families,
                        1949
Rogler, Charles   Comerio. A Study of a Puerto Rican Town,
                        1940
Sereno, R.   Cryptomelanism: A Study of Color Relations
                        and Personal Insecurity in Puerto Rico.
                        Psychiatry 10: 261-269, 1947
Steward, J. H. et al   The People of Puerto Rico, 1956
Stycos, J. M.   Family and Fertility in Puerto Rico, 1955
Tugwell, R. G.   The Stricken Land, 1947
Wolf, K. L.   Growing Up and Its Price in Three Puerto
                        Rican Subcultures. Psychiatry 15:401-433,
                        1952

Notes

1. Sidney W. Mintz, - Worker in the Cane. A Puerto Rican
     Life Story. Yale University Press. 1960. pp. 89-92.
2. Ibid.

Part III

The Puerto Rican Experience on the Mainland:
Conflict and Acculturation

One in five New Yorkers lives in poverty. Estimates based
on the 1960 United States Census, taking into account budget requirements and family size, show that 875,000 whites, 490,000 nonwhites, and 315,000 Puerto Ricans are below the poverty line--a
total of 1,680,000 persons. (Table 1.)

Deprivation is emphasized among Puerto Ricans and nonwhites
relative to other whites (that is, whites other than Puerto Ricans).
One of every two Puerto Ricans and two of every five nonwhites live
in poverty. In comparison, one of every 7.5 other whites lives in
poverty. (Table 2.)

Furthermore, Puerto Rican and nonwhite poverty are concentrated in large families. Of the Puerto Ricans living in impoverished circumstances, 61.9 per cent were in family constellations of
five or more members. Of poor nonwhites 46.0 per cent were in
similarly large families. But only 17.7 per cent of the poor other
whites were in family groups of five or more. Among the other
whites, 57.2 per cent of the deprived lived alone or with just one
other related person. Only 25.4 per cent of the impoverished nonwhites and only 7.9 per cent of the Puerto Ricans were alone or in
such small families. (Table 1.)

The statistics show that poverty among the other whites is
primarily, but not exclusively, a problem of the aged.

For nonwhites, and even more for Puerto Ricans, poverty is a
characteristic of family life--large families including children. It
casts a shadow over the future of a generation of youth...

Newcomers to a complex urban society can accommodate to
it most successfully if they arrive with or quickly achieve the cultural equipment that enables upward mobility in the new society.
Certainly in the United States educational attainment is a vital part
of that equipment, for it is usually educational preparation that enables occupational achievement in an industrial society. And because occupations normally are the chief source of income for urban individuals and families, the link between education, occupation,

127

and income constitutes a cycle of individual development of critical importance.

The cycle is significant between generations also. While family income and father's occupation are by no means perfect predictors of the educational and occupational future of children, they are significant predictors. That is, low occupational status and inadequate family income can constitute powerful deterrents to the

* * * * * * * *

Table 1
Persons Living in Poverty, New York City,
By Size of Family and Ethnic Group
(Thousands)

Persons in Poverty

Ethnic Group	Persons in Families	Ethnic Distribution	One Person	Two Persons	Three and Four	Five	Six and Over
Total	1,680	100.0	320	330	455	195	380
Puerto Rican	315	18.7	5	20	95	60	135
Nonwhite	490	29.2	65	60	140	65	160
Other White	875	52.1	250	250	220	70	85

Persons in Poverty
Percentage Distribution by Family Size

Total			100.0	100.0	100.0	100.0	100.0
Puerto Rican			1.6	6.0	20.8	30.8	35.5
Nonwhite			20.3	18.2	30.9	33.3	42.1
Other White			78.1	75.8	48.4	35.9	22.4

Persons in Poverty
Percentage Distribution by Ethnic Group

Total		100.0	19.1	19.6	27.1	11.6	22.6
Puerto Rican		100.0	1.6	6.3	30.2	19.0	42.9
Nonwhite		100.0	13.2	12.2	28.6	13.3	32.7
Other White		100.0	28.6	28.6	25.1	8.0	9.7

Source: Based on United States Census and budget estimates derived from New York City Welfare Department, United States Bureau of Labor Statistics, and Community Council of Greater New York.

Table 2
Total Population and Persons Living in Poverty[a]
(Thousands)

Ethnic Group	Total Population		Population Living in Poverty	
	Number	Percentage	Number	Percentage
Total	7,780	100.0	1,680	21.6
Puerto Rican	613	7.9	315	51.4
Nonwhite	1,140	14.7	490	42.9
Other White	6,640	85.3	875	13.2

[a]Source: Based on United States Census, and budget estimates
derived from New York City Welfare Department, United States
Bureau of Labor Statistics, and Community Council of Greater New
York.
* * * * * * * *

subsequent achievements of children growing up in deprived circumstances.   The adverse consequences for children and youth, moreover, are augmented when poverty and its associated conditions, such as poor health, housing, and delinquency, are rigidly concentrated in urban ghettos.   For then they grow up in the shadows of failure and despair, isolated from the expectation of success generally characteristic of other parts of the American society.

It is appropriate that we look at the history of Puerto Ricans in the United States from the specific perspective of the education-occupation-income cycle.   We will see if there is evidence of the structural mobility prerequisite to integration or acculturation, and examine indications of obstacles to full and productive contributions by Puerto Ricans to their fellow citizens in New York.

The Migration
In 1960, nearly 900,000 Puerto Ricans--born on the island or in the states to Puerto Rican parents--lived in the United States. Persons born in Puerto Rico were first recorded as residents of the states by the United States Census of 1910, when 1,500 were enumerated.   Their numbers increased so that by 1940 almost 70,000 lived in the 48 states.   However, the great migration began after 1940, with two subsequent censuses showing a very large increase in numbers.   By 1950 Puerto Rican born persons numbered 226,000, and over the decade to 1960 the net gain due to migration from the island amounted to nearly 390,000.   (Table 3.)

The census of 1950 recorded the beginning of the second generation of Puerto Ricans in the United States--those born on the continent to parents who came from the island.   They numbered 75,000 in 1950 and 272,000 ten years later.   By 1960, three of every ten Puerto Rican stateside residents were born on the continent.   (Table 3.)

With the great migration began a reversal of the historic trend of Puerto Ricans living in New York City.   In 1910 only a little more than a third of them in the states lived in New York

City, but by 1940, 88 per cent made New York their home.   Since
then a dispersal to other areas has occurred.   The percentage in
New York City for those born in Puerto Rico dropped to 83 in 1950
and 70 in 1960.   The dispersal probably is continuing, but at this
time Puerto Ricans in the United States still are overwhelmingly
New Yorkers.   More than two-thirds of the migrants and their children live in New York.
* * * * * * * *

Table 3
Persons of Puerto Rican Origin,
Coterminous United States and New York City,
1910 to 1960

| | United States | | New York City | |
Nativity and Year	Number	% Increase	Number	% of total
Puerto Rican birth:				
1960	615,384	172.2	429,710	69.8
1950	226,110	223.2	187,420	82.9
1940	69,967	32.6	61,463	87.8
1930	52,774	346.8	a	-
1920	11,811	680.6	7,364	62.3
1910	1,513	-	554	36.6
Puerto Rican parentage:b				
1960	272,278	261.8	182,864	67.2
1950	75,265	-	58,460	77.7

a. Not available.

b. Born in the United States.

Source: U.S. Bureau of the Census-U.S. Census of Population:
1960.   Subject Reports.   Puerto Ricans in United States.   Final
Report.   PC(2)-1D.   U.S. Government Printing Office, Washington,
D.C., 1963.   Table A, p. viii.
* * * * * * * *
It is with this population in excess of 600,000 Puerto Ricans that
we are specifically concerned.

Age Groups
        The Puerto Ricans are the newest, and the youngest, of New
York City's populations.   More than 47 per cent of the males and
45 per cent of the females were under 20 years of age in 1960.
In contrast, only 38.8 per cent of the male and 34.9 per cent of the
female nonwhites were in the same age category.   The proportions of youth among the non-Puerto Rican whites were even smaller, being 28.6 per cent of the males and 26.0 per cent of the females.
        The aged are few in the Puerto Rican community.   Just 1.5
per cent of the men and 2.5 per cent of the women were 65 or
over in 1960, while among nonwhites 4.5 per cent of the males
and 4.9 per cent of the females were 65 years or older.   New

York's other whites are much older; 11.6 per cent of these men
and 13.1 per cent of the women were 65 years of age and older in
1960.
    As a result of the number of children among them, a rela-
tively small part of the Puerto Ricans are at their best working
ages. Only 51.1 per cent of the men and 52.4 per cent of the
women were aged 20 through 64 in 1960. The nonwhites and other
whites, in contrast, had higher proportions in the 20-64 age group.
For the nonwhite men and women the comparable percentages were
56.7 and 60.2. About 60 per cent of both male and female other
whites were 20-64 years of age. (Table 4.)
    Only 7.9 per cent of New York City's population in 1960 was
Puerto Rican. However, the Puerto Rican proportion among the
younger population is more significant. In 1960, Puerto Ricans
were 11 per cent of all youth aged 15 through 19, 11 per cent of
the boys and girls 10-14 years old, 12 per cent of those 5-9, and
14 per cent of all children under 5. (Table 5.)

Table 4
Ethnic Groups, by Sex and Age,
New York City, 1960[a]

Age	Puerto Rican		Nonwhite		Other White	
	Male	Female	Male	Female	Male	Female
Total:						
Number	296,701	315,873	530,028	611,294	2,892,528	3,135,560
%	100.0	100.0	100.0	100.0	100.0	100.0
0-4 yrs	15.8	14.6	13.2	11.5	8.0	7.1
5-9 "	12.6	11.5	11.0	9.6	7.1	6.4
10-14 "	10.4	9.9	8.6	7.7	7.4	6.6
15-19 "	8.6	9.1	6.0	6.1	6.1	5.9
20-24 "	9.7	10.2	6.5	7.7	5.5	5.8
25-29 "	10.1	10.4	7.5	8.2	6.2	5.7
30-34 "	8.8	8.9	8.3	9.1	6.7	6.3
35-39 "	7.2	6.9	8.5	8.9	6.6	6.8
40-44 "	4.9	5.-	7.1	7.5	6.5	7.1
45-49 "	4.1	4.2	6.1	6.4	7.2	7.8
50-54 "	2.8	2.8	5.1	5.1	7.5	7.7
55-59 "	2.1	2.3	4.4	4.3	7.3	7.2
60-64 "	1.4	1.6	3.1	2.9	6.3	6.5
65 & older	1.5	2.5	4.5	4.9	11.6	13.1

[a.] According to the 1960 census, 24,871 Puerto Ricans--4 per cent
of the total--reported their color as nonwhite. Characteristics of
nonwhite and white Puerto Ricans were not tabulated separately for
New York City in 1960. To estimate the characteristics of whites
other than Puerto Ricans in this table and others which follow, all
the Puerto Ricans, including those who were nonwhite, were sub-
tracted from total whites. The nonwhite Puerto Ricans were not
eliminated from the total nonwhites. This introduced an error

of 2 percent for nonwhites and less than a half of one per cent for
whites other than Puerto Ricans.

Source: U.S. Bureau of Census. U.S. Censuses of Population and
Housing: 1960. Census tracts. Final Report PHC(1)-104. Part
1. U.S. Government Printing Office, Washington, D.C. , 1963.
Tables P-2 and P-5.

                    * * * * * * * *

        In other words, Puerto Ricans are an increasingly larger
part of the upcoming age groups in our youth population. Moreover, large numbers of Puerto Ricans will be among the city's
youth for the near future, unless a radically different migration
flow occurs. The migration has selected young adults, and in 1960,
75 per cent of adult (20 years of age and older) female Puerto Rican residents were in the child-bearing age group of 20-44. There
is a reasonable expectation that this proportion will increase.
(Table 4.)

Educational Attainment
        Puerto Rican adults have the lowest level of formal educa-
tion of any identifiable ethnic or color group in New York City.
Only 13 per cent of the Puerto Rican men and women 25 years of
age and older in 1960 had completed either high school or more advanced education.[1] In other words, 87 per cent of them had
dropped out without graduating from high school. Among New York's
nonwhite (predominately Negro) population, on the other hand, nearly a third had at least completed high school; 68.8 per cent had
left school prior to high school graduation. The other white population (not including Puerto Ricans) was in an even better position.
Slightly more than 40 per cent had at least completed high school.
(Table 6.)
        The deficiency in the educational preparation of the Puerto
Rican population is perhaps more dramatically revealed by the numbers who had not even completed a grade-school education in
1960.[2] More than half--52.9 per cent--of Puerto Ricans in New
York City 25 years of age and older had less than an eighth grade
education. In contrast, 29.5 per cent of the nonwhite population
had not finished the eighth year, and only 19.3 per cent of the other whites had so low an academic preparation. (Table 6.)
        The lag in educational attainment of the Puerto Rican popula-
tion is not entirely a commentary on New York City's educational
establishment. The Puerto Rican population is heavily weighted
with persons born on the island, many of whom undoubtedly ended
school careers before coming to the states. The educational levels
of Puerto Ricans born in the United States differ markedly from
those of Puerto Ricans born in the Commonwealth.
        Table 7 shows for 1960 the percentages of high-school drop-
outs among Puerto Ricans, 20 years and older, born in Puerto Rico
and in the United States, further classified by age and sex. The
males and females born in Puerto Rico at every age level exhibit
very high percentages of school leavers. These range from 84 to
97 per cent. Those born in the United States, however, have considerably lower proportions of school leavers. In the youngest age

Table 5
Age Groups, by Ethnic Background,
New York City, 1960

| | | Percentages for Males + Females | | | |
| | | | Puerto | | Other |
Age	Number	Total	Rican	Nonwhite	White
Totals	7,781,984	100.0	7.9	14.7	77.4
0-4 years	686,717	100.0	13.6	20.4	66.0
5-9 "	505,847	100.0	12.3	19.6	68.1
10-14 "	575,321	100.0	10.8	16.2	73.0
15-19 "	486,851	100.0	11.2	14.2	74.6
20-24 "	482,522	100.0	12.6	16.9	70.5
25-29 "	513,629	100.0	12.3	17.6	70.2
30-34 "	542,769	100.0	10.0	18.3	71.7
35-39 "	546,966	100.0	7.9	18.2	73.9
40-44 "	524,381	100.0	5.8	15.9	78.3
45-49 "	550,310	100.0	4.6	13.0	82.4
50-54 "	534,526	100.0	3.2	10.8	86.0
55-59 "	499,493	100.0	2.7	10.0	87.3
60-64 "	428,825	100.0	2.2	8.0	89.8
65 and older	813,827	100.0	1.6	6.7	91.7

Source: U.S. Bureau of Census. U.S. Censuses of Population and
Housing: 1960. Census tracts. Final Report PHC(1)-104. Part 1.
U.S. Government Printing Office, Washington, D.C., 1963. Tables
P-2 and P-5.

Table 6
Years of School Completed,
Persons 25 Years of Age and Over,
by Ethnic Background,
New York City, 1960[a]

Years of School Completed	Puerto Rican	Nonwhite	Other White
Total: Number	268,524	639,624	4,046,933
Percent	100.0	100.0	100.0
No School Years Completed	8.2	3.2	5.2
Elementary: 1-4 yrs	20.9	8.2	3.9
5-7 "	23.8	18.1	10.2
8 "	17.2	16.3	21.0
High School: 1-3 "	16.9	23.0	19.6
4 "	9.9	21.4	23.0
College 1-3 "	2.2	5.7	7.7
4 " or more	0.9	4.1	9.4

[a.] Includes persons in school at time of enumeration.

Table 6 (cont.)
Source: U.S. Bureau of the Census. U.S. Censuses of Population and Housing: 1960. Census tracts. Final Report PHC(1) 104. Part 1. U.S. Government Printing Office, Washington, D.C., 1962. Tables P-1 P-4, P-5.

* * * * * * * *

group--25 through 34--the differential between the two generations is largest, amounting to 34 percentage points for females and 25 for males. Among this relatively mobile population, birth and present residence in the United States do not necessarily mean that all education was acquired in stateside schools. Moreover, an unknown number of Puerto Ricans educated in New York have returned to the Commonwealth. So differences in educational attainment by place of birth is probably not a satisfactory indicator estimate of the impact of New York's educational system.[3]

If the educational attainment of Puerto Ricans born in the United States is strikingly better than that of those born in the Commonwealth, it so far has small weight in the statistics for the total adult Puerto Rican community in New York City. The numbers in the second generation who have reached adult years is still small, only 6.4 per cent of persons 20 years of age and older in 1960.

* * * * * * * *

Table 7

Percentages of Puerto Ricans 25 Years of Age
and Older Who Had Not Completed High School,
by Age, Sex, and Place of Birth,
New York Standard Metropolitan Statistical Area, 1960[a]

	Place of Birth			
Age	Puerto Rico		United States	
	Male	Female	Male	Female
25-34 years	84.5%	84.0%	59.4%	50.0%
35-44 "	87.1	90.8	67.8	60.3
45-64 "	91.1	93.3	81.5	78.2
65 and over	94.5	96.8	90.2	84.5

a. Includes persons in school at time of enumeration.

Source: U.S. Bureau of the Census. U.S. Census of Population: 1960. Subject Reports. Puerto Ricans in the United States. Final Report. PC(2)-1D. U.S. Government Printing Office, Washington, D.C., 1963. Table 11.

* * * * * * * *

There is evidence that Puerto Rican youth, more than any other group, is severely handicapped in achieving an education in the New York City public schools. A 1961 study of a Manhattan neighborhood showed that fewer than 10 per cent of Puerto Ricans in the third grade were reading at their grade level or above. In comparison, 19 per cent of the Negroes in the same schools and 55 per cent of the others (mostly whites) were reading at grade level. Moreover, the degree of retardation of Puerto Rican youth was extreme. Three in ten were retarded one and one-half years or more

and were, in the middle of their third school year, therefore reading at a level no better than appropriate for entry into the second
grade.   Only one-fifth of the nonwhite children and one in 14 of the
others were so disadvantaged.   (Table 8.)

By the eighth grade the degree of reading retardation was
even more severe.   While 13 per cent of the Puerto Rican youth
were reading at grade level or above, almost two-thirds were retarded more than three years.   In contrast, three in ten of the
Negro youth were at least at grade level, with one-third retarded
more than three years.   More than one-half the others were at
grade level, with only 13 per cent retarded more than three years.
(Table 8.)   City-wide studies are needed to measure reading ability
in other neighborhoods.

Puerto Rican graduates with academic diplomas from New
York City high schools still are rare in New York City.   Of the
nearly 21,000 academic diplomas granted in 1963, only 331 were to
Puerto Ricans and 762 to Negroes.   This is only 1.6 per cent and
3.7 per cent, respectively, of the total academic diplomas.   In contrast, Puerto Ricans received 7.4 per cent of the vocational school
diplomas, and Negroes, 15.2 per cent.   As a result, only 20 per
cent of the small number of Puerto Ricans completing high school
in 1963 were prepared to begin higher academic education.   Of the
Negroes, 22 per cent received academic diplomas, as did 50 per
cent of the other graduates.   (Table 9.)

One critical issue for the Puerto Rican community is, then,
the education of its children in the New York City public schools.
Large numbers of Puerto Ricans are of school age, and they are an
increasing proportion of the public school enrollment in New York
City.   In fact, Puerto Ricans accounted for about 20 per cent of
public elementary school pupils in 1963, compared with 15 per cent
in 1957.   Of the junior high students 18 per cent were Puerto Ricans in 1963, up from 16 per cent six years before.   In addition,
23 per cent in vocational high schools and 29 per cent in special
schools (both upwardly trending proportions) were youth of the Puerto Rican community.   The proportions in academic high schools
were much smaller, changing from 4.6 per cent in 1957 to 7.2 per
cent in 1963.   (Table 10.)

Employment
Since the level of education of New York's Puerto Ricans is
lower than that of any other group in the city and since educational
attainment is prerequisite for entry into many kinds of jobs, employed Puerto Ricans are more than any other group concentrated in
occupations with the lowest pay and status.   In 1960, 70.6 per cent
of the employed Puerto Rican males were in low-income occupations
(operatives and kindred workers, non-household service workers,
private household workers, and laborers), compared with 61.3 per
cent of the nonwhite and 31.4 per cent of the other white males.[4]
(Table 11.)

The differences in the occupations of employed females by
ethnic group show the same pattern.   Of the Puerto Rican employed
women, 78.2 per cent worked in the low-status occupations.   Among
nonwhites and other whites the percentages were 66.6 and 26.8.

Table 8

Reading Retardation, by Grade and Ethnic Group, 1961
(Selected Manhattan Neighborhood)

School Grade and Ethnic Group	Total Number	Percentages by Degree of Reading Retardation[a]							
		Over 3 Years	2.5 to 3.0	2.0 to 2.5	1.5 to 2.0	1.0 to 1.5	0.5 to 1.0	0.1 to 0.5	At Grade Level or Above
Grade 3.5[b]									
Total	2,721		.49	6.68	16.60	25.86	14.23	15.68	21.58
Puerto Rican	1,490		.92	7.12	21.29	30.69	15.85	14.44	9.80
Negro	626		.16	5.43	15.97	27.00	15.02	17.73	18.69
Other	806			1.82	5.45	12.37	9.24	16.33	54.79
Grade 8.5[b]									
Total	862	30.74	3.94	8.24	4.06	6.26	3.83	4.76	38.17
Puerto Rican	235	64.68	2.98	7.66	1.28	4.79	2.55	2.98	13.19
Negro	138	33.33	5.80	11.59	3.62	7.97	3.63	5.07	28.99
Other	489	13.70	3.88	7.57	5.52	6.54	4.50	5.52	52.77

a. Since the academic year is 10 months, scoring intervals consist of five months each.
b. Tested midway through each of these grades.

Source: Research Center, Columbia University School of Social Work.

Table 9
High School Graduates, New York City Public Schools,
by Ethnic Background and Type of Diploma, 1963

Numbers

Ethnic Group	Total	Academic Diploma	Vocational Diploma
Total	38,304	20,729	17,575
Puerto Rican	1,626	331	1,295
Negro	3,434	762	2,672
Other	33,244	19,636	13,608

Percentages

Ethnic Group	Total	Academic Diploma	Vocational Diploma
Total	100.0%	100.0%	100.0%
Puerto Rican	4.2	1.6	7.4
Negro	9.0	3.7	15.2
Other	86.8	94.7	77.4
Total	100.0%	54.1%	45.9%
Puerto Rican	100.0	20.4	79.6
Negro	100.0	22.2	77.8
Other	100.0	59.1	40.9

Source: New York City Board of Education.

Table 10
Pupils Enrolled in New York City Public Schools,
by Type of School, Fall of 1957-1963

Year	Number	Per Cent			
		Total	Puerto Rican	Negro	Other
Elementary					
1957	550,357	100.0	15.2	20.4	64.4
1958	558,749	100.0	16.3	21.9	61.8
1959	557,159	100.0	17.4	23.5	59.1
1960	567,613	100.0	17.9	24.9	57.2
1961	573,122	100.0	18.6	26.2	55.2
1962	581,755	100.0	19.1	27.3	53.6
1963	586,046	100.0	19.8	28.7	51.5

Table 10 (cont.)

Year	Number	Per cent			
		Total	Puerto Rican	Negro	Other

Junior High

Year	Number	Total	Puerto Rican	Negro	Other
1957	169,123	100.0	16.1	18.9	65.0
1958	172,286	100.0	16.0	18.7	65.3
1959	186,595	100.0	16.1	19.2	64.7
1960	185,479	100.0	17.4	21.4	61.2
1961	186,113	100.0	18.3	23.6	58.1
1962	193,293	100.0	18.1	25.7	56.2
1963	208,177	100.0	17.9	26.9	55.2

Academic High

Year	Number	Total	Puerto Rican	Negro	Other
1957	187,282	100.0	4.6	9.3	86.1
1958	192,409	100.0	4.7	10.0	85.4
1959	189,737	100.0	5.0	10.4	84.6
1960	188,795	100.0	5.2	10.7	84.1
1961	198,256	100.0	5.5	11.2	83.3
1962	205,971	100.0	6.2	12.5	81.3
1963	204,075	100.0	7.2	14.7	78.1

Vocational High

Year	Number	Total	Puerto Rican	Negro	Other
1957	41,282	100.0	20.4	23.6	56.0
1958	39,111	100.0	21.1	23.4	55.5
1959	37,920	100.0	21.6	23.2	55.2
1960	38,697	100.0	20.6	22.9	56.5
1961	40,508	100.0	21.6	24.2	54.2
1962	40,223	100.0	21.3	24.5	54.0
1963	40,622	100.0	22.5	25.9	51.6

Special Schools

Year	Number	Total	Puerto Rican	Negro	Other
1957	4,574	100.0	25.1	32.7	42.2
1958	5,310	100.0	26.4	33.7	39.9
1959	6,120	100.0	26.6	37.0	36.4
1960	6,095	100.0	27.7	35.3	37.0
1961	6,266	100.0	29.1	36.9	34.0
1962	6,186	100.0	28.4	37.8	33.8
1963	6.634	100.0	29.1	38.6	32.3

Table 10 (cont.)

Year	Number	Per Cent			
		Total	Puerto Rican	Negro	Other
		All Schools			
1957	952,617	100.0	13.5	18.2	68.3
1958	967,865	100.0	14.2	19.0	66.8
1959	977,531	100.0	15.0	20.2	64.8
1960	986,679	100.0	15.6	21.5	62.9
1961	1,004,265	100.0	16.1	22.8	61.6
1962	1,027,428	100.0	16.5	24.0	59.5
1963	1,045,554	100.0	17.1	25.6	57.3

Source: New York City Board of Education.

Employed Puerto Rican and nonwhite women were concentrated in the low-status occupations to a greater degree than were Puerto Rican and nonwhite males. The other white females, compared to the males, had higher status jobs overall.

The Puerto Ricans employed by agencies of New York's city government also are in the least desirable jobs to a greater degree than are Negroes and others. Three of every four Puerto Rican city employees are at the level of operatives or below, while only three of every five Negroes and one of every three of the others are so employed. In other words, two-thirds of the others, 40 per cent of the Negroes, and only 25 per cent of the Puerto Ricans are employed as foremen, clerical workers, professionals, or officials on the city payroll. (Table 12.)

Furthermore, only 3 per cent of city employees are Puerto Rican, whereas 23 per cent are Negroes and 74 per cent, others. As a result the Puerto Rican proportion in each occupational category is small, the largest being 6.4 per cent of service workers. The most striking differences are between ethnic proportions of the craftsmen-foremen and the managerial categories. Of the craftsmen and foremen employed by New York City, only 3.7 per cent were Negroes and only six-tenths of one per cent were Puerto Ricans: 95.7 per cent of the influential category of officials were whites or other races, only one-half of one per cent (44) were Puerto Ricans. (Table 12.)

Comparisons of 1960 with 1950 show modest changes in the occupations of Puerto Ricans. In 1950, 37.2 per cent of the employed males 14 years old and over were operatives and kindred workers; 28.4 per cent more were non-household service workers; 5.2 per cent were laborers. Among better-paying jobs, 11.1 per cent of these men were craftsmen, foremen, and kindred workers; 10 per cent were clerical, sales and kindred workers; 5.4 per cent were managers, officials, and proprietors; and 2.6 per cent were professionals, technicals, and kindred workers.

The employed women in 1950 were even more highly con-

concentrated in a few occupational categories. Of these, 77.5 per
cent were operatives and kindred workers; 9.2 per cent were
clerical, sales, and kindred workers; 5.9 per cent were non-household service workers; and 2 per cent were professional, technical,
and kindred workers.   None of the other occupational categories
employed as many as 2 per cent of the Puerto Rican females.
(Table 11.)

The percentage distribution of Puerto Ricans among major
occupational groups in 1960 showed changes, even though they remained predominantly in low-status jobs.   For males 14 years and
older the per cent in non-household occupations declined from 28.4
to 20.5; the percentage of managers, officials, and proprietors
dropped from 5.4 to 3.7; professional, technical, and kindred workers declined slightly as a proportion of the total.   However, it
should be remembered that the number of Puerto Ricans in New
York had increased considerably between 1950 and 1960.   Even
though certain job categories showed a drop in the proportions of
Puerto Ricans in them, in every instance the absolute number of
persons increased.   Among the males in 1960, the percentage employed as laborers (5.9) and as craftsmen, foremen, and kindred
workers (11.3) remained about the same as in 1950.   Clerical,
sales, and kindred workers showed a modest increase, from 10 to
12.3 per cent.   The greatest increase, however, was registered in
the category of operatives and kindred workers, in which 44.1 per
cent of the Puerto Rican employed males worked in 1960, compared
with 37.2 per cent in 1950.   In spite of these shifts, the occupational distribution of employed Puerto Rican males overall showed no
improvement in the decade.   In 1950, 70.9 per cent of them were in
the lowest income occupations (operatives, private household workers,
non-household workers, and laborers).   In 1960 the comparable figure was 70.6 per cent.   (Table 11.)

Changes through the decade between censuses were somewhat brighter for employed Puerto Rican females, though at both
points in time they were employed in low-status jobs in greater proportions than were Puerto Rican males.   In 1950, 85.9 per cent of
the employed females were in the lowest income occupations (listed
above) compared with 70.9 per cent of the men.   By 1960, only
73.2 per cent of the females were so employed, compared with 70.6
per cent of the males.   Thus, the occupational differential between
males and females narrowed from 15 to 7.6 percentage points during
the decade.   (Table 11.)

Improvement in the occupational situation of Puerto Rican
women occurred chiefly through their employment as clerical, sales,
and kindred workers.   Of the total, 9.2 per cent were so employed
in 1950; by 1960 the proportion in this category had increased to
15.9 per cent.   A slight gain was also registered by professional,
technical, and kindred workers.   (Table 11.)

Examination of the separate data for the first and second-
generation Puerto Ricans shows even more clearly an improvement
of the occupational status of employed Puerto Rican women relative
to Puerto Rican men.   The employed men and women 14 years of
age and older born in Puerto Rico were, of course, heavily employed in low-status occupations at the beginning and at the end of

Table 11
Occupational Status of Employed Civilian Labor Force,
by Sex and Ethnic Background, New York City, 1950 and 1960

Occupation	Puerto Rican 1950	Puerto Rican 1960[a]	Nonwhite 1960	Other White 1960
Employed Males:				
Number	49,860	127,384	233,584	1,601,904
Per cent	100.0	100.0	100.0	100.0
Professional, technical and kindred workers	2.6	2.2	5.2	13.6
Managers, Officials and Proprietors	5.4	3.7	5.0	14.1
Clerical, Sales and kindred workers	10.0	12.3	16.9	23.1
Craftsman, Foremen and Kindred workers	11.1	11.3	11.6	17.8
Operatives and kindred workers	37.2	44.1	28.4	17.2
Non-household service workers	28.4	20.5	21.1	9.4
Private household workers	0.1	0.1	0.9	0.1
Laborers	5.2	5.9	10.9	4.7
Employed Females:				
Number	34,685	67,518	181,942	860,722
Per cent	99.9	100.0	99.9	99.9
Professional, Technical and kindred workers	2.0	2.9	8.8	13.7
Managers, Officials and Proprietors	1.1	1.1	1.4	4.9
Clerical, Sales and kindred workers	9.2	15.9	21.8	53.1
Craftsman, Foremen and kindred workers	1.7	1.9	1.2	1.4
Operatives and kindred workers	77.5	69.7	25.9	15.8
Non-household service workers	5.9	6.9	18.8	8.2
Household service workers	1.6	0.8	21.2	2.6
Laborers	0.9	0.8	0.7	0.2

[a]Includes Nassau, Rockland, Suffolk and Westchester counties.

Source: U.S. Bureau of the Census. U.S. Censuses of Popula-
tion and Housing: 1960.   Census Tracts. Final Report PHC(1)-104.
Part 1. U.S. Government Printing Office, Washington, D.C., 1962.
Tables P-3, P-4, P-5; U.S. Bureau of the Census. U.S. Census

Table 11 (cont.)
<u>of Population 1950.   Special Report.   Puerto Ricans in Continental
United States.</u>   U. S. Government Printing Office, Washington, D. C.,
1953.   Table 5.   U. S. Bureau of the Census.   <u>U. S. Census of Population: 1960.   Subject Reports.   Puerto Ricans in the United States.
Final Report.   PC(2)-1D.   U. S.</u> Government Printing Office, Washington, D. C., 1963.   Table 11.

Table 12
Occupations of New York City Employees, by
Ethnic Background, 1963[a]

Occupations		Puerto Rican	Negro	Other
Total:	Number	5,404	40,946	130,848
	Per cent	100.0	100.0	100.0
Officials		0.8	2.0	5.7
Professional, Technical and kindred workers		14.6	22.4	42.4
Clerical and kindred workers		8.6	14.1	8.6
Craftsman, Foremen and kindred workers		1.4	1.1	9.4
Operatives and kindred workers		5.3	3.8	4.4
Service workers		54.8	49.7	17.4
Laborers		14.5	6.9	12.1
Officials		0.5	9.9	89.6
Professional, Technical and kindred workers		1.2	14.0	84.8
Clerical and kindred workers		2.5	31.3	66.2
Craftsman, Foremen and kindred workers		0.6	3.7	95.7
Operatives and kindred workers		3.7	20.5	75.8
Service workers		6.4	44.2	49.4
Laborers		4.0	14.6	81.4

[a] Figures do not include all City Departments.   See source publication, Table 3.

Source: New York City Commission on Human Rights, <u>The Ethnic
Survey</u>. (New York City Commission on Human Rights, 1964)
Tables 1.1 thru 1.6.

the 1950-1960 decade. Of the employed Puerto Rican-born men in
1950, 71.9 per cent were in low-status jobs (as defined above).
The number changed only slightly--to 72.4 per cent--by 1960. The
employed women born in Puerto Rico, however, improved their occupational positions to a more striking degree, even though they began (and remained) in a disadvantaged occupational situation relative to the men. In 1950, 89.1 per cent of these women were in
the low-status occupational categories, but by 1960 the percentage
had fallen to 82.3. Thus, due to improvement in the occupations
of females the percentage-point difference between men and women
born in Puerto Rico dropped from 17.2 to 9.9 over the decade.
(Table 13.)

Among the employed Puerto Ricans born in the United
States the females began with occupational distribution more favorable than that of the men in 1950 and they widened their advantage
during the decade. However, the occupational situation of both men
and women improved significantly. In 1950, 57.7 per cent of the
men and 51.7 per cent of the women were in low-status occupations. By 1960 the figures had dropped to 49.4 per cent for the
males and 34.2 per cent for the females. Thus the female occupational distribution improved to a greater degree than did that of the
men. As a result, the female percentage-point advantage increased from 6.0 in 1950 to 14.2 in 1960. (Table 13.)

The occupational advance for both men and women of the
second generation was achieved in similar ways--through increasing
participation as professional, technical, and kindred workers, and
as clerical, sales, and kindred workers. The proportion of men
who were craftsmen, foremen and kindred workers also increased.
The most dramatic increase was of women employed in clerical,
sales, and kindred tasks, which rose from 39.4 per cent in 1950
to 56.0 per cent in 1960. The greatest percentage-point losses for
the men were in the operative category--from 40.9 per cent in
1950 to 24.4 per cent in 1960. (Table 13.)

The occupational distributions do not tell the entire story,
for of the 147,495 Puerto Rican males 14 years old and over in
New York City's labor force in 1960, 14,507--or 9.9 per cent--
were unemployed. Table 14 gives the unemployment rates for the
Puerto Rican males, nonwhite males, and other white males, as they
stood at the time of the censuses of 1950 and 1960. In both periods
one in ten Puerto Rican men was unemployed and looking for work.
Furthermore, the unemployment problem for the Puerto Rican was
significantly worse than that of the nonwhite male or the much better off other white male.

This unemployment was heavily concentrated among youth.
Of the Puerto Rican male labor force 14 to 19 years of age, 19.7
per cent were unemployed, as were 19.0 per cent of the nonwhite
males of the same ages. (The figures for age groups are for New
York City and Nassau, Suffolk, Rockland, and Westchester counties
combined and probably understate the unemployment then prevalent
in New York City.) Among females of the same age group, the
unemployment rate of 14.7 for nonwhites was virtually the same as
the Puerto Rican rate of 15.0. Unemployment was also high among
the labor force 20 to 24 years of age: 10.7 per cent of the Puerto

Table 13
Occupational Status of Persons Born in Puerto Rico
and of Puerto Rican Parentage, by Sex,
New York City, 1950 and 1960

Occupation	Born in Puerto Rico		Puerto Rican Parentage	
	1950	1960a	1950	1960a
Employed Males:				
Number	46,275	118,288	3,585	9,096
Per cent	100.0	100.0	100.0	100.0
Professional, Technical and kindred workers	2.4	1.8	5.4	7.4
Managers, Officials and Proprietors	5.5	3.7	4.4	4.0
Clerical, Sales and kindred workers	9.2	11.4	20.5	23.8
Craftsmen, Foremen and kindred workers	11.0	10.8	11.9	16.3
Operatives and kindred workers	37.4	45.2	35.4	29.7
Non-household service workers	29.3	21.1	16.3	12.5
Household service	0.1	0.1	0.0	0.2
Laborers	5.1	6.0	6.0	6.0
Employed Females:				
Number	31,730	61,625	2,955	5,893
Percent	100.0	100.0	100.0	100.0
Professional, Technical and kindred workers	1.7	2.6	5.6	6.3
Managers, Officials and Proprietors	1.0	1.1	1.2	1.7
Clerical, Sales and kindred workers	6.4	12.1	39.4	56.0
Craftsmen, Foremen and kindred workers	1.7	1.9	2.0	1.7
Operatives and kindred workers	80.8	74.0	40.9	24.4
Non-household service	5.7	6.7	8.6	8.7
Household service	1.6	0.8	1.7	0.5
Laborers	1.0	0.8	0.5	0.6

[a] Includes Nassau, Rockland, Suffolk and Westchester counties.

Source: U.S. Bureau of the Census. U.S. Census of Population, 1960. Subject Reports. Puerto Ricans in the United States. Final PC(2)-ID. U.S. Government Printing Office, Washington, D.C., 1963. Table 11.

Table 14
Male Unemployment, by Ethnicity,
1950 and 1960

Ethnic Group	Per Cent Unemployed	
	1950	1960
Puerto Rican	10.6	9.9
Nonwhite	8.4	6.9
Other White	5.1	4.3

Source: U.S. Bureau of the Census. U.S. Census of Population
and Housing: 1960. Census tracts. Final Report PHC(1)-104.
Part 1. U.S. Government Printing Office, Washington, D.C.,
1963. Tables P-3, P-4, P-5.

Rican males and 12.4 per cent of the females; for nonwhites, 9.7
per cent of the males and 9.2 per cent of the females. Rates of
unemployment at older ages were smaller, but for no male Puerto
Rican age group did it fall below 7.7 per cent. (Table 15.)

Table 15
Unemployment Rates, for Puerto Ricans and Nonwhites, by Sex,
New York Standard Metropolitan Statistical Area, 1960

Persons 14 Years of Age and Over	Puerto Rican		Nonwhite	
	Male	Female	Male	Female
Total	9.7	10.6	6.8	6.5
14-19 years	19.7	15.0	19.0	14.7
20-24 "	10.7	12.4	9.7	9.2
25-34 "	8.5	9.5	6.6	6.7
35-44 "	8.5	9.3	5.3	5.8
45-64 "	8.8	9.5	5.6	4.7
65 years and older	7.7	12.3	7.9	4.6

Source: Manpower Report of the President, 1964. U.S. Government Printing Office, Washington, D.C., 1964. Table 33.

In summary, the occupational statistics for Puerto Ricans in
New York City show that they largely occupied low-status, low-income occupations in 1950 and in general remained in them in 1960.
The overall unemployment rate for Puerto Rican males has consistently exceeded that of any other racial or ethnic group in the city.
A considerable upgrading is apparent in the occupations of the generation born in the United States relative to those who migrated
here. However, the proportion of the second generation that has
reached labor-force age is still small. Among both the first and

second generation a trend is evident for the occupational status of employed women to improve relative to that of the employed men of the same generation. If the trend continues, it may have unfavorable implications for the stability of traditional Puerto Rican cultural patterns of family life.

Income
          In part, a consequence of the low educational attainment of the Puerto Rican population and the consequently low-status jobs at which they work, is the evident poverty of their families. Poverty is significantly more pronounced among Puerto Ricans than among any other identifiable racial and ethnic group in New York City.
          In 1959, 33.8 per cent of Puerto Rican families had incomes of less than $3,000, and more than half (53.7 per cent) had less than $4,000. The nonwhites in the city were better off, although not in an enviable situation. In this group, 27.1 per cent had incomes below $3,000 and 43.6 per cent had less than $4,000. The other whites were least disadvantaged. Only 11.8 per cent of their families had incomes of less than $3,000; 19.2 per cent had less than $4,000. (Tables 16 and 17.)

Table 16
Family Income, by Ethnic Group, New York City, 1959

Income	Percentages of Families with Income[a]		
	Puerto Rican	Nonwhite	Other White
Under $3,000	33.8%	27.1%	11.8%
Under $4,000	53.7%	43.6%	19.2%
$4,000 and over	46.3%	56.4%	80.8%

[a]Not additive. Families with less than $4,000 income includes those with less than $3,000 income.

Source: U.S. Bureau of the census. U.S. Censuses of Population and Housing: 1960. Census Tracts. Final Report PHC(1)-104. Part 1. U.S. Government Printing Office, Washington, D.C., 1962. Tables P-1, P-4, P-5.

          Because of the youthfulness of the Puerto Rican population in comparison with nonwhites and other whites, the children and youth in the Puerto Rican communities are struck more severely than any other group by massive conditions of poverty and deprivation.

Housing
          As newcomers, Puerto Ricans entered the competition for housing later than did the nonwhite and other white populations. This is reflected in the statistics on the year in which household heads moved into the units where they resided in 1960. Among

Table 17
Family Income, by Ethnic Group, New York City, 1959

Income	Percentage of Families with Income			
	Total Population	Puerto Rican	Nonwhite	Other White
Total: Number	2,079,832	140,389	263,963	1,675,480
Percent	100.0	100.0	100.0	100.0
Under $1,000	3.5	6.9	6.3	2.8
$1,000-$1,999	4.9	9.2	8.2	4.0
$2,000-$2,999	6.8	17.7	12.6	5.0
$3,000-$3,999	9.4	19.9	16.5	7.4
$4,000-$4,999	11.2	15.3	14.8	10.3
$5,000-$5,999	13.1	11.3	12.5	13.4
$6,000-$6,999	11.2	7.4	9.0	11.8
$7,000-$7,999	8.9	4.7	6.3	9.6
$8,000-$8,999	7.1	2.9	4.5	7.9
$9,000-$9,999	5.4	1.7	3.0	6.0
$10,000 and over	17.5	3.1	6.3	21.7

Source: U.S. Bureau of the Census. U.S. Censuses of Population
and Housing: 1960. Census Tracts. Final Report PHC(1)-104.
Part 1. U.S. Government Printing Office, Washington, D.C.,
1962. Tables P-1, P-4, P-5.

Puerto Ricans, 46.6 per cent had moved in during the period from
1958 to March, 1960. Only 30 per cent of the nonwhites and 22.8
per cent of the whites had occupied their units so recently. Puerto
Rican heads of households were under-represented in the long-term
occupants of housing units. While just 18.7 per cent of them had
moved into their 1960 unit in 1953 or earlier, 41.1 per cent of the
nonwhite and more than half (53.6 per cent) of the other white
household heads were long-term residents. (Table 18)

Table 18
Year of Occupancy of Housing Units, by Ethnic Group,
New York City, 1960

Year moved into unit	Percentages		
	Puerto Rican	Nonwhite	Other White
Total: Number	156,110	352,554	2,145,781
Per cent	100.0	100.0	100.0
1958 to March 1960	46.6	30.0	22.8
1954 to 1957	34.7	28.9	23.6
1953 or earlier	18.7	41.1	53.6

Source: U.S. Bureau of the Census. U.S. Censuses of Population
and Housing: 1960. Census Tracts. Final Report PHC(1)-104. Part 1
U.S. Govt. Prtg. Office, Washington, D.C., 1962 Tab. H-2, 3, 4.

In a city where owner-occupants of housing units are a distinct minority, families with household heads of Puerto Rican birth or
parentage were least represented in the ownership group. Of the
Puerto Rican families, 95.3 per cent rented the unit where they
lived, compared with 86.8 per cent of those with nonwhite heads
and 75.6 per cent of those with other white heads of households.
(Table 19)

As the lowest-income population in the city, Puerto Ricans
also paid less rent for renter-occupied units, but only slightly less
than did the nonwhites.   The median gross rent (the "middle" rent,
with half the rents less and half exceeding it) for Puerto Ricans
was $62; that for nonwhites was $66.   In comparison, the other
whites in general paid substantially higher rents.   Their median was
$76.   (Table 20)

Table 19
Tenure of Housing Units, by Ethnic Group,
New York City, 1960

Occupied Units	Percentages		
	Puerto Rican	Nonwhite	Other White
Total: Number	156,110	352,554	2,145,781
Per cent	100.0	100.0	100.0
Owner Occupied	4.7	13.2	24.4
Renter Occupied	95.3	86.8	75.6

Source: U.S. Bureau of Census.   U.S. Censuses of Population and
Housing: 1960.   Census Tracts.   Final Report PHC(1)-104. Part 1.
U.S. Government Printing Office, Washington, D.C., 1962. Tables
H-1, H-3, H-4.

The Puerto Rican households are concentrated in the oldest
residential structures in New York City.   Of the households, 87.3
per cent were in structures built in 1939 or earlier, whereas 84
per cent of the nonwhite households and 79.2 per cent of the other
white households were in the older buildings.   (Table 21)   The
Puerto Rican homes also are more frequently in the structures with
larger numbers of units than are the homes of the nonwhites and
the other whites.   Of Puerto Rican households, 85.4 per cent were
in structures with five or more units, compared with 70.5 per cent
for the nonwhites and 61.1 per cent for the other whites. (Table 22)

Though a significant number of Puerto Rican households are
in the large, low-income public-housing projects where physical
standards are maintained, 40.1 per cent of their households were
in deteriorating and dilapidated structures.   Thirty-three per cent
of the nonwhites and just 11.0 per cent of the other whites were so
badly housed.   Furthermore, the differential among the ethnic
groups is dramatic for units classified as "dilapidated"--housing
that "does not provide safe and adequate shelter."[5]   While 10.4
per cent of the Puerto Rican households and 8 per cent of the nonwhites lived in such units, only 1.8 per cent of the other whites were
so housed. (Table 23)

Table 20
Gross Rent, by Ethnic Group, New York City, 1960

Rent	Percentages		
	Puerto Rican	Nonwhite	Other White
Total: Number	148,714	305,098	1,624,078
Percent	100.0	100.0	100.0
Less than $20	0.1	0.1	0.1
$20 to $39	7.7	6.4	4.1
$40 to $59	36.6	30.2	20.1
$60 to $79	37.3	32.3	29.7
$80 to $99	11.3	15.9	18.8
$100 or more	5.1	12.5	25.4
No cash rent	1.9	2.6	1.8
Median rent	$62.00	$66.00	$76.00

Source: U.S. Bureau of the Census. U.S. Censuses of Population and Housing: 1960. Census Tracts. Final Report PHC(1)-104. Part 1. U.S. Government Printing Office, Washington, D.C., 1962. Tables H-2, H-3, H-4.

Table 21
Year Housing Structure Built, by Ethnic Group,
New York City, 1960

Year Built	Percentages		
	Puerto Rican	Nonwhite	Other White
Total: Number	156,110	351,914	2,249,396
Percent	100.0	100.0	100.0
1950 to March 1960	8.8	10.9	13.5
1940 to 1949	3.9	5.1	7.3
1939 or earlier	87.3	84.0	79.2

Source: U.S. Bureau of the Census. U.S. Censuses of Population and Housing: 1960. Census Tracts. Final Report PHC(1)-104. Part 1. U.S. Government Printing Office, Washington, D.C., 1962. Tables H-1, H-3, H-4.

Puerto Ricans residing in these households were crowded for space to a degree not true of the nonwhites and other whites. Of the households with a Puerto Rican head, 38.6 per cent were in units with 1.01 or more persons per room. Among nonwhite households, 22.1 per cent were crowded to this degree, compared to only 8.7 per cent of the other white households. (Table 24)

Thus, the information about the housing of Puerto Ricans parallels that characterizing their population. Just as they are the least educated, most frequently out of a job and looking for work, most concentrated in low-status occupations, and have the least family

Table 22
Units in Housing Structures, by Ethnic Group,
New York City, 1960

| Number of Units | Percentages | | |
in Structure	Puerto Rican	Nonwhite	Other White
Total	100.0	100.0	100.0
1	2.8	9.5	14.6
2	4.2	9.3	15.8
3-4	7.6	10.7	8.5
5 or more	85.4	70.5	61.1

Source: U.S. Bureau of Census. U.S. Censuses of Population and Housing: 1960. Census Tracts. Final Report PHC(1)-104. Part 1. U.S. Government Printing Office, Washington, D.C., 1962. Tables H-1, H-3, H-4.

Table 23
Condition and Plumbing of Occupied Housing Units,
by Ethnic Group, New York City, 1960

| | Percentages | | |
Condition and Plumbing	Puerto Rican	Nonwhite	Other White
Total	100.0	100.0	100.0
Sound	59.8	67.0	89.0
With all plumbing facilities	53.8	57.9	85.2
Lacking some or all facilities	6.0	9.1	3.8
Deteriorating	29.7	25.0	9.2
With all plumbing facilities	24.0	18.6	7.7
Lacking some or all facilities	5.7	6.4	1.5
Dilapidated	10.4	8.0	1.8

Source: U.S. Bureau of the Census. U.S. Censuses of Population and Housing: 1960. Census Tracts. Final Report PHC(1)-104. Part 1. U.S. Government Printing Office, Washington, D.C., 1962. Tables H-1, H-3, H-4.

income of any identifiable ethnic population in New York City, so do they live in housing units that are the most deteriorated or dilapidated, and the most crowded. For this they pay slightly lower rents.

Health
        Puerto Ricans in New York City, as reflected by public health records, consistently maintain an intermediate rate relative to that of nonwhites and other whites. This is shown by statistics on infant mortality, active tuberculosis, and infectious venereal diseases. [6]

Table 24
Persons Per Room in Housing Units, by Ethnic Group,
New York City, 1960

| Persons per Room | Percentages | | |
	Puerto Rican	Nonwhite	Other White
Total: Number of Units	156,110	352,554	2,145,781
Per cent	100.0	100.0	100.0
0.50 or less	11.9	28.6	36.7
0.51 to 0.75	17.7	20.1	28.5
0.76 to 1.01	31.8	29.2	26.1
1.01 or more	38.6	22.1	8.7

Source: U.S. Bureau of the Census. U.S. Censuses of Population
and Housing: 1960. Census Tracts. Final Report PHC(1)-104.
Part 1. U.S. Government Printing Office, Washington, D.C.,
1962. Tables H-1, H-3, H-4.

The mortality rate for Puerto Rican infants--the number of
deaths under one year of age per 1,000 live births--has hovered
around 30 for the past decade. The actual rate for 1963 was 28.4,
but annual fluctuations have produced almost this low a rate in prior
years, followed by higher rates. The nonwhite infant mortality rate
over the same decade has fluctuated around a rate of 40, the latest
being 38.9. The 1963 rate for the other whites was 19.5, continuing the tendency to remain near 20 infant deaths per 1,000 live
births. Thus, the pattern for the decade has been a rate of about
20 for the other whites, 30 for the Puerto Ricans, and 40 for the
nonwhites. (Table 25)
Similar relationships are pointed up in statistics on newly
reported cases of active tuberculosis, all forms, in 1963. Puerto
Ricans comprise 7.9 per cent of New York City's population, but
they comprised 13.8 per cent of new tuberculosis cases. Thus, the
proportion of Puerto Rican cases was not quite twice the Puerto
Rican percentage in New York's population. The proportion of Negro tuberculosis cases was slightly more than three times their
representation in the city's population. Of all new cases 46.5 per
cent were Negro, whereas Negroes account for 14 per cent of the
city's population. In contrast, other whites contributed only 35.7
per cent of new tuberculosis cases--less than half their percentage
of New York City's population. As in infant mortality rates, then,
Puerto Ricans are between the other whites and the nonwhites in
rate of new cases of tuberculosis. (Table 26)
The much less adequate data on rates of infection with syphilis and gonorrhea also show Puerto Rican rates in excess of those
for whites and lower than those for nonwhites. However, these
statistics should be interpreted as suggesting the possibility of ethnic differences in true rates, not as establishing them. In the first
place, the data reflect only the cases diagnosed in public clinics.
It is highly likely that many such cases diagnosed by private physicians are not reported and that this particularly minimizes the rates

Table 25
Infant Mortality, by Ethnic Group
New York City, 1953-1963

| | | Deaths under 1 year per 1,000 live births | | |
Year	Total	Puerto Rican	Nonwhite	Other White
1953	24.4	29.0	40.5	20.8
1954	23.7	28.8	37.2	20.2
1955	25.8	34.9	41.0	21.0
1956	24.5	28.8	38.2	20.3
1957	25.0	30.7	41.9	19.6
1958	26.4	30.8	43.1	20.8
1959	26.5	32.1	43.3	20.3
1960	26.0	28.4	42.4	20.3
1961	25.6	30.3	39.7	19.7
1962	27.3	28.2	43.3	21.1
1963	25.9	28.4	38.9	19.5

Source: New York City Department of Health. Summary of Vital
Statistics: 1962. The City of New York. Table 6; unpublished
1963 tabulation. New York City Department of Health.

Table 26
Newly Reported Cases of Active Tuberculosis, All Forms,
by Ethnic Group, New York City, 1963

Ethnic Group	Tuberculosis Cases	1960 Population
Total: Number	4,779	7,781,984
Per cent	100.0	100.0
Puerto Ricans	13.8	7.9
Negroes	46.5	14.0
Other whites	35.7	77.4
Other nonwhites	4.0	.7

Source: New York City Department of Health, unpublished 1963
tabulation.

for whites. Second, Puerto Ricans are identified only by a judgment that the name on the record "sounds" Spanish. The degree of
error thus introduced is unknown and may be very large. It is
safer merely to state that a serious problem of venereal infection
exists in New York City than to emphasize differences in rates between ethnic groups. (Table 27)
    A recent study indicates that a high rate of mental disability
may exist among Puerto Ricans in New York City. Based on responses to a list of symptoms, rather than past or present treatment for disability, nearly half--48.8 per cent--of the sample of

persons born in Puerto Rico were classified as ranking in the highest of three groups in degree of mental disability.   In contrast, only 27.1 per cent of the Negroes were so classified, and no other
ethnic or religious group approached the Puerto Rican rate. (Table
28)

Table 27

Estimated Rates of Syphilis and Gonorrhea,
by Sex and Ethnic Group,
New York City, 1962[a]

Syphilis

Ethnic Group	Number of Cases		Rate per 100,000 Population	
	Male	Female	Male	Female
Spanish-sounding names	172	64	58.0	20.3
Nonwhites	1,079	525	186.1	78.6
Whites	1,267	192	40.7	5.6

Gonorrhea

Ethnic Group	Male	Female	Male	Female
Spanish-sounding names	824	125	277.7	39.6
Nonwhites	11,221	1,482	1,935.7	221.7
Whites	4,071	438	130.8	12.8

[a] Cases based on public clinic diagnoses.
Source: Provided on request.

Table 28
High Mental Disability Scores, by Ethnic Group,
Area of New York City, 1960-1961

Ethnic Group	Percentage with High Scores
Puerto Ricans (Born in Puerto Rico)	48.8%
Non-Irish Catholics	37.0
Jewish	33.3
Protestants	27.8
Negroes	27.1
Irish	15.5

Source: Edward A. Suchman, Raymond Maurice, Martin Goldman,
and Daniel Rosenblatt, Sociocultural Variations in Illness and Medical Care.   Unpublished manuscript, 1963, p. 14.

The authors of the study themselves state:

While one may question the validity of this instrument as a measure of mental disability, especially when administered to a Puerto Rican-born population, the size of the difference is such as to strongly suggest that in our Puerto Rican population in New York City we are dealing with a group that is experiencing difficult problems of psychological adjustment. [7]

Notes

1. See Table 6, footnote a.

2. Grade school, as used here, refers to eight grades of education.

3. These figures are for the New York Standard Metropolitan Statistical Area and include 16,856 Puerto Ricans living in Westchester, Nassau, Suffolk, and Rockland counties, in addition to those in New York City. Comparable data are not available currently for New York City alone. Puerto Ricans living outside the city limits have somewhat higher educational attainment than those within, so the percentages underestimate the dropout rates characteristic of New York City's Puerto Ricans. The numbers undoubtedly include a few persons still in school in 1960, but it is unlikely that the number of subsequent high-school completions would change the percentages greatly.

4. See footnote a, Table 11.

5. U.S. Bureau of the Census. U.S. Censuses of Population and Housing: 1960. Census Tracts. Final Report PHC(1)-104. Part 1. U.S. Government Printing Office, Washington, D.C., 1962.

6. Statistics for Puerto Ricans are available only when place of birth (or place of mother's birth on birth certificates) is a part of the record. For this reason the variety of statistics for color groups cannot be extended to the Puerto Rican population. Since place of birth is the basis of classification, these statistics are not entirely comparable to the census definition which, in addition to those born in Puerto Rico, includes as Puerto Ricans those born elsewhere but with one or both parents born in Puerto Rico.

7. Edward A. Suchman, Raymond Maurice, Martin Goldman, and Daniel Rosenblatt, Sociocultural Variations in Illness and Medical Care. Unpublished manuscript, 1963, p. 14.

East Harlem cuts deep into Manhattan, on two square miles
of the highest priced rock in the world, running from the East River
to Central Park, and roughly from 96th to 130th Street on Manhattan's east side.

Its borders are always shifting. So are its neighborhoods,
or subareas. Some have their own identity. When the European
immigrants dominated East Harlem they referred to it as "the
neighborhood." It was then more a neighborhood simply transferred from some European town to the New World, with the same
people and the same culture. Though Italians still talk about "the
neighborhood," social workers and the new migrants--Puerto Ricans
and Negroes--know that physical togetherness alone does not make
people neighbors.

The community is divided, says a City Planning Commission
report, into several social areas. A commuter's railroad track on
Park Avenue, the former site of an elevated line, a hill on 102nd
Street are natural borders that create subareas. These may, like
national boundaries, isolate one group from another and give rise
to separate patterns of living. Often the borders separate the more
from the less desirable areas.

Public housing can be a more formidable barricade than
streets, tracks, and lines of transportation. The giant projects
tend, like barbed wire, to shut off communications. Projects midway in East Harlem stretch across its whole width and cut it in two.
To the north and west of this barrier are the dominantly Negro
neighborhoods. To the south on one end is El Barrio, the oldest
Puerto Rican settlement in the states.

Mixed in with El Barrio's Spanish residents are some West
Indians, Irish, Russians, Hungarians, and Negroes. Its nerve center is the enclosed market under the Park Avenue railroad tracks.
Here goods and information are exchanged. Some claim that prostitution and the narcotics trade are rife in El Barrio, on 110th and 111th
Streets, for example, west of Park Avenue. Two active community
groups also work there: the Taft Neighborhood Development Committee and the East Harlem Reform Democrats. Along Fifth Avenue and in a different world is a towering row of public institutions
facing Fifth Avenue and Central Park, their backs turned to the
slum.

The "Triangle" at the northern end of East Harlem between
125th and 130th Streets is probably Harlem's poorest spot. Though it
has a number of stable residents, its present, predominantly Negro

155

population includes many recent arrivals from the rural Deep South.
It stands in a corner by itself, isolated, ignored by many agencies
that tend to the southern tier.   The Triangle is the end of the line
for many hard-core cases.   The bulldozers have pushed them about,
like gravel, from one spot to another, and now they are here,
many of them too down-and-out to qualify for public housing.
Again the bulldozers may push them out.   The next step in their
line of march seems to be the East River.

East Harlem is now brimming with a mixture of dark and
volatile people: Puerto Ricans who give it a Spanish accent (41 per
cent), Negroes (38 per cent), Italians, and others (21 per cent).

The most significant recent population change is the increase
in Negro residents.   Many of them came in with the new public
housing projects.   In 1940 Negroes were only 20 per cent of East
Harlem's population.   In each recent decade Negroes increased by
roughly 10 per cent.   As in other cities, New York City's Negro
population has been dispersing.   The increase of Negro population
now comes mainly from natural increase rather than new migration.
The migrations have merely slowed, not stopped, and newcomers
in undetermined numbers still arrive from the most backward rural
areas of Puerto Rico and the deepest South.

Puerto Ricans have also increased.   They were only 30 per
cent of the total in 1950.   The Italians, until recently dominant,
are still leaving for Long Island and other suburban points.   Both
East and Central Harlem have been losing population very rapidly.
East Harlem's loss was 17 per cent in the 1960 census.   Central
Harlem's was about 14 per cent, most of it in the 21 to 44 age
group.   The young grow up and leave when they marry and start
work.

East Harlem's residents have known upheaval and change.
About half of its population moved from one place to another during
one five-year period.   In Central Harlem only one out of three
moved.

Cultural differences have been rather overplayed in discussions of the disadvantaged.   Idiosyncracies of culture are of more
interest and use to the tourist than to the advocate of progress and
change.   What is most significant about the culture of the disadvantaged is that its essentials are much like those of the advantaged,
minus the material comforts and self-respect that are their by-
products.   A brief tour of East Harlem's culture, here and later in
the book, will suffice, with a pause for a taste of its special Puerto Rican flavor.

"The cultural attitudes of the Puerto Rican and Negro segments toward authority are in direct contradiction to each other,"
Preston Wilcox observed as director of the East Harlem Project.
Puerto Ricans tended "to be submissive toward authority and thus
easily came under the domination of a single leader who did little
to develop their potential.   The Negro segment tended to be aggressive toward authority--the result being that they continued to receive
'guarded' reactions from authority figures with little goal achievement."[1]

Submission from one group, aggression from the other;

neither gets the most out of authority. Puerto Ricans, it is claimed,
favor the "maximal leader," the unquestioned leader that all follow:
a corollary in everyday life is that "If they like you, they'll accept
anything from you." Protest leaders in East Harlem are critical of
Puerto Ricans for accepting social inequities and for their "failure
to join Negroes in protest." It is said that Puerto Ricans are
"more American than Americans," and that anything in the United
States goes with them; they do not complain.

An estimated one-fourth of Puerto Ricans are Negro. Though
Puerto Ricans tend to be racially unbiased, by mainland standards,
the dark-skinned Puerto Ricans say they are treated as the "lowest"
in their families, and it is said that the Puerto Rican drug addict
is almost always the darkest member of his family.

Though conflict is still open, Puerto Ricans are closer in
life style, religion, and attitudes to their Italian rather than their
Negro neighbors. Italians, an exclusive and "cornered" community
in East Harlem, accept neither group, but Puerto Ricans are less
rejected and some intergroup dating and marriage do occur. Only
a few Puerto Ricans and even fewer Negroes are to be seen in the
Italian's last major preserve: La Guardia Neighborhood House. A
mixed dance was once held there (Italian and Puerto Rican), but the
boys fought over mixed couple dancing, and the attempt at friendship through youth socializing was all but abandoned. La Guardia
House still sponsors a fairly active Italian-Puerto Rican friendship
group (which Negroes say should include them too) to reduce violent
conflict and help in neighborhood improvement.

All three groups are fond of music and dancing. While the
Puerto Rican youth retain much of their "folk music," the Italian
youth are almost submerged in the pop music of the larger "youth
culture" and rarely speak Italian or sing Italian songs in public.

Sex is a favorite subject if not activity, though strong re-
straints on girls are found among Italians and Puerto Ricans. One
youth worker, who has lived or worked in East Harlem all his life,
claimed that "all the kids can think of is sex;" he referred to all
three ethnic groups. "No wonder they can't learn anything in
school," he said, "they have sex on their mind 24 hours a day."

One teacher described her Puerto Rican and Negro children
as "very active" physically. "They love to dance and move their
bodies. They can't sit still. The ones that do well in school usually don't like to dance or move around. When I had a group to
my house, they all danced wildly, except one girl who was the best
student in the school. She didn't dance at all."

"The children here," she said, "can do so much on their
own--sewing, and painting, and creative work. The middle class
children always have to be taken care of. They want you to do
everything for them." East Harlem's children tend to take on responsibility and independence at an early age, and to "do for themselves."

Teachers and others claim that Puerto Ricans keep their
children close to home and off the streets, while the Negro children
are permitted much more freedom of the streets and sidewalks.
Puerto Rican girls, in particular, are closely watched and shel-
tered, and are rarely permitted out at night without an adult escort.

This restriction is breaking down with time.   Italian girls too are very closely watched by their parents, and many are continually in trouble with parents about keeping late hours or not being home on time.   Negro girls are given much more freedom.

While Italian youths express open and profound racist feelings, Puerto Ricans, themselves a racial mixture, tend to feel that "everyone is equal" and that they should not talk against Negroes. Some, in unguarded moments, will express fear of Negroes.   One sixth grader said: "The Negro people, they all act tough.   The colored people, if we walk down the street and if a Negro were walking by and we looked at them, they just start a fight.   If we're walking down the street, my grandmother says, and I see a Negro walking down the street, he could talk anything he want, I would look down not to see his face because the Negro people act tough. They say 'what are you looking at?' "

Their relations are better with Spanish Negroes: "Where I used to go there was some nice Negro people.   I used to always be with them and take them to my house and give them candy or anything what I had.   I had a friend, she was real nice with me.   She used to always, you know, stick with me, and another girl named Margie, you know, she was colored people.   Colored, yeah, but she was Spanish, she was just like me.   She lived in the same building and we three used to always stick together.   I think sometime that Negro people are generous too. "

The dark-skinned Puerto Rican child tastes mainland racial prejudice and doesn't like it at all; it helps him understand, however, what American Negroes have to live with.   A sixth grade Puerto Rican girl tells this story of discovery:

"I went to Lane's about two weeks before Easter, and I looked all over the place, and my mother is light skinned and I was with her.   So I looked all over the place like that and I didn't see nobody my color and I said to my mother, 'I'll wait out here,' and she said, 'No, you come in here.'   We went up to the top part to find the hats, so I got on the escalator and there was these light-skinned people on the escalator going down and I was going up and they were looking at me and I had this badge that said about the Beatles 'I like Paul, ' and they looked at me, and this lady stuck her tongue out at me.   And I asked my mother and my mother said, 'You don't live with her, keep walking,' but they were all looking at me and I thought because I was the only dark-skin in there.   I looked all over the place and I was the only one dark skin. "

Race and ethnicity underlie much of the open and hidden conflict in East Harlem, as it always has in the slums of New York's melting pot.   The poor, consumed by conflict with the new poor who are moving in on top of them, often ignore "enemies without" and those at a distance who pull the strings that manipulate their lives.

Typically, in the old tenement housing, these groups will not live together in the same building, though they may live in adjacent buildings or at opposite ends of a block.   In the new public housing projects, they at least share the same roof, however little they may communicate under it.   In the old blocks, one side of the street may be Italian and the other side Puerto Rican.   The melting down of

these new migrants, the effort of learning to talk and share and
work together, is a slow and troubled process.

Politically, the Puerto Ricans in East Harlem have tended to
form alliances with Negroes rather than with Italians within the
Democratic party, and they have now successfully taken over much
of the party's control from the Italians.

The rapidly diminishing Italian community tends to live in
the old row houses rather than the projects; a number of Italians
are home owners who are aging and want to stay in their old neighborhood. Italian youths of dating age are boxed in, constrained
from dating Puerto Ricans and Negroes, and unable to find a big
enough matrimonial field in their own community; Irish boys from
other neighborhoods are desirable to the girls but not very accessible. The Italians are more prosperous than the other groups and
the Puerto Ricans least prosperous. Negroes tend to favor project
living, and they now constitute a fairly large upwardly mobile and
unusually sophisticated group in East Harlem, though there are also
large numbers of destitute people.

The Italian community is tightly sealed against outsiders;
many of East Harlem's "Italians" are Sicilians, some of whom have
been (some claim still are) close to the Sicilian underworld; nobody
talks about it to outsiders. This underworld may have been, in fact,
East Harlem's most earnest "self-help" effort--a community project
that serviced people in a variety of legal and illegal ways, gave assistance, welfare, and protection, enriched some and helped others
rise out of poverty. Neither Puerto Ricans nor Negroes have had
any comparable organization.

The gray poverty of the old Spanish section of East Harlem,
roughly marked by 96th and 112th Streets on the south and north and
Fifth and Third Avenues on the west and east, contrasts with the
green poverty of the homeland, Puerto Rico.

The island, once a U.S. colony, is now a commonwealth.
It elects its own government and pays no taxes to the United States.
Yet it receives the benefits of U.S. citizenship and limited U.S.
federal services and funds. Recent economic growth has made it
the most prosperous Latin American territory, though it is still a
long way from prosperity as we know it.

The Puerto Rican migration to <u>Nueva York</u>, unchecked by
immigrant quotas, is a major source of the island's prosperity. It
upgraded the migrants, converted them from rural to urban people,
relieved the island of some of its labor surplus, and sent lots of
cash back home.

The commonwealth government plays many improvisations on
the mixed economy theme. It built much of the industry on the island and still operates some of it. It also gives substantial tax ex-
emptions to private enterprises that have been brought in from the
states, and feverishly encourages private investment.

In Puerto Rico the outsider is aware of a national spirit
amid residual poverty. A spirit that is busy and buzzing and wide-
eyed rather than shrewd, ruthless, competitive. It is a lyric and
a creative excitement rather than a highly organized or mechanized
one. Many people, very modest people, seem to think it is their
job to do something: first for their people, second for themselves.

It seems the reverse of what they run into in New York City.   The
rural campesinos are still impoverished, however, and 13 per cent
of the labor force is unemployed.

For an industrializing people, many Puerto Ricans have an
incongruous bubbling of good spirits.   Mainland visitors usually love
the island and wonder why Puerto Ricans left this lovely place to
live in El Barrio.

The simple answer of course is poverty.   They left in
search of a job, food, good shoes, a phonograph, a chance to suc-
ceed--just like everyone else.   New York is cold and gray; Puerto
Rico is green and warm, an island paradise.   It is so close to
New York by air coach that Puerto Ricans continue to have some of
the best of two worlds and, unlike any previous migrants, keep one
foot in the green homeland and the other in gray El Barrio or south
Bronx.

The migration to New York City, where 60 per cent of the
migrants (over 650,000) came, is said to have stopped.[2] It is harder to get jobs in the states and easier for those with skills to get
jobs in the island than before.   So many return to their "rich port"
or never leave in the first place.   Some learn skills on the mainland and go home to use them, or acquire capital and go home to
set up a business.

Meanwhile Puerto Ricans helped those back home.   In 1954,
$3 million went from New York to Puerto Rico by postal money
order alone.   In 1940 bank deposits in Puerto Rico were $76 mil-
lion; in 1961, $674 million.   About half the capital invested in new
manufacturing now comes from Puerto Rico itself.   Political power
has changed hands.   Once dominated by sugar lawyers, the legislature came to be heavily influenced by labor leaders and spokesmen.
It is this political change that produced economic change.   The
great Governor Luis Muñoz himself was influenced by the U.S. labor movement, as were many of the new Puerto Rican leaders.

In the 1930s, after some thirty-five years of American colonial status, Puerto Rico was impoverished, illiterate, diseased,
congested.   About one-third of all births were illegitimate.   It was
almost wholly dependent on sugar and had little industry.   In other
words, it resembled most of Latin America.   With its commonwealth status came new life and prosperity.

In El Barrio and New York generally, about half of adult
Puerto Ricans are disqualified from voting by English literacy tests.
Most are literate and could pass tests in Spanish, but not English.
The Puerto Rican's political disfranchisement greatly weakens his
organized strength in New York.

Nominally Roman Catholic, about ten times as many Puerto
Rican children go to public as to parochial school, though the New
York archdiocese has about 250 Spanish-speaking priests.   There
are some 4,000 Puerto Rican-run businesses in New York.

El Diario--La Prensa, a Spanish daily paper in New York
that prints Puerto Rican news, is owned by Roy Chalk, of Trans-
Caribbean Airways, a non-Puerto Rican.   The paper is called the
"patron" of many Puerto Ricans; some say it is a Puerto Rican
equivalent of Tammany Hall.   Others criticize its "conservatism"
and influence on Puerto Rican opinion.

Some Puerto Ricans have moved up rather fast in New York. In 1950, only 24 per cent of mainland-born Puerto Rican women were in sales and clerical occupations. A decade later, 43 per cent held these jobs.

Many Puerto Rican women marry and bear children while they are still children. The birth rate for girls younger than 20 is five times higher among Puerto Ricans and Negroes than among non-Puerto Rican white groups. The effect of the combination of large families and low wages is visible in the ethnic make-up of the New York City Welfare Department's recipients of supplementary assistance, assistance given those who have jobs but whose wages do not cover their minimum needs. One-half of all families in New York who receive this assistance are Puerto Rican. Thus government subsidizes the hundreds of marginal businesses in the city that do not pay a living wage.

Birth control is a big issue with Puerto Ricans, as it is with others. The women so want to keep down family size, says Elena Padilla, in her book Up from Puerto Rico,[3] that "abortions and other forms of discontinuing pregnancies may be attempted," such as castor oil, quinine pills, strong purgatives and teas. Abortions, carried out by women (comandronas) who do them for small fees, "are closely guarded secrets, for, reported one informant, 'a woman who has an abortion can be sentenced to death in the electric chair.' " Sterilization, obtained without great difficulty in Puerto Rico, is said to be preferred to contraception.

Many Puerto Ricans, she reports, regard other Puerto Ricans as "worthless" because of their "lack of unity" and because in New York they do not "help each other as they do in Puerto Rico. "

"Americans" are highly regarded by Puerto Ricans. They are said to be "nice, honest, beautiful, and funny. " "Americans," as defined by Puerto Ricans, are nonimmigrant whites. The second-generation New York Puerto Ricans interviewed gave a "high" rating to Americans, Cubans, Italian, Jewish and other European immigrants; a "medium" rating to American Negroes including West Indians; and a "low" rating to the new Puerto Rican migrant. "For some Hispanos it is openly accepted and unquestioned that Hispanos are undesirable persons. " One Puerto Rican voiced his feelings when he said, "Our race, the Latin race, has spoiled this country by the use of drugs. That is why the Americans hate us. "

Such feelings are not usually reciprocated. Only American Negroes, West Indians, and Cubans rated Puerto Ricans "high. " Italians rated them "medium. " Others rated them "low. "

Though Puerto Ricans are a mixed race, ranging from blonde to black, the "mainsprings of intergroup tensions in the neighborhood lie between recent Puerto Rican migrants and American Negroes. " Puerto Ricans speak of Negroes as "bad, dangerous, and capable of violence against them. " The Negroes and Puerto Ricans who have lived in the neighborhood for years however "have learned to associate with each other in small groups, become close friends, visit each other, and share in real comradeship. "

In East Harlem the beginnings of a close alliance between Negro and Puerto Rican can be seen, but there is still tension and fear. Many Puerto Rican and Negro parents keep their small children close to home or inside the apartment even in hot summer months. The streets are dangerous, they say; they are filled with youths whose parents do not try or cannot keep them home; they are filled with young men who are too old to be told what to do and who, in their tragic idleness, have a way of teaching "bad things" to the young or getting in trouble with other ethnic groups.

Among Puerto Ricans the family is stressed as the "center of an adult's obligations," while individuality and "doing things just for oneself are discouraged as being of no value."

Success and achievement are encouraged only as ways to help the family. The person who does not succeed can expect help from the family. As one person put it: "A good life is when we work and we have the things we need for all the family." Independence and self-reliance "are not to be encouraged in a child." Good children are defined as "obedient, respectful, and docile."

For recent migrants, prized values are: being a "good" worker, formal schooling, learning English while not forgetting Spanish, desiring "progress" and getting ahead ("get the feet off the dish") especially through the education of children, not letting anyone "take you for a ride," being quiet, being careful in choosing friends, and trusting only a few people.

It is considered an essential quality of a good and worthwhile person that he "have sentiment." Women may express grief by an "attack"--loud screaming, shaking, falling to the floor with arms rigidly extended and hands clenched. Attacks are regarded as a "demonstration of intense grief and great affection for the person in danger." A man is not criticized for crying or having an "ataque."

In El Barrio, says a City Planning Commission report, Puerto Ricans "are extraordinarily gregarious and have greatly suffered the loss of the small shop. The bodega, the barber shop, the small Puerto Rican luncheonette and the township club were and are, in the cases of the few remaining ones, the meeting grounds for Puerto Ricans of all ages."

As a group they would rather take "every precaution to hide and shelter a relative for years than reveal the exact number of occupants in an apartment to a building inspector or landlord."

One young Negro, president of a public housing tenant council in El Barrio, complained that Puerto Ricans are hard to talk to about tenant meetings.

"Fear is everything," he said. "It's the only thing that works. I used to go to their door and they'd close it in my face. Now I canvass with a Puerto Rican fellow and they talk to him. He goes to the door and says: 'Do you want to be shot? Do you want to be robbed? If you don't, you'd better support the tenant's council--because we're going to get rid of crime around here. Otherwise, there's no telling what will happen to you.' He signs them up."

Up farther, in the Triangle, organizers say the few Puerto Ricans there are much easier to organize than Negroes and much less afraid. Perhaps Puerto Ricans living in slum housing are less afraid and feel less strange than those living in new projects.

El Barrio's streets and life are tied into the bloodstream of the city. They are not detachable. Many people do not seem to have this clearly enough in mind; East Harlem seems to them almost a separate duchy, which can go it alone.

Even less clear, and further from view, is the connection of the community with the state and federal systems. In these distant centers most of the strings are pulled that manipulate the lives of slum dwellers.

The neglect of the slum, and discrimination against it, come out of the city's neglect by the state and federal systems. The city, and increasingly its suburbs, stand against the state system, which is controlled by rural and business interests. And, when the "state system" and its political conservatism control the federal system, the city stagnates and suffers. It is always in need of massive transfusions from the federal system. Its own money-raising powers are limited by the state, and contributions from anti-city state legislatures are not generous.

Neglect of the city has spawned East Harlem's slums. It has produced massive pathology in the whole city. The wounds of East Harlem and El Barrio will probably never heal while the city's sores are raw.

Notes

1. Preston Wilcox, "Grassroots Participation, a Step Toward Better Mental Health," Realizing the Mental Health Potentials for Children and Youth in City Living. Proceedings of a conference held by the Manhattan Society for Mental Health, October 2-4, 1961, p. 46.

2. About 50,000 Puerto Ricans are going north each year, but there has in the past few years been a great increase in the number returning. The return migration went up to 33,000 in 1963 and is expected to be over 50,000 in 1964.

   In 1960 Puerto Rican per capita income was just below $700 a year, the highest in Latin America, but less than half that of Mississippi.

   Of new professional jobs created in Puerto Rico between 1955 and 1960 (3,000), 28 per cent were taken by returned migrants. Of 6,000 new merchant and commercial openings, 36 per cent were filled by returnees.

3. New York, Columbia University Press, 1958.

Renato Poblete, "Anomie and the 'Quest for Community': The Formation of Sects Among the Puerto Ricans of New York." American Catholic Sociological Review, 21:18-36, Spring 1960. Reprinted by permission.

Immigration and assimilation of immigrants are sociological processes that have long been part of the American scene and have received their share of attention from sociologists. For some years after 1924, legislation restricting entrance to this country resulted in substantially lessening the importance of these phenomena in our midst. However, in recent years such problems have again come to the fore as a result of political conditions in Europe and the attraction of large numbers of migrants from the Commonwealth of Puerto Rico to the continental United States.

The migration of the Puerto Ricans introduces important new elements into the picture of cultural assimilation. First of all, these arrivals are citizens of the United States. Secondly, they arrive at a time when most other groups whose American origin goes back to a similar immigration experience have advanced far along the path of assimilation to general American culture patterns. Thirdly, despite their American citizenship, the Puerto Rican migrants come from a culture that is quite different from that of the people of the mainland. Thus to the discrimination that such arrivals usually meet is added the note of irony that they are in fact legally citizens of the Republic.

A fourth point is of considerable importance. Earlier immigrants clustered together in communities where adaptation to the new situation was eased by the preservation of important elements of the older culture. As time went on, more extreme ideas of rapid acculturation were replaced by the recognition of the vital role of the immigrant community in avoiding the worst effects of social and personal disorganization in the acculturation process.

"In view of this the concept of cultural pluralism became widely accepted. This helped scholars to recognize the importance of the culture of the immigrant, and to recognize that his loyalties and values and customs should be able to exist in America together with the other culture that we have come to call American."[1]

The Puerto Ricans, however, have been attracted chiefly to the eastern part of the country and in large numbers to New York. In New York City, which is our concern here, the Puerto Ricans have found themselves dispersed into almost every section of the city.

"There are noticeably large concentrations of them in East Harlem, in the South Bronx, on the Lower East Side and in downtown Brooklyn. But in considerable numbers they are scattering into almost every section of the city. This is reflected in the large number of public schools that have Puerto Ricans in attendance in large numbers, and in the parishes, so many of which require the

164

assistance of a Spanish-speaking priest."[2]
    There are many factors which are responsible for this dis-
persal. The city is built up and crowded. Public housing projects
often replace older decaying tenements and disperse forming immigrant communities, and the criteria of admission to such projects
when completed make impossible the development of a Puerto Rican
immigrant community in them.
    "In this situation, it is doubtful whether the Puerto Ricans
will be able to form the type of community which earlier immigrants
formed. If they do, they will have done it in circumstances much
more difficult than those faced by earlier immigrant groups."[3]
    The new arrivals come from a culture that may in certain
respects be called "Catholic" and their reception by co-religionists
here on the mainland is therefore of great significance. The official policy of the Archdiocese of New York has paralleled the conditions we have described. There has been no attempt to set up
national parishes but rather to integrate the Puerto Ricans into the
already existing parish structure. Yet in these circumstances "it is
clearly acknowledged that an intermediate process must take place,
that special services must be provided in Spanish, and opportunity
given for the practice of traditional customs and devotions by the
new parishioners."[4]
    In this situation, then, the new arrivals experience cultural
assimilation, a process that is already begun at home in the Commonwealth, for the island has been a United States possession for
over half a century and the people have enjoyed citizenship for four
decades. English was for a time the standard language of instruction and although that is no longer the case it is a compulsory subject at all levels of the educational system. Moreover, the political and also the business integration of the Commonwealth into the
American community have opened other avenues of acculturation.
    This paper is concerned with one element in that accultura-
tion process, a response to conditions of social and cultural uncertainty in terms of religion. Any visitor to a densely populated
Puerto Rican section of New York City will see a large number of
what are often referred to as "store-front churches." These are
religious groups that use as a place of meeting or worship stores
formerly occupied by retail merchants. In one section in East
Harlem, in 24 blocks (between First and Third Avenues, and between
100th and 105th Streets) there are 30 of these store-front churches.
These sects will be our concern here, more specifically, the Pentecostal Sects or the "Asambleas de Dios."

Protestantism in Puerto Rico

    First of all, however, let us look for a moment at the situ-
ation of Protestantism in Puerto Rico. Protestantism began its
activities in that island about fifty years ago. The World Christian
Handbook for 1952 mentioned 522 areas where Protestant activity
was being carried on. Another publication, Midcentury Pioneers
and Protestants, gives the number of Protestant church members
who are active communicants as 46,433 and the total size of the
Protestant group seems to be about 160,000. The study states that

at least ten per cent of the population could be characterized as
Protestant and "probably eighty per cent of the island population
would say they were Catholics if pressed with the question of religious orientation."[5]   According to a study done at Columbia University in 1948, fifty-three per cent of the 5,000 persons who answered the question claimed that they were "religious in my own
fashion."

Such, then, in so far as we know it, is the religious com-
plexion of the Puerto Rican people before migration.   Largely nominally Catholic, with a strong Catholic group and a minority of Protestants.

Protestantism Among Puerto Ricans in New York

The only information we have of a detailed kind on Protestantism among Puerto Ricans in New York City is found in a report
made by the Church Planning and Research group of the Protestant
Council of Churches of New York City in November, 1953.   The
survey covered 146 non-Roman Catholic churches in the seven areas
of heavy Puerto Rican concentration.   Fifty-four Negro churches re-
sponded saying that they had almost complete lack of contact with
the Puerto Ricans.   Fifteen other non-denominational churches said
that Puerto Ricans were attending their groups and listed a total of
134 active members and 217 who only attend services.   Fifteen of
the 43 denominational churches had no contact at all with the Puerto Ricans in their neighborhoods.   The survey revealed that the
Protestant churches in the communities where Puerto Ricans reside
were doing little to welcome them or to evangelize the "unchurched."
The director of the survey has stated that the non-Spanish-speaking
Protestant churches had only an infinitesimal contact with the Puerto Ricans.[6]   This study is now six years old and the situation in
these respects has changed because of the efforts made in an intense campaign to contact and attract Puerto Ricans, but no statistics are available.   In a study of three Bronx communities[7] completed in November, 1956, we find fifteen per cent of the Puerto
Rican population attending Protestant churches.   The figure under-
estimates the actual state of affairs, since many of the small store-
front churches do not turn in any reports of this kind.

What is the situation of the Spanish-speaking Protestant
churches?   It is in fact quite different.

The 1953 survey quoted above admits that it is almost impossible to arrive at an exact figure of the number of such churches
and of their membership.   It has been possible, the survey states,
to draw up a list containing the names of 204 non-Catholic Spanish-
speaking churches in New York City.   Of these, however, only 169
provided sufficient data to permit meaningful study.   Yet this figure
was three times as large as the number located in 1947 by the
Pathfinder Service.   Despite the inadequacy of statistics, the fact
of growth seems indisputable.

Of these churches reported by the Protestant Council, fifty-
five per cent are classified as Pentecostal, but those listed under
the category of "Independent" appear to be very similar and could
without serious distortion of the situation be added to the total of

the Pentecostal Movement.   That would mean that probably seventy per cent of the Spanish-speaking churches can be classified in the Pentecostal category.   This figure is impressive at first sight and a closer examination of what it involves reveals it to be particular-ly significant.   For it is readily seen that "these two groups--Pente-costals and Independents--are largely a real indigenous expression of Protestant convictions.   They receive no aid from denomination-al agencies...they have a strong evangelical spirit and are willing to work with other Protestant Churches towards a limited number of specific short term goals.   Generally they are reluctant to identi-fy themselves with institutionalized efforts for Protestant coopera-tion."[8]

This striking phenomenon of vitality of the Pentecostal groups among people of a Latin culture is not something confined to New York Puerto Ricans.   In Italy such groups had 120 places of worship in 1944.   Ten years later they had 380 places of wor-ship and comprised sixty per cent of all Protestant churches in the country.[9] In Chile the Pentecostals had around 182,000 adher-ents in 1955.[10]   In fact the Pentecostals are the most numerous and active of all Protestant groups throughout Latin America.

In New York the Pentecostal churches have an average mem-bership of 85 persons while the Independents have an average mem-bership of 67 in each church group.   The store-front churches have very little resemblance to the typical denominational church.   The physical layout consists of a small store which is rented and trans-formed into a single large room with seats similar to those in a theatre.   These seats face what had originally been the rear of the store but is now the front of the church.   Here facing the congre-gation is a pulpit from which the Bible is read.   Behind this, sepa-rated from the church by a curtain, is a small room in which mem-bers can go and pray in solitude and in silence.   This is called the "cuarto alto," the upper room.

The Pentecostal groups are self-starting and self-sustaining. They are evangelical and missionary-minded.   They stress a way of life rather than a creed: the emphasis is on intensity rather than universality and they tend to maintain uncompromisingly radi-cal religious attitudes, demanding from their members the maxi-mum in their relationships to God, to the world and to men.   The moral standards are very high and there is a genuine austerity about their attitudes and patterns of living.   This rigorism often ex-presses itself in external details: no smoking, no consumption of alcohol drink, no use of cosmetics for women.   Membership is available only after a probationary period of from six months to one year and upon public confession of a personal religious experi-ence.   There is a high ratio of lay leadership and responsibility. Tithing is a common practice.   One or two collections at one serv-ice are common. A community with 80 to 100 members supports a full-time minister.   One survey found that of 96 churches reporting, forty-five have full-time pastors, that is to say, serving only one church and having no other employment.   Thirty-six have pastors who work at other jobs during the week and fifteen share a pastor with another church.[11]

Theory on Sect and Church

It is interesting to recall here the classic definitions of sect
and church deriving from the work of Ernst Troeltsch and Max
Weber. Troeltsch declares, in his conclusion to his monumental
study of church and sect in Christian history, that "the history of
the Christian Ethos becomes the story of a constantly renewed
search for...compromise, and of fresh opposition to this spirit of
compromise."[12]   Park and Burgess, Simmel, Von Wiese, Becker,
H. Richard Niebuhr and Liston Pope[13] have elaborated this basic
idea.   For these writers a "church or ecclesia is characterized by
the following: (1) membership on the basis of birth; (2) administration of the means of grace and its sociological and theological con-
comitants--hierarchy and dogma;   (3) inclusiveness of social structure, often coinciding with ethnic or geographical boundaries; (4) orientation to conversion of all; and (5) a tendency to compromise with
the world.   The sect, on the contrary, is characterized by (1) sepa-
ratism and defiance of or withdrawal from the demands of the secular sphere, preferring isolation to compromise; (2) exclusiveness,
expressed in attitude and social structure; (3) emphasis upon conversion prior to membership; and (4) voluntary election or joining."[14]
Moreover, the sect is always ascetic and usually attempts to
implement the "priesthood of believers" in an egalitarian social
structure.   From these definitions it is quite clear that the church
is usually associated with settled cultural and social conditions while
the sect is a response of groups that do not for one reason or another fit into the going institutionalized religious bodies of the larger
society.   H. Richard Niebuhr has shown the social sources of de-
nominationalism to be related to the position of deprived social
classes in the total society and Liston Pope has studied the role of
the sect in the adaptation of rural workers to industrial conditions.

In short, it may be said that the sect represents a response
of the restructuralization of religious attitudes and orientations in a
condition of what Durkheim has called anomie.   For Durkheim anomie was characterized by two interrelated elements.   First of all
there is a breakdown of those social structures in which the individual found the psychological support and nurture requisite to personal
and psychological security.   Secondly, there is a loss of consensus
or general agreement upon the standards and norms that previously
provided the normative orientations and existential definitions in
terms of which individual and group life were meaningful.   Talcott
Parsons has shown that the prevalence of anomie was positively related to rapid social change which brought about social differentia-
tion and the upsetting of old standards and relationships in a changing situation, which prevents the crystallization of new attitudinal
and social structures.

It is quite clear that the Pentecostal groups we have described meet most of the criteria of a sect put forward by the classical definitions.   While the theological aspects of sectarianism are
interesting and important, the sociological level of analysis seems
to offer a more fruitful area of research for a fuller understanding

of what these developments really signify.   Over two decades ago
Christopher Dawson suggested something similar with respect to the
history of the Church.   Said Dawson, "Most of the great schisms
and heresies in the history of the Christian church have their roots
in social and national antipathies, and if this had been clearly recognized by the theologians, the history of Christianity would have been
a very different one. "[15]

The Anomie Hypothesis

On the basis of the information which this preliminary and
exploratory study has provided us so far we can safely conclude
that the rise and development of the Pentecostal movement among
the Puerto Rican migrants in New York represents a typical example
of sectarian formation and development.   That it is a serious religious phenomenon is clear to any informed observer.   Moreover,
historically such a development has been found to be associated with
anomie and to be a form of the recrystallization of attitudes and the
re-formation of solidarity in the face of such anomie.   Since we
are dealing here with people who all the available objective evidence
would suggest are suffering the concomitant anxieties of social and
cultural change encumbent upon migration and assimilation to a new
culture, it seems a fruitful hypothesis to suggest that such movements represent precisely such a reaction to the anomie involved
in migration.
It is necessary to recall that one important aspect of anomie
for Durkheim was the disruption of existing social structures.   Certainly removal to a new city under the conditions of dispersal
would suggest that element in the present case.   Moreover, Parsons, following Max Weber, has suggested that the "process of ration-
alization" by introducing impersonal relationships in the place of the
more personal relationships of the older cultures played an important part in undermining personal securities and contributing to the
anomique condition of the people involved. [16]

Sectarianism: A Response to Anomie

The hypothesis to be explored in the remainder of this paper
may be stated as follows.   The development of sectarianism among
New York Puerto Ricans is a response to anomie.   It is furthermore a response that represents a positive quest for community in
the face of the loss of more traditional social structures and the
impersonalization (universalism and functional specificity, in Parsons' terms) of modern American urban society.
The larger frame of reference in which this problem must be
considered is one that includes western civilization as a whole.
Modern man is haunted by the specter of insecurity in consequence
of the many reasons which we have indicated above.   "There is a
decided weakening of faith in the inherent stability of the individual
and in psychological and moral neutrality; individualism has become
in recent decades a term to describe pathological conditions of society. "[17]   The release of the individual from the traditional ties of

class, religion and kinship has made him free, but on the testimony of innumerable works of our age, this freedom is accompanied not by the sense of creative release, but by the experience of
disenchantment and alienation.   Erich Fromm has shown that it may
be accompanied by intense psychological anxiety.[18]   In fact the
theme of uprooted man seeking fellowship is as frequent in our time
as was the theme of the individual's emancipation from tribal or
communal conformity in the past.   Riesman speaks of a new need
for "other directedness" among Americans, and popular magazines
exploit the theme of "togetherness."[19]   The loss of what Durkheim
called consensus is what Nesbit has called a loss of moral certi-
tudes and is followed by a sense of alienation from one's fellow-
man.[20]   Industrial sociology has shown the importance of the work
community for the morale of the individual workman.   Drucker has
commented upon the "end of the economic man."   Since the larger
framework of human orientation includes what Paul Tillich has
called "the ultimate," that such a loss of solidarity and consensus
has religious significance and that the response to it may take the
form of a religious quest is not difficult to see.

Today there is visible a reaction against the heritage of the
immediate past.   Men seem to be seeking integration, status, membership; there is a desire for recognition, for the formation of
small groups, for personal relationships.   This is a reaction against
the impersonalization of a technological society characterized by ur-
banism.   Toennies saw the history of the West as the transformation of Gemeinschaft into Gesellschaft, what in Redfield's terms
may be called the transition from a folk to an urban society.   Today, American society seems to be reacting in an opposite direction.   The much heralded and quite ambiguous revival of religion
seems to be an associated phenomenon.[21]

If religion appears to offer a way out of this situation--espe-
cially to a people whose cultural background is characterized by
important religious elements--the reverse is also true.   Religious
life requires the support and underpinning of social solidarity.
André Brien emphasizes the need of small communities in order
that Catholic people may be able to live the faith.[22]   He refers to
the proliferation of sects in the popular milieu as a sign of the importance of the formation of small communities in the urban world
of today.   These groups, characterized by enthusiasm in the 18th
century meaning of that term, and sometimes to the point of fanat-
icism, are capable of evoking from the impersonalized man of our
age a spirit of unity and sacrifice.   The intense life of the group
exalts the personality; the person caught up in the current of ir-
resistible enthusiasm discovers in himself a force of life which
previously had lain dormant.   This gives the individual a feeling of
participation and consequently of strength and worth.

The Quest For Community

What we have reviewed so far would suggest that anomie is
a fairly general problem in modern urban society and that reactions
against it--attempts to escape it--are far from uncommon.   We

are suggesting that a similar condition is characteristic of the
Puerto Rican migrants in response to the concrete conditions of
their migration. At this point, in view of our general characteriza-
tion of this phenomenon as a quest for community, it will be helpful to consider recent theoretical discussions of the meaning of that
term among sociologists.

George A. Hillery in his study of areas of agreement in the
definitions of community used in sociological literature states that
"a majority of the definitions include as important elements...: an
area, common ties and social interaction."[23] For MacIver a community is a social unity whose members recognize as common sufficient interest to permit the common activities and interactions of
common life.[24] In his book Society, the same author states that
we have community when the members live their lives wholly within
the general group. He stresses community sentiment as the most
important ingredient of community, since modern transport has
made a territorial base relatively unimportant. For MacIver this
community sentiment has three elements: "we-feeling," that is, a
sense of collective participation in an indivisible unity, a sense of
belonging to the group which can use the term "we" with the same
referent; role feeling, a sense of status which consists in the fact
that each person feels he has a part to perform, a function to fulfill in the reciprocal exchange, involving a subordination of the individual to the whole; and dependency-feeling, closely associated
with role-feeling, involving the individual's feeling of dependency upon the community as a necessary condition for his own life. It involves either physical or psychological dependency since the community is the greater home which sustains him. It is the refuge
from solitude and the fears that accompany the individual isolation
so characteristic of modern life.[25]

Toennies found the supreme form of community in what he
called the "Gemeinschaft of mind" implying "cooperation and coordi-
nated action for a common goal."[26] August R. Hollingshead concluded that the term community was defined in at least three different ways in current literature: (a) as a form of group solidarity,
cohesion and action around common and diverse interests; (b) as a
geographic area with spatial limits; or (c) as a socio-geographical
structure which combines the first two definitions.[27]

The elements of these classical and contemporary definitions
of most concern to us would appear to be those stressed in Toennies' Gemeinschaft of mind and MacIver's community sentiment and
represented in other terms in the other definitions.

A Test of the Anomie Hypothesis

Let us restate our hypothesis more fully at this point: The
formation of sects is one of the known ways out of anomie, and the
facts of Puerto Rican life in New York suggest the presence of
such a condition among these new arrivals. The sect represents a
search for a way out of that condition and is therefore an attempt
to redevelop the community in the new urban situation.

In attempting to explore this hypothesis and to prepare for
some kind of observational testing of it, a small area in the South-

ern Bronx was studied.   This area coincides with St. Athanasius
Roman Catholic Parish.   In this area we were able to locate ten
store-front churches and two larger churches of the same type,
the Christian Church of Juan 3:16, at Westchester Avenue, and the
Independent church, Iglesia del Señor, with characteristics quite
like those of the Pentecostals.

These store-front churches did not have more than 60 members each.   They have almost daily meetings with an attendance of
half to two-thirds of the membership present.   It is quite difficult
to get reliable figures on the exact membership since there are always some visitors at the services who either come from other
store-front churches or who may be just curious outsiders.   Each
evening's services are organized by a different sub-group, the
men's group, the women's group, or the youth group.   The service
begins around eight o'clock in the evening and lasts until around
ten.   When a stranger attends he is greeted immediately, given a
song-book and offered a seat.   The amount of cordiality shown to
the visitor is remarkable to the field worker.   The minister or
some person from the congregation reads the Bible and explains
what has been read.   Accompanying the words of the speaker there
gradually develops a kind of spontaneous participation by the congregation.   This takes the form of spontaneous ejaculations such as
Amen, Alleluia, Gloria a Dios, Gloria à Jesus, Dios todopoderoso,
and Alabado Dios.   In this way the group actively participates even
in that part of the service in which a leader has the structured
ascendancy and initiative.

After the sermon, which is punctuated by such exclamations
from the congregation, the whole community sings.   Some of the
melodies are old American folk songs with special religious Spanish
text or are translated Protestant hymns.   Frequently somebody
volunteers to sing a solo or to play an instrument.   The minister
during this period invites people to speak a few words or relate
their own religious experience or the history of their conversion.
Some members of the congregation express gratitude for some favors received, or ask for prayers for some need.   This is followed
by more singing.

Then plans for evangelical work are proposed or reports of
current activities are heard.   At the end everybody prays in a loud
voice and spontaneously.   One can feel the enthusiasm and desire
for the Spirit in the group.   At times an individual manifests the
reception of the Holy Spirit by "speaking with tongues."   When that
happens the members begin to shout incoherently or just to utter
words.   The speech of the person who has the gift of tongues may
be "interpreted" by another member.   Then the members of the
community thank God and pray that all may receive these gifts.

On Sunday, service lasts for two hours.   Here the minister,
either the regular minister or a guest, will have a more important
role.   He will give instruction to the people on the Bible or upon
moral precepts.

In addition to using what sociologists call "participant observation" of these groups, ministers and members were interviewed.
We were able to interview 28 persons.   The interviews were conducted in Spanish by the field worker, for whom Spanish is his

native language. All but three of the twenty-eight were baptized
Catholics. Yet these 25 did not have any real knowledge of the
Catholic Church. There appeared to be no ground to assume that
their conversion was in any intellectual sense a protest against the
Catholic Church. The element of protest was not important in what
they reported about themselves. Moreover, the interviews revealed
that their knowledge of the ideology of the sect was rudimentary.
The Bible is held to be the only norm of life, a point of view that
involves a very fundamentalistic interpretation of the "Word." They
all hold that we have been redeemed by Christ's death. They hold
the importance of two baptisms, one of water and one of the spirit.
There is much emphasis upon a total way of life involving brotherly
love and the rejection of sin. There is no systematic doctrinal
body of beliefs.

The people interviewed talked very frankly about their conversion. They consider the frank revelation of the history of their
conversion as a "testimony": bearing of witness to the Holy Spirit.
The form of such testimonies shows that despite the spontaneity of
communal religiosity there is a degree of stereotyping. It would
appear that each convert has heard many testimonies and makes the
attempt to interpret and fit in his own experience into a normative-
ly desired pattern. They usually go in this way. "I used to drink
...I was a drug addict...I used to run around with women...I was
on the wrong path...but one day I received the Spirit, I got to know
the 'Word.' " They always attribute a great sinfulness to their
previous life. The form of the testimony emphasizes a great experience of sinfulness and the religious experience of being possessed by the Spirit. And the latter appears to give them a certi-
tude of regeneration.

The formal "design" of the testimony reveals consciousness
of sinfulness--conversion--regeneration. While this is not a spontaneous product of subjective personal disposition unaffected by social conformation to an expected pattern, there is reason to suspect
that subjective experience lent itself readily to such conformation.
That is to say, while these testimonies may be elicited in an interview situation without any direction suggested by the interviewer,
the sectarian expectations do in fact act to standardize them. Yet
they also seem to reflect something important of the experience of
conversion which seems in itself (as well as in its retelling) to have
been shaped for subjective awareness by the sectarian stereotype.
Moreover, the original need dispositions of the subjects appear to
have lent themselves to precisely this kind of standardization. Although it would be very difficult to separate the elements analytically and perhaps impossible to observe them empirically, there appears a measure of congruence between the "primitive" experience
and the content of the sectarian stereotype. This bears obvious resemblance to the general sectarian conviction of regeneration and to
that aspect of the world religions that Max Weber referred to in his
treatment of "salvation religions." These people feel saved from
something and incorporated into something new and clean and good.

Conversion--the classical phenomenon of religious psychol-
ogy--is something that follows upon some months of attending services as spectators. When the interviewees were asked why they

first became interested in the sect, their answers also revealed a
degree of uniformity, and possibly one less affected by a cultural
stereotype. "The first time I went there, I was impressed by the
way everyone shook hands with me and the way everybody said
'hello' to me." "I was sick, they came to my home to say a
prayer for me." "I used to go to the Catholic Church, there nobody knew me ...now in my church they call me sister." A very
typical answer was "Me senti como en mi casa." (I felt at home.)
"I was lost here in New York, a friend invited me and I like the
way they sang and that we all could sing." "I like to read the
Bible." "The first time I went, when the service was over, someone came to me and asked my name and invited me to come again."
Participant observation at the meetings confirms the interpretation
of warmth, welcome, and participation related by the converted.

The interviews strongly suggest that isolation is one of the
things from which such people are saved by the salvation experience
of conversion. Isolation appears to be associated with a loss of orientation in life. Thus the material offered by those interviewed
would tend to support the contention that conversion offered a way
out of anomie, both in terms of providing social relationships and
giving meaningful orientations to the converted.

That the sect is a real community according to those elements stressed in the sociological literature is confirmed by both
the content of the interviews and participant observation. For example the three elements of community sentiment stressed by Mac-
Iver are present to a high degree in the Pentecostal sect.

The presence of "we-feeling" is clearly evident in the way
members talk about the sect. The church to which they belong is
not something foreign or removed from them. The service is a
common enterprise; the members support the group with great financial generosity; there is a real conviction of membership in a
brotherhood. They all know each other by name: "hermano Juan,"
"hermana Maria," etc.

"Role-feeling" is also quite evident. Each member has a
role in the community and so marked is such participation that one
report concluded that "it is hard to know to what degree we can call
these churches a lay association."[28] The individual member has
opportunities to direct the service, to tell his troubles, to recount
his religious experiences, to ask for prayers and to give thanks for
prayers said, or to ask for help. The members not only participate in religious services in this way but also take part in such
work as visiting the sick. The minister of the East Harlem Protestant Parish, a parish divided into five small communities following
the example of l'Abbe Michoneau in France, stated to us that the
activity of the layman was in his opinion the clue to the success of
these Protestant sects.

Moreover, MacIver's feeling of dependency is also present.
Each person knows that he is a part of the group, that he needs the
group in order to sustain his regeneration. He feels this dependency at the service when the minister asks the names of those who
are sick, or the names of those whose birthdays fall in the coming
week. If a person give his name, the whole community prays for
him.

It is important to note that the group solidarity appears to the converted not as a loss of individuality but rather as a chance to develop his own personality--to experience a worthwhile fulfillment.

One indication of what has been said concerns the question of size. It would seem that such close in-group sentiment requires small groups and that a larger membership would inevitably introduce secondary relationships with concomitant impersonalization. In this respect it was interesting to find in the area of our study a large Pentecostal church with a membership of 800. This church had been founded in 1935 and began, as all such groups begin, as a small group with a small meeting place. By 1954, it had grown to 500 members and was able to purchase for $70,000 a reconditioned theatre with a seating capacity of 1,800. Now two full-time ministers care for the community. At their weekly meetings they have between 200 and 300 persons. Though this figure in comparison with that of the total membership suggests a lower degree of participation, it is nevertheless remarkable to find there all the characteristics we found in the smaller bodies. H. Richard Niebuhr has developed the Troeltschian theory to show that sects in time also have to make some kind of compromise with the world in which they live and become routinized. Such a routinized sect he calls a denomination. This larger group in our area does not in the opinion of the observer show any impressive signs of such routinization, but our research has not proceeded far enough to answer the important questions in this respect.

While we do not consider our hypothesis unambiguously confirmed at this stage of the game, we do feel entirely justified in stating that a hypothesis based upon such a firm body of sociological theory as this one is provides a very helpful device for understanding the phenomenon with which we are dealing. Moreover, the evidence to date does bear a striking congruence with the hypothesis itself. Since the hypothesis is based upon a body of theory that has considerable congruence with religious life as it has been studied in a multitude of different concrete settings, the congruity of our preliminary material with it gives us greater confidence than would be the case were our hypothesis merely an ad hoc construction unrelated to a larger body of theory and empirical generalization.

Theoretical Suggestions

Following this provisory and tentative confirmation of our hypothesis several questions of importance arise in addition to the need for more data on the points discussed above. Many of them cannot be answered definitively by this study even when it is completed, but what we have uncovered so far makes their formulation possible and worthwhile.

1. Why do some people form specifically religious groups as a way out of anomie?

Some suggestions might be made here in relation to the general religious culture from which these people come. The Pentecostals bear a strong resemblance--and possibly an obscure his-

torical relationship--to the Joachimite enthusiasm of the Middle Ages.
First of all, there is the emphasis upon the Holy Spirit. Secondly,
while the Joachimites expected the "rule of monks" in a third age
of the world, the Pentecostals are in a certain sense monks in the
world. Moreover, during the ages when religion was a dominant
element in the culture of the West in a sense that has long ceased
to be the case, many movements of social and even political
significance found expression in religious forms and with a religious ideology, for example, the followers of Thomas Münzer in
the German Peasant War. With secularization, such movements
found socialistic or syndicalistic forms for expression. Certainly,
the Communist Parties in their period of revolutionary opposition
offer an analogue to the sect in the sphere of political life, while
their becoming a ruling core of functionaries after they take power
shows structural and functional equivalents to the transformation of
a sectarian movement into a church. The Social Democratic Parties appear in many ways similar to denominations, with sectarian
traditions accommodated to the present in a practical way. The
Puerto Ricans, despite the remoteness of institutional Catholicism
from many of their needs, would appear to come from a cultural
situation more like that of Europe before secularization had proceeded very far, than like the culture of urban workers in Europe
today. Hence their needs for orientation and personal security take
on a religious form of expression and become a religious need.

2. If anomie is a result of migration, how do we explain
the success of Pentecostal groups in Puerto Rico and in other Latin
countries as well?

One might suggest that the relation of the institutional church
to the needs of people in certain conditions of life in these countries is worth a good deal of study. It appears that institutional
Catholicism fails to meet these needs and hence people turn elsewhere. The gap between them and the Church would appear to leave
a void that involves some aspects of anomie. Yet the Church has
kept them sufficiently Christian in their outlook so that they seek
the answer in a Christian idiom.

3. How long does regeneration last? What about backslid-
ing?

We have no real information on this important point. Back-
sliding has been an important and ubiquitous phenomenon in American Protestant revivalism, from which the term derives.

4. What are the sociological concomitants of the need for
salvation, or as our interviewees express it, the sense of sinfulness?

Certainly isolation and the concomitant loss of meaningful
orientation are important in this respect. But much more needs to
be known. Certain conditions of life predispose people to certain
needs and attitudes. Which of these are found associated with the
sense of sin?

5. Do social mobility, status, and class, play a role in
these sectarian movements? Does the frugal life of the sectary lead
to worldly success as has so often happened with such groups?
Does regeneration withstand worldly success?

We have as yet no information on these questions.

6. What about the suggested congruence between the stero-
type of sinfulness--conversion--regeneration and the "primitive" experience of needing to be saved from something?

This question is largely a problem for religious psychology,
but it is also important to the sociology of religion, for such experiences bear a relationship to socially structured and shared conditions. For, they are in part at least a response to anomie.

Notes

1. Joseph P. Fitzpatrick, "The Integration of Puerto Ricans,"
   Thought, XXX, No. 118, (Autumn 1955), p. 406.

2. Ibid., p. 413.

3. Ibid., p. 415.

4. Ibid., pp. 415-416.

5. Meryl Ruoss, Midcentury Pioneers and Protestants. A survey
   report of the Puerto Rican migration to the U.S. mainland
   and in particular a study of Protestant expression among
   Puerto Ricans in New York City, Department of Church
   Planning and Research, Protestant Council of the City of
   New York, (New York, 1954), Second Edition, p. 2.

6. Ibid., p. 14.

7. Morrisania, Melrose, Mott Haven, Three Bronx Communities.
   Prepared by Department of Church Planning and Research,
   Protestant Council of the City of New York, (November
   1956), p. 3.

8. Midcentury Pioneers, p. 16.

9. Revista Del Clero Italiano, Rome, (February 1950).

10. Ignacio Vergara, "Los Evangelicos in Chile," Revista Mensaje,
    Santiago, Chile, (August 1955).

11. Midcentury Pioneers, p. 22.

12. Ernst Troeltsch, The Social Teachings of the Christian Church-
    es, Olive Wyon (London and New York: George Allen and
    Unwin, Ltd. and The Macmillan Company, 1931), II, pp.
    999-1,000.

13. Cf. Robert E. Park and Ernest W. Burgess, Introductory to
    the Science of Sociology, (Chicago: University of Chicago
    Press, 1921), pp. 50, 202-3, 611-2, 657, 870-4. Howard
    Becker, Systematic Sociology: On the Basis of the "Bezie-
    hungslehre und Gebildelehre" of Leopold von Wiese: Adapted
    and Amplified. (New York: John Wiley and Sons, 1932),

pp. 624-8. H. Richard Niebuhr, The Social Sources of De-
nominationalism, (New York: Henry Holt and Company,
1929), pp. 17 ff. And Liston Pope, Millhands and Preachers,
A Study of Gastonia, (New Haven: Yale University Press,
1942).

14. Thomas F. O'Dea, "Mormonism and the Avoidance of Sectarian
Stagnation: A Study of Church, Sect, and Incipient Nationality," The American Journal of Sociology, LX, (November
1954), 286.

15. Christopher Dawson, "Sociology as a Science," quoted from the
republication in Cross Currents, IV, No. 2 (Winter 1954),
136.

16. Talcott Parsons, Essays in Sociological Theory, (Glencoe, Illinois: The Free Press, 1954), especially "Democracy and
Social Structure in Pre-Nazi Germany," pp. 104-23 and
"Some Sociological Aspects of Fascist Movements," pp. 124-
41.

17. Robert A. Nesbit, The Quest for Community, (New York: Oxford University Press, 1953), p. 7.

18. Erich Fromm, Escape from Freedom, (New York: Farrar and
Rinehart, 1941).

19. David Riesman, The Lonely Crowd, (New Haven: Yale University Press, 1950).

20. Nesbit, op. cit., p. 11.

21. Will Herberg, Protestant, Catholic, Jew, (Garden City, New
York: Doubleday, 1955).

22. André Brien, "Les petits communautes soustenance de la Foi,"
Etudes, Paris, Vol. 279, (November 1953), 168-86.

23. George A. Hillery, "Definitions of Community: Areas of Agreement," Rural Sociology, XX, (June 1955), 111-123.

24. R.M. MacIver, Community, (New York: The Macmillan Company, 1936), pp. 110-31.

25. R.M. MacIver and Charles H. Page, Society, (New York:
Farrar and Rinehart, Inc., 1939), p. 293.

26. Ferdinand Toennies, Fundamental Concepts of Sociology, tr.
Charles Loomis, (New York: Monthly Review Press, 1940),
p. 40.

27. A.B. Hollingshead, "Community Research: Development and Present Condition," American Sociological Review, XIII, (April 1948), 136-46.

28. Midcentury Pioneers, p. 20.

The Puerto Rican does not see the cop as a friend. He does not feel he can come to the station house for help. To him, the cop is someone who is there to oppress him.--A Puerto Rican leader.

When a policeman comes into an area and he is feared, he can understand that, even though he doesn't like it. But when he is not only feared but hated, then, being human, he sometimes responds in kind--with hatred. --A Police Department official.

Bitter comments like these, made to this reporter, suggest the extent of the gap in human relations between Puerto Rican Americans and the police of this city. Such tensions are not new; in any major city, a minority group, with strange language and customs, tends to stand out from the dominant groups. What is new is that, as a Puerto Rican civil rights expert put it, the Spanish-speaking people in New York "have ceased to sleep" and are reacting angrily to alleged prejudice and brutality on the part of the police.

The tensions erupted into violence last November on Manhattan's West Side after two Puerto Ricans, Victor Rodriguez and Maximo Salero, were shot to death by a policeman in a radio car. The police were taking the men to a station house for booking on a charge of disorderly conduct. They allege that Rodriguez shot at them from the back seat, and that they reacted in self-defense. Scores of Puerto Ricans and sympathizers thought otherwise. They picketed the station house to protest the killings, and marched down Broadway, stopping traffic, in a mood described as ugly and near-riotous.

The two policemen were transferred out of the area. But even while their case was before a grand jury, another killing of a Puerto Rican by the police, on the East Side of Manhattan, again inflamed the Spanish people. Francisco Rodriguez Jr., 18, who had been named a "Boy of the Year" in 1962, was shot dead by an off-duty policeman who said that Rodriguez had slashed his jacket with a knife when he tried to end a scuffle. Puerto Rican Americans picketed the East Side station house, shouting "Assassins!" at the police.

Gilberto Gerena-Valentin, a leader of the new National Association for Puerto Rican Civil Rights, charged that the police were acting as if they were "running a plantation." He did not criticize

180

police officials or the captains of precincts--but Police Commissioner Murphy reacted sharply to what he called the "false sympathy" of
some newspapers for the dead youth. He asked at a press conference: "Shall the police take action (when attacked) or call a psychiatrist? Make up your minds."

What is responsible for this gap in human relations between
the Puerto Ricans and the police? There are a record 25,929 men
on the force today, and in most communities the blue-clad officers
symbolize protection. "But it is also a fact," said a recent editorial in El Diario-La Prensa of New York, "that the police in the
Spanish-speaking neighborhoods...are not seen in this light."

The viewpoints of the Puerto Rican Americans and of the
police are set out clearly in the neighborhood where the two prison-
ers were killed in the radio car: the 24th Precinct of Manhattan's
Upper West Side.

The area, 29.7 miles of streets, from 86th to 110th Streets,
and from the Hudson River to Central Park West, holds 138,190
people--more than many American cities. Wedged in close proximity are 74,693 whites; 49,794 Puerto Rican Americans; 11,987
Negroes; 1,716 "others" (Japanese, Cubans, Indians, etc.)

Once part of historic Bloemendael, or vale of flowers, the
area was, said Washington Irving, "in a sweet rural valley, beautiful with many a bright flower." Edgar Allan Poe often came to the
riverside, to meditate alone for hours. Now neither the riverside
nor Central Park is safe for meditators after dark.

Families range from the poor, many of them existing on welfare payments, to the upper middle-class on West End Avenue and
Central Park West--with very little communication between the two
extremes. A new middle-income housing complex, Park West Village, maintains a private police force, complete with dogs. The
Village forms an odd conclave in the tenement section, abutting
Douglass Houses, a low-cost city housing project.

The large majority of the people are hardworking and law-
abiding and rarely come in contact with the police. But this is also one of the city's 25 high-hazard areas. Some crime figures
give the size of the police problems:

	1962	1963
Murder	9	15
Rape	50	40
Grand larceny	1,213	1,669
Grand larceny (auto)	255	263
Felonious assault	613	498
Narcotics arrest (felony)	101	109
Possession of dangerous weapons	14	21

Of half a dozen youth gangs in the area, two are "boppers"
(fighters). Narcotics addicts clutter sidewalks, entrance halls and
bars--scatter when the police come, only to return when the police
depart. Shopkeepers bitterly complain that business suffers because
"people won't come out at night for fear of the muggings."

The police of the 24th clearly have to face tough and unusual
conditions; in fact, they are saturating "sectors within sectors"
where danger threatens. But over the years, the 24th has also

earned a dubious reputation for roughness.

A police precinct is commanded by a captain, who is, in effect, the chief of police in his area. Here at the 24th he commands 255 patrolmen and 18 sergeants. This is conceded to be a "trial precinct"--that is, a proving ground for captains who expect to become inspectors. Thus the turnover in captains at the 24th tends to be high--with some six or eight different captains in the past five years. Civic workers in the area cynically comment that "captains bucking to be inspectors" have been more interested in arrests than in people.

A precinct spokesman, for example, refers with pride to a patrolman's "reputation for good arrests" built, last year, on 16 felony and 15 "other" arrests. When a visitor asks, "What about a reputation for good community relations?" he answers with a rueful smile: "That's a gossamer."

It is this "gossamer" that many Puerto Rican Americans feel must be replaced with the sturdier stuff of daily effort by certain policemen to live up to their code of ethics.

Few Puerto Ricans interviewed by this reporter tar all policemen with the same brush. Several praised the "good things" that a particular officer had done for their families or children. But many were resentful of "certain cops" who constantly harass them, bully or sneer at them, and, in short, have no respect for them as persons and Americans.

Puerto Rican skepticism about the police goes far back. Some decades ago, there was a universally hated cop named O'Hara, notorious for "beating you up first, then asking questions." Over the years, his name became synonymous for "police"--as La Hara or la jara.

Even today, when a newcomer from Puerto Rico gets on the witness stand in Criminal Court, he frequently begins his testimony with, "When la jara came in..." Often the judge will ask for the meaning of la jara, and the court translator will automatically reply: "The police."

But Puerto Ricans in the 24th will not name the policemen they complain of, nor will they take their grievances to the station house, because, they say, they fear retaliation if they speak up.

"They have discrimination for the Puerto Ricans," a Columbus Avenue shopkeeper says. "I used to work in New Jersey, and the same cop saw me every day. He used to stop me and asked me for my identification every time. Would he do that to an 'American'?"

A young laundry worker says bitterly: "I live around the corner. Me and my friends stand talking on the street and the cop comes to me and pushes me like this, with his stick. 'I'm coming back in a minute,' he says, 'and if you're still here, I'm gonna arrest.' I try to explain that I live at this corner. He say, 'I can't listen to you, you damn spick, move.' I go into my house, but I feel bad."

A Puerto Rican mother of three, living in the 80's, says: "They make many brutalities here. Now they kill another Puerto Rican. I don't feel right with the police. I am afraid. I don't think he is my friend, the police."

Many Puerto Rican businessmen in the area feel that they receive "Sunday summonses" (for opening their shops) while non-Puerto Ricans are bypassed. Others are known to pay graft to be allowed to open on Sundays.

"You stop around here on Sundays and watch the cops going to the Spanish stores on Columbus," a shopkeeper says. "They don't go to the American stores for the money and cigarettes, because the Americans know they're not supposed to give nothing to the cops. Only the Puerto Ricans. Because the Spanish people are afraid. I don't want to give names. I don't have much in my store, but they might come and break my windows if I tell."

Perhaps above all, the Puerto Ricans resent police snooping at their private functions. Not long ago, members of a "home town" club met one Sunday afternoon to celebrate a religious holiday. They sang songs, exchanged gifts, ate such Spanish delicacies as coconut rice and served beer. Nothing was sold. A plainclothesman walked in. When some beer was offered to him, he demanded to "see your license to sell beer." Hotly informed that no beer was being sold, he walked off--but his snooping had dampened the occasion. The people felt that the intrusion had happened only because they were Puerto Ricans. They carried the grudge home with them.

As Oscar Gonzales Suarez, a criminal lawyer, puts it: "Even though we come here as American citizens, many policemen look on us as aliens. We resent this. We feel their contempt in the discourtesies and harassments."

For their part, the police in the area reflect bitterness and some bewilderment. Several point out that, as a new minority, many Puerto Ricans "go around with a chip on their shoulders, more than anyone else," and that they "don't understand the role of the police."

"They don't seem to know," says one spokesman, "that the laws are laid down by the Legislature, and that the police must enforce the laws. Because they're unhappy with the bad housing, the rats and the slumlords, they take it out on us."

There are streets in the area that police frankly fear to walk on. They have to threaten landlords with summonses unless they clear off the rocks and bottles that youths have stockpiled on the roofs. The Police Youth Squad had to be called to remove "Molotov cocktails" (bottles containing inflammable liquid) from one rooftop.

Patrolman Charles Connolly on his night beat says: "The average Puerto Rican worker respects us. There is only a small segment of any group which has no respect for law and order.

"But I feel that the Spanish people don't have a full conception of what they're expected to do as citizens. For instance, we frown on the drinking of beer and wine in the streets. If we point out that it's a violation, they resent being told not to do it. This sort of thing causes friction."

Patrolman Fred Schiele puts in: "If I ever lock someone up, it's because he's a criminal and not because he's a Puerto Rican or anything else." Another young patrolman says, with a shrug: "I

don't have problems. I just lock them up if they refuse to move."
      The language barrier gives both sides trouble, but, the
police aver, the Puerto Ricans often use it to "clam up" or "feign
a lack of understanding" which obstructs police work. The police
blotter shows an increasing number of "1851's" and "1825's"--
charges of interference with arrest, or with a police officer acting
in his official capacity. "This," says Capt. David Fallek, who was
given command of the 24th last May, "should be of more concern to
the public than to the police, since it indicates that the people don't
care."
      Perhaps no one in the 24th is more sensitive on the subject
of civil rights and respect for minorities than Captain Fallek.
"And it's not only because I'm a cop," he says.
      A World War II veteran who holds a law degree (earned at
night) from Brooklyn Law School, Captain Fallek, now 49, has been
with the force for 21 years. He is prominent in American Jewish
Congress affairs in Brooklyn, where he lives with his wife and
three children. His bulking (5-foot-11) figure is familiar throughout the precinct, since he goes on patrol every day ("You can't run
a precinct sitting behind a desk"). These days his reflective manner is edged with worry. The grand-jury findings might touch off
another riot, unless human relationships in the area are vastly improved.
      In his small office in the modern station house on West
100th Street, Captain Fallek examines clip boards marked "Vice &
Gambling," "Work Chart," "Youth Gang Data." To the First Pla-
toon, lined up at 12:01 a.m. for a briefing before its eight-hour
tour of duty, he says grimly:
      "You all know what's going on in the country on civil rights.
You will enforce the law impartially, regardless of race, color or
creed--because it is individuals and not the Puerto Rican people
who are responsible for crimes. I want you to remember that
Police Commissioner Murphy has said that the concept of equality
is the fundamental characteristic of professional police service."
      He pauses to take off his black horn-rimmed glasses, then
he goes on in even tones to brief his men on current crime problems: "I want you to watch the degenerates and the homosexuals.
Lock them up if they're in the park after 12. We've done pretty
well on burglary arrests, but burglaries have been increasing.
Broadway still has the prostitutes. Keep them moving. And narcotics is still the big problem. If you get a pusher, you'll be rewarded with a day off."
      The men march out to their posts. The captain changes in-
to a business suit and follows them, first in a squad car, then, in
the 90's, on foot along Broadway. The movie houses and shops are
closed and dark, but a sandwich bar is brightly lighted. Captain
Fallek glares morosely at the stream of prostitutes, deviates and
junkies--white, Negro and Puerto Rican--flowing in and out of the
place. He and his men serve a health-violation summons on the
owner, who weeps, "It's driving me out of my mind." Whether the
tears are caused by the clientele or the summons is not clear.
      Later, Captain Fallek says acidly: "We are educating our
cops. My question is: Who is educating the Puerto Ricans as to

their responsibilities as citizens? I keep telling the cops how to
get along. Who is teaching the Spanish people? If they're hurt, if
they're bleeding, if there's a fire, if a kid is hit by a car, do we
ask: 'Is he a Puerto Rican?' We do our job impartially. Then
again, what rights have we got? Have I got the right as a cop to
make an arrest without being assaulted?"

The tensions that have been growing between Puerto Ricans
and police throughout the city have stirred leaders on both sides to
action. Deputy Police Commissioner Walter Arm, proud of his
citation from the New York Hispanic Press for his "human concepts,"
has ordered "every cop on the beat" to improve relations. Top police officials are meeting with Puerto Rican leaders to consider a
"task force" that would confer on any situation in which trouble is
brewing. Additionally, captains of all precincts have been told to
reach Puerto Rican leaders at the grassroots, "to try to build relations and improve the police image."

Puerto Rican leaders themselves have offered a 10-point program to the Police Department, because, as Gerena-Valetin puts
it, "they must show faith that they want to work with us." At the
top of the list is a request for a permanent grievance board of civic leaders, such as Philadelphia has, with no former policemen
among its members since their orientation would be unsatisfactory.

Another suggestion is for a citywide committee to meet monthly with the police to examine ways of improving relationships.

In the 24th, one sees the beginnings of such a dialogue taking shape. With Andres Gonzalez, director of a travel agency,
Captain Fallek talks community relations. At the time of the November riots, Gonzalez helped the captain to calm the crowds.
Now Gonzalez, a short, mild and candid man says: "There is a
grudge against the police, but it can be solved with better communication."

The captain urges his cooperation in forming a neighborhood
group to "come and see me personally with any problems they
have." Gonzalez agrees this is essential, adding: "I don't want
Joe Blow from Brooklyn coming into this area again to exploit the
feelings here." (During the November unrest, malcontents from
other areas infested the 24th, distributing circulars that described
the police as "murderers.")

Fallek asks how the police can be of "special help," and
Gonzalez replies earnestly: "I'm telling you as a friend, Captain,
that the Puerto Ricans don't want special favors. They want only
to be seen as one more minority who, however, are Americans.
Their problems should not be separated from the problems of all
minorities."

Later, in a neighborhood school, Captain Fallek meets with
a panel on civil rights. It includes members of the clergy, the
Mayor's office, settlement houses and ordinary folk of the area.
Occasionally, tempers flare. When one Puerto Rican leader excori-
ates police methods--not only in the 24th, but in general--a young
mother speaks up quietly:

"We all have to face the fact that poor people everywhere
are afraid of the police for all sorts of reasons. On some blocks,
it is the poor Puerto Ricans. On others, it is the poor Negroes.

On others it is the poor whites.   The fear, valid or not, is something that is always with the poor.   It is not just a Puerto Rican
problem."

People of goodwill on both sides believe that progress is being made now, if only because the dialogue has begun in earnest.
But many students of the scene believe that much of the trouble
stems from a basic problem.   The city is still frustrated in its
long-range objective--to develop a truly professional police force in
which officers will be skilled also in such areas as foreign languages, the law and sociology.

The Police Academy, which trains recruits, emphasizes good
human relationships.   Various lessons bring up concepts of equality,
personal dignity and the golden rule.   Anthony F. Marra, chief at-
torney for the criminal division of the Legal Aid Society, said recently, "The patrolmen and detectives of today are more intelligent
and of a higher caliber than those of years ago."

But the education of most policemen is limited to four years
of high school or its equivalent.   Few speak or understand Spanish.
The Academy--and the precinct stations--use few civilian social scientists, social workers, psychologists or the like in their training
programs.   Indeed, at the Police Academy, one finds an ambivalent
attitude.   "I have no objection to the civilian," said one spokesman,
"but I don't feel it's necessary."

But Captain Fallek, who must see that his men translate the
Academy's theories and the new headquarters' directives on the
streets of New York, says bluntly: "I think outside help would be
beneficial.   I don't see any harm coming out of using this professional help from civilians.   I would accept help from any such area
or school or community center."

With tensions in some areas boiling over alleged injustices,
the road ahead is not going to be easy.   Perhaps Patrolman Ernest
Malara has the best answer for both sides.

Of Italian background, this youthful, prematurely gray officer
in the 24th, who learned Spanish "by picking it up from the people,"
is so admired by the families on his beat that he is known as the
caballero blanca--"the white-haired gentleman."   At playtime in the
Sol Bloom Elementary School, the Puerto Rican children plow into
him for attention, trying to touch his badge.   Their mothers smile
with pleasure as he answers questions in Spanish.   What is his approach after eight years in this precinct?

"I respect them and they respect me," he says.   "They feel
that I'm here for one reason--to protect their life and their property.   I speak their language, not fluently but enough to get a smile
when I want it.   This is a strange country to them.   They don't
know our ways.   I see it as part of my job to have a helping attitude."

Piri Thomas, "Nightmare in Mi Barrio." New York Times
Magazine, August 13, 1967, p. 16-17. Copyright (c) by
The New York Times Company. Reprinted by permission.

I had left Spanish Harlem early Sunday, July 23, for Lancaster, Pa., to give a seminar and class in creative writing for
underprivileged teen-agers at Franklin and Marshall College. As
I rode the train, I was digging a Life magazine that I had bought.
I guess I must have made a face at the stories describing the rioting in Newark. I decided to "turn off"all this bad news and put my
mind to what I was going to talk about to these kids--like a sense
of their being able to create beauty instead of ugliness and for
them to be able to develop their minds for a sense of harmony instead of disorder.

I arrived in Lancaster and was met at the train by Vinie
Burrows, a beautiful and talented Negro actress, who is a drama
director at Franklin and Marshall, and her husband, Dean, a community worker who had lived through the Newark nightmare. We
chatted happily and yet in our minds and hearts, as in those of
most Americans, we were deeply concerned with the hell that has
been breaking out across this great land.

That night, after chapel, I showed the youngsters a film
called "Petey and Johnny," produced by Time-Life and Bob Drew
Associates and shot on location in Spanish Harlem. It showed
something of life in the ghetto, its violence, its street gangs, and
the work I had done as a street worker with several of the toughest
gangs.

Sunday night and Monday morning I purposely did not read
any newspaper or listen to the radio. Monday afternoon I had to
return to Spanish Harlem to give my weekly class as "author in
residence" at the East Harlem Protestant Parish. At the railroad
station in Lancaster, I picked up a newspaper and felt my skin grow
cold and every damn hair on my body literally stand on end. "My
God, it's hit my Barrio. My people are rioting! No lo creo" ("I
don't believe it"). But there it was, black on white, Puerto Ricans
rioting in El Barrio--the District--Spanish Harlem.

It was now 3 o'clock in the afternoon and I was still in Lancaster. The train was late in coming, adding to my sense of frustration. I called Fay Edwards at the East Harlem Protestant Parish and she said the youngsters in the creative writing class had
been told to stay at home that night since big trouble was expected.
I didn't know what I was going to do in Harlem to help call off the
hell that it was going through. I just knew that I had to be there.

I arrived in New York and immediately called up some of
my boys who work with different antipoverty agencies. "Caramba,
man," I said. "What the hell's happened?"

187

"Some cats decided to call it on," was the reply. "Come
on down. You ain't going to stop it but come on down anyway."
"Man, how bad is it?"
"Baby, they threw bottles at Herman Badillo. They wouldn't
let Jose 'Chewee' Torres talk, not to mention the rest of the community leaders. They even turned their backs on a priest."
I made it to El Barrio about 8 o'clock that night. As I
walked from 103d Street to 125th Street and Third Avenue, I couldn't
help thinking as I looked at broken windows, broken stores and
broken bottles, what kind of a misunderstanding tornado had hit my
Barrio. I walked slowly up and down the streets, 110th Street,
112th Street, 118th Street. I stopped here and there to talk or
wave a greeting in reply to a friendly "Como ésta, Piri? or
"How's it going, baby?"
Every which where there was a hell of a feeling in the air,
like El Diablo was just waiting for nighttime to fall so he could
light up the scene. I saw the young cats making little knots of
themselves on street corners, in the middle of the block, some
playing cards on stoops, others watching domino games in front of
bodegas. I heard the soft wail of a Puerto Rican bolero from an
apartment facing the street which was lost a block later by the wild
swinging sounds of some Latin jazz, something like a boogaloo.
I met Chino and said, "Fill me in, baby. Que paso y como
paso?" ("What happened and how did it happen?") As we sat on
the stoop, this young Puerto Rican sort of smiled, a kind of sad,
resigned smile and shook his head from side to side. His mouth
took on an ugly shape. "It's on," he said. "Like the word is out.
Un policia shot and really wasted one of us Puerto Ricans." I
said, "Yeah, baby, but I heard the cat had a blade and was trying
to mess up that cop."
"Whatever it is," he said. "Like we don't like it. Maybe
the cat had it coming to him and maybe not. But a whole lot of us
have been thinking of all the inocentes that didn't deserve it but got
it anyway in the past."
I decided not to dig into my brother's heart any more because I could sense his growing tension and the wailing anger in his
dark eyes. I left him running his fingers through his thick black
hair. I met another friend on the street and he told me of a meeting that was to take place at the 23d Precinct with Capt. Solomon
Gross and Puerto Rican community leaders.
I walked into the precinct and introduced myself. There
were several community leaders there. I shook hands with them
and sat and listened to the conversation, particularly watching Captain Gross, a giant of a man who looked very, very tired, yet was
employing everything in his power to keep another hell from breaking loose tonight.
I heard his voice planning how to get all the ministers, nuns
and priests from every area of Spanish Harlem to reason with my
people. For he, as well as all of us present, knew that the small
hard core of youngsters who were raising this storm of protest because of past memories of isolated police brutality, would not or
could not differentiate between un policia bueno or un policia malo.
In their mood, anyone with a blue uniform, a badge and a helmet

was el enemigo, especially the ones that had el helmet blanco, the white helmet of the Tactical Patrol Force.

A little later, Deputy Commissioner of Community Relations Theresa Melchionne, a warm, vital person, spoke in a calm voice and I could not help admire the cool way she was handling her role. I called up several ministers that I knew and on my way out, I ran into Willie, a Puerto Rican policeman who grew up with me on 104th Street. We shook hands and for some minutes in the middle of all this tension, reminisced about the old days and our amigos, the few who made it and the many who never had a running start.

I was called back into the precinct and given an arm band so in case I would be out in the middle trying to calm my people down, I would be distinguished by the arm band as not a participant in the expected trouble. I took the arm band, walked out, and very gently folded it into four parts, tucking it into my back pocket, and thought I would do it, the trying to make peace as part of my people, not with an arm band, for that will only set them apart from me and my words like a Grand Canyon.

As I stood on the steps of the 23d Precinct,. Willie, who had changed into civilian clothes, passed by me. "Where are you going?" I asked. "Ven conmigo" ("Come with me"). I said, "What's happening?" "I'm trying to get all the priests, nuns and ministers together so we could have a meeting. Maybe we can hold this damn thing down."

"Thanks, Willie," I said, "but I'm going to move in and out to see what I can do with individuals."

"Okay, Piri, take care of yourself."

"Okay, swinging, you, too."

I watched the smile on his face and dug his words up to me. "Cojelo suave" ("Take it smooth"). I waved my hand, throwing him the same feeling. I looked to my side and saw Eddie Suarez, a young Puerto Rican who has done great work in the past with drug addicts and who is now working with Metro North, a relocation program headed by the Rev. Norman Eddy.

Eddie said, "I heard there is a meeting over here of community leaders." "No, it's just gonna be for the nuns, priests and pastors." Eddie went in to see Captain Gross to check it out and then came out and told a group of men and women who had been with him that the meeting was only for the clergy.

"Where you headed, Piri?"

"I'm gonna cruise and see what's shaking," I answered.

We walked off together up to Third Avenue and it was already starting to happen. Everywhere we looked were policemen. I saw a bottle thrown out of a window. It looked like a star and when it hit the street, it made a long path of bright yellow fire, a Molotov cocktail. Then I saw another, and another, and intermingling with its bright light were defined screams and crystal sounds of what seemed to be thousands of bottles being smashed in. I looked up at long Third Avenue toward 114th Street and saw a large group of youngsters marching toward us. Two of the young people were holding a Puerto Rican flag. At their side marched a young girl, at their rear were youngsters throwing bottles or whatever they could.

It struck me that it was not a race riot but ghetto kids letting off steam from a sense of frustration at their everyday life of
poverty and no way out in sight.   I heard a voice calling my name.
I turned around to see Ted Velez of the East Harlem Tenants
Council, José Torro of the arts and crafts poverty program called
ASPIRA, and Arnold Segarra from Community Development Project.
I said, "We've got to stop this."   Ted Velez's face was sweated
and he replied, "All we can do is try.   You know, Piri, they said
they were going to kill me."

About eight of us formed a line in front of the marching
youngsters and about 30 feet behind us an army of policemen were
forming their barrier.   I threw my hands up and the Puerto Rican
flag was a few inches from my face.   I yelled out, "No tiren mas
botellas ("Don't throw any more bottles").   If you got to march,
march without throwing bottles.   If you hit one of the police, they
may be forced to shoot."

Those in the front lines turned around to scream to those behind them, "Don't throw no more bottles."   Most stopped except
for a few whose pent-up feeling of frustration and past memories
of social injustice made them deaf and blind.   I believe they threw
bottles in sheer anger, not at human beings before them, but at
their sense of hopelessness of a long future living in a ghetto and
at the discrimination by a few who abuse the authority placed in
their hands as an outlet for their own personal prejudices.

They did not advance but rather stood yelling and screaming
at no one in particular, yet to everyone within the range of their
anger and beyond.   I heard one kid screaming, "Why don't they get
bulldozers and tear these slums down?"

Two nuns, dressed in white, approached me.   With them
was a young man.   The youngest nun asked me, "Are you Piri
Thomas?"   I said, "Yes, sister."   She said, "We've come down
here to help in any way we can.   Perhaps the love of Christ can
do something."   I heard someone yelling: "They don't only want us
to live in these slums.   They want us to keep los ratones (rats),
too."

I am a religious man.   But I could not help thinking that if
Christ Himself was crucified for trying to bring beauty and harmony
into the world, what could these two young nuns do.   But hell, I
thought, the only thing anyone can do is try, for trying beats a
blank.

I looked over the shoulder of the nuns and saw the running
of the crowds in and out of the blocks and blocks beyond, and each
time they came back on Third Avenue, more were added.   Just
then, more Molotov cocktails were thrown out of windows and the
sounds of smashing bottles were like weird sounds of a street symphony.   It reminded me of when, as a young boy, I had read Dante's
description of the Inferno.

A package of lit firecrackers hung together on one string was
thrown from a rooftop and it sounded like many guns or perhaps a
machine gun opening up.   I turned around and saw panic begin to
grow.   People were running and the two young nuns with me pan-
icked also, because you see, to get scared is part of being a hu-

man being too. I grabbed each by an arm and told them not to panic, just to get down and squat behind a car.

The youngsters were surging forward again. I ran into Arny Segarra and we threw our arms around each other. He said, "Piri, man, I'm glad you're here, baby." I said, "Where else could I be, baby?" And in the midst of all this confusion, my mind could not help going back to when Arny was a young boy, maybe 16 or 17, a gang leader, a tremendous basketball player, who having won a college scholarship, was not very much interested in it, and how I kept talking to him how important it would be, not only for him but for his people, if he would go and prepare himself, since he is a natural-born leader and, with education, he would be a thousand times more effective.

And this year, while I was walking past the East Harlem Tenants Council, a voice called out to me. It was Arny Segarra and he told me, "I graduated from Paul Smith's College. I got a degree."

I heard what in the distance were shots. You can tell bullets from firecrackers. One has a sound just to make noise and the other a sound that can kill. People were running all over the place. I found myself running with them, talking to one angry kid, his arms carrying 10 bottles. I tried to talk to the crowd. Arny said, "It's no good, Piri." We walked back about three or four blocks toward 104th Street. A policeman was going to stop me and I said, "My name is Piri Thomas, I'm trying to help." "Yes, I know. I saw you on the Alan Burke Show. Is he really as mean as all that?" I had to smile because in the midst of all this anger, a young policeman and a Puerto Rican were having a bit of restful humor.

I remember next being near a police captain. I believe it was Solomon Gross, a brave man, a patient man, and in all sincerity, a just man. I heard him shout, "Don't shoot, don't shoot, don't shoot" and in spite of the barrage of the bottles coming toward them, the police did not shoot.

We knew, the majority of us Puerto Ricans and the majority of the police, that this was not a race riot, but rather an outburst of past memories and of the everpresent reality of the poverty that exists in Spanish Harlem, like crummy tenements, hot and cold running cockroaches and king-size rats.

Eddie Suarez, Arny Segarra and myself walked over to 110th Street, and right next to the library where I used to go as a kid to find an escape from poverty by reading all kinds of books, another little bit of hell broke out. Bottles were being thrown off the roof, some empty and some with soda. Eddie and I were making our way to the corner of Third Avenue when from around the corner, a policeman appeared and said, "Get back."

Eddie and I kept walking toward him and I opened my mouth to identify myself, but the policeman in a very quiet and tired voice, firmly repeated, "I said get back." There was no malice in his voice. He did not know who we were or what was our purpose. He was doing a job and I believe he was doing it to the best of his ability. Eddie and I looked at each other, nodded and went back.

Just then it looked as if half of the candy stores in Spanish Harlem were throwing all their soda bottles down at us. We ducked into a hallway and there I ran into Bobby DeLeon from M.E.N.D. (Massive Economic Neighborhood Development). We sort of smiled at each other and talked small talk, trying to make believe that all this was not happening. But we both knew it was for real.

I heard shots, or was it firecrackers? By this time, nobody knew for sure which was which. I looked around for Arny Segarra but he was gone. I said to Bobby, "Cojelo suave," and he said, "You going out there, you take it easy, baby." "Okay, my brother," I answered. An hour or so later, I heard that Arny had been hit with a bottle. Thank God, it was only a glancing blow. He was released from the hospital, a little shook-up, a patch on the back of his head, but still in there among the people trying like all of us to bring a sanity to a few who were growing more insane with each passing moment.

There was a rumor out that a woman had been shot and every which way you turned, there were kids running back and forth, back and forth, like a centipede, only with a built-in jet motor. It seemed to come from everywhere and go out of nowhere. Some of them had bandaged heads.

I found myself on Lexington Avenue and 108th Street and there was a young policeman talking to six or seven Puerto Ricans and two Negro kids. I heard his words. It was like a brother talking to his little brothers. I had to smile. I looked at him and sort of crinkled my nose up, and said in my heart, "Caramba, thank God, for policia like you."

There were other rumors running like gasoline set afire on water. "The cops killed six cats." "Man, they're breaking heads left and right." But those of us in the know knew that these were agitators. I heard voices yelling out to all those hundreds of running feet, "Keep it hot, baby, keep it hot."

On 105th Street, in one of the big department stores, I saw two young Puerto Ricans smash all the front windows in, making no attempt to loot, but rather, methodically, with sticks in their hands that were longer by three feet than the policeman's night stick, smash with all their fury the heads of the mannequins and then stand inside the store and look out at the crowd, almost as if to say, "World, we are not mannequins, we are human beings."

I saw the fantastic patience of a group of policemen who turned their backs on them. I saw one of the kids step out of the store window and walk over to the police, heard not his words, but understood his gestures. It was as if he were telling them, "Go ahead, man, hit me." I saw one policeman put up his hand in a gentle sort of plea and I sensed his words to be, "Go on home, son. I have a kid just like you."

I had been trying to reason with three or four of the most militant ones near 119th Street and Third Avenue. That must have been half an hour ago or was it a year ago? Time and violence have no essence of minutes, hours, or days. It must have been 11 or 12 o'clock. I remember my having called the Mayor's office as soon as I had got in from Lancaster to find out what was happening from their point of view and to offer my services. Then I remembered

the rumors that started about a quarter to 10 that Mayor Lindsay
had promised to come to El Barrio at 10 o'clock that night. As
the time grew nearer, ugly words began to pour out of kids that
were high on beer, spurred on by others that had no other motive
except blind hate, helped along by others who were in this to get
what they could by looting. "If the Mayor don't get here by 10
o'clock, it's on."

Later, I found out that the Mayor didn't even know he was
supposed to come. He had all of his top aides there at the scene
while he was buried up to his neck in a mountain of paper work establishing a plan along with community leaders to bring peace to El
Barrio, whose people are not only most productive but the most
gentle of people.

It was a living nightmare as I look back on it now, underscored by my sheer amazement as I ducked bottles thrown at me
by my own people. I have lived a life full of violence and yet like
so many of us who have lived such a life, I can still be amazed any
time I see violence and always wonder why it has to be. That
night brought back to mind the Harlem, Bedford-Stuyvesant and Paterson riots in 1964 which I had filmed as a freelance cameraman.

I understand that a human being blinded by injustice and by
poverty that surrounds him works his rage out not by reasoning but
by instincts. But I am glad that the great majority of my people,
and the great majority of the police that night, resorted to reasoning and not to blind savage instinct. I have seen too many wars,
as a young boy in Spanish Harlem, as a young man in prison, as a
merchant seaman in World War II, as a rehabilitated drug addict
working with drug addicts in New York and Puerto Rico, as a former gang leader working with gang kids. Out of my family of seven
children, I have now two brothers and one sister left. Both brothers are professional soldiers who had not seen each other in
years until they ran into each other in Vietnam after a bloody battle.
One was subsequently wounded, but is now recovering. I remember
as a kid reading about some general, Sherman, saying, "War is
hell." I believe that hate is the real hell because if we get rid of
hate and misunderstanding, there will be no more wars.

Two weeks ago, I was invited to testify before the Senate
subcommittee considering a bill to set up bilingual education programs. Senator Kennedy, who had invited me to testify, asked me
what would I do if I had the power.

I say it here not verbatim, but the gist of it was this: if I
had the power, all the races would be as one, and all of us would
speak one tongue. The cause of hate and fear would turn to one of
love and all the world with my Harlem would turn to helping each
other to rise above the ignorance of the mind, where black man,
white man, yellow man, red man, brown man, multicolored man,
any-colored man, can clasp hands one on top of the other in an ever
swinging handclasp of harmony, understanding, and a sense of brotherhood.

Mi Barrio, mi gente, my people, we have given this country,
our country, our respect, our hands, our labor, our talents, and
we are proud to be Americans and proud to honor our Puerto Rico.
We are proud of our heritage, of our many mixtures of blood, of

our songs, our poets, of our statesmen such as Muñoz Rivera and
his honored family. We are proud of our Borough President Herman Badillo, our State Assemblyman Robert Garcia, our Arny Segarra, our Eddie Suarez. We have made a point, we have made a
voice. Out of this trouble, those who are in power are working
day and night to make a better understanding.

    One cause of the trouble has already been settled by having
a Puerto Rican policeman or a Spanish-speaking policeman in every
patrol car in East Harlem. I am very happy that the Police Department had the insight to put out a pamphlet warning against racial slurs being thrown at Negroes, Puerto Ricans, Italians, or any
ethnic group. This is one of the greatest causes of strained relationships between the community and the police. I personally would
like to see the day when any policeman who is found to harbor racial prejudice will be quietly but effectively relieved of his authority.
He alone can cause untold damage in community relations, not to
mention undermining the good work that thousands of his brother officers are doing.

    Since time immemorial, man has tried wars and the only
thing he has ever accomplished is blood baths. It is time now for
us all to sit down and discuss for a better us, for a better Barrio,
for a better America, and even beyond, for a better world. We
must get to know each other or we shall be just an experiment that
was put on earth and became a failure.

    Americans, stop your hate among yourselves or, by God,
you will convert this great land of ours into a holocaust. Americans, no matter your color, share this land, share human dignity,
share so that our children and our children's children will not have
to live in a human jungle. I love my Spanish Harlem, my Barrio,
with all its swinging sounds, music, and its blend of peoples, Puerto Ricans, Italians, Irish, Jewish, Negroes, Polish. But my love
goes beyond to my great America.

    We in the ghetto do not want charity, but a chance to have
the sun light up a place that is dark. Americans, this land belongs
to all of us. Let's make it greater. Let us all walk in a swinging sense of brotherhood, sunlight and beauty.

Clarence Senior, "Puerto Ricans on the Mainland." Américas
13:36-43, August 1961. Américas is a monthly magazine
published by the Pan American Union in English, Spanish
and Portuguese. Reprinted by permission.

Immigrants from other countries have played a tremendously
important role in the growth of the population of the United States.
Almost forty-two million persons have come, mostly from Europe,
to seek a better life. They started as strangers to one another;
they became neighbors.

The movement was slow in getting under way. There were
only 210 settlers from Europe in 1610, when several Latin American countries were already large enough to support thriving universities. They were thinly scattered along the Atlantic seaboard,
merely on the edge of the three million square miles now occupied
by around 180,000,000 inhabitants of the forty-eight continental
states.

But there was land, used, if at all, by only small scattered
bands of seminomadic Indians who numbered perhaps nine hundred
thousand in the entire territory, and who had not developed the advanced social organization of the Aztecs, Incas, and Mayas. There
were timber, adequate and well-timed rainfall, an equable climate
and a long growing season for crops. There were industrial metals
and minerals the working of which required settled communities and
participation by the settlers themselves. There was no gold or
silver found for over two centuries, so that the "hit and run" tactics of the conquistadors who found gold on their initial explorations
were not adopted.

Perhaps as important, or even more important, there was
religious liberty and political freedom (except in those areas in the
South where slavery was established, which still suffer from that
aberration). So immigrants flocked to the new country, attracted
either by economic opportunities or by religious or political freedom.

Fairly exact records are available since 1820. Even the
bare statistics by decades since that time are exciting. Perhaps
they become even more meaningful if we know that six years in
this century saw one million or more arrivals: 1905, 1906, 1907,
1910, 1913, and 1914.

Behind them one can see historical events reflected in the
movement of people: the English and Scottish enclosure acts, the
Irish famines, the agrarian changes in northwestern Europe, the
revolution of 1848, the coming of railroad lines and newspapers to
remote areas of Poland, the distress of farm workers in southern
Italy, all provide a background. The opening of more and more
free land for "homesteading," the discovery of gold in California

Table 1
Immigrants to the United States, 1820-1959[1]

Period	Immigrant Aliens (thousands)	Period	Immigrant Aliens (thousands)
1820-30	152	1891-1900	3,688
1831-40	599	1901-10	8,795
1841-50	1,713	1911-20	5,736
1851-60	2,598	1921-30	4,107
1861-70	2,315	1931-40	528
1871-80	2,812	1941-50	1,035
1881-90	5,247	1951-59	2,250

and silver in the Rocky Mountains, the need for workers in the mines and the growing industries, all acted as magnets attracting the dispossessed or the dissatisfied. The figures also reflect, especially in the 1931-40 decade, the effect of the world-wide depression, and since then, the effects of restrictive immigration legislation.

Economic development did not take place evenly throughout the three million square miles, either geographically or in time. After people settled in one area, many would move to another part of the country that was economically more advanced. The United States census in 1850 found that somewhat over one in every five persons was living in a state different from that in which he had been born (21.3 per cent). It surprises many people to learn that the 1950 census found a slightly higher proportion of the population mobile by the same measure (23.5 per cent)! Figure 1 shows the numbers involved and the direction of the main stream as shown by the 1950 census.

One of the smaller streams is that from the Caribbean island of Puerto Rico, once a colony of the United States and now an associated free state. Puerto Ricans have been coming to the mainland for many years. Almost a century before they became citizens of the United States in 1917 there was a Puerto Rican community in New York City. The net migration of Puerto Ricans to the United States has been recorded since 1908 and is shown in Figure 2.

Puerto Ricans spread across the country just as other newcomers had in the past; the 1910 census found them in thirty-nine states and the territory of Hawaii. They were living in all forty-eight states by 1930.

By the end of 1960 there were about 650,000 persons of Puerto Rican birth living in the mainland United States, plus about 296,000 individuals one or both of whose parents was born in Puerto Rico. The largest single "Puerto Rican city" in the United States was New York, with a total of 720,000 Puerto Ricans, first- and second-generation. This was about three quarters of those in the forty-eight states. The remaining quarter were found widely scattered, with sizable communities in the Chicago metropolitan area; Philadelphia, Pennsylvania; Newark, Camden, Paterson, Perth Amboy, Trenton, and Jersey City, New Jersey; Milwaukee, Wisconsin; Miami, Florida; Bridgeport and Hartford, Connecticut; San Fran-

Figure 1

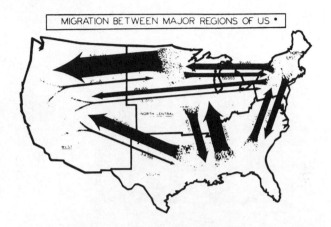

MIGRATION BETWEEN MAJOR REGIONS OF US *

* Persons found in 1950 to be living outside the region in which they were born.

Arrows indicate movement from region of birth to region of residence in 1950.

(Source 1950 U. S. Census of Population 'State of Birth' Special Report PE No 4A)

---

cisco-Oakland and Los Angeles, California; Boston and Springfield, Massachusetts; Buffalo and Rochester, New York; Cleveland, Lorain, and Youngstown, Ohio; Detroit, Michigan; and in dozens of other towns and cities of the mainland, as well as in Hawaii.

The ebb and flow of the Puerto Rican migration is, as can be seen from Figure 2, overwhelmingly dependent on business conditions in the United States. The annual average net migration for the following specific periods also illustrates this point:

1909-1930	1,986
1931-1940	904
1941-1950	18,794
1951-1960	41,212

Reduction in the number of available jobs resulted in a 22 per cent drop from 1948 to 1949 in migration from the island; economic conditions in late 1953 and 1954 caused an over-the-year drop in migration to the mainland of 68.8 per cent. Increased demand for labor began to reflect itself in an upturn in Puerto Rican migration during the third quarter of 1955, and the total for the year was 45,464. Migration during 1956 reflected continued improvement in job opportunities and reached 52,315 for the year.

Figure 2

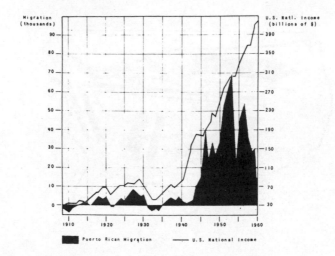

Note how volume of migration from Puerto Rico to mainland reflects changes in U.S. national income.

The downturn which began the next year caused a drop in the flow for 1957 of 28 per cent, to a total of 37,704. A further drop of 27 per cent was registered in 1958, with the figure for that year 27,690. Migration rose only slightly in 1959, with the improvement of job conditions, to 29,989, but unemployment was high in 1960 and the migration fell to the lowest point in fifteen years, 16,298. In other words, when more workers are needed by the economic machinery on the mainland, more Puerto Ricans come; when fewer are needed, fewer come. This was exactly what happened in the case of the voluntary immigrations that built the population of the United States.

The same ebb and flow with the business cycle is found in all of the internal streams of migration in the United States. It is particularly noticeable in the case of migration from such underdeveloped areas of the country as the South, and from the farming sections generally.

Movement back and forth from the farms to the cities is governed by the demand for labor in the cities. The depression decade of the 1930's, for example, showed only a trickle of migration from rural to urban areas. During the prosperity decade 1940-50, on the other hand, some 8,600,000 persons, net, moved off the farms of the United States and settled in the cities. This was almost a third of the entire farm population.

However, people who have lived for years in big cities are likely to lose sight of their own historical past and even to be unaware of the vastness of the internal migration. Every working-class group that migrates is likely to have problems in securing adequate housing, for example. If it is an ethnic group different from that which is in the majority in the receiving area, difficulties that might arise because persons are new to the area are likely to be attributed to differences in ethnic group membership. An understanding of cultural backgrounds is one of the ways of helping speed up the process of adjustment that is always necessary when two groups meet under such circumstances.

Because the United States has often been called "a nation of many nations" it is particularly important that our various ethnic and nationality groups understand each other. We have, in recent years, worked out a goal for the entire nation that is referred to as "cultural democracy" or "cultural pluralism." Those of Spanish, or Italian, or Swedish, or Polish, or other backgrounds are not forced to try to divest themselves of their former cultures. Their songs, poems, plays, customs and costumes, ideas and ideals are no longer thrown into what was once called "the melting pot."

There are hundreds of organizations dedicated to the ideals of "cultural democracy;" to the promotion of better understanding between different racial and cultural groups. Churches, labor unions, civic organizations, service clubs, women's groups, educational systems, all carry on programs with the aim of improving and perfecting our democracy in the field of the relations of one human being with another--on the basis of mutual respect for human dignity. Millions of pieces of literature--leaflets, pamphlets, and books--are dedicated to those aims. My little book is a modest addition to this material.

The Anti-Defamation League asked me to write for the people of the United States an account of the Puerto Rican at home, the advances that have been made by "Operation Bootstrap" (see "Puerto Rico Goes Ahead," by George Meek, Américas, October 1960), the contribution which migration is making toward helping the dramatic advances that have been made in Puerto Rico itself, and the contributions that the bearers of the rich Spanish cultural heritage can and do make in their new homes. The Anti-Defamation League was created forty-eight years ago by a Jewish fraternal organization called, in the Biblical Hebrew language, B'nai B'rith; in English, "Sons of the Covenant." It is a 110-year-old international institution, with lodges all over the Western Hemisphere, as well as in most other parts of the world. It seeks peaceful relations and understanding between all groups and has published a large library of books and pamphlets on intergroup relations.

One of my first problems was to deal with the widespread misunderstanding that there was something new about the experience of the Puerto Ricans. In the book, many illustrations out of the past were given to point up the parallels between the Puerto Rican migration of the present and the experiences of the ancestors of most of our present-day inhabitants.

Then there is the problem of the feeling that there is something different about the Puerto Rican who comes to the mainland to take his place in the economic machinery here. Both history and the data on the vast internal migration taking place today were used to help overcome this feeling. The cosmopolitan character of New

York City today is indicated by the fact that its radio stations carry
programs in twenty-one tongues daily and that its newspapers represent fifty-four languages! Yet it is probably safe to say that the
majority of the citizens of New York City are not aware of how
many languages are used daily, or that there are more in use today in their city than the eighteen that were being spoken on Manhattan Island in 1644 when it was still part of the Dutch Empire.

This language diversity is one indication of the improvement
in attitudes of which our citizens can be proud.

Our Judaeo-Christian tradition counsels us to love the stranger "as thyself." Generally this does not happen. It is more likely to happen if the stranger belongs to our own racial, ethnic, or
nationality group, to our church, to our lodge, to our union, or at
least to our own socio-economic class. This is because he is
somewhat more likely to have been raised as we were raised, to
"talk the same language," to have the same tastes; to have developed the same habits, the same reactions to daily events. In the
vast majority of our daily actions we are creatures of habit; life
would become a mass of intolerable choices in small matters if we
were not. Trouble begins, in a society undergoing rapid social
change, when habits rule decisions on matters vitally affecting democracy and public issues. That is, trouble begins if we have not
deliberately cultivated habits that are consonant with the democratic
way of life in human relations.

Left to their own devices, our habits will often be guided by
an insidious and universal fallacy known to scholars for years as
ethnocentrism. This is an old synonym for "group centeredness."
It has now been described and analyzed by social scientists and is
understood to be part of the "natural" behavior of mankind. It is
by applying intelligence and self- and social control to "natural" actions that man becomes human, however. We now know that we
must become aware of the process by which we acquire our habits,
our feelings, our ideals, our ideas, and especially our assessment
of "strangers." We must become aware of the fact that if a stranger comes from another ethnic, racial, national, religious, or class
group he may well have habits, feelings, ideas, and ideals that do
not coincide exactly with our own. Unless we can find or work out
common ones, a neighborly life will be difficult.

Often in our history this has proved to be a painful process.
It is one of the encouraging signs of a maturing democracy that in
the United States we are working out ways of achieving just such a
solution to our human relations problems.

Another misunderstanding arises from an oversimplified view
of the relationship between population growth and economic development. People in the United States are proud of the fact that Puerto
Rico has done so brilliantly in its efforts to industrialize and otherwise improve its economy and raise levels of living for its people.
They know that life expectancy has been lengthened from forty-six
years in 1940 to seventy years in 1960 and that this one change reflects tremendous progress in cutting down deaths from diarrhea
and enteritis, tuberculosis, pneumonia, and other diseases that men-
ace the lives of peasant and working-class families throughout most
of the world. They read that smallpox and malaria have been abol-

ished as causes of death in Puerto Rico. They hear that over a
thousand engineers, doctors, public administrators, educators, labor leaders, and others come from the "underdeveloped" areas of
the world each year to see how Puerto Rico has made such dramatic advances.

They ask, "What was this miracle that happened in Puerto
Rico? And why, when there has been all this progress, should
workers still wish to migrate to the United States?" Of course,
those who brought it about deny that it is a miracle at all. They
point out that it took hard work, imagination, receptivity to new
ideas, and a willingness to sacrifice immediate gains for future
growth. It also took a governmental apparatus that is both efficient and honest. Crucial as they are, governmental activities tell
only part of the story. Puerto Rican citizens were themselves involved in working out their future.

Briefly, let us consider the historical background of the island's progress.

Colonialism was perhaps the first major obstacle to economic and political development. Spain ruled the island for four centuries, and although it left a rich cultural heritage, it did not leave
much for the average citizen. It failed to establish a public school
system (leaving 90 per cent of the population illiterate), and left
behind it birth and death rates characteristic of an uneducated,
poverty-stricken people, and political machinery designed to serve
outside interests. Resistance to Spanish rule became widespread,
even at the community level. In 1898 there was a change of sovereignty.

Overwhelmingly, Puerto Ricans welcomed United States
troops when we "freed" them, as well as the citizens of Cuba and
the Philippines, from Spanish rule. We were not accustomed to
running an empire, however, and we made many mistakes. It was
not until the latter part of the 1930's that Puerto Rican citizens began sharing the responsibility of working out an extensive program
of social, economic, and political reconstruction.

In 1917 citizenship was granted those Puerto Ricans who
wanted it (only 288 out of 1,223,981 refused it), and the machinery
of internal democracy was somewhat improved. But no further real
progress was made until 1948, when Puerto Ricans elected their
own governor for the first time. The governor chosen then--and
re-elected three times since--was Luis Muñoz Marin, the leading
proponent of a new kind of political status for Puerto Rico--the
"commonwealth." In the 1948 election, the voters were offered
three alternatives for the kind of government to replace the worn-
out colonial system. The tally for the three was: independence,
65,351 votes; statehood, 182,977; and commonwealth, 392,386, or
61.2 per cent of the total ballot. After being approved by the U.S.
Congress and three times ratified by the Puerto Rican voters, this
concept was incorporated into the Constitution of the Commonwealth
of Puerto Rico, which was accepted by Congress and went into effect on July 25, 1952.

The United Nations Assembly voted, in November 1953, by
26 to 16, to recognize that the Puerto Ricans had been "invested
with the attributes of political sovereignty which clearly identify the

state of self-government attained by the Puerto Rican people as an
autonomous political entity." The United States henceforth was not
required to report to the UN each year on developments in this former "dependent area." The commonwealth arrangement has been
applauded as one of the great political inventions of our times.
This is one reason the island is so frequently visited by people
from colonial, semi-colonial, or recently liberated areas of the
world. The transition from dependence to democracy was accomplished without damage to economic or social patterns.

Poverty, with all its attendant ills, was another part of the
Puerto Rican heritage, as it is for three fourths of the peoples of
the world. Lack of resources, plus lack of imagination in using
resources, was a heavy handicap. Agricultural land is scarce on
the mountainous island, where sub-tropical rains have eroded soil
on hilly lands unmercifully. The Puerto Ricans can use only about
one half of an acre of land per person for farming, compared with
about four acres per person in the mainland United States. Forest
resources are practically nonexistent, and no subsoil resources of
any consequence have yet been found. Puerto Rico, in common
with many of the developing areas of the world, suffers from a
heavy population density and from a high birth rate. In 1959 each
of the island's 3,435 square miles of area supported an average of
681 persons, compared with fifty persons per square mile in the
States. In other words, the economy of Puerto Rico has to support
almost fourteen times the population per square mile that the rich
and highly developed economy of the United States supports in its
territory.

"Operation Bootstrap" was launched as an effort to develop
the people themselves as a major factor in raising levels of living.
Agricultural improvement and diversification, industrialization,
greater education, and the knitting together of all these goals by co-
ordinated planning have been the major programs.

Agriculture has been dominated by sugar production, with
coffee and tobacco as secondary crops. The land now produces, in
addition, pineapples, legumes, coconuts, avocados, sweet potatoes,
and bananas, which were not of great importance before. Cattle
raising and dairying have become important sources of income.
Many more persons are landowners now than were two decades ago.
The "500 Acre Law," on the books since 1900, has been enforced
and the land held in violation of it has been expropriated and made
available to landless farm workers in several ways.

The industrialization program has resulted in the erection of
almost seven hundred new factories and an increase of some 800
per cent in income from manufacturing. The new plants are efficient and modern in every detail. It is in exactly this condition
that one of the most critical issues of the industrialization of the
"underdeveloped" areas lies. It is imperative that the issue be understood throughout the world. New, modern, efficient machinery
means more production with fewer workers! Puerto Rico built the
first five plants under its industrialization program at a cost of
roughly $11,000,000. The five plants gave direct employment to
992 workers. Thus one industrial job required an average investment of $11,087. One new job is created in secondary industry or

services for each manufacturing job, but of course with additional
investment needed. Obviously, more workers would be given employment if older, less efficient machinery were to be used. Obviously, also, this would result in higher costs of production, and
then the industry could not survive in competition with those industries that used newer and more efficient machinery. This is one
of the most serious problems facing those developing areas which
are overpopulated. As A.J. Jaffe has pointed out, "there can be
substantial increases in national income without any change in the
overall level of employment."

Puerto Rico's experience has been that, while the national
income has risen spectacularly, the percentage of the labor force
unemployed is still much too high. Improvements in agricultural
techniques are also partly responsible for this. The number of
workers employed in farming in 1940 was 230,000; eighteen years
later it had dropped to 137,000, although income originating in agriculture grew appreciably in the same period.

While manufacturing jobs were increasing at a much slower
rate than income, and while agricultural employment was losing
ground, the rate at which the population grew was itself increasing.
The death rate, reflecting substantial improvements in both levels
of living and health and sanitation services, fell from 18.4 per
1000 in 1940 to 7.0 in 1958, a drop of 62 per cent. The birth
rate, however, fell only 15 per cent, from 38.5 in 1940 to 32.7 in
1958. If there had not been a net emigration of some 600,000 persons during this period, the Puerto Rican population would today be
at least 750,000 more than it actually is, or 3,087,000 instead of
2,337,000. This, in turn, would be reflected in a lower per capita
income and a higher rate of unemployment.

As it is, population pressure is great enough to hamper development plans and interfere with economic and social advance. It
is probable that per capita income, now at about $600, would total
at least $800 if it were not for the effects of overpopulation.

It is, unfortunately, easy to assume from these data that it
is the unemployed Puerto Rican who migrates. Most of those who
migrate, however, leave jobs to go to new jobs on the mainland.
They go seeking better jobs, not jobs as such. And because the
economic machinery there is so highly developed, complex, and
large-scale, their chances of getting a better job are much greater
than if they had remained at home--so long as unemployment is not
too high in the United States. But when unemployment is high and
fewer workers are needed, fewer come. As Figure 2 indicates, in
the three depressions during the 1908-1959 period, more Puerto
Ricans returned to their island homes than came from there.

How is this correlation of migration and opportunity achieved?
Through what I call the family intelligence service. A foreman who
likes the work of a Puerto Rican employee often says "Juan, you
are a good mechanic. Are there any more at home like you?"
Juan is likely to answer, "Sure, my brother José is just as good
a mechanic as I am." So José comes to join Juan. Since family
solidarity is strong in Puerto Rico, even one member working in a
town or city in the United States may result in a thriving, growing
Puerto Rican community within a few years. That is, there will be

a growing community if additional workers are needed.   If not,
there will not be.

Thus the migration of Puerto Ricans to the urban areas of
the mainland is not organized; it is spontaneous and depends on news
of job opportunities.   But the Government of Puerto Rico is interested in helping its people in their endeavor to work out a better
economic future for themselves and their children.   Its Department
of Labor in 1948 opened an office in New York City for this purpose.   Its activities have now grown to the point where it is a full
Division of the Department, with thirteen offices in the United
States and an Orientation Unit operating in Puerto Rico.   It has
printed over five million copies of leaflets and pamphlets, in Spanish and English, to help the migrant or a person considering migration.   The thirty-eight titles include Clima y Ropa, warning against
the bitter cold of northern winters; Nueva York y Usted: Un Guía,
an eighty-page guide; Derechos y Deberes del Inquilino y el Casero,
treating of the problems of living in multifamily buildings, which
often is a new experience for the recent arrival; Usted Necesita
Estos Documentos, listing papers that will be needed, such as birth
certificates, vaccination certificates for children, social security
cards, and so on, without which life in a big city can become even
more complicated than it otherwise is; Use Su Derecho a Votar, re-
minding the Puerto Rican that in his new home he should register
and vote just as he does in Puerto Rico.   The Orientation Unit
works with local mayors' committees on migration in a majority of
the seventy-seven municipios of the island, those from which the
most migrants come, as well as with other departments of the government.

While the government neither encourages nor discourages migration, it realizes that it will take place so long as economic development in the United States affords greater employment opportunities than are found in Puerto Rico.   It therefore wants to help
its people ease the process of adjustment to a new environment and
prepare them to meet new problems.   It also wants to be helpful
to the institutions of the receiving community that can aid the newcomer in making his adjustment.   Its offices offer both the migrant
and the local people the services of employment experts, social
workers, educators, and community organizers.   Radio and television are used both in Puerto Rico and in the United States, as are
newspapers and magazines, speeches, and discussion groups.   Each
week the twenty-nine radio stations throughout the island carry a
program called "Guide for the Traveler," based on the experiences
of earlier migrants.

The entire force of the nine local offices of the Puerto Rico
Employment Service aids in the orientation process, using labor
market information received through U.S. Employment Service channels.   The U.S. Employment Service on the mainland has 1,800
local offices, forty-eight state offices and twelve regional centers
for the gathering and dissemination of employment information.   It
is all available to the prospective migrant, as are the services of
the local offices in job placement, aptitude testing, and counseling
of applicants and employers on various problems that may arise.

There is still another stream of migration from Puerto Rico:

it flows toward the mainland in the spring and early summer and back toward Puerto Rico in the autumn. It consists of farm workers whose seasonal work in Puerto Rico is coming to an end just at the time when demand for farm labor is increasing in the Middle Atlantic and New England states. This is highly organized in comparison with spontaneous urbanward migration. The Secretary of Labor of Puerto Rico requires the employer to sign an agreement that provides more protection than any other farm worker in the United States receives. It requires that the local prevailing wage be paid, but states a floor below which it cannot fall. The worker is guaranteed wages for 160 hours of work per month and acceptable housing, rent free. The employer must insure the worker against occupational accident or illness, a form of protection that is rare for farm workers although universally required in industry. There is also a group insurance plan covering off-the-job accidents and illnesses. The Migration Division of the Puerto Rican Department of Labor maintains a field staff to assure that the agreement will be respected and to iron out any difficulties that may arise. While some fifteen thousand workers have come to the States under the agreement each season for about eight years, there are now probably another fifteen thousand who come "on their own." They feel that their first few years under the agreement have taught them all they need to know about farm work on the continent and that they now can make their own arrangements.

It is from the farm labor stream that dozens of important Puerto Rican settlements have got started. If workers are needed in industrial centers near farming areas in which Puerto Ricans work, the industrial employer often offers jobs at the end of the farm season. The "family intelligence service" takes over from that time on, if more workers are needed.

One of the questions frequently asked by those not directly in contact with the wide range of industries and services in which Puerto Ricans are employed is "Where do the Puerto Ricans work?" Many times those who ask this question have just been served by a Puerto Rican waiter in one of New York City's best hotels. Often they have been waited upon in an exclusive lingerie shop or department store by a Puerto Rican sales clerk. Since the Puerto Ricans are not a separate race but have about the same racial mixture that characterizes Spain, it is often difficult to identify them by bodily characteristics.

The direct answer to the question is that Puerto Ricans work in almost all the trades and professions that are a part of the economic life of New York and many other cities. Some of the better-known Puerto Ricans include José Ferrer of stage, screen, radio, and television; Jesus María Sanromá, Boston Symphony piano soloist and recording artist; Graciela Rivera, opera singer, Olga San Juan, Rita Moreno, and Juano Hernández, of screen fame; Tito Puente and Noro Morales, popular orchestra leaders; and Ruth Fernández, the great interpreter of Caribbean songs. Baseball fans recognize such major league names as Victor Power, Orlando Cepeda, Ruben Gómez, Jim Rivera, Luis Arroyo, Valmy Thomas, Felix Mantilla, Arnold Portocarrero, Juan Pizarro, and Roberto Clemente.   The world's junior welterweight boxing championship was captured in 1959 by Carlos Ortiz. However, most Puerto Ricans, like most of their neighbors, work at the more mundane occupations. The biggest single group of employers in New York City is the needle trades: women's and men's clothing, undergarments, sweaters, millinery, hats and caps, and hosiery. Other industries and services that find the new workers highly satisfactory include: steel foundries and metal fabricators, plastics factories, hotels and restaurants, food-processing plants, electronic equipment manufacturers, optical and surgical instrument plants, jewelry makers, the merchant marine, laundries, hospitals, building maintenance, and welding. New York's forty thousand factories include over three hundred industries, and Puerto Ricans are found in almost all of them. Each month 1,500 new corporations are created in New York City. Three hundred of these are engaged in manufacturing. As the City Commerce Department reported in 1959, "What generates these new businesses and keeps the old ones stable or expanding is the city's labor supply. Its greatest resource is manpower."

The Reverend David W. Barry, Executive Director of the New York City Mission Society, says: "No previous immigrant group so quickly numbered among its members so many policemen and welfare workers, teachers and social workers, office workers, and independent businessmen, and even doctors and lawyers--after barely a dozen years in New York. And the signs of the future are in the substantial enrollment of young Puerto Ricans in the city's colleges and universities."

Dr. Barry's organization has for over one hundred years been helping newcomers in their adjustment to life in the nation's metropolis.

His view is supported by the existence of substantial organizations in the business and professional fields, such as the Spanish Merchants' Association, with its two thousand Puerto Rican members; the thirty-five-year-old Puerto Rican Civil Service Employees Association, which has its own building and successful credit union; the Spanish Club of the New York City Police Department, with 250 members, mostly Puerto Rican; the Association of Puerto Rican Social Workers, with more than one hundred members; and the organizations of lawyers, school teachers, nurses, ministers, electricians, barbers, bar owners, taxi owners and drivers, and baseball umpires.

The Puerto Ricans are also active in union affairs. A recent survey showed that 63 per cent of New York's Spanish-speaking households contain one or more union members. Many are now union officers. They are also active politically. All three political parties in New York City (Democratic, Republican, and Liberal) place great emphasis on work among the Puerto Ricans. Puerto Rican ranks now include two state legislators, a city magistrate, and a number of appointive officials in the executive branch of the city and state governments. The first Puerto Rican elected to the New York State Assembly, in 1937, was a Republican. The next, a Democrat, was elected in 1953 and re-elected in 1954, 1956, 1958, and 1960. He was joined in 1958 by another Democrat.

Democracy depends on far more than simply voting on elec-

tion day, however. The Puerto Ricans have learned this at home
where civic participation is constantly stressed as an indispensable
factor in "Operation Bootstrap." The Puerto Rican who moves to
the mainland shows that he has learned this lesson well. Two years
ago some 150 Puerto Rican civic, educational, religious, business,
labor, recreational, and social groups in New York City organized
the Puerto Rican Self-Help Program, Inc. Its activities are centered primarily on the young people of the community. They include neighborhood meetings of parents, orientation centers, teachers giving Spanish classes to local government workers, an employment service, youths assisting the Fire Department in its fire-pre-
vention campaign, and many others--all on a volunteer basis. Other Puerto Rican organizations run twenty-one "housing clinics"
every week to help solve problems arising from the housing shortage. They have published a Self-Help Manual on Housing Problems
for the use of their own clinics and others that are being formed
to serve non-Puerto Ricans.

The Puerto Rican brings his ideas, ideals, attitudes, and
habits, as did the forty-two million representing other cultures who
came before him, to take part in the building of our nation. In
closing the book, I wrote of their contributions:

"Perhaps the greatest need of the world today is a willingness on the part of individuals and groups to accept other people on
their own terms and not to hold and express the Philistine attitude,
'Thank God I am not as he,' when a member of a different nationality, race, ethnic group, or class passes by. There is among
the Puerto Ricans none of the bitter hatred toward other religious
groups which so marred the record of our democracy in the days
of the Ku Klux Klan and sporadically ever since.

"It is in the field of race relations especially that the Puerto Rican may make a contribution--if we allow him. Puerto Ricans
of dark, light, and white skins have lived together for several centuries without serious discrimination or recrimination, and this
healthy attitude can be a model for us. One of the orientation leaflets issued by the Commonwealth is entitled, in Spanish, the equivalent of 'When in Rome, Do As the Romans Do.' It reminds the
migrant that habits and customs differ and that one should watch his
neighbor or shopmate for clues to proper actions. It ends by telling the reader, however, that there is one outstanding Puerto Rican
virtue: 'We don't discriminate against anybody because of his race
or the color of his skin.... We must continue practicing this
wherever we live.'

"Next, commentators who know the Puerto Rican well stress
the contribution he makes with his strong family life, the kind of
solidarity which is so missing from the city scene today.

"Others are impressed by his warmth, vitality, friendliness,
and hospitality, the great value placed on the non-material side of
life, on artistic expression, on love of music and dancing, on such
indications of cultural values as the fact that the Governor of Puerto Rico is widely known as 'El Vate,' 'the Bard.' He once wrote
poetry and is still proud of it and yearns for the time he might do
it again. The Secretary of Labor is a playwright--and does not
conceal it, as he might likely do if he were a prominent public of-

ficial in the United States!

"Most highly prized of all, and basic to many of the contributions mentioned, is a deep sense of the dignity and worth of the
individual.

"All of these--plus the basic addition to the manpower we
need here and the far-reaching assistance Puerto Rico is giving us
in our international relations--are among the contributions of the
Puerto Ricans."

Note

1. From Walter F. Willcox, International Migrations, Vol. 11,
   New York 1931; U.S. Department of Justice, Annual Report
   of the Immigration and Naturalization Service (1959), Table
   1.

Ethna O'Flannery, "Social and Cultural Assimilation." American Catholic Sociological Review, 22:195-206, Fall 1962. Reprinted by permission.

Following Parsons' distinction between cultural and social systems, a tentative model of assimilation which distinguishes social and cultural assimilation is proposed. This model is tested in an analysis of Puerto Rican migrants to New York City. Both the analytical and empirical data seem to reveal a basis for maintaining that social and cultural assimilation are, to a degree, independent processes.

The adaptation of immigrants to American society has been the object of extensive investigation on the part of sociologists. It will be the purpose of this paper to outline a model of assimilation, as this can be derived from some recent sociological literature, and to apply this model in a modest study of the assimilation of Puerto Rican migrants to American society. It must be emphasized that this formulation is tentative and may require considerable amplification and revision.

The starting-point of this discussion will be the distinction made by Parsons between the cultural and social systems. Culture is defined by Parsons as the "transmitted and created content and patterns of values, ideas and other symbolic-meaningful systems as factors in the shaping of human behavior and the artifacts produced through behavior."[1] The social system, on the other hand, is the "specifically relational system of interactions among individuals and collectivities."[2] The approach to the process of assimilation outlined here will distinguish between the adaptation of immigrants to the social and cultural systems of the receiving society.

Social and Cultural Integration

The need for acculturation among immigrants is obvious and has been well documented in many studies.[3] The acculturation approach to assimilation is devoted chiefly to a consideration of the extent to which the immigrant is socialized into the various values, customs, and behavior patterns of the new society. Here, a distinction is made between the internal and external acquisition of the new cultural complex,[4] and considerable attention is focussed on deviance as an indicator of improper socialization into the new culture.[5]

The study of the integration of immigrants into the social system of the new society has been the subject of far less effort on the part of social scientists, though recently more interest has been

shown in it.   Actually, the need of the immigrant for social integration may initially be greater than the need for cultural integration, for the first effect of migration seems to be, not culture conflict, but an extensive shrinkage in the individual migrant's field of
social relations.   He is detached from many, if not all, his previous primary groups, and his earlier self-image which derived from
the configuration of roles he played in the parent society is severely damaged, if not totally destroyed.[6]   Hence, the immigrant's first
problem is the re-establishment of social relations without which
his individuality is threatened, without which cultural assimilation
might be impeded.   It is at this point that the immigrant community has functions to fulfill for the individual migrant and for the receiving society.   Hence, there will be in this paper a distinction
between cultural and social assimilation.   Further, it will be maintained that, while there can be no social assimilation without some
cultural assimilation and no cultural assimilation without some social assimilation, nonetheless these processes can vary somewhat
independently of each other.   That is, there may be considerable
cultural assimilation without the same degree of social assimilation
and vice versa.

    One of the first analysts to distinguish between social and
cultural assimilation was Peter Munch who studied the adjustment
of Norwegian groups in Minnesota.[7]   According to Munch, immigrants are faced with a need to divest themselves of their old ways
and to adopt American patterns at the same time that they are excluded from association with many groups in the community.   The
result is the continued existence of ethnic groups in American society which are more or less isolated from one another and from
the general American community.   Nonetheless, these ethnic
groups stand out clearly as American in comparison with the original migrating groups.   Munch summarizes the position of these
ethnic groups as follows:

        In some cases, it seems, the immigrant group has made
        a thorough adjustment to the new environment without los-
        ing its identity as an ethnic group.   An almost complete
        cultural assimilation has not been followed by the expected
        social assimilation.[8]

Indeed, the main problem of ethnic groups as studied by Munch
was how to be accepted into the social configuration of the new environment.

    Peter Campisi in his survey of the Italian family in Ameri-
ca reached similar conclusions.   Though the Italian family progres-
sively approached the American ideal of family life, still it could
be identified as Italian even in the third and fourth generations because of its rootedness in the Italian community.[9]

    The most comprehensive statement of the distinction between
social and cultural assimilation to be found among American sociologists is in Ruth Cavan's The American Family.   Cavan distinguishes between the foreign-culture group which has adjusted neither socially nor culturally to American life and the ethnic group
which is mostly American in its culture, but has not been fully absorbed into American institutions and informal group life.   The
ethnic group is marked by a certain residential segregation and so-

cial isolation.[10]

Cultural Assimilation

The next problem that arises is to determine what constitutes cultural and social assimilation in American society. We will consider the question of cultural assimilation first. Obviously, cultural assimilation has not, in fact, involved the adoption of the total value system of American society. Munch and Cavan noted in their studies the persistence among culturally adapted groups of particular ethnic traits. Indeed, Walter Hirsch warns against the confusion of cultural assimilation with cultural homogeneity.[11] If then cultural assimilation does not demand the annihilation of the ethnic culture and its replacement by the dominant culture, what does it entail? An answer to this question has been formulated by S. N. Eisenstadt in his study of immigration to Israel.[12]

Following Linton, Eisenstadt distinguishes three types of roles or values in a society.[13] These are universal roles or values incumbent upon all members of the society, specialties incumbent upon special groups or individuals, and alternatives which offer choice to all members of the society. Theoretically, the total cultural assimilation of an immigrant group would imply that all its members perform all the universal roles, are absorbed in more or less equal proportion by the various special groups, and that all the alternatives are open to them. But a pluralist society such as our own only demands complete fulfillment of the universal roles and allows the emergence of a particularistic immigrant body within the general social structure with special roles allocated to it and a limitation on the scope of alternatives open to it. Eisenstadt points out that "within the limits of such possible alternatives the immigrant group might retain distinct structural characteristics differing from other sectors of the society..."[14] Thus, the immigrants are acculturated to the degree that they internalize and express the major American patterns and values and fulfil the universal roles of the society. They are allowed to retain certain particularistic traits from the old culture. Such traits are, however, themselves modified in their transplantation to American society. For example, certain universal traits in the old society such as festivals or religious observances become alternatives or specialties in the new country. These variations from the dominant culture are allowed to exist as long as they do not put too great a burden upon the institutional framework; as long as they do not endanger the integrity or survival of the receiving social system; and as long as they do not generate tensions which cannot be contained by that system. Thus, cultural assimilation does not demand uniformity in all areas of culture nor does it preclude the existence of subcultural groups within the society.

Social Assimilation

The process of social assimilation is more difficult to describe, mostly because it has received comparatively little attention from analysts. As mentioned previously, one of the immediate ef-

fects of migration is the limitation of the immigrant's sphere of social participation through the loss of roles and through the lack of
the various institutional channels of communication with the larger
society. Initially, therefore, the immigrant is faced with the need
to institutionalize his role expectations in the new society. This institutionalization is achieved when the immigrant's role expectations
are compatible with roles as defined in the new society and are
capable of being implemented in it. This can be accomplished, according to Eisenstadt, only by the interweaving of the immigrant's
basic groups and fields of social relations into the social structure
of the receiving society. Such a transformation of the immigrant's
groups involves, first of all, the development of group values and
aspirations compatible with the absorbing society's values and roles
(an element of cultural assimilation) and the extension of social participation beyond the immigrant group. Such integration of immigrants into the dominant social structure of American society has
usually been manifested first in the political, educational, and occupational spheres. A minimal integration seems to be essential in
the social adaptation of immigrant groups and opens up channels of
communication to the larger society. Moreover, the institutional
participation of the immigrants provides opportunities for the development of new reference groups in terms of which new and broader
identifications can be made. Social assimilation at its extreme
would involve the formation of primary groups and primary relations
with "older" members of the social structure. However, there are
few precise indicators for measuring social assimilation. Only certain minimal standards such as participation in the political, educational, and occupational spheres seem to have been stressed so far.

When the processes of social and cultural assimilation coincide, the process of social absorption may be said to have taken
place. Absorption is defined by Eisenstadt as

> ...the learning of new roles, the transformation of pri-
> mary group values, and the extension of participation be-
> yond the primary group in the main spheres of the social
> system. Only in so far as these processes are success-
> fully coped with are the immigrant's concept of himself
> and his status and his hierarchy of values reformed into
> a coherent system, enabling him to become a fully-func-
> tioning member of society.[15]

From the point of view of society, absorption does not demand the annihilation of the ethnic group. Indeed, it is accelerated
because of the ethnic group. Absorption merely requires that the
ethnic community be "balanced" in terms of the larger society. According to Eisenstadt, this "balance" is achieved by the ethnic community in so far as

> ...its members perform the universal roles of the society,
> its particularist tendency agrees with the normative prem-
> ises of the absorbing social structure, and its structural
> peculiarities fall within the legitimate institutional limits
> of the society. In such a case the various specific associ-
> ations and ethnic leaders serve as channels of communica-
> tion with the legitimate values and symbols of identification

of the society as a whole and as mediators of its wider
roles and values.[16]
Thus, the whole nature of immigrant assimilation or absorption has
been modified. It consists of two elements: cultural and social
assimilation. The cultural assimilation of immigrants in American
society, while ideally it may demand the total displacement of immigrant values by American values, actually requires only the acceptance of the major values, roles, and behavior patterns of American society, and allows considerable variation from customary patterns in secondary areas. Socially, assimilation of the immigrant
involves the participation of the immigrant in the major institutional
spheres of the receiving society. In the United States, these spheres
are the political, the educational, and the occupational. In the extreme case, social assimilation would involve the "complete oblitera-
tion of distinct identities and...institutional dispersion."[17] Actually,
this has rarely happened in the American experience.

The Ethnic Community

It has often been assumed that the mere existence of the ethnic community has been a barrier to the adaptation of immigrants
to the new society. There is considerable evidence to contradict
this assumption. The American experience indicates that the existence of separate immigrant communities has not prevented assimilation. Seventy-five years ago Jacob Riis plotted the existence of
various ethnic communities associated with particular geographic locations in New York City.[18] These immigrant communities go back
at least to the 1830's. Robert Ernst notes that "the...coming of
the Continental Europeans in the thirties transformed the Empire
City into a complex agglomeration of little communities."[19] The
immigrant communities have had a number of positive contributions
to make to the process of immigrant absorption and to the stability
of the resulting social system.
Immigration is often productive of various types of behavior
tending toward the disintegration of social and cultural systems.
Among these strains and tensions is personality disorganization.[20]
As remarked several times earlier, one of the first consequences
of migration for the individual is the destruction of his system of
social relations, especially his system of primary relations. This
leaves the individual isolated and unsure of his self-identification.
The existence of an ethnic community into which an individual can
be integrated serves to moderate some of the disorganizing effects
of the migration experience by a restoration of primary relations
and some accustomed role-expectations. The ethnic community provides the immigrant with a sense of identification, with the "security
of a well-organized social life during the difficult period of transition to a new culture."[21]
The immigrant community functions in other ways to further
the process of absorption. The immigrant community is the media-
tor and transmitter of the new values and roles of the absorbing society. In the process of transplantation, the ethnic community is itself Americanized. The members of the ethnic community are of

necessity integrated to some degree into the political, occupational, and educational spheres of American society. The associational structure internal to the immigrant community also becomes a channel of communication to American society; the churches, parochial schools, mutual aid societies, lodges, etc.--all bring American culture to the immigrant.

First of all, the principle of associational autonomy is itself an American trait.[22] The very functioning of ethnic organizations involves adaptation to American principles. In addition to cushioning the shock of transition for the individual and enabling the migrant to maintain patterns of interaction among his fellows, the immigrant community helps to solve many of the problems arising from Americanization, problems such as care of the aged, selection of marriage partners, etc. The immigrant, within his community, has an opportunity to practice American behavior in a setting where he is accepted before venturing into the more impersonal larger society. Leadership is often developed within the ethnic community which is later utilized in the broader community. The ethnic group provides a framework within which American patterns can be tested and evaluated. Finally, the ethnic community's associations often become the representatives of the group's interests in the community at large.[23] Thus the immigrant community sponsors the advancement of social and cultural integration.

The immigrant communities of past migrant groups to the United States have usually been well-defined and delimited socially and geographically. Indeed many definitions of community emphasize the importance of a common geographical basis. For example, Mercer defines a community as

...a functionally related aggregate of people who live in a particular geographic locality at a particular time, share a common culture, are arranged in a social structure, and exhibit an awareness of their uniqueness and separate identity as a group.[24]

Identity Among Puerto Ricans

However, the newest migrants to New York City, the Puerto Ricans, seem to be deprived of the opportunity to form a community based upon geographical proximity.[25] This is at root an ecological problem. There are simply no undeveloped areas in New York where Puerto Ricans might congregate to form a community without entering into a previously occupied area. This ecological problem is complicated by the housing situation in New York. Puerto Ricans are among those citizens who are most in need of public housing assistance. Since the housing policy of New York is one of non-discrimination and non-segregation, Puerto Ricans who live in city housing projects are further dispersed throughout the city.

Numerous data could be cited to indicate how widespread is the distribution of the Puerto Rican population throughout the city. Puerto Rican children are found, often in substantial numbers, in most of the city's public elementary schools. The number of churches--both established and store-front--which offer Spanish language services or which are totally Spanish-speaking is very large, and these institutions are also scattered throughout the city.

If therefore the Puerto Ricans find it hard to form a cohesive community and if the ethnic community is indeed a valuable instrument for encouraging both social and cultural assimilation, the question arises: what structures, if any, have the Puerto Ricans developed as functional alternatives to the ethnic community? It will be the hypothesis of this paper that the Puerto Ricans are seeking in religious institutions that sense of identity (apparently so essential to social integration in particular) which other migrant groups found in the ethnic community. For the Puerto Rican, the church functions as a substitute for the immigrant community.

The Parish Study

Data to support the plausibility of such an hypothesis were derived from a study of the activities of some of the Puerto Rican members of a large Catholic parish in New York City. The parish involved encompasses an area which was once inhabited almost entirely by Irish immigrants and their children. Today there are a substantial number of Puerto Ricans in the area. In 1950, the Puerto Ricans constituted approximately ten per cent of the population living in the parish.[26] More recent estimates of the Puerto Rican population range from twenty-five to fifty per cent.[27] Within the parish, the Puerto Ricans are not residentially segregated. There is no street which does not have a number of Puerto Rican families living on it.

In 1954, one of the parish curates undertook the care of the Puerto Rican residents as a special project. Since that time, there has been a considerable increase in the religious services offered to the Puerto Ricans. A special "Spanish" Mass is offered each Sunday and a Spanish language Novena is conducted each Wednesday. Baptisms for Spanish-speaking communicants are scheduled for Saturday afternoons and provision is made for Spanish language confessions.

As far as the organizational structure of the parish is concerned, Spanish-speaking groups, paralleling the English language association, have been established. There are Spanish religious instruction classes for adults and adolescents. Pre-Cana and Cana Conferences are offered to the Spanish-speaking parishioners. While there is no Spanish language section in the St. Vincent de Paul Society, there are several Spanish members who handle the needs of the Puerto Ricans. A Spanish translator is available at the meetings of the parish Legal Aid Society. On the whole, therefore, the Puerto Ricans find themselves in the seemingly anomalous position of being segregated in an integrated structure. The question arises as to whether this segregation is voluntary. Moreover, it would be fruitful to consider some of the consequences of this segregation for the adaptation of the Puerto Ricans in the light of the assimilation model presented in this paper.

To explore some of these problems, a brief study was made of one of the Spanish language associations of the parish, the Hijas de Maria. The Hijas de Maria is composed of forty young women between the ages of fourteen and nineteen years. The activities of

the members of the organization consist of attendance at the Spanish
language Mass and Novena, where the girls constitute the choir, and
attendance at weekly meetings.

Interviews were conducted with twelve of the members of the
organization, ranging in age from fourteen to seventeen years. The
subjects were queried with respect to their participation in Church,
school, and purely social activites, their relations with English-
speaking people, and their awareness of the religious situation of
the Puerto Ricans in New York. The questions were general and
open-ended.

From the interviews, certain striking conclusions emerged.
All but one of the girls were perfectly fluent in English. Therefore,
for the members of the Hijas de Maria, language is no barrier to
communication and interaction with the dominant American society.
All lived in residentially integrated neighborhoods and all but one
attended school where mingling with "Americanos" is both common
and necessary. None admitted any difficulty in getting along with
the "Americanos." None reported any sense of rejection on the
part of the American community. Nonetheless, the subjects, when
queried with respect to their associational patterns, indicated a consistent preference for Spanish-speaking persons in their church,
school, and recreational activities. This persisted despite the fact
that there seemed to be very few barriers to successful intermingling with "Americanos," as perceived by the respondents.

The main focus of the girls' associational lives appears to
be the Church. Only one girl held membership in a non-religious
group, and most of their friendships and recreational activities
were located within the context of the parish.

Within the parish, these girls are quite isolated from the
English-speaking parishioners. Despite encouragement and opportunity, the members of the Hijas de Maria refused to join with the
equivalent English-speaking organization, the Sodality. A number
of reasons were cited by the respondents for this. First, the
Spanish-speaking girls feared that the English-speaking girls would
attempt to control the joint organization. Secondly, the Spanish-
speaking girls had certain religious practices, particularly the wear-
ing of a special uniform (which had been newly purchased) on one
Sunday of the month, which they feared they would have to give up
if "integrated" with the English-speaking girls. Thirdly, the Spanish girls indicated a very strong preference to remain among "their
own." This desire to be inconspicuous, to remain within their own
group, was the most common reason verbalized by the respondents
for refusing to participate in the general service of the parish.

Friendship is an extremely important factor in motivating
these girls to participation in religious affairs. Friendships appear
to be both numerous and strong among the members of the Hijas de
Maria. In fact, friends were frequently cited as the channel through
which admission to the Hijas de Maria was gained.

When questioned about the non-Catholic religious activity of
the Puerto Ricans in New York, the respondents indicated that, in
their opinion, Puerto Ricans were attracted to the Protestant
churches, especially the store-fronts, and to the Spiritualist groups
because there they found a sense of belonging, a feeling of accept-

ance, and some of the satisfactions of the family. The non-Catholic religious groups in which the Puerto Ricans hold membership in large numbers were thought by the respondents to be appealing because they offer their members a chance to be "by themselves," to speak their own language, and to participate actively in the services.[28] (These groups appear to offer their members the same protection and satisfactions which the national parishes offered earlier Catholic immigrants.) Here, the only allusions to a sense of rejection on the part of other groups were made when one of the respondents remarked that the non-Catholic churches allowed the Puerto Ricans to conduct their own services without the surveillance of other groups "like the Irish." Finally, the respondents felt that many Puerto Ricans remained outside the Catholic Church in New York because the Church was integrated. The fact that Americans, Irish, Italians, Negroes, etc., worship in the same church makes the Catholic Church less appealing to people who are insecure, who are unsure of the proper behavior in a strange and unfamiliar situation. Apparently, therefore, as Treudley maintains, ethnic institutions do provide the immigrant with an opportunity to become gradually integrated into the new culture before he is expected to perform his roles according to the standards of the new society.

Conclusions

From the above data, certain inferences can be derived with respect to the notion of assimilation presented in this paper. There does seem to be some basis for distinguishing between social and cultural assimilation. The young ladies studied were to some extent isolated from the American community. This isolation was partly voluntary, for the subjects lacked neither the tools nor the opportunity for extensive interaction with "Americanos." However, this isolation was in no sense absolute, for all the girls had links to some of the major institutional structures of American society. These links were located in the educational and religious spheres. Moreover, the girls were members of a strong Spanish-language organization centered around the Church where they found a sense of belonging and identification. The need for solidarity was predicated by the respondents as constituting the appeal of many non-Catholic groups for Puerto Rican migrants. Hence, there seems to be some evidence, though it is by no means sufficient, to suggest that religious groups are providing some Puerto Ricans with many of the satisfactions which the geographically-based ethnic community provided for earlier migrants. (What structures, if any, the un-churched Puerto Ricans are developing as functional equivalents of the immigrant community must await further investigation.)

With respect to cultural assimilation, the data indicate that the girls studied are in the process of adapting to American values. The fact that the girls could perform roles in some of the major institutional realms of American society indicates that they have adopted some of the universal norms and values of the society. Though the girls did preserve some of their traditional patterns and practices within an ethnically-oriented association, still the process of cultural assimilation went on, for cultural assimilation in the American experience allows the retention of particularistic patterns as secondary values. The Hijas de Maria was itself a vehicle of acquaintance with American ideals and norms, because it provided the girls with experience in a democratic, voluntary organization.

This paper has attempted to present a formulation of the process of immigrant adaptation which distinguished between the notions of social and cultural assimilation, both analytically and empirically. It has also attempted to derive a hypothesis by which this model of assimilation might be applied and tested. There are a number of other problems that might be specified within the context of this theoretical approach. For example, it would be profitable to investigate the permanence of the ethnic community and of ethnic associations within the broader community. Is the ethnic community a transitional structure in American society or has it become institutionalized?[29] The attempt to answer this and similar questions may result in the further extension or modification of this formulation.

Notes

1. A.L. Kroeber and Talcott Parsons, "The Concepts of Culture and Social System," American Sociological Review, XXIII (October, 1958) p. 583.

2. Ibid.

3. See, for example, F.J. Brown and J.S. Roucek, One America, New York: Prentice-Hall, Inc., 1952; and Duncan G. Hannibal, Immigration and Assimilation, Boston: D.C. Heath, 1935.

4. S.N. Eisenstadt, The Absorption of Immigrants, Glencoe: The Free Press, 1955, p. 64.

5. For an example of this approach, see Thorsten Sellin, Culture Conflict and Crime, New York: Social Science Research Council, 1938.

6. Eisenstadt, op. cit., p. 11.

7. Peter C. Munch, "Social Adjustment Among Wisconsin Norwegians," American Sociological Review, XIV (December, 1959), p. 780-787.

8. Ibid., p. 786.

9. Peter A. Campisi, "Ethnic Family Patterns: The Italian Family in the United States," American Sociological Review, XIII (May, 1948), p. 367-373.

10. Ruth Shonle Cavan, The American Family, New York: Thomas Y. Crowell Company, 1956, p. 188-215.

11. Walter Hirsch, "Assimilation as Concept and as Process,"
    Social Forces, XXI (October, 1942), p. 35-39.

12. Eisenstadt, op. cit.

13. Ralph Linton, The Study of Man, New York: Appleton-Century,
    1937, p. 792-794.

14. Eisenstadt, op. cit., p. 18-19.

15. Ibid., p. 9.

16. Ibid., p. 19.

17. Ibid., p. 18.

18. Jacob A. Riis, How the Other Half Lives, New York: Saga-
    more Press, 1957, p. 146.

19. Robert Ernst, Immigrant Life in New York City 1825-1863,
    New York: King's Crown Press, 1949, p. 41.

20. Eisenstadt, op. cit., p. 20. For a fuller discussion of some
    of the disorganizing effects of immigration, see Georgene
    Seward, Clinical Studies in Culture Conflict, New York:
    Ronald Press, 1958.

21. Joseph P. Fitzpatrick, S.J., "The Integration of the Puerto
    Ricans," Thought, XXX (Autumn, 1955), p. 402-403.

22. The following discussion is based upon Mary Bosworth Treud-
    ley, "Formal Organizations and the Americanization Process
    with Special Reference to the Greeks of Boston," American
    Sociological Review, XIV (February, 1949), p. 44-53.

23. For an analysis of the representative function of the ethnic com-
    munity and its associations, see William Foote Whyte,
    Street-Corner Society, Chicago: University of Chicago
    Press, 1955.

24. Blaine E. Mercer, The American Community, New York:
    Random House, 1950, p. 14.

25. The dispersion of Puerto Ricans is evident in such studies as:
    Martin B. Dworkis (ed.), The Impact of Puerto Rican Migra-
    tion on Governmental Services in New York City, New York:
    New York University Press, 1958; and Christopher Rand,
    The Puerto Ricans, New York: Oxford University Press,
    1958.

26. United States Department of Commerce, Bureau of the Census,
    Census of Population: 1950. Volume III. Part I: Summary

for the United States, Part 32, New York, Washington, D.C.; United States Government Printing Office, 1951.

27. Morrisania, Melrose, Mott Haven: Three Bronx Communities, New York: Protestant Council of the City of New York, 1956, p. 27-29.

28. Similar conclusions were reached by John J. Maciso, Jr., and Ramon Rivera in their study of The Puerto Rican Store-Front Churches of the Lower Bronx, Unpublished manuscript: Fordham University, 1959, and by Renato Poblete, S.J. and Thomas F. O'Dea, in "Anomie and the 'Quest for Community'; The Formation of Sects Among the Puerto Ricans of New York," American Catholic Sociological Review, XXI (Spring, 1960), p. 18-36.

29. For a discussion of this question which points to the permanence of the ethnic community, see Amitai Etzioni, "The Ghetto--A Reevaluation," Social Forces, XXXVII (March, 1959), p. 255-262.

Joseph Monserrat, "Community Planning for Puerto Rican Integration in the United States." (An address at the National Conference on Social Welfare, Minneapolis, Minnesota, May, 1961.) Reprinted by permission.

During the past twelve years, the Migration Division of the Department of Labor of the Commonwealth of Puerto Rico has conducted an intensive program of community organization.

The experience of those twelve years has taught us that integration of newcomers into the American community is a problem the people of the United States have never fully solved, nor even probed deeply.

Migration is a two-way street. Both the migrant and the community must be prepared to adjust to each other. However willing the migrant may be to adopt new modes of thought and living, if the community itself does not accept the newcomer, integration is impossible. As a Puerto Rican, I can make every effort to become part of the strange new life of the mainland, but if the mainland rejects me, all my efforts have been futile, and my hopes have been mocked.

With this in mind, the Migration Division developed a two-pronged program aimed at both the newcomer and his community. Our goals are (1) to help the Puerto Rican function effectively in his new surrounding, and (2) to help the community respond effectively to the Puerto Ricans. The ideas contained in this paper are drawn from our twelve-year experience in over 100 cities across the country, ranging from small farm communities to giants like New York, Chicago and Philadelphia.

The United States is a community of former immigrants. Its history is one of successive waves of immigration. We knew that many clues to our present day problems could be found in the past. We found, in fact, that all newcomers have faced problems similar to those confronting today's Puerto Rican migrants. Even more striking, we discovered that throughout successive migrations, communities have always felt the same burdens imposed upon them by the newcomers.

These observations have helped us develop the theories that give form and shape to all our programs. Since they come of a universal experience, we think these theories have more than limited application. I want to share them with you, in the belief that they can be of help in dealing with the problems of all newcomers, no matter who they may be, or where they may choose to settle.

First, we discovered that the belief--sincerely held by most Americans--that our country has always stretched forth its arms to the "poor and wretched" masses, is simply not true!

No new group has ever been welcomed with open arms by

221

the nation as a whole. As with any thesis, we must qualify as well
as quantify, but there is abundant evidence to support this as a general statement.

Remember when we whispered about the "Yellow Threat?"
Remember the history of the Know Nothing Party? Do you recall
the reception given the Irish and German Catholics, or the Polish
and Russian Jews? These are but a few of many examples.

Paradoxically, part of America's greatness arises from this
very situation. Despite an initial cold reception, immigrant groups
have produced the "doers" of our society. Nowhere on earth have
so many people from so many different places accomplished so
much in so short a time.

From the basic concept of hostility to newcomers, we developed a second thesis. Throughout our history, the United States
has never solved the problem of the first generation American!

To be sure, the Irish, the Germans, the Swedes, the Italians, in time did become integrated. But when we say "in time,"
we mean that it was the second and third generations who were assimilated, not their first generation elders. The problems of the
second and third generations were, of course, totally different from
those of the first generation.

There is a second paradox here: we submit that the second
generation groups are largely responsible for the fact that each new
wave of immigrants has faced the same problems as those who
preceded them!

Historically, the second generation American seems to become a "one hundred and twenty-five percent American." He has
been an instigator of, and participant in most, if not all, of the
"nativist" movements in the United States. Outside of the south, he
is in the forefront of a good number of the major race riots that
have occurred in our country.

The goal of all second generation Americans has always been
to be accepted as part of the "in-group" of the latest newcomer.
The children of immigrants, who a short time ago were the "out-
casts" and "problems" of our cities, turn against the latest newcomers in the same manner as the children of those who preceded
their parents turned against them. Furthermore, we realized that
in their efforts to be accepted as part of the "in-group" the second
generation youngsters have a need to--indeed must--give up the
"foreign-ness" of their parents. From the reactions of those they
would emulate, the in-group--they have learned that this is something to be ashamed of.

The United States is one of the few countries in the world
where a man can consider himself educated and yet speak only one
language, English. And yet, the United States is perhaps the only
country in the world that has received large groups who originally
spoke all of the world's modern languages.

There are, no doubt, several reasons for this. It could be
argued that, in the words of Walt Whitman, "...here is not a nation, but a teaming nation of nations," and consequently needed one
tongue to bind all people. One might point out that the United States
is not surrounded by foreign speaking countries as is say Switzer-
land, and does not have a practical need to speak more than one

language.

Both these reasons have validity, but we think there may be an even more important cause. To be "foreign" is to be different, and unfortunately, to be different in this sense, means to be inferior. In giving up the "foreign-ness" of their parents--dress, culture, food, perhaps their values--the second generation usually abandons the language before anything else.

From this type of analysis, we began to recognize what we were up against. The Puerto Rican, as the newest newcomer, faced the same unresolved problem of any first generation American group. But there was a major complicating factor. The Puerto Rican came as a full-fledged U.S. citizen, grounded in U.S. history and traditions, and eager to be accepted as such. And yet, he came as a "stranger" speaking a different language. The Puerto Rican migrant, in other words, came as a foreigner to his own country!

Clearly, our job was to help him "integrate" within one generation, and that called for finding a solution to a problem that had never been solved. Many of us in the Migration Division were in the Air Corps during World War II. We are accustomed to doing the difficult immediately. But the impossible takes us a little longer.

In the meantime, we had to plan for the most rapid adjustment possible. We had to keep in mind those aspects of the problem which could be solved only by working directly with the Puerto Ricans, and those aspects of the problem which involved the non-Puerto Rican groups in the community. We had to decide which problems could be dealt with on a "short-term basis" and which could be dealt with on a "long-term basis." Finally we had to identify problems which "only time could cure" and admit that there might be some which were insoluble.

Early in our experience, we realized that Puerto Ricans like other newcomers were what we might call the "product" of the vast internal migration taking place within the United States.

That American were pioneers and "a people on the move" is known to all. What is not generally recognized however, is the fact that there are almost as many people moving within the country today as there were a century ago.

Every year, according to Census Bureau data, 30,000,000 mainland Americans move their homes; among these 5,000,000 move from one county to another within the same state; another 5,000,000 move from one state to another. From 1953 to 1958, an average of 2,726,000 persons a year moved from the South to the North Central States, and from the South to the West. During the past seven years, net out-migration from Puerto Rico has averaged slightly less than 33,000 persons a year--less than one percent of the total of those who moved across state lines.

Important as these figures are to a fuller understanding of the extent of the migration--we at the Migration Division have learned that an understanding of the dynamics of this migration is of even greater importance.

Our migration is primarily economically motivated. Some migrants, as Senior[1] has pointed out, move in search of greater economic success; others move as a result of economic success.

Those who, like the Puerto Ricans, seek economic improvement, move when better jobs are available in other areas. During
recessions fewer migrate and during depressions, there is a return
flow to the area of origin.

Thus, immediately following World War II, Puerto Ricans
began to migrate to New York City in large numbers in response
to New York City's need for workers.

New York City is the largest single labor market in the
United States. It is primarily a service town. There are 390
hotels with 125,000 rooms containing 180,000 beds, for tourism is
a big business in New York with over 14,000,000 visitors a year.
The city's largest single occupation is the garment industry. Some
3,000,000 of the city's population derive their livelihood directly
or indirectly from the needle trades. There is extensive manufacturing, mostly in light industry. I mention only these because these
are the major areas in which Puerto Ricans work.

In the past, workers in these industries were first-genera-
tion immigrants. These workers are now leaving, or have already
left, in large numbers, through death or retirement. Their children have had an opportunity to secure a better education, and can
find better jobs. They do not enter these trades in any large numbers. The Puerto Rican migrant by and large fills the gap. These
jobs pull him to New York.

The constant upward movement within the economic pyramid
of our industrial centers must always be kept in mind if we are to
fully understand the dynamics of migration. Those on the bottom
of the pyramid, the persons with the least desirable and lowest paying jobs constantly seek to better their position and climb higher.
As they move upward they create a vacuum which must be filled if
the entire economic structure is not to crumble.

But, while cities need the newcomers to fill this vacuum,
they are not prepared to meet the needs of the newcomers. Inadequate planning, or formulas based on a blue-print and not on human
needs can not resolve the basic problems of our cities. We know
that the newcomer is a victim of these problems. But, to his
neighbors, he becomes the symbol and the cause of them.

In New York City today, Puerto Ricans are a symbol. They
personify the basic problems of the city. Today, even as one hundred years ago, New Yorkers facing rapid community change are
"rarely in a position to reason abstractly about causes." It is
much easier to point a finger, and the pointing finger moves in the
direction of the Puerto Ricans.

Whoever the migrant may be, he shares the troubles of the
city into which he moves, and he is faced with the necessity of adjusting to the culture of the big city and to the social and economic
conditions in which he finds himself. Just as migration is a national phenomenon, so too, are the problems which migrants face.
There is nothing uniquely "Puerto Rican" about these problems.
The following quotation from a report on migrants to a big city
speaks for itself:

"They [the migrants] are satisfied with poor living conditions...They don't want modern facilities...They won't
use bathtubs...They don't want to change their standards
...They're destructive and overspend money...We've
known about any number of illegitimate children who have
moved into already overcrowded homes with the mother.
I recall a family with thirteen of its own. Sister has
four illegitimate children..." and so on.

Is this New York City? Are these Puerto Ricans? No.
The city is Cincinnati. The migrants are white Southern mountaineers.[2]

In other words, the basic problems confronting Puerto Ricans in New York City and elsewhere throughout the States have
little to do with the fact that Puerto Ricans come from a culturally
different area, and speak a different language. The American Negro, the Southern white mountaineer, the American Indian, the
Mexican-American--to name but some of the 5,000,000 persons
who migrate from state to state each year--are all faced with more
or less the same dilemmas that confront Puerto Ricans. It is quite
obvious that each of these groups has different cultural and language
problems. They also have several things in common:
-- They all need to learn how to live within the complexity
   of a metropolitan area.
-- They all highlight the basic problems existing in the cities
   they migrate to (they reflect these problems because they
   have a high rate of "visibility" resulting from the differences between themselves and the majority groups around
   them.)
-- They all share the bottom rung of the occupational ladder
   in their new communities.
-- They all become the scapegoats for the problems existing in the cities they move to.

Housing is a major need all over the country. In New York
City there is a great need for low-income housing. But there is
little new housing of this type available. Land values are high,
construction costs higher. Private investors will not build houses
in the low-income bracket. The only houses in this bracket are
built by government. Yet, with all the housing that has been built
in New York City under government sponsorship (106,000 units),
and all that is to be built in the foreseeable future (145,123 units),
the shortage will continue. This is true in New York and all other
cities and even in Puerto Rico.

If all Puerto Ricans were to suddenly disappear from New
York City, neither the housing problem nor the other basic issues
confronting the city would be solved. In fact, without the Puerto
Ricans, New York would be faced with one of two alternatives:
either "import" people to do the work done by Puerto Ricans (and
whoever was imported from wherever they might come would have
to live in the very same buildings Puerto Ricans now live in for
the simple reason that there is nothing else); or industries would
have to move to other areas where there are workers, causing a

severe economic upheaval in the city.

Obviously, neither one is a viable solution. Nor will the stagnation of the past resolve our dilemma.

It is important not to let day-to-day frustrations make us forget the basic precepts of social work. We must remember that we can do nothing for a group--not even a migrant group; we can only work with a group and motivate them to do it themselves. There is a dynamic in all such groups, an urge which develops and produces the strongest and most effective kind of organization. These groups are the key to successful adjustment. Once begun, this dynamic reflects itself in new and creative approaches to the whole spectrum of a city's problems. The very concept of "community" takes on new meaning under the impact of the newcomers. City dwellers live in proximity, not in community. The neighborhood is very often the least likely place for a community organization program.

The Puerto Rican, although he comes from a close knit neighborhood in the Commonwealth, has found the best possibility for social action and self-improvement on the city-wide level. The community of Puerto Ricans is not the East Side or the South Side. It is New York City, Lorain, Chicago, Los Angeles, Middletown. City living is learned living. The migrants must be helped to learn the facts of city life and how to function effectively as a pressure group in a pressure group society.

It may appear to city dwellers that they can't live with the migrants, but, in truth, the city would die without them. The challenge, then, to community organization, is to cut through the mass of clichés and ignorance surrounding basic urban problems. Integration of migrant groups demands creative approaches to the ills of our sick cities. Perhaps in this way the vicious cycle of rejection and introversion can finally be broken throughout the country. If the Puerto Rican migration has taught us anything, it is that change is a perennial fact of urban life. The only question is whether or not our cities can guide and shape it in the interests of all our people.

Notes

1. Clarence Senior, Strangers Then Neighbors, From Pilgrims to Puerto Ricans. (Anti-Defamation League, New York City, 1961), p. 14.

2. Report of a Workshop Sponsored by the Mayor's Friendly Relations Committee and the Social Service Association of Greater Cincinnati. Cincinnati: City Hall, Dec. 1954.

Part IV

The Puerto Rican Experience on the Mainland:
Puerto Rican Children in North American Schools

J.J. Osuna, "Report on Visits to New York City Schools." Government of Puerto Rico. Department of Labor & Employment & Migration Bureau, (1948). (Mimeo.) Reprinted by permission.

On February 18, 1948, I visited the office of Superintendent of Schools Jansen and was given a general letter of introduction to district superintendents and principals of schools. February 25 I called on Dr. Clare C. Baldwin, Assistant Superintendent, who gave me a list of schools which he thought I should visit. February 27 I called on Dr. Frank Whalen, Assistant Superintendent, 330 East 152 St., Bronx, who also suggested a number of schools with a large attendance of Puerto Rican children. March 2 I called on Miss Antoinette Riordon, Assistant Superintendent, 223 Graham Avenue, Brooklyn, who took me to visit two elementary schools in her district. Later Miss Riordon made arrangements for visits to other schools. Besides the schools suggested by the three Assistant Superintendents above, I visited other schools upon the suggestion of this office or through personal invitation on the part of the school principals or teachers. Altogether, I visited the following schools:

Bronx -
        P.S. 30 Elementary School
        P.S. 124 Elementary School
        P.S. 25 Elementary School
        P.S. 99 Elementary School
        P.S. 60 Junior High School (Girls)
        Morris High School

Harlem -
        P.S. 57 Elementary School
        P.S. 102 Elementary School
        P.S. 157 Elementary School
        P.S. 83 Junior High School (Boys)
        P.S. 120 Junior High School (Boys)
        P.S. 171 Junior High School (Boys)
        P.S. 101 Junior High School (Girls)
        P.S. 172 Senior High School (Boys)

Lower Manhattan
        P.S. 188 Elementary & Junior High School
        (Coeducational)

Brooklyn -   P. S. 55 Elementary School (Annex)
                  P. S. 36 Elementary School
                  P. S. 168 Elementary School
                  P. S. 148 Junior High School (Boys)
                  P. S. 196 Junior High School (Girls)

Ten of these were elementary schools, one was elementary
and junior high combined, seven were junior high schools, and two
were senior high schools. It is supposed that these schools constitute a fair sampling of those schools in sections of the city where
the Puerto Rican population is concentrated. The enrollment of
Puerto Rican children in these schools varies from 90% in P. S. 57
to about 4% in P. S. 188. My visits to these schools were very
brief, generally a day in each, hence I have not made a thorough
study of conditions in them--I have visited briefly and jotted down
observations.

I was cordially received in all of these schools by principals
and teachers, and was given every opportunity to observe what was
going on and what each school was trying to do in behalf of the
Puerto Rican children.

The Puerto Rican children whom I saw in these schools may
be classified into three groups: (1) those born in the United States
of Puerto Rican parents; (2) those who came to this country very
young and have resided here more than five years; (3) the recent
arrivals. All things being equal, there should be no special educational problem with the first group, not any more than with any
other group of native children of foreign parentage. Those who
came very young, who have been here over five years, and who have
gone through the kindergarten and first grades of the elementary
school, should adjust very rapidly, almost as quickly as the first
group.

The recent arrivals come from all parts of the island--quite
a few from the inland towns such as Caguas, Cayey, Aibonito, Comerio. But the great majority of them come from the large city
areas, San Juan being first and Ponce second; Mayaguez and Huma-
cao follow. The large majority of the children I visited were recent arrivals, that is, generally two years or less in this country.
With some exceptions, they come from the poor and under-privileged groups, economically, socially and educationally. The great
majority of them have not enjoyed full advantage of school facilities
in Puerto Rico. The older ones have attended school on an average of four years or less. I found a few fourteen and fifteen year
olds who had attended school very little and who were illiterate in
their vernacular.

Another phenomenon which must not be overlooked and which
is very prevalent is the fact that a large number of these children
have some home problem. A good number come from broken
homes. Father and mother do not live together--in many cases
the mother is here and the father in Puerto Rico or vice versa.
In many cases there has been divorce and remarriage, with one of
either parents being replaced by a stepfather or stepmother. In
some instances the child is an orphan and lives here with relatives.
Or again, the parents are in Puerto Rico and the children live here
with the grandmother, aunt, sister, or uncle, or what not--all

sorts of combinations. In many cases both parents are here, but they both work, and the children are left to themselves all day long. They generally have lunch in school or somewhere near the school. After school hours they roam the streets or vacant lots playing and sometimes getting into trouble. I mention these cases not only because of the emotional strain under which these children live, which is bound to be reflected in the school, but also because such situations lend themselves to truancy and all the evils derived therefrom. I discovered these facts casually, by talking to the children. I have not made a thorough study of home conditions. It would be interesting to know just how many broken homes are represented in the number of Puerto Rican children attending the New York public schools. These recent arrivals, with all the handicaps they bring from the island, plus the conditions under which they are compelled to live in New York, constitute a real educational problem for the schools of the city.

What are the New York schools doing to meet these problems? The report prepared by a Committee of the Association of Assistant Superintendents entitled "A Program of Education for Puerto Ricans in New York City" tells us what is being done educationally today for the Puerto Rican population here, and makes recommendations for the future. The report is thorough, comprehensive, and above all, most sympathetic, showing genuine, sincere interest on the part of the school authorities in the approach to and solution of the problem. Parts III, IV and V are the most helpful insofar as my visits to the schools are concerned. It is not necessary to repeat here the main facts brought out in that report and the recommendations made therein because copies of the report are available to this office. As far as I have been able to observe in my visits to the schools, an earnest effort is being made by public school authorities and teachers to carry out the recommendations made in that excellent study.

After reading this report and visiting twenty schools among the under-privileged population of the city, it seems to me that critics of the public schools here, including the so-called "Harlem Project," are very pessimistic. Anyone who knows anything about schools knows that no school is perfect. The New York public schools no doubt leave much to be desired--the schools I have seen could be improved greatly in many ways. (However, it is not my purpose to describe here how these schools may be improved, the Superintendent of Schools and his staff are aware of needed improvements.) But the criticism that the public schools of the city are breeding places for delinquency is very unjust. It happens that I have visited some of the very public schools which have been the object of this criticism. After observing the communities where these schools are located, after interviewing principals and teachers and observing the teaching in the classrooms, and the behavior of the children, I have come to the conclusion that these schools, rather than breeding places for delinquency, are the very institutions which are contributing most toward the prevention of delinquency. As usual, the public school must be the scapegoat and answer for the sins and shortcomings of the whole community, plus the neglect of other agencies.

As to the Puerto Rican children attending the public schools which I visited, I have found school authorities, principals and teachers genuinely interested in their problems. In many cases I have found real devotion on the part of principals and teachers toward helping the Puerto Rican children. After hearing so much adverse criticism, I was very pleasantly surprised at the intelligent way the problem is being attacked and the generally sympathetic attitude on the part of the school.

As may be observed in the report of the Assistant Superintendents, the problem of the education of Puerto Rican children in this city is a new problem for administrators and teachers. The city schools are trying various methods of approach and experimentation. The one outstanding concern is the language problem. The various methods being used in the teaching of English are described in the aforementioned report. These methods are being changed in accordance with experience. It is interesting to go from school to school, talk to teachers and hear their criticism of the methods being used in the teaching of English to Spanish-speaking children. It is interesting also to observe the changes these teachers are making constantly, and their explanations for the changes. This attitude shows the interest of the teachers and their desire to find out for themselves the efficiency of the methods recommended.

As I went from school to school, teachers and principals seemed anxious to discuss with me the work they were doing and the problems they were meeting. A perusal of the report of the Association of Assistant Superintendents will show that the New York school authorities are conscious of these problems and are planning intelligently for their solution. There is very little I can add to the recommendations made in this report. Nevertheless, I would like to comment briefly on some of the problems mentioned in this report, which the teachers wanted to discuss with me.

1. The Language Problem

Methods of teaching English to the Puerto Rican children in the schools are described in the report already mentioned. Some teachers do make variations on the methods recommended. Some principals and teachers are afraid of segregation and push their students so as to keep them in the special classes as short a period as possible. Others retain the children longer. As a general rule the policy is that a child should be placed in the regular grade as soon as he can benefit thereby. Of course, a great deal depends on the child's ability, and his previous schooling. I believe this practice is being handled very wisely.

Some teachers seem troubled because their children speak Spanish at every opportunity they have. It is natural for children to use their vernacular among themselves, as it is natural for any group of people to use their mother tongue in preference to a foreign language. That should worry no one. A child learning a foreign language does not use it as a rule in place of the vernacular until he consciously feels the need to do so. This requires discipline on his part because he sees that it is absolutely necessary for him to learn the foreign language. This means that he must abstain from speaking his vernacular and accept the additional burden of speaking the more difficult medium. That resolution does not come to a child until the period of adolescence or later when he realizes the need for his learning the foreign language and the advantages that he will derive from the mastery of it. Then he makes the effort. The environment in which he lives has a great deal to do with the effort that he puts forth. An English-speaking environment would stimulate the effort. I do not think that too much pressure or constant urging helps very much--on the contrary, this may antagonize the child.

Another problem most discussed among teachers is the teacher herself. Should the teacher know Spanish herself? Some believe she should, and many teachers in New York City who teach Puerto Rican children are learning Spanish. In some schools as many as 50% of the teachers can use enough Spanish to get along with the children. Nevertheless, there are some teachers and administrators who feel that the teacher who teaches Spanish-speaking children need not know Spanish. They contend that when the teacher knows Spanish she uses it as a crutch. I have observed teachers who do not know Spanish and I have also observed those who know Spanish very well. In my visits, I have observed teachers without a knowledge of Spanish working very hard and very energetically in order to "put it over" as we often say. At the other extreme I observed a teacher who has an excellent command of Spanish and who used so much Spanish in the classroom that it was more an exercise in translation than an English class. These are the two extremes. On the other hand, in one of the public schools of the city, I visited a young, inexperienced teacher instructing Spanish-speaking children. No one could tell that she knew Spanish until she resorted to that language in order to clear up some slight point and avoid waste of time. In my opinion, this young teacher was using her knowledge of Spanish wisely, at the opportune moment. In the meantime, she used every possible device to make the children use English. Personally, I feel that a teacher teaching children whose native tongue is Spanish could do a better and more intelligent job if she were equipped with a knowledge of Spanish. Such a teacher would not only understand the child better, but would be able to appreciate his linguistic difficulties, because she can put herself in the child's place, and therefore should be able to understand him better than the teacher who does not know Spanish.

Due to the circumstances in the homes and the communities from which the children come, circumstances beyond the control of the school, the child hears and speaks more Spanish than English out of school. Hence the importance of his being in an environment of English when he is in school. I agree that if the Spanish-speaking child in New York City is going to learn English he should be taught in that language. Spanish should be used only when necessary. However, this should not be an argument against the teacher's knowing Spanish as part of her teaching equipment. It is not her knowledge of Spanish which is a liability, but it is the misuse of Spanish as a crutch when it is not necessary. I think, therefore, that knowledge of Spanish on the part of a teacher who teaches children of Puerto Rican extraction is an asset rather than a liability.

2. Materials of Instruction

Another problem which seems to bother the teachers is the
dearth of materials of instruction in English which may be used in
the classes, especially in the junior high school where the children
are retarded and the literature available is inadequate. Some resourceful principals and teachers are developing their own materials of instruction. This seems to be an excellent way to furnish
the schools with reading material in the absence of appropriate literature. Some elementary and junior high schools have already
gathered considerable material which should be mimeographed and
improved in the hope that it will contribute to a fund of literature
much needed for the Spanish-speaking population. The recommendation (4) made by the Report of the Association of Assistant Superintendents is most pertinent. Nevertheless, there should be adapt-
able material in the large amount of literature for children which
is being published constantly by the various publishing firms. It
seems to me that a committee of teachers, together with the school
authorities entrusted with the selection of textbooks for the public
schools, should get together and explore the field, find out what is
being published and what might be appropriate in order to supply
this need. I have examined several publications which should be
interesting to children of Spanish speech. These deal primarily
with Latin American topics. The New York public schools might
have in stock material which may prove suitable. Bibliographies of
children's literature issued by various companies and agencies may
help. The Office of Puerto Rico in New York will be pleased to be
of service in this regard.

3. Placement of Children

Another problem which concerns principals and teachers is
placement of children upon their arrival from Puerto Rico. The
teachers feel that there are no norms or diagnostic tests which
might aid in the placement of these children in the city schools.
Puerto Rico has an American system of education organized on the
6-3-3 plan, with the exception that Spanish is the medium of instruction in the elementary school. The content of the curriculum,
including many of the textbooks, is the same as in the schools on
the mainland. There is, therefore, sufficient similarity in organization and content so that when a Puerto Rican child transfers to
the States, all things being equal, he should have a normal transfer. There is, nevertheless, the language difficulty which has to be
met. At first the language difficulty seems an enormous barrier
because the child apparently does not know English. Due to the
fact that he has lived in a Spanish environment and has been taught
in Spanish, he has had little opportunity to practice English; hence
his ear is not educated to comprehension and his tongue is not educated to expression, and he may appear to know less English than
he really does. It is my firm conviction that a child coming from
Puerto Rico should, as far as possible, be given the opportunity of

normal transfer.   Then, in the special classes in English, he should
have at least two hours a day studying the language.   In six months
he should be doing normal school work in his grade.   This rule
could apply both to the elementary and the secondary school levels.
     The difficulty lies in the fact that the majority of the chil-
dren in the schools which I have visited are recent arrivals, from
underprivileged groups who have not had normal school facilities.
They belong to the large group of children in the island who do not
go to school long enough either to learn English or to receive much
instruction of any kind.   Generally, they are average, of secondary
school level as far as school age is concerned, but very retarded
in school achievement.   It is difficult to place these children in
New York City schools.   I found many in junior high school, but
actually doing primary grade work.   This problem seems to trouble
the teachers and they wonder whether Puerto Rico has a compulsory
school attendance law, and why the children do not know more English when this language is taught from the first grade all through
the public school system.   Here, for teachers instructing recent arrivals from Puerto Rico, is the need for information about the lack
of school facilities in the island; the problem of double enrollment;
the tremendous increase in population; and the inability of the educational system to cope with the educational needs of the population.
The visit of New York City teachers to Puerto Rico this summer
will contribute a great deal toward the comprehension of this problem.   The problem of these under-privileged retarded children is
most serious, not only in New York, but also in Puerto Rico.   It
is difficult to make suggestions based on my brief visits.   It is a
problem which bears further and more extensive study.

4. Test of Academic Achievement and Mental Ability

     Many teachers have spoken to me about diagnostic tests
which might be used in placing children coming from Puerto Rico.
Very little has been done in this field.   The University of Puerto
Rico has done some work in the preparation of a standard test for
the public schools in Puerto Rico.   Quite a great deal was accomplished in the thirties.   Unfortunately, this activity has been neglected in recent years and the tests that we have today are not up
to date.   They may serve, however, as models in case a study of
this kind is undertaken.   The Office of Puerto Rico in New York
will be glad to furnish copies of these tests to the school authorities in case they may help in the construction of new tests.
     Copies of the following tests may be secured at the Office of
Puerto Rico:
     1. Spanish American test of English
        Form 1-A for Grades 2, 3, 4, 5.
     2. "TEST" Hispanoamericano de Habilidad y Aprovechamiento
        Forma 1-A para grados 3, 4, 5.
     3. Spanish American test of English
        Form II-A for grades 6, 7, 8, 9.
     4. "TEST" Hispanoamericano de Habilidad y Aprovechamiento
        Forma II-B para grados 6, 7, 8, 9.

5. University of Puerto Rico
   General Ability Test for Grades 8-12
   Form A (Revised)
6. University of Puerto Rico
   General Ability Test for Grades 8-12
   Form B
7. University of Puerto Rico
   General Ability Test for Grades 8-12
   Form C
8. University of Puerto Rico
   General Ability Test for Grades 8-12
   Form X

California has done some work in the preparation of tests for children of Spanish speech. I am not acquainted with these tests but copies may be secured from the State of California, Bureau of Examinations, 5916 Hollywood Boulevard, Los Angeles, California. This test was translated into Spanish by the personnel of the Department of Education of Puerto Rico.

The Inter-American Test: The Committee of Modern Languages of the American Council on Education, of which Professor Robert H. Fife, of Columbia University, is chairman, has been interested in the construction of tests for children in bilingual situations. In 1940 Dr. Fife and Dr. H.T. Manuel of the University of Texas, visited Puerto Rico under the auspices of the American Council on Education. As a result of their visit it was decided that they should prepare a battery of tests which should be parallel in English and in Spanish for measuring achievements in these languages. With the cooperation of the Department of Education of Puerto Rico, the University of Puerto Rico, the Ministry of Education of Mexico and the University of Texas, the test construction project was begun. Copies of the test were completed in 1942.

The tests included general ability at the primary, intermediate and advanced levels; reading (vocabulary and comprehension) at the primary, intermediate and advanced levels; language usage (active vocabulary and expression); vocabulary and interpretation of reading material in the natural sciences; and vocabulary and interpretation of reading material in the social studies.

The test administration in Mexico and Texas began in 1943, and in the spring of that year the tests were administered to nearly 20,000 pupils in the schools of Puerto Rico. The final test, revised and standardized, will be ready for use before the end of this year. Copies may be secured from the Educational Testing Service, Rosedale Road, Princeton, New Jersey, or from the American Council on Education, 744 Jackson Place, N.W., Washington, D.C. These tests should prove useful in New York.

Irrespective of what aid may be found in these tests mentioned above, I believe that the New York public school authorities should as soon as possible put into effect Recommendation No. 5, page 103, of the Report of the Association of Assistant Superintendents, and, that personnel be prepared in the construction and administration of tests to handle this situation; that other personnel be equipped with

the linguistic preparation necessary to handle the problem and that
the same personnel be attached to the Division of Test and Measurement of the Bureau of Reference, Research and Statistics of the
Public Schools of New York. It is obvious that people doing this
work should know Spanish well. It may be that the University of
Puerto Rico would be willing to lend the services of a member of
the staff of the Department of Educational Psychology to aid in the
initiation of such a program. Dr. H.T. Manuel of the University
of Texas has had a great deal of experience with children of Spanish speech and may be available for consultation.

4. Teacher Training Program

Inasmuch as the language problem is recognized by all to
be the pivot point around which revolve many of the educational difficulties of the Puerto Ricans in New York, it would seem advisable
to implement the recommendation of the Report of the Association
of Assistant Superintendents to the effect that "courses for teachers
in methodology and instructional materials for teaching non-English
speaking pupils should be organized and staffed by experts." Much
has been done in recent years in the preparation of teachers for the
teaching of English as a modern foreign language. Several universities have recognized the need of preparing teachers to meet the
language needs of non-English speaking children. The outstanding
institution in this new field of language teaching has been the English Language Institute at the University of Michigan. Teachers
College, Columbia University, has also established a program.
New York University is planning to establish courses of this nature.
It may seem advisable for the Board of Education, in accordance
with the recommendation of the report already quoted, to establish
a teacher-training program in the teaching of English as a foreign
language, select those teachers who have been successful with Puerto Rican children and equip them with the knowledge and techniques
necessary to meet the needs of the non-English speaking pupils.

5. The School and the Home.

In my visit to the public schools I took special interest in
inquiring about the relationship between the school and the home and
what is being done to bring the two together. All of the schools
have Parent Teachers Associations. In some of them, such as
P.S. 124, Bronx, the PTA is a strong organization. A Puerto Rican mother happens to be President. She has been instrumental in
securing the cooperation of Puerto Rican parents. I was informed
in other schools that Puerto Rican parents were members of the
Board of Directors of their Parent Teachers Associations, but in
many schools I found the PTA rather weak, and as a general rule
the participation of Puerto Rican parents in the activities of the
PTA was poor.

Housing and health conditions among the Puerto Rican population are substandard in many instances. The report cited, pages
25-27, gives a description of these conditions. Also the report
"Puerto Ricans in New York City," prepared by a committee of the

Welfare Council, gives (pages 30 and 33) a fine description of housing and sanitation facilities available to Puerto Ricans. Most of
the parents living in these homes work and it is difficult for them
to attend meetings. Mothers are overburdened with housework and
large families, and this, plus the fact that the mothers as a general rule do not speak English and cannot understand what is going
on, keeps them from attending the PTA meetings. It is not difficult to understand why Puerto Rican parents are not more active in
the PTA in view of the above.

Some principals and teachers spoke about irregularity in
school attendance on the part of Puerto Rican children. Sometimes
they attend only half a day and sometimes they are absent all day.
In some schools the problem is more serious than in others. The
children play hooky and there is a need for someone to act as a
connecting link between the home and the school. This person is
generally a man and is called "Attendance Officer." Some devote
all their time to this job, while others have other duties. The attendance officers whom I met are very fine men and some of them
genuinely interested in the children. Yet the attendance officer is
looked upon by the children more as a policeman, as the one that
goes after the delinquent child, as the one who goes for the child
after he has done something wrong. He is, therefore, someone to
be afraid of, to be avoided, to run away from. Recommendation
13, page 107 of the report mentioned, reads as follows:

A community relations teacher should be assigned to districts where there are large concentrations of Puerto
Ricans.

School-community coordinators should be attached to the
Assistant Superintendent's offices to facilitate adjustments
and to further efforts for the establishment of more favorable school and community relations. These workers
should be trained and supervised by the Bureau of Community Education. Their assignments should be made on
the basis of local need in areas which have large numbers
of Puerto Rican residents. The ability to speak Spanish
should be one of the prerequisites in the selection of personnel for such assignments.

There is very little that I can add to this recommendation. The
time is ripe to have these community coordinators in sections
where the Puerto Rican population is concentrated, especially when
the home falls so far short of cooperating with the school. The
present system does not prevent the child from becoming delinquent.
The community coordinator or community relations teacher would
prevent delinquency. The community coordinator would be an agent
of adult education among the parents. Benjamin Franklin High
School already has employed a fine young lady of Puerto Rican extraction with excellent command of both languages, well educated in
one of the city colleges. The services of this young lady are invaluable to Dr. Covello, the Principal. He should have not only one
community coordinator but as many as the needs of the school demand. A school such as P. S. 57, East Harlem, with a Puerto Rican enrollment of about 90%, could well use several community

workers or community coordinators. I am sure the Puerto Rican
parents would cooperate better if such a coordinator, with a knowledge of Spanish, were to work among them. The Social Welfare
section of this office might well be of help in the selection, training and orientation of community coordinators.

6. Vocational Guidance

Most of the Puerto Rican children attending public schools in
New York will leave school as soon as it is legally possible and
will go to work. The schools must have a vocational guidance program to orient children in useful and gainful occupations upon leaving school. The Board of Education also has a cooperative education program. Boys and girls under eighteen years who visit our
office seem to be unaware of the existence of a guidance program.
I have generally referred the cases that have come to this office to
the school principals. I would like to learn more about the vocational guidance program of the public schools of New York City,
the facilities available and the number of Puerto Rican children who
take advantage of these facilities. I have not had time to look into
this part of the school system. The majority of the boys and girls
of Puerto Rican extraction will either become unskilled, semi-
skilled or skilled laborers. The school should be able to guide
them into vocational training in accordance with their abilities. I
think that the section of Education in this office should be equipped
to cooperate with the public schools in furnishing guidance to boys
and girls who are preparing to learn a trade or profession.

Puerto Rico's Part

What should Puerto Rico do? As soon as a person from
Puerto Rico transfers to New York City and establishes his residence here, he thereby becomes a citizen of New York and an heir
to all the privileges and responsibilities to be found here, and is no
longer a problem for Puerto Rico. Nevertheless, due to the unusual circumstances of population, migration, language, economic status and problems of adjustment, Puerto Rico cannot lose interest in
her citizens on the mainland who may be in need. To a certain
extent Puerto Rico does have a responsibility, if only because of
her population problem. She should cooperate with the States in the
adjustment of her citizens who transfer to the continent. What
should she do?

1. Children of School Age. - New York City has a compulsory school law whereby every child under eighteen years of age must
attend school full time until he is sixteen years old, and part time
under special arrangements during the last two years of compulsory
school attendance. Therefore, the Department of Education of
Puerto Rico could help the New York school authorities by facilitat-
ing school records and any check that the Department may have on
the children's abilities, such as records of intelligence tests or any
other pertinent information. It would help a great deal if children
transferring to New York schools were informed about New York

and the educational opportunities in the city. This should not be
difficult for the Department, and the New York school authorities
would no doubt be willing to furnish information for dissemination
among those transferring to New York.

2. Materials of Instruction. Puerto Rico is beginning a new
epoch in her educational history. For fifty years the Federal Government has actually set the pattern which Puerto Rico was to follow in her educational development. This year Puerto Rico will
elect her own Governor who in turn will appoint a Commissioner of
Education. In other words, Puerto Rico after fifty years since the
American occupation, is going to take over the school system and
run it her own way. She will be free to develop an educational
philosophy and to implement it as she thinks best. An educational
survey will soon be made of the school system. No doubt these
events will be followed by much activity in the field of education.
Puerto Rico has done little in the development of materials of instruction suitable to her peculiar problem in dealing with two languages and two civilizations. Great activity is already in progress.
The results will no doubt encourage the development of materials
of instruction and methodology. New York City is also working intelligently in the development of materials of instruction. There
should be an exchange of materials and experience which will aid
mutually in the solution of many problems.

3. Exchange of Personnel. This summer several teachers
from New York City are visiting Puerto Rico and observing the
schools at work. Puerto Rican educators have visited the New York
schools and are interested in the education of their fellow citizens
here. I believe the time has come to go further and think of exchanging personnel for a semester or a year. The people working
on English at the Department of Education should spend a season in
New York finding out what the schools here are doing, and some
educators from New York interested in the problems of Puerto Rican children could spend half a year or a year observing what
Puerto Rico is doing. This exchange of personnel should prove beneficial to the two parties concerned. Members of the University of
Puerto Rico staff may aid in this program.

4. The Teaching of English. Puerto Rico should intensify
the teaching of English so that the transfer of children to the mainland and their adjustment here may be made easier. The Puerto
Rican child should practice hearing and speaking English. He knows
a great deal of English, but his ear does not catch on and his
tongue is tied. Emphasis should be given to pronunciation.

5. Preparation for Migration. The Department of Education
should facilitate as far as possible the preparation of workers,
through courses in the public schools and vocational schools, either
during the regular sessions or in evening classes and summer
schools. The new School of Industrial Arts of the University can
do much in this regard. There is a great demand for household
services in this country. Candidates should be well selected and

should be instructed in household work techniques of the mainland. There is a great demand on the continent for skilled laborers, who receive excellent wages. Intensive courses in English should be offered to those preparing to work in the states, with special emphasis on what we might call vocational English, i.e., the English mostly used in connection with the trade or duties the migrants will perform upon their transfer to the mainland. I think the time has come for the Office of Puerto Rico in New York, in cooperation with industry, to take upon itself the responsibility of establishing adult education programs among Puerto Rican workers in the states and follow up work begun in Puerto Rico.

6. Control of Migration. As far as possible something should be done in Puerto Rico to discourage migration of people who do not have occupations to go into upon their arrival in this country, or of children whose parents live in Puerto Rico and who have no home in New York. Too many people are coming, hoping that they may find work and thereby better themselves economically, and in the case of the children, educationally. It is laudable that they take the chance, but the experience of the past teaches us that as far as possible, people should not come to the continent until they have secured employment here.

In closing I would like to express through you my deep appreciation to Superintendent Jansen, assistant superintendents, principals and teachers, for their courtesies and many acts of kindness during my visits to schools. They are all doing an excellent job worthy of Puerto Rico's gratitude.

Cándido Oliveras, "What Are the Educational Needs of Puerto Ricans Who Come to New York?" Address, New York University, January 14, 1961. Reprinted by permission.

I fully appreciate the invitation extended to me by the authorities of New York University to participate in this Conference on the education of the Puerto Ricans who migrate to New York City. For a long time I have devoted my life in the public service to the effort of raising the economic and cultural standards of my people. Now, as Secretary of Education of Puerto Rico, I am particularly pleased to speak before this group of distinguished educators and statesmen interested in discussing ways and means to help the Puerto Ricans realize their fullest potential.

On the subject of the educational needs of Puerto Ricans who come to New York, I can claim neither originality nor completeness. Other fellow-workers from Puerto Rico and from the mainland have made significant contributions in this field, in various forms, ranging from the formulation of possible basic policies to the study of specific problems in various areas, including the preparation of curriculum materials for teaching the Puerto Rican children in the States. Further, the subject is so vast that it precludes any attempt at full treatment before the job of full research is accomplished.

It would be presumptuous on my part to tell you specifically what the educational needs of Puerto Rican migrants are. Or, having suggested some or all of those needs, to try to come up with specific suggestions to take care of the needs. The case is similar to that of a patient who calls on a doctor. Through adequate examination the physician may be able to come up with an accurate diagnosis. After that, he may be in a favorable position to prescribe the required medical treatment. However, before starting on the physical examination the physician usually finds out what the clinical history of the patient is. If the patient cannot supply these answers, somebody ought to do it.

In connection with the educational needs of Puerto Ricans who come to New York City, you are in a better position than we to make the final diagnosis and prescribe the treatment. But we may help as a source of facts in order for you to be able to write the full clinical history of the patient. Hence, most of my talk today will be devoted to supplying this type of information.

I shall first talk about the contributions made by the Puerto Rican Study undertaken a few years ago under the sponsorship of the Board of Education of the City of New York with a grant-in-aid from the Fund for the Advancement of Education. At this time, I should like to mention some of the steps that, according to the Report, must be taken in order to accelerate the learning and adjustment of first and second generation Puerto Ricans and other non-

English speaking pupils in New York City. They were:
> Recognize and define the school's responsibility to
> assist, counsel, and cooperate with the parents of
> non-English-speaking pupils in all matters pertaining
> to the child's welfare.

> Take a new look at the school's opportunity to acceler-
> ate the adjustment of Puerto Rican children and their
> parents through advice and counsel to parents on prob-
> lems normally considered to be outside the conventional
> functions of the school.

> Staff the schools to do the job: to help the new arrival
> to make good adjustment to school and community; to
> help the non-English-speaking child to learn English and
> to find his way successfully into the main stream of the
> school's program.

> Take a new, hard look at the psychological services
> provided for non-English-speaking children, especially
> for Puerto Rican children.

One significant statement of basic policy of the Puerto Rican
Study was that we should accept it "not as something finished but
as the first stage of a larger, city-wide, ever-improving program
for the education and assimilation of non-English-speaking children."

Those proposals cover some of the outstanding areas of research and action in which definite programs can be planned. They
embody original ideas and approaches for the solution of unique new
situations, yet not unlike similar ones that you faced in the past
with respect to other minority migrant groups.

I will not elaborate on the educational needs of Puerto Ricans who migrate to New York and other parts of the mainland.
This has been the subject of numerous conferences and seminars
both here and in Puerto Rico. Any account of such needs must,
however, take into consideration the academic, social and vocational needs, and it must deal in part with the problems of adult education. I feel that you will be in a better position to discuss the subject by including an analysis of the social and cultural forces now
prevailing in Puerto Rican life. As all of you know, Puerto Rico
is at present undergoing a profound economic, social and cultural
transformation. Although I may not be able to add any significant
data to what has already come to your attention, I am sure you will
readily understand how the Puerto Rican effort of the last twenty
years is affecting in various forms the character, the culture, the
education and the adaptive potential of the Puerto Ricans who will
migrate to New York.

Under its Commonwealth status, Puerto Rico is a self-governing country in voluntary and close association with the United
States of America based on common citizenship, common defense
and free trade. In a historic resolution adopted by the General Assembly of the United Nations on November 3, 1953, this Commonwealth was solemnly recognized as a self-governing political body.

The fact that it preserves its partnership with the Union represents
a unique feature of world-wide significance and may eventually have
its impact on the ways of dealing with international relationships.
As a house of freedom it will necessarily have its imprint on the
migrants who come to New York. It has been said that a good culture must be flavored with both local and world-wide values.   It
is, thus, quite understandable that an observer might say this is
precisely what the Commonwealth of Puerto Rico is trying to do,
as exemplified by the terms "free" and "associated."   In the present day culture of Puerto Ricans the average child and the average
adult are increasingly learning the lesson of democracy and will
thus be able to contribute with their own values to the life of their
fellow-citizens on the mainland.   After all, we must never forget
that, in spite of the so-much publicized cultural differences between
New Yorkers and Puerto Ricans, we have much in common inherent
in our common Western and Christian heritages.

The effort being made by the Commonwealth of Puerto Rico
toward economic development will also affect the character of the
Puerto Rican migrant.   Due to its dynamic economic development
program, Puerto Rico is no longer a predominantly agricultural
country.   In 1959-60 the net income from manufacturing was $289
million; that from agriculture $177 million.   Income from manufac-
turing exceeded income from agriculture for the first time in 1955.
The number of factories established with government help reached
a total of 629 in June 1960.   During the decade between 1949-50 to
1959-60 the Commonwealth's gross product rose from $750.5 mil-
lion to $1,572.6 million.   As a result of all this economic growth,
the per capita income is now the highest in the Caribbean area and
the second highest in all Latin America (exceeded only by oil-rich
Venezuela).   However, it is still only about one-half that of the
poorest U.S. state.

One interesting feature of this economic growth is the fact
that it has been planned in a democratic climate.   The Puerto Rico
Planning Board, created by the Legislative Assembly, has been the
basic instrument in this connection.   This Planning Board has developed a master plan which includes a set of plans each dealing
with a particular aspect of the island's development.   This master
plan continually adjusts its "guide lines" in accordance with the
emerging needs and goals.

As a result of its economic development, Puerto Rico is undergoing a rapid transition from a rural to an urban way of life.
The social transformation resulting from urbanization will be a factor in determining the educational needs of all Puerto Rican migrants.   It will obviously increase the adaptiveness of the Puerto
Rican to the patterns of living in New York.

This, gentlemen, is a tight summary of what is happening
in Puerto Rico in the political, economic and social spheres.   As
to the impact of these recent developments on the Puerto Rican migrant, no one is better qualified to describe it than Governor Luis
Muñoz Marin, who, in an address to a labor convention in Atlantic
City, New Jersey, concluded:

　　When you meet a Puerto Rican in the streets of New
　　York, Chicago, Los Angeles, or on the farms of New

Jersey, Connecticut or Minnesota, no matter how un-
adapted he may seem to his new environment, think of
him as a member of a human group that is trying to be
useful to freedom; remember that there is a little more
to him than meets the eye. Back in his Commonwealth
he has a background of democracy and kindliness, a
simple and sincere regard for his fellow-beings--no matter of what race, color or nation. This may be invisible
at first, but it also migrates with him.

Education, of course, has played a very significant role in
the Puerto Rican transformation. At the present time well over
a third of the island's population is receiving some kind of formal
education, ranging from kindergarten to college and adult education.
A United Nations publication (1957) reported this as the world's
highest proportion, and this is undoubtedly a measure of Puerto
Rico's faith in education. One-third of all government outlay is
devoted to educational services of various kinds.

The stronger effort, just started, for the coming ten years
has been very appropriately labeled "The Decade of Education."
The economic, social and cultural goals adopted by the Commonwealth give rise to new demands and present new challenges to our
educational system. These have to do not only with our manpower
needs for further economic growth, but also with all the problems
and needs generated by a rapidly changing society in a very exacting period of its history.

During the last twenty years, we have witnessed an unprecedented educational growth in quantitative terms. The number of
classrooms and teachers have increased spectacularly but are still
insufficient. This has indeed been a remarkable achievement, but
is only a first important stage. This effort must be continued but
at the same time we have started on a new phase in which quality
more than quantity will be our main concern. The present educational reform movement gives special attention to factors that condition the teaching effort. We have been able to make free, universal education a reality in Puerto Rico; we are now starting to con-
solidate this achievement by providing at least the minimum requisites for efficient instruction in all our schools.

At present, 61 per cent of all children in elementary grades
attend schools organized under a double enrollment plan, which provides only 3 hours of instruction per day, and 10 per cent attend
schools organized under an interlocking plan, providing for a 5-hour
school day. At the junior and senior high school levels, 37 per
cent and 18 per cent, respectively, are attending schools organized
under the interlocking plan. Out of a total of 572,000 pupils in our
public schools, 241,000 are in double enrollment. This means that
over two-fifths of our students receive only three hours of schooling
daily. It is thus obvious that our new reform effort needs to be
directed toward the complete elimination of this inadequacy, representing, as it does, not only a handicap to the normal quality of
performance but also a limit on the actual extension of educational
opportunities. We have set this as a goal to be attained within the
next four years.

Closely related to the quality of instruction is the problem of providing suitable textbooks and teaching aids in adequate quantities to meet the needs of all our students at all instructional levels. We have made considerable progress in this direction during the last ten years, thanks to the appropriations of our Legislative Assembly, but we still have a long way to go. We are producing a sizeable quantity of books especially designed to meet our educational needs and we have established our own printing facilities. We will continue to avail ourselves of United States textbooks, but we will also continue to produce increasing numbers of books, manuals, guides, courses of study and various other teaching materials adapted to our present day trends and conditions.

The number of pupils a teacher can handle in any ordinary teaching situation without impairing teaching efficiency is another problem receiving our attention. A heavy teaching load precludes the possibility of individual attention. This situation is responsible for a prevailing instructional pattern in which teaching is geared to the less than average performances, thus depriving the most capable students of the challenges to which they are entitled in a truly democratic educational system. We have, therefore, begun to organize special courses for talented students, including college level courses for twelfth grade students. We have also organized pilot classes for retarded but educable pupils.

We are strengthening our mechanisms for evaluating results. For this we are preparing achievement tests to be administered at the various teaching levels to ascertain the degree of performance in terms of the goals previously set. The results of this evaluation will show us the deficient areas in which remedial action should be taken. In general, this will also be a concrete way of assessing the effectiveness of our public education for which so much money is being spent.

We have already started on other projects which, because of lack of time, I will not describe on this occasion. I have outlined only those which might be of special interest to you at this Conference. I should like to assure you that we in the Department of Education of the Commonwealth of Puerto Rico will give our wholehearted support to the recommendations made by the Fourth Migration Conference held in June 1960 here in New York. In that Conference it was recommended that the Board of Education of New York City and the Department of Education of Puerto Rico establish a joint committee to coordinate their activities in several areas of mutual concern; among these I mention the following: further implementation of the program for the teaching of English as a second language in Puerto Rico; the development of workshops for Puerto Rican teachers and supervisors to be held in New York; improvement of procedures for the exchange of pupil information and school records; exchange of information on methods of working with parents as part of community education and parent participation; continuation of efforts to develop valid tests to aid in the grade placement of pupils; re-activation of the program for the exchange of teaching personnel between Puerto Rico and New York; exchange and further development of teaching materials; and the continued development of educational and vocational guidance activities and of vocational train-

ing aimed at further encouraging Puerto Rican students to enter
professional and technical fields.

This joint committee has already been organized and our
permanent committee in collaboration with New York school authorities has currently under consideration a supervisory exchange proposal recommended by its sub-committee on the teaching of English
as a second language. I hope soon to give special attention to matters concerning the joint action of this New York-Puerto Rico committee. In the meantime, we are continuing the projects that I have
already outlined and these will eventually have their impact on the
education of all Puerto Ricans, including the migrants to New York
and other parts of the Union.

In closing, I would like to say that I have complete confidence in the results of this important conference sponsored by the
educators of New York University. As co-workers we are rededi-
cating ourselves to the unity of the Western Hemisphere. Puerto
Rico and New York provide a remarkable example of what should be
done on behalf of a better understanding among all the peoples of
the world.

"Puerto Rican Pupils in American Schools."   Mayor's Committee
on Puerto Rican Affairs in New York City.   Report of the
Sub-Committee on Education, Recreation and Parks.   (New
York, 1951), pp. 12-20.   Mimeograph.   Leonard Covello,
Chairman.   Reprinted by permission.

There are numerous important nuclei of Puerto Ricans outside the familiar "barrio" (community) in East Harlem: Lower
Bronx, northwestern Manhattan, "south" Brooklyn, etc.

***

In the 75 schools under discussion (i.e. with the heaviest
percentages of Puerto Rican pupils), there are over 25,000 pupils
listed as Puerto Rican.   There are, of course, thousands more in
schools not included in this study.

The city has 8 assistant superintendents whose districts are
included in this study; in the city over 26% of the entire school population is Puerto Rican.   One superintendent's group of districts has
over 49% Puerto Rican pupils; another has over 42%.

***

In the schools whose total school population is over 26%
Puerto Rican, only 5% of the teachers claim any skill in use of
Spanish.   "In districts having 49% and 42% Puerto Ricans, we find
that only 7.6% and 6.1 respectively of the teaching body can communicate with the pupils or their parents in a common language."

"The need for teachers who can speak Spanish is urgent.
If...increased proportionately to the Puerto Rican school population,
we should need approximately 1000 real Spanish-speaking teachers
..."

"Almost one-third of schools reporting have no Spanish-
speaking teachers."

"We disagree with the viewpoint that the teacher's use of
Spanish in the classroom serves as a crutch.   If we accept as our
basic goal the child's adjustment to his new environment, it is important that he communicate...in Spanish until he is able to express
himself somewhat adequately in English."   (It may be added that
this is particularly true in the case of adolescents, recently arrived
from Puerto Rico, who have attained some measure of mental and
emotional maturity.)

***

"The Puerto Rican parent must be made to feel that his child
is being accepted with the same status as that of the Continental
child..., that his home life is not being held up to criticism."

"A special effort should be made to involve parents in the
school program."

"All communications for parents should contain a Spanish
translation."   (It may be of interest to know that schools are be-

246

ginning to use report cards in duplicate with translations in Spanish.)

***

"Active participation in the recreational life of the community will accelerate the Puerto Rican's acculturation... It will give
him a sense of belonging."

"Contact with other community groups in experiences which
help relieve tensions will undoubtedly stimulate the desire to learn
English."

"Schools should be kept open a maximum number of hours
summer and winter for recreational and vocational purposes."

***

"The Elementary Division has appointed a group of 10 Puerto
Rican (bi-lingual) teachers (Substitute Auxiliary Teachers) to
schools having the largest concentration of Puerto Ricans...to assist
in the orientation of these children (and to) serve as liaison between
the school and the community."

"If the purposes for which "C" classes were originally introduced...are to be fulfilled, the register should not exceed 15.
"C" classes are special classes required for non-English speaking
pupils and new arrivals from Puerto Rico.

***

"The number of "C" classes is disproportionately small...
No school area has even half as many as it needs."

***

"There is need for a Curriculum Bulletin on each level...
which will collate materials in existence." "The dearth of suitable,
adequate teaching and learning materials is a major problem."

***

"The kindergartens are crowded and there is an additional
40% waiting for admission."

***

"The attendance problems which are causing great concern
...will be appreciably lessened if an adequate mental hygiene policy
were pursued."

***

"Sixty of 75 schools...find totally inadequate medical and
health resources, including those services offered by health agencies..." "The conditions under which they live (on the island and)
in New York City...have made the Puerto Ricans more vulnerable
to disease."

***

Recommendations

This survey, encompassing all schools in the city with Puerto Rican children and including all areas of the total school and
community program, has served to highlight the magnitude of the
task which confronts educational and social agencies in New York
City.

On the basis of the responses to the survey questions, the
following recommendations are indicated.

I. Registration
       A. The first contact between the school and the Puerto Ri-
can parent should be made a pleasant experience. The Puerto Rican parent must be made to feel that his child is being accepted
with the same status as that of the Continental child. He must be
made to feel that his home life is not being held up to criticism
and to scrutiny.
       B. The attitude of principal, clerks and other school person-
nel acting as receptionists will set the tone for future rapport.
       C. There is no doubt that a Spanish-speaking person on the
staff will facilitate this initial contact with the schools. Many questions that arise in the mind of the parents concerning the school
program, routines and special services offered by the school as
well as many questions that arise in the minds of the school personnel concerning important aspects of the child's previous schooling and background, will be resolved through the medium of the foreign language.
       D. Short welcome booklets that explain the school program
pictorially have been used effectively and should be made a universal practice.
       E. All pre-registration and registration forms should contain
a Spanish translation. These translations, however, do not obviate
the necessity for a Spanish-speaking person since many parents cannot read or write.

II. Placement
       The emotional security and need for belonging that we recog-
nize as fundamental for optimum school adjustment, are ensured to
a great extent with the proper grade placement of the Puerto Rican
child. Although more time-consuming, all placement done on an individual basis will effect more satisfactory adjustment. The following factors should be taken into consideration in order of importance:
       1.   The age of the child
       2.   Social maturity
       3.   Physical appearance (a child who is very small due
            to nutritional deficiency may be placed in a lower
            grade, where his classmates would most nearly ap-
            proximate his stature)
       4.   Previous schooling

       When the grade has been determined on the basis of the
four points listed above, the class chosen should be one where
there are other Spanish-speaking children. Criteria for selection
of the teacher may include a knowledge of Spanish and an understanding attitude.
       The above considerations obtain in cases of placement below
the third year and where there are no "C" classes.
       The child should remain with this group until he shows abil-
ity to adjust to a regular class.

III. Organization

In schools where there are large numbers of Puerto Rican children, maximum registers in all regular classes in the school should not exceed 25. For even after the initial period of orientation, there is still a great need for individualized instruction and guidance, e.g. in the development of communication skills so that the child may participate more fully in class and school activities; in speech improvement and in intonation patterns.

If the purposes for which "C" classes were originally introduced into the schools are to be fulfilled, the register should not exceed 15.

IV. Teachers

A. Use of Spanish-speaking teachers

We disagree with the viewpoint that the teacher's use of Spanish in the classroom serves as a crutch, retarding the child's English language development. If we accept as our basic goal the child's adjustment to his new environment, it is important that he communicate with others in Spanish until he is able to express himself somewhat adequately in English.

The objection that the child will not feel the need of learning English if the teacher understands his Spanish, is not a valid one; the child's desire and interest in learning the second language will be stimulated by participation in meaningful classroom experiences and activities.

The Spanish-speaking teacher may be utilized in all phases of the school program:

1. For registration
2. For translation of forms and letters
3. As interpreter for parents and children
4. As teacher of "C" or Remedial Language classes
5. As liaison with the community
6. As school guidance counselor
7. As speaker at parents meetings
8. As instructor of Spanish In-Service Courses
9. To advise parents and children in the areas of health, safety, nutrition, sanitation and community resources.
10. To assist school, district and city personnel, who come to render special services (Bureau of Child Guidance, Attendance Coordinators, Psychologists, etc.)

It is suggested that special examinations be given for the purpose of licensing people with a knowledge of Spanish, to serve both in the classroom and in the capacity stated above.

B. The Orientation of Teachers

Teachers should be assisted in meeting the challenge of this latest migration. The following minimum suggestions are offered:

1. The principal should arrange for faculty conferences dealing with the background of the Puerto Rican and with problems of Puerto Rican adjustment here. Resource people should be invited to contribute the benefit of their experience.

2. Workshops should be set up in each school to examine existing materials and to develop additional units of work.

3. A Spanish-speaking teacher in the school or in a neighboring school should give instruction in Conversational Spanish.

4. There should be a center which would serve as a clearing house for ideas, units, materials of instruction that have been found useful. This project would serve as a means of articulation between the different levels of the system.

5. There must be time set aside for periodic conferences between the Remedial Language (O.T.P.) and the regular teacher. Learnings, knowledge, skills and attitudes as they are gained in one class may be reinforced in the other by a mutual exchange of ideas and materials.

6. Teachers who are known to have evolved special procedures and techniques with Puerto Rican children, should be encouraged to give demonstration lessons for other teachers.

7. Provision should be made for inter- and intra-visitation.

8. Bulletins dealing with the bilingual children from other sections of the country should be studied and evaluated for adaptation to the New York City situation.

V. Textbooks and Supplies

Summaries of the answers to this question show such wide variations in the amount of extra money made available to the schools for the Puerto Rican program as well as in what the schools actually required that a special study is evidently needed in this area.

VI. Teaching and Learning Materials

The dearth of suitable, adequate teaching and learning materials is a major problem confronting supervisors and teachers.

There is a need for a Curriculum Bulletin for elementary, junior and senior high schools.

1. This Bulletin should represent the cooperative effort of teachers of Puerto Rican children, of Curriculum Research Assistants, of personnel from special divisions at the Board of Education and Community Agencies.

2. This Bulletin should suggest additional experiences, activities, procedures and practices for the Puerto Rican children.

3. The Bulletin should be based on the principles of child growth and development which are the foundations of the current school program in New York City.

4. The Bulletin should emphasize the experiences, activities and concepts which the Puerto Rican child will find useful in his daily life, in the home, school and community.

5. The Bulletin should evaluate carefully such methods as the Ogden Method, or the Fries Method, adapting these to the situation of Puerto Ricans in New York City. These methods might assist teachers to supplement and vary certain aspects of the teaching situation.

6. The Bulletin should make suggestions for all teachers of Puerto Rican children. The regular teacher with some Puerto Rican children has as much need for this type of material as the

"C" or Remedial Language teacher.

There is need for materials in all areas geared to the social maturity level of the children but with a vocabulary level simple enough for their limited knowledge of English. Material may be prepared locally.

Audio-visual materials which develop and fix concepts and which vitalize instruction should be part of the regular school equipment. Existing audio-visual materials should be examined in light of these children's needs.

Strip films and slides which allow for informal, spontaneous discussion during their showing are to be preferred to more elaborate movies.

A special differential should be allowed not only for texts, but also for craft and art supplies, for manipulatory activities and art experiences which contribute to the emotional security of the Puerto Rican child. These offer to the Puerto Rican child the opportunity: 1. to express himself in media other than language and 2. to utilize his native abilities. He will thus acquire status in the eyes of his classmates.

VIII. Methods of Instruction

All formal learning should be deferred until the child feels secure. The development of learning should follow the pattern suggested below:

1. Utilization of the child's background.

2. Provision for experiences which familiarize him with the school and community and which stimulate the desire to learn English.

3. Utilization of the language arts program of the natural sequences of communication arts: activities--oral communication--reading--writing.

The approach to formal reading should be through experiential charts.

All means of expression, music, art, puppetry, dramatic play should be an integral part of the school day.

IX. Tests and Measurements

Tests for these children should be developed and standardized according to our knowledge of their background in Puerto Rico and the emerging cultural pattern in the new environment.

The tests, to be conducted by trained Spanish-speaking personnel, should be administered in small groups and in an informal atmosphere so that the maximum potentialities of the child can more accurately be gauged.

Results of group standardized tests should not be the decisive factor in grade placement. Wherever questions arise, individual non-language tests should be given.

X. Health

An intensified health program for children and adults is vitally important. Instruction in the areas of sanitation, nutrition and safety should be emphasized through actual experiences in and out of the classroom. Discussions and actual demonstrations on these and similar topics should be held for parents. Spanish translations of available health materials should be made. Home visits by social and welfare personnel, although very costly in time and money, are desirable. Parents should be made aware of existing public or private health services.

It would be advisable to carry on a "readiness" program which would help the child to accept the foods served in the school lunch program. One effective means of doing this would be to introduce new foods together with the familiar foods.

XI. Mental Health or Child Guidance

Every school should have a well-planned guidance program with fixed responsibility, resting upon a person assigned for that specific purpose. This person should speak Spanish. The entire staff, however, should be made aware of the problems facing the children and of the necessity of adapting the curriculum to meet the special needs of these children.

The attendance problems which are causing great concern at the present time will be appreciably lessened if an adequate mental hygiene policy were pursued.

XIII. Recreational Facilities

All city agencies should be involved in planning for adequate recreational facilities.

Many Puerto Rican mothers work because it is easier for the woman to find work than the man. Provision for all-day care of children at all age levels should be made to insure the health and safety of the children and to eliminate any incipient juvenile delinquency.

Summer camp facilities should be extended.

In all cases, the personnel should be especially trained to work effectively with these children.

Schools, strategically located and equipped for adult afternoon and evening programs, should be kept open a maximum number of hours summer and winter for recreational and vocational purposes.

XIV. Community Relations

A.   Efficient and responsible operation of the program requires fixed responsibility. Trained personnel should be licensed to assume full charge of community centers.

B-1.   Optimum functioning requires a procedure where tested experiences could be reported to a central agency, and guidance funneled out from central headquarters to all workers in the field. This can be the case only if one agency, such as the Board of Education, assumes responsibility for the appointment of all the Puerto Rican field or staff workers recommended above.

B-2.   Uniform qualifications for service should be established in terms of the needs of such a position rather than depending on the haphazard selection now evident.

B-3. Part-time or on-the-run responsibility cannot cope with a
      problem of the magnitude of the Puerto Rican orientation and
      assistance program. There is need for a full-time staff
      worker distributing his time among teaching Puerto Rican
      students, serving as a counsellor to this group, and working
      with parents and community agencies for the welfare of
      these people.

C.   While the indicated attempt to convey the aspects of the Puerto
      Rican program to parents and community is commendable,
      there is no evidence of a procedure to evaluate most effec-
      tive techniques developed for such purposes. Here, too, a
      central overall responsibility in the Board of Education might
      be able to set up central evaluation procedures.

XV.   Adults

A special effort should be made to involve parents in the
school program so that they will understand the aims and the functions of the schools. One effective means of obtaining parent cooperation is to assist them.

Group meetings of parents should be so arranged that the
Puerto Rican parents are made to feel an integral part of the proceedings. Topics for discussion at these meetings should be carefully selected on the basis of an awareness of their needs--needs
as we may see them and as they express them. There is no doubt
that other participating groups will profit from discussions of nutrition, health, employment opportunities and community resources.

All communications for parents should contain a Spanish
translation.

XVI.   Teacher Training

In addition to the recommendations of the Subcommittee, the
training of teachers is one of the basic areas which should be developed and strengthened. Accordingly, the following four recommendations should receive the special attention of the educational
system and the teacher-training institutions:

1. Separate training and examination for bilingual teachers
with ability to speak Spanish fluently, and with knowledge of Puerto
Rican social backgrounds and special methods of teaching English
to Puerto Ricans.

2. Stimulation at all teacher-training institutions for above
qualifications for use in student-teaching, with credit for practice
teaching.

3. Stimulation for all teacher-trainees looking toward teaching careers to take majors in Spanish and guidance.

4. Intensification of In-Service credit courses for teacher-
training in the above services.

Leonard Covello, "Recommendations Concerning Puerto Rican
    Pupils in Our Public Schools." Benjamin Franklin High
    School, May 1, 1953. (Mimeo.) Reprinted by permission.

A number of recommendations concerning the Puerto Rican
Program in our public schools have been presented at various times
by the following:
    I. The Committee of the Association of Assistant Superin-
tendents of the Board of Education of the City of New York. (August 1947) Dr. Clare C. Baldwin, Chairman.
    II. The Committee of Puerto Ricans in New York City of
the Welfare Council of New York City. (1948)
    III. The report on "Education of the non-English speaking
and bi-lingual (Spanish) pupils in the Junior High School of Districts
10 and 11 Manhattan submitted by Assistant Superintendent Clare C.
Baldwin, June, 1952.
    IV. The suggestions presented by Dr. Francisco Collazo,
Associate Commissioner of Education for the Commonwealth of
Puerto Rico. (1953)
    V. Recommendations of the report of the Subcommittee on
Education, Recreation and Parks of the Mayor's Committee of Puerto Rican Affairs. (1951) "Puerto Rican Pupils in New York City
Public Schools" directed by Dr. Leonard Covello.
    All of the most important recommendations are summarized
below. The Roman numerals I, II, III, IV and V appearing in
parentheses at the end of each recommendation indicate the source
of the recommendation in accordance with the listing of the sources
above.
    You will note that these recommendations come from social
agencies of the city and the supervisory and teaching staffs of our
public schools--groups who are in daily contact with the problem
and who are working actively with Puerto Rican children and their
families.
                              Leonard Covello
                Principal, Benjamin Franklin High School

I. School Organization:
    A. Special classes (C) should be allowed to schools in the ratio
       of a teacher for each 15 pupils newly admitted from Puerto
       Rico. (I)
    B. A special differential in class size should be provided in
       schools enrolling Puerto Rican pupils in proportion to the num-
       bers on register. Class registers with a large representation
       of these pupils should not exceed 25. (I) (II) (III) (IV)
    C. Kindergarten opportunities should be provided for four and five-
       year-old children in schools located in Puerto Rican communi-
       ties. (I)
    D. Junior High Schools should be reorganized as co-educational

      schools. (III)

E. Fifteen and sixteen year old children who are new arrivals should be directly admitted to senior high schools without restrictions as to the length of time of previous schooling or reading achievement, or the tenth year should be added to the Junior High School for those children who are close to 16 and 17 years of age. (III)

F. Eleven and twelve year old children who are new arrivals should be kept in the elementary schools until they are thirteen years old in order to ease the adjustment to new surroundings. (III)

G. In the reorganization report in June, schools should be permitted to leave at least one class in each grade unfilled for the new admissions in September so that we may eliminate a condition which is virtually a reorganization in September. (III)

H. No person licensed in Spanish should be appointed to the Junior High Schools unless requested by the principal. (III)

I. Principals of Junior High Schools should be given the privilege of selecting all the teachers for their schools. (III)

J. The allowance of teacher's time should be increased for remedial instruction in English and mathematics and for health counseling. (III)

K. The by-laws should be waived to permit appointment to our schools of teachers licensed to teach English to foreigners to tide us over a critical period. (III)

L. An additional assistant to principal should be provided for the supervision of teachers of non-English speaking children. (III)

M. Additional clerks should be assigned to prepare stencils and to mimeograph materials made in the schools. (III)

N. The Puerto Rican children should be placed in schools on an individual basis to effect a more satisfactory adjustment. (V)

II. Textbooks and Supplies

A. A special differential in textbooks and supply allotments should be made to schools enrolling Puerto Rican pupils in proportion to the numbers on register. (I)

B. An increased allotment should be granted for auxiliary instructional materials such as projectors, film strips, recorders and players. (III)

C. Report cards printed in Spanish should be made available for ordering from the general supply list. (III)

D. A special study should be made to determine what allotment for textbooks and supplies should be authorized for schools with a large concentration of Puerto Rican students. (V)

III. Curriculum

A. Under the direction of the Division of Curriculum Research, a study should be made of existing curriculum materials and methodology with a view toward devising new courses of study and teaching materials appropriate to the instruction of Puerto Rican pupils on various school levels. (I) (V)

B. There should be more English classes for all age groups. (II)

C. The curriculum for children classified as CRMD should be
   reviewed by the department. (III)
D. The curriculum should be broadened to include pre-vocational
   training for 15 and 16 year old pupils. (III)
E. A program for the correction of foreign accent and improvement of slovenly speech should be planned by the Department
   of Speech for use with bi-lingual pupils. (III)
F. Uniform teaching procedures should be used in the schools
   having a large number of beginners in English until such time
   as the need for special instruction in English is no longer so
   urgent. (III)
G. There should be continuous teaching of English in the schools
   of Puerto Rico. (IV)
H. There is a need for a curriculum bulletin for elementary,
   junior and senior high schools suggesting additional experiences, activities, procedures and practices for Puerto Rican
   children. (V)

IV. Tests and Measurements
   A. Under the direction of the Division of Educational Research,
      a study should be made of present tests of academic achieve-
      ment and mental ability and appropriate instruments of meas-
      urement should be developed for Puerto Rican pupils. (I) (V)
   B. No standardized tests should be given to any children who
      have not had at least five years of attendance in our schools
      until such time as valid tests are available. (III)
   C. A program for aptitude testing should be introduced for the
      15 and 16 year old students. (III)

V. Health
   A. Special medical services should be provided in schools having
      a large proportion of Puerto Rican pupils. (I) (V)
   B. A dental clinic should be set up in one of the schools for the
      exclusive use of junior high school pupils in each school dis-
      trict.
   C. Increased time should be given by the school nurse and doc-
      tor. (III)
   D. More welfare aides should be assigned as escorts for pupils
      to clinics. (III)
   E. More psychiatric services should be made available. (III)

VI. Registration
   A. Teachers who are expert interpreters of Spanish should be
      assigned during the period of registration to schools in the
      Puerto Rican neighborhoods to assist in the registration of
      new pupils. (I) (III)
   B. Spanish-speaking teachers should be used for all phases of
      the school program such as registration, for translation of
      forms and letters, as interpreters, as liaison with the com-
      munity, etc. (V)

VII. Adult Education
   A. A study should be made to determine the adequacy of the

present program of adult education for Puerto Ricans. (I)

B. The special educational needs of the Puerto Rican people are the following:
  a. To learn English
  b. To learn a marketable skill, trade or vocation if they arrive in New York without one and are beyond school age.
  c. If they are parents they need to learn:
    (1) Nutrition and marketing facts.
    (2) Child care and child care facilities available to them in the city, such as baby health stations, playgrounds, school requirements and services.
  d. To be oriented in urban living as to consumer problems, civic problems, sanitation and institutional assistance available. (II) (IV)

C. There should be local parent education on a full time basis. (II)

D. There should be a vital adult education program in areas where many Puerto Ricans live. (II)

E. Personnel should be assigned for parent education and work with mothers' clubs to meet during school hours and as part of the regular work of the schools. (II)

F. Instructions to parents on education and attendance laws should be printed in Spanish and be made available to the schools. (III)

G. There should be broader and more intensive instruction in English in Puerto Rico for the prospective adult migrant. (IV)

H. There should be more adequate information about living conditions in the continental United States in the social science program of Puerto Rican schools. (IV)

I. The prospective migrant in Puerto Rico should be provided with graphic information on the entire United States by means of films on life in all sections of the country in order to break down concepts limited to the New York area alone. (IV)

VIII. Teacher Training

A. Orientation courses for teachers on Puerto Rican culture and in conversational Spanish should be organized. (I) (II)

B. Courses for teachers in methodology and instructional materials for teaching non-English speaking pupils should be organized and staffed by experts. (I)

C. The eligibility requirements for all licenses should be expanded to include at least one course in the principles and methods of teaching English as a foreign language. (III)

D. In-service courses should be given in the techniques of selecting and writing materials for Puerto Rican pupils. (III) (V)

E. During the year there should be a series of district-wide institutes of all teachers of the schools having large numbers of non-English speaking pupils with a view toward exchanging ideas, experiences, new materials and to improve our way of educating for citizenship. (III)

F. The junior high school program of articulation with the elementary schools should be extended to include areas of methodology, materials, curriculum and community problems related

to the education of non-English speaking children. (III)
G. A committee of supervisors and teachers of the junior high
   and elementary schools should be organized to explore the
   possibilities for broadening the base for articulation and
   guidance and for exchange of experiences. (III)
H. Special examinations should be given for the purpose of
   licensing people with a knowledge of Spanish to serve in the
   classroom and to assist with other special services. (V)

IX. Guidance
    A. Insular, federal and city authorities should attempt to divert
       the flow of Puerto Rican emigrants from the overcrowded areas
       of New York into other sections of the city and elsewhere with
       some regard to the adequacy of housing accommodations and
       to occupational opportunities. (I)
    B. There should be more child guidance work in areas of spe-
       cial needs. (II)
    C. A Spanish-speaking teacher or social worker should be as-
       signed to each school for work with parents and children.
       (II) (III)
    D. Pupils entering high school from Puerto Rico require special
       vocational and individual guidance. (II)
    E. Each school should be assigned a full time attendance officer.
       (III)
    F. Each school should be assigned a full time guidance counsel-
       or. (III)

X. Community Relations
   A. A community relations teacher should be assigned to districts
      where there are major concentrations of Puerto Ricans. (I)
   B. There should be closer liaison between school and out of
      school social agencies. (II) (IV)
   C. A publicity program should be initiated by the schools adver-
      tising guidance and educational services available in this city.
      This should be in Spanish. (II) (IV) (V)
   D. Three pilot community centers should be established in Man-
      hattan, Brooklyn and the Bronx under the Board of Education
      to include recreation, English classes, family case work, etc.
      (II) (III) (V)
   E. More outdoor play yards should be set up in Puerto Rican
      districts under the supervision of duly licensed teachers. (III)
   F. A youth council with pupil representation from each school
      should be established with a view toward directing continuing
      attention to community problems and to affecting joint action
      in the improvement of the community. (III)
   G. A plan should be developed with social agencies for the co-
      ordination of activities. (III)

XI. Vocational Training and Guidance
    A. Free vocational training should be provided beyond the age of
       17 years. (II)
    B. The plants and teaching staffs of the vocational training
       schools should be open at night for the training of young adults

in vocations for which there is a demand as indicated by the state employment services. (II)

C. There should be vocational training of prospective workers in public and vocational schools and orientation of students towards useful and gainful occupation upon leaving school in Puerto Rico. (IV)

XII. Coordination

A. There should be coordination of the activities of the Department of Education of Puerto Rico, the Board of Education of the City of New York, and the Migration Division of the Puerto Rican Department of Labor. (IV)

B. There should be a continuous exchange of personnel between the Board of Education of New York and the Department of Education of Puerto Rico for on the spot study and training. (V)

Joseph Monserrat, "School Integration: A Puerto Rican View."
Address, Teachers College, Columbia University, May 1,
1963. Reprinted by permission.

I welcome this opportunity to discuss with you what has been
called a "Puerto Rican View of School Integration." This title
would seem to imply that Puerto Ricans view the question of school
integration somewhat differently from others. As a matter of fact
--we do!
To understand how we see this issue of integration and why
we see it as we do--what integration means and does not mean to
us--requires an understanding of our experiences and conditioning
as well as our view of the total issue. It is equally necessary and
important to bear in mind clearly the experiences and conditioning
of the American Negro if we are to fully understand all the issues
inherent in the struggle for integration in New York City and the
rest of the nation.
The present struggle for desegregation and for integration in
schools is not just a struggle to secure truly equal educational opportunities for members of the Negro community of America. At
this particular moment in the history and dynamics of this struggle,
the pertinent sentence of the Supreme Court decision is not the one
that reads, "Segregation with the sanction of the law has a tendency
to retard the educational and mental development of Negro children
and to deprive them of some benefits they would receive in a racially integrated school system." The really pertinent and significant
statement of the May 17 decision now, at this moment, is the one
that reads, "To separate them (Negroes) from others of similar age
and qualifications solely because of their race generates a feeling
of inferiority as to their status in the community that may affect
their hearts and minds in a way unlikely ever to be undone."
The judicial tempering of this statement by saying "may affect" could have been left out. The fact of history clearly demonstrates that this type of segregation, along with all other types of
segregation, has in fact affected the "hearts and minds" of our
American Negro community in a way that most certainly would "unlikely ever be undone" if it were not for the affirmative action being taken by the Negro in America today, a century after the sign-
ing of the Emancipation Proclamation.
Segregation as practiced in our society against the Negro can
be understood only as a part of his tragic history in America; it
can be understood in terms of how he came to the United States
and how he has been dealt with by the majority society since his
arrival.
The stigma of inferiority became a means of enforcing a
negative self-evaluation upon the victims. It also provides the justi-

260

fication for the oppressiveness of the oppressors, and while this stigma has been and still is used against others in America, its greatest effect has been against the Negro.

Unlike the Puerto Rican of today, or the Irish, the German or the Jew of yesterday, the Negro did not come here as a free man seeking to better his opportunities in a new environment. His relationship with his homeland, its history and civilization, its language and forms of worship was forcibly broken. He was not just disarmed physically--he was disarmed psychologically.

That tremendous and untold damage has also been done to the majority group--including not only the old-line Americans, but the millions of others who followed and who, though citizens of the United States today, were born in other countries yesterday or are children of those who were--is also implicit in the Supreme Court opinion. It can be said--more, it can be both quantified and qualified if we will--that damage has been done "to the hearts and minds" of the majority which, if we are not careful, may "unlikely ever be undone." It may well be that the majority group, unlike the Negro, was not disarmed physically, but it has most certainly been somewhat deranged psychologically; for how else would one explain adults spitting upon children, pushing lighted cigarettes into the ears of a diner sitting quietly at a lunch counter, or shooting a mailman peacefully walking his self-appointed round in the dead of night?

The heroic efforts being made to integrate public schools in New York City or New Rochelle; Gary, Indiana, or Englewood, New Jersey; Mississippi or Georgia must first of all be clearly understood to be a part of a national movement on all fronts on the part of both Negroes and whites to undo this damage to both groups which in fact has been so long left undone. It is first of all a basic part of the struggle of the American Negro to secure the self-respect and dignity due him as a human being and as a creature of God. It is part of a basic fight whose battle cry, as Dr. Martin Luther King points out, is contained in three words: --all, here, now.

The Negro seeks all of his rights. He seeks all of his rights here--in New York City, in Georgia, Alabama, Maine or California --wherever he may be. He seeks all of his rights here and he seeks them now, not tomorrow or next year or in ten years. He has waited long enough. He can not and will not be a Job any longer.

Segregated schools, whether de facto or de jure, whether they provide equal educational facilities and high educational standards--indeed even if they were to provide the Negro child with a better education than that received by his white peer--would, in my view, still be unacceptable to the Negro in America today. They would be unacceptable because they symbolize, as do all other forms of segregation, the inferior and unequal status in which the Negro, simply because he is a Negro, is held by the white, simply because he is white.

The segregated school is but one of the many ways in and through which the one group is continuously reminded by the other that the first is inferior and the other superior. It also represents one of the means through which the Negro child is conditioned to recognize his "inferior" status and the white child conditioned to understand his "superior" one--for each must be carefully though subtly taught.

That this is the first and basic issue involved in the entire matter of school integration may very well be clear to most of those attending this conference--but it is not so clearly nor so broadly understood as it should be. In fact, it was the absence of any consideration of this point in Dr. James Conant's "Slums and Suburbs" that may have made many of us concerned with this crucial issue, fail to accord the book the serious attention it deserves.

For the Negro--indeed, for all Americans--there can never be truly equal educational opportunities; there can never be an eradication of the damage done to the hearts and minds of both majority and minority groups until--and unless--each and every single and individual Negro is seen first of all as a human being, equal in dignity and potential to all human beings. He must first be judged and evaluated as an individual, solely on the basis of his ability and potential <u>as</u> an individual, and <u>not</u> on the basis of his being Negro.

I believe that in fighting against segregation, the Negro is fighting for his right to be a Negro. In fighting for his right to be a Negro, he fights for his right to <u>be</u>, for he can only be <u>as</u> a Negro. He can not be anything else--nor should he be--or want to be--nor should anyone else want him to be otherwise.

In a multi-cultured democratic society such as ours, integration must not and can not mean submerging or forgetting the specific content and values of one's own past, either as an individual or as a member of a group. In a multi-cultured democratic society such as ours, integration must mean:

a) That we recognize and respect the differences among us; and, that difference means just that--different; it does not mean that the factor of being different makes some people better and others worse. These values must be judged on the basis of individual ability and potential.

b) That the right to be different must not be detrimental to the whole nor to those parts of the whole who may wish to or must (because of their visibility) remain different.

c) That the whole can not discriminate against an individual or a group because of the desire or need of that individual or group to remain affiliated with what they consider a special value.

In other words, integration is in fact the fulfillment of the American dream of unity without uniformity.

If I may be permitted a parenthetical note on the affairs of our country in our international dealings, the struggle for the survival of the democratic concept in today's world, in my view, may perhaps depend more upon our success with the issues involved in integration as I have outlined them, than on any other single factor, for democracy cannot truly flourish unless there is a respect for and an appreciation of the worth, dignity, difference between men, and value of each individual man.

If I seem to belabor this point I do so for two reasons. First, because it can not be said often enough; second, because only by keeping these factors clearly in mind can we understand what I am about to say relative to integration and the Puerto Ricans.

In discussing the issues of integration in New York City schools, Negroes and Puerto Ricans are referred to constantly almost as if they were one and the same. They are not.

Unlike the Negro, we Puerto Ricans are not a race. We are, at most, an ethnic group. As such, some of us are "white," some of us are "Negro" and some of us are so-called "mixed."

Puerto Rico was discovered by Christopher Columbus in the year 1493. It was settled by Juan Ponce de Leon, the first Puerto Rican migrant, in 1508. The island's original Indian population was rapidly overcome and soon disappeared as a separate discernible ethnic group. With the virtual disappearance of the Arawak Indian as a source of labor, the Spaniards turned to Africa. From 1511 to 1530 some 1500 African slaves were brought into Puerto Rico. From 1530 to 1555, some 15,000 more slaves were brought to the Island.

The bloodline of the Puerto Rican comes from many sources. Its base is Spanish. There was some early mixture of Spanish with the few remaining Indian women, some of whom were concubines and others wives. Europeans from many lands came next as soldiers, adventurers and pirates. In 1511 slaves began to arrive. The revolution of Toussaint L'Ouverture in Haiti drove many French families into Puerto Rico. The Louisiana Purchase in 1803 brought other hundreds of families to the Island.

Ruth Gruber, in her book "Puerto Rico--Island of Promise," writes:

> The bloodstreams of all these migrants fused to make the Puerto Rican of today. He is not a Negro, although 20 percent of the population is Negro. He is not Indian, yet the golden skin, the high cheek-bones, the aquiline nose, the gentleness and hospitality of the Indian are a common trait all over the island. He is not a Spaniard, yet he may have the blond hair of Northern Spain or the pure white skin of Barcelona.

But these, at least to my mind, are but the superficial differences between the Puerto Rican and the Negro. The real differences come from other factors. They come from our experiences, our conditioning, and our history as a people.

In our history as a people we have never had what we call in the United States a "minority group." In Puerto Rico the only people who are called a "minority" are those members of the political parties that fail to win an election. Puerto Ricans, therefore, whether Negro, white or mulatto, have not received the same conditioning in this regard as have both the American Negro and white.

This is not to imply that there is no prejudice among us Puerto Ricans. As members of the human race we, too, suffer from this disease. However, in our history as a people prejudice has been limited primarily to relations between individuals. In our

history of more than 450 years, we have never had a broad scale
system of institutionalized discrimination de facto or de jure.

Puerto Rico was the only area in the Caribbean where the
Negro slave did not rebel against his master, for right from the
beginning there was a strong movement to free first the Indian and
then the Negro.   Slavery was abolished finally in Puerto Rico in
1873, at which time only 4.2% of the total population were slaves.

In 1812, of a total population of 150,426, the slave population totalled 17,536 Negroes, having remained substantially the same
as in the year 1794.   In addition to the 17,536 Negro slaves, there
were also 12,872 free Negroes living in Puerto Rico.[1]

Puerto Ricans, whether Negro or white, have never had to
bear the horrendous burden of having to fight those who would make
them feel or believe that they were lesser human beings than others
because of skin pigmentation--or for that matter, for any other
reason.

There has never been a race riot in Puerto Rico.

Dr. Melvin Tumin of Princeton (and one of the discussants
at this conference) and his colleague, Dr. Arnold Feldman of the
University of Delaware, conducted a field study among 1,000 heads
of households, scientifically selected from all social strata in Puerto Rico.   Their trained interviewers classified these 1,000 heads of
households as follows: 608 white, 307 mulatto, and 80 Negro.   On
the other hand, the respondents classified themselves thus: 537
white, 397 mulatto, and 55 Negro!

"The evidence," say Tumin and Feldman, "urges us to the
conclusion that skin color is considerably less important in Puerto
Rico than in the United States; that it is virtually of no significance
whatsoever in many important areas of life; that the majority feel
that people of darker color are not blocked from major opportunities by their color. . ."   There is no doubt that, as Tumin and
Feldman point out, there are areas of problems around color in
Puerto Rico.   However, as they indicate, ". . .it is fair to say
that color discrimination in Puerto Rico is a subtle and minor theme
in Puerto Rican life."

This, then, is one of the major differences between the Negro and the Puerto Rican in the United States: that all Puerto Ricans are not colored, and that even among those who are, color is
not a major issue in Puerto Rican life.

Another significant difference is that Puerto Ricans represent a whole, unlike the Negro, who represents a part or minority
of a whole.   For this reason, Puerto Ricans are accustomed to
seeing other Puerto Ricans at work at all levels, from low-income
farm workers to the rich landowners who hire them; from the
teacher who teaches them to the Rector of the University; from the
district political leader to the Governor, the members of his Cabinet, and all the members of the House and Senate.

I repeat:

"The Puerto Rican by experience, conditioning, and history is
not a member of a minority group.   He is both a part of the whole,
and the whole itself--despite existing differences of class and race."

The Puerto Rican parent of the Puerto Rican child in New

York City schools--and, indeed, many of the children themselves--
were in Puerto Rico accustomed to attending school or seeing others attend school where all in attendance are Puerto Rican. The
child of the Negro parent has also attended all-Negro schools, but
unlike the Negro, I do not believe any Puerto Rican ever gave
thought to whether his schools were integrated or not.

In other words, in Puerto Rico the Puerto Rican in a "racial" sense has--and has had--ALL of his rights; he has--and has
had--all of his rights HERE (i.e., wherever he has lived in all parts
of the Island); and he has--and has had--them NOW! For almost
four centuries the Puerto Rican has possessed what the Negro now
is fighting to attain.

We are fully aware of the fact that we, upon arrival in New
York City and elsewhere, are seen by our fellow citizens as an-
other--a new--minority group. We are also aware of the fact that
we are seen by our neighbors as being "non-white." Since the question of color has not been a major theme in our experience or our
history, we at first paid little attention to this designation. However, we learned fast. We learned that in the states a new dimension had been added: the dimension of "color." We found that skin
pigmentation could determine where we could live and work. In
fact, many Puerto Ricans soon learned that color was only part of
the restriction they were facing: they were rejected as soon as
they identified themselves as Puerto Ricans. I recall vividly the
almost traumatic shock of one blue-eyed "pure white" Puerto Rican,
(whose ancestors on both sides descended from a long line of titled,
German nobles) when he came to grips with this problem. In applying for an apartment, he had been refused, because he was Puerto Rican!

We realize that prejudice and discrimination in America are
not wholly a matter of color and race. They are a state of mind--
a state of mind brought about (among other things) by fear, which
in turn often engenders hate.

We therefore reject the designation of "non-white." We reject it not because those of us who are in fact non-white are in any
way ashamed of being of color; we reject it because we reject the
state of mind behind it which, in referring to us as "non-white," is
really telling us that we are not equal to others--that we are "inferior." To accept their value would be to become inferior. Human beings are only inferior to others when they acknowledge themselves to be so. In so acknowledging we reinforce the belief of
those who consider themselves superior. This we will not do!

We will not do this not only because man's scientific knowledge has demonstrated that one group of humans is not superior to
another; we will not do so because for us to do so would be to retard the fight for equality which is moving forward on all fronts
everywhere in America today. For, as I indicated earlier, the
struggle for school integration in New York City and elsewhere in
America at this stage is "first of all a basic part of the struggle
of the American Negro to secure the self respect and dignity due
him as a human being..." This self respect and this dignity in
this sense have been ours for centuries. They are ours now in
Puerto Rico (a part of the American union), and we insist on keep-

ing them wherever we go.

How to do this--how to keep our self respect and dignity as human beings both in our own eyes and in the eyes of our neighbors--is the real problem confronting us. It is from this point of view--the point of view of keeping, not acquiring--that we must deal with the problem of integration in schools.

We Puerto Ricans have joined, are joining, and will join in ever-growing numbers with our Negro neighbor and with all others who seek to eliminate segregation in schools and in every other walk of life. We do so because to us integrated living has not been a far distant goal--it has been our way of life! And, if we are to maintain this way of life--and yes, eradicate whatever vestiges of prejudice and discrimination yet remain with us, we must promote our way of life. The realization of this is being pressed upon more and more of us. As a result more and more of us will participate more actively in promoting and maintaining that which up to now we had taken for granted.

We believe there is a distinction between the significance of a Puerto Rican child attending a school in which most or all of the children are of Puerto Rican background and of a Negro child attending a school in which most or all of the children are Negro. From a "racial" point of view, the all-Negro school is in fact completely segregated. On the other hand, because of the racial background of the Puerto Rican child, an all-Puerto Rican school may well be, from a "racial" point of view, the most integrated of schools. The real difference, however, is that the Negro feels that he is segregated because of his race (as, in fact, he is in most instances), while the Puerto Rican by and large does not feel this.

However, we have said that segregation and discrimination, particularly in the North, is more a state of mind and emotion than a matter of race.

Therefore, we recognize that the effect of the segregated school on the Puerto Rican child and on the Negro child is to a high degree almost identical when measured by the final result of their education, their achievement scores and reading level. We also recognize that this type of school and the present values that create and maintain it indeed generate a feeling of inferiority as to our status in the community which certainly affects the hearts and minds of our children.

At this time the Negro and Puerto Rican child both--even if for different reasons--by and large are not accepted into the middle-class society or its schools. They are excluded. Their education is a different one, geared to a different product from the education of the children who are members of the middle-class society.

Ours are the children of the outside group, and as such they are dealt with in our educational processes. Their occupational opportunities are considered to be limited, and these limitations are the framework of the educational process especially prepared for them. They are the "unfortunate" in our society, and the well-meaning teacher, not to speak of the prejudiced teachers, wants to help them to go through school with as few problems as possible, prepared to accept willingly the menial jobs which may be waiting for them and which many conclude a priori to be their lot.

The Negro today militantly refuses to accept this situation any longer. The Puerto Rican, not having the experience or conditioning of the Negro in this type of situation, has for some years lived in blissful ignorance--a dupe of circumstances. For although Puerto Ricans were recorded as far back as the 1910 census as living in 39 States, the majority of the some 800,000 of us living in the United States today have lived here less than 20 years.

Actually, as we look back we discover that in 1940, although there were over 70,000 Puerto Ricans living in the States, mostly in New York City, there was at that time no "Puerto Rican problem."

It was not until after 1946 that we became a "race," that an identifiable descriptive stereotype had been created for us. In 1954 we discovered that our children, along with Negro children, were being described as "X" children who attended "X" schools. There also were some other children who were called "Y" children and they attended "Y" schools.

We also learned at that time, that when the "X" schools were compared with the "Y" schools it was discovered that the "X" school buildings were older and somewhat less well equipped than the "Y" school buildings; also, that there were fewer regular teachers in the "X" schools. That is, that a disproportionately high percentage of the teachers teaching in the "X" schools as compared with the teachers of the "Y" schools were teachers who for a variety of reasons did not meet the minimum standards established by the Board of Education for licensing a teacher--a prerequisite for becoming a regular teacher.

We also learned that the children in the "X" schools were not "achieving" at a par with the children of the "Y" schools. And, we suddenly realized that many of these "X" children were our children. With this realization came awareness of the segregated school and the fact that we could ignore neither its meaning nor its result. Thus, too, New York City realized that it could no longer ignore what a number of concerned citizens, most of them Negroes, had been aware of for many years--namely that New York City had many de facto segregated schools.

I realize that this description may be thought of by some as being either facetious or cynical or both. I assure you I mean to be neither. I am simply trying, to the best of my limited literary ability, to describe in words the awakening process of a group of people whose entire history and experience left them without the necessary "malicia," as we say in Spanish, to see what was happening before their eyes or to fully understand the implications and meaning of what they did see.

I am trying to explain to those who wonder, why the Puerto Rican has not been as militantly concerned as has the Negro over the problems and issues of integration and the segregated school. He has not, because he does not have (at least not quite yet) the same motivation as, or seek the exact same immediate goal the Negro does. Furthermore, his entire experience, conditioning and history have made him slow to realize the threat and danger that segregation poses not only for his children but for his very way of life. The irony of it all is, of course, obvious. The experience,

conditioning and history of the Puerto Ricans which has resulted in
a way of life that has made him unable to perceive as quickly and
clearly as he should have, what was and is happening to him, is
the very way of life we here in the states seek in the struggle
against segregation!

But much has happened since 1954. The symbols "X" and
"Y" used in a scientific study are rather impersonal, as they should
be and are intended to be. However, when the symbol "X" school
is changed to read first "problem" school, then "difficult" school
and now "subject" school, we leave the realm of the impersonal
and become quite personal and very understandable. Thus we now
clearly understand that "problem" school--"difficult" school--"subject" school really means problem children--difficult children--sub-
ject children. And many of the children thus being described are
ours. As parents we know some of our children are "problems"
and are "difficult." But, are all of our children problems?--are
they all difficult? This we would find hard to believe--and indeed
we are assured by teachers and other educational authorities that
they are not. We are assured that there is no intent to label, be-
little or stigmatize our children when these school designations are
made. But, intended or not--we have now reached the point where
we must begin to question seriously not necessarily the intention--
for if it were bad intent, bad as that would be, we could at least
understand; but the appalling lack of sensitivity, understanding or
perception on the part of those either in education or the Behavioral Sciences responsible for devising such names is beyond comprehension. Children attending schools with pathological labels are
labeled and marred; this is not good for children, it is not good
education, and it is not good for education.

Yes, much has happened to us and to our understanding of
the issues involved since 1954. Today we are able to say--and do
say--that this type of labeling of the children attending specific
schools in specific areas, whether intended or not, is another way
of differentiating minority group children from majority group children, and is another means of re-enforcing the concepts of group
superiority and inferiority. This is racism--as a state of mind--
in its most damaging and subtle form.

Puerto Ricans are particularly adept at devising nicknames
--"apodos," we call them in Spanish. Some of these "apodos" are
so obviously descriptive of the peculiarities of the individual being
so baptized that I say, perhaps not altogether facetiously, that this
may be one of the as yet unknown and unmeasured motivations for
migration.

Pitirim Sorokin in his monumental work, "The Fluctuation
of the Arts," describes, if I remember correctly, how different
art forms are dominant in a given culture at a given time. In
Puerto Rico the most highly developed art form has been, and no
doubt still is, poetry. To be poetical one must, among other things,
possess a feeling for words and their nuances, as well as the ability to verbalize concepts. There may be those who might say that
this is the reason for our concern over names. They may also
feel that this is why we are also greatly concerned over the current set of all-encompassing slogans such as "culturally deprived,"

"socially disadvantaged," or the "culture of poverty." It may be, but I think not, because many non-Puerto Ricans are also concerned over the implication inherent in these pseudo-social scientific terms. In fact, many of those who use them admit they do not really mean what they suggest.

I ask: is a culture that has for four centuries been able to maintain the individual dignity, value and worth of all its members (despite differences in race and class) a deprived or disadvantaged culture when compared with one that has been striving to achieve these values and has as yet not been able to do so?

If it is a disadvantaged and deprived culture it can only be so judged if the values used to "measure" it are values which support the concept of segregation--of the superiority and inferiority among and between groups of man.

If this is the value to be used in judging which culture is deprived and which is not, then let us come forth and say so clearly and openly. If it is not--and I know all here would agree it is not --then let not the educators or the social scientists be guilty of appearing to believe it is by creating, adopting, promoting and defending concepts and theories which in fact do reenforce the notion of the superiority of one group and the inferiority of another.

But you insist this is not what is meant when it is said that Puerto Ricans are culturally deprived. What is meant is that because of his background he is not properly motivated to take advantage of those things in our society which will enable him to raise his standards in life.

Here there are many questions I would ask if time permitted. I will ask just a few.

Are we sure that a culture that puts more value on status, prestige, symbols, and material possession, that makes of material things an end in and of themselves rather than a means to an end, a culture which in fact recognizes the great need to change some of its present basic values, is this a culture to be emulated so that in so doing we continue to perpetuate that which many agree needs to be changed?

Is the child of a minority group culturally deprived because the majority group has established norms which a priori assume that most of the minority group members will not be able to attain the majority values, position or education and then proceeds to prove this hypothesis by providing a school system which is by and large geared to prevent him from achieving middle class majority levels?

I am aware of what those who talk about the problems of the "culturally deprived," of the "socially disadvantaged" are trying to say and point up. However, while I am not a semanticist, I believe that in the emotionally charged atmosphere of today's struggle for integration the use of what I have already termed pseudo-social scientific terms filled with ambiguities can only lead to the raising of questions like those I have raised and many more I could raise which, while of great importance, address themselves only to part of the problem. Discharging emotionally and value laden words into an emotionally charged atmosphere will most certainly result in thunder. At best, we can expect only an occasional flash of heat lightning. What we need is a constant bright light.

As we Puerto Ricans look at the total problem of school integration and equal educational opportunities for all, we are only too aware of the vastness of the problem. As a people with a culture, with history and with an experience we do what others do--we seek answers to present problems by falling upon our experience of the past.

In Puerto Rico proper, we Puerto Ricans have a living functional reality of the "proof," if you will, of our ability to both achieve and attain. "Operation Bootstrap," the program developed by the people of Puerto Rico to pull themselves out of a 19th century existence into a 20th century reality, is known round the world. Thousands of people from over 112 nations have come and are still coming to see how we do it--to help us--and to learn from us.

It is the brothers and sisters, fathers and mothers, sons and daughters, cousins and the former neighbors in Puerto Rico of the Puerto Ricans in New York, and indeed many of the New York Puerto Ricans themselves, who are responsible for this achievement.

If time permitted, we could also dwell on "Operation Commonwealth," through which the people of Puerto Rico are hard at work on one of their most difficult of problems--namely the development ofa new and creative political status.

We could also discuss another bold conception of the people of Puerto Rico, "Operation Serenity." Simply put, Operation Serenity represents the attempts of a people to husband their expanding economy, its means of production as well as its products in such a way that these means remain means and not become ends in and of themselves. In other words, the tools of society should remain just that, tools, and man must remain the master not become the slave of his tools. Only in this way can man remain conscious of the value of man and not superimpose over it and give greater value to the things man produces.

But because of time we can only give passing mention to these areas. But, we remind you that we have this experience to fall back on as we look for a solution to our present problems. And, I repeat, we recognize only too well the enormity of our educational problems, after all, we are one of its main victims.

Nevertheless, we recall that against tremendous odds we in Puerto Rico are well on the way toward resolving our educational problems--as much as man can ever resolve these.

In Puerto Rico just 65 years ago only one Puerto Rican in every 41 attended school. Eighty percent of the population was illiterate--there were only 600 teachers. Some 40 years later, in 1940, with twice the population we had 286,113 students attending schools even though many were dilapidated. But we still did not have enough schools for all of our children. By 1960 almost all of our grade school children were in schools, in fact, over 700,000 persons are receiving some kind of education in Puerto Rico today!

We now have almost 15,000 teachers. By the end of this, what we have termed the decade of education, we will have acquired an educational system equal to any.

We function from the belief that no one knows the potential

of any child until that child is given every opportunity to develop whatever ability he may have. We therefore set out to provide for each child the highest education possible. We are fully aware that there are individual differences between and among children, and that each will develop according to these differences; but we start out by affording to each child the maximum of opportunities we are able to provide. We do not a priorily decide which child or group of children should or should not receive these benefits. They are available to all.

If it is new concepts that we seek in order to solve our serious and pressing educational problems, we should begin by assuming that each child, given every opportunity, will in fact develop to his full personal ability. If any doubt exists, it does not exist in the minds of the young people--it exists only in the minds of adults.

Can there be doubt when we think of the young American Negro of today, a product of a so-called socially deprived culture, the product of the culture of poverty, who has taken his destiny into his own hands and is staging one of the most profound and significant social revolutions ever seen in the United States.

In carrying out this revolution he has adapted a technique which, while conceived by an American, Thoreau, was put into practice only in Africa and India. This technique, based upon the concept of non-violence, fortified with love, requires the highest type of motivation and the most stringent self-imposed discipline.

Can we possibly say that there is no hope for the Negro youth of America in the face of all this, or must we admit that it is we who lost faith and lost hope?

As Governor Muñoz Marin of Puerto Rico once said in discussing the problem of developing the under-developed countries, "In the final analysis, the great resource which must be tapped... is people. The great task is to unleash their creative energies, and the great first step is reached when they join together to work with enthusiasm and purpose, armed with adequate technical tools to achieve their own salvation."

It is this that the Negro youth of today is doing.

To quote Governor Muñoz again "...the great engines of creative energy in peoples are hope and pride...if you can find the touchstones to spur their hope and pride you will unleash their creative capacities and energies, and a new dynamism will enter into their lives before which even stubborn obstacles will fall."

Notes

1. U.S. War Department, Report on Puerto Rico Census, 1899 (U.S. Printing Office, Washington, D.C., 1900)--Diario Económico de Puerto Rico, March 21, 1814--as quoted in Historia de la Esclavitud Negra en Puerto Rico by Luis M. Díaz Solar, published by the University of Puerto Rico.

Eugene Bucchioni, "Home Atmosphere and Success in School."
<u>A Sociological Analysis of the Functioning of Elementary</u>
<u>Education for Puerto Rican Children,</u> (Unpublished Doctoral
<u>Dissertation, New School for Social Research, 1965), pp. 55-</u>
66. Reprinted by permission.

Most Puerto Ricans in New York City live in the least desirable residential areas of New York, either in slums or in public
housing projects that are rapidly deteriorating into slums. Individuals who live in a slum area and who are members of lower classes
are apt to have little orientation to success at school. Frequently,
residents of slum areas, especially Puerto Ricans, encounter much
discrimination socially and occupationally because of their ethnic
origin, even if they have secured some education. This tends to
discourage further schooling.

Another important factor affecting home atmosphere and success at school is the fact that the integrated social norms of the
larger North American society do not function well in a slum; residents of slum areas have their own norms, nevertheless they are
expected to accept the norms of more privileged groups in society
and reflect those norms in their behavior; yet the realities of the
immediate social and cultural milieu and life chances of Puerto Ricans in slums have resulted in norms and values that are at variance with and seemingly contradict the norms and values of other
groups in the society.

What are the realities of life in a slum for Puerto Ricans?
What norms and values have developed that conflict with those of
middle class groups? Many Puerto Ricans live in crowded and dilapidated old-law tenements; some live in low income housing projects that are deteriorating rapidly. High rates of unemployment
and of unstable employment as unskilled laborers result in chronic
economic insecurity. A disproportionate number of broken families
is characteristic. In Puerto Rican homes, there is likely to be an
almost complete absence of books, magazines, and toys for the
children. Walls are frequently adorned with images of Christ in
his various manifestations such as the Bleeding Heart, the Cruci-
fixion, the Resurrection, or the Ascension. The Virgin Mary in
her various manifestations, or the family's favorite saints are likely to appear either as pictures on the walls or as the focal point
for a family altar. The normal home objects such as the family
furniture, including usually a radio and television, however, generally furnish the main contents of a Puerto Rican home.

There exists a pattern of life for children that exposes them
to a mere minimum of direct contact with the central issues of
North American middle class culture. On the contrary, the everyday problems of living such as dealing with economic insecurity,

272

coping with many children in a crowded apartment, cooking the various meals and making them stretch in order to provide for the family and unexpected guests, leave little time for adults to assist their children in exploring the local and the larger world and their relationship to it.

For many Puerto Rican children, the street becomes the playground where very much is learned. Fearlessness, bravery, daring physical prowess, machismo are among the norms learned in a Puerto Rican slum. One learns to be independent, tough, and to outsmart others, especially the police or other representatives of middle class authority. The authority figure becomes the hijo de puta (son of a bitch), the one responsible for having caused the individual to become jodido (screwed). A search for excitement, thrills, involving some degree of risk or danger, occurs with considerable frequency. Aggression is more often physical than verbal, and when it is verbal, obscenities in Spanish predominate. While the consequences of one's behavior are sometimes recognized, one's general situation is frequently attributed to la suerte (meaning both luck and fate) or to the will of God (como Dios quiera), or to the intervention or interference of a middle class authority.

The attitudes, values, and norms of the slum dweller are designed to strengthen, reinforce, and affirm his way of life. When these patterns are sharply different from the norms and values of middle class culture, they may be interpreted as malicious, evil, deliberately non-conforming and downright threatening by the middle class teacher. In school, the Puerto Rican child is expected to accept the conflicting norms of the larger society, and he is penalized if he does not. What is tolerated in a home in a slum is not always tolerated in other segments of the society, especially in school. Inappropriate behavior of the Puerto Rican child is penalized in many ways, and the resulting punitive atmosphere in school contributes to the lack of successful achievement.

An additional variable affecting success at school is the educational level of the parents and the image they have of the school. Mills found that most of the migrants in his sample were poorly educated.[1] The average number of years completed was 6.5. He also discovered that 8% of the total number of migrants in his sample were illiterate. The lack of sufficient parental education, coupled with the resulting inadequate understanding of the role of the school, hinders Puerto Rican children in their school careers. Parents are unable to assist their children with school work when necessary. In addition, parents are frequently unable to motivate their children or encourage them in their work at school because of their inadequate understanding of what the school is attempting to do.

Schools, in addition to teaching the traditional "Three R's" and providing instruction in the other subjects, also attempt to stimulate individuality in pupils, encourage self-assertiveness, initiative, self-expression, and creativity. These additional tasks of the school do not always coincide with the conceptions that Puerto Rican parents have concerning the role of the school. Puerto Rican parents expect their children to be quiet and submissive and respectful. Boys should develop into men of character and get an

education that will enable them to get good jobs. This will help
boys to become good parents and, later, persons respected by the
family and others in their social group. A girl should develop into
a quiet, modest, and virtuous woman, one who has some education
so that she can secure employment if this should become necessary.
    All this is part of the home atmosphere; and all this con-
flicts with what is taught in the schools and with what parents think
should be taught. What is of importance here is the fact that parents believe the school should reinforce what they are teaching the
children at home. This represents a conception of education that
differs very sharply from that held by the teachers, principals, and
the Board of Education.
    Education has served as an instrument of upward mobility
for many North Americans who were able to secure better employment and whose life chances were improved as a result of their
education: children from these families were motivated to succeed
in school because of the evident success of their parents. Puerto
Rican children have no such motivation. Expressed differently,
Puerto Ricans are not school-oriented because of the various factors discussed above; this lack of school orientation contributes to
academic retardation and inadequate educational achievement. Inadequate educational achievement makes difficult, if not impossible,
the continued education which could contribute to the improvement
of the life chances of Puerto Ricans.

Home Atmosphere and the Curriculum

    For Puerto Rican children there is little relationship between
the curriculum and the complex of social and cultural patterns characterizing their lives. There can be little enthusiasm for the subjects and experiences of the curriculum, little motivation to succeed at school, when children are ill, hungry, poorly housed, from
broken families, and when they do not speak or understand the language in which they are taught.
        The school bears little relationship to the streets around
        it, where the policeman is the killer of Georgie Martinez,
        the milkman a legend of an older era of brownstone fronts
        and horse-drawn carts whose product is now too expensive
        for many of the families who live here largely on water
        and rice and beans. The children fed with those staples
        may qualify for the health class, where they take home
        lists of diets that are often impossible to fulfill...The
        schools have been of little help to the children of Spanish
        Harlem in escaping the realities of its streets, or in
        changing those realities to something like the promise of
        the posters that smile from the classrooms. The schools,
        in fact, have blocked out the possibilities of the world be-
        yond even more profoundly than the tenement buildings
        around them.[2]

    This discrepancy between the realities of Puerto Rican life
in New York and the school curriculum becomes especially clear
when analyzed in terms of what Puerto Rican pupils learn on a

day-to-day basis. Textbooks, for example, advise Puerto Rican
children as to what they ought to eat:

> Your food for the day should include foods from each of
> the seven groups you have already learned about. Can
> you name them? Let's review them. You know that milk
> makes a difference in health and growth. Milk and the
> many foods from milk are the best sources of calcium.
> They supply excellent protein and vitamin A.

> The world's most wonderful engine--your body--runs well
> on the food energy from bread and cereal. Whole grains
> and enriched white bread and cereals supply vitamin B,
> phosphorous, and iron. They are a good source of pro-
> tein, too. They are one of our cheapest foods. Meat
> and fish and eggs supply excellent protein and phosphor-
> ous...Citrus fruits and tomatoes...give us all the vitamin
> C we need...Butter or fortified margarine is high in food
> energy and in vitamin A. A little fat goes a long way.
> We should not eat too much of it.[3]

Recommendations as to what specific meals should contain
are also made:

> Do you feel strong as a tiger or weak as a mouse?
> What kind of breakfast do you have at your house? You
> can't eat like a bird and work like a horse. Do you get
> that tired feeling before the morning is half over? Per-
> haps it is because you're a breakfast skipper. Do you
> have a 'four-star' breakfast every day? The four stars
> are (1) citrus fruit, (2) whole-grain or enriched cereal
> or bread or both, (3) milk, (4) butter or vitamin A mar-
> garine. If you have an orange or tomato, or half a grape-
> fruit, at another meal, you may omit the citrus fruit for
> breakfast.[4]

> A good lunch to take to school contains the Big Three--
> (1) cereal or bread, (2) milk or cheese, (3) fruit or
> vegetables. Your lunch box might contain some food
> from each of the following groups, which include the
> seven basic foods:
> Group 1: Sandwiches having any of the following kinds
> of filling: finely chopped boiled eggs mildly seasoned;
> peanut butter; dried fruit paste made by grinding raisins,
> dates, figs or other fruits and nuts; chopped chicken
> liver; chopped meat; various kinds of cheese...
> Group 2: Fresh fruits of all kinds, ripe tomatoes, and
> pieces of raw carrot are easily carried. Applesauce
> and other kinds of stewed fruit may be carried in small
> jars with screw tops.
> Group 3: A sweet such as a jelly sandwich, sponge cake,
> cookies, cup custard, dates or figs, or fruit candy.
> Group 4: A milk or fruit drink. If possible, bring a
> pint bottle of milk or fruit juice or a thermos bottle of
> hot milk, soup or cocoa. At least take a drink of water.[5]

The appropriate way in which to serve food is also part of
elementary school health instruction.

> Food that looks and tastes good helps digestion. It
> "makes the mouth water." The digestive juices in the
> mouth and in the stomach, too, flow faster when the
> food looks good, smells good, tastes good. If you were
> helping to get breakfast, dinner, or supper, what could
> you do to make the food look good? Did you think of
> these things? See that the table cover is clean. A
> clean, bare table, painted, is pretty, too. See that the
> dishes and silverware are clean. Put the food neatly on
> plates. Put a bowl of fruit or a small plant or fresh-
> cut flowers on the table. Serve hot foods hot and cold
> foods cold. Plan to have some color in your meal - a
> green salad, orange carrots, a red tomato.[6]

The above selections represent the kind of health teaching
that takes place in the elementary schools. Children learn during
health instruction about a balanced and nutritious diet, one containing a wide variety of foods, many of which Puerto Rican children
have not eaten previously, nor would they eat such foods considering the cultural background of their parents and their economic
status as well. Frequently, children bring home detailed lists of
foods that comprise a well-balanced diet, lists which often must be
signed by parents and returned to school.

The social studies curriculum is equally unrelated to the
Puerto Rican experience in New York City. In classroom studies
of different communities within the United States, both farm and
suburban life are emphasized. In contrast, little attention is given
to studies of urban life.

The suburban community is especially stressed through a
careful presentation of the suburbs as a complex of one family
houses with one or more bathrooms, one or more automobiles,
supermarkets where one drives to in order to make the necessary
purchases, and trees, lawns, flowers, and new modern schools.
Puerto Rican pupils thus learn early to desire these symbols of respectable middle class status. The unreality of this goal becomes
most pronounced when considering the racial identification of Puerto
Ricans that will probably prevent them, even if they secure adequate funds, from residing in such suburban communities.

Other social studies teaching includes studies of community
helpers: the milkman, policeman, fireman, grocer, street cleaner,
and the like, and their contributions to society. In the second
grade, for example, the child should "develop the concept that the
policeman is a friend and protector of children."[7] In order to develop this concept, the following basic experiences are prescribed:
getting to know the policeman who serves the school; learning to
call him by name; talking to him; making friendly gestures like
writing notes; sending greeting cards; inviting him to visit class.[8]

The "community helpers" are generally depicted in a manner
that bears little resemblance to the realities of the experience of
Puerto Ricans with them. The policeman, for example, is idealized as one who helps and protects those in need of his assistance.

Policemen assigned to slum areas, however, are not always sympathetic to residents, and in many instances, the Puerto Rican's experience with the police has been the reverse of the image presented in school.

Other social studies teaching is equally unrealistic. Puerto Rican children are taught that the United States provides them with many opportunities that are available in no other country in the world. The United States is the one nation where all people are free and equal, and where all people can get ahead if they work hard enough.

> The people of the United States have much to be thankful for. Most of them are living longer, healthier, and more comfortable lives than their ancestors did. Within their free nation Americans have made use of the knowledge, experience, and arts they inherited from Europe, to create their own art, music, literature--their own way of life. Because of their arts, natural resources, industries, skilled labor, and inventions, the people of the United States have more wonderful things and more time in which to enjoy them than any other people in the world. But greatest of their blessings are the freedoms of their democracy, which makes all other things possible. This democracy has been won, increased, and protected by the courage and hard work of many generations of Americans. The people of the United States will have to continue to work hard to keep and protect it.[9]

The curriculum, in calling for the kind of teaching illustrated above, excludes all reference to the realities of poverty, discrimination, and hostility which are the lot of many Puerto Ricans and their children. This type of teaching does not interest nor motivate Puerto Rican pupils who know through their experience and that of their families that often the reverse is true, especially where differences in race, color, and culture are involved.

Notes

1. C.W. Mills, The Puerto Rican Journey, New York: Harper, 1950, p. 32.

2. Dan Wakefield, Island in the City, New York: The Citadel Press, 1960, p. 157.

3. W.W. Charters, et al., Habits Healthful and Safe, New York: The Macmillan Company, 1955, p. 214.

4. Ibid., p. 215.

5. Ibid., p. 218.

6. Ibid., p. 221.

7. Resource Units for Classes With Puerto Rican Pupils in the
      Second Grade, p. 33.

8. Ibid., p. 33.

9. M.G. Mackey, et. al., Your Country's Story. New York:
      Ginn, 1953.

Eugene Bucchioni, "The Daily Round of Life in the School."
A Sociological Analysis of the Functioning of Elementary
Education for Puerto Rican Children, (Unpublished Doctoral
Dissertation, New School for Social Research, 1965), pp.
73-151. Reprinted by permission.

The curriculum is but one of many factors affecting life within the classroom. Daily, in the classroom, the teacher, in discharging her professional duties and responsibilities, attempts to
implement the curriculum and its numerous provisions by making
available the suggested experiences and activities, by utilizing the
recommended materials and methods of instruction, and by observing the required time allotments. Children arrive early in the
morning, their attendance is taken, and the acting out of the curriculum then begins.

Concurrently with the acting out of the curriculum, however,
other things occur as well. Along with the mandated experiences
and activities of the curriculum, children talk, become noisy, and
are reprimanded accordingly. There are many requests for permission to get drinks or to use the toilets. The pencil sharpener
and the waste paper basket become the crowded sites of frequent
small meetings as children approach these locations, ostensibly to
sharpen their pencils and discard paper but instead remain to chat
or to laugh and play. Questions and answers, the playing of games,
singing songs, recess periods for milk, classroom monitors performing their roles, the giving of homework assignments, fire
drills, getting on line, standing up and sitting down are all significant components of classroom life.

The combination of the interaction of various curriculum requirements and these patterns of child behavior in the classroom result in an intricate round of life that is repeated daily, weekly and
monthly in each elementary school. But this round of life, as varied and highly complicated as it is, becomes still more complex
as Puerto Rican children interact with it and act out their several
roles as children in elementary school, and as young members of
lower classes and participants in Puerto Rican culture.

Miss Dwight, the Curriculum, and los Niños Puertorriqueños[1]

Miss Dwight was seated at her classroom desk handscoring
her fourth grade class's achievement tests when the 8:45 bell rang.
She clipped the papers and arranged them in a neat pile on the
metal file cabinet to her right, put out the room lights, and locked
the door after her.

The third grade and other fourth grade teachers had begun
to gather inside the side entrance to the building and took the op-

portunity to talk among themselves for a few minutes before admitting their lines of classes into the building.

Miss Dwight joined the group and said, "I've just been marking the achievement tests and I wish they hadn't been given."

"I know what you mean," said Mrs. Maran.

"How can almost everyone of the children miss a simple question like the one about musical instruments?"

"The Puerto Ricans seem to learn absolutely nothing--either here or at home."

"Yes," said Miss Dwight, "all they seem to care about is sleeping, eating, playing, and having parties."

"But you know...the ones in my third grade class are very well behaved. Authority means something to them."

"Too bad they have to grow up!" said Miss Dwight. "Things sure take a turn for the worse then."

"Something's wrong somewhere," said Mrs. Maran.

"Well, we'd better get the children."

Miss Dwight moved to the door, beckoned her class to enter the building, and led the double line to their classroom. She held the keys out to Juan, who opened the door and switched the lights on quickly before another classmate, running to the switch, could beat him to it.

The children talked quietly among themselves as they went past the bookcase to hang their coats on the hooks in the closets. The two coatroom monitors took their stations in the closet at either end and saw that no one remained there longer than necessary. They also made certain that the children entered the closet at the left side and went out at the right.

Maria was watering the plants which sat on the long shelves built in front of the windows. She took particular care of the cactus plants and consulted with Miss Dwight as to the proper amount of water to be given them. Antonio adjusted the shades so that the bright morning sunlight did not streak across the desks and into eyes.

The bulletin board on the wall opposite the windows was filled with samples of children's written work, arranged in columns, some papers boasting glittering colored stars while others were devoid of similar commendation. To one end of the bulletin board were charts with colorful pictures illustrating words that begin with different consonants. The remainder of the bulletin board was devoted to a crudely drawn map, water-colored by the children, with street names indicated, of a twenty block radius around the school. Cracked, yellowed plaster hung from almost all of the room's wall space. The lighting for the room came from two rows of three huge globes that were suspended from the ceiling by long chains.

Miss Dwight finished looking over the plans she had written for the day's work. She took the classroom in with a glance and noticed that about half the class was already seated and ready for the day's work with a notebook and pencil on most desks.

"Children," she said, "please get to your seats now."

As the children moved to obey, some a little slowly, some more rapidly, Miss Dwight called the name of each child in the first seat across the room for the attendance of each row. The names of the boys and girls absent were called out and Miss Dwight made the appropriate notations in her attendance register.

As she closed the book, about to put it in its place in the metal file cabinet, Dolores and Jesús entered the room, late. Miss Dwight glanced at them, made the necessary corrections in her register, and asked, "Do you have a note for being late?"

Dolores replied breathlessly, "Maestra, el reloj despertador se rompió y..."

"Dolores, speak in English please. You know that I don't understand Spanish."

"Si, maestra. ¡Como no! Deh alarrme clock. Eet broken bery bad. My mama say..."

"Please, Dolores. We've taken enough of the class's time for this. Furthermore, if it's not your alarm clock, it's having to go to the store, or helping dress your brother or some other excuse. You will have to learn to come to school on time. You too, Jesús! You have been coming to school long enough to realize that one of the important rules is to be early in the morning. And another thing, you are to bring a note each time you are late or absent. I expect a note from each of you tomorrow morning. And I'm tired of changing my attendance report every time you both come in late."

Miss Dwight turned to the class and asked for two volunteers to be Mr. and Mrs. America for the opening exercises. She looked at the many hands that were raised in her class of thirty-three children, and selected Alan and Carmen. Carmen smiled as she walked quickly to the front of the room. She joined Alan in asking the class to rise for the pledge of allegiance to the flag. Miss Dwight also rose, faced the flag, and helped to lead the class over such words as allegiance, republic, indivisible, and justice.

During the first few months of school the class sang America, but Miss Dwight had recently advanced them, after much drilling, to The Star Spangled Banner. Miss Dwight winced when she heard such phrases as "was so proudly we held" and "bought estripes and bri destars." Other words were also unintelligible: perilous, proof, ramparts.

Some of the children moved to seat themselves after the song. Miss Dwight stared in the direction of several of them, folded her hands, bowed her head, and followed Alan and Carmen as they led the class in prayer.

"Almighty God, we acknowledge our dependence on Thee. We beg Thy blessings on us, our parents, our teachers, and our country."

The children seated themselves and Miss Dwight looked at her planbook briefly. Some of the children talked with each other, a few looked through their desks for various papers and books, and others slumped down in their seats.

"Class, please open your number books to page 46. Henry, would you start reading the instructions at the top of the page."

Henry read the title, " 'Learning more about subtraction.' These are problems that ask how many are left. To find the answer you must subtract."

"Helena, please read the first problem aloud."

"Dere were seex duckes esweemin een a pon. Two a dem eswam away. How many were lef?"

Miss Dwight said, "Helena, that's not quite right. You're not pronouncing the words correctly. Say, there were six ducks swimming in a pond. Two of them swam away. How many were left?"

Helena repeated the question incorrectly. Miss Dwight said, "That's better. Now, how many do you have left?"

Miss Dwight called on Juan. He tilted his head to the side and stared ahead, as Miss Dwight waited for an answer. Several children raised their hands to be called on, and others buried their heads in their books or rummaged through their desks.

"Juan, do you or don't you understand this problem?"

He did not answer. His grip tightened on the book as he continued to peer into it.

"Juan, I asked you a question and I expect an answer."

"Maestra, dees word I donno.   Qué quiere decir?"

"Spell the word for us."

"S-w-i-m-m-i-n-g."

"That's swimming. To move in the water."

"Nadando," called out Manuel in explanation.

Juan looked into his book again and Miss Dwight waited in silence, keeping the class quiet by glancing around and resting her gaze on those who talked or fidgeted in their seats.

Manuel raised his hand and asked to go to the boys' room. "No, Manuel, you will have to wait until I take the entire class at ten o'clock."

Manuel turned to his neighbor, Pedro, and spoke rapidly and not too softly. "Pero Tengo que ir al baño ahora mismo," Miss Dwight heard him say.

"No talking, Manuel! Juan please read the problem aloud to the class."

"Dere were seex duckes esweeming to..."

"To-geth-er," said Miss Dwight.

"...to-ged-der een a pon. Two a dem eswam away. How many were lef?"

"What is it, Juan?"

"Lef? No comprendo lef. What mean lef, teacha?"

"It means how many stayed together after the two ducks went swimming away."

"Ah, sí, ahora comprendo," he said rapidly, sitting taller in his seat.

He looked into his book and his lips began to move as he re-read the problem silently. Miss Dwight said, "Juan, we have taken a long time on this problem. Do you know how to solve it?"

"Seex...takaway two."

Manuel shouted, "Seis menos dos."

"Quiet, Manuel," said Miss Dwight. Juan turned his head to the window. "Juan, please try to pay attention. Take out your squared material and work it out. And," she addressed the class, "if you do not have the answer, I want you to do the same."

The children, some quickly, and others more slowly, searched in their desks for the arithmetic materials. Books from

overstuffed desks fell onto the floor and some children took this opportunity to walk to the basket with crumpled scrap paper they
found in their desks. Others went to the pencil sharpener that was
attached to the side of the bookcase where they conversed in soft
tones.

"Get to your desks," called out Miss Dwight. "This moving
about has got to stop!" When order was restored, she continued,
"Class, how many ones' squares do you need to solve this problem?"

The same few hands that were raised previously went up
again. Miss Dwight ignored these offers of assistance. The remainder of the class looked back into their books at the problem.
More hands were raised.

"Juan, how many do you need?"

"Seex."

"Fine. Now take them out of your holder and place them
separately on your desk. Now, how many should you take away?"

Again, heads turned to page 46.

"Two," Juan answered, as he picked up two squares of
paper.

"How many are left?"

"Uno, dos, tres, cuatro," he answered as he tapped each
square that remained.

"No, Juan. One, two, three, four."

Miss Dwight took a deep breath and adjusted her posture.
She then read the second problem to the class. She called on Marvin for the solution and received an immediate correct answer.

"Children, these problems go on to the next page. When
you have free time today, you are to do these two pages. Otherwise, they are part of your homework. Make an example of each
one. And now, put all your arithmetic materials away. It's ten
o'clock, and we must go to the lavatories and then to the basement
for physical education. Row one, line up. No talking."

The children began to talk loudly. Miss Dwight said, "Sit
down, children. We will have to stay here if you do not line up
quickly and quietly. And Manuel and Pedro, school is no place for
you to be leaping out of your seats and racing others to the front
of the room. Behave yourselves."

"Now, let us try again. And keep quiet on line. Row one,
stand. Walk to the front of the room. Row two."

Miss Dwight gave each row time to move slowly and then
called the rest of the class in the same manner. She gave the keys
to Juan, watched him lock the door and turn off the light switch,
tried the door handle to make certain it was locked, and reminded
him to pull the door closed after the class was out of the room.
He nodded and gave her a grin as he said, "Sí, maestra."

Miss Dwight led the class to the end of the hallway and lined up
the boys in front of the boys' toilet and the girls at theirs. "Hurry,
boys, three at a time. Girls, four at a time. Please don't waste
time as it's ten past ten and we have the basement only until it's
ten thirty."

As a boy or girl came out of the lavatories, another child
went in. Miss Dwight opened the door to the boys' room frequently and could see, through the mirror to the left, the boys standing

at the urinals. "Wash your hands, boys, and if you are ready,
come out so that the others might come in."

Antonio was out as fast as he had gone in. Miss Dwight
felt his dry hands and sent him back to wash them. The girls were
finished and standing on line. Miss Dwight said, "Girls, I'm sure
you remembered to wash your hands. If anyone has forgotten,
please go back and do it now."

Four girls returned to the girls' room and came out com-
plaining that there was no soap in the dispensers. "Well, girls,
we have soap in our room. You can wash your hands later. Now,
class, let's be on our way."

Miss Dwight walked to the left of her class line and kept at
about the middle. In this way, she was able to control the strag-
glers at the end of the line and watch for talking in the hallway.
The line leaders stopped at the end of the next hall, waiting for instructions to make a turn to the left. There was some talking, but
Miss Dwight restored silence and then instructed the line leaders to
continue. She moved to the front of the line when they reached the
staircase, and led them slowly down to the basement.

"Children, this morning we are going to continue with the
square dance. You remember that I explained that this is an early
American dance that the first settlers in this country used to do.
Today, many people still enjoy doing this kind of dancing. I need
eight children; four boys and four girls for the first set."

Most of the children showed eagerness to participate by waving their hands and calling out, "Me!" or by shouting, "Pleez,
teacha!" Some children hopped up and down and a few took their
partners' hands and skipped about. Miss Dwight asked the class to
calm down, selected some of the more eager children, and told the
rest of the class to sit on the benches along the wall.

She arranged the four boys opposite the girls and gave brief
instructions as to how to begin the dance. She put the Virginia
Reel on the record player and started the record. The children
danced in time to the rapid music. Miss Dwight took the arm of
different children at times to help them with directions and to lead
them to the new partners during the successive phases of the dance.

"Miss Dwight," complained Arthur, "Carmen doesn't know
how to do this dance. She is always going the wrong way and getting me all mixed up."

"Arthur, be patient. You did this dance last year. And besides, Carmen is just learning our language. It is not easy to be
new to everything all at once and maybe she doesn't understand directions."

Miss Dwight's attention was suddenly diverted to the children
seated on the benches. They were talking, some were pushing and
teasing others, some were laughing, and some were just moving
about. She asked the children who had danced to sit down, then
asked for quiet, and proceeded to select the next group of eight.
She chose the children who had been making the most noise and disturbance, gave them the necessary instructions, and played the record once more. When the group had gotten halfway through the
dance, another class entered the basement. Exclamations of an-
noyance came from those who had not yet danced. Miss Dwight

lined up her class and spoke with Mrs. Frazier who had led her class to the benches.

"Hi, Mary. Boy! What a waste this morning has been. Two arithmetic problems and only half the class danced."

"Same here. All I do is give directions and explain, explain, explain! You'd think that by the time they get to the sixth grade they'd be able to read ten science pages by themselves."

"But we haven't even got enough texts, even if they could read them. It's a joke. I'm supposed to find time today for social studies, reading, language arts, writing, and health. Not to mention art and music."

"The third month of school and nothing across yet," said Mrs. Frazier.

"Yes, and I don't dare question most of the children about their work. I'm sure that most of what I say has gone out of the window. Most of them listen quietly and never ask a question, except now and then. Well, see you at lunch, Mary."

Miss Dwight reorganized her class and led them back to the classroom. Felipe came up to her at her desk and asked to go to the boys' room. "No, Felipe, you were there only twenty minutes ago."

"But, teacha, I deen have to make den."

"All right, but this will be the last time you leave the room this morning. And don't call me teacher. I have a name. Learn it!" Felipe left the room quickly. When he returned, the class was ready to begin a social studies discussion of the neighborhood.

"Yesterday, class," said Miss Dwight, "we talked of the block you live on. Many of you told us about your own block: what the houses look like, where you play, where you go to buy your groceries, drugs, and candy, and where your library, church, and police station are located. Today, let us talk about different neighborhoods right here in New York City and decide whether the differences make people live in different ways than you do. Who can tell me what the five boroughs of New York City are?"

Ronald, Frieda, and Stephen raised their hands. Some children opened their notebooks to find their listing of the boroughs, but other children went to the pencil sharpener or waste paper basket.

"Boys and girls, sit down and keep still." "Now what is the answer?"

Miss Dwight called on Frieda who answered, "Manhattan, Brooklyn, Queens, Bronx, and..." She could not think of the fifth borough, and Stuart completed the answer with, "Staten Island."

"Children, please sit up tall," said Miss Dwight. "Your feet belong on the floor, and not on the rungs of your desks. And everyone should be listening. Some of you do not look as if you are paying attention. To continue, let us talk about the borough of Queens where I live. I'll write a list on the blackboard of points of comparison that we can make between your neighborhood and an average neighborhood or suburb of Queens. Now, what things can we compare?"

Many hands were raised, and a list was developed:

kinds of houses
places to shop for food and clothing
churches
schools
libraries
playgrounds

Miss Dwight explained, "Many of the houses in my neighbor-
hood are two family houses. One family lives on the first floor
and another family lives upstairs."
Jesús asked, "Each family--they have their own baño?"
Miss Dwight asked, "Baño?"
Jesús replied, "Sí, where you go to wash yourself."
"You mean bathroom," said Miss Dwight. "Yes, they do."
"Dees I like, " said Jesús. "The same baño the odder
people use, we use too. And sometimes I cannot get een dere neb-
er. For dat, I am een the morning late."
María added, "I too. And mama rrush me when I trry to
take a bat. Me she tell not to make people in the beeldeen wait.
Dice que no tengo derecho a hacer que espere tanto a la gente."
"English, children," requested Miss Dwight. "You will find,
children, that many families have houses all to themselves, with
sometimes two bathrooms upstairs--one for each bedroom and one
on the first floor too."
"Only bery rreech peepool leebe een doz places," said Juan.
"Not exactly rich, Juan. But they do work hard, and every
day."
"My papa, he say he work hard, every day--eben on Sunday.
Sometime he don habe to work on Sunday. He get a day to estay
home." Juan added, "And heem I hear say, and my mama say
too, neber weel we be able to move to a more better place to
leebe."
"It is difficult, sometimes, to earn enough money to do
everything we want. It's important for you to remember that your
work in school will some day help you to get a better job, earn
more money, and live in a good home. This is why I am here:
to help you live better. But let us remember that while we work
toward something better, we must accept what we have now and try
to appreciate the good things we have. For instance, what do you
have that is good in your way of living?"
Faces took on various expressions and mixed comments were
made.
"A lot--we gotta a lot een weech to play."
"I habe a bedroom weed my brodder."
"And neber I am hungry like de oder keeds in my beeldeen
who are bery hungry all dee days."
"Yes, when we have these basic comforts, we do have something to be thankful for. And that reminds me that it is time for
our milk. Will the people we chose to give it out this week please
do that now? And if you brought cookies, you may get them."
Miss Dwight sat at her desk and worked on the achievement
tests while the children drank their milk and chatted. She over-
heard a few children make complaints about their living conditions.

There was some talking in Spanish. When the milk containers had
been discarded, she resumed their social studies lesson. Marvin
began to tell of his cousin who lives on Long Island.

"My uncle drives my cousin, Raymond, to school every day.
And I saw his school. It's not big like this one. And it's new.
They have a gym with everything in it. They even have one of
those things that they use in the circus to jump on. There's a big
cafeteria and they have flowers and trees in front of the school.
And the walls in the room are pretty colors."

"Long Island, children, is not in New York City. It is an
island, almost 800 miles long, right outside of New York City.
Many people have moved there because it is like the country, and
they have built new modern schools and they have shopping centers
where you have all the stores you need all together. There are
very few apartment houses. Almost every family has its own house.
The people who live near each other often get together for parties
and dinner."

"Dat we'll do neber. My papa say eet ees too hard to
change. Peepool won let you."

"No, Juan. That is not always true. If you study and work
hard, and show people that you want to do what is right, they will
let you improve yourself. It takes time and patience. We've seen
today, children, that people in different places live in different ways,
and I hope to continue this discussion tomorrow. For homework,
I would like you to bring in pictures of houses, schools, churches,
and playgrounds. And tomorrow, we will try to decide what kind
of community these pictures fit into and compare them with your
own. We have a half hour before lunch. Please open your notebooks to the English section and write a heading for today's work.
I would like you to write a paragraph about our discussion today in
social studies. Elsa, why is it taking you so long to find a page
to write on?"

"An emty page, I cannot fin, teacha."

"How many times have I told you to keep at least five blank
pages in each subject section of your notebook?"

"I don have no more paper."

"Well, why don't you ask your mother to buy you some?"

"I deed. Friday she say."

"But tomorrow is Tuesday. That means that you will have
to borrow paper from a classmate for the entire week."

Several children were quick to offer Elsa paper. She accepted a few sheets and inserted the pages into her book. Miss
Dwight walked around the room and stopped at many of the desks to
help pupils in their work and to prod others to begin. Several children asked for the spelling of certain words. Miss Dwight stopped
at Pedro's desk.

"Pedro, not 'Today we learn about new york.' It's 'learned'
with an 'ed' ending to mean past time. Also New York is capital-
ized because it is the name of a place."

"I teenk New York ees only where I am."

"No, Pedro, you live in Manhattan which is only a small
part of our state, which is also called New York."

Pedro shrugged his shoulders and Miss Dwight moved a few

desks away and read, silently, the paragraph that Juan had written:
I libe in nu yor city and so do oder
many pipul who hab ril jauses
i wil not oways lib were I
lib because i wil studi in escool.

Miss Dwight smiled and pointed out the spelling, punctuation,
and capitalization errors. "Juan, this is a very good beginning.
I hope you will add a few details to show in what ways other people
live differently than you do."
        "Sí, maestra, cómo no." He took his pencil and proceeded
to the next sentence.
        "Tomás, please stop holding your head up and get your el-
bow off the desk. What time did you go to bed last night?"
        "Carajo," whispered Tomás. "Twelve o'clock, teacha."
        "Why so late?"
        "My moder and fader had a party. Eet was een de room
where I esleep."
        "Well, couldn't you have slept in your parents' room until
the party was over?"
        "No, on de bed were too many coat. We don habe no room
in de closet for de coat of de peepool."
        "Well, Tomás, I hope you will go to bed early tonight so
that you are rested tomorrow."
        "Sí, maestra, I am bery tired."
        "Children it is time to get ready for lunch. Will those chil-
dren who are going home for lunch get their clothing?"
        The children made much noise as they got their clothing and
moved back to their seats. Most of the class remained in school
for lunch, and Miss Dwight called them, row by row, to get their
clothing. At the sound of the bell, she dismissed those who were
leaving the building, and after having reminded them to go directly
home and to be back before the late bell, then called the remainder
of the class on line.
        "Children, the principal made a definite point of telling the
teachers that the behavior and noise in the lunchroom is terrible.
I hope I can be proud of you and that you will behave as you should,
get your food quietly, eat quickly, and clean your places before
you leave."
        Juan took care of the lights and door and Miss Dwight led
the class through the crowded hallways to the lunchroom. She
stopped at the entrance and observed the actions of many of the
children as they pushed each other, called out to friends, approached
their tables at a half run, and slammed the metal trays down. She
saw many children who had already finished eating return their trays
with salads and vegetables untouched. She turned to enter the
teachers' room.
        She poured herself a cup of coffee, chose a seat next to
Mary Frazier, and began to unwrap her sandwich. The teachers'
room was not large and was undecorated, except for a small bulletin board with leaflets tacked to it and notes and letters from teachers who had either left or were on leave. There was a brown
leather couch along a small wall space and three matching easy

chairs along another side. Teachers from all grades filled the
three tables. Conversation ranged from fashions to housework to
theater to curriculum.

"How was the rest of your morning, Frances?" Mary
Frazier asked Miss Dwight.

"Not too bad. I did some social studies and a little English.
But I must tell you about Juan."

"Before you do," interrupted Mary, "why not get your coffee
and relax a little?"

Frances Dwight went to the small kitchen in the teachers'
room and poured herself a cup of coffee. Edith, who sat opposite
Mary said, "What's the use of worrying about these kids? Between
their lousy way of living and their Spanish, we're lost before we
begin."

Frances returned to the table in time to hear Edith's remark and said, "That's just what I mean about Juan. This morning we had a class discussion in social studies and he told how his
father works so hard. His parents are sure they'll never get anywhere. It's sad."

"Well," said Mary, "how can they when they don't know anything, go anywhere, or read anything?"

"That reminds me," said Edith, "of a story I heard of a kid
who had an assignment to collect pictures of colorful gardens from
magazines. He came in the next day without any pictures. When
his teacher asked why he replied, 'All we got home is love 'n mur-
der.' Really, I can't wait to get away from these dirty kids.
Sometimes, I could faint when I get close to them."

"Edith," said Mary, "let's face it. We are in a slum neighborhood, and as far as the Puerto Ricans go, only the lower class
has migrated here."

"True," said Frances. "They're told about the wonderful
opportunities for them in America. If they knew any better, they
wouldn't live the way they do."

"They act like animals, too. But they're worse in high
school. I wouldn't teach there if you doubled my salary."

"You'll have tenure this year, won't you?" Mary asked
Edith.

"Yes, and then the hell with all this. No more of this for
me."

"But," said Mary, "what if all the teachers felt the way you
do. I get discouraged too, but they are in this country and we have
a job to do. They are American citizens you know, and we have
to teach them how to live here."

"So far, they've been useless," said Edith. "All you see in
the newspapers are gang wars, dope addicts, and rapes. You know
it is so dangerous here that we have to walk to the subway together."

"Oh, Edith, it's not really as bad as all that," said Frances.

"No, it's worse. It was bad enough when we had the Negroes. Now the goddamn spics too. Why even the Negroes des-
pise these damn Puerto Ricans."

"Look," said Mary, "we've got them, so let's do the best
we can."

"Another thing. What can you do with all this experience

learning?" asked Edith. "If you fit in all these experiences,
there's no time left to teach. These kids need good old-fashioned
drill and lots of it. And what child can count from five to ten without fingers or one's strips?"

"What really bothers me," said Frances, "is all the talking
in Spanish. And I'll flip if just one more child calls me 'teacha'
today."

"When they speak Spanish, they really prattle like monkeys.
I'm sure they're not even trying to learn English," said Edith.

"Wait," said Mary. "Remember that Spanish is natural to
them. How would you like the pressure of learning a new language
and new subjects all at the same time?"

"Mary," said Edith, "you're entirely too sympathetic. You
live in a dream world. Do you really think for one minute that
these kids will ever amount to anything? In ten years you'll be unable to recognize New York because there will be so many Puerto
Ricans here."

"Well," said Mary, "I can't help feeling sorry for these
people. They are so persecuted from all sides and they need help,
and lots of it."

The bell rang and the teachers cleared their places at the
table and filed out to the yard to get their classes. Miss Dwight
called her class into the building, led them to the room and Juan
opened the door. The children seated themselves and Miss Dwight
called them, row by row, to put their clothing away. She attempted
to keep the children quiet by alternately saying, "Quiet, boys and
girls," or "Keep still, children."

"I noticed, children, that the lunch didn't go over too well
today. I saw many salads and vegetables untouched. Would someone care to explain why?"

María raised her hand. "Si, maestra, the corn eet habe no
taste, and the sald was just lechuga."

"Lettuce," called out one of the children.

María continued, "My mama she make a sald dat taste so
good."

"Well, we all do have different ways of preparing food so
that it tastes good to us, but isn't it necessary to have a variety of
foods each day?"

The class showed no response to this query. Miss Dwight
continued, "Let us discuss a proper breakfast."

"Who has a suggestion?"

Roger and Antonio began to talk and Miss Dwight asked them
to pay attention. They glanced at each other and smiled. Roger
looked at the clock and then stared ahead, while Antonio picked up
a pencil and started to scratch a groove deeper in his desk.

"Antonio, that is not your property that you are ruining.
Many children will use that desk after you. I think you should
leave it as you found it. Now put the pencil down and stop this
nonsense. Do you hear?"

Antonio uttered a Spanish obscenity. He did not lower his
voice when making this remark. Most of the children looked at one
another, showing shock, and some giggled.

"Antonio, what did you say? In English!"

He repeated the obscenity.

"Antonio, stand up and tell me in English what you said."

Antonio did not answer. He looked away from her.

"I'm waiting for your answer, Antonio. What does that mean?"

He stared at Miss Dwight.

"Would anyone in the class care to translate for me?"

"Maestra, it ees a bad teeng he say. We cannot say."

"Thank you, Juan." Miss Dwight turned to Antonio and suggested, "Perhaps you would like to repeat it to your mother at a conference."

"No, teacha, I am bery sorry. I do not mean eet. No more will I say eet."

"All right, Antonio, I will believe you. And I hope you will control your feelings better in the future. People just don't burst out and call each other names whenever they feel like it. You must learn how to cooperate more with others. We have to live with many people in this world, and it's time you've learned that everything does not always go the way you want it to. Now sit down and behave yourself."

She turned to the class. "Now, what is a food that we should eat at breakfast time?"

Marvin said, "Cereal."

"Fine. What else should you have for breakfast?"

"Café," answered another child.

"Coffee? No, coffee does not nourish you. It doesn't help you to grow strong. What can you drink that is good for your bones and teeth?"

Several children called out, "Milk!"

"Yes, milk. Milk has calcium in it. There is one more thing you should have at breakfast time."

David interrupted, "Miss Dwight, what is calcium?"

"I'm glad you asked, David. Children, I wish more of you would ask me to explain words that you don't understand. Calcium is a mineral. Our bodies need minerals and vitamins, just as a car needs gas and oil. Without the different minerals and vitamins, our bodies would break down and become sick. Each vitamin has a special job to do. Calcium makes our bones and teeth strong. Now what else besides milk and cereal should we have at breakfast time?"

She paused for a suggestion. None came, so she added, "Orange juice. Orange juice is for vitamin C."

María raised her hand. "What ees beetameen C?"

"Each vitamin has a letter and that is a vitamin we get from citrus fruits. I'll make a list of these items on the blackboard while you are making a heading for today in the health section of your notebooks and copy the list. Perhaps you can show the list to mother so that she, too, will understand what the best foods are for you and the family. Now, what are other foods that we should eat each day?"

"Bread?"

"Yes, and whole wheat or rye bread is better than white because the   flour has not been whitened. That means that there is more food value in these other breads."

"Meat?"

"Good. Each day you should have some meat or eggs or cheese. These are called protein foods and they help to build your bodies. What goes with meat?"

"Tomatoes?"

"Well, yes. Also, vegetables that are green. Can you name some?"

"Espeenach?"

"Peas."

"Fine. We have others, too, cabbage, stringbeans, broccoli, asparagus, and many more. Every day you should have a salad, too. If you have these foods each day, you are sure to be getting all the vitamins and minerals that your body needs and you will be healthier and stronger."

Manuel raised his hand. "Teacha, my mama she cook so deeferent. Our beshtabools are oways jellow and white, like corn and rrice. We habe beans, too. But mama don make doz oder teengs. Neber I heard of some of dem."

"This is why we are making a list, Manuel. Perhaps your mother will be interested in trying some of these foods. I think your family might find it fun to eat different foods. Children, why not ask mother to give you, each day, one of these foods on the list? And if you like it, she can serve it again. Little by little, you will have a balanced diet.

"It's almost one-thirty and we had better get into our reading groups. I'll work first with the Bluebirds. While I do that, I want the Little Red Group to finish the reading exercises you started yesterday, and the Thunderbirds can work on the paragraphs you started this morning in social studies. Bluebirds, bring your chairs and reading books up to the front of the room."

Some children pushed their chairs and Miss Dwight told them to carry them. Others who were talking were told to stop or they would be given additional homework assignments. Miss Dwight wrote a list of words on the board and said to the children, "Today we are going to read a story about a little boy and girl just your age who go with their uncle to a wharf. As I say the words on the board, you look at them and try to remember them. 'Wharf, trawler, pier, cabin, galley, stern, aft, salmon.' Now I want you to look these words up in the dictionary that is in the back section of your reading books and be prepared to tell me the meaning of each word."

She then addressed the children of the Little Red Group. Some were still working on the exercises in the reading workbooks. Three children who had finished this work were standing at the bulletin board before a world map and appeared to be discussing anything but geography.

"Will the children in the Little Red Group take your workbooks and chairs to the back of the room now?" The ten children followed directions and Miss Dwight started the review of the first exercise. "Vera, read the first sentence with your answer."

" 'Fran has a ...' I don't know that word."

" 'Ewe.' You pronounce it like the word 'y-o-u.' "

" '...ewe lamb.' "

"Yes, that is right.   José, do the next."

"I couldn't do eet, teacha."

"Why not?"

"I deen read de story. I was home."

"Don't you know that you are supposed to catch up on your
reading when you come back after being absent?"

"Sí, but I deen habe not enough time."

"Well, take the book and go to your seat and read it now."

Miss Dwight looked over the Bluebird group. "Bluebirds, if
you continue to talk, I will have you write the meanings of those
words and write them in sentences of your own. Continue your
work quietly."

She turned back to the Little Red Group. "Susan, do the
second one."

"The name of the ewe lamb is Fluffy."

"Correct. Antonio, the next."

"I don know what eet mean."

"Linda, read it please. Read it without the answer so then
Antonio can answer it."

" 'Jerry works in a ...' "

"Antonio, finish the sentence."

He looked into his notebook. Miss Dwight asked, "Antonio,
do you know where he worked?"

"No."

"Get the book and look for the answer."

Antonio went to his desk for the book, came back to his
chair, and turned the pages slowly, trying to find the story.

"Antonio, why don't you use the table of contents?" You can
find the story very quickly this way."

He turned back to the table of contents, found the page number and after several moments, found the story.

"Now, look quickly," Miss Dwight said, "for the part that
tells where Jerry works."

He used his finger to underline the sentences as he began to
look methodically down the first page.

"Antonio, we read the story only yesterday. Can't you remember that the first few pages are about the lambs? You will
find your answer further on in the story. There is no time to wait
for you to find it now. Continue to look for the answer when you
return to your seat. Children, we will finish this exercise tomorrow. Make sure that you have completed all the questions, so that
we will be able to review this rapidly."

She spoke to the third reading group. "Thunderbirds, we
have no time for reading today, I will start with your group in the
morning. Bluebirds, go back to your seats now. We will start to
read our new story tomorrow."

The children moved noisily. Miss Dwight ignored the mo-
mentary confusion while she continued to consult the planbook at her
desk.

"We just have time before the bell rings to talk about our
Christmas party. First, we need to divide the class into committees for entertainment, decorations, and refreshments. I'll write

the committee titles on the blackboard and you decide which ones
you want to be on."

Many children raised their hands. When Miss Dwight had
finished writing on the board, she turned to see almost every hand
waving energetically and voices grew louder as children began to
call out. When Miss Dwight called for silence and asked each child
for his and her preference, many more hands went up. The lists
of names were noted on the blackboard.

"Each committee will have a special assignment and special
things to do. Today, let's decide what the decoration committee
will do."

Suggestions were shouted out from different parts of the
room. The voices resounded. Miss Dwight raised her voice.
"Children, if you continue to call out like this, we will have no
party. We studied in our language arts lesson yesterday about how
to hold a discussion. Please try to remember this discussion and
all the rules we talked about, and be courteous so that you will all
have a chance to be heard."

The class quieted down and Miss Dwight nodded to different
children for their suggestions.

"Let's make baskets for our candy."

"I can make a Santa Claus for the door."

"Esnow for de weendo."

"Paper Christmas trees for the bulletin board."

"Fine. Those are enough ideas for now. Tomorrow, the
decoration committee can meet and plan the work to be done. Let
us give the entertainment committee something to work on."

Again, there was much rapid talk while the children offered
suggestions and decided upon a program. The class soon developed
a long list of dancers and singers.

"I can see that we will need several more hours for our
party than we have planned in order to fit in all of this entertainment. The bell is about to ring! I will write your homework on
the blackboard after I explain the assignment. Copy it and be sure
to take home all the books you need. Do spelling unit number ten,
part B. Look at the new words carefully and write the answers to
all the questions. If you did not finish your social studies paragraphs today, finish them for homework. And last, I want each of
you to find at least three pictures from magazines and newspapers
of different kinds of homes, schools, churches, and communities."

Miss Dwight called the class row by row to get their coats.
When they were ready to leave, she asked the first person in each
row to go down the row and point out papers and pencils left on the
floor so that they might be picked up. She then walked around the
room for a final check and called the class to line up. She led the
children to the outside door where many wishes for a pleasant afternoon were exchanged between her and the children. The children
burst through the door to the street where they shouted, talked,
laughed, and ran.

The Culture of the Classroom

The preceding account of Miss Dwight's fourth grade class portrays the range of experience of Puerto Rican pupils and their teacher in an elementary school classroom. Extensive observations indicate that Miss Dwight and her class represent the typical situation encountered in Puerto Rican schools. The daily round of life is similar. In these schools, the acting out of the curriculum, the interaction of teachers and pupils as they act out their particular roles, and the contact with Puerto Rican culture traits and lower class social patterns form a culture that is characteristic of them.

The school day began with the arrival of Miss Dwight and her pupils in the classroom. The children immediately placed their coats and other belongings in the closets at one side of the room. Whispering, loud talking in both Spanish and English, laughing and moving about characterized the informal opening moments of the day. Some children busily attended to certain housekeeping chores such as watering plants or dusting about the room. Other children worked on class assignments not completed the day before. Others read books that they had taken from the library table in the room. A few pupils just sat in their seats and stared out the window or at the teacher or other children.

Miss Dwight soon called her class to order. Attendance was taken and the routine opening exercises--the salute to the flag, the singing of the Star Spangled Banner, and the recitation of the Regents' Prayer--were held. Then the day's lessons and other activities began. They included arithmetic, recess, square dancing, social studies, milk time, English, lunch, health, reading, and discussion of plans for a party. Miss Dwight included these activities in her day's program because, as a teacher, it was her responsibility to assist her pupils to learn to read and write and acquire the other basic skills represented by the other lessons and activities held. Along with instruction in the fundamental academic skills, however, her pupils were learning other things.

They were learning, for example, to participate in certain rituals and ceremonies. In addition, Miss Dwight encouraged her Puerto Rican pupils to accept and internalize certain norms and values that were defined as appropriate by the teacher; her pupils were then expected to regulate their conduct in the classroom accordingly. Miss Dwight's pupils also learned that sanctions were applied to those who deviated from the moral rules and codes of behavior prescribed in the culture of the classroom. In short, the Puerto Rican pupils in Miss Dwight's class learned much that was not always explicitly formulated in her lesson plans for the day's instruction. They were learning, in general, the middle class definitions and interpretations of life and of the world.

Ritual Behavior in the Classroom

The elementary school includes, as a highly integral component of its culture, a wide variety of complicated and elaborate ritual behavior. Frequently, the recurring rituals can be defined and described by the teacher, and explanations of their manifest functions can be given without too much difficulty. Yet many of these rituals have functions and meanings other than those stated and recognized by the teacher, functions that are especially significant in the education of Puerto Rican children.

In Miss Dwight's classroom, children enter the class coatroom by the left door and leave through the right. Monitors are carefully stationed at each side to prevent children from deviating from the prescribed manner of entrance into and departure from the coatroom. Teachers state that this particular cultural arrangement, and others that are comparable, permit children to move quickly. Such an arrangement has certain pragmatic utility. Less time is wasted as each child enters one door, places his coat on his hook, and leaves by another door. This is a regular, orderly, and steady movement in one door and out the other.

This ritualistic behavior, however, does more than save time. The one-way traffic through the narrow coatroom prevents children from quarrelling and fighting with one another. It prevents the development of a critical situation that might occur if a child wishing to enter the coatroom and one wishing to leave arrive simultaneously at the same door. The ritualistic pattern of one way coatroom traffic from which deviation is not permitted functions to prevent the likely occurrence of conflict. A fight could result, there might be shouting and crying, and the teacher would then be responsible for terminating the fight, determining its cause, placing the blame, and administering appropriate punishment. A conflict of this kind and its consequences obviously threaten the social order of the classroom, a situation that most elementary teachers wish to avoid.

In the elementary school, equilibrium is ascribed a positive value, and teachers attempt to secure this equilibrium and preserve it at all costs. Furthermore, noise, disorder, and chaos--the probable consequences of a fight in the classroom--are difficult for the teacher to cope with, and yet class disorganization must be attended to immediately. The restoration of the stability of the social order in the classroom becomes the paramount aim. Both teachers and principals consider the breakdown of stability in the classroom, and the failure or inability to re-establish it, an indication of incompetency on the part of the teacher involved. Such a teacher is then likely to be criticized by other teachers or admonished by supervisors and principals.

The calling of the class row by row to line up, and the line itself pausing at specific locations in the halls to wait for the necessary permission before proceeding to its destination, represent another form of ritualistic behavior designed to avoid conflict among children and protect the highly valued social equilibrium of the classroom. Each child has his place on line. There is no pushing or fighting to be first on line because there are specially designated leaders. Line leaders have higher status in the culture of the classroom; children desire this status and consequently strive to be good, to live up to the expectations of the teacher, in order to be appointed leaders.

The stopping at fixed intervals for the required permission to proceed represents an act of deference to the teacher and her

socially ascribed authority. Through the frequent stopping for permission to continue the trip through the corridors, the teacher im-
presses upon her class the significant fact that she is the possessor
of important authority which must be respected by all.

The children, in stopping, recognize and acknowledge the superordinate status of their teacher; they obey the teacher by stopping and waiting, not only because it is the right and fitting thing to
do in the culture of the classroom, but also because imminent mis-
fortune--in the form of appropriate sanctions imposed by the
teacher--threatens if they do not.

A threat to impose sanctions helps to secure the careful exe-
cution of complicated ritual behavior, behavior that contributes to
the maintenance of the equilibrium of the classroom and the authority of the teacher. Authority is asserted frequently by elementary
teachers, for it is easily lost and weakened in the classroom, especially through failure to assert and exercise it with sufficient
frequency.

The daily opening exercises in Miss Dwight's classroom constitute another important form of ritualistic behavior. It is legally
mandated that the salute to the flag be recited daily in elementary
classrooms. The singing of the National Anthem or some other appropriate song is also required. Teachers and principals say that
these procedures help children to develop and strengthen a feeling
of patriotism.

These rituals, however, become especially important when
lower class children or children of differing ethnic backgrounds are
in attendance. The salute to the flag and the singing of a suitable
patriotic anthem help to promote a sense of identification with the
society as a whole. Puerto Rican as well as other children participate in this unifying ceremony together, without regard to race,
color, religion or culture. In this manner, the ritual functions to
overcome, to some extent, ethnic group divisiveness. This ritual
also tends to obscure economic differences. Even those who are
poor are Americans. They too salute the flag and sing the National
Anthem in a ceremony that renders homage to the nation, a nation
in which even the poor are important participants.

Miss Dwight, in common with most elementary school teachers, holds various additional ceremonies throughout the school year
that honor the nation and its heroes. Lincoln's birthday, for example, is commemorated. It is a school holiday, and in the days
preceding this event, elementary school children are told about Lincoln, Honest Abe; about how he gave his life for the nation and
freed the slaves; and about his rise to the presidency even though
he was a poor boy of humble origin who was born in a log cabin.
The stress upon this particular image becomes especially important
in schools attended by lower class children. They learn, in this
manner, that anyone can get ahead, if only he perseveres and works
hard enough.

Celebrations of Washington's birthday, Armistice Day (now
called Veterans' Day in the schools), Memorial Day, and Thanksgiving are also held. Through these celebrations and the periodic

retelling of the relevant national myths and legends, Puerto Rican
and lower class children are taught to identify with the nation, to
accept and respect its heroes, myths, legends, and values. By inculcating this sense of identification with the society as a whole,
the schools contribute to the development of an important and profound sense of unity, one which tends to obscure and overcome divisiveness because of ethnic or social class differences and which,
equally important, precludes the development of conflicts arising
from these differences.

Rituals honoring the nation and its heroes are only one component of the daily opening exercises. Miss Dwight's class also recited the Regents' Prayer,[2] a prayer authorized for use in the public schools by the New York State Board of Regents.* In this prayer, the class jointly affirms its dependence upon God. In this public affirmation of its dependence upon its deity, the class is almost
like a society begging the blessings of its gods upon its ancestors
(parents) and its ruler (teacher). Puerto Rican children, Negro
children, Catholics, Protestants, and Jews, the indigent and those
who can make ends meet, all pray together. All affirm jointly
their dependence upon and the nearness of God. This collective expression of common social values symbolizes the unity of Miss
Dwight's class and ultimately of the larger society.

Another type of ritual in Miss Dwight's classroom and in
other elementary school classrooms is the morning trip to the
toilet, followed by games or dances comprising the physical education period. During the course of the morning, children frequently
request permission to go to the toilets. Occasionally, children are
given permission immediately, while at other times, children are
reminded that the entire class will be leaving the room for the
toilets at a specified time and that they must wait until that time.
There is no apparent consistency in the granting or withholding of
permission.

The fixed daily toilet period represents more than time given
to children to attend to their physical needs. Physical needs are
secondary, for if they were otherwise, the permission needed to
leave the room would probably be granted when requested; furthermore, it is highly unlikely that all children in a class will need to
eliminate at a specified time during the school day.

During the school day, there are many reprimands and
scoldings, lectures and warnings, all of which contribute to the
building up of a considerable degree of tension in the classroom.
Given the pressures inherent in the atmosphere of the elementary
school classroom, any break in routine, even a hurried trip to the
toilet, is welcome, and can function to provide much needed relief
of the accumulated emotional and social tensions. Children and
teachers are separated from the classroom and each other for several moments. Then they proceed to the basement for games and
dances, a further break in the routine of the classroom. Children
can laugh and talk and move about to a degree not permitted in
class. Much of the informal conversation at such times is in Spanish, another illustration of the permissiveness that prevails at this

* This was true at the time Dr. Bucchioni was writing. [Ed.]

time, in contrast to the situation in the classroom where the use
of Spanish is discouraged.

During classroom observations, there was less general disorder in those rooms where the mid-morning trip to the toilet and
the basement for physical education was a daily procedure. In
these classrooms, children were sometimes warned that disobedience, disorder or noise of any kind would result in the cancellation
of the recess period. In those classrooms where the mid-morning
recess was not observed, teachers stated that the failure to have
recess was the result of a lack of time or of the imposition of
sanctions.

Most teachers, including Miss Dwight, stated that the mid-
morning recess provides welcome relief from the pressures of the
morning. "It's a break from the rat race." "It gives me a breathing spell." One teacher explained that the recess provided her the
opportunity to "recharge her battery because the long morning is
such a drain of her energy." During the physical education period,
Miss Dwight had the opportunity to speak to another teacher about
the first half of the morning, providing additional relief of tension.
Without the alleviation of the pressure and tension that accumulate
very rapidly, it is quite possible that many teachers and children
might not be able to function as expected for the remainder of the
morning in school. Inattention, noise, disorder and restlessness
might also develop more readily and the attempt to preserve order
would result in a classroom climate even more punitive and repressive.

Social Behavior of Puerto Rican Pupils

The social behavior of Puerto Rican children in elementary
school generally presents very little serious difficulty for the teacher insofar as classroom management and control are concerned.
Puerto Rican children, for the most part, respect their teachers,
do whatever they are requested to do, and generally attempt to be
good in the sense of the word as used by teachers. There is little
severe or uncontrollable disorder, few fights, and no attacks upon
the teacher. Children strive to be good because they fear punishment by the teacher and their parents if they deviate to any great
extent from the patterns of behavior expected in the classroom.
Teachers do encounter some difficulties, however, and Puerto Rican children are frequently reprimanded. There are, for example,
occasions of minor disorder, usually consisting of talking and the
noise resulting from movement in and about the classroom; sometimes obscenities in Spanish are heard.

To a great extent, these difficulties encountered by the teacher derive from the conflict arising from differences in the values
of middle class teacher and those of her slum dwelling pupils. The
elementary school teacher is a transmitter of the culture, and she
transmits, along with a variety of academic skills and other cultural
traits, the values of the middle class group to which she belongs.
When the elementary teacher teaches lower class pupils, as Miss
Dwight does, value conflicts are likely to occur. The educational
process then reflects the conflict in values both within the school

and the social and cultural milieu of the surrounding community.

Most elementary school teachers are drawn from middle or lower middle class groups.[3] In these groups, the traditional values are emphasized. There is, for example, much emphasis placed upon success, especially success in school, and upon the belief that hard work and the deferment of immediate advantages and satisfactions are the means to its achievement.

Saving is stressed as well as the care of personal possessions and private property. Neatness, etiquette, and politeness are important. Respect for and obedience to authority are also important, and appropriate deference to the police, parents, and teachers is encouraged. The control of aggression, except perhaps in self-defense, is emphasized, and in most instances, when aggression does occur, it tends to be verbal. In general, middle class groups value their good reputation and conventionality and are quite concerned with what others think of them.

Lower class groups, in contrast, tend to prefer immediate satisfaction and gratification. There is little or no long range planning. Missing school is not always penalized and education is not generally ascribed much importance in the lower class scheme of things. It is important to get a job, and to get it early. There is no special emphasis upon neatness, politeness, or etiquette.

Early sex experience occurs with considerable frequency among lower class individuals, and there are few restrictions placed upon overt aggression either within or outside the family. Aggression tends to be physical rather than verbal. Lower class individuals tend to be hostile to middle class authority, to parents, teachers, and police. One achieves success through smartness and through the ability to get away with things. In general, lower class individuals tend to have little concern with the opinions of middle class individuals. These factors represent points of potential conflict with the middle class values that elementary school teachers attempt to transmit. Conflicts do occur, of course, but many teachers attempt to prevent the development and outbreak of conflict by consistently striving to maintain equilibrium or order through the establishment of a disciplinary ceremonial that is resorted to both before and after violations of the normative order occur.

Miss Dwight and the Normative Order

In Miss Dwight's classroom, as in almost all elementary school classrooms, certain recurrent requests or demands were observed. "No talking," "Quiet down," "Get back to your seats," were among the statements and commands made by Miss Dwight in defining and enforcing certain norms that she considered important in regulating the conduct of her pupils.

In attempting to avoid conflict and to prevent disruption of her classroom, Miss Dwight, in common with most elementary teachers of lower class Puerto Rican children, referred frequently to the framework of middle class values and norms that made up the normative order within her classroom. That is, Miss Dwight strived to affirm at all times, and in a variety of ways, the norms and moral rules of her classroom, and attempted to develop syste-

matic, consistent, and methodical behavior which she considered
fitting and proper in the culture of the classroom.

Like many other teachers, Miss Dwight displayed charts
labelled, "How We Should Act in School," "Things We Should Do,"
and "Do's and Don'ts." In addition, in Miss Dwight's classroom,
various rote procedures and rituals were emphasized. Spontaneity
was not encouraged and was at a minimum. The general classroom atmosphere was impersonal and inflexible, and the children
were kept under rigid control. Certain types of behavior were prohibited, while other kinds were encouraged.

After several observations in Miss Dwight's classroom, the
following norms became evident, either through prominent display
on the charts referred to previously, or because they were expressed through periodic statements, reminders, group discussions,
reprimands, or lengthier scoldings:

No chewing gum
No speaking Spanish
No talking loudly
No talking when you're not supposed to
No pushing
No fighting
No fooling around
To speak English
No calling out
No throwing around books or anything else
To pick up paper or anything else on the floor
No copying
To raise hands during discussions
No passing notes
No writing on walls
No running in halls
No cursing
To say thank you and you're welcome
To come to school on time
Not to make noise
No taking things that don't belong to you
Not to interrupt when the teacher or someone else is talking
To get your work done on time
To do your work neatly and quickly
To pay attention to the teacher
To come to school neat and clean.

Many of the explicitly stated norms in Miss Dwight's classroom prohibit aggressive behavior, verbal or physical, as well as
any other type of behavior that might result in conflict that would
threaten the equilibrium in the classroom. Thus children are frequently reminded that pushing, fighting, fooling around, throwing
things, and the like are prescribed. Other norms refer to the appearance of school work and the punctuality with which it is done.
Still other norms are concerned with personal hygiene and cleanli-
ness, care and appearance of the classroom, standards of courtesy,
and prohibitions of swearing, obscene language and the use of Spanish.

Controls and Sanctions

The maintenance of order seems to be an essential prerequisite for a group to attain its objectives. The elementary school classroom is no exception in this respect in that the preservation of order is necessary if it is to function smoothly, continuously, and with a minimum of disruption. To prevent deviation from the patterns of equilibrium and order expected and demanded by the normative order of the elementary school classroom, various disciplinary measures are devised and utilized by teachers. Pupils are required to enter and leave the classroom in straight, double lines. If children wish to speak or use the toilets they must raise their hands and wait for recognition by the teacher. Spontaneous or otherwise unauthorized conversation among pupils is not usually permitted. Lengthy and involved reminders and discussions of the kind of behavior appropriate to the decorum of the classroom occur with considerable regularity. If there are no major disturbances in class, little noise or talking, and if children sit in an orderly and attentive posture, answer questions promptly, and if they express the respect and deference due to their teachers as people in authority, then there exists good, strong discipline in the frame of reference of the elementary school teacher. Inattention, talking, fighting, playing or any other indication of disorganization in the classroom or deviation from the prescribed norms shows poor control and weak discipline, a situation that could easily cast reflection upon the professional competency of the teacher.

When the continuance of the order and equilibrium of classroom is endangered through talking, playing, fighting, and the use of Spanish, or any other deviation from the expected patterns of behavior implicit in the established normative order, retribution is almost automatic and immediate. There are stern and frigid glances directed without delay at the offender. Sharp reprimands and long scoldings consitute a major portion of the sanctions applied, and children are frequently commanded to apologize for their offenses.

Sanctions may also include the isolation of the offending pupil. He may be sent to the classroom of a teacher of a lower grade, or he may be sent to stand in a corner of the classroom or outside the door of the room. There may be long classroom discussions on the ethics appropriate to the particular situation and grade level. Threats are made to notify the principal or to hold a conference with the parents of the offender. Elementary teachers frequently shorten or cancel recess periods or classroom parties when the normative order of the classroom is seriously violated. In some instances, teachers shake children, pull their hair, or humiliate them verbally in the presence of the entire class.

All the systems of control portrayed here involve domination of the children by the teacher. Children must learn to respect authority. They must be obedient and carry out orders. Disobedience, disorder, disruption of any kind must be punished with a degree of severity appropriate to the offense. In the culture of the classroom, consistent strictness and severity are essential, for if you give the children "an inch, they'll take a yard." In light of the systems of control used in most elementary school classrooms, the elementary school appears to be a highly authoritarian organization where things must be made tough, where the power and authority inherent in life must be forcefully demonstrated, and where to "spare the rod, is to spoil the child." In the elementary classroom, the social order is established and maintained through coercion and force, and through general domination by the teacher and submission by the children.

Teachers of Puerto Rican children operate within the framework of controls portrayed above. They state that rigid and inflexible regulations must be applied and enforced at all times if Puerto Rican children are to be controlled, and if the business of teaching and learning are to proceed properly and without undue interruption. The resulting classroom atmosphere is essentially punitive and repressive in nature.

Miss Dwight's sanctions and controls were similar to those characteristic of most elementary classrooms, although she was not observed applying corporal punishment as a sanction. When Jesús and Dolores arrived late as was their practice, Miss Dwight scolded:

If it's not your alarm clock, it's having to go to the store, or helping dress your brother or some other excuse. You will have to learn to come to school on time. You, too, Jesús. You have been coming to school long enough to realize that one of the important rules is to be early in the morning. And another thing, you are to bring a note each time you are late or absent. I expect a note from each of you tomorrow morning. And I'm tired of changing my attendance report every time you both come in late.

During the mathematics lesson when some of the children became restless and inattentive, Miss Dwight glanced at the class and fixed her gaze upon those children who were the most obvious offenders. At about the same time, Manuel volunteered, in Spanish, the definition of the word swimming for Juan who did not understand the word in English. Miss Dwight reprimanded, "No talking, Manuel!" A few moments later, when Manuel requested permission to go to the boys' toilet, Miss Dwight said, "No, Manuel, you will have to wait until I take the entire class at ten o'clock." This refusal of a request is another type of control used by Miss Dwight, who seems to be saying, in effect, that if you want certain privileges, you must live up to the rules of the game.

Miss Dwight used many additional reprimands. She said to inattentive Juan, "Juan, please try to pay attention." When several children went to the pencil sharpener and waste paper basket during the mathematics lesson, and some general noise broke out, Miss Dwight ordered, "Get back to your desks. This moving about has to stop." At recess, she commanded the class to "calm down." During the social studies lesson, when a short procession found its way once more to the pencil sharpener and waste paper basket as had happened during the mathematics lesson, Miss Dwight demanded, "Boys and girls, sit down and keep still." At the same time she ordered, "Children, please sit up tall. Your feet belong on the floor and not on the rungs of your desk. And everyone should be listening." When children spoke in Spanish, she reminded them, "English, children." "You know I don't understand Spanish." She

told Tomás, who was resting his elbows on his desk and holding
his head with his hand, "Please stop holding your head up and get
your elbows off the desk. What time did you get to bed last night?"

Particularly sharp rebukes were directed at Antonio. When
Miss Dwight caught him attempting to scratch a groove in his desk,
she stated forcefully:

> Antonio, that is not your property that you are ruining.
> Many children will use that desk after you. I think you
> should leave it as you found it. Now put the pencil
> down and stop this nonsense. Do you hear?

Antonio's rejoinder was to utter a most insulting Spanish
obscenity. Miss Dwight did not know the meaning of this Spanish
obscenity and ordered, "Antonio what did you say? In English!"
She continued:

> Antonio, stand up and tell me in English what you said!
> ...I'm waiting for your answer, Antonio. What does
> that mean?

After having been informed that it could not be translated because "eet is a bad teeng he say," and having received subsequently an apology from Antonio, Miss Dwight's scolding continued:

> All right, Antonio... And I hope you will control your
> feelings better in the future. People just don't burst out
> and call each other names whenever they feel like it.
> You must learn how to cooperate more with others. We
> have to live with many people in this world, and it's time
> you've learned that everything does not always go the way
> you want it to. Now sit down and behave yourself.

In addition to reprimands, scoldings, refusals of requests,
and threats to inform parents, Miss Dwight also held group discussions about problem situations, such as the noise in the children's
lunchroom.

> Children, the principal made a definite point of telling
> the teachers that the behavior and noise in the lunch-
> room is terrible. I hope I can be proud of you and
> that you will behave as you should, get your food
> quietly, eat quickly, and clean your places before you
> leave.

A further technique of control was the threat to cancel recess, and later in the day, the threat to cancel the Christmas party.

> Sit down, children. We will have to stay here if you
> do not line up quietly.

> Children, if you continue to call out like this, we will
> have no party.

Miss Dwight also used the imposition of additional school
work as a sanction. During the reading lesson, Miss Dwight
threatened, "Bluebirds, if you continue to talk, I will have you
write the meanings of those words and write them in sentences."

In Miss Dwight's classroom and others like it, the extremely me-
ticulous attention given to sanctions, techniques of control, and other
disciplinary measures, has, of course, its obvious pragmatic utility.
Classrooms are expected to be quiet and orderly. Children are expected
to accept and internalize the norms set before them, and the elaborate
disciplinary ceremonial encourages them to do so, and penalizes them
if they do not. But the sometimes complicated disciplinary reminders
and rituals involving the expression of norms and the application of
sanctions have other functions as well.

Most Puerto Rican children are not able to follow directions and
classroom instruction quickly and accurately because of their lack of
sufficient fluency in English. In addition, according to the elementary
teacher, Puerto Rican pupils are limited in their intellectual abilities;
their I.Q.'s are low, and they are, consequently, extremely slow in
school work. Little seems to be accomplished in the classroom for one
reason or another, and this fact is acknowledged by teachers of Puerto
Rican children. Mrs. Maran, a colleague of Miss Dwight, stated that
"Puerto Rican pupils seem to learn nothing--either here or at home."
Miss Dwight agreed.

The elaborate disciplinary ceremonial, however, consumes much
time; in a sense, it helps to pass time, and as such conveys the impression to all concerned that at least something is learned. While academi-
cally little is achieved, in terms of improved behavior much seems to
be accomplished. This was acknowledged in a conversation between
Mrs. Maran and Miss Dwight. When a brief discussion of the lack of
academic progress had been brought to a conclusion, Mrs. Maran stated,
"But you know...the ones in my third grade class are very well behaved.
Authority means something to them."

In the teacher's definition of the school and her own role in it,
there is, or there ought to be, much teaching and learning; but in teaching Puerto Rican pupils, however, teachers observe that little learning
occurs for a variety of reasons. Miss Dwight observed that Puerto Rican children do not learn because "all they care about is sleeping, eating, playing, and having parties." During lunch in the teachers' room,
other teachers suggested possible reasons for the lack of academic progress. Edith, for example, referred to their "lousy way of living" and
the use of Spanish. Another teacher expressed her conviction that Puerto Ricans will not "get anywhere," because "they don't know anything,
go anywhere, or read anything."

The teacher's definition of the reality of the school situation and
her own self-esteem are thereby challenged. She is supposed to teach
her pupils; she at least attempts to teach them. She prepares her lessons, refers to her lesson plans, provides the necessary books and instructional materials, and becomes fatigued at the end of the day. Yet
the children seem to have learned little as the result of her endeavors.
She is seemingly a failure in her job.

In this situation, the elaborate disciplinary rituals function to resolve satisfactorily this challenge to the self-esteem and professional
reputation of the teacher by making it appear that something is, after
all, occurring, if only the frequent acting out of the various rituals that
help to convey an impression of successful teaching and learning.

Use of Spanish in the Classroom

When Antonio was reprimanded by Miss Dwight because he had scratched a groove into his desk, he shouted out an obscenity. This use of obscenities in Spanish occurs in many instances, especially in the upper grades. It represents the defiance of a child who can no longer accept what he views as intolerable... * * *

The use of Spanish, however, is not restricted to the utterance of obscenities. Puerto Rican pupils also speak Spanish when they are embarrassed, nervous, or angry, or when they are reprimanded. When Dolores arrived late and Miss Dwight asked for an explanation or a note from her parents, she replied in Spanish, "Maestra, al reloj despertador se rompió y..." ("Teacher, the alarm clock broke and...") When Manuel was refused permission to go to the boys' room and was told by Miss Dwight that he would have to wait until ten o'clock when the entire class would have recess, he said, "Pero tengo que ir al baño ahora." ("But I have to go to the toilet now.") In discussing one and two family houses and their private bathrooms, Dolores explained rapidly and excitedly that when she tries to take a bath her mother tells her "not to make the people wait." Dolores then added quickly, "Dice que no tengo derecho a hacer que espere tanto a la gente." ("She says that I have no right to make the people wait so much.")

Spanish is also used when the required English words or phrases or answers to questions are unknown. During the mathematics lesson, Juan did not know the meaning of "swimming." He asked, "Que quiere decir?" ("What does it mean?") Manual assisted him by calling out, "Nadando." ("Swimming.") When Juan did not understand the problem "six minus two," a neighbor suggested "seis menos dos." ("Six minus two.") In a health discussion Maria said that the salad at lunch consisted only of "lechuga." ("Lettuce.")

The primary function of language is communication, and in this sense, the use of Spanish by Puerto Rican pupils represents an attempt to communicate effectively when the alternative vehicle of communication is foreign, inadequately understood, and poorly spoken. The use of Spanish, however, in addition to serving as a means of communication and relatively safe way of expressing defiance and hostility, especially through the use of obscenities that are not understood, functions to assist Puerto Rican pupils in maintaining contact with the familiar in an unfamiliar, frequently hostile, environment.

Spanish is, for these Puerto Rican children, a symbol of their solidarity. As a means of communicating, the use of Spanish assists Puerto Rican children in sharing their experiences and thoughts with one another. But as a symbol of solidarity, the language helps to define the social situation in the classroom. It establishes a degree of rapport among the Puerto Rican children present physically in the classroom. Its use symbolizes the cultural understanding and unity of Puerto Rican pupils, especially when confronted by an outsider, one who is not a member of the group, and one who represents the imposed authority and control of a superordinate group. What is said in Spanish is not really important; the importance of its use lies in the fact that it is spoken in a hostile and unknown environment, and one's enemies cannot understand it.

In the classroom, the children speak Spanish while the teacher does not. They can use the language when they do not wish to have the

teacher understand what they are saying. They are able to communicate
with one another in a language known only among themselves. This use
of another language distinguishes very sharply between the children who
speak it and the teacher who does not. In this manner, language, as an
important symbol of cultural differences, emphasizes the solidarity of
the Puerto Rican pupils in the classroom.

When Antonio shouted out in defiance of Miss Dwight, Juan,
in spite of the teacher's request, refused to translate the obscenity because "it was too bad to say." He was, of course, refusing to inform or "tattle." But this refusal to translate represented
another significant factor: Juan was, in a sense, acknowledging his
membership in a particular social group. He could not explain that
the teacher and her mother, members of an out-group, were verbally attacked in a manner the full significance of which is known
only to Puerto Ricans, in a manner representing intense hatred,
utter scorn, and challenge. Even more significant, however, is
the fact that the refusal to translate also symbolized the determina-
tion not to weaken the solidarity of the group by sharing its accumulated cultural understandings with outsiders. If Juan had explained
the obscenity, assuming that he was capable of doing so, he would
have permitted an outsider, an enemy, to share the secrets of his
group, thereby weakening its solidarity and unity.

Puerto Ricans, Lessons, and Life Adjustment

The daily lessons in the elementary schools conform in both
content and time allotments to the prescriptions of the authorized
curriculum. Frequently, however, lessons are begun, but never
completed; they are terminated abruptly when the scheduled time has
run out. Thus Miss Dwight brought her arithmetic lesson to a sudden end when time was up.

Children, these problems go on to the next page. When
you have free time today, you are to do these two pages.
Otherwise, they are part of your homework. Make an
example of each one. And now, put all your arithmetic
materials away. It's ten o'clock and we must go to the
lavatories and then to the basement for physical education.

The reading lesson was concluded in the same manner, even
though all of the children had not had the opportunity to read.
Thunderbirds, we have no time for reading today. I
will start with your group in the morning.

Questions and answers, and some discussion, composed Miss
Dwight's teaching methods as they do for many elementary school
teachers. A child is asked to read a passage in a book, and then
he is asked one or more questions based upon his assigned reading.
There is little or no explanation. Occasionally, concrete materials
are used to clarify problems, such as in the arithmetic lesson
which utilized squared materials, a mathematics device designed to
help the child count, add, and subtract by actually performing these
computations with small squares of paper.

Teachers encourage Puerto Rican pupils to participate in these and other lessons, but when they wish to have the correct answer given immediately, perhaps to save time, perhaps because of impatience, they call upon non-Puerto Rican children.

There emerges from the subject matter and teaching methods a pattern of teaching based upon a concept of education as life adjustment, implying resignation to the prevailing conditions and pressures; also implied is a lack of self-reliant aggressiveness in meeting challenges.

Children of elementary school age are generally very unself-conscious. They express quite candidly much dissatisfaction with their living conditions. Teachers, as Miss Dwight did, emphasize that "we must accept what we have now and try to appreciate the good things we have." Children are questioned as to what is "good in your way of living." In the culture of the classroom, there is something good in every child's life, something for which each child can be grateful. When Puerto Rican children are taught to appreciate and be thankful for what they have, they are taught to accept and adjust to the situation in which they find themselves. Even though the teacher states that she is in school "to help the children live better," there is much, nevertheless, for which to be thankful.

In the elementary school, a program of education based upon the conceptual framework of life adjustment and resignation to prevailing conditions does not emphasize the acquisition of the various academic skills essential to continued education. In addition, the subject matter and teaching methods are unrealistic; they do not motivate Puerto Rican children because of their irrelevance to the present status and general life experience of these pupils. Widespread discouragement and frustration occur, but are alleviated by the advice to accept and be thankful for what one has.

Observations indicate that many teachers, Miss Dwight included, have accepted life adjustment teaching. With the general acceptance of life adjustment teaching and the concomitant attitudes of acceptance and gratitude, education for failure, or alternatively expressed, education in attitudes of acceptance of failure, is the result. The teacher, in light of the general academic failure of Puerto Rican pupils, in reality attempts to appease and condition them to the point of resignation to their life situation. The teacher's objective then becomes that of sending her pupils into the world, resigned and adjusted, but also with the belief that if they but work hard enough, they will be able to improve their life chances.

What Do Puerto Rican Children Learn?

Academic learning among Puerto Rican children is limited, but these pupils do learn, in spite of the social, cultural, and other factors preventing successful academic progress, much that is not explicitly suggested in the curriculum or acknowledged by teachers. Much of the teaching during a typical day contains frequent allusions to the language of Puerto Ricans, to their food preferences, and to other characteristic social and cultural patterns. They speak Spanish. Their preferred foods are considered unhealthful. Their hous-

ing accommodations are drastically unlike the more desirable arrangements of middle class North Americans. These factors are
frequently contrasted unfavorably with the social and cultural patterns
of the North American middle classes. In this manner, Puerto Rican children develop a strong consciousness of themselves as Puerto Ricans and as members of a particular social group; thus,
Puerto Rican children very quickly learn that they constitute a group
apart from and different from North Americans.

As an essential component of this developing group consciousness, Puerto Rican pupils learn who their antagonists are: the
teacher who constantly scolds and reprimands and the principal who
supports the teacher in her attitudes, both of whom represent the
dominant middle class groups. Furthermore, these other groups
possess the highly desired symbols of the preferred and superordinate status. They have better schools, better housing, better jobs,
and more money. They are the teachers and principals; and they
control the schools in which Puerto Rican pupils are in attendance.

The Puerto Rican child must attend school because of compulsory school attendance laws. But to continue to attend school
when his ego is threatened and weakened by constant and often derogatory reference to his culture requires an adjustment by the
Puerto Rican child that will enable him to survive the elementary
school experience.

This adjustment, with a few notable exceptions, consists of
a passive submission to and acquiescence in the school's demands.
Puerto Rican pupils generally sit quietly in class. Teachers frequently complain that they are always "daydreaming." Puerto Rican children usually carry out whatever requests the teacher makes.
They develop the technique of extreme, exaggerated courtesy as
part of their social equipment for survival. The excessive courtesy
helps the child to avoid further attacks upon his social and cultural
status by his teacher, for teachers are less likely to reprimand or
attack those who are polite and who accord them the proper deference.

Another technique of survival is the development and strengthening of group solidarity. Puerto Rican children do not inform upon their classmates. They do not reveal the names of children who
may have caused some disturbance on the school playground, or in
the classroom or lunchroom. If an obscenity is heard in the classroom, the translation, if requested, is not given. Puerto Rican
children develop, in this manner, patterns of mutual aid and support
when confronted by individuals of higher social status and differing
cultural background.

Conclusion

The culture of the classroom represents a design for living,
and it includes all the behavior patterns and thought ways of teachers
and pupils. In Miss Dwight's classroom, pupils were guided to certain methods and techniques of accomplishing objectives. Children
were also subject to certain rules, to certain do's and don'ts for
living in the classroom. That is, the classroom culture provided
for a complex of evaluations as to what is permitted or prohibited,

appropriate or inappropriate, or good or bad in the elementary
school scheme of living. This complex of evaluations, however, included consideration of ultimate values as well as immediate values,
especially as manifested in various religious and patriotic rituals
and ceremonies.

The elementary school can be considered the institution
where the child learns to read and write and acquire other skills
fundamental to literacy and continued education. Nevertheless, in
a much broader sense, elementary education can be interpreted as
socialization. Thus Miss Dwight's role can be viewed as including
the guiding or directing the socialization process for her Puerto Rican pupils so that they might become accepted adults in middle
class North American society. Miss Dwight provided her pupils
with a set of definitions of various social and cultural situations,
and these definitions included values and norms representing the
general society and culture as well as those unique to the school
and classroom. Miss Dwight's classroom, however, became the
scene of a conflict in values, a conflict between the values of middle
class North Americans and lower class Puerto Ricans. As a manifestation of this conflict, children became inattentive, uninterested,
restless, talkative, and sometimes disorderly, and scoldings, repetitions, reprimands, reminders, moral rejoinders, and threats were
commonplace and time consuming. In effect, much time, attention,
and energy were given by Miss Dwight to the presentation, explanation, and enforcement of certain values and norms. Conversely,
less time and attention were directed to the acquisition of academic
skills and knowledge, also a phase of the socialization process.
This differential time allotment is a factor affecting the academic
achievement of Puerto Rican pupils.

Notes

1. The data presented in this chapter, including incidents within the
   classroom, teacher attitudes, etc., were derived from an
   extensive series of observations made in various classrooms.
   Observations revealed the occurrence of similar events and
   incidents in each of the classes observed. Since curriculum
   content, teaching methods, and reactions to these were essentially similar in each of the classes, one such classroom
   was then selected for detailed discussion. Miss Dwight, her
   pupils, and the other teachers to whom reference was made
   are real persons; the names of both teachers and pupils were
   changed to conceal their identities. Several details concerning other incidents occurring within the classroom on the
   same day were eliminated in order to prevent a repetitive
   discussion; the details eliminated include classroom routines
   such as distribution and collection of materials, collection
   and correction of homework, several interruptions by children with messages from other teachers, much informal conversation among children during the transition from one subject to another and when lining up, and a fire drill.

2. The Regents' Prayer: "Almighty God, we acknowledge our de-

pendence upon Thee.   We beg Thy blessings upon us, our
parents, our teachers, and our country." On June 25, 1962
the recitation of this prayer in the public schools was de-
clared unconstitutional by the United States Supreme Court.

3. William Lloyd Warner, et al., Who Shall Be Educated? New
York: Harper and Brothers 1944, Chapter VIII. See also,
Robin J. Williams, Jr., American Society, New York:
Alfred A. Knopf, 1951, p. 286 and
Robert Riehey and William Fox, An Analysis of Various Fac-
tors Associated with the Selection of Teaching as a Vocation,
Bulletin of the School of Education, Division of Research and
Field Services, Indiana University, May, 1948.

A. Anastasi and C. De Jesús, "Language Development and Non-Verbal I.Q. of Puerto Rican Preschool Children in New York City." Journal of Abnormal Psychology 48:357-366, July 1953. Copyright 1953 by the American Psychological Association. Reprinted by permission.

Psychological studies of Puerto Ricans have been relatively few, probably because of the bilingualism which complicates the testing of such a group both in Puerto Rico and elsewhere. Three studies on Puerto Rican children in New York City (1, 3, 7) suggest that on language tests, whether administered in English or in Spanish, the Puerto Ricans are markedly deficient.[1] Such a deficiency extends to any test involving language, even when the items are themselves nonverbal but require fairly extensive oral instructions (1). The inferiority appears to be less pronounced, however, on nonlanguage and performance tests. In fact, one study on first-grade children found the Puerto Rican children to equal the American norms on three such tests (7). In an investigation conducted in Puerto Rico with the Pintner Nonlanguage Mental Ability Test, the Puerto Rican children excelled the American norms in grades three to five, but fell below these norms in grades six to eight (14).

Tests administered to various ethnic groups in Hawaii (15, 17) showed the Puerto Rican children to rank lower than any of the other groups in both language and nonlanguage tests. One of the investigators calls attention to the disproportionately large number of zero scores obtained by the Puerto Rican children, which suggests "that the majority of the group were artificially blocked at the beginning of the tests through failure to understand what was required" (17, p. 66). Reference is also made to the "good natured apathy that this group displayed toward following directions" (17, p. 66), an attitude which was likewise observed in the case of New York City Puerto Rican school children (1).

When considered in the light of certain educational and other cultural factors in the environment of the Puerto Rican, the psychological test results obtained with Puerto Rican children suggest certain hypotheses regarding their intellectual development. The first of these hypotheses pertains to the bilingualism of the Puerto Rican. The native language of the Puerto Rican is Spanish. English, however, is taught in the Puerto Rican schools, either as a separate language or as the language of instruction, the policy in this regard varying from time to time and from one academic level to another. For many Puerto Ricans, such a combination of languages has served only to make them "illiterate in two languages" and to create educational difficulties and confusion (13, p. 12).

The New York City Puerto Rican who may have some Negroid features, moreover, finds that by remaining Spanish-speaking

312

he enjoys higher social status than is accorded to the English-speaking American Negro (13, p. 87). This factor, together with the strong feelings of group identification which characterize Puerto Rican communities, encourages the Puerto Rican migrant to retain Spanish as his principal language. Upon school entrance, therefore, most New York City Puerto Rican children know little English, and they continue to speak Spanish with their classmates and with most children and adults outside of school. Since school instruction is conducted entirely in English, these children tend to learn one language in one set of situations, represented by the school, and another language in another set, represented by the home and community. Such "linguistic bifurcation" provides an inadequate mastery of either language and may account for the inferior language test performance of Puerto Rican children in both English and Spanish.

The second hypothesis, which concerns the Puerto Rican child's attitude toward school, is in fact related to the first. Upon entering school, the Puerto Rican child who lives in New York City or in Hawaii is suddenly thrust into an exclusively English-speaking environment at a time when he knows almost no English. This initial school experience seems to produce a sort of "psychological insulation" to whatever goes on in school. Passive and unresponsive habits gradually become the child's characteristic reaction to school (cf. 1). Performance on psychological tests, especially tests of a relatively abstract nature, is seriously handicapped by this passivity and lack of motivation for academic tasks. It should also be noted, of course, that the child's scholastic progress and his general intellectual development are likewise impeded by the attitudes and work habits resulting from his early linguistic confusion. Perhaps a similar though less pronounced effect is produced in the Puerto Rican schools by the introduction of a second language at an inappropriate time or in a confusing manner. In all such situations, the child's poor emotional adjustment to the school could account for his increasing deficiency in test performance from the lower to the upper grades, a deficiency which becomes apparent only after prolonged exposure to the school environment.

A consideration of the two hypotheses outlined above suggests that it would be of special interest to investigate the performance of Puerto Rican preschool children with both linguistic and nonlinguistic measures. At such ages, the Puerto Rican child is predominantly Spanish-speaking and has not yet been exposed to the sharp linguistic bifurcation of the school child. Similarly, he has not had the opportunity to develop negativistic or passive attitudes toward tasks associated with the school environment. Accordingly, the present study is concerned with the language development of a group of New York City Puerto Rican preschool children, as well as with their performance on a nonlanguage test, the Goodenough Draw-a-Man Scale. The scores of the Puerto Rican children will be compared with published norms on American children, as well as with the scores of samples of Negro and white preschool children tested in New York City in a study by Anastasi and D'Angelo (2). For this reason, the procedure of the present study has followed closely that of the earlier investigation.

Table 1
Description of the Sample*

Item	Boys	Girls
Child's birthplace		
New York City	15	15
Puerto Rico	5	9
Father's birthplace		
New York City	1	1
Puerto Rico	19	21
Cuba	0	1
Mother's birthplace		
New York City	0	0
Puerto Rico	20	24
Number of Siblings		
None	4	6
One	5	7
Two	4	8
Three or more	7	3
Median Number of Siblings	2	1
Father's occupation+		
1. Unskilled	1	4
2. Slightly skilled	8	7
3. Semiskilled; minor clerical	7	4
4. Clerical; skilled trades	1	3
5. Semiprofessional; managerial	0	0
6. Professional	0	0
Unknown or Unemployed	3	6
Median Occupational Level	2.44	2.21
Number of Employed Mothers	8	13
Mother's Occupation+		
1. Unskilled	6	8
2. Slightly skilled	1	2
3. Semiskilled; minor clerical	1	2
4. Clerical; skilled trades	0	0
5. Semiprofessional; managerial	0	1
6. Professional	0	0
Median Occupational Level	1.17	1.31
Median Educational Level: Father	7.70	6.83
Median Educational Level: Mother	7.75	6.75
Place of Father's Education		
New York City	1	2
Puerto Rico	19	21
(none)	0	1
Place of Mother's Education		
New York City	2	3
Puerto Rico	18	21

* Data based on 44 completed questionnaires (20 boys and 24 girls).

+ Classified in terms of the occupational scale given by Goodenough and Anderson (9).

Method

The subjects (Ss) of the present study included 25 boys and 25 girls attending day-care centers[2] in Manhattan's Spanish Harlem, where approximately 70 per cent of New York City's Puerto Rican migrants are to be found (cf. 13). The children were all within six months of their fifth birthdays, the mean ages of the boys and girls being 59.64 and 60.16 months, respectively.

In order to obtain additional background information, a questionnaire was administered in Spanish to the parents, either orally or through the mail.[3] Completed questionnaires were obtained for 88 per cent of the Ss, the missing cases including 5 boys and one girl. Since home environment is such an important factor in the language development of preschool children, the questionnaire replies have been summarized in Table 1. It will be noted that the large majority of the 44 children on whom questionnaire data are available were born in New York City, the rest in Puerto Rico. All mothers and all but three fathers were born in Puerto Rico. The number of siblings varies from none to seven, the median number being two for boys and one for girls. As in other surveys on Puerto Ricans of New York City, occupational level is very low, both the median and mode of the fathers' occupations falling in the slightly skilled category. Slightly less than half of the mothers were employed outside the home, their occupational level being on the whole even lower than that of the fathers. The median grade reached in school is between the seventh and eighth for both parents, the large majority having received their education in Puerto Rico.

One of the questionnaire items was concerned with the proportion of Spanish and English spoken at home. The replies, tabulated in Table 2, indicate that in the large majority of families, more Spanish than English was spoken, and in 8 only Spanish was spoken. Only one respondent checked more English than Spanish, while none reported exclusively English. It might also be noted that all day-care center personnel were English-speaking, as were several of the children attending the centers. The Puerto Rican children, however, tended almost always to cluster together and to converse in Spanish. At the time of testing, the children had attended the nurseries for approximately one year or less.

Table 2
Languages Spoken at Home

Sex	Always Spanish	More Spanish than English	Half & Half	More English than Spanish	Always English
Boys	4	12	4	0	0
Girls	4	12	7	1	0
Total	8	24	11	1	0

Procedure   4
        All testing was conducted by a Puerto Rican examiner,
each child being tested individually in a quiet room with no other
person present. The examiner spoke Spanish exclusively to the
child, although the child's speech was recorded in whichever language was employed by the child. The procedure followed in obtaining the language sample was essentially that developed by Mc-
Carthy (11) and employed by several other investigators (4, 5, 11).
A collection of 22 small, attractive toys was presented in a suit-
case, from which the child was permitted to remove all that ap-
pealed to him. These were the same toys employed in the study by
Anastasi and D'Angelo (2).[5] The S was simply told that the toys
were for him to play with. As in the earlier study (2), two picture
books were also available, but were used only when a child was
very shy or when he looked at the toys briefly and seemed to need
something else to hold his attention. The examiner often engaged
the child in conversation to get him started, but simple answers to
questions were not included in the language sample.

        Sixty consecutive responses or "sentences" were recorded
for each child, all scoring being based on the last fifty. The rules
followed in determining sentence division were those described by
Davis (4). The language responses were analyzed with respect to
proportion of English and Spanish words and sentences, mean sentence structure. Mean sentence length for each S was the mean
number of words in his last fifty recorded responses. In making
the word count, the rules outlined by McCarthy (11) were applied
with reference to contractions, hyphenated and compound nouns,
and other special problems, although only a few of these problems
arose in scoring the Spanish language material (cf. 6). The analysis of sentence structure was based upon the procedures of Mc-
Carthy (11) and Davis (4), with slight modifications suggested by the
findings of the same authors. For every S, each of the fifty
scored responses was classified into one of the six sentence types
described below, and the percentage of each type of sentence was
determined for S.

        1. Simple sentences without a phrase.

        2. Simple sentences containing a phrase or a compound sub-
ject, object, or predicate.

        3. Compound and complex sentences.

        4. Elaborated sentences, which include: (a) simple sentences
with two or more phrases, or with compound subject or predicate
and a phrase, (b) complex sentences with more than one subordinate
clause, or with a phrase or phrases, and (c) compound sentences
with more than two dependent clauses, or with a subordinate clause
or phrase.

        5. Functionally complete though structurally incomplete re-
sponses. In this category are included naming, expletives, answers
in which the missing parts are implied because they were included
in a previous remark, etc.

        6. Incomplete responses. These are characterized by omis-
sion of any necessary part, such as subject, verb, preposition, etc.

        The examiner's classification of each sentence in the pres-
ent study was independently checked by a Spanish-speaking graduate
student in the Department of English.

        Immediately after the language sample had been obtained
from each child, the Goodenough Draw-a-Man Test (8) was administered. The standard oral instructions for this test were given in
Spanish. The test was scored on the basis of the 51 points described by Goodenough, and the MA and IQ were computed by the
use of Goodenough's age norms. In order to check on the possible
operations of any response set or constant error on the part of the
scorer, a random sample of 10 drawings from the present study
was scored by D'Angelo (cf. 2) and 10 drawings from the Anastasi
and D'Angelo study were scored by the present examiner. Each
scorer proceeded without knowledge of the scores obtained by the
other. The results showed very close scorer agreement, only
three of the 20 drawings yielding a scorer discrepancy of one point
and the direction of these differences being inconsistent with reference to the two scorers.

Results

        Throughout the analysis of results, comparisons will be made
between the present group and the Negro and white preschool children tested in day-care centers of the Department of Welfare in
New York City by Anastasi and D'Angelo (2). It will be recalled
that special efforts were made to keep the procedure identical in
the two studies. With reference to background characteristics, it
should be noted that the Puerto Rican sample differs from both the
Negro and white samples primarily in the educational and occupational level of parents. The median educational level of both Puerto Rican fathers and mothers is approximately four years lower
than that of the Negro and white parents. Similarly, the median
occupational level of both Negro and white fathers falls within the
semiskilled and minor clerical classes, while that of the Puerto Rican fathers falls into the slightly skilled category. The group discrepancy is even greater when occupational level of the mothers is
compared. At the same time, the proportion of employed mothers
is much less in the present group, being 48 per cent among the
Puerto Ricans in contrast to 78 and 89 per cent for the Negro and
white samples, respectively.

Goodenough Draw-a-Man Test

        In Table 3 will be found the mean Draw-a-Man IQ's of boys
and girls in the Puerto Rican, Negro, and white samples, each mean
being based on 25 cases.[6] In order to determine the significance
of differences among these means, an analysis of variance was conducted. When tested for homogeneity of variance by the L_1 test
(cf. 10), the six subgroups yielded $L_1 = .8995$. With k= 6 and f=24,
p falls between .05 and .01. Since the decision regarding the hypothesis of homogeneity of variance thus appears to be doubtful, the
possibility of unequal variances will be considered in the analysis
of these data.

Table 3
Mean IQ on Goodenough Draw-a-Man Test
(Data on Negro and white samples from [2]).

Ethnic Group	Boys	Girls	Total
Puerto Rican	88.88	102.52	95.70
Negro	96.88	103.28	100.08
White	99.00	105.64	102.32
Total	94.92	103.81	99.37

The results of the analysis of variance are given in Table 4, all F ratios having been computed with the within-group variance as the error term. As in the earlier study (2), neither ethnic group nor the interaction of ethnic group and sex yielded significant F ratios. The F ratio for sex, however, is significant at the .01 level, the girls excelling the boys in all three ethnic groups. This finding is in line with the results of other studies employing the Goodenough Draw-a-Man Test, and is probably attributable to the standardization procedure (cf. 8, pp. 56-57). Because of the doubt regarding homogeneity of variance, the sex difference within the Puerto Rican sample was separately checked by a t ratio based on 48 degrees of freedom and separately computed variances for Puerto Rican boys and girls. These variances did not differ significantly from each other (cf. 18). Under these conditions, the t ratio of the Puerto Rican sex difference in mean IQ is significant at the .02 level, thus substantiating the general conclusion regarding sex differences on this test.

Table 4
Analysis of Variance: Goodenough Draw-a-Man IQ

Source	Sum of Squares	df	Variance Estimate	F
Ethnic	1133.77	2	566.89	2.01
Sex	2965.92	1	2965.92	10.49*
Ethnic x Sex	422.82	2	211.41	0.75
Within-group	40710.32	144	282.71	
Total	45232.83	149		

*$p < .01$

It is noteworthy that the Draw-a-Man IQ's of both Puerto Rican boys and Puerto Rican girls are more variable than those of Negroes or whites of either sex. The IQ's of the Puerto Rican boys range from 58 to 124, with an SD of 18.76; those of the Puerto Rican girls range from 58 to 158, with an SD of 23.62. When the separate variances are tested by F ratios, the Puerto Rican girls are significantly more variable than the Negro girls at the .01 level and more variable than the white girls at the .05 level, while

the Puerto Rican boys are more variable than the Negro boys at
the .05 level. The difference between the variances of Puerto Rican and white boys, though failing to reach significance at the .05
level, is in the same direction.

It is possible, of course, that the Puerto Rican population
under investigation is more heterogeneous than the Negro or white
population in the abilities measured by the Draw-a-Man Test. Another factor to consider, however, is the resistance to this test encountered among the Puerto Rican children. Although excellent
rapport was observed during the language recording, when the child
was free to play with the toys and say what he pleased, many of
the children appeared to be disturbed by the specific task of drawing a man. Three Ss for whom language records were easily obtained had to be eliminated from the study because of failure to
draw a man. Six others had to be given a second trial because
they drew some other object. Verbal refusals, crying, and other
signs of emotional disturbance were likewise observed. No such
general resistance was encountered among the Negro or white children (2). Whatever the reasons for the negativism on the part of
the Puerto Rican children, this condition may have served as an
additional error factor to increase the variability of their test performance.

Proportion of English and Spanish in Language Sample

The percentages of English and Spanish words and of English, Spanish, and mixed sentences in the language responses of the
Puerto Rican boys and girls are reported in Table 5. It is clearly

Table 5

Percentage of English and Spanish Words and of English, Spanish,
and Mixed Sentences Spoken by Puerto Rican Boys and Girls

Sex	Words		Sentences		
	English	Spanish	English	Mixed	Spanish
Boys	3.66	96.34	1.76	6.72	91.52
Girls	1.24	98.76	0.16	5.76	94.08
Total	2.45	97.55	0.96	6.24	92.80

apparent that the language samples were almost wholly Spanish,
only about 2 per cent of the individual words and about 1 per cent
of the sentences being English. The occurrence of slightly over 6
per cent of mixed sentences reflects the beginning of a trend which
becomes more marked in older Puerto Ricans and which also characterizes most immigrant groups in America. Certain words are
adopted from the American culture and incorporated into the migrant's foreign speech in everyday conversation. Such words as
"teacher," "cowboy," and "baby" were among those occurring most
frequently in otherwise Spanish sentences spoken by the children. It
is interesting to note that the boys tended to use more English

words and sentences than did the girls. Such a sex difference suggests a greater tendency for acculturation on the part of the boys,
even at the preschool age. Similar evidence for such a sex difference has been found among older Puerto Rican children in New York
City (1).

Mean Sentence Length

The data on mean sentence length are given in Tables 6 and
7. The variances of the six subgroups can be regarded as homogeneous, since $L_1 = .9520$; with $k = 6$ and $f = 24$, $p > .05$. The results of the analysis of variance are summarized in Table 7. It
will be noted that the F ratio for ethnic groups is significant at the
.001 level. The F ratio for overall sex difference is obviously
negligible, while the Ethnic x Sex interaction yields an F ratio
slightly lower than would be required at the .05 level. With reference to the ethnic group differences, the Puerto Rican mean is significantly higher than both the Negro and white means, the t ratios
of the two differences being 5.38 and 3.79, respectively (df = 144).

Table 6
Mean Sentence Length
(Data on Negro and white samples from [2].)

Ethnic Group	Boys	Girls	Total
Puerto Rican	5.42	5.23	5.33
Negro	4.56	4.13	4.35
White	4.46	4.83	4.64
Total	4.81	4.73	4.77

Table 7
Analysis of Variance: Mean Sentence Length

Source	Sum of Squares	df	Variance Estimate	F
Ethnic	25.42	2	12.71	15.31*
Sex	0.28	1	0.28	0.34
Ethnic x Sex	4.23	2	2.12	2.55
Within-group	120.06	144	0.83	
Total	149.99	149		

*$p < .001$

In interpreting the higher mean sentence length found in the Puerto Rican sample, a question immediately arises regarding possible differences between the Spanish and English languages. In order to check on this factor a random sample of 200 English sentences from the Anastasi and D'Angelo study (2) were translated into Spanish, and a random sample of 200 Spanish sentences from the present study were translated into English. The results are summarized in Table 8. It will be noted that the translations in both languages average significantly longer than the originals. Although every effort was made in the translation to adhere to the original childish form of expression, the adult experimenter apparently could not completely prevent his more mature habitual speech from influencing sentence length. From a methodological standpoint, such a finding indicates the need for translating sample responses in both directions when making such linguistic comparisons, a practice which has not heretofore been followed (cf., e.g., 16). When the entire set of 400 sentences is combined, the mean number of words in the Spanish and English sentences is virtually identical. Thus structural differences between the two languages do not appear to provide an adequate explanation for the superiority of the Puerto Rican children in mean sentence length. Other hypotheses will be considered in the next section, following an analysis of the data on sentence structure.

Sentence Structure

The 50 language responses analyzed for each S were classified under the six previously described sentence types, and the percentage of each sentence type was determined for the individual. The means and SD's of these percentages for the Puerto Rican boys and girls are given in Table 9. For comparative purposes, the corresponding means and SD's for Negro and white boys and girls have been included. The t ratios of sex and ethnic differences are presented in Table 10. In interpreting the results on sentence structure, it should be noted that, in general, the first four sentence types listed have been found to increase in frequency with age among young children, while the last two tend to decrease (4, 5, 11). The former may therefore be regarded as relatively "mature" sentence types, the latter as relatively "immature." To be sure, this generalization requires some further study at specific age levels. For example, simple sentences increase in frequency with age among very young children, but are gradually replaced by more complex types among children within the age range of the present study. The frequency of occurrence of simple sentences is thus less diagnostic in the present age group than are the frequencies of the other sentence types.

Reference to Table 10 shows, first, that none of the sex differences within the Puerto Rican group is significant. When considered together wtih the similar finding on sentence length, these results indicate that Puerto Rican boys and girls do not differ in

Table 8

Mean Length of Spanish and English Translations of
Sample Sentences

Measure	English Sentences	Spanish Translations	English Sentences	Spanish Translations
Mean	4.84	5.02	5.38	5.64
SD	2.33	2.60	2.82	2.73

r = .95   r = .88

σ diff. = .058 σ diff. = .094

t = 3.10   t = 2.77

p < .01   p < .01

Combined Mean: English, 5.24;
                  Spanish, 5.20

Table 9

Means and Standard Deviations of Per Cents of Each Sentence Type
(Data on Negro and white samples from [2].)

Sentence Type		Puerto Rican		Negro		White	
		Boys	Girls	Boys	Girls	Boys	Girls
1. Simple	M	41.84	40.56	38.16	35.20	41.52	44.12
	SD	11.13	13.62	12.85	13.90	8.88	11.40
2. Simple with phrase	M	20.88	20.88	15.84	11.20	15.52	15.96
	SD	7.04	7.15	8.41	8.43	7.55	6.35
3. Compound and complex	M	11.76	10.08	3.44	3.76	4.72	6.08
	SD	7.09	8.13	3.47	3.89	3.34	5.11
4. Elaborated	M	7.12	8.48	2.72	2.24	3.36	5.04
	SD	6.32	9.78	2.76	2.21	3.08	4.84
5. Functionally complete	M	14.08	13.52	26.24	34.56	24.88	23.12
	SD	8.48	6.15	18.15	21.72	7.90	11.02
6. Incomplete	M	4.32	6.48	13.60	13.04	10.00	5.68
	SD	5.20	5.44	6.84	8.54	10.37	3.99

Table 10

Significance (t Ratios) of Sex and Ethnic Differences in Sentence Structure

Sentence Type	Puerto Rican Sex Differences +	Puerto Rican vs. Negro‡			Puerto Rican vs. White‡	
		Boys	Girls	Boys	Girls	
1. Simple	.36	1.06	1.35	.11	-.98
2. Simple with phrase	.00	2.25*	4.28***	2.55*	2.52*
3. Compound and complex	.76	5.17***	3.43**	4.40***	2.04*
4. Elaborated	-.57	3.12**	3.04**	2.61**	1.55
5. Functionally complete	.26	-2.97**	-4.56**	-4.58***	-3.74***
6. Incomplete	-1.40	-5.30***	-3.17**	-2.40*	.58

+ Negative values indicate smaller male mean.
‡ Negative values indicate smaller Puerto Rican mean.
  * p < .05.
 ** p < .01.
*** p < .001.

language development within the age range tested. In this regard,
the Puerto Ricans resemble neither the white nor the Negro sample,
since in the former the girls excelled and in the latter the boys excelled in language development (cf. 2).

Comparison of the Puerto Ricans with the Negro and white
samples in sentence structure also corroborates the findings on sentence length in so far as the Puerto Ricans again excel both of the
other samples. As would be expected with five-year-old children,
the frequency of simple sentences shows no clear-cut trend. All
other sentence types, however, present a highly consistent picture
of group differences, the "mature" sentence types occurring more
frequently and the "immature" types less frequently among the Puerto Ricans. If simple sentences are excluded, all differences between Negro and Puerto Rican boys, Negro and Puerto Rican girls,
and white and Puerto Rican boys are significant; all but two of the
differences between white and Puerto Rican girls are significant.
The differences between the Puerto Rican and Negro groups are
larger than those between the Puerto Rican and white groups, but
the latter differences are also well above chance expectancy.

Consideration of the linguistic characteristics of Spanish and
English suggests one difference which should be taken into account
in this connection, viz., the possibility of omitting the subject in
certain Spanish sentences, since the subject is understood in the
verb form. Such a condition would probably make it less likely for
a Spanish sentence to fall into the "incomplete" category and might
account in part for the predominance of "mature" sentence types in
the Puerto Rican language samples. It is doubtful, however, that
all the differences in favor of the Puerto Ricans in sentence structure can be explained on this basis.

Other hypotheses regarding the Puerto Rican children's superiority in language development may now be considered. First,
the sample attending day-care centers may represent a superior selection, since it could be argued that only the more intelligent and
enlightened parents will avail themselves of such facilities. The location and nature of the centers at which Ss were obtained do not,
however, provide strong support for such a hypothesis. It should
be recalled, moreover, that in comparison with the white and Negro
samples, the present Puerto Rican sample is decidedly inferior in
both educational and occupational level of parents.

A second hypothesis concerns the fact that the Puerto Rican
children had the opportunity to utilize both English and Spanish in
the language sample and might thus have benefited from their bilingualism. In this connection it should be noted, however, that in
the study by Smith (16) on several national groups in Hawaii the bilingual children used shorter sentences and less "mature" sentences
than the monolingual, even when both languages were recorded in
the speech samples. Rapport is a third possible explanation of the
superior linguistic performance of the Puerto Rican children. In
the relatively strange nursery environment, with its exclusively
English-speaking adults, such children reacted with genuine pleasure
and enthusiasm to a Spanish-speaking Puerto Rican adult who offered them toys and put no constraint upon their behavior. That
they became very loquacious under such circumstances was apparent.

For the white and Negro children, on the other hand, the examiner was accepted more nearly in the role of regular nursery personnel. Whether such differences in rapport could affect the maturity of linguistic expression remains a moot point.

A final hypothesis which may be considered pertains to the home environment of the Puerto Rican child of preschool age. Although unfavorable from many points of view and often characterized by extreme poverty and squalor, such an environment usually involves close proximity with many adults. The single small apartment unit often houses an "extended family" of close and distant relatives and perhaps a boarder or two (cf. 13, p. 94). The much smaller proportion of working mothers in the Puerto Rican group, in comparison with the Negro and white samples, would likewise provide more adult contact for these children. It should be noted in this connection that degree of adult contact has been found to be one of the most significant factors in early language development (12).

In conclusion, the consistent and significant superiority of the Puerto Rican sample in measures of linguistic development may have many explanations. Perhaps the most noteworthy finding of the present study, however, is that these children were certainly not inferior to the white American norms (cf. 4, 11). This is in sharp contrast to the marked inferiority reported for older Puerto Rican groups on all language tests. The present findings would thus seem to support the hypotheses outlined in the opening of this paper.

Summary

Measures of language development and Goodenough Draw-a-Man IQ's were obtained on 25 Puerto Rican boys and 25 Puerto Rican girls attending day nurseries in New York City's Spanish Harlem, all Ss being within six months of their fifth birthdays. Comparisons were made with the performance of 50 white and 50 Negro five-year-old children tested by the same procedures in an earlier study by Anastasi and D'Angelo (2). The language sample was recorded in both Spanish and English, according to the language spontaneously employed by the child. Spanish was used almost entirely, however, only about 2 per cent of the words and less than 1 per cent of the sentences being spoken in English.

Although the Puerto Rican sample was inferior to the Negro and white samples in educational and occupational level of parents, the Puerto Rican children did not differ significantly from the white or Negro groups in Draw-a-Man IQ, and they excelled both white and Negro groups in mean sentence length and in maturity of sentence structure. The greater extent of adult contact in the home environment of the Puerto Rican children is suggested as one possible factor to account for their superiority in early linguistic development.

Notes

1. For a more detailed report of these and other psychological studies on Puerto Ricans, cf. (1).

2. Most of these cases were obtained at Casita Maria, the excellent cooperation of whose staff is gratefully acknowledged.

3. A copy of this questionnaire, together with its English translation, will be found in (6), pp. 55-56.

4. All Ss were tested by the junior author. Thirty-six of the 50 cases employed in the present study were tested in connection with an MA dissertation submitted in the department of psychology, Fordham University (6). A more detailed report of testing and scoring procedure will be found in (2) and (6).

5. The writers are indebted to Miss D'Angelo for making these materials available and for cooperating in the study in a number of other ways.

6. Since the white group in the Anastasi and D'Angelo study (2) contained 26 boys and 24 girls, one white boy was eliminated at random and one comparable white girl was examined in both Draw-a-Man Test and language sample for the present purpose.

References

1. Anastasi, Anne, and Cordova, F.A. Some effects of bilingualism upon the intelligence test performance of Puerto Rican children in New York City. J. Educ. Psychol., in press. [44:1-19, January 1953. Ed.]
2. Anastasi, Anne, and D'Angelo, Rita Y. A comparison of Negro and white preschool children in language development and Goodenough Draw-a-Man IQ. J. Genet. Psychol., 1952, 81, 147-165.

3. Armstrong, Clairette P., Achilles, Edith M., and Sacks, M.J. Reactions of Puerto Rican children in New York City to psychological tests. In Report, Special Comm. Immigration and Naturalization, N.Y. State Chamber of Commerce, N.Y., 1935.

4. Davis, Edith A. The development of linguistic skill in twins, singletons with siblings, and only children from age five to ten years. Univer. Minn., Inst. Child Welfare, Monogr., 1937, No. 14.

5. Day, Ella J. The development of language in twins. Child Develpm., 1932, 3, 179-199, 288-316.

6. DeJesús, C. A study of language development and Goodenough IQ of Puerto Rican preschool children in New York City. Unpublished MA dissertation, Fordham Univer., 1952.

7. Dunklin, Laura D. A study of the intelligence of some recent

Puerto Rican immigrant children in a first grade in a New
York City school. Unpublished MA dissertation, Teachers
College, Columbia Univer., 1935.

8. Goodenough, Florence L. Measurement of intelligence by drawings. Yonkers-on-Hudson: World Book Co., 1926.

9. Goodenough, Florence L., and Anderson, J.E. Experimental
child study. New York: Century, 1911.

10. Johnson, P.O. Statistical methods in research, New York:
Prentice Hall, 1949.

11. McCarthy, Dorothea. The language development of the preschool child. Univer. Minn., Inst. Child Welfare, Monogr.
1930, No. 4.

12. McCarthy, Dorothea. Language development in children. In
L. Carmichael (Ed.), Manual of child psychology. (2nd Ed.)
New York: Wiley, in press.

13. Mills, C.W., Senior, C., and Goldsen, Rose K. The Puerto
Rican journey. New York: Harper, 1950.

14. Monroe, P. A survey of the public educational system of
Puerto Rico. New York: Bureau of Publications, Teachers
College, Columbia Univer., 1926.

15. Porteus, S.D. Racial group differences in mentality. Tabulae
Biologicae, 1939. 18, 66-75.

16. Smith, Madorah E. Some light on the problem of bilingualism
as found from a study of the progress in mastery of English
among preschool children of non-American ancestry in Hawaii. Genet. Psychol. Monogr., 1939, 21, 119-284.

17. Smith, S. Language and non-verbal test performance of racial
groups in Honolulu before and after a 14-year interval.
J. gen. Psychol., 1942, 26, 51-93.

18. Snedecor, G.W. Statistical methods. (4th Ed.) Ames, Iowa:
Iowa State College Press, 1946.

Anne Anastasi and Fernando A. Cordova, "Some Effects of Bilingualism upon the Intelligence Test Performance of Puerto Rican Children in New York City." Journal of Educational Psychology, 44:1-17, January 1953. Reprinted by permission of AMS Press, Inc.

Bilingualism is generally recognized as a serious difficulty in the comparative psychological testing of many groups. Although not restricted to this country, the problem is especially cogent in America, with its variety of foreign-speaking subcultures. Many studies on American Indians and on European and Asiatic immigrant groups in America have compared the test performance of bilingual children with that of monolingual, English-speaking children within the same national or racial groups, as well as with the American norms (cf. 1, pp. 717-725; 3; 4; 29). Such investigations have consistently demonstrated that the substitution of a non-verbal for a verbal test reduces the inferiority of the bilinguals. In some instances, the inferiority disappears completely with the use of the non-verbal test. The relative position of the groups may even be reversed, the bilingual excelling the monolingual on such a test. The latter result is especially likely to occur when the non-verbal test is of the performance type (cf, e.g., 15).

The interpretation of such findings on bilingualism is complicated by a number of factors. In the first place, it cannot be assumed that verbal and non-verbal tests measure the same functions. The specific abilities called into play by these two types of tests may, and probably do, differ. Do bilinguals score higher on performance than on verbal tests only because their insufficient mastery of English handicaps them on the latter tests? Or does the difference in score reflect inequalities in the relative strength of verbal and spatial abilities in the particular group? The bilingual group under investigation may have been reared in a culture which selectively fosters the development of spatial aptitude (or some other ability or combination of abilities involved in the performance test), while discouraging the development of verbal skills.

A second and closely related point to consider is that bilingualism is often correlated with other differences in cultural background which may influence test performance. The bilingual is likely to differ from the American normative population in his general information, work habits, interests, and motivation. The degree of bilingualism, moreover, is probably related to the amount of deviation in these other cultural factors. There is evidence, too, that in certain situations more personal maladjustment occurs among bilinguals than among monolinguals (30). To be sure, such maladjustment appears to result primarily from the cultural conflict confronting a second generation immigrant group, but the bilingualism makes

the conflict more acute, since it serves as a symbol and constant
reminder of such conflict.

A third complicating factor is to be found in the possible influence of bilingualism upon rapport in the testing situation. The
bilingual may score higher when tested in one than when tested in
the other of his two languages. In a study of Spanish-speaking
school children in Arizona, for example, the children obtained higher IQ's on a non-verbal test when the oral instructions were given
in Spanish than when they were given in English (24). Such a difference may result from a more complete mastery of the one language. But it could also arise, wholly or in part, from a more
favorable emotional response toward the examiner who speaks the
language with which the individual identifies himself more closely.
There is evidence to suggest that both Negro and white children perform better on intelligence tests when the examiner is a member of
their own race than when he is a member of a different race (6).
Like skin color, language may serve as a reduced cue for group
identification and it may influence the examiner-subject relationship
in a similar manner.

Finally, it should be noted that bilingualism itself may be of
more than one type. Whether or not bilingualism constitutes a
handicap, as well as the extent of such a handicap, depends upon
the way in which the two languages have been learned (26, 31). In
immigrant families, the child often learns one language at home and
another at school. The result is a sort of 'linguistic bifurcation,'
whereby one language develops in one set of situations and the other
in another set. Mastery of both languages is thus limited. It is
not the interference between the two languages so much as the restriction in the learning of each to certain areas that leads to handicap. In such cases, the extent of the child's vocabulary as well as
other aspects of his linguistic development will be inferior in both
languages (5, 28). By contrast, the individual who learns to express himself in all types of situations in at least one language will
probably suffer no handicap from learning a second language. Such
a situation might be described as 'bilingual parallelism,' since the
second language provides a parallel means of expression in some or
all situations, depending upon the thoroughness of its mastery.

The present investigation is concerned with the role of bilingualism in the intelligence test performance of Puerto Rican children in New York City. The native language of the Puerto Rican is
Spanish, although English is taught in the Puerto Rican schools.
Unfortunately, an ill-advised educational policy with regard to the
way in which English was introduced into the Puerto Rican schools
has served only to make many Puerto Ricans 'illiterate in two languages,' and has prejudiced them against English, which they blame
for their educational difficulties and confusions (23, p. 12). The
dark-skinned Puerto Rican migrant, moreover, is encouraged to remain Spanish-speaking, since as a foreign-speaking Negro he tends
to enjoy higher status in the United States than does the native
American Negro (23, p. 87). Such a hybrid Puerto Rican prefers
to be identified as a 'Latino' rather than as a Negro. For these
and other reasons, the Puerto Rican migrant makes little use of
what English he knows. Consequently, Puerto Rican children in

New York City are virtually monolingual until school entrance, having had little or no opportunity to learn English in their own home or community. This persisting linguistic barrier is a handicap in the child's school adjustment and in his educational progress. The language problem is also undoubtedly a major reason for the scarcity of psychological data on this large and rapidly growing immigrant group.

A recently completed sociological survey by Mills, Senior, and Goldsen (23) provides some information on the cultural background, socio-economic level, living conditions, interests, and outlook of New York City Puerto Ricans. Strong in-group feeling, low occupational level, and a widespread pessimism regarding the chances of improving their status were characteristic of the sample of 1113 respondents interviewed in this survey. Similarly, an analysis of 188 Puerto Rican first admissions to all New York State mental hospitals during a single year indicated low educational and socio-economic status and a relatively high proportion of cases with subnormal intelligence (22).

Only two investigations have been reported in which psychological tests were administered to Puerto Ricans within continental United States, both having been conducted in New York City. The earlier of the two was carried out by Dunklin (16) in 1934-1935. Thirty-five Puerto Rican public school children enrolled in a special section of the first grade taught entirely in Spanish, were given a Spanish translation of the Pintner-Cunningham Primary Test, the Pintner Non-Language Primary Test, the Pintner-Paterson Performance Scale, and another performance test developed by the author. On the two individual performance tests and on the Pintner Non-Language Test, the median IQ of the Puerto Rican children was virtually equal to the American norms, but on the Pintner-Cunningham it was only 73.

The other psychological study of New York City Puerto Ricans was that of Armstrong, Achilles, and Sacks (2), reported in 1935. The Army Individual Performance Test was given to 240 Puerto Rican public school children in grades four to six, most of whom were between the ages of nine and fourteen. In addition, the Otis Test of General Ability for grades four to eight was administered in English to 129 of the fifth- and sixth-grade children. As a 'control group,' the authors employed a sampling of over 400 nine- to fourteen-year-old public school children drawn from Manhattan and Westchester County. On both the performance and the verbal test, the mean scores of the Puerto Ricans were lower than those of the control group, the critical ratios of these differences being 7.099 and 9.504, respectively. From these findings, the authors drew rather sweeping conclusions regarding the inferiority of Puerto Rican intelligence, their report arousing considerable controversy (cf., e.g., 11). Chief among the difficulties in the way of interpreting the results of this study may be mentioned language handicap, problems of rapport and test motivation, and lack of comparability of Puerto Rican and control groups, especially with reference to socio-economic level.

It may be of interest to consider also some results obtained from the testing of Puerto Rican children outside of continental

United States. Porteus (27) reports mean Stanford-Binet and Porteus Maze IQ's of 71.72 and 74.87, respectively, for a group of
429 Puerto Rican children tested in Hawaii. The subjects were all
clinic cases, brought to the Psychological Clinic of the University
of Hawaii, and included delinquent, educationally retarded, mentally
defective, and dependent children, from the lower half of the socio-
economic scale. Within this group, the Puerto Rican children
scored lower than any of the other national samples tested. There
is no indication of how the language problem was handled, if at all.
Moreover, the possibility of differential selection of various national subgroups within the clinic population needs to be taken into account. An extensive and better controlled investigation was conducted in Puerto Rico under the direction of The International Institute of Teachers College, Columbia University, and reported in
1926 (25). In addition to island-wide testing with school achievement tests given both in English and in Spanish, this study included
the administration of the Pintner Non-Language Mental Ability Test
to 1000 children in grades three to eight. In the latter test, the
Puerto Rican children excelled the American norms in grades three,
four, and five, but fell below these norms in the next three grades.

Procedure

In the present investigation, Puerto Rican children in the upper three grades of a New York City elementary school were tested
with the Cattell 'Culture Free' Test, Forms 2A and 2B, designed
for ages eight to twelve and unselected adults (7, 8, 9, 10). This
is a non-verbal test, all items being perceptual or spatial. Cattell
maintains, moreover, that the oral instructions for this test can be
translated without altering the validity of the test (9, p. 3). It
should be added that for the present purpose no assumption has been
made that this test is actually 'culture free.' No test can be completely 'culture free,' nor even 'culture constant,' since the content of any test will tend to favor one or another culture. The
elimination of specific culturally limited information from a test is
only a partial and superficial solution. Each culture stimulates the
development of certain abilities and interests, and inhibits others.
The resulting psychological differences will inevitably be reflected
in test performance, as in any other behavior of individuals reared
in diverse cultural settings. In the Cattell test, for example, the
items consist almost exclusively of abstract geometric forms and
patterns; and the test is, of course, of the paper-and-pencil variety.
Individuals having relatively little interest and practice in intellectual games and those who have developed antagonistic or discouraged
attitudes toward purely academic activities would quite probably be
at a disadvantage on such a test, which provides little practical appeal.
            The plan of the present experiment was to administer Form
A in English to one half of the subjects (Group 1), and Form A in
Spanish to the other half (Group 2). After an interval of two weeks,
Form B was given with a reversal of the two languages, Group 1
now receiving the instructions in Spanish, and Group 2 in English.
The basic experimental design was thus a 2 x 2 latin square, as

shown below:

Test Session

	I		II	
Group 1	Form A: English		Form B:	Spanish
Group 2	Form A: Spanish		Form B:	English

Both forms of the test were employed with each language in order
to balance out any possible differences in the difficulty level of
Forms A and B. Although Cattell reports (9, p 3) that the two
forms are equal in difficulty, such equivalence might not hold for
the present population. The study was therefore set up in such a
way as to make the assumption of equality of forms unnecessary.

The Spanish translations of the instructions were prepared
by the junior author, who is himself a bilingual Puerto Rican, and
were independently checked by a Spanish-speaking reader. All tests
were likewise administered by the junior author, with the assistance
of classroom teachers. The children were tested in groups containing from thirty-five to forty-nine subjects. Preliminary introductory remarks, as well as replies to subjects' queries, were made
in the same language as the instructions during any one test session.

Subjects

The subjects tested in the present study included 176 boys
and girls in the sixth, seventh, and eighth grades of a parochial
school. The school was situated in the principal area of residence
of Puerto Ricans in New York City, where the two earlier studies
on New York City Puerto Ricans, described in the first part of this
paper, had also been conducted. Of the total group of 176, thirty-
two were omitted owing to absence from one of the testing sessions,
seven because they were not Puerto Rican, and three because of a
zero score on one or both forms of the test. The three last-men-
tioned subjects had made no effort to put any marks on the test
items. The remaining 134 cases were employed in determining the
reliability coefficients of each form of the test. A further reduction in number was made prior to carrying out the analysis of variance, in order to have an equal number of cases in each subgroup.
For this purpose, the number of cases retained was 108, consisting
of twenty-seven boys and twenty-seven girls in Group 1 and the
same numbers in Group 2. Within each school grade, individual
subjects were assigned to Groups 1 and 2 by the experimenter in
such a way as to equate the two groups as nearly as was practicable
in relevant background characteristics.

At the end of the second testing session, each subject filled
out a personal data form. This questionnaire was written in English, but the examiner read each question aloud in both English and
Spanish, explaining how it should be answered and giving individual
attention to subjects who raised questions or required assistance.
The results of this questionnaire served as the basis for describing
the sample under investigation, as well as for determining how
closely Groups 1 and 2 had been equated. The questionnaire data
are reported for only the 108 subjects used in the analysis of variance, since it is on this group that the major conclusions of the

study are based.

In age, the group ranged from eleven to fifteen years, with a mean of thirteen. Nearly all parents were born in Puerto Rico, only one or two fathers or mothers in each subgroup having been born in other Spanish-speaking countries or in the United States. Among the children, nearly half were born in Puerto Rico, the rest in New York City; nearly all had lived in New York City over three years. Since Puerto Ricans make frequent return trips to their native island, questions were also inserted to cover the number and duration of such visits. Nineteen of the 108 children reported such trips, but only four of these had remained in Puerto Rico over one year during their visits. As in other surveys of Puerto Rican migrants, the occupational level of the present group was very low. When classified according to the Goodenough and Anderson (17) occupational scale, none of the parents fell into the professional, semi-professional, clerical and skilled trades, or farmer categories. The majority were engaged in semi-skilled and slightly skilled occupations.

Nine of the eighteen items in the questionnaire were concerned with the extent of the subject's bilingualism. These items were selected and adapted from a bilingualism scale developed by Hoffman (20). In replying to each question, the subjects checked one of the following alternatives: (a) always in Spanish; (b) more in Spanish than English; (c) about half and half; (d) more in English than Spanish; (e) always in English. Most children reported that they spoke Spanish and English about equally often with their families, a larger number clustering at the all-Spanish than at the all-English end of the scale. The rest of the family, however, most often spoke Spanish among themselves. Reading by the family scatters widely over the scale, as does letter-writing, although Spanish predominates in the latter. The children themselves employ predominantly English in their reading and writing, a fact which undoubtedly reflects the influence of the school. English language movies are the more frequently attended, although Spanish movies are well represented in the group. Radio listening shows a more even distribution of Spanish and English, with a slight predominance of English. Finally, a clear majority of the children indicated that they 'think' in both languages; and as between the two ends of the scale, a larger number fell at the English than at the Spanish end of the scale on this item.

The four subgroups proved to be closely equated in all of the above background variables, with only the following minor exceptions: the Group 2 boys included a slight excess of New York-born cases, were somewhat superior in parental occupational level, and reported a little more frequent use of English. Because of longer residence in this country, the families of these boys may thus have made a more effective adjustment to the American environment, both economically and culturally. That this subgroup difference was, however, too slight to have appreciably influenced the results of the present study is suggested by the fact that in overall test performance the Group 1 boys excelled those in Group 2. The only clear sex difference noted in the questionnaire data is a greater tendency for the girls to report attendance at Spanish movies. This difference may result in part from the greater restriction of the girls' activities in Puerto Rican families, which would delay their assimilation to the American culture. But it may also be related to the nature of Spanish films, which are more often the 'romantic' type and would thus appeal more to girls than to boys at the pre-adolescent and adolescent level.

Results

Test reliability.--Split-half reliability coefficients were computed separately for Forms A and B, in both the English and Spanish versions. These coefficients were obtained by finding each subject's score on the odd items (a), the even items (b), and the total test (t), and applying the following formula (13, 19):

$$r_{11} = 2 \left(1 - \frac{\sigma a^2 + \sigma b^2}{\sigma t^2} \right).$$

The reliability coefficients, together with the number of subjects on whom they were computed, will be found in Table 1. As a

Table 1. - Split-Half Reliability Coefficients

Test Form and Version	N	r_{11}
A - English	61	.92
A - Spanish	73	.84
B - English	73	.88
B - Spanish	61	.88

check on the applicability of an odd-even reliability technique to the present test, the degree to which the scores depended upon speed was determined. This information was also of direct interest in so far as there are cultural differences in the emphasis placed upon speed. Such differences would be reflected in performance on a speed test.

As an index of speed, the following measure developed by Cronbach and Warrington (14) was computed for each subtest within each form and version of the test:

$$\frac{\sigma^2 f(a) \Sigma x^2 \lambda p}{N \sigma x^2}$$

In this formula, σ_x^2 is the total variance of the test scores, and $\sigma^2 f(a)$ is the variance of the number of items attempted. To find $\Sigma x^2 \lambda p$, each person's score on the last two items attempted is averaged, the average is squared, and this quantity is then summed for all persons. Adjustments are also made for any persons who may have completed the test before time is called. Essentially, this index is based upon the extent of individual differences in number of items completed, as well as upon performance on the last two items attempted. Thus an individual who failed the last two items attempted would probably not raise his score appreciably if given time to try more, and harder, items. An estimate of the lower bound of the reliability coefficient of a speed test can be found by subtracting this index from the obtained reliability coefficient.

Table 2. - Index* Showing the Contribution of Speed To Scores on Each Subtest

Sub-test	Form A English	Form A Spanish	Form B English	Form B Spanish
1	.0513	.6068	.0358	.0278
2	.0093	.3114	.0011	.0021
3	.0308	.0681	.0000	.0218
4	.0038	.0000	.0000	.0003

* Computed by formula of Cronbach and Warrington (14, p.175).

The results of the speed analysis are given in Table 2. On the whole, the values reported in this table are quite low, all but two falling between .0000 and .0681. The two exceptions are subtests 1 and 2 of Form A administered in Spanish. Scores on these two subtests were evidently influenced to a considerabl extent by speed, probably because most subjects were slow in starting after receiving the instructions. For the present purpose, only total scores on all subtests are of interest. It is likely that the reliability coefficient of .84 obtained for Form A-Spanish has been spuriously raised to some extent through the contribution of speed to scores on two of its four subtests. In all other forms, however, it is apparent that speed played a negligible role.

Analysis of variance.--The mean scores of boys and girls in Groups 1 and 2 during each of the two testing sessions are reported in Table 3. It will be recalled that in Group 1, the first

Table 3. - Subgroup Means of Test Scores

Testing Session	Group 1 (A-English; B-Spanish)		Group 2 (A-Spanish; B-English)	
	Boys	Girls	Boys	Girls
Session 1: Form A	20.93	15.93	15.70	18.30
Session 2: Form B	24.52	22.19	21.89	25.07

testing session was conducted in English and the second in Spanish, while the reverse order was followed in Group 2. In order to evaluate the contribution of language, session, order, and sex to test performance, the data were submitted to an analysis of variance. The type of analysis employed is essentially the same as that described by Grant (18) for a 2 x 2 latin square, except for the addition of the sex variable and the computation of the interaction of sex with each of the other three variables. The interactions among language, session, and order are confounded and lost, as in all 2 x 2 latin squares.

In order to determine the applicability of analysis of variance to the present data, the eight subgroups were tested for homogeneity of variance by the L_1-test (cf. 21, pp. 82-86). The obtained value of L_1 is .9687; with f = 26 and k = 8, we find that P> .05. Hence the variances may be treated as homogeneous.

The results of the analysis of variance are summarized in Table 4. In computing the F-ratios, the subject x session interaction was used as the error term; in one case, a second F-ratio

Table 4. - Analysis of Variance

Source of Variation	df	Sums of Squares	Variance Estimate	F-ratio
1) Order	1	22.686	22.686	1.152
2) Session	1	1756.741	1756.741	89.202*
3) Language	1	32.667	32.667	1.659
4) Sex	1	8.167	8.167	.415
5) Session x Sex	1	35.852	35.852	1.820
6) Language x Sex	1	14.518	14.518	.737
7) Order x Sex	1	580.166	580.166	29.459*
				9.908*
8) Subjects (within order-within sex)	104	6090.074	58.558	2.973*
9) Error (subjects x session)	204	2048.222	19.694	
10) Total	215	10589.093		

* Significant at .01 level.

was found with another error term, as will be explained below. It will be noted that of the four principal factors investigated, viz., order, session, language, and sex, only session yielded a significant F-ratio. This ratio, 89.202, is considerably greater than the value of 6.90 required for significance at the .01 level, with 1/104 df. Such a finding indicates a large and significant practice effect, all groups scoring much higher in the second session regardless of language used. Of the 108 subjects, eighty-five improved on the retest. Since this group was taking its first psychological test, the role of test sophistication and rapport is strongly suggested by these results. Whereas in the test manual Cattell allows one point for test sophistication when Form B follows Form A (9, p. 8), the present group showed a mean rise of 5.71 points. Cattell elsewhere (8, p. 157) cites evidence to suggest that gains between Forms A and B tend to be greater for individuals with higher IQ's. In the present group, however, overall level of performance, or IQ, was low in terms of the Cattell norms, while retest gains were relatively high. This is what would be expected when initial scores are spuriously lowered by failure to understand directions, poor motivation, and the like.

The language in which the test was administered had no significant effect upon performance. Translating the directions evidently offers no solution to the testing of these subjects. The bilingualism encountered in this group appears to be of the bifurcated variety, the children's mastery of either language being restricted

and inadequate. The teachers report that these children show a
reluctance to speak English. Yet in Spanish, the majority are ilit-
erate. In connection with the present testing, a number of the children told their teachers that the Spanish used by the examiner was
'too correct' for them. Nor could this objection refer to regional
differences in Spanish idiom or accent, since the examiner was a
native Puerto Rican. Another interesting illustration of the linguistic bifurcation of these subjects is the difficulty which many experienced with the word 'subrayar' (to underline), which they had more
often encountered in the English-speaking school situation than in
the Spanish-speaking home setting. It should also be noted that the
linguistic bifurcation provides a further reason for the improvement
upon a retest, since by the second session all subjects had heard
similar instructions in both languages, and thus had a better opportunity to complement their inadequate understanding of either language. It is clear that in future testing of Puerto Rican migrants,
the best procedure is either to use exclusively non-language tests
or to present the instructions in both languages.

There was no significant sex difference in overall performance, but the sex x order interaction was significant at a high level
of confidence. Such a significant interaction could result either
from the differential effect of order upon the two sexes, or from
the fact that the subjects differed widely among themselves, since
each order was employed with a different sampling of subjects. As
a check on these alternative explanations, a second F-ratio was
computed for the sex x order interaction, using the subject variance
as the error term.[1] This F-ratio also proved to be significant at
the .01 level. Hence the significant interaction could not be attributed to sampling fluctuations which might have made the Group
1 girls inferior or the Group 1 boys superior by chance. The obtained interaction effect indicates that the testing order which began
with English favored the boys, while that beginning with Spanish
favored the girls. Such a sex difference probably reflects differences in the degree of acculturation of the two sexes. Several questionnaire items suggested that the boys were more highly Americanized than the girls. This difference may be due in part to the
slight excess of New York born boys in the total sample. Another
and more general explanation is to be found in the greater freedom
traditionally allowed to boys in Puerto Rican families, while girls
are more closely restricted to the family circle.

It is interesting to note that the language x sex interaction
was not significant. Neither sex did significantly better in one language than in the other. The Spanish instructions proved as difficult as the English for all groups, probably because of the unfamili-
arity of key words resulting from the subjects' linguistic bifurcation.
At the same time, the initial use of Spanish or English by the examiner may have influenced rapport, an influence which would carry
over to the second test session. The boys may have felt more cooperative and at ease with an initially English-speaking examiner,
the girls with an initially Spanish-speaking examiner. The sex difference would thus be a matter of attitude rather than linguistic
comprehension.

Comparison with normative sample.--The overall perform-

ance of the present group fell considerably below the norms reported in the test manual (9, p. 9). For this comparison, the
Form B scores of the total sample of 108 children were converted
to standard score IQ's. The Form B norms, as given by Cattell,
are based on the assumption that Form A was taken prior to Form
B, as was done by the present subjects. Moreover, Cattell recommends that, with subjects lacking in test sophistication, Form B
scores are a more satisfactory measure of performance, Form A
serving as a practice test (8, p. 156). The median standard score
IQ obtained by the present sample was 70. The range extends
from two top IQ's of 124 down to three scores indicating chance
performance, i.e., raw scores below 9.2 (8, p.157). The distribution of IQ's is significantly skewed, with a piling up of scores at
the lower end.

In interpreting these standard score IQ's, it should be noted
that they are based on a standard deviation of 24 points, as contrasted with the more familiar 16- or 15-point σ in use in such
scales as the Stanford-Binet and the WISC. Thus the median IQ of
70 is 1.25σ below the norm of 100, and would correspond to an
IQ of approximately 80 or 81 in terms of the more familiar units.
The nature of the normative sample must also be taken into account. The norms were obtained on 3297 British and American
children, ranging in age from six to seventeen. Cattell reports
that "a substantial fraction of the (normative) population...was taken
either from two Midwestern university towns of population about
twenty-five thousand each, or from a British industrial city of population about two-hundred-forty thousand" (8, p. 156). Both Midwestern towns were rated above average in cultural and social status in
the survey conducted by E. L. Thorndike (cf. 8, 32). Parental occupation is not reported by Cattell, but it is almost certain that the
normative sample is of much higher socio-economic level than the
present group. The low socio-economic status of the Puerto Rican
children, as indicated by parental occupation, is undoubtedly one
factor to consider in evaluating their poor test performance. Their
language handicap, limiting their mastery of both Spanish and English, is another important factor.

Even more conspicuous as a reason for the inferior test performance of the present group is the children's attitude toward the
testing. A large number of factors, including lack of test sophistication, little or no motivation to excel in a competitive intellectual
situation, and lack of interest in the relatively abstract and academic content of the test contributed to this attitude. The characteristic reaction to the testing was a mild confusion, followed by amuse-
ment and indifference. Such attitudes, moreover, are closely related to the poor emotional adjustment which this group makes to
the school. The children were described by their teachers as 'un-
ambitious,' many just sitting in the classroom without understanding
what goes on. Their initial school experiences, involving sudden
placement in an exclusively English-speaking environment at a time
when they knew almost no English, seem to have produced in these
children a sort of 'psychological insulation' to what goes on in
school. The passive and unresponsive habits thus established have
remained their characteristic reaction to school. A solution of the

language problem early in the child's school career would thus seem
to be an essential first step for the proper education of these children. Not only test performance, but also the general intellectual
development which the tests are designed to gauge, are seriously
handicapped by the attitudes and intellectual habits resulting from
the child's early linguistic confusion.

It may be of interest to reexamine the findings of Dunklin
(16) and of Armstrong et al. (2) in the light of the present results.
The subjects in the Dunklin study were first-grade children and
were attending a special section taught in Spanish. Thus these
children had not yet developed the passive, unresponsive attitudes
characteristic of the older school children. Rapport was also better because the teacher, as well as the examiner, spoke to them in
the more familiar Spanish. Under these conditions, Dunklin found
no inferiority to the American norms on three of the tests. The
inferiority on the Spanish translation of the Pintner-Cunningham may
be attributed to the fact that the Spanish which the children had acquired in their own homes failed to provide the type of vocabulary
required to understand psychological test instructions. In the Armstrong et al. study, which was conducted on fourth- to sixth-grade
children, consistently poor scores were obtained on both verbal and
performance tests. Although no language was employed on the performance test, the inferiority of the Puerto Rican children on this
test was probably due partly to poor rapport in the testing situation
and partly to the cumulative effects of four to six years of unsuit-
able schooling.

Summary

The Cattell Culture-Free Intelligence Test, Forms 2A and
2B, was administered to 176 Puerto Rican children in grades six to
eight of a parochial school in the Spanish Harlem area of New York
City. One half of the group received the test instructions in English during the first testing session (Form A) and in Spanish during
the second session (Form B); the order of the languages was reversed for the other half of the group. The split-half reliability of
Forms A and B in the English and Spanish versions ranged from
.84 to .92. Speed played a negligible part in the scores obtained.

An analysis of variance was conducted on 108 of the subjects,
including twenty-seven boys and twenty-seven girls in each of the
two language-order subgroups. Significant F-ratios were found for
two variables, subjects and session, and for the interaction of order
x sex. The most conspicuous finding was the marked improvement
from first to second testing session, regardless of language. Although there was no overall sex difference in score, the girls performed better when the testing order was Spanish-English, the boys
when it was English-Spanish. This order x sex interaction was attributed principally to rapport, the more highly Americanized boys
responding more favorably to an initially English-speaking examiner,
while the more restricted and less acculturated girls achieved better
rapport with an initially Spanish-speaking examiner.

The overall performance of the present group fell considerably below the test norms reported by Cattell. Among the reasons

for such a discrepancy are the very low socio-economic level of the Puerto Rican children, their bilingualism which makes them deficient in both languages, their extreme lack of test sophistication, and their poor emotional adjustment to the school situation. In so far as this maladjustment itself appears to have arisen from the children's severe language handicap during their initial school experiences, a solution of the language problem would seem to be a necessary first step for the effective education of migrant Puerto Rican children.

Notes

1. It will be noted that the subject variance is itself significant, when tested against subject x session interaction as the error term. This simply means that, despite marked improvement from first to second session, subjects tended to maintain their relative status in the group. In other words, differences among individuals were significant and persisted throughout the experiment.

References

1. A. Anastasi and J. P. Foley, Jr. Differential Psychology (Second Ed.). New York: Macmillan, 1949, p. 894.

2. C. P. Armstrong, E. M. Achilles and M. J. Sacks. "Reactions of Puerto Rican children in New York City to psychological tests." Rep. Spec. Comm. on Immigration and Naturalization, New York State Chamber of Commerce, 1935, p. 9.

3. S. Arsenian. Bilingualism and Mental Development. Teachers College, Columbia Univ., Contrib. to Educ., 1937, No. 712, p. 164.

4. ----. "Bilingualism in the post-war world." Psychol. Bull., 1945, 42, 65-86.

5. E. M. Barke and D.E.P. Williams. "A further study of the comparative intelligence of children in certain bilingual and monoglot schools in South Wales." Brit. J. educ. Psychol., 1938, 8, 63-77.

6. H.G. Canady. "The effect of 'rapport' on the IQ: a new approach to the problem of racial psychology." J. Negro Educ., 1936, 5, 209-219.

7. R. B. Cattell. "A culture-free intelligence test: I." J. educ. Psychol., 1940, 31, 161-179.

8. ----. "Classical and standard score IQ standardization of the I.P.A.T. Culture-Free Intelligence Scale 2." J. consult. Psychol., 1951, 15, 154-159.

9. R. B. Cattell and A. K. S. Cattell. Culture-Free Intelligence Test. Scale 2. Handbook. Champaign, Ill: I.P.A.T., 1949, p. 9.

10. R. B. Cattell, S. N. Feingold and S. B. Sarason. "A culture-free intelligence test: II. Evaluation of cultural influences on test performance." J. educ. Psychol., 1941, 32, 61-100.

11. P. A. Cebollero. Reactions of Puerto Rican Children in New York City to Psychological Tests. An Analysis of the Study by Armstrong, Achilles, and Sacks of the Same Name. San Juan, P.R: The Puerto Rico School Review, 1936, p. 11.

12. F. A. Cordova. A Comparison of the Performance of a Bilingual Group on a "Culture Free" Test Administered in English and in Spanish. Unpub. M.A. Disser., Fordham Univ., 1951.

13. L. J. Cronbach. "Coefficient Alpha and the internal structure of tests." Psychometr., 1951, 16, 297-334.

14. L. J. Cronbach and W. G. Warrington. "Time-limit tests: estimating their reliability and degree of speeding." Psychometr., 1951, 16, 167-188.

15. N. T. Darcy. "The effect of bilingualism upon the measurement of the intelligence of children of preschool age." J. educ. Psychol., 1946, 37, 21-44.

16. L. D. Dunklin. A Study of the Intelligence of Some Recent Puerto Rican Immigrant Children in a First Grade in a New York City School. Unpub. M.A. Disser., Teachers College, Columbia Univ., 1935.

17. F. L. Goodenough and J. E. Anderson. Experimental Child Study. New York: Century, 1931, p. 546.

18. D. A. Grant. "The statistical analysis of a frequent experimental design." Amer. J. Psychol., 1949, 62, 119-122.

19. L. Guttman. "A basis for analyzing test-retest reliability." Psychometr., 1945, 10, 255-282.

20. M. N. H. Hoffman. The Measurement of Bilingual Background. Teachers College, Columbia Univ., Contrib. Educ., 1934, No. 623, p. 75.

21. P. O. Johnson. Statistical Methods in Research. New York: Prentice-Hall, 1949, p. 377.

22. B. Malzberg. "Mental disease among Puerto Ricans in New York State." Psychiat. Quart. Suppl., 1948, 22, 207-218.

23. C. W. Mills, C. Senior and R. K. Goldsen. The Puerto Rican Journey. New York: Harper, 1950, p. 238.

24. A. J. Mitchell. "The effect of bilingualism in the measurement of intelligence." Elem. Sch. J., 1937, 38, 29-37.

25. P. Monroe. A Survey of the Public Educational System of Porto Rico. New York: Bur. Publ., Teachers College, Columbia Univ., 1926, p. 453.

26. R. Pintner and S. Arsenian. "The relation of bilingualism to verbal intelligence and to school adjustment." J. educ. Res., 1937, 31, 255-263.

27. S. D. Porteus. "Racial group differences in mentality." Tabulae Biologicae, 1939, 18, 66-75.

28. M. E. Smith. "Measurement of vocabularies of young bilingual children in both of the languages used." J. genet. Psychol., 1949, 74, 305-310.

29. D. T. Spoerl. The Adjustment at College of Students Who Were Bilingual in Childhood. Unpub. Ph.D. Disser., Clark Univ., 1942.

30. ----. "Bilinguality and emotional adjustment." J. abn. soc. Psychol., 1943, 38, 37-57.

31. W. A. Stark. "The effect of bilingualism on general intelligence: an investigation carried out in certain Dublin primary schools." Brit. J. educ. Psychol., 1940, 10, 78-79.

32. E. L. Thorndike. Your City. New York: Harcourt, Brace, 1939, p. 204.

Sophie E. Elam, "Acculturation and Learning Problems of Puerto
Rican Children." Teachers College Record, 61:258-264,
February 1960. Reprinted by permission.

Many studies have been made and much has been said about
the Puerto Rican child in cities. Although there are characteristics common to Puerto Rican children, these are by no means very
different from those of other minority and emigrant children in the
lower economic range. Problems of acculturation of emigrant
groups are not new in our society, but invariably there is an ur-
gency about them which is reflected in the many problems in the
school and the community.

Perhaps as we look back at other migrations and note how
these have been assimilated it is possible to reflect that people who,
like the Puerto Ricans, have recently come out of a rural peasant
cultural pattern of living find acculturation more difficult than those
who come from an urban center. It may well be that rural peoples
tend to be tradition-oriented while those from metropolitan communities are more other-directed so that they more readily respond to
the cues available to them in our culture.

Acculturation is basically a problem of accommodation to a
whole new set of patterns and being. It is actually the change-
over from one culture to another. Culture is primarily a learning
which is begun at birth and which provides the base for living. It
permeates all behavior, from the simple fundamentals of eating and
dressing and talking to the more complex and involved patterns of
communication, use of symbols, and the development of a value system. Culture is also considered to be a determinant of the way
one perceives oneself and others. It involves the totality of living
from the biological to the social and intellectual. And the greatest
complexity of the adjustment lies largely in the social sphere:
"...under situations of stress or strain, of rapid change and consequent disorientation there is likely to be an increase in manifest ill
health."[1]

Despite the vast network of our communications in mass
media each emigrant group maintains almost intact its social constructs. For the adult who is already completely oriented to a way
of life and whose whole gamut of responses is organized around the
expected cues in his culture, the transition is difficult enough. He
must select from the new what has resemblance to the familiar and
add to this repertoire by trial and error the new learnings as they
are needed. He tends to remain in his own ethnic and cultural
clusters, both in industry and in neighborhood living, as witness
the conclaves of Puerto Ricans in our cities.

But for the child who is still in the process of learning his
social role and the inherent responses, the transition--often in only

a few hours from the known to the unknown; from the simple to the complex environment; from rural areas to the cosmopolitan city-- creates an even greater problem. It is the children who manifest the greatest degree of maladjustment.[2]

When the culture process is interrupted or suddenly changed, learning seems to cease. The new setting often destroys the foundations of security. It is, therefore, little wonder that the child who is an emigrant has not completely learned the culture of the land of origin before he is thrust into the new world with a brand-new set of learning conditions to deal with. He is also usually the child of a family that is socially and economically disadvantaged and is therefore heir to all the insecurity, fears, and instabilities of our society to a larger degree than others. Both he and the adults in his family pursue a day-to-day existence with the attendant problems of inadequate housing, clothing, and nourishment. His parents too are caught in the crosscurrents of adjustment: to find jobs though they may be unskilled; to find housing at a cost they can afford when there is little available; to hold onto their own culture in a setting which neither understands nor is able to accept this.

The Puerto Rican child is thus caught between the two cultures, that of his people and the one which he must meet every day in the school. Sometimes he must respond to one that contradicts his own. The little girl who has been compliant is now expected to be active and responsive, to take the initiative, to face new people and situations on her own. In the schoolroom she is expected to talk and play with boys and to socialize more freely with her peers. There are rewards in our culture for this, but when she goes home she is forbidden to go out on the street to play. At home there is no reward for enterprising deeds, but rather the awaited and expected punishment. The emigrant child's age and sex roles and his developmental tasks are not the same as ours. If he adjusts to one, he negates the other, and as a result may lose his sense of identity with his family. The rewards we offer for these "disloyalties" are perhaps not as satisfying, nor can they be easily integrated into the patterns of the home and the other culture. We do in fact, tend to create "culture conflict"--the battle of the supremacy of cultures in the family and the clash of roles between parents and children.[3]

Parents play the primary role in transmitting culture to the child. This is part of the socialization process. The child identifies with the parent and internalizes the learnings. In the new environment the parent is no longer in tune with the prevalent culture. He cannot command his child's involvement, since the new society does not value his contribution to the socialization of his own child. The dichotomies and dualisms we create tend to whip the dog we taught to eat.

I

Such a situation is evident in the story of Ana, the sixth of eight children in a family. She was eight years old when she came to the mainland. Ana's mother is the strong and managing figure in the family--a traditional Puerto Rican mother who holds her

daughters in rigid control. They are not allowed out on the street;
they must not talk to other people, particularly boys. Even the
older girls are kept in this strict regimen. Ana could perhaps
have developed some ease in interchange, but the mother's restrictions were so forceful that the girl's only recourse was to deny all
contact. As a result, no one was able to reach out to Ana. She
went on to junior high school, where she is barely passing. In addition, she has developed even more reticence and isolates herself.
She has frequent headaches and stomach upsets, and is absent from
school very often.

This is a rather extreme example of the frequently found
conflict in social roles particularly in reference to the upbringing
of girls. Since the neighborhoods in which these families settle are
often socially disorganized, there is a kind of justification for the
fears of the parents which further constricts the life of the girls
and the younger children. It is important in working with Puerto
Rican parents to help them find ways to protect their children without completely depriving them of social interchange. However, the
traditions are so firmly imbedded in the structure of their living
that this is difficult to achieve. It is equally difficult to help growing children find the channel between outright rebellion and complete
submission, hence they live in an atmosphere of conflict and inde-
cision. It is at this point that they either compliantly submit and
lose the ability to relate to their own peer group, or completely
leave their families and join the peer group, thereby losing the support which they still need so much.

The language disability which pervades all these problems is
very real. It is also a measure of the emotional stability of the
person at this time of pressure. The differential rates of language
learning are not only the result of age differentials and intelligence
levels (the younger child learning more rapidly than the older and
the brighter child learning faster than the duller) but also cues to
the general level of the individual's emotional adjustment and the
resolution of cultural identification and conflicts. Language is one
of the tools for learning which the emigrant child lacks. He is left
with only the cues he can obtain from nonverbal communication; the
expressive gestures which may convey some meaning for him.
Here too, however, a facial expression or a gesture may mean
something else to him, since gestures are also a language and are
richly colored by each culture with specific meanings. Meanwhile
he must manage without the necessary cues for directing his behavior.

As a result of these handicaps the child begins to feel inadequate. He cannot solve all the problems of adjustment to a new
land, new language, new living, and new culture. He cannot seek
support from his parents since they too are faced with the identical
problems and with the added responsibility of founding their families
in this new land. Therefore, if the child fails he suffers further
indignity. He may reason that it is better not to try. Then one
has not failed. Or better still, it is possible to remain so indifferent, uninvolved, and apathetic that one evades all responsibility for
functioning in a setting fraught with failure and with many demands
that one cannot meet.[4] This kind of "culture shock" is frequently

found in great or small degree in many of our children and families.

The school is brought face to face with all these problems. There may be some variation in the nature of these difficulties in different families or individuals, but the total problem is present in every child the school works with who has recently arrived from Puerto Rico. Neither the school nor the teacher has been trained to see behavior in the light of these causes. Rather, they tend to meet each situation separately either as a discipline question or as an education problem. Our training practices in education have dealt chiefly with the child who is native to our land and has no outstanding language problem. The child of the lower economic and social strata is also rarely dealt with in our academic courses. Most of our textbooks are written by middle-class professors for middle-class teachers of middle-class children. We tend to think of education as primarily establishing literacy and the ability to deal with the daily technics of middle-class living in urban centers.

Education, although drawn from many other disciplines, for a long time tended to ignore the findings in anthropology, social psychology, and clinical psychology. Or at least it has not found a way to integrate these findings into the educational and developmental sequence usually taught in the teacher-preparation courses. We tend to divide sharply our disciplines at the college level, thus making it more difficult to provide an interdisciplinary approach to problems that the school faces. It seems hardly necessary to point out that if we are to work with a large number of children from a given culture we must, at the very least, learn something of the specifics of that culture, and of how it pervades the entire personality and its perceptions in new situations. Learning how Puerto Rican children dance or play ball or count in Spanish will not make the teacher aware of how Puerto Rican children view their inadequacy in learning the fundamentals of arithmetic or how and why it is so difficult for them to retain the fact that three and four are seven or remember that our j does not sound like h. There needs to be rather the concept of "fundamental education to cover the whole of living; to teach not only new ways but the need and the incentive for new ways."[5]

How does it feel to be unable to comprehend the cues in this new setting? How does it feel not to understand what people are saying? How do anxiety and insecurity affect a child's readiness to learn? How do people acquire a new culture without stress and destruction to their sense of well-being? The findings and skills of anthropology, sociology, and social and clinical psychology will help us interpret this kind of defeat and better still to learn to look for these problems. They will perhaps also sharpen our focus and help us find the educational methods which are best employed for reaching these children who really so desperately want to achieve. The individual caught in the maelstrom of conflicting cultures and feelings can be helped to move from inadequacy and near panic (as in "culture shock") to independence and courage.

II

In our work we encounter many children who reflect these problems. Rafael, a boy of two, saw his father migrate to the states. His mother left when he was three. When he was four his younger sister was sent to the mainland to join the family. He and his grandmother lived in Puerto Rico until he was seven. All these years of separation seemed to have given him the feeling of being unwanted. When he arrived here his mother was again unavailable to him, since she worked long hours away from home. During his first two years in this country he made few friends, and seemed to his teacher unable to learn. Carmen, his younger sister, was much more competent than he, and carried on much of the interchange for him and other members of the family with the new and strange world. Rafael was frequently sick and remained at home with his old grandmother to care for him. In the third year of his stay he seemed able to come to terms with his new country--to emerge from his chrysalis. Now he is lively and takes an interest in what goes on around him. He greets adults and children alike with warmth and friendliness, and his work at school has begun to show the real potential that he possesses.

Elsa is another child who experienced the privation of her mother's departure. When Elsa was two, her mother left for the United States, leaving her children to the care of their maternal grandmother. At three Elsa was brought to the mainland, but since her mother was working the children were left in the care of a woman living in the same apartment house. Elsa's initial adjustment to school was so poor that when she was in the second grade the school notified the mother that something had to be done. The child was hyperactive, inattentive, and created too much distraction in the classroom. The mother sent Elsa back to Puerto Rico to live with an aunt for a year. When Elsa returned, her adjustment to school, and her learning achievement were no better. At this time Elsa is being referred to a child guidance clinic.

These are only two cases among the many which we encounter in the schools. The pattern of emigration here depicted is usual in the Puerto Rican family. Early deprivation of the mother creates social and emotional problems which are very difficult to overcome, even with care and concern by the school and other agencies.

Many Puerto Rican children arrive after a period of separation from their mothers or both parents. Thus the emotional concomitants are disabling before the schools in this country even begin to work with the children. Exploration of conditions in each of the new families might alert the schools to the problems and perhaps gear the school situation to help these children. The syndrome of this difficulty has already been fully described by such writers in this field as John Bowlby and Lauretta Bender. It includes a range of behavior: apathy, lack of social responsiveness, depressed intellectual functioning (discussed by William Goldfarb), inability to form meaningful relationships, hyperactivity, aggression, and lowered intellectual potential.

III

The Alvarez family presents a different picture, yet it also
has within it all the problems of adjustment to a new environment.
There were four children in this family, who lived originally in a
rural community on the island.   The father worked in the sugar
cane fields; they had a small house, a cow, and chickens.   Miguel,
the father, migrated to the United States eight years ago.   Two
years later, Rosa, the mother, leaving the children on the island,
came to set up the new home.   After a few months of separation
all the children were brought to the mainland.

The father had no skills, but he found employment as a dish-
washer and has remained in that work.   He is always employed but
does not earn enough to care fully for his growing family.   Two
children were born here and the entire family lives in a partly
furnished apartment (they have never been able to save enough to
buy the requisite furniture).   The Department of Public Welfare
helps to subsidize the family, but even with this help the budget is
too small to provide adequate bed linen, blankets, and warm winter
clothing.   All the children are slender and the school records indicate poor nutrition for all the school-age children.

Frequently the members of the family are prey to the upper
respiratory illnesses so common to Puerto Rican families.   Maria,
the thirteen-year-old daughter, must then remain at home to help
care for the mother and children.   She had so many absences from
school that the teachers complained they could not really help her.

Maria is a tall, stoop-shouldered girl with large dark eyes,
pale olive skin, and a slow, hesitant manner.   She attended an
after-school club program for three years but always remained on
the outskirts of the group, although nearly all the club members
are of Puerto Rican background.   She uttered hardly a word.   When
she was ten Maria had the first of a series of minor epileptic attacks and is now attending the Seizure Clinic regularly.   (This is
another common ailment among newly emigrant families, who refer
to this illness as "attaques."   It may be another manifestation of
the somatic effects of the stress in adjustment.)

Maria has repeated the sixth grade and even now has
achieved a reading level of only third grade.   Her ability in mathematics is even lower than her reading level.   This girl saw herself
as completely inadequate in every aspect of her living.   She never
undertook anything for fear of failure.   It was only after a year of
intensive work with Maria and her family, using nearly every resource in the community, that Maria gained any sense of competence.

There were many health problems in the family for which
nursing, nutritional guidance, and hospital care had to be obtained.
Fortunately, though the mother speaks no English and is completely
illiterate, she is deeply concerned for her children, has much
warmth and affection to give, and is eager to help her family adjust
to the new environment.   She is able to overcome the traditional
patterns and encourages Irma to participate in clubs and activities.

The problem of family finances was partially solved by additional funds allotted for special diets for several of the children.

The family was encouraged to make application for public housing. The social service resources were made available for Maria by the Catholic Big Sisters, and Maria is now assured of a permanent relationship to meet her emotional needs.

A special program was set up to give Maria opportunities for relationships with children in the group club program, and a special worker was assigned to act in a supportive role for the child as she began to make the transition to active participation. A remedial program in reading was also arranged. From the start it was felt that Maria had much more potential than her low IQ indicated. She seemed quite creative with art materials. As all this enrichment was made available she began to awake from her long passive role and to look out and see people. She clamored for help in her school work; she wanted to achieve. She began to take a more active role with her peers. Even her slow, hesitant manner and walk changed. She ran now and jumped; she had a close friend; and she had abandoned her role on the periphery of the group.

Although there are still many problems in the Alvarez family and Maria has a long way to go, we have already some sense of the potential of the child and the possibility that she can move more rapidly now toward the achievement of a large part of that potential. She will probably never achieve all that is possible for her. But having studied Maria we can continue with the other children and help each one of them. They are younger and there may be a better chance to bring to fruition more of their potential. Perhaps the second generation of this family will achieve greater self-actualization.

The school has to meet the needs of many children. Now it is the Puerto Rican child, as it was once the Irish, the Italian, the Jewish groups in other tides of emigration. In each child there will be problems which stand in the way of learning. It is only as the school and the community come to know the family and its needs that these newcomers can be helped in their development. It will be through the school, together with many other agencies and with a view to the totality of the child and his family, that the acculturation will come about.

Notes

The cases described above are derived from the operation of a training program for undergraduates in Education at the City College of New York. Students serve as leaders for groups of children in a community group work program. The names of all cases described here are fictitious.

1. Margaret Mead, Cultural Patterns and Technological Change. New York: Mentor Books, 1955.

2. Ibid., p. 281.

3. Ibid., p. 254.

4. A. Anastasi and F. A. Cordova. "Some Effects of Bilingual-

ism upon the Intelligence Test Performance of Puerto Rican Children in New York City." Journal of Ecucational Psychology, 44:1-19. [1953]

5. Margaret Mead, op. cit., p. 253.

Francesco Cordasco. "The Puerto Rican Child in the American
School." Journal of Negro Education, 36:181-186. Spring,
1967. Reprinted by permission.

The Migration

In 1960 some 900,000 Puerto Ricans lived in the United
States, including not only those born on the island but also those
born to Puerto Rican parents in the states. Until 1940, the Puerto
Rican community in the United States numbered only 70,000, but by
1950 this had risen to 226,000, and over the decade to 1960 the net
gain due to migration from the island amounted to nearly 390,000.
The census of 1950 began the recording of second generation Puerto
Ricans (those born on the continent to island born parents) and
counted 75,000; in 1960, the figure stood at 272,000, so that by
1960 three out of every ten Puerto Rican residents in the United
States were born in the states.

Although there has been a dispersal of the migration outside
greater New York City, the overwhelming number of Puerto Ricans
are New Yorkers; the 1960 census showed 612,574 living in New
York City (68.6 per cent of the United States total). New York
City's proportion had dropped from 88 per cent in 1940 to 83 per
cent in 1950 and to 69 per cent in 1960.[1] If there is no serious
setback in the American economy the dispersion will undoubtedly
continue.[2]

The Commonwealth of Puerto Rico neither encourages nor
discourages migration. As an American citizen, the Puerto Rican
moves between the island and the mainland with complete freedom.
If his movement is vulnerable to anything, it fluctuates only with
reference to the economy on the mainland. Any economic recession
or contraction graphically shows in the migration statistics.[3] It is
at best invidious to suggest that "The Puerto Rican migration to
Nueva York, unchecked by immigrant quotas, is a major source of
the island's prosperity," but there is truth in the appended observation that the migration "...upgraded the migrants, converted them
from rural to urban people, relieved the island of some of its labor
surplus, and sent lots of cash back home."[4]

For the American schools, the Puerto Rican migration presented a distinct and yet in many ways a recurrent phenomenon.
With the imposition of immigration quotas in the early 1920's, the
non-English speaking student had gradually disappeared. The great
European migration and its manifold educational problems had in a
manner been resolved. With the increasing Puerto Rican migration
and the recurrent pattern of the ghettoization of the new arrivals,
the migrant child, non-English speaking and nurtured by a different
culture, presented American schools with a new yet very old challenge.[5]

Puerto Ricans and Mainland Schools

The Puerto Rican "journey" to the mainland has been (and continues to be) the subject of a vast literature.[6] For the most part, the Puerto Rican child reflects a context of bitter deprivation, poor housing, high unemployment, and a record of disappointing educational achievement. It is the poverty context to which the Puerto Rican community has been relegated in our cities that explains its problems and graphically underscores its poor achievement in the schools. Not only is the Puerto Rican child asked to adapt to a "cultural ambience" which is strange and new, he remains further burdened by all the negative pressures of a ghetto milieu which educators have discerned as inimical to even the most rudimentary educational accomplishment.[7]

How the Puerto Rican child has fared in the mainland schools is best illustrated in the experience in New York City, where Puerto Ricans have the lowest level of formal education of any identifiable ethnic or color group. Only 13 per cent of Puerto Rican men and women 25 years of age and older in 1960 had completed either high school or more advanced education. Among New York's nonwhite (predominately Negro) population, 31.2 per cent had completed high school; and the other white population (excluding Puerto Ricans) did even better. Over 40 per cent had at least completed high school.[8]

In 1960 more than half (52.9 per cent) of Puerto Ricans in New York City 25 years of age and older had less than an eighth grade education. In contrast, 29.5 per cent of the nonwhite population had not finished the eighth grade, and only 19.3 per cent of the other whites had so low an academic preparation.[9]

If the schools in New York City were to correct all of this (the numbers in the second generation who have reached adult years is still small, only 6.4 per cent of persons 20 years of age and older in 1960), there is still evidence that Puerto Rican youth, more than any other group, is severely handicapped in achieving an education in the New York City public schools. A 1961 study of a Manhattan neighborhood showed that fewer than 10 per cent of Puerto Ricans in the 3rd grade were reading at their grade level or above. The degree of retardation was extreme. Three in ten were retarded one and one-half years or more and were, in the middle of their third school year, therefore, reading at a level only appropriate for entry into the second grade. By the eighth grade the degree of retardation was even more severe with almost two-thirds of the Puerto Rican youngsters retarded more than three years.[10]

Of the nearly 21,000 academic diplomas granted in 1963, only 331 went to Puerto Ricans and 762 to Negroes, representing only 1.6 per cent and 3.7 per cent, respectively, of the total academic diplomas. In contrast, Puerto Ricans received 7.4 per cent of the vocational school diplomas, and Negroes, 15.2 per cent. For the Puerto Rican community, these figures have critical significance since Puerto Rican children constituted in 1963 about 20 per cent of the public elementary school register, 18 per cent of the junior high school register. In keeping with long discerned trends, Puerto Rican youngsters made up 23 per cent of the student body in vocation-

al schools and 29 per cent of that in special (difficult) schools.[11]
    Clearly, the critical issue for the Puerto Rican community
is the education of its children, for the experience in New York
City is a macrocosm which illustrates all the facets of the mainland
experience.[12]

Educational Programs to Meet the
Needs of Puerto Rican Children

    In the last decade a wide range of articles have reported
special educational programs to meet the needs of Puerto Rican
children;[13] although many of these have been of value, the more
ambitious theoretic constructs have largely come from the school
boards and staffs which have had to deal with the basic problem of
communication in classes where a growing (and at times preponder-
ant) number of Spanish-speaking children were found. As early as
1951 in New York City, a "Mayor's Advisory Committee on Puerto
Rican Affairs" turned its attention to this major problem of communication;[14] and this problem was periodically re-examined during the years which followed.[15]
    In New York City (as in other cities)[16] the Board of Educa-
tion turned its attention to the Puerto Rican child because communication had to be established, and (in this context) the most ambitious study of the educational problems presented by the Puerto Rican
migration became (for New York City) "...a four-year inquiry into the education and adjustment of Puerto Rican pupils in the public
schools of New York City...a major effort...to establish on a
sound basis a city-wide program for the continuing improvement of
the educational opportunities of all non-English speaking pupils in
the public schools."[17]
    If the major emphasis of The Puerto Rican Study was to have
been the basic problem of language (English), its objectives were
soon extended to include the equally important areas of community
orientation and acculturation. The Study's objectives were summed
up in three main problems: (1) What are the more effective ways
(methods) and materials for teaching English as a second language
to newly arrived Puerto Rican pupils? (2) What are the most effective techniques with which the schools can promote a more rapid
and more effective adjustment of Puerto Rican parents and children
to the community and the community to them? (3) Who are the
Puerto Rican pupils in the New York City public schools?[18] For
each of these problems, The Puerto Rican Study made detailed
recommendations (Problem III, largely an ethnic survey, resulted
in a profile of characteristics of pupils of Puerto Rican background
and fused into Problems I and II).[19]
    Problem I: How to teach English effectively as a second lan-
guage. The Puerto Rican Study concluded that an integrated method
(vocabulary method, structured or language patterns method, and
the functional situations or experiential method) was to be employed,
and it developed two series of related curriculum bulletins, keyed to
the prescribed New York City course of study.[20] But in the course
of its considerations, it dealt with the ancillary (and vital) need
"...to formulate a uniform policy for the reception, screening,

placement and periodic assessment of non-English speaking pupils."[21] It recommended (until such time as the Bureau of Educational Research may find or develop better tests or tests of equal value) the use of The USB Test--Ability to Understand Spoken English; The Gates Reading Test--Primary and Advanced; and The Lorge-Thorndike Non-Verbal Test. It proposed, too, three broad categories of class organization, considered the need of adequate staffing (Substitute Auxiliary Teachers [SAT], Puerto Rican Coordinators, School-Community Coordinators and Other Teaching Positions [OTP], and guidance counselors, particularly in the senior high schools), and found essential the "...coordinating [of] efforts of colleges and universities ...to achieve greater unity of purpose and effort in developing both undergraduate and graduate programs for teachers who will work with non-English speaking pupils..."[22]

Problem II: How to promote a more rapid and more effective adjustment of Puerto Rican parents and children to the community and the community to them. In its recognition of this problem, The Puerto Rican Study struggled with providing answers to the basic anxieties and preoccupations of a group of people beset with problems of housing, adequate employment, health, and "assimilation." That the Study found difficulty in providing answers is perhaps explained by its inability to relate the answers it found most effective to the mandate of the school. If it was possible to revise curricula and discern the problems implicit in the learning experience of the Puerto Rican child, it remained an altogether different matter to attempt the solution of broad socio-economic problems, or to attempt the amelioration of community ills. In essence, the following statement suggests how far the schools have retreated from the community:

> On the relation of Puerto Rican parents to schools, The Puerto Rican Study holds that because Puerto Rican parents are preoccupied with problems of learning English, finding apartments, finding employment, and with problems of providing their families with food, clothing, and proper health protection, they are not ready to set a high priority on their children's school problems. The schools can't wait until they are ready.[23]

If The Puerto Rican Study is not thought of as a finished guide to the solution of the problems it investigates but rather as a beginning, it must be characterized as the best assessment of the educational challenges which the Spanish-speaking child poses to the American school. In this sense, it is both a guide and a blueprint for effective reform.

A Postscript

Basically, the Puerto Rican child is not a newcomer to the American school. In many ways he presents himself to a school and a society whose very nature is heterogeneous and variegated and to which the non-English speaking child is no stranger. In this sense, the acquisition of English for the Puerto Rican child (if necessary and inevitable) is not a great problem; certainly, it is a soluble problem to which the American school brings a rich and successful experience and The Puerto Rican Study affirms how successful and resourceful American schools can and have been. What is more important to the Puerto Rican child (and to American society) is the process of acculturation. How does the Puerto Rican child retain his identity, his language, his culture? In substance this remains the crucial problem, and in this crucial context, the role of the school in American society needs to be carefully assessed. If the Puerto Rican child is sinned against today, the tragedy lies in the continued assault against his identity, his language, and his cultural wellsprings. In this sense, his experience is not fundamentally different from that of millions of other children to whom the American school was a mixed blessing. This is in no way a deprecation of the egalitarianism of the American "common school," but rather a reaffirmation of the loss of the great opportunity that a free society afforded its schools to nurture and treasure the rich and varied traditions of its charges. The "melting pot" theory is at best an illusion measured against the realities of American society and a true discernment of its strengths.[24]

In another light, the Puerto Rican child is the creature of his social context, its opportunities or lack of opportunities. If his needs are to be met, they can only be effectively met insofar as the needs of this context are met. A school which is not community-oriented is a poor school. If this is so for the middle-class suburban school, it is even more so for the urban school which is the heir of the myriad complexities of a rapidly deteriorating central city. More important than the Puerto Rican child's lack of English, is the lack of that economic security and well-being that relate him to a viable family structure. If the Puerto Rican child's major disenchantment does not result from the segregated schools into which his poverty has placed him,[25] still one would have to deplore the school's inability to cope with the alienation that segregation spawns, and the bitter destitution that poverty brings to its children. Perhaps, the "great society" really emerges from a strengthening of the school by its joining hands with all the creative agencies of the community.

Notes

1. U.S. Bureau of the Census. U.S. Census of Population: 1960. Subject Reports. Puerto Ricans in The United States. Final Report, PC(2)-1 D. U.S. Government Printing Office, Washington, D.C. 1963.

2. The 1960 census reported Puerto Rican-born persons living in all but one (Duluth-Superior) of the 101 Standard Metropolitan Statistical Areas of over 250,000 population. Particular concentrations were reported (1960) as Chicago, 35,361; Paterson-Clifton-Passaic (N.J.), 6,641; Los Angeles-Long Beach, 7,214; San Francisco-Oakland, 4,068. For an illuminating study of Puerto Rican dispersal in New Jersey, see Max Wolff, Patterns of Change in the Cities of New Jersey: Minorities--Negroes and Puerto Ricans Affected by

and Affecting These Changes, N.Y. mimeo., 1962.

3. See in this connection migration figures for 1953-54. The best source on Puerto Rican Migration is the Migration Division of the Department of Labor, Commonwealth of Puerto Rico, which maintains a central mainland office in New York City and offices in other U.S. cities. It also maintains an office in Puerto Rico to carry out a program of orientation for persons who intend to migrate to the states.

4. Patricia Sexton, Spanish Harlem: Anatomy of Poverty. New York: Harper & Row, 1965,p. 15.

5. Although one of the greatest achievements of the American common school has been the acculturation and assimilation of the children of non-English speaking immigrants (largely European), it has received little study. See F. Cordasco and L. Covello, Educational Sociology: A Subject Index of Doctoral Dissertations Completed at American Universities, 1941-1963. Metuchen, N.J.: Scarecrow Press, 1965. Of over 2,000 dissertations listed, only a few clearly concern themselves with the non-English immigrant child, or generally with the educational problems of the children of immigrants.

6. One of the best accounts is Clarence Senior, The Puerto Ricans, Chicago: Quadrangle Books, 1965, which includes an extensive bibliography. See also Christopher Rand, The Puerto Ricans, New York: Oxford, 1958; Don Wakefield, Island in the City, Boston: Houghton-Mifflin, 1959; Elena Padilla, Up From Puerto Rico, New York: Columbia University Press, 1958; Jesus Colon, A Puerto Rican in New York And Other Sketches, New York: Mainstream Publications, 1961; an older but invaluable documented study of Puerto Ricans in New York City is that of C. Wright Mills, Clarence Senior, and Rose Kohn Goldsen, The Puerto Rican Journey, New York: Harper and Row, 1950.

7. For a graphic commentary on the debilitating environmental pressures and the "ghetto milieu" see David Barry, Our Christian Mission Among Spanish Americans, mimeo, Princeton University Consultation, February 21-23, 1965. The statistical indices of Puerto Rican poverty (and the related needs) are best assembled in The Puerto Rican Community Development Project, New York: The Puerto Rican Forum, 1964, p. 26-75.

8. See The Puerto Rican Community Development Project, p. 34.

9. Ibid., p. 34-35.

10. Ibid., p. 39. The study was undertaken by the Research Center, Columbia University School of Social Work.

11. Ibid., p. 41, and tables, p. 43-44.

12. The situation would not be significantly different in other cities
    where the Puerto Rican community is encapsulated in poverty,
    e.g., Camden (N.J.), Philadelphia, Chicago. A different
    dimension would be added in the educational problems pre-
    sented in those areas where Puerto Rican migrant workers,
    contracted for agricultural labor, live for varying periods of
    time. The best source of information on the Puerto Rican
    agricultural migrant worker is The Migration Division, Com-
    monwealth of Puerto Rico. See footnote no. 3, supra. The
    N.J. Office of Economic Opportunity completed a study of
    the needs of migrant workers in that state in terms of its
    projected programs.

13. Typical is Jack Cohn, "Integration of Spanish Speaking New-
    comers in a 'Fringe Area' School," National Elementary
    Principal (May 1960) p. 29-33. See also F. Cordasco,
    "Helping the Language Barrier Student," The Instructor,
    XLXXII (May 1963), 20; S. E. Elam, "Acculturation and
    Learning Problems of Puerto Rican Children," Teachers
    College Record, LXI (1960), 258-264; James Olsen, "Chil-
    dren of the Ghetto," High Points, XLVI (1964), 25-33;
    John A. Burma, "Spanish Speaking Children," in Eli Ginz-
    berg, The Nation's Children, III (1960), 78-102.

14. "Puerto Rican Pupils in the New York City Schools, 1951."
    The Mayor's Advisory Committee on Puerto Rican Affairs.
    Sub-Committee on Education, Recreation and Parks. This
    was a survey of 75 elementary and junior high schools as
    well as a report on day classes for adults, evening schools,
    community centers and vacation playgrounds. The report
    was directed by Dr. Leonard Covello, principal of Benjamin
    Franklin High School in East Harlem. See in this connec-
    tion, Covello's The Heart Is the Teacher, New York: Mc-
    Graw Hill, 1958, passim.

15. See Martin B. Dworkis (ed.), The Impact of Puerto Rican Mi-
    gration on Governmental Services in New York City, New
    York: New York University Press, 1957.

16. Particularly Philadelphia, Chicago, Newark, and Camden (N.J.).

17. J. Cayce Morrison, Director, The Puerto Rican Study (1953-
    1957); A Report on the Education and Adjustment of Puerto
    Rican Pupils in the Public Schools of the City of New York,
    New York: Board of Education, 1958, p. 1.

18. Ibid. See New York City Board of Education, Summary of
    Recommendations Made by the Puerto Rican Study For the
    Program in the New York City Schools, December 8, 1958.

19. The profile was separately published in 1956, and reprinted in

the final report (1958).

20. A series of nine Resource Units and four Language Guides.
    Each Resource Unit bulletin contains three or more resource
    units. See Puerto Rican Study (Publications of the Puerto
    Rican Study) for list.

21. See Summary, supra, p. 3.

22. Ibid., p. 5.

23. Ibid., p. 7.

24. See Milton M. Gordon, Assimilation in American Life: The
    Role of Race, Religion and National Origins, New York:
    Oxford University Press, 1964; and review, F. Cordasco,
    Journal of Human Relations, XIII (Winter 1965), 142-143.

25. See Joseph Monserrat, "School Integration: A Puerto Rican
    view." Conference on Integration in New York City Public
    Schools. Teachers College, Columbia University, May 1,
    1963.

Elsie Wolk, "The Teaching of English as a Second Language in the Schools of New York City." Hispania, 49:293-296, May 1966. Reprinted by permission.

Many are startled to learn that we have over 67,000 pupils in the public elementary schools of New York City who are in the process of learning English as a second language. What may be even more of a surprise is that most of these children were born in New York City but enter our schools with little or no facility in the English language. An added complexity in our situation is the diverse national background of the language learner. An informal survey conducted in 155 out of the approximately 600 elementary schools indicated that there were 5,089 such language learners representing 74 locales in the world other than Puerto Rico and speaking 32 distinct languages. The overwhelming majority, however, were from Spanish-speaking countries.

Certain assumptions underlie the basis for our program. These are that:

The elementary school child will learn English better if he is placed in a class where the majority of the children are English-speaking. This arrangement builds into the language learner's day a natural and forceful motivation for speaking English as well as many native models of English speech to which he may listen and respond.

The language learner's classmates should be English-speaking children of average and above average academic ability in order to give him a verbally stimulating environment and classmates whose attitudes toward learning are positive.

The language learner will adjust better if he is placed as closely as possible and desirable with his age peers, regardless of his previous schooling.

English will be learned best if taught by a native speaker of the language.

The classroom teacher needs special assistance in acquiring the skills of teaching English as a second language as well as additional instructional aids.

Teachers who have an understanding and appreciation of the cultural heritage of their language learners are more apt to relate better to their pupils and thus establish a better climate for the teacher-learning process. Children

360

who are learning English as a second language should
not be referred to as "culturally deprived" regardless
of the economic status of their parents. The term "culturally diverse" appears to be more accurate.

The Teachers

To assist us we have 322 non-classroom teachers who function in three categories. One group, numbering 166, are known as
non-English Coordinators. These teachers are regularly appointed,
experienced classroom teachers who are taken out of the classroom
and are given the major responsibility for coordinating the instructional program for the language learner.

A second group, numbering 142, are known as Auxiliary
Teachers. These teachers hold a special Auxiliary Teacher license.
They have the same salary schedule as the classroom teacher and
non-English Coordinator and are regular members of the staff. The
Auxiliary Teacher is bilingual in Spanish and English and serves in
a liaison capacity between the school and the Spanish-speaking child,
parent and community.

Our third group of teachers are known as Operation Understanding Teachers. We have an interchange program with Puerto
Rico. Fourteen New York City elementary school teachers spend a
year in Puerto Rico serving as resource people in several elementary schools of Puerto Rico. In addition to interpreting mainland
culture to the Puerto Rican children and community, they assist in
the English language program there. The fourteen Puerto Rican
teachers who serve in the New York City schools are additional resource people. They acquaint our children with the history and culture of Puerto Rico. They teach Spanish to all first grade children
in the schools to which they are assigned and conduct after-school
clubs in Spanish on four days of the week.

What happens in the classroom is of paramount importance.
In addition to possessing the personal attributes of warmth, friendliness, kindness, empathy for the language learner and an abiding
understanding of his needs in a bewildering environment, the classroom teacher has to make specific adjustments in the organization
of his teaching program. For thirty minutes each day, the classroom teacher gathers the language learners into a small group and
gives these children what we in New York City call a "language emphasis" lesson. During this period, the teacher gives specific, systematic instruction in the English language, using appropriate techniques for the teaching of the English language as a second language.

The methods and materials we use are those initially developed by the Puerto Rican Study. The Puerto Rican Study was a
four-year research project directed by Dr. J. Cayce Morrison of
the New York State Department of Education under a grant-in-aid
from the Fund for the Advancement of Education and the New York
City Board of Education.

A key feature of our program is that the English content to
be taught and practiced during the thirty-minute language emphasis
lesson is drawn from an ongoing curriculum area. It also means
that the language learners' group may be assembled in a different

part of the room. The group may meet, for example, around the
science table, or in the rear of the classroom where some maps,
and a globe or other realia are easily available or near the housekeeping corner if the grade is a primary one. The important factors
are that the language learners meet with the teacher in a small
group and that the lesson is conducted in a setting which is more
informal and which brings teacher and pupil closer together for the
essential practice.

Each classroom teacher is provided with two types of printed
materials. One is a Resource Unit related to the curriculum of the
grade. The Resource Unit is divided into a series of themes based
upon the social studies program for the grade.

The other type of printed material is the Language Guide.
This bulletin includes, inter alia, several chapters describing methods of teaching English as a second language, a section contrasting
word order and sentence structure in English and Spanish, and a
listing of specific sound, rhythm, and intonation problems in English for the speaker of Spanish. The major part of the Language
Guide is devoted to descriptions of the experiential settings growing
out of the basic experiences referred to in the Resource Units and
to listing the suggested vocabulary and language patterns to be taught
in connection with these experiences.

The Language Lesson

The language emphasis lesson itself has certain distinguishing characteristics. For one thing, it includes a few minutes of
what we call "free conversation." The teacher motivates the conversation by referring to the basic experience in which the whole
class had been involved. During this time the language learners
will talk informally about the activity. No attempt is made to control the vocabulary or the structural patterns the children use to
express themselves. In fact, if the child hesitates, the teacher will
quickly supply the needed word or phrase or make an unobtrusive,
quick, casual correction.

Other features of the thirty-minute language emphasis lesson
include the direct teaching of specific vocabulary and structural patterns. The teacher will always present a model before each choral
and individual response. Teachers are asked to avoid exaggerations
of pronunciation, tempo, rhythm and stress and are encouraged to
use a natural style of speech. There will be numerous repetitions
of the language items being taught. Each lesson will include review
of previously learned material and a variety of meaningful drills.
Attention is given to the correction of sounds, rhythm, intonation
and stress. Through drill, pupils are given practice in audio discrimination and oral production of vowel sounds, natural rhythm,
intonation and accurate stress.

Throughout the lesson there is maximum opportunity for the
children to practice orally. To avoid tension which might develop
from the concentrated practice, the teacher will include some type
of oral exercise for relaxation. This might take the form of a
game, a song, a song play, the recitation of a favorite poem or
the review of familiar items such as a previously learned dialogue.

An effort is made to provide for a functional application of newly
learned items through a game, a dramatization, a dialogue or the
preparation of a summary of what was learned in the form of an
oral "report" to be given to the rest of the class. The latter technique is used as a means of unifying the class and of building the
native speakers' respect and admiration for the language learners'
special task and accomplishment.

Public Information and Teacher Training

For our Spanish-speaking community we conduct a weekly
radio program in Spanish on Station WADO entitled "Julio and Ana
Garcia Discuss the Education of Your Child." Two Auxiliary Teachers impersonating Mr. and Mrs. Garcia engage in an informal conversation during which they discuss an educational problem of interest to parents. These topics may relate to such matters as attendance regulations in our schools, cultural opportunities available
to pupils and parents, summer camping programs, recreational facilities in the city, specialized schools, the teaching of reading or
other subjects and so on. The content of the radio program is
based upon questions parents have frequently asked or procedures
needing clarifications as indicated by principals or other school personnel. In addition, the local radio and television stations have
conducted pertinent, general descriptive programs in English of interest to the community at large.
Our teacher training projects include the production of a
sound color film entitled Bienvenidos which gives an overall description of the program for the non-English-speaking child and the organization of several types of in-service courses for teachers.
Each semester we offer courses in methods and materials for
teaching English as a second language. The use of television, in
addition to making it possible to reach a larger number of teachers,
has been an effective means of demonstrating specific techniques as
well as of conducting interviews with experts in the field. The
telecasts, thirty minutes in length, are then used as a basis for
discussion at the workshop centers set up throughout the city and
conducted by the non-English coordinators.

The Ultimate Goal

New York City has for years been a port of entry for the
millions who for a multitude of reasons have come to our shores.
In generations past, thousands upon thousand of children have had
to learn English as a second language and to adjust to the American way of life. Throughout, their teachers, using whatever methods were known to them or, in some cases, just following procedures that seemed instinctively right to them, contributed to this
enormous process of welding the diverse language and cultural
groups into one. Community agencies and civic groups played their
part. Even today, in our schools, we are enriched by the voluntary service of the Public Education Association School Volunteers
group who come into several of the schools on a regular schedule
and work on a one-to-one basis with some of the language learners.

The fact that New York City, despite its polylingual population, is an English-speaking city is its own tribute to the success of all who have shared in the process.

What we are trying to do is to improve our techniques with one great difference. Whereas previously those who learned English as a second language tended to discard their first language and to diminish their understanding and appreciation of their own culture, today we recognize that the teaching of English as a second language includes the responsibility for inculcating the love and regard for the other languages and cultures of the world. This is truly an exacting challenge but one which may not be by-passed. Such a deep broad human goal will shatter the silences imposed by a commitment to monolingualism, will open the channels of communication and will bring us closer together in the world community of man.

Emilio L. Guerra, "The Orientation of Puerto Rican Students in
    New York City." Modern Language Journal, October 1949,
    pp. 415-420. Reprinted by permission.

The past year has witnessed a considerable influx of Puerto
Ricans into the city of New York, which was made possible by the
easing of wartime travel restrictions. Perhaps the chief reason
for this modern hegira has been the upsetting of the Island's economic balance by the pressure of growing population. Puerto Rico
has an area of 3,423 square miles and a population of 1,869,255
persons. Of these, 1,302,898 are living in rural areas.[1]
    Although the Jones Act of 1917 made Puerto Ricans citizens of
the United States, the Puerto Rican migrant who arrives in New
York City is faced with problems very similar to those that were
encountered by our foreign immigrant forbears when they arrived
in New York harbor.
    If he should arrive during the winter months, our Puerto Ri-
can fellow American will undoubtedly be greeted by a chill wind
that he never experienced in the benevolent tropical climate of his
enchanted isle. He will also find himself compelled to express himself in a language which is not his normal vehicle of communication because, although Spanish customs have been modified considerably, Puerto Rico is still more Spanish than American. A rich
culture of over four hundred years simply cannot be erased in thirty
years through a legislative enactment.
    The Puerto Rican migrant generally has lived all his life in
a rural area with a slower tempo of life and a friendly atmosphere.
Upon his arrival in New York he is suddenly thrust into a highly
industrialized community where competition is the byword. His
lack of adequate previous vocational training for work in this type
of community makes it difficult for him to meet this competition.
In addition, he is forced to live in crowded quarters where housing
conditions are inadequate and where an intolerant attitude is often
displayed by other, non-Puerto Rican residents.
    Another obstacle for the Puerto Rican migrant to overcome
is his lack of adequate previous educational preparation. According
to Rodriguez Bou,[2] during the academic year 1944-1945, 46.69 per
cent of the children of school age in Puerto Rico were not in school.
That is, out of two hundred children of school age, approximately
one hundred were not in school. Of the hundred children who entered school, fifty-two per cent left school from the first to the
third grade. Thus, of each hundred children, fifty-two had about
a year and a half or less of instruction.[3]
    Rodriguez Bou[4] states that, although illiteracy has been di-
minishing in Puerto Rico since 1890, it can well increase from now
on because of the great number of pupils who are not in school

each year. At present there are more than half a million illiterates over five years of age. Of each hundred persons ten years of age and older, sixty-four can be classified as natural or functional illiterates (having less than a fourth grade education).

The legal school age in Puerto Rico is five to eighteen years of age. The compulsory age is from eight to fourteen years. Rodriguez Bou[5] estimates that fifty-one per cent of the pupils in urban zones and fifty-nine per cent of the pupils in rural zones are over the normal age for the grade in Puerto Rico. The loss in expenditure of effort and money involved in the high percentage of school failure could be avoided, according to Rodriguez Bou, by providing better school buildings, better equipment, better and more textbooks and better prepared teachers. Fifty per cent of teachers now teaching in the schools of Puerto Rico have an academic and professional preparation inferior to that of a normal school diploma.[6] Also, some towns with twice the number of pupils of other towns have fewer teachers assigned to their schools.

For some time the educational authorities of the city of New York have been aware of the necessity of making adequate provision to meet the needs of our fellow Americans, the Puerto Ricans, so that their adjustment to their new milieu may be as rapid as their natural capabilities warrant. Accordingly, a committee of assistant superintendents was appointed to conduct a survey of conditions and to make the necessary recommendations for the implementation of a program that would meet the needs of our Puerto Rican pupils.

According to the findings of the Committee,[7] in June, 1947, there were 13,914 pupils enrolled in the public elementary and junior high schools of the city who originally came from Puerto Rico. After making a careful study of conditions, the Committee stated in its report:

> There is no doubt but that many pupils coming from Puerto Rico suffer from the double handicap of unfamiliarity with the English language and lack of previous educational experience, sometimes approaching complete illiteracy. Malnutrition and other health deficiencies contribute to the educational problem of the schools. The overcrowding at home and the restlessness on the street carry over into the school in the form of nervousness, extreme shyness, near tantrums, and other behavior characteristics which are the more difficult for the teacher to understand because of the language barrier.

> The essential thing to remember, however, is that these boys and girls have the same capacity to learn, the same rights to education, the same desire for security, and the same basic loyalties to our country as any other citizens of the United States. They present a challenge to our schools to see that full educational opportunity is given them to understand and share these rights, and privileges."[8]

As a result of its study, the Committee of the Association of Assistant Superintendents made the following recommendations:[9]

(1) Special classes ("C") should be allowed to schools in the ratio of a teacher for each fifteen pupils newly admitted from Puerto Rico.

(2) A special differential in class size should be provided in schools enrolling Puerto Rican pupils, in proportion to their numbers on register.   Class registers in schools with a large representation of these pupils should not exceed 25.

(3) A special differential in textbook and supply allotments should be made to schools enrolling Puerto Rican pupils, in proportion to their numbers on register.

(4) Under the direction of the Division of Curriculum Research of the Bureau of Reference, Research and Statistics, a study should be made of existing curriculum materials and methodology, and new courses of study and teaching materials be devised, appropriate for the instruction of Puerto Rican pupils on the various school levels.

(5) Under the direction of the Division of Tests and Measurements of the Bureau of Reference, Research and Statistics, a study should be made of present tests of academic achievement and mental ability, and new and appropriate instruments of measurement be developed for Puerto Rican pupils.

(6) Special medical services should be provided in schools having a large proportion of Puerto Rican pupils.

(7) Teachers who are expert interpreters of Spanish should be assigned during the period of registration to schools in the Puerto Rican neighborhoods to assist in the registration of new pupils.

(8) A study should be made to determine the adequacy of the present program of adult education for Puerto Ricans.

(9) Orientation courses for teachers in Puerto Rican culture and in conversational Spanish should be organized.

(10) Courses for teachers in methodology and instructional materials for teaching non-English speaking pupils should be organized and staffed by experts.

(11) Insular, federal, and city authorities should attempt to divert the flow of Puerto Rican emigrants from the overcrowded areas of New York into other sections of the city and elsewhere with some regard to housing accommodations and to occupational opportunities.

(12) Kindergarten opportunities should be provided for all four and five year old children in schools located in Puerto Rican communities.

(13) A community relations teacher should be assigned to districts where there are large concentrations of Puerto Ricans.

In general, teachers in the elementary schools have found that younger children are more easily assimilated.   Primarily it is the language difficulty which differentiates the Puerto Rican pupil from his classmates.[10]

Wherever possible, the "buddy system," in which a Puerto Rican child who knows English accompanies the child who does not, is used.   Special provision has been made for pupils nine to twelve years of age.   These children are placed in homogeneous groups ("C" classes) and taught Basic English.   They are also given op-

portunities to associate with other pupils in many activities. When
ready, they are transferred out of "C" classes to regular grades.
Special abilities are recognized in the arts and crafts program,
and medical and dental attention is provided.

Lectures are given to teachers on the Puerto Rican background so as to render them sympathetic toward Puerto Rican children. Excursions to places of interest are planned for the children.

In the junior high schools, teachers play phonograph records,
plan exhibits and teach units in social studies to bring about a sympathetic understand of Puerto Rican culture on the part of non-Puerto Rican pupils.

Puerto Rican pupils are placed in regular classes with other
pupils but are segregated in groups of twenty-five for two consecutive periods each day for intensive study of English. Each English
teacher has three groups of pupils graded according to their knowledge of the English language.

Spanish-speaking teachers explain the school program to pupils and their parents. Simple instruction dealing with the geography and history of New York City is given, and pupils are taken on
trips to places of interest in the city.

Special instruction in nutrition is given, and medical examinations are provided.

A committee of junior high school principals of the district
was organized to discuss problems which arose in connection with
the Puerto Rican program.

Benjamin Franklin High School, located in East Harlem,
probably has the largest concentration of Puerto Rican pupils of any
academic high school in New York City. The program at Franklin
revolves about the special "orientation classes" for newly arrived
Puerto Rican students. These classes are conducted entirely in
Spanish because those boys who are placed in the classes cannot express themselves adequately in English, although they may understand a little English if it is spoken slowly. The orientation class
attempts to make the pupil's adjustment to his new environment a
pleasureable experience during which his customs, traditions and
language are treated with a sympathetic understanding that makes it
unlikely that the pupil will experience those frustrations which are
generally the cause of maladjustment. With his dignity and prestige assured, the new arrival is asked to fill in a questionnaire (in
Spanish) through which the teacher attempts to determine what the
pupil's previous educational experience has been and also to learn
something about his home background. Then a non-verbal intelligence test (in Spanish) is administered. This is followed by an
achievement test to determine literacy in Spanish.

In general the aim of the course is to orient the Puerto Rican pupil to the school community, to East Harlem, to his city,
state and nation; to explain the duties and responsibilities of the
good citizen and to acquaint him with the educational and vocational
opportunities offered by the school and the city. The major emphasis in the course is on attitudes and skills rather than on purely
factual understanding.

Some of the subjects treated during the orientation class

period are:

(1) The organization of the Benjamin Franklin High School: school regulations, functions of key personnel and extra-curricular activities.

(2) Educational guidance: courses of study, college requirements, how to study, the use of the library and reading the newspaper.

(3) Vocational guidance: requirements of various vocations and how to secure working papers.

(4) Our community: the geography and history of New York City, our present city government, health and safety, housing in New York City, the state and federal government under which we live and the responsibilities of the citizen toward his government.

During each class period due patience must be exercised by the teacher in answering innumerable questions which may appear to be extraneous to the subject at hand but which are an essential part of the orientation process.

In addition to the above, part of each lesson is devoted to the reading of an easy Spanish text whose selections serve as a basis for free discussion and composition. Moreover, the students are taken on excursions to places of interest about the city.

Important elements in the orientation program are the "Club Borinquen" and the Puerto Rican Parents' Association. These two organizations are conducted in Spanish.

Besides being enrolled in the orientation class, the new arrival is also scheduled for a special English class. The remainder of his program is the same as that of non-Puerto Rican pupils in the school.

Lack of space has made it impossible to go into greater detail in describing the special programs for Puerto Rican children that have been initiated on three levels of instruction. No one would claim that the present programs are the last word. Much remains to be done. However, it is to be hoped that with their customary faith and zeal our teachers will be able eventually to arrive at a program which will provide richer opportunities for our fellow Americans, the Puerto Ricans.

Notes

1. The Office of Information for Puerto Rico, Puerto Rico Handbook (1947), p. 39.

2. Rodriguez Bou, Ismael, Problemas de educación en Puerto Rico, p. 26. Universidad de Puerto Rico, San Juan, 1947, pp. 288.

3. Because of the system of doble matricula and "interlocking," sixty-eight pupils of each hundred in urban schools and eighty-two of each hundred in rural schools had only a half day of instruction in 1944-1945.

4. Rodriguez Bou, op. cit., p. 33.

5. Ibid., p. 34.

6. Ibid., p. 82.

7. Board of Education, New York City, A Program of Education for Puerto Ricans in New York City (1947), p. 28.

8. Ibid., p. 32.

9. Ibid., pp. 94-99.

10. Ibid., p. 33.

Claudia Lewis, "Some Puerto Rican Viewpoints." Childhood Education, 43:82-84, October 1966. Reprinted by permission.

"But will I be able to teach the Puerto Rican children?" Every supervisor preparing student teachers in New York City today hears this question and feels a strong responsibility to help the student answer "Yes." Teachers and administrators continue their efforts to meet the challenge of children who come from a different culture.

Twelve Puerto Rican families living on Manhattan's Upper West Side were interviewed as part of a larger interview program in a study of parent-teacher communication.[1] My object in the interviews was to talk informally with mothers about their expectations of public schools; the extent of their involvement with the schools; their hopes, ambitions, frustrations.

In this school district lived old residents with as many newcomers from the Caribbean and the South, representing a wide range of racial backgrounds and economic conditions. As I went from house to house I became aware that the mothers of Puerto Rican origin, though differing in family circumstances and backgrounds, were stressing approximately the same core of values about child-rearing. A clear-cut picture emerged of values that not only contradict some of the common sterotypes about Puerto Ricans but are so traditional that they are somewhat in conflict with those of the dominant trend in the American culture of today. It is partly this conflict that has created problems for both teachers and children in the schools.

An Interview with One Family

Let me describe an interview with one family we will call the R. Family. It was here that I found the values I refer to most clearly embodied. The family consisted of mother, father, and two daughters aged thirteen and eight. The parents had been in New York eleven years. Their apartment was in a low-income housing project. I arrived without any previous arrangement and knocked. The door was opened only a crack. The thirteen-year-old girl peered through cautiously, her mother standing behind her. The purpose of the visit was explained and the child translated it in Spanish to her mother. When I was finally admitted, it was the little girl--dainty, neat--who led me into the living room, her mother silently following. I was much impressed by the child's ability as she conversed with me and interpreted for this mother who did not attempt one word of English.

The apartment was decorated in a style characteristic of all but two of the twelve homes, even those in the most dingy build-

371

ings. The moment the door is opened, one is in a different world
--a light, airy, flowery, spotless world. It seems that the attempt
has been to create an outdoor summer environment with light cur-
tains and furniture and linoleum, delicate embroidered organdy
hangings, and large bouquets of artificial flowers.

The interview began, and the eight-year-old child sat with
us for a while. She was absolutely self-effacing, turning her head
away self-consciously when I looked directly at her. (In seven other homes there were young children present during the interview,
and in all but one case this same self-effacing behavior was the
rule, even in children as old as fourteen.)

Mrs. R., a neatly groomed woman in her thirties, indicated
that her time was spent in homemaking chores and in chaperoning
her children to and from their separate schools each day, to church
on Sunday and occasionally to the public library. She had gone a
few times to the younger child's school--with an older daughter or
a friend to interpret--to see the teacher and the principal, "to ask
them to teach more and to make the children have more respect...
The teaching is not exactly second grade. When I was in second
grade I had more."

She was especially concerned about a recent incident. A
little boy had been "bothering" her child--breaking her pencil, kick-
ing her table, hitting her outside of school--and the teacher had not
contacted the boy's parents. Just yesterday her husband had gone
to see the parents and they had not known a thing about it. "The
teacher was wrong not to contact the parents and tell them." (Here,
I thought, was one of those clashes of values--the mother wanting
the parents notified at once about misbehavior, whereas the teacher
may well have believed that childish kicks and hits were fully within her province to handle in school.)

Mr. R. came home from work about halfway through the
interview. Since he could speak English with some ease, he took
his wife's place after a few words in Spanish with her; she retired
to the kitchen. "Teachers should let us know more about how
things are going in school," he said. "They should send notes. In
Puerto Rico you miss one class and right away they let the parents
know. And in Puerto Rico they break your neck if you act up."
In the town where he had lived, the mayor used to go to the school
meetings. "They get one thousand people to come to these meetings. They really care about kids. The mayor talks to the teachers about how to have the kids behave. Then the teacher can say
to the kids, 'You got to do this because the mayor said so."

I found the emphasis on "respect" typical for the twelve
families--the wish that children would respect the teacher more
than they do. One mother even commented, "Why, I myself always
bow to my mother when she speaks to me, no matter how old I
am."

The desire for more communication, usually expressed in
terms of "notes from the teachers," was mentioned spontaneously
by five of the interviewees. Three others who felt it important to
know what was going on indicated that they were being well informed
and appreciated it. "If my daughters don't go to school, I know
about it right away. They send me a note."

There was variation in the amount of contact the parents were actually having with the schools. Reasons given for staying away included the mother's busyness with her house and children, inability to understand what is said at meetings, and lack of interest. As one mother stated, she had been to Open School meetings but felt "the purpose was not for the teacher to talk with the parent; she doesn't know your case; she doesn't tell you things." Another mother said of the parents who came to the Parent Association meetings, "They were not Spanish people, or the poorer ones, who came. They were the higher ones. They don't really get the ones who should come."

Three of the more educated parents suggested that mothers should be used by the schools to help with the problems of communication. "The Board of Education could use these parents, really train them to help. Every school should have a counselor just to work with the neighborhood. People need that pat on the back. They need a chance to express their problems. It's difficult here for teachers to go to the home. And the Puerto Ricans don't know when to open the door. But if they hear a Spanish voice..."

Implications for Teachers

What are the implications for teachers? Surely it does not follow that a teacher should feel an obligation to stress the Puerto Rican version of "respect" in the classroom if some of its elements run counter to his concept of the teacher-child relationship that best promotes learning. Perhaps, though, he will move cautiously and with compromises toward the less authoritarian controls he believes in to avoid confusing both children and parents. And certainly he will go out of his way to show the interest that will enable him to communicate in an accepting way with the parents and perhaps eventually arrive at a common understanding.

Does this imply more and more "notes"? Possibly it does --but what kind of notes? Must they be about misbehavior and poor work? Surely out of his knowledge of what profits a child the creative teacher might devise an entirely new kind of note to reach and satisfy parents and convince them of the school's wholehearted interest in their children. New ways might be found, also, to bring about more personal contact. The old apparatus involving the expectation that parents will come to the school to large meetings may be inappropriate. Possibly the calling together of small groups of mothers for common purposes might be more feasible. Or perhaps that mother was on the right track who suggested that Spanish-speaking liaison workers might be trained to go to the homes. Have the potentials of television been sufficiently explored? And still other avenues might be opened up by administrators and teachers who feel the challenge of making changes to meet the tide of new conditions.

Notes

1. Conducted by a research team from Bank Street College of Education, New York City, under the direction of Donald Horton, with the aid of a grant from the Field Foundation.

"Summary of Recommendations Made by the Puerto Rican Study for the Program in New York City Schools." Board of Education, City of New York. 1958. (Mimeo.) Reprinted by permission.

I. Introduction

The Puerto Rican Study is a four-year inquiry into the education and adjustment of Puerto Rican pupils in the public schools of the City of New York.

People want to know:
How to assess their ability to learn English?
How to group for instruction?
How to teach them English?
How to reach their parents?

The Study's objectives are summed up in three main problems:
First--What are the more effective ways (methods) and materials for teaching English as a second language to newly arrived Puerto Rican pupils?
Second--What are the most effective techniques with which the schools can promote a more rapid and more effective adjustment of Puerto Rican parents and children to the community and the community to them?
Third--Who are the Puerto Rican pupils in New York City's public schools?

II. What are the effective methods and materials for teaching English as a second language to newly arrived Puerto Rican pupils?

A. The study found such a great diversity in approach toward teaching English that it decided to experiment to determine which approach was best. Three methods are singled out for experimentation, the vocabulary method, the structured or language patterns method, and the functional situations or experimental method.

The conclusions arrived at were:
1. The experiential approach leads to greater gains in ability to understand English than does the vocabulary approach.
2. The vocabulary and structural approach lead to greater gains in ability to write English than does the experiential approach.
3. The vocabulary approach leads to greater gains in ability to speak English than does the experiential approach.

374

4. None of the methods leads to significant gains in ability
   to read English.
The Puerto Rican Study, therefore, recommends an integration of all three approaches plus a more direct attack on reading.

B. To integrate the several methods described above the Puerto Rican Study developed two series of related curriculum bulletins, keyed to the prescribed New York City course of study. These are the series of nine Resource Units and the four Language Guides. Each Resource Units bulletin contains three or more resource units.

The units and guides for use in the Junior High Schools were prepared on a needs rather than on a grade basis. These are the orientation, extended orientation and transition stages.

The need for continuous evaluation of these bulletins with an eye towards their revision and improvement is strongly emphasized. Also emphasized is the need to develop pupil reading material keyed to these Resource Units.

The bulletins, "A Doorway to Science," and "A Guide to the Teaching of Science," are supplements to the course of study in Science in the Junior High Schools for use with Puerto Rican pupils not ready for the regular stream, who are still in the process of learning to read English. They are geared to help these children adjust to their new environment and cover such basic areas as safety, health, and nutrition.

The Junior High School bulletins are also recommended for use with orientation pupils in the High Schools. In addition, to meet the needs of orientation pupils in High Schools, the "Resource Units for Puerto Rican Pupils in Teaching Occupations" were developed.

For the kindergarten class, the Study experimented with the bulletin, "Directing Language Learning in Early Childhood." Further development or revision of this bulletin as experimental use might dictate was left to the Bureau of Curriculum Research.

C. In 1955, it was decided that more precise information was needed as to the numbers, characteristics of Puerto Rican pupils, distribution by age, grade, and need for instruction in English. Forms were prepared and filled out. From these a seven-point rating scale as to English ability, A to G, was developed. This scale has a high degree of validity for use in formulating city-wide policy and programs for improving the educational opportunities of Puerto Rican pupils.

D. Practices helpful to adjustment and learning of non-English-speaking Puerto Rican children in the primary grades are:

1. Themes should be closely related to children's own experiences.
2. Pupils need physical and motor activity.
3. Children need time to explore the classroom and to use materials and equipment.
4. Children need to hold and manipulate objects. Possession means so much.
5. Occasional periods of silent watching and socializing are needed.
6. Where children's initiative, spontaneity and active interest are at a high level, they make great strides in language learning.
7. Cultural differences in the interest in toys and games exist. Puerto Rican children need toys and games, but different ones, sometimes, than mainland children. Teachers must bridge these cultural differences.
8. There is need for a continuity of experiences between kindergarten and first grade, first grade and second grade.
9. A great deal can be done within the classroom to improve cultural social adjustment if the teaching load is not overwhelming and if teachers are given additional help.
10. Sympathetic school supervisors and warm, understanding teachers are crucial to the success of the program.

E. Further conclusions and recommendations to achieve continuing improvement of methods and materials are listed below:

1. The elements of vocabulary, structure, quality of speech and experiences in learning English as a second language are interrelated.
2. The aural-oral approach is essential until the child gains some skill in the oral use of English.
3. A daily period of direct teaching of English in an experiential setting plus continuing attention to pupils' use of English throughout the school day are two elements of method essential to learning.
4. Non-English-speaking children learn much from their peers, therefore, the content and method of instruction should be organized to promote learning through association with English-speaking children.
5. Knowledge of Spanish is useful but not essential to the successful teaching of English to non-English-speaking classes.
6. The resource units are designed for use in mixed classes as well as in classes made up wholly of non-English-speaking pupils.
7. In addition to the need for preparing informational and recreational type reading material for non-English-speaking pupils, there is a need to gather audio-visual aids such as tape-recordings (for use with individuals and groups to improve speech), films, film strips, radio and television. There is also the need to develop a guide to the social and cultural background of all non-English-speaking pupils as cultural information for pupils and teachers.

8. The use of the core program (combining the English and Social Studies periods) is recommended for non-English-speaking pupils in High Schools. Additional Resource Units, keyed to the maturity and experiential background of pupils, should be developed for the High Schools.

III. There is a need to formulate a uniform policy for the reception, screening, placement and periodic assessment of non-English speaking pupils. The alternative is to continue the present high rate of retardation and perennial orienteeism.

A. Instruments for assessment:
   1. The Study found the following instruments useful and suggests that they be used regularly in screening and assessing progress of non-English-speaking pupils until such time as the Bureau of Educational Research may find or develop better tests or tests of equal value:
      a. The USE test--Ability to understand spoken English
      b. The Gates Reading test--Primary and Advanced
      c. The Lorge-Thorndike Non-Verbal Test.
   2. Forms were developed to help screen and place non-English-speaking pupils.

B. The Puerto Rican Study proposes three broad categories of class organization.
   1. The regular class--mainland pupils and bilingual pupils rated A or B on the Scale of Ability to Speak English. Bilingual pupils rated C, who have demonstrated ability to carry the work of the regular class, may be admitted.
   2. The mixed class--mainland pupils and non-English-speaking pupils rated C, D, E or F on the Scale of Ability to Speak English.

   It is desirable that these classes should not exceed 25 in ADA (average daily attendance) and that the non-English-speaking group should not exceed from one-fifth to one-third of the class register (that is from 5 to 9). In general, provision should be made to transfer pupils who show marked improvement to regular classes. Such transfer may be made at any time during the year.

   3. The orientation class--made up entirely of non-English-speaking pupils needing aural-oral instruction in English, that is, pupils rated C through G.

   Here, too, it is desirable that the class register should not exceed 25 or 22.5 ADA. Should the majority of this class fall in E-F-G categories, a class standard not to exceed 20 ADA is recommended.

   Opportunities must be provided pupils in orientation classes to associate with mainland children. This is partly achieved through the daily use of the curriculum materials

prepared by the Puerto Rican Study. The goal may be
further achieved through association with mainland children
in the lunchroom, the gymnasium, the playground, club activities, assembly programs, and other school activities
that cut across class and grade lines.

C. Other types of special class organizations approved by the
Puerto Rican Study are:
   1. The CRMD class for the educable mentally retarded pupils.
      It is assumed that non-English-speaking children would
      qualify for admission to these classes in about the same
      proportion as do mainland children.
   2. The reception or C class--to serve only the needs of the
      newly arrived non-English-speaking pupils.

      These classes should be set up only where a school has a
      considerable number of new arrivals. Only C through G
      rated pupils should be assigned. The teaching should be
      highly individualized and pupils transferred out as rapidly
      as they show evidence of ability to carry the work of the
      regular classes.
   3. The transition class--for retarded language learners.
   4. The core class--for non-English-speaking pupils in the
      High Schools. These are double period classes, combining
      social studies and language arts, taught by a single teacher.

D. Staffing

   Schools with non-English-speaking pupils must be adequately
   staffed. The Puerto Rican Study found the use of Substitute
   Auxiliary Teachers (SAT's), Puerto Rican Coordinators,
   School-Community Coordinators and Other Teaching Positions
   (OTP's) in both elementary and junior high schools essential.
   The functions of the OTP to be stressed are specifically de-
   fined.

   In the Senior High Schools, teachers of English to non-English-
   speaking children and Guidance Counselors are needed.

   After describing the service the holders of these positions
   may be expected to perform, the Puerto Rican Report specifies
   that when an Elementary School has 100 non-English-speaking
   pupils or 10% of its total registration is non-English-speaking,
   an SAT should be assigned. If the school has less, then it
   should be provided with the services of an SAT on a part-
   time basis. If the school has more, a coordinator of the program for non-English-speaking pupils is needed. As the number of non-English-speaking children increases other OTP positions will be required. When a junior high school has 75
   or more non-English-speaking pupils rated C-G, a Coordinator
   should be assigned. When such schools have 500 or more
   non-English-speaking pupils, a School-Community Coordinator
   should be assigned to them as well as OTP personnel.

To help the district superintendents' office counsel and assist schools with their problems as well as to coordinate the services, a coordinator from the Bureau of Community Education should be assigned to the office. The Study suggests that this be tried in three districts.

At headquarters, the Puerto Rican Study recommends the continuation of the Puerto Rican Planning Committee; the placing of responsibility for the smooth operation of the Puerto Rican Program in the hands of the associate superintendent in charge of the Curriculum Division; the assignment of a Puerto Rican Coordinator in each of the three operating divisions--Elementary Schools, Junior High Schools, High Schools.

Following are proposals affecting the staffing of bureaus:
1. A full-time staff member, qualified in audio-visual instruction and in the education of non-English-speaking pupils, be added to the Bureau of Audio-visual Instruction.
2. WHYE should be staffed to develop radio programs specifically keyed to the resource units and language guides prepared by the Puerto Rican Study for use in teaching non-English-speaking pupils.
3. The Bureau of Child Guidance needs a minimum of three terms of two persons each--one a psychologist, the other a social worker of Hispanic background, to examine those difficult cases where language is a barrier between examiner and pupil.
4. The Bureau of Community Education will need one or more additional supervisors to develop a more adequate program (method and content) for teaching English to Puerto Rican adults, in addition to the junior high school-community Coordinator and the assistants in the offices of the district superintendents for the development of leadership and social affiliation of ethnic groups.
5. In the Bureau of Educational and Vocational Guidance is needed personnel to provide the High Schools with competent counseling and testing by bilingual examiners working in close cooperation with teachers. Such personnel should be assigned to each High School on a full or part-time basis.
6. The Bureau of Educational Research must provide two types of service not now available to schools. One is in the area of testing non-English-speaking children, the other is an expansion of the Bureau's psychological service. This calls for additional personnel.

E. Problems of Teacher Education. The Puerto Rican Study recommends:
1. A carefully organized series of seminars for training teachers assigned to work with non-English-speaking pupils.
2. Summer workshops in Puerto Rico to promote a better understanding of Puerto Rico.
3. A re-examination and revision of in-service credit for

teachers who work and help carry out the Puerto Rican
program.
4. Coordinating efforts of colleges and universities within the
metropolitan area in cooperation with the Board of Education to achieve greater unity of purpose and effort in developing both undergraduate and graduate programs for
teachers who will work with non-English-speaking pupils,
and to promote the mutual interests of Puerto Rico and
New York City in developing a program that will be helpful to people everywhere confronted with similar problems
of education and social assimilation.

IV. What are the most effective techniques with which the schools
can promote a more rapid and more effective adjustment of
Puerto Rican parents and children to the community and the com-
munity to them, and
Who are the Puerto Rican pupils in the New York City Public
Schools?

A. The Puerto Rican Study, through an ethnic survey, obtained a
profile of characteristics of pupils with Puerto Rican background. The findings were published in 1956 and repeated in
this final report.

B. A considerable amount of up-grading and down-grading of
pupils transferring from Puerto Rico was found in New York
City classes. These pupils present so many different patterns
of educational history in relation to their age that they present
serious problems in identifying, screening and placement to
our schools. Schools must have a diversity of educational
programs to meet the needs of so heterogeneous a group.

C. The Study divides pupils into four categories, (A) island-born,
island-schooled, (B) island-born, mainland-schooled, (C) mainland-born pupils of Puerto Rican parentage, and (D) mainland-
born pupils of non-Puerto Rican parentage. This includes
pupils one or both of whose parents were born in a foreign
country or whose parents were mainland born.

The Study concludes that there is a steady, progressional
change from group to group as measured by the time spent in
New York City or on the mainland, with respect to intactness
of the family unit, the employment status of the father, reduction of crowded living quarters, and in the percentage of
homes where English is used wholly or in part.

The apparent differences between the groups may be credited
primarily to changes taking place in the social-cultural outlook of the home. Therefore, one potential means of accelerating the social-cultural adjustment of Puerto Rican pupils is
to find ways and means of helping to facilitate the social-
cultural adjustment of the parents.

D. Widespread public opinion holds that the incidents of poor attendance, truancy, disciplinary problems, and welfare status of Puerto Rican pupils to be most discouraging. Frequently, analysis of school records produces quite a different picture. The Study concludes that:

1. Like other children, Puerto Rican children tend to become about as good or as bad as the children or youth with whom they associate.

2. While the proportion of Puerto Rican pupils who get free lunch exceeds the proportion of non-Puerto Rican children, we must keep in mind that free lunch is part of the educational pattern in Puerto Rico and that it is not a true measure of need or reliance on public welfare.

3. The record of school attendance in New York City of Puerto Rican children is quite comparable to that of mainland children. This is a great credit to them when we consider the degree of cultural deprivation under which so many of them live--the language barrier, the different climate in New York City as compared to Puerto Rico and the fact that there is no compulsory education law in Puerto Rico. Yet, when they become truants, they are more inveterate truants.

4. Illness is not the major cause of absence among Puerto Rican children.

5. Truancy is more prevalent in Junior High Schools than in Elementary Schools.

6. Non-Puerto Rican children exceed Puerto Rican children in the number of court referrals.

E. Findings of special studies on adjustment in schools made by Puerto Rican pupils follow:

1. Many newly arrived Puerto Rican pupils were not participating in classroom activities, were not learning but were quietly and unobtrusively "sitting-out" their allotted school time.

2. There are no shortcuts to understanding the progress of the individual child. No simple background factors can be isolated as explaining a child's difficulty or ease in adjusting to school or neighborhood. Many areas must be studied. Included among these are inter-family relations and the personality structure of the child.

3. Can the Puerto Rican pupils learn English?

The records show that they can be expected to repeat the experience of other migrant groups and become well assimilated by the third generation. Their performance tends to improve each succeeding year spent in New York City schools. The rate of improvement decreases after the fourth year. Even their I.Q. goes up--which shows they adapt to our culture in time. The third generation should be able to compete on equal terms with their peers of like socio-economic background. Their progress would be accelerated if the best that we know were applied in teaching and guiding them.

But even with the best teaching and guidance in the school, there would still be need for obtaining the active cooperation of the home in learning English and for helping children at all levels to find social acceptance.

F. On the relation of Puerto Rican parents to schools, the Puerto Rican Study holds that because Puerto Rican parents are preoccupied with problems of learning English, finding apartments, finding employment, and with problems of providing their families with food, clothing, and proper health protection, they are not ready to set a high priority on their children's school problems. The schools can't wait until they are ready. The Study ran into varied responses to its questions as to how far schools should be expected to help the parents. The Study states the following:

1. The schools are important to the newcomers. They do come to school for guidance and such help as referrals to hospitals, clinics, welfare agencies, to get letters written for them and for advice on family problems.

2. The Puerto Rican parents tend to transfer the anxieties of living in new surroundings to fears and suspicion of their neighbors--even Puerto Rican neighbors.

3. Puerto Rican parents are timid rather than aggressive. They are not responsive to notices of parent meetings and school functions. Those who do attend are shy and non-participating. Meetings as usually conducted do not meet their needs.

4. Puerto Rican parents must be dealt with individually rather than in groups.

5. Puerto Rican parents come to see their children perform in assembly programs and to give help with trips, bazaars, cake sales, health drives, clerical work, sewing, as resource persons, and as interpreters. A few become leaders.

6. When meetings are well advertised and have Puerto Rican speakers, Puerto Rican parents attend.

7. Clubs are more successful than big meetings.

8. Schools have tried to work with parents in many ways. They have tried using a school-community coordinator and extending the services of SAT's. These have found personal, informal contact of most help. From this beginning, they have developed mothers' clubs and gotten them to work with parent associations on school functions. Given time and scope to work informally, they can build friendly relations with the schools.

G. On factors in financing the education of non-English-speaking children, the Puerto Rican Study reports that in 1956 the state legislature voted additional state aid for this purpose. The State Education Department accepted the Puerto Rican Study's Scale of Ability to Speak English. A rating of C or below makes one a non-English-speaking child. The additional costs in educating non-English-speaking pupils justifying state aid are described:

1. Cost of special staff (SAT, Puerto Rican Coordinators, School-Community Coordinators, OTP's, SAT Officers, High School Counselors).
2. Cost of special classes with lower registers.
3. Cost of keeping accurate additional records and follow-up measures necessitated by high mobility.
4. Cost of producing special teaching material.

The Commissioner of Education recognized three types of special classes:

a. A class with 100% non-English-speaking children
b. A class mixed with 50% non-English-speaking children
c. A class that meets for special instruction one period a day, but in other periods these children are in regular classes.

The 100% non-English-speaking class must be composed of fewer than 25 ADA (Average Daily Attendance), which means 27 as an average class register. All must be in C-G category on the rating scale and must work as a class group the full day or at least 80% of the school day under a single teacher or several departmental teachers.

Classes of fewer than 10 may be included with special permission of the Commissioner.

The Board of Education may fix a minimum class standard between 10 and 25 ADA. This helps in setting up classes with open registers for reception or orientation of new arrivals anticipated in June.

The 50% mixed class must have fewer than 25 ADA, half of whom are non-English-speaking. This type of class should be used with discretion because during its three years of experimental work the Puerto Rican Study found that where there are 1, 2, or 3 non-English-speaking children in a class, they are forgotten. As the concentration approaches 50 per cent, the teacher tends to divide the class in half, leading towards segregation. A concentration of thirty to thirty-five per cent was considered best. Therefore, there is need to have the Commissioner change the fifty per cent in ADA to allow for twenty or thirty per cent and still get one-half of the state aid.

V. Next Steps: Where The Puerto Rican Study Leads

Like other groups that have entered New York City, the Puerto Ricans, in the normal course of events, will become socially and educationally assimilated by the third generation. Neither we nor the Puerto Ricans can afford to wait that long. We must find ways and means of accelerating the learning and

adjustment of first and second generation Puerto Rican and
other non-English-speaking pupils. Twenty-three lines of attack on many fronts towards the aforementioned goal are
listed:

1. Accept the Puerto Rican Study, not as something finished,
   but as the first stage of a larger, city-wide, ever-improving
   program for the education and assimilation of non-English-
   speaking children. To translate proposed measures into
   practice will take three to five years at the very best.
2. Take a new look at the philosophy governing the education
   of non-English-speaking children in New York City schools.
   Does educating them involve helping them to forget the language of their fathers? Does it involve creation of barriers
   between them and their parents? What attitudes are we
   inculcating?
3. Recognize that whatever is done for the non-English-speaking child is, in the long run, done for all the children.
   The schools' program must be adapted to the ability and the
   need of each individual.
4. Use the annual school census as a basic technique in planning the continuing adaptation of the schools to the needs of
   the non-English-speaking pupils. The probabilities are that
   the characteristics of Puerto Rican pupils will change within a decade or generation and that these changes will prove
   even more challenging to educational planning than their increase in number and distribution.
5. Recognize the heterogeneity of the non-English-speaking
   pupils. Part of the difficulty in learning English and in
   assessing their abilities stems from their different cultural
   background. This needs to be explored further.

   (The Puerto Rican children are heterogeneous with respect
   to their native intelligence, prior schooling, aptitude for
   learning English, general scholastic ability, etc.) This
   heterogeneity must be taken into account in almost every
   contact the school has with the pupil.

6. Formulate a uniform policy for the reception, screening,
   placement, and periodic assessment of non-English-speaking
   pupils. Putting the proposals made by the Study into effective operation in all schools is a major undertaking.
7. Keep policies governing the grouping of non-English-speaking pupils flexible. Place the emphasis upon serving the
   needs of the individual pupil. Discourage the practice of
   grouping new arrivals with grossly retarded language learners. Encourage the practice of a reception class for new
   arrivals where each pupil is given individual attention and
   is helped to achieve his best. These classes will require
   small registers, and teachers skilled in teaching and guidance of non-English-speaking pupils. Every teacher of a
   non-English-speaking child has a right to a profile of his
   prior schooling, his achievement, and his potential abilities.

Practices and proposals for grouping vary with different
school levels.

8. Place special emphasis on reducing the present backlog of
retarded language learners.
9. Recognize "English as a second language" as an area of
specialization that cuts across many subject areas. It
starts with the aural-oral approach leading gradually into
reading and writing.
10. Use the curricular materials developed by The Puerto Rican Study to achieve unity of purpose and practice in teaching non-English-speaking pupils.
11. Capitalize on the creative talent of teachers in finding
ways and means of supplementing and of improving the program for teaching non-English-speaking pupils. Develop
materials to supplement those prepared by the Puerto Rican Study. Set in motion processes that will improve future editions of established courses of study.
12. Recognize and define the school's responsibility to assist,
counsel and cooperate with parents of non-English-speaking
pupils in all matters pertaining to the child's welfare.
There is too wide a range of theory and practice on this issue.
13. Take a new look at the school's opportunity to accelerate
the adjustment of Puerto Rican children and their parents
through advice and counsel to parents on problems normally considered to be outside the conventional functions of the
school.
14. Staff the schools to do the job.
15. Staff the proper agencies of the Board of Education to
maintain a continuing program for the development and improvement of curricular materials and other aids to the
teaching of non-English-speaking pupils.
16. Staff the proper agencies of the Board of Education, and
set in motion the processes to maintain a continuing assessment or evaluation of techniques, practices and proposals.
17. Take a new, hard look at the psychological services provided for non-English-speaking children, especially for
Puerto Rican children.
18. Through every means available, make it clear that the
education of the non-English-speaking and their integration
in an ever-changing school population is the responsibility
of every member of the school staff.
19. Maintain, improve and possibly expand the program of in-
service preparation initiated through the Puerto Rican Study
for training special staff to assist in accelerating the program for non-English-speaking children.
20. In cooperation with the colleges and universities of Metropolitan New York, create a dynamic program to achieve
unity of purpose and more adequate coordination of effort
in the education of teachers and other workers for accelerating the program in the schools.
21. Use the varied opportunities available to develop an ever-

improving cooperation between the Department of Education in Puerto Rico and the Board of Education in New York City. Maintain the practice of operating summer workshops, consider more effective use that might be made of participants, develop a system of exchange of teachers between New York City and Puerto Rico, hold annual conferences of officials alternately in New York City and in Puerto Rico to examine practices, common interests and generally to promote the educational program for the Puerto Rican pupil.

22. In cooperation with the responsible representatives of the government of the State of New York, continue to explore the mutual interests and responsibility of the city and state for the education and adjustment of non-English-speaking children and youth.

23. Think of the City of New York and the Commonwealth of Puerto Rico as partners in a great enterprise.

Joseph O. Loretan, "Problems in Improving Educational Opportunities for Puerto Ricans in New York." High Points, May 1963, pp. 23-31. Reprinted by permission. (Address delivered at the Third Annual Conference for New Yorkers of Puerto Rican Background.)

I am grateful to New York University for its invitation to open this Third Annual Conference. Today two vital forces of the educational community--the university and the public schools--have called together members of the teaching profession, the university faculty and students, and the esteemed members of our Puerto Rican community in New York City to discuss the practical ways in which all of us in cooperative effort can improve the education of Puerto Rican students of all ages in our metropolis.

We are here because we wish unceasingly, ardently, and honestly to learn. In the process of examining our findings and evaluating our methods, our materials, and our techniques, we may differ in opinion. But this is all to the good, for we know that we are united in purpose and in motive.

Our spirit is contained in the cogent thought of John Milton, an idea as valid and as powerful today as it was when it touched men's minds from the pages of the Areopagitica; namely, that: "Where there is much desire to learn, there of necessity will be much arguing, much writing, many opinions, for opinion in good men is but knowledge in the making."

Results of The Puerto Rican Study

For the curricular aspects of our work with all our Puerto Rican pupils, the necessary background and foundations are, of course, contained in The Puerto Rican Study. Without doubt everyone present today is familiar with the study. It would, therefore, constitute a laboring of the obvious to mention at this point the particulars of the origin of the study, its duration, its workings. Yet we may, very briefly, recall the three principal areas of the study's concern: effective methods and materials, effective school adjustment of Puerto Rican youngsters, and an analysis of the Puerto Rican school population. Everyone here believes, as I do, that the outcomes of The Puerto Rican Study have been, for the most part, monumental. I am sure that every teacher here today has, with benefit, used the Curriculum Bulletins born out of the findings of The Puerto Rican Study. Every teacher and supervisor here today has used the seven-point rating scale suggested by The Puerto Rican Study for consideration in formulating programs for the teaching of Puerto Rican pupils.

Problems Still Exist

Yet, after all these years, all of us are aware that there
still exist problems--even in connection with the study. Our attitude in the analysis of problems and of needs must be one which
was so eminently described by Walter Pater as "maintenance of a
kind of candid discontent in the face of the very highest achievement." We have accomplished some remarkable things--the very
highest achievement indeed--in the education of Puerto Rican pupils
of all ages. However, in a free society which aims constantly toward the good, we must--on the side of intellectual honesty--main-
tain that "candid discontent" which is the motivation at the core of
all real growth.

More Flexible Individual Programming

Some problems emerge which this conference of educators
might profitably consider. How can the materials of The Puerto
Rican Study be extended? What new materials might be added to
the original guides and bulletins emanating from The Puerto Rican
Study? On what level in particular are such materials needed?
Let me be specific. Let us take the case of a Puerto Rican pupil,
admitted to Grade 8 in one of our junior high schools on his arrival
from the Island. After six months of satisfactory work and cooperation in an Orientation Class, the pupil is placed in a program in the
"normal stream" of the school. The youngster finds himself lin-
guistically able to participate in much of the work, but, immediately,
he realizes that he is behind his peers in the mastery of the content of the various subjects. Does there not appear here a real
need, a practical demand, for adding to the orientation materials
suggested by The Puerto Rican Study such material as upgraded
syllabi in the various subject areas geared to the "transition" Puerto Rican pupil? Are not more flexible and ingenious methods of individual programming needed for these youngsters? The pupil who
is bridging the gap between the Orientation Class and the "normal
stream" class is sometimes lost. His zeal to learn is diminished.
He begins to think of dropping out of school.

The Need for Help in Subject Content

School administrators have noted with appreciation the efforts
of the Non-English Coordinators on all levels to devise means for
providing "special language emphasis" for pupils leaving the Orientation Classes. Yet, while such emphasis on language as tool is
essential and must by all means to be continued, the problem still
remains. Must we not provide help in language as content in order
to bridge the gap occasioned by the pupil's need to spend a certain
period of time in the Orientation Class?
At this point, a very interesting tangential problem opens up.
Shall this help in language as content be provided in the pupil's
native language? Only a week ago, in Puerto Rico, it was my
privilege to observe a most exciting project being planned to help
educate youngsters of Puerto Rican extraction who have recently

returned to the island.

The Problem in Reverse

On this visit, Commissioner Oliveras arranged for me to visit the Ponce School System. Superintendent Longo assembled twenty-five New York Puerto Rican youngsters and representative teachers and supervisors. We talked for a while about the problem of the students in getting adjusted to Ponce, especially to learning Spanish. For here the problem we have is reversed. These New York students spoke English with facility. But they were failing in content subjects since they were all presented in Spanish.

Superintendent Longo then presented her ideas concerning an experiment. She would assemble all such New York junior high school students at a central school in Ponce. She would teach the basic subjects: mathematics, science, social studies, in English plus two periods of Spanish. May I comment parenthetically that I visited a dozen schools and observed some of the best teaching I have seen anywhere any time.

In scope and objective, the program is very similar--it seems to me--to something we are embarking upon in science and Spanish in the Junior High School Division--experiments which we shall present later in this talk.

Supplying Individualized Materials

In connection with the need for good, extended materials for the non-English pupil in the transition stage, we might also consider this question: What has been our response to the challenge presented by such recent techniques as programmed materials for pupils who have left the Orientation Class and are now in the "normal stream?" Are we availing ourselves, for instance, of the potential made in this area by the latest findings in the field of reading? The need for supplying individual materials indeed constitutes a tremendous challenge, a real one, to all school people. Can't we also destroy the myth which prevents teachers from illustrating a concept or phrase in the native tongue of the learner of a second language? In this regard I must point out a special project being conducted by Aspira, a Puerto Rican Civic Group, in which college volunteers are teaching Puerto Rican students to improve their reading.

Involving the Local Puerto Rican Community

The second major problem which I should like to point up today concerns our entire metropolitan community. It is this: the urgent need for the schools to involve the local Puerto Rican community more fully and more actively in educational life and work. Is there not a need for the school to develop more imaginative ways of appealing to our Puerto Rican parents, of making our Puerto Rican parents aware of how integral and vital a part we feel they are of each and every one of our public schools?

We, in the schools, know how very much we need the cooperative assistance of the Puerto Rican parents and the expression

of their ideas in the formulation of school-community plans and
processes. In every Parent-Teacher Association, we need the presence of the cultural tone and personality of the Puerto Rican parent
community as a corollary to the particular racial, cultural values
already being contributed by the various other peoples who form the
parent groups in our schools--all our schools. We need to make
the Puerto Rican parents aware of the special, necessary, unique
contribution they alone can make to school groups in the area of
interracial and intergroup understanding. And do we not all hope
that, from association with our present parent groups, our Puerto
Rican parents will carry out to the larger Puerto Rican community
of our city the knowledge of the workings of our school system and
the desire to participate in those workings?

The greater involvement of our Puerto Rican parents in our
schools does, indeed, seem to constitute a problem for educators
to tackle with vigor. The involvement of our Puerto Rican parents
will increase the active and intelligent workings of that real and
practical democracy which is the pride of our school system in New
York.

We have tackled our problems intelligently and effectively in
the past. From such honest effort, the results which have developed have been most rewarding to us as educators and most beneficial to our pupils.

Operation Understanding

We have been talking about problems. There are some active, ongoing projects on which we can report real progress. First,
there is Operation Understanding, an exchange program of teachers
between the New York schools on the elementary level and comparable Puerto Rican schools. This year there are twelve Puerto Rican teachers working in our elementary schools among Non-English
classes while twelve New York teachers have taken some of the
classes of their Puerto Rican colleagues on the Island.

Dr. Gross, Dr. Senior, Dr. Donovan, Dr. King, and I had
dinner in San Juan with these New York teachers. A similar meeting with our Puerto Rican Operation Understanding teachers should
prove rewarding. The insights these New York teachers are developing are invaluable. They will be meeting jointly soon with their
Island colleagues who are working in New York. Plans are being
made now for next year. Teachers from junior high schools and
senior high schools are to be part of this Operation for the next
school year. A nucleus of teachers from the original group of this
year will be retained to help orient newly involved ones. It is also
planned to coordinate the activities of the summer workshops of the
National Conference of Christians and Jews with this Operation.

Superintendent of Schools Gross shares with Commissioner
Oliveras and Dr. Senior, both of whom have been leaders in bringing the top level administrators of the Island and New York City
together, the idea of regular meetings for purposes of planning and
evaluation. The positive, constructive fruition of this type of professional exchange is conveyed in the naming of the project, Operation Understanding. The wealth of implications, professional and

cultural, generated by this enterprise is an earnest of great good for our teachers and pupils both here and in Puerto Rico.

Other Projects on J.H.S. Level

On the junior high school level, there are several other projects of which we are all very proud. In the light of the need for intellectual leadership in the space-age world, we are now initiating an experiment in the implementation of the new science curriculum in selected schools which have classes of Non-English children. Here, instead of general science, we are using laboratory materials and techniques in dealing with blocks of subject matter and concepts in chemistry, biology, physics, and earth science. Parallel to this modernization of our science curriculum, further work involving advanced instruction in the Spanish language is underway in one of our junior high schools in Manhattan. Such an experiment has been going on for the past two years with Spanish-speaking youngsters who have come to our schools with a good foundation in this language. These youngsters have been encouraged to continue their study of Spanish on an advanced level in the 7, 8, and 9 years, a program which has culminated in their taking the Three-Year-Spanish Regents instead of a two-year exam. The results have been remarkable. This "advanced standing" enables the pupils to enter high school with a superior record of achievement. Moreover, it enables them to start studying another language in high school. We have reason to believe it also helps their understanding of English. We are also planning a further experiment in which we contemplate teaching some of the subject areas (probably mathematics, social studies, and science) in Spanish. By the time of the Fourth Annual Conference at New York University next year, we may have some interesting findings.

The Career Guidance Project

For less successful pupils, some of whom are in the Non-English program, the Career Guidance Project was begun in 1958. It had been apparent for a long time that the needs of a significant segment of the junior high school population were not being met by the modifications and adaptations of the existing curriculum, even with the addition of corrective services. These pupils were not succeeding in their studies, and their records indicated strong dropout possibilities. To cope with this problem, Career Guidance was begun. From 1958 to '62 we experimented. In September 1962 we moved into a large scale program. We find that many of our discouraged pupils from Non-English classes have been salvaged, some towards graduation and others towards successful vocational adjustment. The chief feature of this program is its concentration on restoring a student's faith in himself and in developing his self esteem. It is occupational education centered and includes intensive personal guidance, many opportunities to visit industrial plants and commercial centers, and many visits by leaders of science, industry, and labor. In this program, 90 to 100 pupils in a ninth year department within a school are taught and guided by eight selected teachers. A counselor sees each pupil once a week. A modernized program of industrial arts patterned on industry is another feature of the program. Programmed materials developed by our math coordinators are being used, and such individualized material in reading, similarly prepared, is in the process of being duplicated for use in September. This World of Work centered curriculum is worth watching.

Effect of New Graduation Policy

It is also heartening to be able to report that the new promotion and graduation policies, especially at the junior high school level, have benefited many pupils from the Non-English, as well as from the "regular stream," classes. As you know, it is possible for a junior high school pupil, on the completion of the ninth year, to receive either a diploma or a certificate. Last year, the requirements were modified so that pupils who received certificates on completion of the 9th grade could return to receive diplomas after having been in high school one or more terms. This is dependent, of course, among other requirements, upon the pupil's ability to meet the reading requirements (not lower than 7.0). Among the 407 who, in 1962, returned to their junior high school, took the reading tests, and were able to replace their certificates with junior high school diplomas, many were former pupils of the Non-English program. This valuable opportunity to replace a certificate by a diploma should be explained to all Non-English classes. The effort to obtain a diploma should be seconded and encouraged.

Teaching English as a Second Language

Another successful project which might be of interest to all of you involved in teaching English as a second language is the very effective use of the school language laboratories being made by some of the Coordinators. In the laboratories the implementation of audio lingual techniques has expedited the pupils' handling of the English language as a tool of communication.

In still another school, the system followed at such eminent language schools as Middlebury in Vermont and the University of Wisconsin is employed in order to facilitate the pupil's use of English at all times. Several teachers of the Non-English classes volunteer to sit in the school cafeteria with the youngsters at lunch time. In this relaxed situation, it is agreed that only English will be spoken. The results have been splendid.

Teacher-Training Projects

All teachers on the junior high school level of Non-English instruction participated in the teacher-training project conducted for the group last year in science, mathematics, and language arts, and particularly composition. To supplement such inservice training, a course is being offered this semester over WNDT Channel 13, every Wednesday from 4-4:30, followed by discussion workshops in some 28 centers. This televised course is carefully structured

to cover all aspects of the Non-English teaching program on all
levels. The manual which accompanies the course is a veritable
source book of material for all persons in the field. This type of
professional enrichment will continue to be given for the benefit of
the teachers and, ultimately, of all Non-English class pupils.

Our present program and our future plans are indeed growing in their scope of service to our children of Puerto Rican background. This growth demonstrates our educational vitality and dynamism. We must sustain these, for we have some 65,000 youngsters
in the Non-English program on the elementary level, some 35,000
on the junior high school level--all involved in the Non-English program. We will not let them down.

Virginia Anderson, "Teaching English to Puerto Rican Pupils."
High Points, March 1964, pp. 51-54. Reprinted by permission.

An English teacher in New York City whose class consists
of a large percentage of children of Puerto Rican background must
be aware that the mental health of the children is at least as important an objective of education as is the inculcation of subject
matter.
Every teacher is faced with the task of guiding the personality formation of his pupils. He must help them become well-ad-
justed happy persons who can live with themselves comfortably and
get along well with others. Another important function of the teacher is to help children learn the traditions and customs of the new
culture and acquire skills which will help them become self-sustaining members of society.

The Best of Both Worlds

The teacher of Puerto Rican pupils has the difficult task of
guiding them so that they will accept unfamiliar manners and morals
without discarding the valuable elements of their native folkways.
He also has the task of seeing that the newcomers are understood,
accepted, and appreciated by their classmates. An English teacher,
therefore, not only must be familiar with both cultures but must see
to it that his mainland-born students learn something about our
American Commonwealth in the Caribbean while they are acquiring
and perfecting the techniques of listening, speaking, reading, and
writing English. The teacher is in a position to make the experiences involved happy and fruitful ones, and to foresee and prevent
experiences that could have a negative effect on personality development.

Praising Admirable Puerto Rican Ideals

In her book, Teaching English as a Second Language, Dr.
Mary Finocchiaro tells us that it is important to give status to students of a new language by developing pride in their own cultural
heritage. One of the most rewarding methods which the teacher of
English to Puerto Rican pupils might use is that of recognizing and
praising, as early as possible in the term, those elements in the
Puerto Rican culture which the mainlander can do well to admire.
In 1960, the Popular Democratic Party of Puerto Rico sponsored serenidad, or "serenity." It was described as a proposal to
teach the people that "the production of wealth is a technique; the
use of wealth is an art." This aim of convincing the Puerto Ricans

that artistic and spiritual qualities mean more than material wealth
is an old value which we, in New York, are accused of ignoring.
Any teacher who points out the virtues of serenidad and deempha-
sizes materialism will not only be helping the Puerto Rican children
make a better adjustment by starting with something familiar but
will also be helping the English-speaking children in his class aspire
to one of the old American beliefs that have fallen away due to a
rising worship of material goods.

Many people in our mainland society pay lip service to the
democratic ideal of accepting a person regardless of his color. We
are having difficulties all over the country because that concept of
brotherhood is disregarded. The Puerto Rican people, by and large,
are not as prejudiced as their fellow citizens on the mainland.
This is another excellent element in their culture that can be
stressed by the teacher for the benefit of the entire class.

Pride in Their Literary Heritage

In the teaching of speech, another way of moving from the
familiar to the unfamiliar is to use cognate words. If the teacher
carefully prepares several lessons in which the majority of the
words used are cognates, the students will be reinforced in their
reading-readiness by their success in reading and understanding a
new language.

A unit could be devised, according to the level of development of the class, on the literature of Puerto Rico. There are not
many places on earth where poetry is as popular as it is in Puerto
Rico. The countryman, or jibaro, is a great baseball fan; but he
is equally fond of poetry. The governor, Luis Munoz Marin, is a
sensitive poet and is called El Vate by the people. With an advanced class the teacher might go into the interesting origin of this
word. Plato, in De Legibus, tells us that poetry was originally of
virtuous intent. He mentions the solemn feasts called Panegyrica
where the poets used to compete once every five years. The
greatest and ablest of the old bards, who was prophet and sooth-
sayer as well as poet, was called vatem. The lesser versifiers,
who wrote of lighter matters and were not as inspired or inspiring,
were called poets.

The décima, Puerto Rico's folk poetry form, is a variant of
the classical Spanish stanza form used in drama by Lope de Vega.
The English teacher should pay some attention to the poems of Luis
Pales Matos, who was first recognized in the 1920's, and to the
first important Puerto Rican literary work, the distinctly original
El Jibaro, by Manuel Alonzo, published in 1949.

The Importance of Saving Face

We not only must try to give status to new language students
by developing pride in their cultural heritage but must avoid em-
barrassing them and taking away the pride they already possess.
It is possible that some teachers, ignorant of the Puerto Rican culture and lacking the understanding of why Puerto Ricans react in
certain ways to our culture, have been partially responsible for the

development of hatred or inferiority complexes in their students.
Dr. George N. Shuster, in The Puerto Ricans, cautions us against
voicing requests in a negative manner. We should encourage the
use of English, not discourage the use of Spanish. Dr. Michael
Bonomo, in his language classes at Hunter College, uses a method
that takes into consideration the student's pride. He never calls
upon a student to respond unless he has repeated the word or
phrase several times himself; until he has had the entire class respond as a unit, followed by a response by each half of the class
separately. Then after repeating the item carefully himself, he
asks for volunteers or calls upon a student who he knows is doing
well. Thus, the poorer student has had the opportunity of having
heard the new word or phrase pronounced correctly several times
before the class. This saving of face is especially important with
children of Puerto Rican background who have a strong belief in la
dignidad de la persona, or the unique dignity and worthiness of respect of each individual, and who have been raised in a land where
machismo, the masculine-virility complex, is an important cultural
component. Any little boy might be embarrassed by not doing well
before his feminine classmates. To the Puerto Rican boy, this
loss of face can have an even deeper emotional impact.

The Aburrido and Mañana Complexes

The English teacher must be prepared to deal with two problems in the reaching and teaching of his Puerto Rican pupils. One
is caused by the aburrido, or "boredom complex." The program
must be varied and lively with many changes of technique in order
to make up for their short attention span. The other problem is
attributable to the "manana complex." In a city such as New York,
where the tempo is bustling and everyone is harried, rushing to get
things done and no one has any time for graceful social living because he is always "too busy," the teacher will have to make advance preparations for homework assignments; but she should be
wary of trying to force the artificial pressures of our society on a
relaxed and happy people. If the teacher occasionally permits the
Puerto Rican children to entertain the class on a holiday such as
Christmas (Three Saints Day) with a piñata, guitar music, and dancing, they will be more amenable to the basic drill work required in
language study. The teacher who manages to make the learning
situation a pleasurable one will have the attention and co-operation
of the class. In the chapter of her book (mentioned above) entitled
"Creating a Desirable Classroom Atmosphere" Dr. Finocchiaro gives
us many excellent methods for the development of rapport between
teachers and pupils.
A teacher who is humane, friendly, understanding, patient,
and capable; who is aware of the implications of the mental health,
or "success approach" to teaching will be rewarded in seeing that
the personalities of her pupils are developing in a healthy manner
and in observing their acquisition of the language arts and skills
which will enable them to become self-sustaining members of society.

Elaine Berkowitz. "Family Attitudes and Practices of Puerto Rican and Non-Puerto Rican Pupils." High Points, March 1961, pp. 25-34. Reprinted by permission.

The primary purpose of this study was to present a comparison of the family attitudes and practices among Puerto Rican pupils with those of continental-American-born pupils. This comparison should provide a basis for modifying the home economics course of study to give practical experiences to the Puerto Rican pupil. The differences that exist in the homes of her pupils are of concern to the home economics teacher because they affect the way individuals and families live. If education for family living is to be of interest to the pupil and carried over into life activities, what is taught must be related to the lives of the pupils.

The Problem

In the past eight years the number of Puerto Rican children enrolled in the public schools of New York City has increased from about 40,000 to over 100,000. The teaching of these children presents difficulties because of their language handicaps and differences in cultural background. Dealing with these difficulties is more than a matter of devices and materials. It is also important for the teacher to have a sympathetic understanding of the environmental factors affecting these children. This insight is the sine qua non of both tolerance and patience, so necessary for effective teaching. The school program can be used to help ease the adjustment of these children only if it is planned with an understanding of their background and needs.

For example, if the difficulty which Puerto Rican children have in adjusting to our meal patterns is known, the home economics program can be used to orient them towards whole grain breads, to introduce them to available vegetables instead of expensive imported vegetables, and to provide information regarding the variety of mainland foods that can be prepared in a fashion similar to their native island foods.

Scope of the Study

This study was made at Junior High School 263, Brooklyn, New York. The specific technique employed was a questionnaire. Copies were made in English and Spanish. The questionnaire was distributed to home economics pupils, all of whom were girls. Two hundred and forty-seven questionnaires were completed, 120 of which were answered by Puerto Rican pupils and 127 by non-Puerto Rican pupils.

The selection of characteristics for study was directed toward those elements which might reveal family relationships, agreement between parent and child, and the conditions under which the students live.

> We are conducting a survey to see how girls feel about the following items. People feel differently about each item. There is no general agreement. There are no right answers. We would like your honest opinion on each of these statements. Do not put your name on this paper. Read each sentence, and then check the answer which best expresses your feeling about the statement.

1. Home is the most pleasant place in the world
   Agree _____
   Disagree _____

2. Parents expect too much from their children
   Agree _____
   Disagree _____

3. A person should discuss important plans with members of her family
   Agree _____
   Disagree _____

4. In making plans for the future, parents should be given first consideration
   Agree _____
   Disagree _____

5. A man should be willing to sacrifice everything for his family
   Agree _____
   Disagree _____

6. Parents too often expect their grown-up children to obey them
   Agree _____
   Disagree _____

7. A girl cannot find as much understanding at home as elsewhere
   Agree _____
   Disagree _____

8. So far as ideas are concerned, parents and children live in different worlds
   Agree _____
   Disagree _____

9. A person owes her greatest obligation to her family
   Agree _____
   Disagree _____

10. People in the family can be trusted completely
    Agree _____
    Disagree _____

11. A girl becomes nervous at home
    Agree _____
    Disagree _____

12. The joys of family life are much over-
    rated   Agree _____
                                   Disagree _____

13. A girl's parents usually treat her fairly
    and sensibly   Agree _____
                                   Disagree _____

14. A girl should confide fully in members
    of her family   Agree _____
                                   Disagree _____

15. A person feels happiest at home
                                   Agree _____
                                   Disagree _____

16. Family ties are strengthened when
    times are hard   Agree _____
                                   Disagree _____

17. Parents are too old-fashioned in
    their ideas   Agree _____
                                   Disagree _____

18. Members of the family are too
    curious about a girl's personal affairs
                                   Agree _____
                                   Disagree _____

19. Parents keep faith in their children even
    though children cannot find work
                                   Agree _____
                                   Disagree _____

20. Parents are too particular about the
    kind of company one keeps
                                   Agree _____
                                   Disagree _____

21. Obligations to her family are a great
    handicap to a young girl today
                                   Agree _____
                                   Disagree _____

22. Here is a list of things girls sometimes
    do at home. Think of all the things you
    have done during the past week. Then
    read the list and check each thing which
    you have done at some time or other.

    Made the bed _____   Swept _____
    Dusted _____   Washed dishes _____
    Mended _____   Set the table _____
    Cooked supper _____ Baby-sat _____
    Shopped for food _____ Others (please list) _____
                                   _____
                                   _____

23. Which of these things has your family done together
    during the past month? Please check only those things
    which the family has done together.
    Read out loud together _____
    Sang or played music _____

Question 23 (continued)
Went to the movies _____
Went to church or temple _____
Watched TV _____
Played games together _____
Went shopping _____
Went visiting _____
Others (please list)_____

_____
_____

24. Is your family of Puerto Rican descent? Yes___ No___

25. Please check all of the following people who live in your home now
Father_____ grandfather_____ mother_____
sisters (how many?)____ brothers (how many?)_____
grandmother_____ aunts (how many?)_____
uncles (how many?)____ cousins (how many?)_____
others (please list)_____

_____
_____

26. How often have you moved?
_____never
_____once every four years
_____once every three years
_____once every two years
_____once a year
_____more than once a year

27. What kind of work does your father do?_____

28. What kind of work does your mother do?_____

29. What language is spoken at home?_____

30. How many rooms does your apartment have?_____

Note:
Items 1-21 are "The Scale of Family Adjustment" of the standardized Minnesota Scale for the Survey of Opinions.

Summary of Findings

The basic similarities and differences between Puerto Rican and non-Puerto Rican pupils as revealed by the survey are summarized below. With such a picture in mind it is possible to define what are the basic needs of the pupils, and, from these, to formulate their implications for education.
Family Attitudes: The attitudes held by both groups were similar in that:

1. The majority of both Puerto Rican (59.1%) and non-Puerto Rican pupils (57.3%) have favorable attitudes toward the family.

2. Both groups indicate disagreement with parents on ideas held.

3. Both groups feel that the home places too much responsibility on them.

4. Both groups feel a sense of obligation to the family.

5. Both groups feel that their parents treat them fairly but that too much is expected from the children.

6. Both groups feel a sense of trust in the family.

7. Both groups feel that members of the family are too curious about their personal affairs.

However, the non-Puerto Rican pupils on the whole are more contented at home than are the Puerto Rican pupils:

1. 69% of the Puerto Rican pupils in contrast to 45.6% of the non-Puerto Rican pupils feel that they cannot find as much understanding at home as elsewhere.

2. 55.8% of the Puerto Rican pupils feel that the joys of family life are much overrated in contrast to 44.2% of the non-Puerto Rican pupils.

3. 50.8% of the Puerto Rican pupils find it difficult to keep a pleasant disposition at home in contrast to 41.6% of the non-Puerto Rican pupils.

Tasks Performed at Home: Both groups perform similar tasks. These include making the beds, dusting, shopping for food, sweeping, and washing dishes. The most frequently performed tasks are the making of beds and dishwashing. More non-Puerto Rican pupils than Puerto Rican pupils cook supper and babysit. The non-Puerto Rican pupils also perform more tasks at home than do the Puerto Rican pupils.

Activities Shared by Families: Puerto Rican families share more activities than do non-Puerto Rican families. This would include such activities as going to church or temple, shopping, going to the movies, visiting, watching television, etc. The activity most frequently shared by both groups is visiting. The activities least frequently shared by both groups are car-riding, watching television, and reading out loud.

Composition of the families: About three-fourths of both groups reported living with both father and mother. However, there are differences in family groups for the remaining one fourth.

1. 6.1% more of the non-Puerto Rican pupils than Puerto Rican pupils are living with only one parent. For both groups the parent is usually the mother.

2. 7.5% of the Puerto Rican Pupils are living with neither parent as compared to only 0.77% of the non-Puerto Rican pupils.

Size of Household Groups: Slightly more than half of both groups are living in groups of five or fewer persons.

1. The average size of the Puerto Rican household groups is 6.34 persons as compared to 5.6 persons in the non-Puerto Rican household.

2. Slightly less than one-fourth of the Puerto Rican pupils are living in groups of six to seven persons, and slightly more than one-fourth are living in groups of eight or more people.

3. For the non-Puerto Rican pupils these figures are reversed. Slightly more than one-fourth live in groups of six to seven people, and slightly less than one-fourth live in groups of eight or more people.

4. The Puerto Rican household group is about 0.74 persons larger than the non-Puerto Rican.

Concentration of Persons in the Home: Although Puerto Rican pupils live in more crowded living quarters than do their non-Puerto Rican classmates, the difference is not so great as some might believe.

1. Of the non-Puerto Rican pupils, 84.18% live in quarters housing two persons or fewer in contrast to 79.93% of the Puerto Rican pupils.

2. However, more non-Puerto Rican pupils indicate homes with a relatively high concentration of more than two persons per room than do the Puerto Rican pupils, 11.01% and 7.46%, respectively.

3. Neither group indicates significant percentages living in homes with more than three persons per room.

Mobility of the Family: Pupils of Puerto Rican background have a much higher household mobility rate than do non-Puerto Rican pupils. The number of Puerto Rican pupils moving on the average once a year or more frequently was more than double that of the non-Puerto Rican pupils, 24.9% and 11.76%, respectively. Of the non-Puerto Rican pupils 38.58% have never moved, in contrast to 24.1% of the Puerto Rican pupils.

Parental Wage Earners in Intact Families: The most common pattern for both groups is for the father to be the sole parent working. The next most common pattern is for both parents to be employed. There are more non-Puerto Rican working mothers (30.51%) than Puerto Rican (24.7%). There are more Puerto Rican fathers unemployed (32.6%) than non Puerto Rican (21.1%). There is more parental unemployment among the Puerto Rican parents (19.1%) than among the non-Puerto Rican (1.05%).

Language Spoken at Home: English is spoken to some extent in the homes of only 39.1% of the Puerto Rican pupils in contrast to 100% of the non-Puerto Rican pupils.

Comparison of Family Life in Puerto Rico and That in the Puerto Rican Families Surveyed Herein

An interesting comparison can be made between the results of Roberts and Stefani's survey in Puerto Rico[1] and the results of this present project:

1. The average size family of 6.34 is larger than that of 5.4 members reported on the island.

2. Although the Puerto Rican children here live in more crowded homes than do the non-Puerto Rican children, these conditions are far superior to those found on the island. Roberts and Stefani report that 71.0% of the households averaged more than two persons to a room; our figure is 12.77%. They report 32.4% of the households have people sleeping alone in a room or sharing it with but one other person; our figure is 50.8%.

3. With regard to a working mother, conditions faced here

in New York City do not differ too greatly from those to which the pupils are accustomed on the island. Roberts and Stefani report that 25.1% of all mothers were gainfully employed; our figure is 24.7%.

4. It would appear that families are more intact here than in Puerto Rico. Roberts and Stefani report that 61.1% of the children are living with both their mother and father; our figure is 74.1%.

However, the larger percentage of children living with only their mother here (16.6%) than in Puerto Rico (10.4%) would not seem to be easily explained.

Conclusions

Much has been written and said about the difficulties encountered in teaching children of Puerto Rican background and about the challenge in adapting the regular courses of study to their needs to aid in promoting the adjustment of these children to the New York City community. Since home economics is the one field of education whose sole purpose is the improvement of home and family living, all home economics programs should be appraised in the light of meeting the needs of the families that they serve. From the results of this survey, it would appear that there are no major differences in family attitudes and practices among Puerto Rican pupils and among those of continental-American-born pupils.

It would appear that both groups of pupils, Puerto Rican as well as non-Puerto Rican pupils, need help in the typical concerns of youth at the adolescent level. If there are any differences they would appear to be the following:

The Puerto Rican pupils more than the non-Puerto Rican pupils need help in the area of family relationships.

The Puerto Rican pupils need help in improving facilities for living within the home and for carrying on normal family life. Since they are living under more crowded conditions, emphasis needs to be on providing some kind of privacy for the members, and help in sharing limited facilities.

Since there is more unemployment among the Puerto Rican group, help must be furnished in the better use of the money they have and in achieving individual competence and independence through earning and spending money.

The non-Puerto Rican pupils more than the Puerto Rican pupils need help in the appreciation of the companionship of the family group.

The non-Puerto Rican pupils have to assume more responsibility for household management because there are more working parents in this group. Therefore, they have an immediate need to learn how to accept and perform the responsibility of food selection and preparation and of child care.

However, the above differences are not significantly great.

Modification of the home economics course of study would appear to be necessary only in terms of general education: placement of pupils and grouping for instruction; bridging the gap between prior schooling and the grade to which their age would en-title them; acquiring verbal facility in English; the need for non-verbal activities in which to work and learn; developing mutually accepting relations between Puerto Rican and non-Puerto Rican pupils; providing for social growth through the selection of content.

For both groups, evaluation of the curriculum should be made on the broad concepts of education for home and family living. Goals should not be too far beyond what the pupils might some day hope to attain, and emphasis should be on the things about which they can do something. The purpose of family life education is to help young people of all backgrounds to develop attitudes and acquire knowledge and judgment for establishing stable, happy, and well-managed homes.

Note

1. Lydia J. Roberts and Rosa Luisa Stefani, Patterns of Living in Puerto Rican Families, University of Puerto Rico, 1949.

Patricia Sexton, "Schools: Broken Ladder to Success." Spanish
Harlem: Anatomy of Poverty, New York: Harper & Row,
1965, pp. 47-70. Reprinted by permission.

School administrators have been under fire in East Harlem
and elsewhere. In New York's Lower East Side, school principals
locked horns with the area's Mobilization for Youth project; charges
and demands for resignation were made on both sides. The principals claimed they were being harassed by the parents.

Such parent arousal is new to these schools. Formerly, the
word of the school authorities was gospel. The new vocal chords
that parents in slum schools are exercising are hard to manage.
The new voice comes out loudly at first, louder than intended as the
bottled up complaints burst forth. Then parents learn to speak in
normal tones. In the meantime schoolmen will probably continue to
take a verbal beating and perhaps worse. Many have asked for it;
some have not.

Parents blame the school for the child's failure to achieve.
The school blames the parents, directly or by implication. In
some cases the blame is harsh: "They (the poor) are animals.
They don't care about their children. How can we be expected to
do anything?" More often the "blame" takes the form of pity rather than accusation: "They are so poor and deprived and apathetic
that they can't do anything. The families are broken, the children
have no fathers. What can the school do?"

Both pity and accusation have the same effect: the abandonment of hope and responsibility for achievement and change. While
some schoolmen have now turned from low IQ scores to conditions
and "deprivation" in the home as explanations of failure, few have
turned to the school for explanations. Those asking for change have
favored a "different" program of instruction for the poor. A good
idea, but what it has often meant in practice is "easy learning" or
detours around mastery of academic skills.

A composition written by a sixth grade Puerto Rican boy in
East Harlem, and reproduced exactly as written, reveals the size
of the problem:

"I would like to have good teachers because some teachers
like to hit the children so the children don't come to school
because of that. Some of the classmates like to pick on the
children that don't like to fight so the classmates pick on
them. Some school don' give good lunch and some of the
window are broken. The chairs aren't good the desk are
bombing and you can't write on it and some of the hallway
are written with chalk or crayon. Some teachers don't teach
us in every subjects. So the children don't learn a lot. So
the teachers leave them back."

405

We, the Puerto Rican people, in our way of life, do not
practice separation of race either by law, by custom, by
tradition or by desire. Notwithstanding this and suspectedly
because of this, in the nomenclature of race relations on the
Continent, we are designated neither White nor Negro, but a
special group denominated Puerto Ricans.

This objectivity, aggravated by our distinctiveness of culture,
has made us the victims of the same type of discrimination
and social persecution that is visited upon the Negro group
of this Country. The result has been to make us more conscious of the justice and righteousness of the cause of the
Negro in America today. We therefore, feel impelled to
identify ourselves with the Negro's struggle and lend him our
support, while at the same time conserving our own cultural
integrity and our way of life.

We, therefore, launch ourselves into the arena of today's
struggles for a full and complete education alongside the
Negro with the full knowledge that by so doing we are advanc-
ing our own cause.
-- Preamble to the "Draft Resolution on the Education of the
   Puerto Rican Child in New York City," issued by The National Association for Puerto Rican Civil Rights, February
   6, 1964.

East Harlem schools are segregated schools in the sense
that, in all but four schools, 90 per cent of the students are Negro
and Puerto Rican. They are not segregated in the sense that Central Harlem's schools are segregated. The Puerto Ricans, a large
percentage of them light skinned, make the difference. East Harlem's schools do not look segregated. Indeed, if the "nomenclature
of race relations" designated Puerto Ricans as white, the schools in
East Harlem would be fully integrated.
    The Puerto Ricans' feelings about segregated schools are
very different from the Negroes'. They do not have the history and
the sense of exclusion that Negroes have, and, because many of
them are in fact white, they have much less trouble "integrating."
    When the first city-wide school integration boycott in New
York came along, the citizens' school committee of East Harlem
hesitated. Puerto Ricans were not strong for protest or integration,
the feelings of whites were mixed, and strong Negro sentiment was
not forthcoming for various reasons. After lengthy debate, led
mainly by whites on both sides, the school committee finally supported the boycott. On the day of the boycott, its support was, like
Central Harlem's, more than 90 per cent effective.
    Whatever else it did, the boycott sparked parent and com-
munity interest in East Harlem. Parents and youths poured into
the preboycott rally, and the older hands who had been begging parents to attend meetings asked, "Where did they all come from?"
They came to protest. They had grievances, and they came to air
them. For many of these parents it was the first time at a school

meeting. Few Negro or Puerto Rican men attended, but the women came, and a number of white men.

School integration achieved by busing, a method championed in New York mainly by middle-class Negroes in the ghetto, has had less appeal in East Harlem than in other places. Puerto Ricans have held back from the integration and civil rights struggle, and many whites in East Harlem school groups feared that busing would remove the active parents from the schools. These whites seem to have one object: to build East Harlem into a real community. Both urban renewal and bused integration run contrary to their goal when they threaten to disrupt the community and remove the more "participating" citizens.

When East Harlem turned out for the integration boycott it was the first time in the community's history, or the city's, that Puerto Ricans joined with Negroes in protest and pursuit of a common goal.

Even the militant CORE youths, committed to organizing and building in the neighborhood, were lukewarm to busing anyone out of the community. They wanted to upgrade the neighborhood schools and tended to read citizen sentiment as also indifferent to bused integration. One Negro organizer said:

> The people in the community are not interested in integration. They just want better schools and better teaching for their kids. In Central and West Harlem there are many people who have a slightly better income level, slightly better earning capacity, and are more articulate than people in East Harlem and want integration.

And a white organizer joined in:

> The integration issue is irrelevant if you're trying to beat the rats off your children at night. We're not up to that point yet. You have to be above the survival level--I shouldn't speak not being black--you haven't got much energy left. Not only that, integration is a horrible experience for people. If your children are limited in the education they get, you really put them through a terrible experience by sending them elsewhere.

Still, East Harlem went all out for New York's first integration boycott...but not for the second.

A powerful argument for school integration is found in the transfer of eighty-three students from East Harlem to white, middle-class Yorkville.

"We found children who improved in many ways following transfer," a report said.[1] "In one, or two, just a handful of cases, there was little noticeable change, but in the majority of cases the children showed dramatic improvement in their school work, in their attendance and, generally, they showed renewed vigor and interest in school."

After parent protest, these East Harlem children had been bused to white schools to relieve overcrowding and promote integration. Only 7 per cent of eligible children in one school and 2 per

cent in the other signed up to transfer. Of these, fifty-eight were
Negroes, twenty-two were Puerto Ricans, and three were Chinese.
    Both the parents and children were far from being the most
destitute in these schools. Of the 83 who transferred, 34 were
reading on or above grade level. Most parents set high educational goals for their children. Sixty-seven parents planned that their
children complete high school; 39 that they attend college; and another 14 favored college if other conditions were met. Only 16
had not attended parent meetings in school. Fifty of the parents
had attended high school, 21 were high school graduates, and 4 had
some college. Fifty-two of the children had fathers at home:
forty-one did manual labor, 11 had professional or white collar
jobs. Only 10 mothers were employed full time.
    What happened to student conduct at the integrated school?
There were 13 changes reported, all improvements. As for interest in school, 47 showed an increase, one a decrease. There were
13 changes in attendance records, all improvements. There were
52 changes of "work habits;" 51 were improvements and one was a
decline. Only 5 parents said they were disappointed with the transfer; 11 were "pretty well satisfied;" and 55 said that they were
"well satisfied."
    Some people complained that the most interested parent lead-
ership "had bused their children out and were lost to East Harlem's
schools." For this reason they opposed further bused integration.
    It appears much easier to integrate schools that are not co-
educational. In 1959 East Harlem's Benjamin Franklin High School
was all boys. It was 29 per cent Negro, 28 per cent Puerto Rican,
and 43 per cent "other," i.e. white. When it became coeducational,
in 1960, the "others" dropped from 43 per cent to 20 per cent.
Catholic schools that are sexually segregated are, for this reason,
easier to integrate racially.
    Increasingly, both whites and Negroes are leaving the public
school integration crisis and transferring to Catholic parochial
schools. Both go to escape mounting Negro enrollment in public
schools. Before World War II, one in twelve students in the United
States was enrolled in Roman Catholic schools; now the ratio is one
in eight. Catholic school enrollment between 1945 and 1962 increased 129 per cent (to 5.5 million students), while public school
enrollment grew only 69 per cent (to 38.8 million students). The
integration conflict seems to be swelling parochial schools.
    Some Catholic schools in East Harlem provide a common
meeting place where racially mixed youth groups have relatively
familiar contact. There are few such places in East Harlem.
    The Catholic schools are strictly disciplined, and parents
are virtually required to attend school meetings. East Harlem's
St. Cecilia's Church bulletin, in a message to parents, said, "After
a short business meeting the parents will meet the teachers and receive their report cards." Report cards are one insurance that
parents will come. The Catholic school is better able to handle integration than the public school for at least three reasons; segregation of the sexes in many Catholic schools, the natural and sometimes arbitrary controls of ethnic mixture, and centralized church
authority.

In New York about half of all Negro and Puerto Rican children go to public schools that are at least 10 per cent "other"
(white).   It is not known what proportion of these integrated minority
children are Negro.   In New York the biggest integration hurdle is
the primary school.   Secondary school students can travel on their
own to integrated schools.   Small children cannot, and their parents
(both Negro and white) are often reluctant to have them bused outside the neighborhood.   A state education department report proposed educational parks as a long-range integration solution and,
for the short term, an integrated "middle school," starting in the
fifth grade (5 through 8), to which children would be bused if necessary.   The purpose of these proposals is to make integration possible by drawing students from a larger and more heterogeneous
area.   The feasibility of these parks is unknown since few people
have much experience with them.

The Quality Issues

>We're asking for a new school.   It will be a ghetto school,
>but we can improve the educational level and move them
>downtown.   For four years they say, "Well, you'll have
>your school this year."   Then they say, "We can't fit it
>into the city budget."

>They said they had no money for repairs.   Then after three
>boycotts, they sent some men around to build a garbage bin
>and they also built some partitions around the toilets.   They
>think that way!   You bug them and they put up a board
>around the toilet which is in the lunchroom.
>-- An eighteen-year-old CORE organizer.

Education is said to be a ladder for the poor to climb up,
but in East Harlem it is rickety and many steps are missing.   Of
the sixteen elementary schools in East Harlem, twelve have over-
capacity enrollment.   Four out of five junior high schools are overcrowded.[2]   The result is a short school day for students who
should have a long one.

Educators stress nursery and early childhood education.   Yet
only a few of East Harlem's schools had a full five-hour first
grade.   About one out of three or four children, it is estimated,
enter first grade without kindergarten.   Space for kindergarten
classes has been in short supply, and the schools have seldom recruited among parents for enrollment.   Often there has been a long
waiting list for kindergarten.   In New York children who have gone
to kindergarten are usually put automatically in top "ability groups"
in first grade, where they tend to stay throughout school.

New schools in East Harlem came slowly and never kept up
with demands made by new housing projects and population.   Schools
should be included in the ground floors of new projects in order to
keep pace with population growth and integrate the school into the
community.

"Tear down the armory, and put up a school" was the slogan
of an East Harlem mass demonstration.   The site demanded was an

"integrated" one within white territory to the south. The armory
has been used, among other things, as a polo ground by wealthy
East Siders and as a police stable. Citizen demands have per-
suaded the board to earmark funds for a school on the site.

One school that would send pupils to the proposed new school,
had three different principals in five years and a 90 per cent turnover of teachers. While the average teacher-turnover in New York
City as a whole has been 10 per cent, the turnover in East Harlem
has been 20 to 25 per cent.

In one recent year, 57 per cent of East Harlem's school
teachers had permanent licenses, 25 per cent were substitutes, 18
per cent had probationary licenses. In the junior highs, 44 per
cent had permanent licenses and 43 per cent were substitutes.
Many licensed teachers in junior highs taught subjects they were not
licensed to teach. Many with only elementary licenses were teaching in junior highs.[3]

Reading and IQ scores of East Harlem children decline with
age. In the third grade, students in one district scored 2.8 on a
reading test compared with the city average of 3.5. By the eighth
grade, the East Harlem students were two full years below grade
level.

By the eighth grade their IQ score was 83.2, compared with
103.4 for the city. In the third grade it had been 91.2, compared
with 98.8 for the city.

In the junior high schools, 12 per cent of students were
reading above grade level, 8 per cent on grade level, 10 per cent
one year below grade level, and 70 per cent more than one year
below grade level.

As for what the children think about school, the compositions
of sixth grade students, quoted exactly, describe some of their
wishes and needs: A Puerto Rican girl wrote:

> I would like to be change is to have a better playground
> where the children could enjoy. Or perhaps a big swim-
> ming pool and around it many fountains. Or to have
> better clean Bathrooms and to have better teachers that
> could teach you all different languages, all maybe a better
> auditorium where many people of all over the world could
> come and make us happy, and in the auditorium could have
> better comfortable seats, all maybe better hallways.

A Negro girl wrote:

> I would like to have more teachers in the school where the
> children could have different subjects everyday. And the
> school need more bathrooms because they have one each
> bathroom on each floor, they need at least three bathrooms
> on each floor. And they need a bigger auditorium because
> this auditorium is too small for this many children that
> they have here.

The children are inclined to blame themselves for their failure to learn. And, on the top of their mind always is fear or concern about physical abuse. Sixth graders commented:

> Suppose you were the teacher and you explained something

and I said, "I wasn't listening" and you explained it again,
and I wasn't listening again.   You would get mad, right?
Some of the kids are real bad.   Some of the teachers don't
know how to hit kids.   You hit with a ruler.   You should
see the Catholic school.   You talk to somebody and the sister she tell you to stand up and she takes the ruler and she
hits you real hard two times on each hand.

If a person wants to learn, he will concentrate, and he
wouldn't get whipped, because by whipping a person he'll
just go on and do it again.   Like my brother, he's real
bad.   He do everything in his classroom.   He pull up
girls' dresses.   He knock down chairs.   This teacher hit
my brother, and he was all black and blue and he was
bleeding.   The teacher has no right to hit no child, they
should send for his mother.

My father says if I get too much unsatisfactory, he's gonna
whip me.   Because if my mother waste her time getting up
at 7 o'clock to wake me up, for me to do nothing, it's my
fault.   I admit it.   I don't listen to nothing what my teacher
says.

I think the teachers should treat us better, you know.
We're young, we don't hardly know nothing.   You know,
when you tell them something, they say, "Where'd you get
that strange story or something."   You tell them the truth
but they don't believe you or nothing.   But I think it's not
the teacher's fault.   It's up to you.   True.

Teacher's Comment

Some teachers try and succeed.   Others try and fail.   Some
don't try, at least not very hard; they give up almost before they
start.   One East Harlem teacher of a "medium slow" fifth grade
(not a "bottom" class) was having trouble and, like many others,
was at the point of throwing in the sponge:

I won't try to teach them something like social studies.
They don't have the basic concepts.   This is true even in
reading.   You can't relate to them.   When they do hit a
story that means something there is a dramatic difference
in their comprehension.   I can't say why some stories
mean something and others don't.   Social studies is a complete loss.   Probably the only thing you can do is tell them
social studies through a story, but this is not social studies.
It is nothing like how laws are made or why a railroad was
built in a certain place.   You shouldn't call story telling
social studies...

This teacher had found one clue to her pupils' learning--
that there was a "dramatic difference in their comprehension" when
a story meant something to them, but she didn't know where to take

this clue, how to find stories and social studies material that had meaning.

Another teacher of a "slow" sixth grade had found many other clues and had a different approach and attitude to her students:

> By demanding correct speech at all times I have found their
> Spanish accents have just about disappeared by now. Their
> vocabularies have begun to enlarge. They must give reports
> orally, without a paper. They must know what they have
> written so well that they can remember the main ideas. At
> the beginning of the year I read aloud to them a great deal
> of the time, pointing out to them what I thought about pitch,
> timbre, pace, etc. Then we used a tape recorder and im-
> mediately they became self-critical, saying things like
> "That isn't me, is it?" and "I didn't say it that way, did
> I?" I didn't let them do any written work at first. After
> a few trips we would start to have open discussions. For a
> few weeks we did almost only talking. I tried to move them
> from specifics to abstracts. ...Then we were ready for writ-
> ing...During the Panama crisis they did sequential pictures
> of why we went there in the first place, how the situation
> grew during the years, and how things began to deteriorate.
> I put the pictures up for a week. Then we discussed what
> the pictures meant. We had discussed the Panama crisis so
> thoroughly that the students seemed to feel personal about it
> by the time they sat down to divide up the topic for the il-
> lustrations.

Though this teacher had a "bottom" group, she had succeeded, according to her story, in teaching the children something about so-cial studies, even in such remote places as Panama, and she had successfully modified their accents. Another teacher said:

> Things just don't make an impression on these children.
> We haven't found the way to teach them. For some reason
> they don't relate to school. The reason is that their whole
> culture is different. The only way to teach them is to re-
> peat things 25 times unless for some reason it means some-
> thing to them. They are not motivated at home. They can't
> learn unless they see the specific reason for doing some-
> thing.

Another teacher feels the children have a problem of "how to get along," and that they are learning this even up until the third grade. Not until the fourth grade are they ready to learn concepts. "They play too much. Discipline of themselves is a problem--per-haps it is at the root."

One East Harlem teacher felt that "Negroes and Puerto Ri-cans have incorrect perception. They probably see only vague out-lines. This would explain why they do so poorly in reading."

Many teachers complain about administrators and say that they stand in the way of learning. One said: "Administrators are

my main problem as a teacher. They are not creative. They think
the slow child won't get things. I don't think this is fair. For example: going to the World's Fair. Only the top three classes will
go. The children feel this and think they should live up to the expectations that they won't catch on to things."

Another teacher complains that beginning teachers are not
properly briefed, that they should be told "how far down these children are." Teachers have to keep "starting over at a lower level."
New teachers never get "concrete help." Administrators give
teachers the wrong books; "the books are too high;" and many are
"worthless." There is no communication between teachers; there
should be "some way for new teachers to get rex-o-graphed materials that more experienced teachers have drawn up."

One experienced and highly rated teacher in an East Harlem
school explains her monitor system for keeping order, her attitudes
toward the children and the rewards they need:

> I appoint monitors at the beginning of the year. I make it
> clear that I will change an appointment if they are not worthy.
> I give awards each month based on conduct, grades, appear-
> ance, and manners. I jot down things that are outstanding
> for each child--good or bad. I used to give an assembly
> award for dressing but now the whole class dresses right so
> I had to give it up. They must be given recognition. For
> instance, right now I have left them alone for this interview.
> It lets them know that I trust them. I don't have monitors
> to take names. There is no tattletaling in my class. One
> way I helped built up this spirit was by taking them on trips
> and doing things together. They know they must act a cer-
> tain way in order to do these things.

Knowledge, at its most useful, is an accumulation of wisdom
and experience from the past. Teachers, custodians of this accumulated knowledge, have virtually no access to the accumulated experience of the thousands of other teachers who have been out in
combat with the same problems, and who have through trial and
failure worked out some successful methods. Neither the colleges
of education nor the school administrators have done much to help
the novice teacher who leaves her middle class cocoon to venture
out into the slum school. The schools of East Harlem are filled
with these novice teachers, most of them eager but lost.

Dr. Kenneth Clark has said: "The concept of the culturally
deprived child is a new stereotype, a new excuse, a new rational-
ization for inadequate education of minority group children. Instead of those responsible for their education being made to teach
them, all sorts of alibis are provided. The only thing that will
really matter is the total reorganization of the educational system
in these communities.

"On the evidence available to date," he went on, "one is
forced to conclude that the major reason why an increasing number
of Central Harlem pupils fall below their grade levels is that substandard performance is expected of them. For this, the schools,
principally its administrators, must shoulder the major responsi-

bility, although the community must share some of the blame."[4]
Dr. Clark cited the data below in support of his statement:

Table II.
Assessment of Pupil Potentials in Central Harlem

	Principals	Assistant Principals	Teachers
1. Per cent reporting that one-fourth or less of the pupils have college level potential.	45	62	53
2. Per cent expecting one-half or fewer of their pupils to finish high school under present conditions.	32	57	46
3. Per cent expecting one-half or fewer of their pupils to finish high school under conducive conditions.	4	19	3
4. Per cent stating that greater learning potential in their students was a major change necessary to carrying out professional duties.	9	14	4

The Rev. Milton Galamison, leader of New York's school
boycott, has contended that "in the Negro school the child is not
being taught. The basic problem we are fighting in the segregated
school is one of attitude, which expresses itself in low expectations
on the part of middle-class teachers whose concept of a human being is not met by these children. The most liberal teacher will
say, 'If the Negro child had an equal economic, cultural and social
background, he could learn as well as other children.' This if-ism
results in 'not much teaching and not much learning.' "
Puerto Ricans have also reacted to the schoolman's concept
of "cultural deprivation," but in a different way. The Puerto Ricans are proud of their culture. Joseph Monserrat, of the Commonwealth of Puerto Rico, asks:
Is a culture that has for four centuries been able to maintain the individual dignity, value and worth of all its members (despite differences in race and class) a deprived or
disadvantaged culture when compared with one that has been
striving to achieve these values and has as yet not been
able to do so?

Some of the dispute has to do with word meaning. The term
"culturally deprived" suggests the negative aspects of low income
culture. In some cases, as in Dr. Frank Riessman's excellent
book, The Culturally Deprived Child,[5] the positive aspects of this
culture are stressed. This emphasis tends to boost rather than
depress teacher morale and expectation.
Another version of the deprivation theme has entered the
arena, put there by psychoanalysis. The school gets the child too
late, the argument goes, after the early, formative years, and
therefore can do very little either by integrating or improving the

quality of education for the disadvantaged. While the argument has strong points, suggesting that much more attention should be given to nursery schools and the child-rearing education of parents, it also suggests what is not proven, that most Negroes and other disadvantaged adults are deficient in the affection, care, or instruction they give to infants. It also ignores the achievements of older children under ideal school conditions and the regenerative effect on older youths and adults of civil rights activity.

What is observed in East Harlem and other slum schools is that children compare favorably in their achievement until the third and fourth grades, when they begin a relative decline. This might indicate that the critical period for the child is in these years rather than the preschool years.

Recognizing the importance of the infant years, however, it is essential that the schools reach not only the child but the mothers as well. On the assumption, true or not, that there are remediable deficiencies in parental care, the parent becomes as much an object of instruction as the child. One hypothesis that should be examined is that the children of the poor are typically put out on their own and given weighty responsibilities at an early age. The parents are burdened, and they are forced to pass on these burdens to young children. Families are often large, and children follow fast after one another. The mother of the large, impoverished family has no help with her chores and no time for the child who is no longer an infant who needs her continuous attention. The child is put on his own and given responsibilities for the care of other children. In short, the child may not be given the individual attention he needs for growth. He becomes a small adult at an age when more advantaged children are just beginning to emerge from infant dependency.

In this sense also, "deprivation" has a double edge. The "deprived" child, because of his early adulthood, knows a great many things that the advantaged do not, too much perhaps. If the schools were able to make use of this knowledge, the "deprived" child might be at an advantage rather than a disadvantage in school.

East Harlem is split into two school districts, as it is split into two police precincts and two political (assembly) districts. The district in the north section also includes schools in Central Harlem. The southern district includes many white, middle class schools, and Martin Mayer, one of the country's leading writers on the schools, has been chairman of its local school board, a group whose functions and powers are rather like those of parent-school groups. Both boards are said to be hard-working and close to the people. They have formed a closer link between citizen and school.

Whites tend to dominate East Harlem schools. All school principals are white and so are almost all administrators. Negroes and Puerto Ricans, in fact, have little to say officially about what goes on in East Harlem's schools. Even unofficially, as parents, they take a back seat and are usually silent. The chairman of the East Harlem Schools Committee, the main citizen group, has been a white woman whose Negro husband operates a small business. Whites usually do most of the talking and leading in the committee.

There is little true integration in parent groups. "In every

school," says Mrs. Nora Bowens (a white woman who works full
time on schools for the East Harlem Project), "there is one major
ethnic group dominating the parent groups. There is seldom a mixture." In recent years a number of Negro and Puerto Rican leaders have come forth, and active parent groups are found in some
schools.

The Schools Committee, from its inception in 1954, had
spurts of energy. Until the first integration boycott, the committee was for a time at low ebb. It did not know what to do next.
Its initial job had been to get new schools for East Harlem. Now
many feel the committee should branch out into the troubled area
of curriculum, an area that has in the past been held as the exclusive jurisdiction of schoolmen.

In East Harlem the major parent demand on curriculum is
that the children improve reading and academic skills. They do
not ask for dreary drills or any particular "method" of instruction.
They want only improved learning. The schools are touchy about
intrusions into curriculum. According to Preston Wilcox of the
East Harlem Project, the worst verbal beating he has gotten from
the schools came after he asked the question at a meeting: "How
can we get parents involved through curriculum?"

The Parent-Teacher Associations are criticized by many active people in East Harlem because they seldom take on any real
issues. Some feel that the PTA's do only what the principal tells
them to do--money-raising, cake sales, socials--and are upset
when curriculum is raised.

Ellen Lurie gave much of the initial drive to the Schools
Committee in the early 1950's. The first act of the committee was
to petition for new schools. Ninety parents gathered and went to
the Board of Estimate with proposals. "Women sat up nights working on their speeches; and Negro and Puerto Rican parents did
things they never thought they could do," said Mrs. Lurie. The
new schools came, but they did not automatically bring quality education. Hence, the new desire of East Harlem parents to take up
curriculum and quality issues. The committee's demands for quality include: academic achievement, smaller class size, preschool
programs, full five-hour first grades, remedial reading in grades
3 to 6 rather than junior high, "gifted child" classes in each school
rather than in one separate school, separate classes with "positive
programs" for children who are discipline problems, involvement
of parents in the educational process as school aides. [6]

Negroes and Puerto Ricans also want the history of their
people to be taught in the schools, and not just to their own children. One young Negro CORE organizer put it this way: "I said
to the history teacher, 'Why are you showing me a book where
there's only one paragraph about Negro history. You mean to tell
me 400 years, with only one paragraph.' The teacher told me,
'Sit down. Lincoln freed the slaves and you should be glad you're
in this part of the book.' Look in the index and look at page 389,
one paragraph, 'Negroes.' The kids don't like this at all. Some
books don't even have a paragraph. They just put down a few
people like Joe Louis and Marian Anderson."

Some citizens in East Harlem are now raising questions, not

only about curriculum but about the "power structure" of the
schools.   They want more Negro and Puerto Rican representation
at high levels in the schools.   As it is, of more than 1,200 top-
level administrative posts in New York's school system, only about
four are held by Negroes.   Of some eight hundred principals, only
several are Negro.   Out of a nine-man city school board, only one
is a Negro; and there is no Puerto Rican member--in a city where
40 per cent of public school children are Negro and Puerto Rican.

What do East Harlem's children think about school?   They
are seldom asked.   When they are, they express little interest in
what they are learning in school.   The reasons they give for going
to school and doing well almost always bear on future prospects,
not on the rewards of learning but on other rewards that school can
offer.   These remarks of sixth grade Negro and Puerto Rican boys
are typical:

> You go to school to get an education so when you grow up
> you can get a decent job, and you can have a high school
> diploma.   You can go to a decent junior high, and then you
> can go to a decent high, and go to a decent college, and
> get a decent job.   When we grow up it'll be the nuclear
> age, and we couldn't do the jobs our fathers do.   They'll
> be done by machines.

> If you don't go to school you'll be a nobody.   You'll be a
> drifter all your life.

> School's OK, cause when you get a job you got to count
> things in your mind, not on your fingers.   If you don't go
> to school you grow up to be dumb.   You won't be able to
> get a job.

> Whenever I wake up I say, you better study, you know, to
> get a better education.   If you study now, you could become
> something big.   When you grow up you get a good job.

A Perspective

Citizen unrest usually moves in an upward spiral.   Among
the poor it has moved in the past few years, during the peaks of
the civil rights revolt, from apathy to agitation, then back to some
midpoint of constructive criticism and interest.

In New York City--big, anonymous, and noisy--a person with
a grievance must make a loud noise to be heard.   The school boycotts and the rent strikes were that loud noise.   They made the
conditions of the poor at last visible and audible.   But the momen-
tum of the revolt (the agitation cycle) was slowed by many related
factors and may not move on again for some time.   Among these
factors were: a presidential election, the civil rights and poverty
bills, the summer ghetto riots that injured only Negroes but frightened everyone, the inability of Negro leaders to bargain their demands and to work in unity, the white backlash, the fatigue of Negro and white activists who wearied of danger and street demonstra-

tions, the northern liberal retreat when the demonstrations came
into the back yard, the failure of the demonstrations to produce immediate and visible results.

More than anything, the school boycotts and the demands for
bused integration of de facto segregated students in New York
brought the civil rights struggle to the door of the white middle
class liberal and caused him to withdraw support from direct action and demonstration.   These liberals, most of whom genuinely
seek equality and integration, balked at busing and dropped away
from groups like CORE, leaving their future as exclusively direct
action groups in doubt.

The loudest and most racist "busing backlash" came from
conservative organizations (Parents and Taxpayers) in middle class
Queens.   A quieter, more moderate, and sadder backlash came
from sections of the Jewish community, which more than other
groups in New York, have been in contest with Negroes and Puerto
Ricans over scarce facilities in the public schools.   Many liberals
have, furthermore, been reluctant to acknowledge the presence of
unequal educational opportunities for Negroes and Puerto Ricans in
the North.   Their response has been: We did it despite discrimination, why can't they?

Having reached this cyclical plateau, very little mass agitation over schools can be expected in the nation's northern ghettos.
This will not mean much in East Harlem since it was a reluctant
partner in the boycotts in the first place, and since the Puerto
Ricans keep it from being a Negro ghetto.

The integration boycott has undoubtedly had a positive effect
on the schools of East Harlem.   It has brought public attention and
extra aid to the schools.   It has clearly informed schoolmen that
parents are dissatisfied with the progress of their children in
school.   Above all, it aroused parents and citizens in East Harlem
to a new interest in the schools and showed them that they could,
through their own actions, influence school policies.   Schoolmen
have traditionally complained that parental apathy is responsible for
low achievement in slum schools.   The boycott aroused many parents from this "apathy."

Insofar as East Harlem has held back from direct action in
the schools, however, it seems likely to get less from the schools
and from new aid programs than Central Harlem, Brooklyn, and
other more "militant' communities.   The wheel that squeaks loudest
usually gets the most grease.

East Harlem schools need a lot more grease.   New schools,
relief from crowding, experienced teachers, preschooling, a suitable curriculum and texts, belief in the children, contact with parents, small classes--all are visible needs.   Integrationists claim it
is impossible to have quality education in segregated schools.   This
may be true, but the claim is unproved, either way.   The effect of
quality education on achievement in ghetto schools is unknown because it is virtually untried.   Only in the last few years has much
serious experimentation with teaching methods and curriculum for
the disadvantaged been tried.   And only now are some suitable reading materials being prepared.

Concentrated research and development in education, com-

parable to the R&D that in the technological and scientific worlds
are regarded as essential to progress, should be supported by public and foundation funds. This educational R&D should pull together available knowledge about successful methods in educating the
disadvantaged, and develop new techniques and curriculum.

It is unlikely that quality education can be brought to the
slums until members of disadvantaged minorities are brought into
the schools--many of them, at high and low levels, as board members and as educational aides either in the schools or outside them.

The schools need new ideas and new energy. One way to
get them is to democratize decision-making and bring in teachers,
parents, and children on decisions and planning. The organization
of teachers into unions and parents into citizen groups is already
beginning to bring the knowledge and wisdom of these two vital
groups to bear on educational decision-making. Their participation
so far has mainly taken the form of protest, brought on by their
general exclusion from school decision-making.

In the money-versus-method controversy, some experts say
that only money, lots more of it, will make any difference in slum
schools. On the other hand people like Martin Mayer say that
money will make little or no difference, that new methods and new
approaches must be found. Both money and methods are needed.
About half as much money is being spent on New York's slum child
as on the child in the better suburbs of New York. With such expenditures, the poor could, without question, be given quality education. The point is, money will not be forthcoming in such amounts,
even though the nation can afford it. So the question becomes:
What are the most efficient and economical ways to give top-quality
education to the poor?

The complaint made by Negro leaders that the schools expect too little of Negro and Puerto Rican students is well taken.
Many schoolmen do not really expect that the poor could, with
proper instruction, learn as much and do as well as middle class
students. This may, indeed, be the major flaw in the slum school:
low expectations on the part of administrators, teachers, children,
parents. This does not mean, however, that the disadvantaged can
always start at the same place as the advantaged. The imposition
of impossibly difficult texts and assignments on children inevitably
leads to frustration and failure. But, with suitable methods and
extra help, these children ought to be able to end at the same place
as other children.

In East Harlem and similar communities there are, then, at
least three routes to change in the schools: (1) change of attitude,
motivation, expectation from failure to success; (2) new instructional and organizational methods; (3) community arousal and the
power and pride it can provide to impoverished citizens.

One solution to the teacher shortage and the general shortage of educated leadership in the slum community would be to offer
special housing buys to teachers in the neighborhood schools. If
the housing offered were good enough, it would not only attract and
hold teachers in the community, but would provide a needed link
and understanding between school and community. These teachers
would also provide community leadership. In East Harlem, for ex-

ample, one of the most active minority group leaders and two of
the most active white parents are also teachers who live and work
in East Harlem. For the most part, however, teachers in slum
schools are "absentee professionals" who leave the school and
neighborhood promptly at three o'clock.

A very heavy burden has been put on slum schools. It is
put there because there are so few other services and institutions
in the slum community. So the school must tend to the intellectual, emotional, recreational, organizational, etc., needs of children
and adults in the community--or at least it is asked to try. Other
groups and agencies should be brought in to help carry this heavy
weight. In particular, a massive volunteer program of youths and
adults, recruited from the community, universities, women's clubs,
church groups, etc., should be drawn in to help with tutorials,
trips, and other instructional needs.

Though the problems of East Harlem's schools are glaringly
visible, it should be said that in many schools the impression is
one of health, not sickness. Teachers can be found in every school
who are creative and effective and who like and respect the children. Most of East Harlem's children seem to like school, and
most are well treated. Moreover, most of the children appear well
dressed, clean, happy, and healthy. It is striking to the stranger
who may be expecting tattered urchins or a scene from Oliver
Twist or The Blackboard Jungle. This is perhaps the neglected
part of the story. The better known and more tragic part is that
so much is wrong; so much is needed and so little received.

It is the same as in the neighborhood. Health and disease
live alongside each other--great strength and serious weakness.
We tend to pick on the soft spots, the weaknesses, because they
need attention. At the same time the strengths need to be seen,
credited, and built upon.

Notes

1. Releasing Human Potential, prepared by the East Harlem Project and the New York City Commission on Human Rights,
1961.

2. The total overload is 2,700 in the elementary schools and 440
in the junior highs as of the end of 1963.

3. Source: Bureau of Educational Research, Board of Education.

4. Harlem Youth Opportunities Unlimited, December 12, 1963.

5. New York: Harper & Row, 1961.

6. At the time of the first school boycott, a new Puerto Rican civil
rights group issued its first detailed manifesto of school demands. Its five stages of demands were:
Language: Spanish should be part of the curriculum of all
elementary schools, and all teachers should have a working
knowledge of Spanish. High schools: Vocational high schools

as they currently exist should be abolished, along with the
general course diploma.   All junior highs should be integrated within a year.   Reading retardation: A five-hour
daily instruction period should be guaranteed; IQ tests should
be abolished; changes should be made to "reflect the specialized learning problems of Puerto Ricans;" a "positive image
of the Puerto Rican child and his culture must be fostered
to enhance the child's motivation for learning."

Teacher training and recruitment: Since there are only 230
Puerto Rican teachers out of 40,000 intensive recruitment
should be undertaken, teachers with Spanish accents should be
accepted.   Teachers should be taught greater understanding
and appreciation of Negro and Puerto Rican culture, "not in
sterile terms of Brotherhood but aimed at handling specific situations that destroy the dignity and morale of the
Puerto Rican youngster."

Puerto Rican Representation: "Neither white dominant
groups nor the Negro minority can speak for the Puerto Rican who must speak for himself."   An effort should be made
"to insure Puerto Rican parent participation in the process
of decision-making which will influence at all levels the future of his child's education, and that such participation be
received in a courteous, dignified manner."   A Puerto Rican should be appointed to the next school board vacancy.

Appendix I

A Summary in Facts and Figures

(From Puerto Rico; Size and Population. San Juan, Commonwealth of Puerto Rico. Department of Labor, Migration Division, 1966.)

Puerto Rico is more than 11 times as densely populated as the United States. If the U.S. had as many people per square mile as Puerto Rico, its population would include nearly everybody in the world.

Area (in square miles)	3,435
Population (July, 1965)	2,633,000
Population per square land mile	766
Population of Continental U.S. (July 1, 1965)	192,854,000
Population of Continental U.S. per square land mile	65

Puerto Rico's Population Growth

Puerto Rico's population has grown rapidly since the first census in 1765. Since 1940 it has increased 40.9 percent. The island's population growth has been offset in recent years by migration to the United States.

Year	Population	Change over Preceding Census	
		Number	Percent
1765	44,883	---	---
1775	70,250	25,367	56.5
1800	155,426	85,176	121.2
1815	220,892	65,466	42.1
1832	330,051	109,159	49.4
1846	447,914	117,863	35.7
1860	583,308	135,394	30.2
1877	731,648	148,340	25.4
1887	798,565	66,917	9.1
1899	953,243	154,678	19.4
1910	1,118,012	164,769	17.3
1920	1,299,809	181,797	16.3
1930	1,543,913	244,104	18.8
1935	1,723,534	179,621	11.6
1940	1,869,255	145,721	8.5
1950	2,210,703	341,448	18.3
1960	2.349,544	138,841	6.3
1961 (a)	2,400,900	51,356	2.2
1962 (a)	2,454,600	53,700	2.2

Puerto Rico's Population Growth (cont.)

Year	Population	Change over Preceding Census	
		Number	Percent
1963 (a)	2,513,200	58,600	2.4
1964 (a)	2,572,200	59,000	2.3
1965 (b)	2,633,000	60,800	2.4

(a) Estimated as of July 15.   Changes are over preceding year
(b) Puerto Rico Department of Health, July 15, 1965

* * * * * * * *
Puerto Rico--Vital Statistics

Year (a)	Annual Birth Rate (b)	Annual Death Rate (b)	Rate of Natural Increase (b)
1887-1899 average	45.7	31.4	14.3
1899-1910 average	40.5	25.3	15.2
1910-1920 average	40.4	24.0	16.4
1920-1930 average	39.3	22.1	17.2
1930-1935 average	39.0	20.1	18.9
1936-1940 average	38.9	19.1	19.8
1940	38.5	18.4	20.1
1941-1945	40.6	15.8	24.8
1946-1950 average	40.9	11.6	29.3
1951-1955 average	36.1	8.5	27.6
1956-1960 average	33.3	7.0	26.3
1961	31.4	6.8	24.6
1962	31.2	6.8	24.2
1963	31.4	6.8	24.6
1964	30.9	6.8	24.1
1965 (c)	27.5	6.7	20.8

(a) 1887-1940, intercensal years. 1940-1964, calender years.
(b) Per 1,000 population
(c) Puerto Rico Dept. of Health, July 15, 1965.

* * * * * * * *
Progress in Public Health
Infant Mortality Rate (a)

Year	Rate	Year	Rate	Year	Rate
1940	113.4	1950	68.3	1960	43.7
1941	116.2	1951	67.1	1961	41.3
1942	103.4	1952	66.6	1962	41.6
1943	95.3	1953	63.3	1963	44.2
1944	99.5	1954	57.8	1964	51.7
				1965 (b)	43.8
1945	93.4	1955	55.1	(a) Deaths of children un-	
1946	83.8	1956	55.4	der 1 yr of age per 1,000	
1947	71.5	1957	50.3	live births.	
1948	78.5	1958	53.7	(b) Puerto Rican Dept. of	
1949	67.6	1959	48.1	Health, July 15, 1965.	

Death Rates
From Principal Causes in 1965

Rate per 100,000

Cause	1940	1965 (a)	Change %
Diarrhea and enteritis	405.2	39.3	-90.4
Tuberculosis	260.2	17.2	-95.6
Pneumonia	169.2	30.3	-85.4
Heart Disease	125.4	138.6	+14.3
Nephritis	108.4	5.7	-95.3
Malaria	98.6	0.0	100.0
Cancer	51.7	84.2	+68.0

(a) Puerto Rican Dept. of Health, July 15, 1965

* * * * * * * *

Demographic Statistics
Changes: 1940 to 1965 (c)

Increase in population (1940-65)	40.9%
Decrease in death rate	63.6%
Decrease in birth rate	28.3%
Increase in rate of natural population increase	.7%
Decrease in infant mortality rate	62.0%
Increase in life expectancy (1940-65)	52.2%

Comparisons With Continental U.S.

Death Rate, 1965: (a)
Puerto Rico	6.7
Continental U.S.	9.4

Birth Rate, 1965: (a)
Puerto Rico	30.3
Continental U.S.	19.7

Infant Mortality Rate, 1965: (b)
Puerto Rico	43.9
Continental U.S.	24.9

Life expectancy at birth, 1965:
Puerto Rico	70 yrs.
Continental U.S.	70.2 yrs.

(a) Per 1,000 population.
(b) Deaths of children under one year of age per 1,000 live births
(c) Puerto Rico Department of Health, July 1965 and U.S. Department of Health, Education and Welfare, October 1965.

Life Expectancy at Birth

1910	38 years
1940	46 years
1950	61 years
1955	68 years
1960	70 years
1963	70 years*

* Data indicates life expectancy will continue to be 70 yrs.

* * * * * * * *

Progress in Public Education

Education is given high priority in Puerto Rico; 32.3 percent of the Commonwealth's total budget in 1963-64 was spent for educational purposes. In 1940, Puerto Rico's schools were able to accommodate only 51 percent of the school-age population; by 1964 they were accommodating 84 percent.

	1939-40 (a)	1958-59 (b)	1962-63 (b) (c)	1964 (b) (c)
Enrollment	303,729	646,039	668,949	793,149
Number of classroom teachers	6,294	12,647	16,000	16,891
Instructional staff	n.a.	13,853	17,258	18,893
Number of classrooms	5,201	11,430	13,608	14,068
Expenditures, in millions of $	$ 7.7	$63.0	$ 91.0	$ 128.9
Cost per student in average daily attendance	$ 28.40	$ 115.81	$ 171.00	$ 206.77
Enrollment, University of Puerto Rico	4,987	17,644	22,958	24,800

(a) Includes public day and evening schools, vocational classes, educational program for veterans, and the University of Puerto Rico. Excludes private schools.

(b) Includes public and private kindergarten, elementary, junior and senior high schools and the University of Puerto Rico, and night students.

(c) Puerto Rico Planning Board.

* * * * * * * *

Transportation and Communication

	1939-40 (a)	1963-64 (a)	Percent Increase
Number of registered motor vehicles (b)	26,847	285,516	976.6
Number of telephones (b)	16,778	171,869	924.4
Number of television sets imported since March 1954 (when TV began in Puerto Rico)			300,000(b)
Number of households per TV set			1.6

(a) Data for fiscal year
(b) Economic Development Administration of Puerto Rico.

* * * * * * * *

Puerto Ricans in the U.S. Armed Forces

Puerto Rico's 65th Infantry Regiment of the U.S. Army has gained fame in two World Wars and in the Korean Conflict. Over 65,000 Puerto Ricans participated in the Second World War, and over 43,000 in the Korean War.

Korean Conflict: June 20, 1950 to July 25, 1953

91.2 percent of the total Puerto Rican participants in the Korean Conflict were volunteers.

Total Puerto Rican participants	43,434
Total who volunteered for service	39,591
Total Puerto Rican casualties (dead, wounded, and missing in action)	3,540

One out of every 42 casualties suffered by U.S. troops in the Korean Conflict was a Puerto Rican. Puerto Rico suffered one casualty for every 660 inhabitants of the Commonwealth, as compared with one casualty for every 1,125 inhabitants of the continental United States.

* * * * * * * *

Economic Development ... 1940-1964

Per capita income, although only about one-half that of the poorest U.S. state, is now the highest in the Caribbean area and second highest in all of Latin America (exceeded only by oil-rich Venezuela).

Family income in 1964 reached $3,818. The income of the working man is keeping pace with the development of the economy as a whole.

426

Income from manufacturing: Puerto Rico's net income from manufacturing rose from $291 million in 1960 to $486 million in
1964, an increase of 67 percent. Much of this gain is
traceable to the manufacturing activities of plants promoted
by our Economic Development Administration.

Over 1,066 new factories have opened since 1947, directly creating
68,410 new jobs, plus another 60,000 to 70,000 indirectly
in services and trade.

Employment has increased in all sectors of the economy except
agriculture, where mechanization is taking place, and home
needlework, where low-paying jobs are declining and being
replaced by new factory jobs.

Unemployment, still a serious problem, has been decreasing
steadily since 1940.

Trade with the U.S. shows that on a per capita basis, Puerto Rico
continued to be the United States' number-one customer,
spending $3,066,301 per day for goods and services from
the continental U.S.

	1939–40 (a)	1963–64 (a)	Percent Change
Production (Gross Product) (b)			
In current prices (millions $)	287	2,532	782.2
In 1954 prices (millions $)	499	2,027	306.2
Per capita in current prices ($)	154	1,003	551.3
Per capita in 1954 prices ($)	269	803	198.5
Net Income (National Income) (b)			
In current prices (millions $)	225	2,097	832.0
In 1954 prices (millions $)	400	1,783	345.8
Per capita in current prices ($)	121	830	586.0
Per capita in 1954 prices ($)	218	706	223.9
By Economic Origin (millions $)			
Agriculture	70.5	205	190.8
Manufacturing	26.7	486	1,720.2
Construction	2.6	144	5,438.5
Transportation, public utilities	18.2	195	982.2
Trade and services	47.3	598	1,164.3
Government (b)	44.8	275	513.8
Other (c)	24.7	136	450.6
Wages and Salaries			
In current prices (millions $)	125.2	1,463	1,068.5
In 1940 prices (millions $)	125.2	781.2	534.0

427

	1939-40 (a)	1963-64 (a)	Percent Change
Net Profits of Business Enterprises			
In current prices (millions $)	99.0	721	628.3
In 1940 prices (millions $)	99.0	385	288.9
Manufacturing			
Number of establishments	798 (d)	2,045	156.3
Employment	25,758 (d)	100,700 (h)	290.9
Agriculture			
Value of production (millions $)	84	279	232.1
Employment (thousands)	230 (f)	151 (g)	-34.3
Banking (millions $) (h)			
Bank deposits	76.3	1,133	1,384.9
Private checking accounts	27.9	295	958.3
Private savings accounts	17.4	282	1,520.7
Government accounts	27.2	148	444.1
Other	3.8	408	10,636.8
Loans	33.1	844	2,449.8
Debits	73.1	1,417	1,838.4
Assets	92.7	1,205	1,199.9
Investments	4.1	229	5,485.4
Electric Power Production			
In millions of kilowatt-hours	166	3,403	1,950
Exports and Imports			
Total exports (millions $)	92.3	895.	869.7
Per capita exports ($)	49	313.7	540.2
Total imports (millions $)	107.0	1,353.5	1,165.0
Per capita imports ($)	57	486.1	752.8
Exports to U.S. (millions $)	90.9	864.7	851.3
Imports from U.S. (millions $)	100.5	1,119.2	1,013.6

(a) Data for fiscal year except where otherwise indicated.
(b) Data for 1939-40 exclude income of U.S. military personnel
    stationed in Puerto Rico; but include income of Puerto Ricans
    in U.S. armed forces stationed outside Puerto Rico. The re-
    verse is true of the 1960-64 data.
(c) Included finance, real estate, and miscellaneous, less net inter-
    national flow of capital returns.
(d) Census data for 1939.
(e) Census data for 1958.
(f) Data for April 1940.
(g) Data for April 1964.
(h) Data for June 30, 1964.

* * * * * * * *

Labor Force

	1939-40 (a)	1963-64 (a)	Percent Change
Total in labor force (thousands)	602	734	+21.9
Employed (thousands)	512	654	+27.7
Unemployed (thousands)	90	80	-11.1
Percent unemployed	15.0	10.8	-28.0

* * * * * * * *

Industrial Distribution

	Number (a)		Percent		Percent Change
	April 1940	April 1964	April 1940	April 1964	
Total Employment (b)	512	654	100.0	100.0	+27.7
Agriculture (c)	229	139	44.7	21.3	-39.3
Manufacturing (except home needlework)	56	106	10.9	16.2	+89.3
Home needlework	45	7	8.8	1.1	-84.4
Construction	16	57	3.1	8.7	+256.3
Wholesale and retail trade	54	115	10.5	17.6	+113.0
Transportation, communication, and public utilities	20	42	3.9	6.4	+110.0
Services (d)	86	176	16.8	26.9	+104.7
Other	6	12	1.2	1.8	+100.0

(a) In thousands.
(b) Figures may not add to total due to rounding.
(c) Since April represents the peak of the agricultural season, these figures give a greater preponderance to agriculture than would annual averages (which are not available by industrial breakdown for 1940).
(d) Includes government.

* * * * * * * *

Selected Data on Puerto Rico,
April 1960

Percent in Labor Force (14 years old and over):

Males	71.5%
Females	22.1%
Males per 100 females	98.0
Median age	18.5

429

Selected Data on Puerto Rico,
April 1960 (cont.)

Percentage Distribution of Employment by Major Industry Groups:

Agriculture	26.5%
Manufacturing	16.1
Trade	17.2
Transportation, communication and public utilities	6.8
Services including government	23.8
Others	9.5

Percentage Distribution of Employment by Major Occupation Groups:

Professional workers	5.1%
Semiprofessional workers	1.2
Farmers and farm managers	6.8
Proprietors, managers and officials, except farm	9.3
Clerical, sales and kindred workers	15.3
Craftsmen, foremen and kindred workers	8.4
Operatives and kindred workers	17.2
Private household workers	2.9
Protective service workers	1.5
Service workers, except private household and protective	6.4
Farm laborers and foremen	18.6
Laborers, except farm	7.4

Literacy (for persons 10 years old and over)

Literacy (for persons 10 years old and over)	83.0%
Percentage urban population	44.2

* * * * * * * *

Puerto Rican Migration to the Continental United States
Annual Averages

1909-1930	1,986	1941-1950	18,794
1931-1940	904	1951-1960	41,212
		1961-1965	6,319

Each Year 1946-1965

1946	39,911	1956	52,315
1947	24,551	1957	37,704
1948	32,775	1958	27,690
1949	25,698	1959	29,989
1950	34,703	1960	16,298
1951	52,899	1961	-1,754*
1952	59,103	1962	10,800
1953	69,124	1963	-5,479*
1954	21,531	1964	1,370
1955	45,464	1965	16,678

* The minus figure represents a net outflow.

* * * * * * * *

Puerto Rican Population
of Continental U.S.

Date	Total	Puerto Rican Birth	Puerto Rican Parentage
Apr. 1, 1960	855,724*	596,280*	259,444*
Apr. 1, 1950	301,375	226,110	75,265
Apr. 1, 1940	n.a.	69,967	n.a.
Apr. 1, 1930	n.a.	52,774	n.a.
Jan. 1, 1920	n.a.	11,811	n.a.
Apr. 15, 1910	n.a.	1,513	n.a.

* Does not include data for Puerto Ricans in Arizona, California, Colorado, New Mexico, and Texas, which list persons with Hispanic surnames.

* * * * * * * *

Puerto Rican Migration
to New York City

During the 1940's 90 percent or more of the migrants were settling in New York City, the world's largest labor market. Since then, as new job openings have created an increased demand for workers in other areas of the U.S., the proportion of those settling in New York has declined steadily and seems to be leveling off at about 60 percent or a little less.

Year	Estimated Migration to New York City	Percent of Total Migration
1950	29,500	85
1951	42,300	80
1952	45,500	77
1953	51,800	75
1954	16,100	75
1955	31,800	70
1956	34,000	65
1957	22,600	60
1958	17,000	60
1959	18,000	60
1960	9,600	60
1961 (a)	-----	--
1962	6,500	60
1963	-----	--
1964	822	60

(a) During the course of this year net migration was away from the States.

* * * * * * * *

431

Puerto Rican Population of
New York City

Date	Total	Puerto Rican Birth	Puerto Rican Parentage
Apr. 1, 1960	612,574	429,710	182,864
Apr. 1, 1950	245,880	187,420	56,460
Apr. 1, 1940	n.a.	61,463	n.a.
Apr. 1, 1930	n.a.	44,908	n.a.
Jan. 1, 1920	n.a.	7,364	n.a.
Apr.15, 1910	n.a.	554	n.a.

* * * * * * * *

Puerto Rican Population of
New York City by Boroughs, 1960

	Total Population	Puerto Rican Population	% of Total Population	% Distribution of Puerto Rican Population
New York City	7,781,984	612,574	7.9	100.0
Manhattan	1,698,281	225,639	13.3	36.8
Bronx	1,424,815	186,885	13.1	30.5
Brooklyn	2,627,319	180,114	6.9	29.4
Queens	1,809,578	17,432	1.0	2.9
Richmond	221,991	2,504	1.1	0.4

(The Migration Division estimate of the Puerto Rican population of
New York City projected for 1965 is 730,000. It was based on
average increase by birth since 1960 plus the percentage of the net
migration that is estimated to remain in the city.)

* * * * * * * *

Puerto Rican Population by States
and Selected U.S. Cities (a)

Alabama	663	Florida	19,535
Alaska	562	Miami	6,547
Arizona	1,008	Georgia	2,334
Arkansas	207	Hawaii	4,289
California	28,108	Honolulu	3,129
Colorado	844	Idaho	60
Connecticut	15,247	Illinois	36,081
Bridgeport	5,840	Chicago	32,371
Hartford	2,307	Indiana	7,218
New Haven	1,169	East Chicago	2,889
Waterbury	1,027	Gary	2,946
Delaware	773	Iowa	226
District of Columbia	1,373	Kansas	1,136

Puerto Rican Population (cont.)

Kentucky	1,376	Buffalo	2,176
Louisiana	1,935	New York City	612,574(b)
New Orleans	1,010	Rochester	1,990
Maine	403	North Carolina	1,866
Maryland	3,229	North Dakota	68
Massachusetts	5,217	Ohio	13,940
Boston	995	Cleveland	4,116
Michigan	3,806	Lorain	3,799
Minnesota	387	Youngstown	1,814
Mississippi	301	Oklahoma	1,398
Missouri	940	Oregon	233
Montana	53	Pennsylvania	21,206
Nebraska	333	Bethlehem	1,145
Nevada	179	Philadelphia	14,424
New Hampshire	212	Rhode Island	447
New Jersey	55,351	South Carolina	1,114
Camden	3,759	South Dakota	124
Hoboken	5,313	Tennessee	499
Jersey City	7,427	Texas	6,050
Newark	9,698	Utah	473
Paterson	5,123	Vermont	108
Passaic	1,713	Virginia	2,971
Perth Amboy	2,718	Washington	1,738
Trenton	1,803	West Virginia	252
New Mexico	433	Wisconsin	3,574
New York	642,622	Milwaukee	2,820
		Wyoming	50

(a) 1960 Census Population: Subject Reports PC(2): Puerto Ricans in the United States.

(b) The Migration Division estimate of the Puerto Rican population of New York City projected for 1965 is 730,000. It was based on average increase by birth since 1960 plus the percentage of the net migration that is estimated to remain in the city.

* * * * * * * *

Sources

Page 422   Puerto Rican population: Puerto Rico Department of Health.   U.S. population: U.S. Bureau of the Census.

Puerto Rican population, 1765-1960: Puerto Rico Statistical Yearbook, 1962; San Juan, Puerto Rico Planning Board; Puerto Rican population estimates. Puerto Rico Department of Health.

Page 423   Data for 1887-1940: Harvey S. Perloff, Puerto Rico's Economic Future; Chicago, University of Chicago Press, 1950; p. 197. Data for 1940-1965: Puerto Rico Department of Health. Annual Report on Vital Statistics.

Infant mortality, 1936-65: Puerto Rico Department of Health, Annual Report on Vital Statistics, 1965.

Pages 424-25   U.S. rates and life expectancy: Trends; U.S. Department of Health, Education, and Welfare. Puerto Rican life expectancy: Puerto Rico Department of Health.

Puerto Rico Department of Education. Puerto Rico Planning Board.

Page 426   Puerto Rico Planning Board. Economic Development Administration of Puerto Rico

Report of Teodoro Vidal, Military Aid to the Governor.

New factories: Puerto Rico Economic Development Administration. Employment, unemployment, and wage earners' family income: Puerto Rico Bureau of Labor Statistics. Other data: Puerto Rico Planning Board.

Page 427   Puerto Rico Planning Board, Net Income and Gross Product, Puerto Rico, and unpublished reports. Net income by economic origin adjusted to new series from previous data.

Page 428   Puerto Rico Planning Board.

Page 429   1939-40 data: Puerto Rico Planning Board. 1960-64 data: Puerto Rico Bureau of Labor Statistics.

Labor force data: Puerto Rico Department of Labor, Bureau of Labor Statistics. Schooling, sex proportions, median age, literacy, and urban population: 1960 Census of Population.

Page 430   Puerto Rican migration: U.S. Immigration and Naturalization Service, op. cit.

Pages 431-33   Puerto Rican population of U.S., census data for 1910-1960. Puerto Rican population of New York City, census data for 1910-1960. Migration to New York City: Estimated by Migration Division.

Puerto Rican population by states and selected cities: Bureau of the Census.

434

STUDIES OF PUERTO RICAN CHILDREN IN AMERICAN SCHOOLS
A Preliminary Bibliography

Compiled by

Frank M. Cordasco
(Professor of Education, Montclair State College;
Educational Consultant Migration Division,
Commonwealth of Puerto Rico)

and

Leonard Covello
(Educational Consultant Migration Division,
Commonwealth of Puerto Rico;
Former Principal, Benjamin Franklin High School,
East Harlem, New York City)

Introduction

A clear need exists for a convenient handlist of
studies on Puerto Rican children and their experiences
in American mainland schools. The compilers of the present
bibliography intend it as a preliminary list and contemplate its continuing up-dating. It is not intended as a
complete list of studies, and inevitably some significant
studies will have unfortunately been overlooked. We
invite suggestions and additions.

We have not attempted a general bibliography on
Puerto Ricans in the United States, although we have
included a short bibliographical note on those titles
which constitute a working list for the over-all study
of the migration and experience of Puerto Ricans on the
American mainland. Since the bibliography is essentially
limited to the Puerto Rican experience in mainland
schools, neither annotation (the individual titles are
generally a clear indication of concern) nor subject
captioning appeared to be practicable or necessary.

Since the Puerto Rican child is usually found in a
context of severe socio-economic deprivation, many of the
titles on the "disadvantaged child" deal (although very
briefly) with Puerto Rican children in the context of
poverty. These titles (in a burgeoning literature) we
have not attempted to list, but we call attention to the
Catalog of Selected Documents on the Disadvantaged: A
Number and Author Index (OE 37001) and a Subject Index
(OE 37002), Washington: U.S. Government Printing Office,
1966, which the Education Research Information Center
(U.S. Office of Education) assembled as "a collection of

1740 documents on the special education needs of the disadvantaged - in support of the Elementary and Secondary
Education Act of 1965 (P. L. 89-10)". An excellent review
of the literature in the field is Harry Miller's Education
for the Disadvantaged (New York: Free Press, 1967), and
good guides to programs for disadvantaged children are
Doxey A. Wilkerson, "Programs and Practices For Compensatory Education For Disadvantaged Children", Review of
Educational Research, vol.35 (December 1965), pp.426-440;
and Edmond W. Gordon and Doxey A. Wilkerson, Compensatory
Education For the Disadvantaged: Programs and Practices:
Pre-School Through College (New York: College Entrance
Examination Board, 1966).

The Covello Papers, which contain a vast amount of
material reflecting the experience of the near quarter-
century tenure as principal at Benjamin Franklin High
School in East Harlem of Leonard Covello, constitute an
invaluable repository of source material on the Puerto
Rican experience both in the community and the school and
are presently being catalogued.

The problems of Puerto Rican children in American
schools are in many ways analogous to those faced by non-
English speaking children in other eras; and in this
connection, Leonard Covello's recently published study
of the Italo-American child* presents a broadly analogous
tableau of the social deprivation, ethnicity, language
handicap and different cultural identity which the child
brought to the American school. Nor should the literature
on the Mexican-American child and his educational needs
be neglected (in five states of the American Southwest
there are some 1.75 million school children with Spanish
surnames).**

General Bibliographical Note

The best source on Puerto Rican migration is the
Migration Division of the Department of Labor,

---

* Leonard Covello, The Social Background of the Italo-
  American School Child: A Study of the Southern Italian
  Mores and their Effect on the School Situation in Italy
  and America, edited and with an Introduction by F.
  Cordasco (Leiden, The Netherlands, E.J. Brill, 1967)
  xxxii, 488 pp.
** See Herschel T. Manuel, Spanish Speaking Children of
  the Southwest: Their Education and the Public Welfare
  (Austin, University of Texas Press, 1958); and "Bi-
  lingualism and the Bilingual Child: A Symposium",
  Modern Language Journal, vol.49 (March-April 1965),
  pp.143-239.

436

Commonwealth of Puerto Rico, which maintains a central mainland office in New York City and offices in other United States cities. It also maintains an office in Puerto Rico to carry out a program of orientation for persons who intend to migrate to the states. See Joseph Monserrat, Puerto Ricans in New York City (Migration Division, Commonwealth of Puerto Rico, 1967); and Bibliography on Puerto Ricans in the United States (ibid., April 1959). In 1964, the New York City Department of Health placed the Puerto Rican population in New York City at 701,500, representing a 9.3 per cent of the city's population. A projection of this study by the Migration Division of the Puerto Rican Department of Labor estimates the 1966 Puerto Rican population at 762,000.

A vast literature exists on Puerto Rico. Generally, good sociological and anthropological studies are easily available. Among these are Theodore Brameld, The Remaking of a Culture: Life and Education in Puerto Rico (New York: Harper, 1959); Melvin M. Tumin and Arnold Feldman, Social Class and Social Change in Puerto Rico (Princeton, 1961); Julian H. Steward, ed., The People of Puerto Rico (University of Illinois, 1956); 2nd pr., 1966; Kurt W. Back, Slums, Projects and People: Social, Psychological Problems of Relocation in Puerto Rico (Duke University, 1962); Gordon K. Lewis, Puerto Rico: Freedom and Power in the Caribbean (New York: Monthly Press Review, 1963); James R. Bourne and Dorothy P. Bourne, Thirty Years of Change in Puerto Rico: A Case Study of Ten Selected Rural Areas (New York: Praeger, 1966); and E.J. Berbusse, The United States in Puerto Rico, 1898-1900 (University of North Carolina, 1966).

For Puerto Ricans in the United States, see Dan Wakefield, Island in the City: Puerto Ricans in New York (Boston: Houghton Mifflin, 1959); Patricia Sexton, Spanish Harlem: Anatomy of Poverty (New York: Harper, 1965); Clarence Senior, The Puerto Ricans: Strangers - Then Neighbours (Chicago: Quadrangle, 1965); Elena Padilla, Up From Puerto Rico (Columbia University, 1958); Nathan Glazer and Daniel P. Moynihan, Beyond the Melting Pot (M.I.T. - Harvard, 1963); and Oscar Lewis, La Vida (New York: Random House, 1966).

An invaluable source of research studies is Jesse J. Dossick, Doctoral Research on Puerto Rico and Puerto Ricans (New York University, School of Education, 1967).

I. <u>Unpublished Materials</u>*

Baldwin, Clare C. "Education of the Non-English Speaking and Bi-Lingual (Spanish) Pupils in the Junior High Schools of Districts 10 and 11, Manhattan." June, 1952, 131 pp.

"Basic Education Facts of the Puerto Rican Educational System." n.d., 10 pp.

Bureau of Applied Social Research of Columbia University. "Letter to Governor Jesus T. Pinero Summarizing the Principal Findings of the Study of Puerto Rican Migrants in New York City which the Bureau has been Conducting since November, 1947." June 15, 1948, 15 pp. In the Covello Papers - Personal Files.

Committee of the Association of Assistant Superintendents. "A Program of Education for Puerto Ricans in New York City." 1947, 107 pp.

"Commonwealth of Puerto Rico, Department of Labor, Migration Division. Puerto Rican Migration to the United States." 1 p.

_____. "Puerto Rican Population by States (according to the 1960 Census)." May 20, 1964, 1 p.

_____. "Puerto Rican Population by States and Cities." 8 pp. (Based on 1960 U.S. Census.)

Community Council of Greater New York. Research Department. Bureau of Community Statistical Services. "Population of Puerto Rican Birth or Parentage for New York City, by Borough: 1960." April 13, 1962, 1 p.

Covello, Leonard. "Recommendations Concerning Puerto Rican Pupils in Our Public Schools." May 1, 1953, 9 pp.

Covello Papers. Files on Puerto Rican Program at Benjamin Franklin High School. [see "Introduction", <u>supra</u>]

Covello Papers. Personal Files.

Covian, Sherrill. "The Effect of Unemployment and Under-employment on the Puerto Rican Male in New York City." October 27, 1965, 23 pp.

"Demographic Tables" (for East Harlem). X Appendix. September, 1964. Unpaged.

---

* Most of these materials are in the <u>Covello Papers</u>. See "Introduction", <u>supra</u>.

East Harlem Neighborhood Study Club. "Report of Operations, 1965 Summer Session." 11 pp.

"Educational Background in Puerto Rico." n.d., 28 pp.

"Factors Affecting Pupil Registration: Day Schools -
Migration Balance in the Movement of Pupil Population to
and from Places Outside New York City - School Years
1953-1954 to 1962-1963 (and) Day Schools - Migration
Balance in the Movement of Pupil Population to and from
Places Outside New York City, by School Group and Borough
- School Year 1962-1963." 1 p. (Statistical)

Fitzpatrick, Reverend Joseph P., S.J. "Delinquency and
the Puerto Ricans." Address given to Fordham University
School of Business, October 8, 1959. 18 pp.

Kouletsis, Greg. "Guidance Follow-Up Study, Spring, 1964
(Comparative Study - JHS 13 M & JHS 117 M)." Spring,
1964. Unpaged.

Mayar, Frank. "Puerto Rican Pupils in New York City Public
Schools: A Comparison of the Effects of Two Methods of
Instructional Grouping on English Mastery and Attitudes."
A Ph.D. dissertation for Teachers College, Columbia
University. 1954, 73 pp.

Mayor's Committee on Puerto Rican Affairs in New York
City, Sub-Committee on Education, Recreation and Parks.
"Study on Puerto Rican Pupils in Senior and Vocational
High Schools." May 1, 1953. Unpaged. [L. Covello, chair-
man]

_____. "Questionnaire on Puerto Rican Pupils in Our
Schools." May 1, 1953, 6 pp.

"Memorandum Re: Day Care Centers." November 30, 1950, 1 p.

"Migration Balance: Day Schools - Migration Balance in
the Movement of Pupil Population to and from Places Out-
side New York City, by Borough and Geographic Area -
School Year 1962-1963 (and) Day Schools - Migration
Balance in the Movement of Pupil Population to and from
Places Outside New York City, by Geographic Area -
School Years 1953-1954 to 1962-1963." 1 p. (Statistical)

Morris High School and the Commonwealth of Puerto Rico,
Department of Labor, Migration Division. "Study of Puerto
Rican Students who were Graduated from Morris High School
- June 1961." June 21, 1963, 23 pp.

New York City, Department of Welfare, Press and Public Relations. "Statement by the Honorable Raymond M. Hilliard, Welfare Commissioner of the City of New York upon his Arrival in Puerto Rico, August 21, 1950." 3 pp.

New York University, School of Education. "Proceedings of the Annual Conferences for Puerto Rican Citizens of New York: 1961, 1962, 1963, 1964." Unpaged.

Oliveras, Candido (Secretary of Education of Puerto Rico). "What Are the Educational Needs of Puerto Ricans who come to New York?" An address given at the New York University Puerto Rican Conference, January 14, 1961. 11 pp.

Pennisi, Guy V. "Some Suggestions for Helping Non-English Speaking Children, Manual for P.S. 33 Manhattan." Prepared by Guy V. Pennissi (Graduate Student, New York University) under the direction of Principal Morris C. Finkel, P.S. 33. November 23, 1949. Unpaged.

Puerto Rico, Department of Labor, Employment and Migration Bureau. "Progress Report on the Puerto Rican Migrants." April 11, 1950, 10 pp.

_____. "Report on Visits to New York City Schools Submitted to Mr Manual Cabranes, Director, by Dr J.J. Osuna, Educational Consultant." 1948, 9 pp.

Rausehenbush, Winifred. "New York and the Puerto Ricans." (Manuscript of article for _Harpers_) 23 pp.

Sanguinetti, Carmen. "Adapting Science Instruction in New York City Schools to the Needs of Puerto Rican Background Pupils." A Ph.D. dissertation for Teachers College, Columbia University. 1956, 163 pp. [See Dossick, _infra_, generally]

Senior, Clarence. "The Newcomer Speaks Out: What Puerto Ricans want and need from Voluntary Agencies and the Public." A paper delivered at the National Conference on Social Welfare, Atlantic City, June 1960. 17 pp.

Shields, Osceola, _et al_. Teachers College Course S 200 FA. "Los Boricuas - Our Newest Neighbors." (Excerpts from a Group Report) 26 pp.

Three hundred eighty-one cumulative record sheets of the Graduates of Benjamin Franklin High School, June, 1963.

Welfare Council of New York City. "Educational Background in Puerto Rico." 1947, 28 pp.

_____. Letter to Dr Leonard Covello from Adrian P. Burke, Chairman. Committee on Puerto Ricans, January 8, 1951, 1 p.

_____. Letter to Dr Leonard Covello from Coverly Fischer, President, September 25, 1950, 1 p.

_____. Letter to Dr Leonard Covello from James R. Dumpson, Consultant, May 21, 1951, 2 pp.

Welfare Council of New York City, Committee on Puerto Ricans in New York City. "Changes to be Made in Draft of Report." December 17, 1947, 1 p.

_____. Sub-Committee to Implement Recommendations. "Summary of Minutes: November 17, 1950." 2 pp.

_____. "Puerto Rican Children: Some Aspects of Their Needs and Related Services." June 30, 1949, 12 pp.

_____. "Report." Submitted January, 1948, 69 pp.

_____. Sub-Committee on Education. "Agenda: May 2, 1947." 2 p.

_____. Sub-Committee on Questionnaire. "Summary of Minutes: March 20, 1951." 2 pp.

_____. Letter to Dr Leonard Covello from James R. Dumpson, Consultant and Secretary, November 2, 1950, 1 p.

_____. Sub-Committee on Education. "Summary of Minutes: May 2, 1947." 4 pp.

_____. Sub-Committee to Evaluate Reports. "Summary of Minutes: November 10, 1950." 4 pp.

_____. Sub-Committee to Survey Progress on Puerto Rican Report. "Agenda: March 20, 1951." 13 pp.

_____. "Summary of Minutes: Tuesday, November 18, 1947." 5 pp.

_____. "Summary of Minutes: Wednesday, December 3, 1947." 2 pp.

_____. "Sumary of Minutes: November 1, 1950." 3 pp.

II. Published Materials

Abrams, Charles. "How to Remedy Our 'Puerto Rican Problem'," Commentary, Vol.XIX, No.2 (February, 1955), pp.120-127.

"Activaran La Ensenanza Del Inglés Basico en las communidades Boricuas," La Prensa, February 23, 1952.

Alcala, Roberto de. "Nueva York - Ciudad Hispana," Temos (February, 1953), pp.7-8.

Anastasi, Anne and Fernando A. Cordova. "Some Effects of Bilingualism upon the Intelligence Test Performance of Puerto Rican Children in New York City," The Journal of Educational Psychology, Vol.XLIV, No.1 (January, 1953), pp.1-17.

Anderson, Virginia. "Teaching English to Puerto Rican Pupils," High Points (March, 1964), pp.51-54.

"Antonio Gonzalez es Nombrado Miembro de La Junta Escolar No.18," El Diario De Nueva York, May 7, 1952.

"Aumentan Los Fondos Para Comedores De Escuelas Publicas De Puerto Rico," El Diario De Nueva York, August 1, 1952, p.3.

Baldwin, Clare C. "Program Outlined for Puerto Ricans," The New York Times, December 5, 1947.

Bell, John. "Puerto Rican Influx Jams Crowded Schools," New York World Telegram, May 3, 1947.

Berkowitz, Elaine. "Family Attitudes and Practices of Puerto Rican and Non-Puerto Rican Pupils," High Points (March, 1961), pp.25-34.

Berle, Beatrice B. Eighty Puerto Rican Families in New York City. New York, Columbia University Press, 1958.

Biddick, Mildred L. and Esther A. Harrison. "Spanish-American Children Receive Help in Achieving Status," School Management (August, 1947).

"Bi-Lingual Problems in Puerto Rican Study," Curriculum and Materials, Vol.XI, No.2 (February, 1948), pp.1-2.

Blourock, Barbara. "Aspira in the Junior High School," High Points (February, 1966), pp.53-55.

Brameld, Theodore. The Remaking of a Culture. New York, 1959, 478 pp.

Briggs, Frances M. "As Five Teachers See Themselves," Educational Forum, Vol.XXVIII, No.4 (May, 1964), pp.389-397. [reprinted by Migration Division, Commonwealth of Puerto Rico, 1965]

Burma, John. Spanish Speaking Groups in the United States. Durham, N.C., Duke University Press, 1954.

Calitri, Charles J. "A Puerto Rican Story," American Unity, Vol.XV, No.1 (September-October, 1956), pp.19-24.

"Campaña De Saneamiento En Harlem," El Diario De Nueva York, June 20, 1949, p.3.

Cannon, Antoinette. "The Puerto Ricans," Interpreter Releases, Vol.XXIV, No.37 (August 28, 1947), pp.296-304.

Cebollero, Pedro. A School Language Policy for Puerto Rico. San Juan, 1945, 133 pp.

"The Challenge in Working with Puerto Rican Families," Pathways in Child Guidance, Vol.II, No.3 (April, 1960), pp.3-6.

Chenault, Lawrence R. The Puerto Rican Migrant in New York City. New York, 1938, 190 pp.

"Children from Puerto Rico," Curriculum and Materials (May-June, 1954), 16 pp.

"City College Da Satisfaccion a Maestra Boricua," El Diario De Nueva York, July 30, 1952, pp.1, 17.

Citizens' Committee for Children of New York. Do You Understand? N-E Program in the New York City Schools. New York, Citizens' Committee, 1961, 23 pp.

"Cívicas Y Culturales: Asociacion de Padres," El Diario De Nueva York, June 13, 1952, p.8.

"Cívicas Y Culturales: Centro Cultural Chileno, Inc.," El Diario De Nueva York, June 13, 1952, p.8.

"Cívicas Y Culturales: Conferencia Sobre Educación Escolar," El Diario De Nueva York, May 21, 1952, p.13.

"Cívicas Y Culturales: Reunion Civica," El Diario De Nueva York, June 2, 1952, p.5.

443

"Cívicas Y Culturales: Escuela Publica De La Calle 109 (Oeste) Abre su Matricula Para Kindergarten," El Diario De Nueva York, May 7, 1952.

Collazo, Francisco. The Education of Puerto Rican Children in the Schools of New York City. San Juan, Department of Education Press, 1954, 14 pp.

"Columbia Plans Study of Puerto Rican Migration to N.Y.C.," PM, October 14, 1947.

"Comprension Por Conocimiento." (Editorial). El Diario De Nueva York, May 27, 1952, p.9.

Cordasco, F. and Leonard Covello. "Schools and the Spanish Speaking Community," Congressional Record, June 12, 1962, pp.A4322-A4323.

Cordasco, F. "Helping the Language Barrier Student," Instructor, Vol.72 (May 1963), p.20.

_____. "Spanish Harlem: The Anatomy of Poverty," Phylon: The Atlanta University Review of Race and Culture, Vol.26 (Summer 1965), pp.195-196.

_____. "The Puerto Rican Child in the American School," Congressional Record, Vol.CXI, No.195 (October 19, 1965), pp.26, 425-26.

_____. "Florence Nightingale in the Ghetto: Patricia Sexton's Spanish Harlem," Journal of Human Relations, Vol.13 (4th Quarter 1965), pp.572-574.

_____. "Nights in the Gardens of East Harlem: Patricia Sexton's East Harlem," Journal of Negro Education, Vol.34 (Fall 1965), pp.450-451.

_____. "The Puerto Rican Child in the American School," American Sociological Association. Abstracts of Papers (61st Annual Meeting), 1966, pp.23-24.

_____. "The Puerto Rican Child in the American School," Kansas Journal of Sociology, Vol.II (Spring 1966), pp.59-65.

_____. "Studies in the Disenfranchised: The Puerto Rican Child," Psychiatric Spectator, Vol.III (November 1966), pp.3-4.

_____. "The Puerto Rican Family and the Anthropologist: Oscar Lewis, La Vida, and The Culture of Poverty," Urban Education, Vol.III, No.1 (1967), pp.32-38.

444

_____. "Puerto Rican Pupils and American Education,"
School and Society, Vol.95 (February 18, 1967), pp.116-119.

_____. "The Puerto Rican Child in the American School,"
Journal of Negro Education, Vol.36 (Spring 1967), pp.181-186.

_____. "The Puerto Rican Family and the Anthropologist,"
Teachers College Record, Vol.68 (May 1967), pp.672-675.

_____. "Educational Programs for Puerto Rican Pupils,"
New York Times, May 30, 1967.

_____. "The Non-English Speaking Child in the American
School: Continuing Challenge to Education in a Democratic
Society." Statement and testimony before the General
Education Sub-Committee of the U.S. House of Represent-
atives. June 29, 1967. Washington, 11 pp. (H.R. Bill
9840).

_____. "The Puerto Rican Family and the Anthropologist:
Oscar Lewis, La Vida, and the Culture of Poverty,"
Congressional Record, July 18, 1967, pp.H8914-H8915.

_____. "The Non-English Speaking Child in the American
School: Continuing Challenge to Education in a Democratic
Society." Testimony before the Senate Sub-Committee on
Bilingual Education, July 21, 1967. Washington, 11 pp.
(Senate Bill 428).

_____ and Louis Roederer. "Modern Languages and Modern
Living," in Joseph S. Roucek, ed., Changing Aspects of
the Foreign Language Teaching in the United States.
New York: Philosophical Library, 1967.

Covello, Leonard, with Guido D'Agostino. The Heart is the
Teacher. New York, 1958, 275 pp.

"Crearan un Fondo de Becas para los Boricuas Residentes
en N.Y.," El Diario De Nueva York, December 9, 1951, p.14.

"Cree Jansen Que El GBno. Federal y El Estatal Deben
Ayudar A Boricuas," La Prensa, February 1, 1954.

Crozier, Emmet. "Puerto Rico: Frontier of Enterprise,"
New York Herald Tribune, June 10, 1948.

Darcy, Natalie T. "The Performance of Bilingual Puerto
Rican Children on Verbal and on Non-Language Tests of
Intelligence," Journal of Educational Research (March,
1952), pp.499-506.

"Las Declaraciones de Osuan," El Diario De Nueva York, October 29, 1948.

Denny, M.C. "Chicago Meets San Juan," Instructor, Vol.76 (February, 1967), pp.38-39.

Diaz, Eileen. "A Puerto Rican in New York," Dissent, Vol.VIII, No.3 (Summer 1961), pp.383-385.

Dossick, Jesse J. Doctoral Research on Puerto Rico and Puerto Ricans. New York, New York University, School of Education, 1967. ("Education," pp.12-19).

Dworkis, Martin B., ed. The Impact of Puerto Rican Migration on Governmental Services in New York City. New York, 1957, 74 pp.

"Educadora Boricua Llevara a las Cortes Al City College de N.Y. Alega es Victima de Discrimen," El Diario De Nueva York, April 24, 1952.

Education-in-the-News. A monthly clip sheet for the use of U.S. editors and radio commentators. New York, Puerto Rican Public Relations Committee, Inc., April 1, 1949, 3 pp.

"Education in Puerto Rico." San Juan Review. Special Education Issue, Vol.II, No.5 (June, 1965), 88 pp.

"Education is Sparking Puerto Rico's Industrial Growth," The New York Times (Special section on Puerto Rico), November 7, 1965, p.18.

"Education of Puerto Rican Children in New York City," The Journal of Educational Sociology, Vol.XXVIII, No.4 (December, 1954), pp.145-192.

"Educacion y Orientación en el Plan de Beneficencia Aqui," La Prensa, November 28, 1947, pp.1, 5.

Elam, Sophie E. "Acculturation and Learning Problems of Puerto Rican Children," Teachers College Record, Vol.61 (February 1960), pp.258-264.

Emery, Helen T. "How the City's Schools Greet Puerto Ricans," New York World Telegram and Sun, November 4, 1953.

_____. "Schools Here Aid Progress of Migrants," New York World Telegram and Sun, June 28, 1956, p.34.

_____. "Schools Weigh Problems of Puerto Ricans," New York World Telegram and Sun, February 11, 1953.

446

_____. "Seward HS Makes Americans," New York World Telegram and Sun, May 11, 1956, p.34.

Entman, Frederick. "Our Puerto Rican Children: One School's Approach," Strengthening Democracy, May, 1955, pp.3, 5.

"Un Esfruerzo Encomiable." (Editorial). El Diario De Nueva York, February 18, 1954, p.13.

"El Espanol en Clinicas de la Ciudad," El Diario De Nueva York, February 17, 1954.

"Existe el Proposito de Contratar 500 Maestros Hispanos Mas para N.Y.," El Diario De Nueva York, February 16, 1954, p.6.

Feigenbaum, Lawrence. "Teaching English to Puerto Rican Youth," High Points (January, 1952), pp.45-48.

Fernos Isern, Antonio. "The Role of Puerto Rico and Its People in the Americas," The Journal of Educational Sociology, Vol.35 (May, 1962), pp.397-401.

Finocchiaro, Mary. "Puerto Rican Newcomers in Our Schools," American Unity, Vol.XIV, No.3 (January-February, 1956), pp.12-17.

_____. "Our Schools Must Meet the Challenge of a New Migration," High Points (March, 1953), pp.29-33.

_____. "A Suggested Procedure in the Teaching of English to Puerto Ricans," High Points (May, 1949), pp.60-66.

_____. Teaching English as a Second Language. New York, 1958, 335 pp.

Fitzpatrick, J.P. "Oscar Lewis and the Puerto Rican Family," America, Vol.115 (December 10, 1966), pp.778-779.

Flicker, Jeanette. "Classes for Spanish-Speaking Children," High Points (November, 1947), pp.58-62.

Fox, Rosa Rudami. "Puerto Ricans in Your Town," American Unity (A monthly educational guide), Vol.XI, No.5 (May-June, 1953), pp.3-8.

Galindez, Jesus de. "Cronicas desde Nueva York: Hispano-America en las Universidades Norteamericanas," El Diario De Nueva York, August 28, 1951, p.8.

"$160,000 Gift Here Aids Puerto Ricans," The New York Times, August 28, 1953, p.18.

Glazer, Nathan and Daniel Moynihan. Beyond the Melting Pot. Cambridge, M.I.T. Press, 1964, 360 pp.

Greenberg, Benjamin B. "1955 Puerto Rican Workshop," Puerto Rico Es Su Casa, Vol.I, No.1 (June, 1955), p.1.

Greenstein, Marvin N. "Puerto Rican Children," Pathways in Child Guidance, Vol.II, No.4 (June, 1960), pp.1, 3.

Guerra, Emilio L. "Orientación de los Estudiantes de Puerto Rico in la Ciudad de Nueva York," El Diario De Nueva York, March 28, 1949, p.6.

_____. "The Orientation of Puerto Rican Students in New York City," Modern Language Journal (October, 1948), pp. 415-420.

_____. "The Role of the Teacher of Spanish in the Orientation of Non-English Speaking Pupils," Hispania, Vol. XXXII, No.1 (February, 1949), pp.59-63.

"Guidance Is Asked for Puerto Ricans," The New York Times, October 28, 1947.

Gurren, Louise. "A Special Class for Puerto Rican Students," High Points (February, 1948), pp.77-80.

Handlin, Oscar. The Newcomers, Negroes and Puerto Ricans in a Changing Metropolis. New York, Doubleday, 1962, 177 pp.

"Hay 46, 85: Ninos de P.R. en Escuelas de New York," El Diario De Nueva York, February 19, 1953, p.4.

"Hay Tres Nuevas Divisiones en Instruccion," El Mundo (San Juan, P.R.), July 16, 1947.

"Helping Puerto Rican Pupils to Achieve Status," Strengthening Democracy, Vol.V, No.6 (May, 1953), pp.4-5.

"El Hogar Y La Escuela." (Editorial). El Diario De Nueva York, November 14, 1951, p.9.

"Home-School Project Drawn," New York Sun, August 6, 1948.

"How to Teach Puerto Ricans," New York Herald Tribune, February 13, 1951.

"Incidente Lamentable." (Editorial). El Diario De Nueva York, February 24, 1954.

Ingraham, Leonard W. "Our Puerto Rican Students Must Become a Part of All the Children," High Points (February, 1951), pp.11-17.

El Instituto Profesional de 1948. November, 1948, 2 pp.

"The Integration Movement in Education," Curriculum and Materials, Vol.XVIII, No.3 (Spring, 1964), p.1.

"Iran a Puerto Rico 20 Trabajadoras Soci Lespor Invitacion del Rector," El Diario De Nueva York, May 23, 1952, p.2.

Jaffe, Abraham J., ed. Puerto Rican Population of New York City: A Series of Papers Delivered Before the New York Area Chapter of the American Statistical Association, October 21, 1953. Bureau of Applied Social Research. January, 1954, 61 pp.

"Joven Damita Hace Honor a Los Boricuas en el Bronx," El Diario De Nueva York, March 5, 1952, p.7.

Juncal, Hernan Poza. "La Escuela Norteamericana y Nuestros Ninos," Plus Ultra, October 10, 1948.

Jusino, Gonzalo. "La Organizacion Civica Puertoriquena," El Diario De Nueva York, April 17, 1952, p.11.

Kahnheimer, Leah W. "A Program in Social Living for Puerto Rican Pupils," High Points (June, 1954), pp.58-68.

Kaufman, Maurice. The Effect of Instruction in Reading Spanish on Reading Ability in English of Spanish-Speaking Retarded Readers. Unpublished Ph.D. Dissertation. New York University, 1966.

Kelly, Mary. "English in U.S. as 2nd Language," Christian Science Monitor. Reprint. October 21, 1963, 3 pp.

Kihss, Peter. "Gains Made by Puerto Ricans Here"; and "City Relief Roll Held Down Despite Job-Hunter Influx." Two articles from The New York Times, May 31, 1957 and June 2, 1957. Reprinted by Commonwealth of Puerto Rico, Migration Division, Department of Labor, 3 pp.

_____. "Puerto Rico and Us." Three articles from The New York Times, February 23-25, 1953. Reprinted by Department of Labor of Puerto Rico, Migration Division, 8 pp.

Kleban, Evelyn. "Thanksgiving: An Orientation Project for Newcomers," Strengthening Democracy, January, 1963, pp.3, 6.
449

Klein, Woody. Let in the Sun. New York, 1963, 297 pp.

Kosinski, Leonard U. "A New Look at the Bilingual Student," Senior Scholastic, Vol.82 (October 4, 1963), p.14.

Landy, David. Tropical Childhood: Cultural Transmission and Learning in a Rural Puerto Rican Village. New York, Harper, 1965.

"Lawyers Association Exposes Untruths about Puerto Ricans," The Daily Compass, March 31, 1952, pp.2, 13.

Lewis, C. "Some Puerto Rican Viewpoints," Childhood Education, Vol.43 (October, 1966), pp.82-84.

Loretan, Joseph O. "Problems in Improving Educational Opportunities for Puerto Ricans in New York," High Points (May, 1963), pp.23-31.

Lorge, Irving and Frank Mayans, Jr. "Vestibule vs. Regular Classes for Puerto Rican Migrant Pupils," Teachers College Record, Vol.LV, No.5 (February, 1954), pp.231-237.

"Maestra Boricua Hace Llamamiento a Los Padres Hispanos Del Bronx," El Diario De Nueva York, April 16, 1952, pp. 6-7.

Massimine, E. Virginia. "The Puerto Rican: Citizen of New York," The Journal of Pi-Lamda Theta (New York University) (April, 1950), p.2.

Mataresi, Felicia. "No Debe Segregarse a Los Estudiantes de Puerto Rico," El Diario De Nueva York, January 19, 1954.

Mayor's Advisory Committee on Puerto Rican Affairs in New York City, Sub-Committee on Education, Recreation and Parks. The Puerto Rican Pupils in the Public Schools of New York City: A Survey of Elementary and Junior High Schools. New York, 1951, 102 pp.

McCuen, John J. "Puerto Rican Survey Seeks Best Methods," New York World Telegram and Sun, April 7, 1954, p.42.

"Meeting the Needs of Puerto Rican Pupils in New York City Public Schools (Facts and Figures)," Staff Bulletin. (Special supplement). March 23, 1964, 4 pp.

"Melting Pot Boils in This High School," The New York Times, December 14, 1952, p.45.

Menton, Seymour. "Teaching English to Puerto Rican Students," High Points (November, 1952), pp.67-70.

Messer, Helaine R. The Puerto Rican Student in the New York City Public Schools: 1945-1965. Unpublished M.A. dissertation. Columbia University, 1966.

Miller, Henry. "New York City's Puerto Rican Pupils: A Problem of Acculturation," School and Society, Vol.LXXVI, No.1967 (August 30, 1952), pp.129-132.

Mills, C. Wright, Clarence Senior, and Rose Kohn Goldsen. The Puerto Rican Journey. New York, 1950, 238 pp.

Mirkin, Sydney. "The Puerto Rican Problem," Daily News, January 3, 1955, pp.3, 29.

_____. "The Puerto Rican Problem: Island Fights for Better Living," Daily News, January 5, 1955, pp.2, 32.

_____. "The Puerto Rican Problem: They Change Her, Island Feels," Daily News, January 4, 1955, pp.3, 24.

Monserrat, Joseph. School Integration: A Puerto Rican View. San Juan, Commonwealth of Puerto Rico, Department of Labor, Migration Division, 1963, 16 pp.

_____. "A Puerto Rican Family," Natural History (April, 1967). On Lewis's La Vida.

Montag, Jennie and Mary Finocchiaro. "Guidance and Curriculum for Puerto Rican Children," High Points (January, 1951), pp.32-42.

Montes, Marta. "La Primera Escuela Puertoriquena en la Ciudad de Nueva York," La Prensa, September 17, 1961.

"More Classes Set for Adults," New York Sun, November 25, 1947.

Munoz Marin, Ines Maria Mendoza De. "Identidad Puerto-riquena," La Prensa, July 30, 1961.

Narvaez, Alfonso. "Beleaguered High School," New York Herald Tribune, December 26, 1965, p.32.

"Need of the Puerto Rican Child," New York Teacher News, November 8, 1952, p.3.

"Nuevo Metodo Para la Ensenanza de Idiomas," El Diario De Nueva York, February 26, 1952, p.4.

New York City. Board of Education

A. Unpublished Materials

"Annual Report of the Commissioner of Education."
n.d., 4 pp.

"Board of Education Statement on the Decentralization
of the New York City School System." June 14, 1965,
7 pp.

Bureau of Curriculum Research. "Puerto Ricans in New
York City," 1965, 8 pp.

_____. "A Resource Unit: Understanding Our Fellow
American Citizens, the Puerto Ricans." n.d., 9 pp.

"Comparison of Special Programs, Classes, and Materials
for Puerto Rican Students in Eighteen Schools." n.d.,
8 pp.

"Curriculum Development: Notes for Discussion at
Principals' Inservice Course." New York Board of
Education, 1943.

Department of Speech Improvement. "Speech Problems of
Puerto Rican Children." A Report of the Committee on
Individualization. November, 1948, 13 pp.

Division of Elementary Schools. "Education of the Non-
English Speaking Child." New York, 1962, 2 pp.

_____. "Highlights of the N-E Program." New York, 1963,
3 pp.

_____. "Proposed Revision of Policy on Operation
Understanding." New York, 1963, 9 pp.

_____. "Record Sheets, Rating Sheets, and Instructional
Aids for the Education of the Non-English Speaking
Child," 11 pp.

Division of Elementary Schools. "The Substitute
Auxiliary Teacher." 1958, 4 pp.

Division of High Schools. "Number of Candidates for
Graduation - June, 1962." 5 pp.

_____. "Report on Graduates - January 1962." 2 pp.

_____. "Non-English Program, Schools Having 25 or More
Students Rated as Non-English Speaking in the Census
of October 1958, October 1959, October 1962, October
1963." 30 pp.

New York City, Board of Education (cont.)

_____. "Some Resources Recommended for Use in the
Education of Non-English Speaking Students." May, 1960,
9 pp.

Division of Junior High Schools. "Minutes of a Conference Related to an Educational Program for Puerto
Rican Children." February 10, 1953, 3 pp.

_____. "The Puerto Rican Bulletin: An Aid to Teachers
and Supervisors of Puerto Rican Children." n.d., 30 pp.

_____. "Some Facts and Figures about Puerto Rico and
Puerto Ricans." 1952. Unpaged.

Donavan, Bernard E. and Benjamin J. Stern. "Memorandum
of Pupils Whose Native Language is not English." March
20, 1953.

Finocchiaro, Mary. "The Role of the Foreign Language
Teacher in an Educational Program for Puerto Rican
Children." n.d., 6 pp.

In-Service Course, Spring Term 1963, Course C - 886.
"Practical Techniques for Teachers of Spanish Working
with Puerto Rican Pupils, Questions Submitted by
Members of the Class." 11 pp.

News Release, July 12, 1965, 2 pp.

_____. July 13-14, 1965, 2 pp.

_____. July 21, 1965, 3 pp.

The Puerto Rican Study. Announcements, correspondence,
minutes. In the Covello Papers - Personal Files.

The Puerto Rican Study. "Follow-Up Study of the
Graduating Classes of Two Junior High Schools." A
report prepared by Maria Luisa Rodriguez. September
20, 1955, 34 pp.

_____."Project for Transitional-Stage Puerto Rican
Pupils in the High School, Helping the Transitional
Stage Pupil in the Subject Class." May 16, 1956, 6 pp.

_____. "The Puerto Rican Study News Exchange," No.1.
November 4, 1954. Unpaged.

_____. "The Puerto Rican Study News Exchange," No.2.
December 8, 1954. Unpaged.

New York City. Board of Education (cont.)

_____. "The Puerto Rican Study News Exchange," No.6.
April 21, 1955. Unpaged.

_____. "A Report on School-Puerto Rican Parent
Relations, 1955-6." A report prepared by Frances Low.
New York, 1957, 61 pp.

_____. "Who are the Puerto Rican Pupils in the New
York City Public Schools? Report No.1: Educational and
Familial Background." A report prepared by Samuel M.
Goodman. New York, 1954, 27 pp.

Sanguimetti, Carmen. "The Puerto Rican School Child in
Puerto Rico and in New York City." An address given at
in-service course for teachers of Puerto Rican adults.
New York, November 17, 1960, 9 pp.

"Special Census of School Population Classification of
'Non-English Speaking' Pupils, October 31, 1963." A
report prepared by Bertha Leviton. May, 1964, 13 pp.

"Statistics on Regular Day Schools - Pupils Newly
Arrived from Places Outside New York City and Leading
Sources of Immigration." 1955, 3 pp.

Union Settlement. "College Readiness Program." 1965,
1 p.

Wolk, Elsie. "A Summary Report of Reading Disabilities
of Children Learning English as a Second Language."
New York, 1963, 4 pp.

B. Published Materials

Bureau of Curriculum Research. Foreign Language
Revision for Secondary Schools, Spanish, Level 5.
1965, 47 pp.

Division of Elementary Schools. Handbook, 1963-1964.
221 pp.

_____. Handbook, 1964-1965. 268 pp.

_____. Teaching Children of Puerto Rican Background in
New York City Schools: Suggested Plans and Procedures.
1954, 76 pp.

Donavan, Bernard E. Implementation of Board Policy on
Excellence for the City's Schools. April 28, 1965,
34 pp.

New York City. Board of Education (cont.)

Educating Students for Whom English is a Second Language. December, 1965, 105 pp.

A Five-Year Crash Program for Quality Education. October 22, 1964, 16 pp.

Hillson, Henry T. and Florence Myers. The Demonstration Guidance Project, 1957-1962: Pilot Project for Higher Horizons. 1963, 31 pp.

Interviewing Puerto Rican Parents and Children in Spanish: A Guide for School Personnel. n.d., 10 pp.

Landers, Jacob. Higher Horizons: Progress Report. January, 1963, 109 pp.

Portals to the Future, Annual Report of the Superintendent of Schools, 1959-1960. 78 pp.

Puerto Rican Profiles. Curriculum Bulletin No.5. 1964-1965 Series. 96 pp.

The Puerto Rican Study, 1953-1957. J. Cayce Morrison, Director. 1958, 265 pp.

The Puerto Rican Study. Developing a Program for Testing Puerto Rican Pupils in the New York City Public Schools. 1958, 143 pp.

_____. A Letter to Friends of Puerto Rican Children. October 1, 1955, 8 pp.

The Puerto Rican Study. The Future is Now. n.d., 32 pp.

_____. Our Children from Puerto Rico, A Report on Their Island Home by the Visiting Puerto Rican Workshop of 1955. 1957, 72 pp.

_____. Resource Units for Classes with Puerto Rican Pupils in the First Grade. 1955, 145 pp.

_____. Resource Units for Classes with Puerto Rican Pupils in the Fifth Grade. 1956, 174 pp.

_____. Resource Units for Classes with Puerto Rican Pupils in the Fourth Grade. 1955, 143 pp.

_____. Resource Units for Classes with Puerto Rican Pupils in the Second Grade. 1956, 119 pp.

455

New York City. Board of Education (cont.)

_____. Teaching English to Puerto Rican Pupils in Grades Five and Six. 1957, 274 pp.

_____. Teaching English to Puerto Rican Pupils in Grades Three and Four. 1957, 216 pp.

_____. Who Are the Puerto Rican Children in the New York City Public Schools? 1956, 88 pp.

Report of the Joint Planning Committee for More Effective Schools to the Superintendent of Schools. May 15, 1964, 19 pp.

School Districts 11 and 18, Benjamin E. Strumpf, Assistant Superintendent. Your American Pupil from Puerto Rico... September 1956, 12 pp.

Sixtieth Annual Report of the Superintendent of Schools, City of New York, Statistical Section, School Year 1957-1958. 1959, pp.69-72.

Toward Greater Opportunity. A Progress Report from the Superintendent of Schools to the Board of Education, Dealing with Implementation of Recommendations of the Commission on Integration. June, 1960. 196 pp.

Working with Pupils of Puerto Rican Background. A Guidance Manual. 1965, 87 pp.

New York State Commission for Human Rights. Division of Research. The Puerto Rican Populations of the New York City Area: Populations of New York State: 1960 Report No.2. May, 1962, 22 pp.

"Niños Boricuas Usurán Aqui Libros Preparados en la Isla," El Diario De Nueva York, March 6, 1951, p.1.

"N.Y.U. Rinde Homenaje a Dos Puertoriquenos." (Editorial). El Diario De Nueva York, April 17, 1952, p.11.

"New York: World They Never Made." Reprinted from Time (June 12, 1950), 2 pp.

"Oportunidad de Estudiar Inglés que Puede Malograrse por Indiferencia." (Editorial). La Prensa, January, 1954.

Osuna, Juan J. A History of Education in Puerto Rico. Rio Piedras, P.R., 1949.

Ortiz, Ernesto, et al. Letter. "En Defensa de los Niños Puertoriqueños," El Diario De Nueva York, April 15, 1954.

Padilla, Elena. Up From Puerto Rico. New York, 1958, 317 pp.

"Parents, Children to Attend School," The New York Times, June 25, 1949, p.8.

Passow, Harry A., ed. Education in Depressed Areas. New York, 1963, 359 pp. [See "Introduction", supra]

Perlman, Ruth. "The American School: Cultural Crossroads," The Elementary School Journal (November, 1958), pp.82-86.

La Prensa. Suplemento Educativo. September 17, 1961, 8 pp.

Probst, Nathan and Sophia A. Olmsted. "The Rising Puerto Rican Problem," Bar Bulletin (New York County Lawyers Association), Vol.IX, No.5 (March, 1952), pp.5-12.

"Program de Orientación Educativa para Niños Hispanos," El Diario De Nueva York, September 30, 1951, pp.4, 14.

"Proponen Intensificar la Ensenanza de Ingles," La Prensa, January 16, 1961, pp.3, 9.

"Puerto Rican Adults Taught," New York Sun, November 13, 1947.

"Puerto Ricans Bid for More Schools," New York Times, August 6, 1967.

"The Puerto Rican Child," New York Teachers' News, November 29, 1952, pp.2, 7.

"The Puerto Rican Child," Teacher News (November 29, 1952), p.227.

"Puerto Rican Children," New York Teachers' News, April 3, 1954, p.4.

"Puerto Rican Committee Reactivated," Better Times, Vol. XXXII, No.10 (December 1, 1950), p.1.

Puerto Rican Community Development Project: A Proposal for a Self-Help Project to Develop the Community by Strengthening the Family, Opening Opportunities for Youth and Making Full Use of Education. New York, Puerto Rican Forum, 1964.

"Puerto Rican Conference on City Needs," New York Times, April 17, 1967.

The Puerto Rican Forum, Inc. <u>Aspira</u>. 1965, 4 pp.

<u>Puerto Rican Graduates of Morris High School, June, 1961</u>.
Migration Division, Commonwealth of Puerto Rico, 1963,
23 pp.

"Puerto Ricans and Inter-American Understanding," <u>The
Journal of Educational Sociology</u>, Vol.XXXV, No.9 (May,
1962), pp.385-440.

"The Puerto Ricans in New York City: Background Information for Teachers," <u>Curriculum and Materials</u>, Vol.XVIII,
No.3 (Spring, 1964), pp.6-7.

"Puerto Rican Migration," <u>Real Estate News</u>, March, 1949,
1 p.

"Puerto Ricans Pose Problems in Education," <u>The Sun</u>,
November 12, 1947, pp.1-39.

"Puerto Rican Problem Cited," <u>Daily News</u>, November 11,
1947.

"Puerto Ricans Seek Better Jobs Here," <u>The New York Times</u>,
June 16, 1948.

"Puerto Ricans Start Up Labor Ladder," <u>Business Week</u>.
Reprint. (May 2, 1953), 3 pp.

"Pupils from Puerto Rico," <u>The Elementary School Journal</u>
(November, 1958), p.74.

Quintero, Babby. "Del Ambiente Hispano," <u>La Prensa</u>
(December 4, 1951), p.3.

Raisner, Arnold. "New Horizons for the Student of Spanish-
Speaking Background," <u>High Points</u> (February, 1966), pp.
19-23.

Rand, Christopher. <u>The Puerto Ricans</u>. New York, 1958,
178 pp.

"Report on Puerto Rico Schools: McCloskey Describes
Difficulties and Accomplishments of Island Educators,"
<u>New York Sun</u>, July 24, 1948.

Riessman, Frank. <u>The Culturally Deprived Child</u>. New York,
1962, 140 pp.

Rogers, Melvin L. "For Puerto Rican Pupils: Crash Program
in Reading," <u>The Elementary School Journal</u> (November,
1958), pp.87-89.

Samuels, Gertrude. "Puerto Rico: Land of Paradox," The New York Times Magazine, October 30, 1955, pp.18, 62, 64, 67.

Sanchez, Jose M. "Más Maestros Hispanos," El Diario De Nueva York, June 15, 1952, p.7.

Sayers, Raymond S. "New York Teachers in Puerto Rican Schools," High Points (November, 1957), 12 pp.

Santolala, Irene Silva. "Los Padres y el Escolar," El Diario De Nueva York, June 15, 1952, p.7.

"Schools to Develop Puerto Rican Programs," New York World Telegram and Sun, August 28, 1953, p.40.

"Se Crea Comité de Padres Hispanos de la Escuela No.29 de Brooklyn," El Diario de Nueva York, June 22, 1952, p.7.

"Seek Better School Program for NYC Puerto Rican Youth," New York Teachers' News, May 31, 1952, p.4.

"La Semana de la Educación," La Prensa, November 1, 1953.

Senior, Clarence. "Schools, Newcomers and Community," Problems and Practices in New York City Schools. 1963 Yearbook of the Society for the Experimental Study of Education. Parts II and III, pp.107-111. New York: Society for the Experimental Study of Education, 1963.

_____. The Puerto Ricans: Strangers - Then Neighbors. Quadrangle Edition. Chicago, 1965, 128 pp.

Sexton, Patricia Cayo. Spanish Harlem: Anatomy of Poverty. New York, 1965, 208 pp. [See Cordasco, supra]

Shaw, Frederick. "A Follow-Up Study of the 1963 High School Graduates," High Points (November, 1965), pp.31-56.

Slotkin, Aaron N. "The Treatment of Minorities in Textbooks: The Issues and the Outlook," Strengthening Democracy, Vol.XVI, No.3 (May, 1964), pp.1-2, 8.

Smith, Richard C. "This School Solves Its Own Problems," The Elementary School Journal (November, 1958), pp.75-81.

"Spanish Endorsed For U.S. Schools," New York Times, July 22, 1967, p.54 (Senate Bill 428).

"Special Study for Migrants: Arts and Crafts Material for Puerto Ricans," New York Sun, December 16, 1947.

459

"Speech Training for Migrants," <u>New York Sun</u>, June 23, 1948.

"Sra. Collazo Dice Son Totalmente Falsas Palabras que se le Atribuyen," <u>El Diario De Nueva York</u>, July 30, 1952, p.4.

"Statement of Policy: 'Excellence for the Schools of New York City'," <u>Staff Bulletin</u>. (Special supplement). May 7, 1965, 4 pp.

"Superintendente Escuelas de N.Y. Pide Mas Respeto Para los Boricuas," <u>El Diario De Nueva York</u>, January 16, 1961, p.2.

Taylor, Carol. "A Better Era for Puerto Ricans: Obstacles of Mass Migration Are Disappearing for Our Newest New Yorkers," <u>New York World Telegram and Sun</u>, May 23, 1963, Second Section, p.17.

"Teaching the Puerto Rican Child," <u>New York Teachers' News</u>, February 24, 1953, p.3.

"Teaching Puerto Ricans in New York," <u>The New York Times</u>, December 17, 1950.

"10 Maestros para 11,900 Alumnos en Escuelas N.Y.," <u>El Diario De Nueva York</u>, April 10, 1952.

Treatman, Paul. "Operation-Understanding for Principals," <u>K-Six Magazine</u>, Issue 2 (1963-1964), pp.19-24.

"Una Noche en P. Rico," <u>El Diario De Nueva York</u>, March 2, 1953, p.6.

Wakefield, Dan. <u>Island in the City</u>. Boston, 1959, 278 pp.

Weales, Gerald. "New York's Puerto Rican Dilemma," <u>The New Leader</u>, March 7, 1955, pp.8-10.

Weitzman, Judy. "Reheating the Melting Pot," <u>The New Leader</u>, June 28, 1954, pp.11-12.

Welfare Council of New York City, Committee on Puerto Ricans in New York City. <u>Puerto Ricans in New York City</u>. New York, 1948, 60 pp.

White, Trumbull. <u>Puerto Rico and Its People</u>. Stokes, 1937.

Wolk, E. "The Teaching of English as a Second Language in the Elementary Schools of New York City, " <u>Hispania</u>, Vol. 49 (May, 1966), pp.293-296.

Young, Marguerite. "Schools in City Fit Courses to Puerto Ricans." Reprint. <u>The New York Herald Tribune</u>, November 16, 1947.

Index

463

464